OUTLINE

OF

ROMAN HISTORY

FROM

ROMULUS TO JUSTINIAN

(INCLUDING TRANSLATIONS OF THE TWELVE TABLES, THE INSTITUTES OF GAIUS, AND THE INSTITUTES OF JUSTINIAN),

WITH SPECIAL REFERENCE TO THE

Growth, Development and Decay

OF

ROMAN JURISPRUDENCE.

BY

DAVID NASMITH, Q.C., LL.B.

AUTHOR OF THE "INSTITUTES OF ENGLISH LAW," ETC., ETC.
JOINT TRANSLATOR OF "ORTOLAN'S HISTORY OF ROMAN LAW."

THE LAWBOOK EXCHANGE, LTD.
Clark, New Jersey

ISBN 978-1-58477-612-3

Lawbook Exchange edition 2006, 2019

The quality of this reprint is equivalent to the quality of the original work.

THE LAWBOOK EXCHANGE, LTD.
33 Terminal Avenue
Clark, New Jersey 07066-1321

Please see our website for a selection of our other publications and fine facsimile reprints of classic works of legal history:
www.lawbookexchange.com

Library of Congress Cataloging-in-Publication Data

Nasmith, David, 1829-1894.
Outline of Roman history from Romulus to Justinian (including translation of the Twelve tables, the Institutes of Gaius, and the Institutes of Justinian), with special reference to the growth, development and decay of Roman jurisprudence / David Nasmith.
p. cm.
Originally published: London : Butterworth, 1890.
Includes bibliographical references and index.
ISBN 1-58477-612-9 (alk. paper)
1. Roman law. 2. Roman law--History. 3. Rome--History. I. Lex duodecim tabularum. II. Gaius. Institutiones. III. Institutiones. IV. Title.

KJA147.N37 2005
340.5'4--dc22

2005025027

Printed in the United States of America on acid-free paper

OUTLINE

OF

ROMAN HISTORY

FROM

ROMULUS TO JUSTINIAN

(INCLUDING TRANSLATIONS OF THE TWELVE TABLES, THE INSTITUTES OF GAIUS, AND THE INSTITUTES OF JUSTINIAN),

WITH SPECIAL REFERENCE TO THE

Growth, Development and Decay

OF

ROMAN JURISPRUDENCE.

BY

DAVID NASMITH, Q.C., LL.B.

AUTHOR OF THE "INSTITUTES OF ENGLISH LAW," ETC., ETC.
JOINT TRANSLATOR OF "ORTOLAN'S HISTORY OF ROMAN LAW."

LONDON:
BUTTERWORTHS, 7, FLEET STREET,
Law Publishers to the Queen's most excellent Majesty.
DUBLIN: HODGES, FIGGIS & CO., GRAFTON STREET.
CALCUTTA: THACKER, SPINK & CO. MELBOURNE: G. ROBERTSON & CO.
MANCHESTER: MEREDITH, RAY & LITTLER.
EDINBURGH: T. & T. CLARK; BELL & BRADFUTE.
1890

LONDON:
C. F. ROWORTH, GREAT NEW STREET, FETTER LANE, E.C.

TO

THE RIGHT HONORABLE

HARDINGE STANLEY BARON HALSBURY,

Lord High Chancellor of Great Britain,

THIS BOOK

IS, WITH PERMISSION,

RESPECTFULLY DEDICATED

BY THE AUTHOR.

PREFACE.

No people with whom the modern world is acquainted are so well known to it as are the Romans. Admitting that legend rather than history tells us of their origin and early days, yet in that legend it is not impossible to sever the real from the unreal to such an extent as to justify the assertion that we know the Romans better than any other people—their birth, their maturity, and their death.

That the study of the organisation and development of the Roman institutions must be one, not merely of interest, but of profit, is necessarily obvious to all who recognise the fact that each generation benefits or suffers by the doings or omissions of its predecessor, and that from the experience of those who have gone before, all learn, or ought to learn, how to steer their future course.

The importance of the study of the Romans and their institutions has long been and still is universally admitted by the learned. There are many and most valuable books on Roman History. There are many and most valuable books on Roman Law. Speaking generally, however, the writers of the former practically ignore the existence of Roman law, and the authors of the latter that of Roman history: by so doing they, to a great extent, deprive their readers of the pleasure of being able to trace cause and effect—the very essence of the value of history. To be told that a particular military enterprise was advantageous or disastrous to the Romans is a historical fact of interest, and one worth the learning, but, when the result of that enterprise was a great and lasting modification of the Roman law, the omission of mention of that fact is serious.

To dilate on a particular Roman institution, for example, that styled the *patria potestas*, in any other than chronological form, is simply absurd; for the *patria potestas* of one period was no more like that of another than was the English feudal system of William I. like that of its namesake abolished in A.D. 1660.

The object of this sketch is to make that which is ordinarily understood as Roman history go hand in hand with the chronological changes in Roman law, and to furnish the reader and myself with an outline or pegs so arranged as to enable us easily and accurately to store our future acquisitions.

Concerning Roman law many strange things have been said, not merely by others, but by some of the Romans themselves.

Prior to the publication by Grotius in A.D. 1625 of his "*De jure belli et pacis*," law in modern Europe had practically no pretension to the rank of a science. The laws, such as they were, of each State, were doubtless more or less diligently studied by the legal practitioners of the period and place, but the notion that law meant anything other than a collection of arbitrary rules does not appear to have entered the minds of those who only saw sovereigns and subjects in the light of masters and servants.

Grotius said, "It is too narrow a view to say that 'utility' is the mother of rights: the mother of rights is human nature taken as a whole, with its impulses of kindness, pity, sociality, as well as its desire of individual pleasure and fear of pain. Human nature is the mother of natural law, and natural law is the mother of Civil or Instituted law." (Art. 16.)

It is true that the learned were more or less acquainted with the works published in the name, and during the reign, of Justinian, but it was not till A.D. 1819, when the Institutes of Gaius were discovered, that modern Europe became alive to the fact that there had been in Rome men like Grotius—true jurists. It was then that the learned became somewhat sceptical concerning their Justinian idol, and began to doubt whether the Romans really were, except during a comparatively brief period of their existence, the great lawyers they had been pictured. A comparison of the Institutes of Justinian with those of Gaius, imperfect as is our copy of the latter, almost instantly demonstrates the fact, that, whereas Gaius was a jurist in the true sense of the term, the author of the Institutes of Justinian was not. As an instance, the author of the Institutes of Justinian says—"Jurisprudence is the knowledge of things divine and human, and the exact discernment of what is just and unjust." (Just. Inst. l. 1.) Again, "The law of nature is not a law to man only, but likewise to all other animals, whether they are produced on the earth, in the air, or in the water. Hence proceeds the conjunction of male and female, which we among our own species style matrimony: whence arises the production of children, and our care in bringing them up. We perceive, also, the rest of the animal creation are regarded as having a knowledge of this law, by which they are actuated." (Just. Inst. l. 11.)

It is inconceivable that such and many other like passages findable in Justinian, could have emanated from a jurist. Nothing in the faintest degree resembling them is to be found in Gaius.

That the Romans from very small beginnings became a mighty nation and afterward dwindled to nothing, is matter of common knowledge. The answer to the question: Why?—is and always has been doubtful, and far from satisfactory.

The decline and fall of the Roman Empire was not due to one, but to various causes. Those causes are, I trust, sufficiently indicated in this sketch.

Why the Romans, whose legal instincts were, from the first, singularly acute, should have fallen from the juristic height of Gaius and the men of his time—Papinian being the greatest—to the depths of the Justinian era, it may not be easy to explain. Should anyone venture to say—"The Romans never did so fall—Justinian and his colleagues were not Romans," it might be somewhat difficult to refute him. When all that gives character and individuality to a people, or to a person, has faded away, the bare name can neither inspire awe, nor respect.

To say that the law of the period of Justinian was in some particulars less harsh than that of the period of Gaius, conveys no real lesson. Of course it was: the law of the period of Gaius was less harsh than was that of Rome two hundred years before his time. All legal growths mollify as they ripen, and apparently continue to do so till they begin to decay. The question is, had decay attacked the Roman law at the time of Justinian? My contention is, that it had, and that to a very serious extent.

Law is one thing, religion is another, and morality is a third. They are the three inseparable bonds of human society. To confound, however, the province of the Church with that of the Law—the Secular power —is fatal alike to the Law and to the Church. The experience of the Romans sufficiently demonstrates that fact.

It is not to the substitution of Christianity for the ancient Roman faith, as has been suggested by some, that the degeneration of the Romans is to be ascribed, for modern nations professing that faith have prospered and flourished to a degree unequalled by nations holding any other faith: except, indeed, in those instances where the Christian church has been suffered to usurp the attributes and functions of temporal sovereignty.

The history of any people necessarily involves the study, *inter alia*, of two things: Geography and Chronology. Where and when did they exist and act? Everything in this world is relative. That which is possible at one period, and in one place, is impossible at another period, and at another place, if not even in the same place. Neither the Romans nor any other people could now do what the Romans once did. Their successes were mainly due to the fact that their great struggles were either with nations effeminated by luxury, or with barbarians who lacked their military skill. Their subsequent failures were largely due to their own effeminacy.

There is one fact to which reference must not be omitted, that is, the mention by me of the names of the emperors who were either useless or worse than useless to the Romans. The reader may say—"Why not pass them over in silence?" My answer is this:—"It appears to me to be no less the duty of the historian to hold the vicious up to execration than the virtuous to admiration. The history of a people demands knowledge of the bad as well as of the good. A vicious or worthless ruler is a nation's curse."

This survey, which covers a period of about 1300 years, presents an ascending and a descending course, the brow of the hill being two centuries—that immediately before, and that immediately following A.D.

The work is divided into three separate parts, viz.:—The Outline: The Institutes of Gaius: and The Institutes of Justinian. It is so divided for the convenience of the reader, who, thereby, can readily compare Gaius with Justinian.

The Outline is divided into twelve chapters, which, with the aid of the chronometrical chart, will, it is believed, keep every period and event chronologically accurate: and, by the device resorted to in the map and numbers, the reader will, almost without reference to it, feel himself in touch of each place as it is mentioned. The locality rather than the exact spot is that which is needed by the historian. However, I have also made an alphabetical geographical index. The chart and map are in the pocket of the back cover.

The translation of Gaius is derived from the text; the translations of M. Pellat, published in 1844; Dr. Abdy's Gaius, published in 1870, and Mr. Poste's Gaius, published in 1885: that of Justinian is the translation by Dr. George Harris, published in 1811. I know of no better. The student who can possess himself of a copy of that work will be delighted with the Latin text and the notes. In the case of Gaius, though at the risk of some grammatical peculiarities, I have substituted the Latin technical terms for their translations, being of opinion that the Latin, even when not strictly in accord with the English context as to case, &c., is far less likely to mislead than is the best translation: there are, in fact, many terms that cannot be translated though they may be explained. Gaius is remarkable for the way in which he explains the technical terms used by him.

Considerable care has been bestowed on the index, by the aid of which, and the table of contents, constructed on somewhat novel lines, it is hoped that the reader will, without difficulty, be able to turn up any point in either of the three sections of the book.

I acknowledge with sincere gratitude the valuable assistance of my learned friend, Mr. Edward Rolland, who read my manuscript and made several valuable suggestions, and also revised the proofs.

4, Brick Court, Temple.
February, 1890.

TABLE OF CONTENTS.

OUTLINE OF ROMAN HISTORY FROM ROMULUS TO JUSTINIAN, IN TWELVE SHORT CHAPTERS.

CHAP. I.

THE REGAL PERIOD.

A.U.C. 1 TILL A.U.C. 244;—B.C. 753 TILL B.C. 510.

CHAP. II.

THE REPUBLIC.—1ST PERIOD.

A.U.C. 244 TILL A.U.C. 354;—B.C. 510 TILL B.C. 400.

N.B.—For the convenience of reference, the page, and where possible the date, is added to each event referred to in the Table of Contents.

CHAP. III.

THE REPUBLIC—*continued.*

THE FOURTH CENTURY B.C., *i.e.*, A.U.C. 355 TILL A.U.C. 454;—
B.C. 399 TILL B.C. 300.

CHAP. IV.

THE REPUBLIC—*continued.*

THE THIRD CENTURY B.C., *i.e.*, A.U.C. 455 TILL A.U.C. 554;—
B.C. 299 TILL B.C. 200.

The Orators, Historians, Philosophers, Poets, &c. of the Period.

Chap. V.

THE REPUBLIC—*continued.*

THE SECOND CENTURY B.C., *i.e.*, A.U.C. 555 TILL A.U.C. 654;—
B.C. 199 TILL B.C. 100.

The Orators, Historians, Philosophers, Poets, &c. of the Period.

Chap. VI.

THE REPUBLIC—*continued.*

THE FIRST CENTURY B.C., *i.e.*, A.U.C. 655 TILL A.U.C. 753-4;—
B.C. 99 TILL A.D.

The Orators, Historians, Philosophers, Poets, &c. of the Period.

THE ROMAN EMPIRE.

A.U.C. 723 TILL A.U.C. 753-4;—B.C. 31 TILL A.D.

CHAP. VII.

THE EMPIRE—*continued.*

THE FIRST CENTURY OF THE CHRISTIAN ERA, *i. e.*, A.U.C. 753-4 TILL A.U.C. 852;—A.D. TILL A.D. 99.

Emperors—Jurists—Orators, Historians, Philosophers, Poets, &c.

CHAP. VIII.

THE EMPIRE—*continued.*

THE SECOND CENTURY, *i.e.*, A.U.C. 853 TILL A.U.C. 952;—A.D. 100 TILL A.D. 199.

Emperors—Jurists—Orators and Writers.

CHAP. IX.

THE EMPIRE—*continued.*

THE THIRD CENTURY, *i.e.*, A.U.C. 953 TILL A.U.C. 1052;—
A.D. 200 TILL A.D. 299.

Emperors—Jurists—Orators and Writers.

CHAP. X.

THE EMPIRE—*continued.*

THE FOURTH CENTURY, *i.e.*, A.U.C. 1053 TILL A.U.C. 1152;—
A.D. 300 TILL A.D. 399.

Emperors—Division of the Empire—Orators and Writers.

Chap. XI.

THE EMPIRE—*continued.*

THE FIFTH CENTURY, *i. e.*, A.U.C. 1153 TILL A.U.C. 1252;—
A.D. 400 TILL A.D. 499.

Emperors of the West—Emperors of the East—No Jurists—One Prose Writer.

Chap. XII.

THE EMPIRE—*continued.*

THE SIXTH CENTURY, *i. e.*, A.U.C. 1253 TILL A.U.C. 1352;—
A.D. 500 TILL A.D. 599.

The Emperors of the East till A.D. 565.

THE INSTITUTES OF GAIUS.

THE INSTITUTES OF JUSTINIAN.

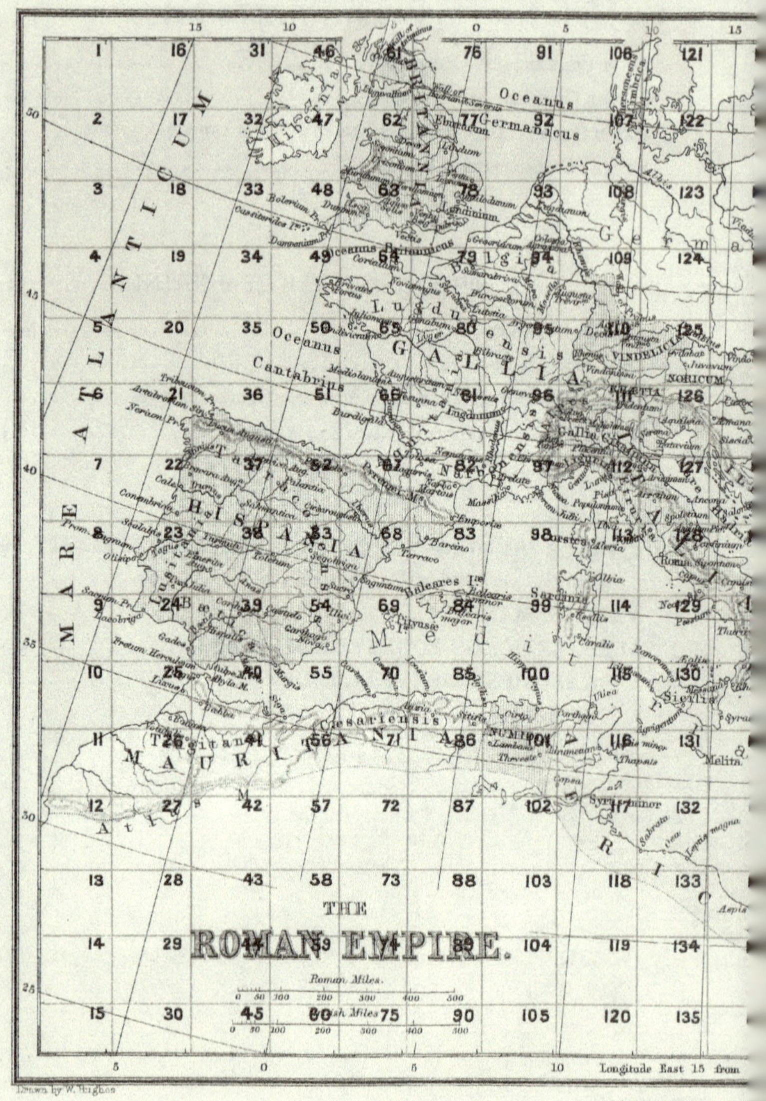

THE
ROMAN EMPIRE.
MARE ATLANTICUM
Oceanus Germanicus
Hibernia
BRITANNIA
Eboracum
Londinium
Oceanus Britannicus
Oceanus
Cantabricus
GALLIA
Lugdunensis
Belgica
Germania
VINDELICIA
NORICUM
RHAETIA
Massilia
HISPANIA
Carthago Nova
Gades
Baleares Ins.
Sardinia
Corsica
Roma
Sicilia
Melita
Caesariensis
Tingitana
MAURITANIA
NUMIDIA
AFRICA
Syrtis minor
Roman Miles.
English Miles
Longitude East 15 from
Drawn by W. Hughes
GEORGE PHILIP & S

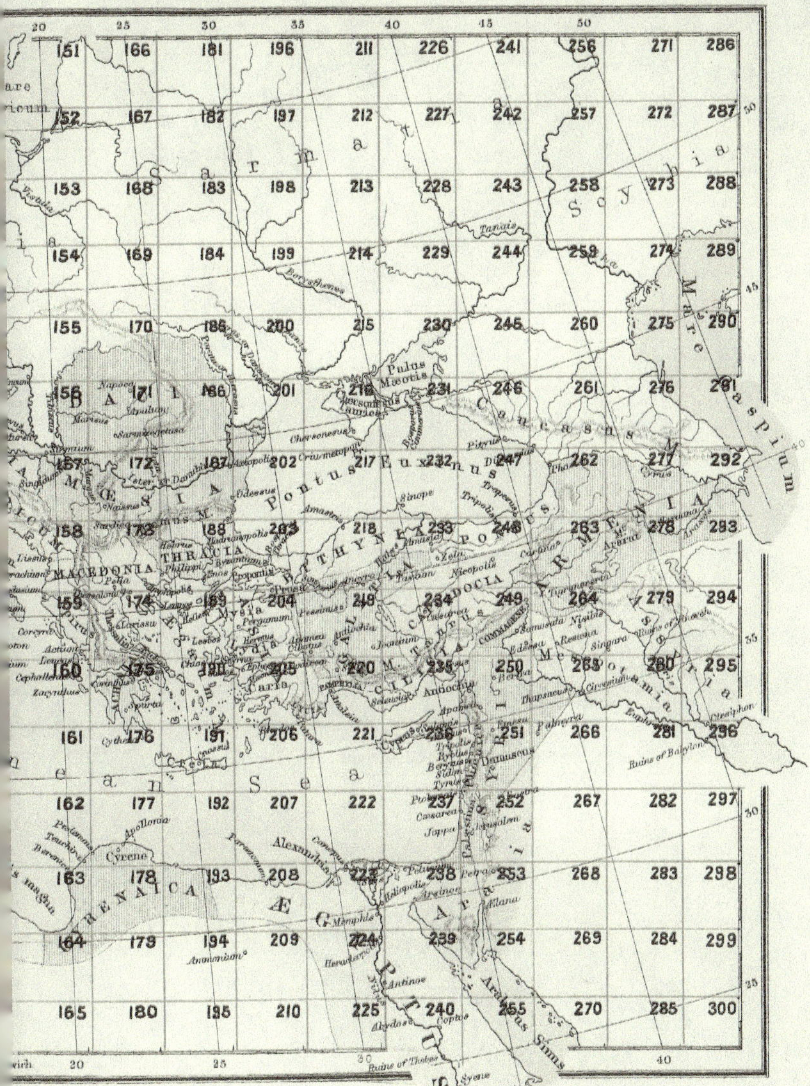

20 25 30 35 40 45 50

151	166	181	196	211	226	241	256	271	286
152	167	182	197	212	227	242	257	272	287
153	168	183	198	213	228	243	258	273	288
154	169	184	199	214	229	244	259	274	289
155	170	185	200	215	230	245	260	275	290
156	171	186	201	216	231	246	261	276	291
157	172	187	202	217	232	247	262	277	292
158	173	188	203	218	233	248	263	278	293
159	174	189	204	219	234	249	264	279	294
160	175	190	205	220	235	250	265	280	295
161	176	191	206	221	236	251	266	281	296
162	177	192	207	222	237	252	267	282	297
163	178	193	208	223	238	253	268	283	298
164	179	194	209	224	239	254	269	284	299
165	180	195	210	225	240	255	270	285	300

Sarmatia
Scythia
Tanais
Borysthenes
Palus Mæotis
Mare Caspium
Caucasus M.
Pontus Euxinus
DACIA
MŒSIA
THRACIA
MACEDONIA
Chersonesus
Odessus
Sinope
Trapezus
BITHYNIA
GALATIA
PONTUS
CAPPADOCIA
ARMENIA
Mesopotamia
Assyria
Mysia
Lydia
Caria
Pergamum
Lesbos
Chios
CILICIA
Antiochia
Tarsus
COMMAGENE
Edessa
Nisibis
Singara
Palmyra
Damascus
Tyrus
Sidon
Joppa
Jerusalem
Ctesiphon
Ruins of Babylon
Euphrates
Alexandria
Cyrene
CYRENAICA
Apollonia
Ammonium
Memphis
Heliopolis
Arabia
Petra
Arabicus Sinus
Antinoe
Abydos
Coptos
Ruins of Thebes
Syene
Berenice
Nilus
ÆGYPTUS
Cnossus
Larissa
Pella
Philippi
Byzantium
Sardica
Naissus
Napoca
Apulum
Sarmizegetusa

20 25 30 35 40

LONDON & LIVERPOOL.

OUTLINE OF ROMAN HISTORY.

ITALY in B.C. 753.

In the year B.C. 753 (A.U.C. 1), the commonly accepted date of the foundation of Rome, Italy and Gaul were peopled by the descendants of three principal races—the Iberians, the Kelts or Gaels with their kindred Cimbri, and the Iones. Among the subordinate nationalities of Italy existing at the date in question there were three of more immediate interest to the Roman historian than the rest, viz., the Latins,[1] the Sabines,[1] and the Etruscans.[1] These three nationalities, or rather a detachment from each, by common consent located themselves at the spot since known as Rome. Though united in one common object—the foundation of an independent state—they to a certain extent retained their original tribal distinctions.

From Romulus, the chief of the Latins, one tribe acquired the name of *Ramnenses;* from Tatius, the chief of the Sabines, another that of *Tatienses;* and from Lucumon, the chief of the Etruscans, the third acquired the name of the *Luceres.*

Thus the Romans from the earliest period and for a long time were divided into three tribes—the Ramnenses, the Tatienses, and the Luceres. Of these three, the Ramnenses (Latins, Romans), and the Tatienses (Sabines, Quirites), appear to have

[1] 128. N.B.—The number indicates the square on the map where the place in question will be found on any large map, if not on that accompanying this book.

been the most important, and, in short, to have been the founders of Rome, by whom the Luceres were subsequently admitted, though when is doubtful. Hence, though the tribes long remained distinct, the collective people were styled "*Populo Romano Quiritibusque,*" and at a later date "*Populus Romanus Quiritium,*" whereas the Etruscan element, when specifically referred to, was styled the third part of the Roman people, "*pars tertia populi Romani.*" Between these three tribes the original Roman territory (*ager Romanus*) was divided into three parts, one being allotted to each. The members of a tribe were styled "*tribules.*" Each tribe was divided into 10 *curiæ*, the result being that the entire populace was divided into 30 *curiæ*. The members of a *curia* were styled *curiales*. Each *curia* had its tutelary deity, its peculiar creed, sacrifices, priests, fates, and festivals.

The dominant characteristics of the Romans of this period—The men of the lance—is conveyed in two words "Religion," and the "Lance." *Romulus*, their founder and first king, was of divine origin. The son of Mars by a vestal virgin guided and protected by heaven during a reign of thirty-seven years was at last borne to heaven by his divine father. Such was the early and long-cherished Roman belief. Whether public or private, no enterprise of importance was undertaken by the Romans without first seeking divine guidance and a divine blessing. The Romans had no idea of right save the "divine will," and "might." By their lance they acquired their territory, their first wives, and their slaves. What then more natural than the notion that their wives, their children, and their slaves, were alike property to be dealt with at the pleasure of the owner?

Romulus.—It is said that for centuries the Romans never doubted the miraculous conception and ascent to heaven of Romulus the founder of their city. The account in brief runs thus:—Procas, king of Alba, of the family of the Silvii, had two sons, Numitor and Amulius. Before his death he appointed Numitor his eldest son to be his successor. Amulius, however, deprived his brother of the throne, put his brother's son to death, and compelled his daughter Rhea Silvia to become a vestal virgin. He, however, suffered Numitor to enjoy his father's private estates. Resolved to avenge the wrong of this unhappy family and to raise a state before which Alba and the Latins should fall prostrate, the divine Mars overpowered the timid virgin Rhea Silvia and then consoled her with the promise of illustrious children. Silvia gave birth to twins. Amulius ordered her to be put to death, and her children to be drowned in the river Anio. A she-wolf, however, rescued the babes, carried them to her den, and there suckled them, till they were discovered by a shepherd, who carried them to his wife, Acca Laurentia, who became their foster-mother. Grown to manhood and informed of the wrongs of their family, the brothers Romulus and Remus, joined by faithful comrades, attacked and slew Amulius, and restored Numitor to the throne. Romulus and Remus then resolved to build a town on the spot where they had passed their infancy. This they did with the assistance of their former companions. It is said that Albans, Latins, and even some nobles descended from the Trojans, joined in the enterprise.

Disputes arose between the brothers, some say as to the site of the new city, others as to which should rule over it. Here heaven again interposed. It was left to the gods to decide by augury. Remus saw six vultures fly overhead. Romulus declared that he saw twelve. Remus was reluctantly compelled to yield. Romulus traced out and built the city wall. Remus, still chafing over his supposed wrong, leaped over it in scorn. For this insult he was slain, some say by one Celer, others by his brother Romulus, who, they say, exclaimed, "So shall die whosoever ventures to leap over my wall." The burst of passion over, Romulus was filled with remorse; he refused to eat, and could not be comforted till informed by Faustulus, his foster-father, that the shade of Remus had appeared to him and promised to be reconciled to his brother, provided Romulus would institute a festival for the souls of the dead. Romulus willingly acceded, and instituted the Lemuria. As a further mark of honour to the deceased, he set up a second throne by the side of his own with a second sceptre and crown.

When the city was built, it was found that the small community was not sufficiently numerous to resist the attack of probable enemies. To increase the population, Romulus threw the city open to all comers. Freemen, exiles, and runaway slaves flocked to it. One element was still wanting. There were no women at Rome. The attempts of Romulus to conclude treaties with neighbouring peoples, whereby marriage between them should be made lawful, failed. Romulus resolved on stratagem. He proclaimed a great festival, the Consualia; the neighbouring Latins and Sabines were invited. Numbers with their wives and children flocked to Rome. On a given signal the Romans fell upon the visitors, seized and carried off their women. The captured maidens were soon appeased, not so their angered relatives. The Sabines rose in arms and marched against Rome. Treachery enabled them to enter the city. The fight grew desperate. The Sabine women rushed between the combatants, peace was concluded. The two people became one —*Populo Romano Quiritibusque.* Each, it was agreed, should retain its own king, but all temples and religious rites were to be common to both. As Romulus was established on the Palatine, T. Tatius built on the Capitoline and Quirinal. Matters of importance were discussed between the two kings in the plain between the Capitoline and the Palatine. T. Tatius, a few years after, was slain by some Laurentines. No successor to him was appointed: Romulus became sole king. After a reign of thirty-seven years, and on the nones of Quintilis, while the king was reviewing his people in the plain near Lake Capra, the sun withdrew his light, the earth was covered with darkness, Mars descended in a tempest and bore his son to heaven. Subsequently, the glorified king appeared to Proculus Julius in a vision, and promised to watch over his people, the Romans, as the god Quirinus.

In the year A.U.C. (B.C. 753), and for some considerable time after, Rome had practically but one class of population, its founders, patricians, at the head of whom was the *king*, who united in himself the three functions of Commander-in-Chief, High Priest, and Chief Justiciary.

The success of the young state early attracted foreigners to it. A ready welcome appears to have been extended to them, though equal rank with the *patricians*, except in rare cases which did exist, but about which we are not well informed, was denied them. The new-comers became and remained distinguished from the patrician founders of the city and their posterity by the style of "*Plebeians*." They had no share in the government, nor were their civil rights equal to those of the patricians.

In addition to persons who went voluntarily to Rome, many of the conquered foes of Rome were dragged to the city as the *slaves* (*servi*) of their conquerors, and were either employed by them in domestic service, or distributed through the *ager Romanus* as the tillers of the soil.

By the year A.U.C. 100, the plebeians had grown numerically strong. By the year A.U.C. 200, they found themselves in the possession, not merely of civil rights little inferior to those enjoyed by the patricians, but of many important political rights. In the year A.U.C. 244 (B.C. 510), they combined with the patricians, and overthrew the hereditary regal republic, and substituted for it an aristocratic republic, with annually elected *consuls* at its head.

In order rightly to appreciate Roman history, it appears to me necessary, in addition to what has already been said, to have just and clear notions on the following points, viz.:—

I. The fundamental principles on which the Roman kingdom was established had little or nothing in them that was then novel in Italy, which, so far as we know, appears to have been split up into little kingdoms, each constructed upon practically the same lines. Gaius says, however, that the *patria potestas* was peculiar to the Romans, by which he must be taken to have intended that the *patria potestas* of the Romans differed, so far as he knew, from that of every other nation.

II. Throughout Italy, service in the army of any of its little kingdoms was a privilege reserved to its patrician class.

III. It was a universal Italian notion that success in war entitled the victor either to slay the vanquished, or to preserve and subordinate him to his use. Those, therefore, who were thus preserved were styled *servi*, *i.e.*, preserved, whence it is obvious that the word *servi* represents a class of persons widely different from those understood by the modern word "slaves" or by the word "serf." They, in many instances, were persons who, at the time of their becoming *servi*, were as well born and educated as their victors and masters, if not better. What their posterity became is another matter. That depended upon circumstances: some attained honourable and high positions; others became the scum of society, more discreditable, perhaps, to the system under which they lived than to themselves.

There were, however, as we shall see, sources of slavery other than war.

IV. Neither the "*commercium*," *i.e.*, the right to trade, nor *à fortiori* the "*connubium*," *i.e.*, the right to intermarry between the people of distinct Italian sovereignties, ever existed, unless by virtue of express treaty; nor did the *connubium* exist in any of those states between the patrician and plebeian members of it, except by special enactment of that state. Slaves never married, they simply cohabited. They were regarded in law rather as cattle than as human beings.

V. There never was such a thing as we understand by the expression a "United Italy." Rome, Regal Rome, the Roman Republic, the Roman Empire, are expressions that from time to time, and till the separation of the Eastern from the Western Empire, were used to convey one idea—Rome—the sovereignty—the mistress of all within its sway. As Rome conquered town after town—the land attached to each was regarded as an annex—it gave to each, according to circumstances, the privileges of *municipia*, first, second, or third class, or those of *coloniæ*.

CHAPTER I.

THE REGAL PERIOD.

A.U.C. 1 till A.U.C. 244;—B.C. 753 till B.C. 510.

CHRONOLOGY OF THE KINGS.

A.U.C.	B.C.	
1	753.	The foundation of Rome.
1—37	753—717.	Romulus.
39—81	715—673.	Numa Pompilius.
82—113 . . .	672—641.	Tullus Hostilius.
114—137 . . .	640—617.	Ancus Martius.
138—175 . . .	616—579.	Lucius Tarquin (Tarquinius Priscus).
176—219 . . .	578—535.	Servius Tullius.
220—244 . . .	534—510.	Tarquinius Superbus.

THOUGH I have indicated as above the names of the seven kings, and the alleged term of the respective reigns of each, it is not my intention to deal with them as individuals, except wherein they may be necessary for the purpose of this sketch of the development of the Romans as a people.

The Inhabitants of the Roman State.—I have selected this heading to avoid the error into which the English reader is not unfrequently led by the expression "*Populus Romanus.*" If we divide the inhabitants of the Roman state under the kings into—(i.) Royalty; (ii.) Aristocracy (Patricians); (iii.) Commonalty (Plebeians); (iv.) Slaves (Servi, Mancipii); (v.) Freedmen (Libertini); (vi.) Foreigners (Peregrini); we have practically before us all the individuals, though not with all their appellations, with whom we are concerned, save and except the *Dediticii* who, as will hereafter appear, occupied a peculiar position.

Populus Romanus.—This expression is a generic term. It was used by the Romans to designate the collective body of patricians and plebeians, and those only.

Royalty.—See *post*, "King."

Aristocracy—(*Patricians, Patres, Patricii*).—The patricians were those who could trace their ancestors through an unbroken line of *ingenui* (*qui patrem ciere possent, id est, nihil ultra quam ingenuus*). The Senators were *Patres*, their descendants were *Patricii.* The term "*Patres*" was not, however, synonymous with senators. The senators were selected from the *Patres.*

Plebeians.—The plebeians were those who were not members of any patrician *gens*—*Plebes, in qua gentes civium patriciæ non insunt.*

Gentes—Ingenuus.—The entire body of the Patricians was divided into artificial families styled "*gens.*" The fundamental principle of a *gens* was the fact that in tracing the descent to the ultimate stock, no instance could be found of an ancestor having ever been in any kind of vassalage. (*Quorum majorum nemo servitutem servivit.*) One born in a *gens* and who could consequently trace a pure lineage was said to be *ingenuus.* At a later date the *gens* seems to have assumed the character of a clan rather than that of a family, for it appears that a *gens* might then consist of different families, *e.g.*, the Cornelia *gens* contained the Scipios and the Sullæ. The members of a *gens* were styled *gentiles*, from which word we have the modern "Gentilhomme," "Gentilhuomo," "Gentilhombre," and "Gentleman." To each *gens* were attached two subordinate classes, viz., the clients of the *gens*, including their descendants, and the enfranchised of the *gens*, including their descendants.

Clientage — *Patron and Client.* — Ortolan says that it is almost capable of demonstration that in the first ages of Rome, all the plebeians, not already enfranchised, were distributed among and attached to the several patrician houses by the bond of clientage.

Patrons—(*Patroni, Clientes*).—The patrons were the secular and spiritual governors of the state. Next to the name of father that of patron stood highest. He was the ultimate tutor and heir of his clients and their descendants, as also, of their enfranchised and their descendants.

Patron's Duty.—It was the duty of the patron to protect his client's interests when present or absent, and to instruct and assist him in litigation.

Client's Duty.—It was the duty of the client to ransom his patron or his patron's son from captivity, and to provide marriage portions for his daughters. The burden of public charges, *e. g.*, the expenses connected with magisterial offices, the payment of fines, the cost of unsuccessful litigation, and the maintenance of public roads and buildings were theirs.

Reciprocal Duties.—Neither patron nor client could be the accuser of, or witness against the other, nor could either render assistance to the enemy of the other; to do so made him liable to be sacrificed to the gods (*sacer esto*). The name of the *gens*, with a peculiar termination, was the name of the client, so of the enfranchised. The religious rites and sacrifices peculiar to the *gens* (*sacra gentilitia*) were his. All the members of his particular *gens* were his *gentiles*, He was a member of the family (*familia*), a familiar (*familiaris*) of his patron.

The Calendar.—It is said that before the time of Numa, the Roman year, like that of the Albans, consisted of ten months only, the first being March; and that Numa added January and February, making a year of, in all, 354 or 355 days, *i.e*, from ten to eleven days less than the solar year. This discrepancy necessitated periodic re-adjustments of the calendar. The duty of re-adjusting was one of the functions of the pontiffs. To appreciate the importance of this function it is necessary to bear in mind two facts, viz.: 1. Many, and indeed all important acts must be done on days and within hours that were *fastus*, otherwise they were invalid. 2. Like modern communities the Romans divided their days into what, for the sake of expressing the idea, we may style week-days (*dies fasti*), on which it was lawful to transact business (*fari licet*); and Sundays (*dies nefasti*), on which it was not lawful to transact any business of a legal character (*fari non licet*). In addition to which, like the Jews, they had days, part of which might be devoted to secular matters and part of which was reserved for spiritual affairs. Such days were termed cut or divided days (*intercisi*). They were *nefasti* in the morning and evening, *i.e.*, at the time of the immolation of the sacrificial victim in the morning, and its solemn sacrifice in the evening, whereas between the two periods they were fasti.[1] In addition to these there were fixed and movable holy days (*dies comitiales*) upon which alone the *comitia* could be held and many other acts done, whether public or private. It is therefore evident that the control of the calendar gave to the pontiffs great power and influence; for, till the publication A.U.C. 450, B.C. 304, of the book of working days (*fastorum libri*) they could, at pleasure, stop any important measure by simply declaring that the day was "*nefastus.*"

The Priesthood.—It was chiefly from an Etruscan source that the Romans derived their religious theories and practices. Cicero, in his book, *De Divinatione* (lib. I. 841), tells us that the Senate decreed that six children of the first patrician families should be confided, one to each of the different Etruscan communities, to be educated in the mystery of divination. The priesthood formed a college of which the king was chief, and as such was styled *Pontifex Maximus.* Though the sacerdotal function was a privilege exclusively enjoyed by the patricians, it was in no way inconsistent with secular dignities and offices, nor did it in any way necessitate departure from the ordinary habits of social life.

Augurs.—The special function of the augurs consisted in presaging the result of contemplated enterprises by the means

[1] It is interesting to note that not merely is Sunday an universal institution, but that there is not, so I have read, one day in the week that is not a Sunday somewhere. Sunday is Sunday with the Romanists and Protestants, Monday with the Greeks, Tuesday with the Persians, Wednesday with the Assyrians, Thursday with the Egyptians, Friday with the Turks, Saturday with the Jews.

of celestial phenomena:—observations upon the entrails of the sacrificial victims, attention to the flight, the song, or the appetite of birds.

Legislative Assemblies—*Comitia Curiata.*—The most ancient, the most aristocratic, and by far the most important of all Roman legislative assemblies was the *comitia curiata*—the meeting of the 30 curiæ held in the centre of the city at the spot known as the *comitium*. It was convoked by the lictors.[1] It selected the king, and elected to the highest sacerdotal, civil, and military offices. It enacted the law of investiture—*lex curiata*—by which the *imperium* or right to command was conferred. By it the composition of families was determined, and testamentary succession regulated. The *comitia curiata* could not assemble, however, unless convoked by patrician magistrates, acting under the order of the senate; and when convoked could only deliberate on one matter, viz., that for which they had been convoked. The presence in their midst of the augurs was indispensable. The augurs could at any moment stop the deliberation and disperse the assembly by the mere utterance of the formula "Another day" (*alio die*). As without the *lex curiata*, no official elect had *imperium*, so without the confirmation of the senate no decree of the *comitia curiata*—

[1] "Lictors, in Rome, were the public servants, who attended upon the magistrates to fulfil their commands. Their name (*lictores*) was derived from their binding offenders hand and foot previously to the punishment of scourging. The office was borrowed by Romulus from the Etruscans, whose chief magistrates were attended by servants, bearing axes tied up in bundles of rods, which were called *fasces*. Romulus was himself always preceded by twelve of them. When the regal dignity was abolished at Rome, the royal pomp was retained, and on this account, consuls, prætors, and other important officers—the censors excepted—were all attended by lictors. When a magistrate of high rank appeared in public, the lictors preceded him in a file, following each other. It was their duty to clear the road of the populace, that the consul, or other officer, might not be impeded in his progress, and this was effected by the cry, 'The consul (or prætor, &c.) comes! Make way for the consul.' When he returned to his own house or entered another, the lictors struck the door with their *fasces*. They also took care that proper respect should be shown to the person of the magistrate. A horseman who met the consul was obliged to dismount. Everyone uncovered his head as he passed, left him free passage, &c. The lictors were the executioners of punishments. They were free men, but chosen from among the lowest classes, and were often freedmen of the magistrate whom they attended.

"The dictators were preceded by twenty-four lictors; the consuls, decemvirs, and tribunes of the soldiers, by twelve; the prætors and master of the horse, by six; and the vestal virgins by one only."—*Popular Encyclopædia.*

the *lex curiata* excepted—was law. The reciprocal action of the two bodies is expressed by Cicero thus:—*potestas in populo, auctoritas in senatu sit.*

The Senate.—The senate styled by Cicero the royal council (*regium consilium*) consisted, at all events at the time of Tarquinius Priscus[1], of 300 members selected from the patricians, apparently on account of their age and experience. Aristocratic birth and age were therefore the two indispensable qualifications of senator. Florus says that they were styled *patres*, on account of their power, and *senatores* on account of their age (*qui ex auctoritate patres, ob ætatem senatus vocabantur*). The 300 senators were divided into thirty senatorial decuriæ.

The senate deliberated on public matters, and on questions to be submitted to the people in the *curiæ ;* by its counsel and authority the king reigned. Cicero, speaking of Romulus, says, "*Multo etiam magis Romulus patrum auctoritate consilioque regnavit.*"

Whether the senators were present at the nomination of the king and the election of the *curiæ* is matter of uncertainty; the better opinion, however, is that they were.

The Feciales.—The college of the *feciales* was composed of twenty-one members. They were the judges of treaties, peace, truces, embassies, and the like; it was they who declared war; it was to them that all questions of international law were referred; they were the guardians of Rome's honour abroad. When a foreign power had done, or was supposed to have done, a wrong to Rome, a member of the college—at times more than one—advanced into the foreigner's territory, and demanded reparation. If satisfaction was not given within thirty-three days, the matter was referred to the senate; if war was resolved

[1] It is said that prior to his reign the senators were only 150 in number. That owing to the great influx of aristocratic foreigners to Rome, and their dissatisfaction at the status allotted them, Tarquinius elevated 100, or 150 to the patriciate and gave them a place in the senate. To distinguish them from the original families, whose pride refused to receive them on absolute equality with themselves, they were styled "*minores gentes*"; the others being subsequently described as "*gentes majores.*"

on, the member returned to the hostile frontier, and, thrusting his lance into its soil, made the solemn declaration of war. The figure of a pig was one of the Roman military insignia. The conclusion of a treaty of peace was always accompanied by a solemn sacrifice; the pig was the sacrificial offering. The words of the officiating priest were, "May Jupiter smite the Roman people, on the day that they shall break this treaty, as I this day shall smite this pig." ("*In illo die, Jupiter, populum Romanum sic ferito, ut ego hunc porcum hic hodie feriam.*")

The King.—Nominated by the curiæ, the election of the king was confirmed by the *auctoritas* of the senate,[1] after which sovereign power was vested in him by the *lex curiata* (*lex rege*). He was the chief spiritual, military, and judicial functionary. He was, as already stated, high priest (*pontifex maximus*), commander-in-chief, and chief justice.

The Census, B.C. 566,—A.U.C. 188 (*temp. Servius Tullius*).—Hitherto the history of Rome has been a mere development of the principle of its foundation. Servius Tullius was the first innovator. He appears to have had little or no sympathy with the patrician element of the community, and to have set himself cautiously but studiously to the task of subverting it. By his order a census of the inhabitants of Rome was taken; it showed 80,000 souls. The head of each family was required, so we are told, to make a written statement on oath of the number of persons composing his family and a schedule of his property of every description, the fair estimated value of each article being stated. The penalty for omitting any article was its confiscation. From this period, the census was taken every fifth year. When the census was completed, the entire population passed in review through the Campus Martius, and underwent the ceremony of purification (*populum lustrare*). Females, males under sixteen

[1] Servius Tullius, A.U.C. 176—219, was the first king who became such without the previous election by the Senate or sanction of the curiæ. His elevation to the throne was secured by subterfuge. Having ascended the throne, however, he solicited and obtained the *imperium* by the *lex curiata*.

who had not exchanged the prætexta for the *toga*,[1] and slaves, were indicated by number merely, and not by name.

After Servius Tullius had thus taken the census, he divided the people into six parts, *i.e.*, into five classes, determined by their income, and a residuum consisting of those who, by reason of their poverty, were relieved from all taxation. This act secured to the king the goodwill of a numerous body, and made the memory of Servius immortal. Each class was taxed differently, and in proportion to its rank, so as to secure contribution to the national expenditure proportionate to the wealth of the individual. The following table according to Livy as to Classes I. to IV., and according to Dionysius as to Class V., shows, in Roman *asses* and English money, taking the *as* at 1*d.* the various classes.

CLASS.	ASSES.	English Money.
I.	100,000	£400.
II.	75,000	£300.
III.	50,000	£200.
IV.	25,000	£100.
V.	12,500	£50.

The members of each of these classes were bound to render fully equipped military infantry service free of cost to the state;

[1] "*Toga* (from *tegere*, to cover) the garment of wool, which, in time of peace, Roman citizens wore in public. Latterly it was worn almost exclusively by the male sex. Under the Emperors the *toga* went out of fashion. As only free-born citizens were permitted to wear the *toga*, it was an honorary garment, and at the same time distinguished the Romans from other nations; hence *gens togata* is used for Roman people. As the *toga* was worn only in peace (the warrior wore the *sagum*), the word *toga* is sometimes used as a metaphor for peace, or peaceful citizens. The *toga* was thrown over the left shoulder and passed over the right arm which thus remained entirely free. From the breast downwards it was sewed together, and, as the Romans had no pockets, the hollow called *sinus* in front of the breast was used to put small articles in. The variety, the colour, the fineness of the wool, and the ornaments attached to it, indicated the rank of the citizen. Generally it was white (*toga alba*). Rich persons wore wide *togæ*, the poor, narrow ones. Candidates for office wore a pure white *toga*. The mourning *toga* was black. Persons prosecuted at law wore a dirty, or old, or grey, or in general unsightly *toga* (*togæ sordidæ*). If it was ornamented with a purple stripe, it was called *toga prætexta*. Such was worn by all superior magistrates and priests. This ornamental *toga* was also worn by boys and girls, the former till their seventeenth, the latter till their fourteenth year, after which the former changed it for the *toga virilis*, *i. e.*, the common simple white *toga*, which was also called *purra* and *libera*. The *triumphatores* wore a *toga* adorned with gold and purple (*toga picta*, also *palmata*)."—*Popular Encyclopædia.*

the most costly branches of that service being allotted to Class I., and so on downward. The residuum were also liable to military service, but at the cost of the state. As to the residuum, however, the authorities are not agreed.

The Franchise.—As Servius taxed the people according to their individual means and arranged them in classes according to their wealth, so he endeavoured to fix the franchise upon rational and equitable principles. For that purpose he distributed the members of the various classes into what were termed centuries—in this instance, the word century signifies division, not 100; some say of 194, others of 199. Each century had one vote. Livy gives the following distribution:—

	CENTURIES.
Cavalry (Knights)	18
Infantry—	
1 Class Seniores	41
Juniores	41
2 Class Seniores	10
Juniores	10
3 Class Seniores	10
Juniores	10
4 Class Seniores	10
Juniores	10
5 Class Seniores	15
Juniores	15
Accensi. Velati	1
Buglers, etc., Seniores	1
Juniores	1
Proletarii and capite censi	1
	194

The military duties of the *seniores* (*æt.* 46) were confined to the defence of the city. The *juniores* were compelled to serve abroad.

Though in all cases, as will be seen, the *seniores* had the same number of votes as the *juniores* of the same class, yet the century of *seniores* in each instance was composed of fewer members than the corresponding century of *juniores*. The intention and effect was to neutralise the undue influence of numbers, to balance numerous youth by less numerous but more experienced age, and the comparative poverty of the many by the wealth of the few. The assembly of the centuries was styled the *comitia centuriata.*

Comitia Centuriata.—These assemblies were held in the Campus Martius, and were convoked by the sound of the bugle. While one section went to vote, the remainder watched in arms on the Janiculum. The suffrages were taken and calculated by centuries beginning with the knights, and then the classes in their order.

It is obvious from an inspection of the above table that if the knights and the sections of the first class all voted one way, voting by the rest was useless. Livy says that it was rarely necessary to call upon the second class. (*Liv. lib.* 26. 2.)

The Comitia Curiata and Comitia Centuriata, concurrent.—The institution of the *comitia centuriata* was not in substitution for, but in addition to, the *comitia curiata.* What attributes belonged, or were supposed to belong properly, to the *comitia centuriata* when first instituted, history does not show. In the course of time, however, the making of laws, determining criminal charges, and the creating of magistrates, became theirs. As their functions increased, those of the *comitia curiata* proportionately decreased.

The local tribes (*ex locis*).—The great increase in the population induced Servius to extend the dimensions of the city. This he did by enclosing the seven hills, after which he divided the whole into four tribes :—the *Palatina*, *Collina*, *Esquilina*, and the *Suburana.* The districts assigned to the first three were those occupied by the three ancient tribes. These four urban tribes expanded with the growth of the city, but were never increased in number, with these tribes *ex locis* the ancient tribes *ex generibus* were consolidated. Henceforth the word tribes signifies the tribes *ex locis.* It was by tribes the taxes were levied, and the legions recruited. Each tribe had its peculiar religious system and sacrifices. The members of a tribe styled their fellows *tribules, tribulis meus.* In the course of time these tribes acquired political importance.

The Knights (*Equites*).—As the knights, though at first mere cavalry soldiers, were destined to become of considerable political importance, in short, to hold the political ground between the senators on the one hand and the body of the plebeians on the other, this appears a convenient place to direct attention to them.

Tradition tells us that the guard of Romulus was called *celeres*, that it consisted of 300 cavalry, 100 being derived from each of the three original tribes, by the name of which its members were respectively known.

We are told that Lucius Tarquin (A.U.C. 138—175) added three new centuries to the knights, composed of the youth of the wealthy and newly made patricians—the *minorum gentium*—and that by Servius (A.U.C. 176—219) twelve other centuries, recruited from the then most wealthy plebeian families, were further added. These eighteen centuries of cavalry marched at the head of the classes and were the first to vote.

That innovations such as have been described must have been distasteful in the extreme to the patricians, need hardly be said. That the popularity of Servius with the rest of the community was certain to have been great, seems equally clear.

Servius was murdered by the emissary of his son-in-law and successor at the instance of his own daughter Tullia.

Tarquinius Superbus, A.U.C. 220—244 (B.C. 534—510).—After the murder of Servius Tullius, L. Tarquinius, subsequently styled Superbus (the proud), ascended the throne without being either elected by the senate and the people, or sanctioned by the *curiæ*. The rights and privileges conferred upon the plebeians by Servius were abolished. The patricians rejoiced, but only for the moment. Tarquinius surrounded himself with a body guard, usurped all power, and took the entire administration into his own hands. He never condescended to consult, or even to assemble the senate.

By the force of his arms he overcame and captured Suessa Pometia,[1] a wealthy Volscian town with a fertile and luxurious domain. By force or treachery, he made Gabii,[1] a Latin town,

[1] 128.

his own. All Latium was made to bow before the majesty of Rome. In order to enable him to complete the building of the magnificent temple of Jupiter on the Capitoline Hill, which his father, during a struggle with the Latins, had vowed to erect, as also to execute other public works of magnitude, he not only exhausted his treasury, but oppressed and failed to pay his labourers.

Discontent began to speak aloud. He resolved on the capture of Ardea,[1] a wealthy town of the Rutulians, as a means of recouping his exhausted exchequer, and satisfying the discontented workmen. Siege was laid to the town. Meanwhile, the vile son of the king, Sextus Tarquinius, overcame the chaste Lucretia. By the threat that, unless she yielded to his lust, he would murder her, and lay a slave with his throat cut beside her body, he accomplished his foul purpose. She immediately after sent messages to her husband and her father, begging them to visit her, accompanied by trusted friends. They went. She saw them, told her tale of woe, called upon them to avenge her, and then thrust a dagger to her heart. The facts noised abroad excited universal execration. The king was deposed, and he, together with the whole *gens* of the Tarquinii, was exiled. Regal Rome was no more. (A.U.C. 244,—B.C. 510.)

The annihilation instead of the reformation of royalty has by many been regarded as Rome's fatal error. From the moment that royalty was abolished, the distinction between patrician and plebeian became illogical. Theoretical equality was the necessary consequence: actual equality is an impossibility.

[1] 128.

Chapter II.

THE REPUBLIC.—1st Period.

A.U.C. 244 till A.U.C. 354;—B.C. 510 till B.C. 400.

The establishment of the Consulate and the Rex Sacrificulus, or Rex Sacrorum, A.U.C. 245,—B.C. 509.—On the expulsion of the Tarquins, it was resolved that no one thereafter should bear in Rome the title of king, and that, with the exception of the king's pontifical duties, all his powers should vest in two consuls, who should be annually elected, and who should alternately, for one month at a time, during the year, hold the *fasces*, the emblem of the *imperium*.

The king's pontifical duties were vested in an officer styled the *rex sacrificulus*, or *rex sacrorum*. The institutions of Servius were restored. The senate was again raised to its full numerical strength—300. As the new senators were taken from the equestrian order they were in many instances plebeians.

To distinguish the new from the old senators, the new were styled *conscripti;* hence, from this period the senate was addressed as *patres conscripti*, *i.e.*, *patres et conscripti*.

The two first consuls were Brutus, who fell in battle when resisting an attempt of Tarquinius to regain the throne, and Valerius who, subsequently, for his public spirit, was surnamed *Publicola*.

Leges Valeriæ, A.U.C. 245, 246 (B.C. 509, 508).—The consul, Valerius Publicola, reduced to written law and extended to the plebeians the patrician custom of *provocatio ad populum*, by which any citizen condemned by a magistrate to be put to death, scourged, or even fined, had the right of appeal to the people (*provocatio ad populum*). He defined the position and powers of the *quæstores parricidii*, and created a new magistracy styled *quæstores*, whose duty it was to collect the public taxes. He further enacted that any one convicted of aiming at royalty, or assuming authority not vested in him by the people, should, with all his substance, be devoted to the gods.

Valerius concluded the first treaty that Rome had with Carthage[1] (A.U.C. 246, 247,—B.C. 508, 507). Rome, at the instance of her exiled king, was besieged by Porsenna, the king or lord of Clusium[2] in Etruria, who ultimately concluded a treaty with Rome. In A.U.C. 253 (B.C. 501) the Romans became involved in a serious war with the Latins.

A Patrician Dictator (*Magister Populi*), A.U.C. 253 (B.C. 501).—In order the more effectually to enable the Romans to cope with the Latins, all other officers were suspended, and absolute power was vested in the hands of T. Larcius. From his decision there was no appeal. He marched on foot at the head of the infantry, preceded by twenty-four lictors. Larcius was succeeded by others. A. Postumius was dictator at the battle of Lake Regillus,[2] A.U.C. 258 (B.C. 496).

The results of the war were plebeian poverty; the necessity of borrowing from the patricians; inability to repay; the adjudication of the debtors to their creditors as bondsmen—*addicti;* cruel treatment by their masters, and general plebeian discontent.

In B.C. 495 an old man who had served in many wars rushed into the forum and showed the bleeding stripes on his back, the doing of his cruel patrician creditor. The plebeians rose in insurrection. The Volscian army was marching against Rome. The patricians promised the plebeians justice. The plebeians enlisted; the Volscians were defeated. The patricians were faithless. The plebeians rose in open revolt. The Sabines threatened Rome. The plebeians said, "Let them come, we fight no more." M. Valerius was made dictator. He was a just man; he promised the plebeians redress; they enlisted; the foe was repulsed.

This period is specially noteworthy, it being generally accepted as the end of Roman tradition and the commencement of the historic period.

[1] 115. [2] 128.

Tribuni Plebis, A.U.C. 260 (B.C. 494).—Two plebeian tribunes were appointed. In A.U.C. 283 (B.C. 471), the number was raised to five, *i.e.*, one for each class, and in A.U.C. 297 (B.C. 457), that number was doubled. Their persons were declared sacred. Their houses, open day and night, were refuges to which any one who considered himself injured might fly. They presided in the assemblies of the plebeian tribes. They had the right to intercede (*intercessio*) with the senate or a magistrate. They could veto the act of either. Thenceforth the senate may be regarded as the guardian of patrician interests, the tribunes as the guardians of those of the plebeians. The tribunes were elected by the *centuries*. Their appointment was ratified by the *curiæ*.

Owing to the secession of the plebeians having taken place during the autumn of B.C. 493, the land had been completely neglected. There was a famine. Corn was imported from Sicily.[1] A patrician, one Coriolanus, suggested that the plebeians should not be allowed to have it, except in barter for their newly acquired privileges. The senate declared the suggestion inhuman.

Comitia Tributa, A.U.C. 265 (B.C. 489).—The first sitting of this assembly was held with the concurrence of the senate, and for the purpose of trying the patrician Coriolanus. He failed to appear, and, in his absence, was condemned.

This assembly was solely composed of plebeians convoked by tribes. It was convened without the consultation of augurs. Though, in law, the entire population was divided into local tribes, in fact, the constitution of these assemblies by tribes was purely plebeian.

Plebeian Ediles (*Ædiles Plebeii*).—Another consequence of the plebeian secession was the appointment of two plebeian ediles, whose duty it was to superintend the details of the police administration; they also acted as judges in cases referred to them by the tribunes.

In B.C. 486, Sp. Cassius, in his third consulship, concluded a

[1] 130.

treaty offensive and defensive between the Romans, the Latins, and the Hernicans. He also proposed an agrarian law. Its object was the removal of a rapidly growing abuse. The fact is, that large portions of the *ager publicus*, which having been conquered in war belonged by law to all, were then in and were gradually increasing in the hands of private patricians. Cassius proposed that part of it should be taken from the patricians and distributed among those plebeians who had no landed property. The patricians took the alarm, and circulated the report that Cassius aimed at royalty. He was tried, condemned, and put to death, B.C. 485.

In B.C. 479, Kæso Fabius, who had taken part in the condemnation of Cassius, but who was now popular with the plebeians, proposed that the lands taken in war should be distributed in equal proportions among the plebeians. "For," said he, "it is but just that those should have them, by whose sweat and blood they have been gained." Fabius was treated by the patricians as a renegade. The Fabii, 306 in number, with 4,000 clients, emigrated; one member of the family alone remained to continue the race at Rome.

Unaided, the Fabii waged war against Veii.[1] Success made them careless. The Etruscans, from their ambush, fell upon them. They were all massacred, B.C. 477. The consul, T. Menenius, could have saved them, but would not.

A Consul impeached by Tribunes, A.U.C. 278 (B.C. 476).—During a truce with the Etruscans two of the tribunes impeached T. Menenius for having neglected to save the Fabii on the Cremera.[1] He was fined. Impeachments by the tribunes became a practice.

The Lex Publilia.—In A.U.C. 282 (B.C. 472), the tribune, Publilius Volero, proposed that the tribunes should be elected in the *comitia tributa;* and in B.C. 471, in conjunction with C. Lætorius, he proposed that the *plebeian ediles* should also be elected in the *comitia tributa*, and that the resolutions of the

[1] 128.

plebeians (*plebiscita*) should extend to matters affecting patricians as well as plebeians, and should be binding on all alike. The patricians in vain endeavoured to prevent those propositions being put to the vote. Violence was resorted to to break up the plebeian assembly. The consul sent his lictors to seize the tribune Lætorius. Lætorius sent his men to arrest the consul. The plebeians seized and occupied the Capitol. The senate yielded. The proposals of the tribunes were carried; they were sanctioned by the senate, and were known as the *lex Publilia.* For the time being that law was a dead letter, but the seed of an ample crop was sown. In the year 463 B.C. Rome was ravaged by a fearful pestilence, thousands perished. In B.C. 462 the tribune, C. Terentillius Arsa, for the purpose of reforming the state, proposed that five competent persons should be appointed to frame a code of laws binding on all citizens. The suggestion was violently opposed by the patricians year after year, till ultimately, in B.C. 453, the patricians yielded, and an embassy, it is said, was sent to Greece[1] to study the working of the laws of that country.

The Decemviri, A.U.C. 303 (B.C. 451).—For the double purpose of making the law uniform, and known to all, consuls, tribunes, quæstors, and ediles laid down their power for a period of one year, or rather their collective power was vested in a body of ten patricians styled decemviri. These ten worked well during their year of office, and at its close published ten tables of law, which were publicly exhibited. Their successors added two tables; but having abused their power they were overthrown, and the former offices re-established. Two of the ten perished in prison, the remaining eight were sent into exile, and the estates of all were confiscated B.C. 449 (A.U.C. 305). Of these twelve tables Cicero speaks in the most enthusiastic terms. For ages they were regarded as the *carmen necessarium*, and were committed to memory by the Roman youth. Unfortunately fragments only of them are in our possession. These fragments have been collected from different authors, throughout whose pages they are scattered. They have been recon-

[1] 175.

structed in part by conjecture and in part by certain indications given by Cicero and Dionysius. As so reconstructed they are as follows :—

Table 1. Treats of the Summons before the *Magister*.
2. Judicial proceedings.
3. Executions.
4. The rights of a Father.
5. Inheritance and Tutelage.
6. Dominion and Possession.
7. Real Property Law.
8. Torts.
9. Public Law.
10. Sacred Law.
11. Marriage (supplement to the first five tables).
12. Supplement to the last five tables.

The following is a concise statement of the provisions of the Twelve Tables arranged under the heads respectively of— 1. Public substantive law; 2. Private substantive law; and 3. Adjective law.

THE TWELVE TABLES.

PUBLIC SUBSTANTIVE LAW.

Generally.—All previous enactments inconsistent with the provisions of these tables are hereby annulled (Tab. 12. 5). All laws must be general. No law shall be enacted that affects one private individual merely (9. 1). No law that inflicts capital punishment—*i.e.*, deprivation of life, liberty, or citizenship—can be enacted by any person or persons other than the *comitia centuria* (9. 2).

Roads, &c.—Roads must be at the least 8 feet broad and 16 feet at the turning at the end (7. 6). A space of $2\frac{1}{2}$ feet at least must be left between adjacent buildings for the purpose of ventilation (7. 1). A space of 5 feet must be left between adjacent fields for the purpose of access and the turning of the plough; this vacant land cannot be acquired by *usucapio* (7. 4). (*Provisions regulating Plantations, Excavations, and Erections on neighbouring Plots of Land* (7. 2).)

Burial.—It is unlawful to burn or bury the dead within the city (10. 1), or to erect any funeral pile or sepulchre within 60 feet of another man's house, except with his consent (10. 10). Neither the sepulchre nor its vestibule can be acquired by *usucapio* (10. 11). The flute-players at a funeral must not exceed ten in number. The dead must not be buried or burned in more than three robes or in more than three fillets of purple (10. 3). Women must not tear their hair nor make immoderate wailings (10. 4). The bones of the deceased must not be collected for the purpose of subsequent funeral, except in the case of death in battle or in a foreign country (10. 5, 8). (*Provisions prohibiting the Embalming of the Bodies of Slaves, Funereal Banquets, expensive Libations, Coronal Garlands, and the Erection of Incense Altars* (10. 6).) If the deceased has either personally, or by his slaves or horses, obtained any public trophy, he shall be entitled to the honours it confers (10. 7). Gold must not be buried with the dead, but if the teeth are fastened with gold that may be either buried or burned (10. 9). The wood of the funeral pile must not be smoothed (10. 2).

When lawful to Kill.—It is lawful to kill any one committing a robbery by night (8. 12). A thief surprised during the day must not be put to death unless he attempts to defend himself with arms (8. 3).

The Penalty of Death.—Death shall be the penalty for:—

(1) Exciting an enemy against the Roman people (9. 5).
(2) Delivering a citizen to the enemy (9. 5).
(3) For seditious gatherings by night in the city (8. 26).
(4) For the acceptance of a bribe by a judge or arbitrator (9. 3).
(5) For arson of a house or haystack near a house. In this case the death shall be by fire and preceded by scourging (8. 10).

(6) For depasturing, or cutting a neighbour's crops by night, when the offender is of the age of puberty; if under that age, scourging at the discretion of the magistrates, and fine of double the value of the damage done shall be substituted (8. 9).

(7) For fraud by a patron on his client. Let him be sacrificed to the gods, *sacer esto* (8. 21).

(8) For the practice of enchantment or the use of poisonous drugs (8. 21).

(9) For perjury. The perjured shall be thrown from the Tarpeian rock (8. 23).

(10) For homicide (8. 24).

(11) Libellers and public defamers are liable to capital punishment (8. 1). A person whose limb is broken by another may retaliate unless compensation is offered (8. 2).

Theft.—Theft is divided into two classes, viz., *furtum manifestum* and *furtum nec manifestum* (8. 15).[1]

A freeman taken in the act of theft shall be scourged and made over by *addictio* to the person he has robbed. A slave shall be scourged and thrown from the Tarpeian rock. Those under the age of puberty shall, at the discretion of the *magister*, be scourged and condemned in damages (8. 14). A theft of private property may be treated as a tort merely, or be settled between the parties. (See *post*, "Theft" and "Adjective Law.")

Usury.—The highest legal interest shall be 8½ per centum per annum. The penalty for exceeding is the quadruple (8. 18).

PRIVATE SUBSTANTIVE LAW.

Societies.—The members of a corporation or college (*sodales*) are free to make what rules binding upon themselves they may think fit, provided that they do not contravene the law (8. 27).

Marriage.—Marriage between patricians and plebeians is forbidden (11. 1). The marital power over a woman may be acquired by *usus* (6. 4), *i.e.*, by cohabitation for one year. By absenting herself from her husband's house for three successive

[1] The distinction between *furtum conceptum*, *oblatum*, and *non exhibitum* had reference to the accidental circumstances attending the act, and the particular action to which each gave rise. See Index "Furtum."

nights in each year, a woman can prevent her husband ever acquiring marital power over her (6. 4). A child born more than ten months after the death of its reputed father is illegitimate. Monstrous or deformed offspring are to be at once destroyed (4. 1). So long as a child is in the *patria potestas* the father may imprison, scourge, sell, or even take his life (4. 2). Three consecutive sales of the son by the father shall release the son from the *patria potestas* (4. 3). All females, vestals alone excepted, are in perpetual tutelage. A vestal is free both from tutelage and from the *patria potestas* (5. 1). *Res mancipi* of females cannot be acquired by *usucapio,* except when delivered to the possessor by the woman herself with the sanction of her tutor (5. 2).

Idiots.—The custody of an idiot and his property, there being no curator (*custos*) belongs to the *agnates,* and in default of *agnates* to the *gentiles* (5. 7).

Usucapio.—Possession by a citizen for two years in the case of land, and for one year in the case of other property, vests it in the possessor (6. 3). Possession by an alien, however long, cannot vest in him the property of a citizen (6. 5). Title to stolen goods cannot be acquired by *usucapio* (8. 17).

Contracts, Purchase and Sale.—In the case of things sold the property does not pass till payment (6. 10).

Nexum and Mancipium.[1]—In the case of *nexum* and *mancipium,*

[1] By the Roman law, as by most other legal systems, all *things* are, as to their alienability, divided into two classes, viz., those that may be alienated by simple handing over, and those the alienation of which must be evidenced by certain formalities. These classes were respectively designated by the expressions *res nec mancipi* and *res mancipi.* The *res mancipi* were lands, houses, slaves, and ordinary beasts of burden, while all other things taken separately, and not as a *universitas,* were *res nec mancipi.* The solemn form required in the case of *res mancipi* was either *mancipatio* or *in jure cessio.* The persons present were—the contracting parties, an independent intermediary, the balance holder (*libripens*), and five witnesses. That form of contracting was styled "by the brass and balance" (*per æs et libram*). As every contract must be for actual or assumed valuable consideration, that consideration was supposed to be placed in the scale, and to balance the value of that for which it was given. It in fact, however, was the reciprocal promise that bound either party. It was the *libripens* and the witnesses who made the bargain binding by their ability to testify as to what it was. A contract, accompanied by the ceremony *per æs et libram,* was styled *nexum.* The only other method of alienating *res mancipi* was by a formal ceremony before a magistrate, styled *in jure cessio.*

the words used at the time of the weighing out constitute the contract—the law (6. 1). Either party subsequently denying that he used the language actually used renders himself liable to a penalty of double the amount of the value of the subject of the contract (6. 2).

Rights in Alieno Solo.—When a road is rendered impassable, the owner of a right of way may cross where he pleases (7. 6). Branches of trees over-hanging adjoining property must be pruned up to fifteen feet from the ground (7. 8). The owner of adjacent property is entitled to a guarantee against threatened damage from the aqueduct and other works of his neighbour (7. 7). The proprietor of fruit has the right to go on to his neighbour's land to pick up the fruit that falls thereon from his trees (7. 9).

Succession.—A father may by will dispose of his entire property as he pleases, and may appoint such tutors as he may think fit (5. 3). In default of appointment of a tutor the *agnates* are the legitimate tutors (5. 6). In the event of intestacy the property of the deceased goes to the *suus hæres;* in default of *suus hæres*, it goes to the nearest *agnate* (5. 4); in default of *agnates*, to the *gentiles* (5. 5). The inheritance is divisible among the heirs. Division may be enforced by the *actio familiæ erciscundæ* (5. 9 and 10). The patron succeeds to the inheritance of the enfranchised dying without *hæres suus.*

ADJECTIVE LAW.

Generally.—*In jure cessio* and *mancipatio* are confirmed (6. 11). Every citizen has the right to institute an action to remove a suspected tutor. The penalty upon a tutor convicted of defalcation is double the value of the property abstracted (8. 20). Any one who, being summoned *in jus* (commonly translated, before a *magister*[1]), refuses to go, may, should he attempt flight, be

[1] *Magister.*—The term *magister* has various significations in Roman law, viz.: a dictator was styled *magister populi;* the head of the cavalry was styled *magister equitum;* when the empire was divided by Constantine into four prætorian præfecturates, the expression *magister militum* designated

arrested in the presence of witnesses and detained by force. If the defendant is infirm or ill, the plaintiff must provide a conveyance, but is not bound to provide a covered conveyance. When the parties cannot come to terms, the action must be entered for trial either in the *comitium* or in the *forum* (a place where justice was administered) before midday. If the case is not finished before sunset it shall be adjourned, in which case bail for the future attendance may be demanded. A rich man must be *vindex* (*bail*) for another rich man. Any one may be bail for a *proletarius* (Tab. 1). Serious illness, or an engagement with a *peregrinus*, is ground for adjournment. Witnesses must be summoned twenty-seven days before the hearing. No trial can commence till each party has deposited the *sacramentum* (Tab. 2).

Interim Possession.—In an action to try the right to property (*manuum consertio*) the *magister* may, pending the litigation, give the possession to which of the litigants he shall think fit. In the case of a claim to liberty, the *magister* shall give the interim possession in favour of liberty (6. 6).

Wrongful Conversion.—Specific chattels, the property of one in the possession of another without the owner's consent, may be recovered by *vindicatio*. Timber of one wrongfully attached to a building of another, or used to support a vine, cannot be removed, but the owner may bring an action against the user to recover the double value (6. 7, 9).

Boundaries.—In the case of dispute as to boundaries, it is the duty of the *magister* to appoint three arbitrators to settle the matter (7. 5).

Right to Chattels.—In the case of disputed right to possession of a chattel the *magister* shall appoint three arbitrators to hear

the commander of the infantry; at times it is almost equivalent to our term "trustee in bankruptcy"; as here used, it indicates a legal functionary, but not a judge (*judex*), for it is never, I believe, used as synonymous with *judex*. When not used as a technical legal term, the context commonly suffices to indicate the sense in which it is used.

and determine. The measure of damage is a sum equal to double the profits (12. 3).

Bodily Injuries.—The measure of damages in the case of the fracture of a bone (of a tooth) of a freeman, shall be 300 asses; in the case of a slave, 150 (8. 3). In the case of the slightest bodily injury, the measure of damages shall be 25 asses (8. 4).

Theft.—In the case of *furtum nec manifestum* the penalty shall be double the value of the thing stolen (8. 16). For theft or damage by a slave his master must be sued by an *actio noxalis* (12. 2).

Fraudulent Bailee.—A fraudulent bailee shall be liable to a penalty equal to double the amount of the damage sustained (8. 19).

Damage to Trees.—The penalty for wrongfully felling the tree of another is 25 asses (8. 11).

Depasturing.—An action lies for depasturing on a neighbour's land (8. 7).

Pignoris Capio.—When a beast has been let on hire for the express object of devoting the hire money to the purposes of sacrifices, or when a beast has been sold for the purpose of being sacrificed, and the purchaser in the one case, the hirer in the other, omits to pay the vendor or bailor, the latter shall be entitled to the *pignoris capio* [1] (12. 1). The penalty for consecrating anything that is the subject of a suit is double its value (12. 4).

[1] *Manus injectio* and *pignoris capio* were words of execution—the former on the person, the latter on the goods of a debtor. *Pignoris capio*, the seizure by a private person of property of his debtor, was only lawful in a few defined cases, and that on the ground of public policy: *e.g.*, the property of one who had bought a beast for sacrificial purposes, but had not paid for it, might be seized by the vendor of the beast to satisfy its price; tax-gatherers might seize property for the purposes of securing taxes; soldiers might seize the property of their paymasters for the purpose of securing their pay, &c. (*æs militare, æs equestre, æs hordiarium*). (See INDEX.)

Negligence.—In the case of damage done through negligence, damages are recoverable for the damage sustained (8. 5). When the wrongdoer is too poor to make good the damage done, *e. g.*, by setting fire to the house of another, he shall be liable to moderate chastisement (8. 10).

Animals.—In the case of damage done by a quadruped, compensation may be recovered from its owner, or the animal be forfeited (8. 6).

Witnesses.—One who has been a witness, or who has acted as scalebearer (*libripens*), and refuses to testify to the facts, shall be branded as infamous, and declared incapable of giving or receiving testimony (8. 22).

Judgment Debtors.—A judgment debtor, in a case of money lent, shall have thirty days' grace within which to pay, or give security; on default, the judgment creditor may forcibly (*manus injectio*) take the debtor before the *magister* again. If he then neither pays nor gives security, his creditor may keep him in chains for two months, during which period the debtor may live as he pleases, at his own cost. If he is destitute his creditor must supply him with one pound of bread daily. If the debt is not then paid, the *magister* shall pass the sentence of *addictio* (by which the debtor became the absolute property of his creditor), after which the creditor may either sell his debtor to any foreigner resident beyond the Tiber,[1] or may kill him. If the debtor has more than one creditor, his creditors may divide his body between them (Tab. 3).

Appeal.—A right of appeal to the people in the case of any penal sentence appears to have been given (9. 4).

It is said that, by the provisions of the twelve Tables, all the patricians and their clients, as well as the plebeians, thenceforth became members of the local tribes: be that as it may, the consuls Valerius and Horatius secured, or, perhaps more correctly, endeavoured to secure to the *plebiscita* a force they had not previously enjoyed.

Lex Valeria Horatia—De Plebiscitis, A.U.C. 305 (B.C. 449).—This law enacted that the *plebiscita, i. e.*, the laws promulgated by the plebeian assembly, the *comitia tributa*, should be obligatory on all citizens (*ut quod tributim plebes jussisset, populum teneret*).

The Canuleian Law—De Connubio Patrum et Plebis, A.U.C. 309 (B.C. 445).—At the instance of the tribune Canuleius, the provision in the Twelve Tables prohibiting marriage between the patricians and the plebeians was abrogated.

The colleagues of Canuleius also proposed that thenceforth one of the consuls should be a plebeian. The opposition of the patricians led to a compromise.

Military Tribunes (*Tribuni Militum*), A.U.C. 310 (B.C. 444).—Military tribunes with consular power (*tribuni militares consulari potestate*) elected from either order were declared eligible, in lieu of consuls, at the discretion of the senate.

The patricians, fearing that the plebeians would shortly lay claim to the consulship, resolved to sever from it one of the most important of the consul's functions, and to create as a distinct office that of *censor*.

The Censors (*Censores*), A.U.C. 311 (B.C. 443).—The censors, two in number, were elected by the *comitia centuriata* from the members of the senate (patricians). The same senator could not occupy the post twice. The term of office was five years, *i. e.*, from census to census. They were the guardians of the public and private morals. The census determined the rank of every citizen and his status in society. The duration of the office was reduced in B.C. 434 to eighteen months, so that, from that date, in every *lustrum*, or period of five years, there were three and a half years during which there were no censors.

In B.C. 440, famine drove many of the poor to commit suicide.

In B.C. 439, L. Q. Cincinnatus was appointed dictator. In B.C. 426, the Romans were defeated before Veii.[1] Nothing but wars of little note marks the history of Rome till the year B.C. 407, when the senate, unsolicited, issued a decree that thenceforth the soldiers should receive pay from the public treasury. In B.C. 405, Veii[1] was besieged.

[1] 128.

CHAPTER III.

THE REPUBLIC—*continued.*

THE FOURTH CENTURY B.C.

i. e., A.U.C. 355 till A.U.C. 454;—B.C. 399 till B.C. 300.

IN B.C. 396, after a siege of nine years, Veii[1] succumbed to the Romans, then led by the dictator Camillus. The Veientine territory was distributed in lots of seven *jugera* each among the plebeians.

Regarding themselves as invincible, the Romans refused satisfaction to the Gauls for a wrong done to them by the Roman ambassador. Fabius Brennus at the head of 70,000 Gauls marched on Rome. The Romans went out to meet him, but at the little river Allia,[1] seeing the strength of the foe, the Romans threw down their arms and fled on the 18th July, B.C. 390 (*dies Alliensis*). The Gauls seized Rome and burned it to the ground. The Capitol alone stood out, defended by 1,000 men, till, pressed by hunger and disease, many of the Gauls retired from Rome. It is said that at the moment that Rome was weighing out the 1,000 lbs. of gold for which Brennus had promised to depart, Camillus, recalled from exile, appeared before Rome at the head of an army by whom the Gauls were defeated; there, and again on the road to Gabii.[1] Neither Polybius nor Diodorus makes any mention of this alleged interposition of Camillus. With the exception of the Sabines and some Latin towns, all the neighbouring towns and tribes endeavoured to recover their independence in the hour of Rome's distress. Between this period and B.C. 376 Rome practically recovered her external

[1] 128.

influence. Within, however, the poverty of the lower orders, consequent on the destruction and rebuilding of Rome, had revived the old cry—the oppression of the rich.

In that year (B.C. 376), L. Licinius Stolo and L. Sextius were elected tribunes. They proposed three laws, viz.:—I. That the interest already paid by debtors should be deducted from the principal debt, and that the remainder should be paid off by three yearly instalments. II. That no one should be allowed to possess more than 500 *jugera* of the public land. III. That thenceforth consuls should be elected instead of consular tribunes, and that one of the consuls should always be a plebeian. These propositions were stoutly resisted by the patricians, and at their instance by the other tribunes. Licinius and Sextius were re-elected year by year.

In B.C. 369, the tribunes were equally divided as to the propositions, when Licinius brought forward a fourth bill, suggesting that instead of the two patricians who till then had been entrusted with the keeping of the Sibylline books,[1] ten

[1] "*Sibyllæ*, certain women said to have been inspired by heaven with the knowledge of futurity. They flourished in different parts of the world, but their number is unknown. Plato speaks of one, others of two, Pliny of three, Ælian of four, and Varro of ten, an opinion which is universally adopted by the learned. These ten Sibyls generally resided in the following places: Persia, Libya, Delphi, Cunæ in Italy, Erythræa, Samos, Cumæ in Ælia, Marpessa on Hellespont, Ancyra in Phrygia, and Tiburtis. The most celebrated of the Sibyls is that of Cumæ in Italy, whom some have called by the different names of Amalthæa, Demophile, Herophile, Daphne, Manto, Phemonoë, and Deiphobe. It is said that Apollo became enamoured of her, and that, to make her sensible to his passion, he offered to give her whatever she should ask. The Sibyl demanded to live as many years as she had grains of sand in her hand, but unfortunately forgot to ask for the enjoyment of the health, vigour, and bloom of which she was then in possession. The god granted her her request, but she refused to gratify the passion of her lover, though he offered her perpetual youth and beauty. Some time after she became old and decrepit; her form decayed; melancholy, paleness, and haggard looks succeeded to bloom and cheerfulness. She had already lived about 700 years when Æneas came to Italy, and some have imagined she had three centuries more to live before her years would be as numerous as the grains of sand which she had in her hand. She gave Æneas instructions how to find his father in the infernal regions, and even conducted him to the entrance of hell. It was usual for the Sibyl to write her prophecies on leaves which she placed at the entrance to her cave, and it required particular care in such as consulted her to take up these leaves before they were dispersed by the wind, as their meaning then became incomprehensible. According to the most authentic historians of the Roman Republic, one of the Sibyls came to the palace of Tarquin the Second, with nine volumes which she offered to sell for a very high price. The monarch disregarded her, and she immediately disappeared, and soon after returned,

custodians should be appointed, of whom one-half should be plebeians. This proposition was to meet the patrician objection that the plebeians, not having the same auguries as the patricians, nor, consequently, the knowledge necessary to enable them to interpret the will of the gods, were not qualified to become consuls.

The existing siege of Velitræ[1] was the excuse offered for postponing the discussion of these propositions. That siege over, the tribunes returned to the charge. The Gauls reappeared: M. Furius Camillus, appointed for the fifth time dictator, defeated and dispersed them. Licinius and Sextius were re-elected for the tenth time. The rogations became law.

The Licinian Law—Plebeians admitted to the Consulate, A.U.C. 387 (B.C. 367).—L. Sextius was elected the first plebeian consul, B.C. 366. The patricians had, however, secured a compromise. Consular power was again lessened. To whom, it was asked, must the knowledge of the law and the right of interpreting it belong? According to the patricians, there could be but one answer:—To them, and to them alone. The judicial functions of the consuls were therefore vested in a new officer—a *prætor*.

when she had burned three of the volumes. She asked the same price for the remaining six books, and when Tarquin refused to buy them, she burned three more, and still persisted in demanding the same sum of money for the three that were left.

"This extraordinary behaviour astonished Tarquin; he bought the books, and the Sibyl instantly vanished; and never after appeared to the world. These books were preserved with great care by the monarch, and called the Sibylline verses. A college of priests was appointed to have the care of them, and such reverence did the Romans entertain for these prophetic books that they were consulted with the greatest solemnity, but only when the State seemed to be in danger. When the Capitol was burnt in the troubles of Sylla, the Sibylline verses, which were deposited there, perished in the conflagration; and to repair the loss which the public seemed to have sustained, commissioners were immediately sent to different parts of Greece, to collect whatever verses could be found of the inspired writings of the Sibyls. The fate of these Sibylline verses, which were collected after the conflagration of the Capitol, is unknown. There are now eight books of Sibylline verses extant, but they are universally reckoned spurious. They speak so plainly of our Saviour, of his sufferings and of his death, as even to surpass far the sublime predictions of Isaiah in minuteness of description; and therefore from this very circumstance it is evident that they were composed in the second century by some of the followers of Christianity, who wished to convince the heathen of their error, by assisting the cause of truth with the arms of pious artifice."—*Lempriere.*

[1] 128.

The First Prætor Urbanus, A.U.C. 387 (B.C. 367).—According to Pomponius, this officer was styled *urbanus* because of his administering the law in the city, "*qui urbanus appellatus est, quod in urbe jus redderet.*" He was nominated by the centuries, and selected from the patrician order. He convoked the senate, and presided over it. He assembled a *comitia*, and presented to them suggestions as to new laws.

Lex Licinia—De Modo Agrorum, A.U.C. 387 (B.C. 367).—This law prohibited the possession by any one man of more than 500 *jugera* of land under a penalty of 10,000 *asses*. It appears to have required the sale by the rich of all the land possessed by them over 500 *jugera*, and to have prescribed the mode in which it should be sold; the object being to bring land by purchase within the reach of the poorer classes.

Licinius was the first who was sentenced for the violation of his own law. He had 1,000 *jugera*, 500 of which, in order to conform to the letter of the law of which he was the author, he placed in his son's name. He was fined 10,000 *asses*.

Lex Licinia—De Ære Alieno, A.U.C. 387 (B.C. 367).—This law enacted that money already paid under the head of interest should be taken in reduction of the capital, and that the surplus should be paid by equal instalments within three years. Though of undoubted benefit to many, this law was insufficient to meet the case, for we find that in B.C. 357 the legal interest was fixed at ten per cent. per annum; that in B.C. 347 it was reduced to five per cent.; and that various expedients were subsequently resorted to to relieve the poor.

Lex Licinia—The Sibylline Verses, A.U.C. 387 (B.C. 367).—The Sibylline books or verses were entrusted to the custody of ten persons, of whom one-half were plebeians.

Ædiles Curules, A.U.C. 388 (B.C. 366).—Two patrician *ædiles* were appointed along with the plebeian *ædiles*, with whom they shared the criminal jurisdiction in annual rotation. They had analogous but superior functions. In addition they had the superintendence of the police, the temples, and the great festivals.

First Plebeian Dictator.—B.C. 356 saw the first plebeian dictator.

First Plebeian Censor.—B.C. 351 saw the first plebeian censor.

Between B.C. 362 and B.C. 343 Rome waged war against the Hernicans,[1] the Tiburtines,[1] the Etruscans of Tarquinii,[1] the Faliscans,[1] the Privernatans,[1] and the Gauls, in each instance with ultimate success. These may be regarded as the schools in which Rome learned the art of war, the Gauls being her best teachers.

Rome's first great military enterprise is to come—the Samnite[2] war. The Samnites were at that time the most powerful and warlike nation in Italy. Lucania[2] and Campania,[2] though then independent nations, had been Samnite colonies.

In B.C. 343 war was declared. Two consular armies took the field against the Samnites. M. Valerius Corvas met the Samnites on Mount Gaurus, in Campania. The struggle commenced which was to determine whether Rome or Samnium should have the sovereignty of Italy. Such was the position of the ground taken by the Romans that between victory and annihilation there was no choice. Both armies fought throughout the day, resolved to conquer or to die. The night was fast approaching, thousands had fallen on either side. The Romans made a final and desperate attack. The Samnites were routed. Cossus, thanks to the tactics of the intrepid F. Decius Mus, came up to the other Samnite army. It is said that 30,000 of the foe were cut to pieces.

The next year the Roman garrison at Capua[1] revolted. Debt and its horried consequences were the alleged causes. Valerius appeased the insurgents by a general cancelling of debts.

Rome or Latium? B.C. 340—338.—Next came the question as to whether Rome should be a mere Latin town, or sovereign

[1] 128. [2] 143.

of the whole of Latium.[1] The Latins demanded that one of the consuls and half of the senate should be Latins. Rome declared war. Her armies were successful. The Latin confederacy broke up. The towns surrendered one after another. The Latin domain lands were distributed among the Romans. The *connubium* and the *commercium* among the Latin towns were abolished. The inhabitants of some of the towns were raised to the rank of Roman citizens, other towns were weakened and humbled.

Leges Publiliæ, A.U.C. 415 (B.C. 339).—The dictator Publilius Philo, a patrician, and an exceedingly popular man, was, according to Livy, the author of three laws favourable to the plebeians and adverse to the patricians (*secundissimus plebei, adversus nobilitati*), viz.:—I. That the censors should be plebians; some say, that one of them should be. II. That the *plebiscita* should be binding on all—*ut plebiscita omnes quirites tenerent.* This law appears to have been in the same terms as the Valerian law of B.C. 449, and the subsequent Hortensian law of B.C. 287. III. That the *curiæ* should confirm the decision of the *centuries* previously to voting; in other words, it abolished the veto of the *curiæ* on laws passed by the *centuries.*

First Plebeian Prætor.—A.U.C. 417 (B.C. 337), saw the first plebeian prætor.

Lex Petillia Papiria—De Nexis, A.U.C. 428 (B.C. 326).—The practice of debtors assigning themselves *per æs et libram* to their creditors as security, or satisfaction, for debt was declared illegal. The servitude of the *nexi* was thus abolished.

The Second Samnite[2] War.—The years B.C. 326 and B.C. 304 are respectively given as the date of the beginning and close of the second great struggle between the Romans and the Samnites for supremacy. Of all the battles fought between them during these twenty-two years, that which stands out most conspicuously

[1] 128 [2] 143.

was fought in the narrow valley of Caudium (*furculæ Caudinæ*) B.C. 324. Hemmed in on every side the Romans were completely defeated and compelled to capitulate. One-half of that Roman army was cut to pieces. The survivors were compelled to pass under the yoke, the then ordinary mode in Italy of disgracing a defeated army. The noble-hearted C. Pontius, the Samnite general, proposed terms of peace, which were accepted and sworn to by the consuls; but, when they, with the remnant of their army returned to Rome, the whole population put on mourning. The senate refused to ratify the peace; they not merely resolved to sacrifice the 600 hostages left by the consuls, but decreed that those who had been parties to the treaty should be delivered up to the Samnites as persons who had deceived them.

Samnium was not the only matter on the Roman hands during those twenty-two years; they had several minor wars, in addition to which the Etruscan[1] war broke out in B.C. 311.

Appius Claudius the Blind, A.U.C. 442 (B.C. 312).—In B.C. 312, Appius Claudius, who had been elected censor in B.C. 313, distributed the whole body of the lower order among the tribes, possibly to increase the number of those entitled to serve in the army. Freedmen, as such, were not eligible. He also excluded from the list of senators the names of a large number of patricians, and substituted for them sons of freedmen. This list of senators was, however, set aside in the following year. He built the road from Rome to Capua, called "The queen of roads," and named after him *via Appia*. He built an aqueduct eight miles long—the oldest at Rome—the *aqua Appia*. He raised Cn. Flavius, a scribe, the son of a freedman, to the *curule ædileship*.

Jus Flavianum, A.U.C. 450 (B.C. 304).—Cnæus Flavius published a book, or list of the *dies fasti* and *nefasti*, called the "*fastorum libri*," and caused it to be exhibited in the forum on a tablet covered with gypsum. By this act, as Cicero expresses

[1] 127.

it, "he put out the crows' eyes" (*qui cornicum oculos confixerit*). By which we may take it to be intended to be understood, that he put an end to patrician mystery, not to say imposition, in relation to the *dies fasti* and *nefasti*.

In addition to this calendar, he made and published a collection of the *formulæ* of the *legis actiones*, which theretofore had been handed down by tradition and kept as knowledge peculiar to the patricians.

First Plebeian Pontiff and Augurs—Lex Ogulnia, A.U.C. 454 (B.C. 300).—To the tribunes Q. and C. Ogulnius the plebeians were indebted for the removal of the last trace of their political inferiority. These tribunes carried a law by which the number of the augurs was increased to nine, and that of the pontiffs to eight in addition to the *pontifex maximus*. The law provided that four of the pontiffs and five of the augurs should always be plebeians.

CHAPTER IV.

THE REPUBLIC—*continued.*

THE THIRD CENTURY B.C.

i.e., A.U.C. 455 till A.U.C. 554;—B.C. 299 till B.C. 200.

The Orators, Historians, Philosophers, Poets, &c., of the Period.

NEVIUS (CNEIUS), poet, first half of the third century.

PLAUTUS (MARCUS ACCINO), comic writer, flourished about B.C. 20.

CATO, orator and prose writer, born B.C. 232, died B.C. 148.

ENNIUS (QUINTUS), poet and historian, born B.C. 239, regarded by the Romans as the father of Roman poetry.

LIVIUS ANDRONICUS, the first Roman dramatist of whom we have any knowledge; is said to have been taken prisoner at the capture of Tarentum, B.C. 272, and carried to Rome.

IN B.C. 299, an army of Gauls, induced by their countrymen who had settled in Italy, crossed the Alps and, at the instance of the Etruscans, marched into the Roman territory. The Romans allowed their territory to be laid waste by them. Laden with booty, the Gauls returned to their homes. The Romans wreaked their vengeance on the Etruscans.

The Third and Last Samnite War.—Between B.C. 298 and B.C. 290, the third and last Samnite War was waged with varying success, ultimately terminating in the triumph of the Roman arms, and the practical annexation of Samnium to Rome. In B.C. 290, the Sabines revolted, were subdued, many made prisoners, and large tracts of land were annexed. Rome was now the mistress of central Italy.

That these perpetual wars should bring in their wake famine, poverty, disease, and consequent discontent, was but natural.

The plebeians once more, and for the last time, seceded, and encamped on the Janiculum, B.C. 287. Q. Hortensius was appointed dictator.

Lex Hortensia—De Plebiscitis, A.U.C. 468 (B.C. 286).—This law enacted that the *plebiscita* should be binding on all Romans. (*Ut plebiscita omnes quirites tenerent.*) From this date that law appears not to have been questioned. Previous laws apparently to the same effect, viz., the *Lex Horatia* and the *Lex Publilia*, had either fallen short of the terms of the *Lex Hortensia* or had been disregarded. It would appear that the *Lex Hortensia* abolished the veto of the senate upon legislative measures passed by the plebeian assembly.

Rome Mistress of all Italy.—Between B.C. 286 and B.C. 266, Rome made herself mistress of the whole of Italy proper (*Italia propria*), *i. e.*, that portion of Europe which is washed by the waters of the Mediterranean and the Adriatic, south of a line drawn overland between, and connecting, the little streams Macra [1] and Rubicon.[2]

Italy (*Italia*) in the wider sense of the term, that in which it was understood in the days of imperial Rome, comprehended the whole of the territory south of the Alps.

It was in B.C. 281, that Pyrrhus, King of Epirus,[3] one of the greatest generals of antiquity, the author of a work on military tactics, crossed over into Italy to aid the Tarentines [4] against Rome. It was he who, after a victory over the Romans on the banks of the Siris,[4] when congratulated on his success, said:—"One more such victory, and I shall be obliged to return to Epirus without a single soldier." Again, referring to the Roman army, he said:—"With such soldiers, the world would be mine, and it would belong to the Romans if I were their commander."

In B.C. 275, Pyrrhus was completely defeated by Curius

[1] 112. [2] 127. [3] 159. [4] 144.

Dentatus. His camp was taken, two of his elephants were killed, and four that were captured alive adorned the consul's triumph.

The Fourth and Last Samnite Rising.—In B.C. 268, the Samnites rose for the fourth and last time. It was but a feeble effort.

Though at this period the Romans had no literature of their own, it is said that they were familiar with that of Greece. Architecture, sculpture, and painting, however, had made considerable strides at Rome.

The First Punic War, B.C. 264 to B.C. 241.—(Punic from *Pœni*, Phœnicians—Carthage [1] was a Phœnician colony.) The first Punic war covers a period of twenty-three years. It was Rome's first great departure. It was the foundation of Rome's world-wide greatness. The patricians and the plebeians were at one.

Rome had no other Italian foe to conquer. To exist without some military enterprise on hand appeared to the Romans an impossibility. The republics of Rome and Carthage had long regarded each other with jealousy. Excepting the little kingdom of Hiero of Syracuse [2] and the north-eastern district governed by the Mamertines of Messana,[2] the whole of the fair island of Sicily [3] was under the sway of the Carthaginians. Hiero had declared war against the Mamertines. The Mamertines were divided among themselves; one section besought the aid of Rome, the other that of Carthage. Hiero made peace with Messana. Rome coveted Sicily, and made war on the Carthaginians B.C. 263. Hiero became the ally of Rome. Rome had no fleet: Carthage had a fine fleet, but only mercenaries.

Hannibal defended Agrigentum; [3] but, after a siege of seven months, he was compelled to surrender to the Romans: 25,000 captives are said to have been sold into slavery. The Carthaginian fleet ravaged the coasts of Italy. The senate resolved

[1] 115. [2] 145. [3] 130.

to build a fleet and to fight the Carthaginians on their own element. 130 ships were built. Each quinquereme had 300 rowers and 200 marines. The Carthaginians laughed at the Roman fleet. C. Duilius furnished each of his ships with a boarding bridge. The Carthaginians hastened to the battle as to certain victory. Duilius grappled his boarding bridges. Thirty of the Carthaginian ships were captured in the first attack, others soon followed; 3,000 Carthaginians were killed and 7,000 were taken prisoners.

In B.C. 259 a Carthaginian fleet, under Hannibal, was destroyed. The Carthaginian Hamilcar defeated the Romans on land. In B.C. 257 nearly half of Sicily was in the hands of the Carthaginians. In B.C. 256 the greatest naval action that the then world had witnessed was fought between the Romans and the Carthaginians off Ecnomus.[1] The Carthaginians were defeated. The Romans landed in Africa. Xanthippus, of Sparta,[2] was engaged in the Carthaginian service. He taught them the use of elephants. He defeated the Romans under Regulus, and, loaded with rich presents, prudently returned to his own country.

The Roman fleet, of between 200 and 300 vessels, sailed to the rescue of the garrison of Clypea.[3] It encountered and overcame a Carthaginian fleet, but finally perished in a storm. A new fleet of 260 vessels was built. In B.C. 252 the consuls again descended upon Africa, but, returning with their booty, 150 of their ships were wrecked. In B.C. 250 the consul Metellus defeated the Carthaginians at Panormus:[1] 104 of their 130 elephants were taken in triumph to Rome. In B.C. 250 Rome ordered the building of a new fleet of 200 ships. In B.C. 249 P. Claudius Pulcher was defeated at Drepana[1] and lost ninety-three of his ships. The Carthaginians, for the time being, regained the ascendancy in Sicily. Hannibal captured the Roman provision ships at Panormus.[1] Carthabo pursued a convoy of 800 transports; he destroyed a large number of them and seven ships of war. C. Junius, the Roman consul, lost all his fleet, save two ships, in a storm. In B.C. 248 Carthabo landed and ravaged various parts of Italy. Hamilcar, entrusted

[1] 130. [2] 175. [3] 115.

with the supreme command of the Carthaginian forces, completely paralysed the Romans, and never lost an opportunity of damaging them. In B.C. 243 Hamilcar was defeated by C. Fundanius. In B.C. 242 it was decreed for a third time that a Roman fleet should be built. The Republic lacked the means. The money was borrowed. The Carthaginians were defeated, 120 of their ships were sunk, the rest dispersed; 14,000 of their men were killed, 32,000 of them were taken prisoners. This victory, gained on the 10th of March, B.C. 241, decided the issue.

The Carthaginians sued for peace. It was granted to Hamilcar on the conditions, *inter alia*, 1st, that the Carthaginians should evacuate Sicily and all the islands between Sicily and Carthage; 2nd, all Roman prisoners should be restored without ransom; 3rd, Carthage should pay 3,200 Eubœan talents. Such are some of the incidents of the first Punic war, during which Rome lost no fewer than 700 ships. There were men in those days in the Roman world.

It is not pleasing to be compelled to take note of another phase of contemporaneous Roman life. But what, we ask, had been going on at Rome during this desperate and glorious struggle? In the year B.C. 264, or the next, the state ceased to defray the cost of the public festivals and games. That burden was thenceforth cast on the shoulders of the ædiles, as none but the wealthy could bear it, and as the higher dignities could only be reached by those who had served as ædiles, Rome placed wealth before blood or virtue. In short, Roman honours were put up at auction and knocked down to the highest bidder —cash down for place. The most popular candidates for the highest offices were those most lavish in their expenditure on the public games.

Gladiatorial Exhibitions, A.U.C. 490 (B.C. 264).—It was to Junius Brutus that Rome was indebted for the introduction at the obsequies of his father of the most brutal, sickening, and degrading of all Roman institutions—the gladiatorial exhibitions.

First Plebeian Pontifex Maximus, A.U.C. 501 (B.C. 253).—Tiberius Coruncanius enjoyed the privilege of being the first plebeian who attained the dignity of *pontifex maximus*. He was also the first plebeian who devoted himself to the public profession of the law. He died B.C. 245.

Prætor Peregrinus—The Jus Gentium, A.U.C. 507 (B.C. 247).—The importance of this date, and the facts for which it is memorable in the history of Rome, can scarcely be over-estimated. It was the duty of this new judge to hear and determine all cases of magnitude between foreigners, or between a Roman and a foreigner, and it was his duty to determine such cases by the doctrines and principles of the *jus gentium* as distinguished from those of the *jus civile*. Reason and equity, in the true sense of the term, were then made to take the place of the old civil law in every case in which a foreigner was interested. It is obvious that the Romans could not long rest satisfied with anything less for themselves. This change appears to be the foundation of the science of law, to which no nation ever contributed more largely than did the Romans.

Lex Silia—Condictio, A.U.C. 510 (B.C. 244).—This, the fifth of the *actiones legis*, lay for the recovery of specific sums of money (*certæ pecuniæ*). We know but little of the details of the forms of the *condictio* beyond the fact that it was so called because the plaintiff announced (*denutiabat*, *condicabat*) to his adversary that he would have to appear before the magistrate, in order that a *judex* might be appointed. Its date is not certain.

Lex Calpurnia, A.U.C. 520 (B.C. 234).—By this law the *Lex Silia* was extended to every species of obligation that was of a definite character. (*De omni certâ re.*)

The Second Punic War.—Between B.C. 218 and B.C. 201, the second Punic war, which Livy says was the most memorable that was ever waged, had as its field Spain, Italy, Sicily, and Africa.

In B.C. 218 Hannibal, at the head of his Carthaginian army,

crossed the Alps and descended into Italy, where he fought the battles of Ticinus[1] and the Trebia.[1] In B.C. 217, on the rocky shores of Lake Trasimenus,[2] he came up with and defeated the consul C. Flaminius: 15,000 Romans are said to have perished, among whom was Flaminius. A new Roman army was formed in which freedmen were enlisted.

On the 2nd August, B.C. 216, the Roman army of 80,000 foot and 6,000 horse attacked Hannibal on the banks of the river Aufidus, near the little town of Cannæ.[3] They were defeated: 47,000 Romans, and almost as many allies, covered the field of battle; among them were the consul Æmilius Paulus, 80 senators, and many other high officials. The surviving Romans capitulated and surrendered on condition that Hannibal sent messengers to Rome to negotiate the ransom of his 3,000 Roman prisoners. The senate bade his messengers return.

The Romans offered sacrifices to the gods. It is said that among others they offered up two pairs of human beings—a male and a female Gaul, and a male and a female Greek. Hannibal's success at Cannæ induced many Italian cities and towns to abandon the cause of Rome and join the Carthaginians. Hannibal wintered at Capua.[4] It is suggested that his army became corrupted in that effeminate city. It is certain that his losses must have necessitated recruiting. It is probable that his new soldiers were inferior to his old.

By almost incredible exertions Rome raised new and mighty armies; 8,000 slaves were purchased by the state on credit, and formed into two regiments; gladiators were enlisted and allowed to serve in their usual arms.

In B.C. 215, though Hannibal pitched his camp in the immediate neighbourhood of Rome, he only ravaged the country and returned to Rhegium.[5]

It was in B.C. 214, that the great Archimedes took part in the defence of Syracuse.

In B.C. 211, P. Cornelius Scipio, a haughty and dictatorial but thoroughly able man, then only twenty-four years of age, offered to take the command in Spain. The command was

[1] 111. [2] 127. [3] 143 [4] 128. [5] 145.

given to him with the title of proconsul. While at Rome he went ostentatiously every morning to pray in the temple of Jupiter, on the Capitol. His piety made him immensely popular with the people. The vulgar credited him with special divine favour. He re-organised the army in Spain. New Carthage,[1] Astapa,[2] and many other towns were taken by him. He defeated Masinissa, whose force was three times as great as his own. Hasdrubal, the brother of Hannibal, quitted Spain to assist his brother in Italy. His army was routed and he killed. His head was thrown into his brother's camp. From that time Hannibal maintained himself on the defensive.

When Hasdrubal quitted Spain, the Carthaginians, deprived of their leading spirit, soon succumbed to Rome, who became mistress of Spain.

In B.C. 206 Scipio went over to Africa, concluded a treaty with Syphax, returned to Italy, was made consul, and raised a volunteer army. In B.C. 204 he landed in the neighbourhood of Utica,[3] in Africa, with an army of 17,000 foot and several thousand horse. In B.C. 202 Hannibal, recalled, landed in Africa. Scipio and Hannibal met for the first time. It was on the river Bagradas.[3] It is said that each gazed on the other in silent admiration. They discussed the terms of peace; a truce was concluded between them. Ambassadors were sent to Rome to obtain its ratification. The Carthaginians, though counselled by Hannibal to the contrary, changed their minds, and resolved on another battle. It was fought at Zama,[3] B.C. 202. The Carthaginian army was cut to pieces and its remnant dispersed. Peace was concluded B.C. 201. Italy, Sicily, Sardinia, Corsica, and a great part of Spain were now subject to Rome. Carthage and Numidia[4] were not independent of it.

Scipio's soldiers were rewarded, but the bulk of the middle classes of Italy were ruined. The gulf between the wealthy and the poor was wide. The gold that had been carried to Rome from Sicily, from Spain, and from Carthage, made war for the sake of plunder tasteful to not a few.

[1] 54. [2] 39. [3] 115. [4] 101.

The Sumptuary Law of the Tribune C. Oppius, A.U.C. 539 (B.C. 215).—It is said that this enactment forbade any woman to wear more than half an ounce of gold, gay-coloured dress, or to ride either at Rome or in any other town and its immediate vicinity in a carriage drawn by two horses except on great religious occasions. The ladies clamoured. The law was repealed B.C. 195.

First Macedonian War.—In B.C. 215 the first Macedonian war was commenced. Philip of Macedonia,[1] fearing the growing power of Rome, concluded an alliance with Hannibal. At that time the Greeks were split into parties. The Romans fostered the discord. Philip began to be looked upon by many as the national protector of the Greeks. A Roman army landed at Dyrrhachium.[2] The Epirots[3] became tired of the war. A peace was concluded between the Romans and Philip in B.C. 205. Athens was at that time in a state of decay, and its inhabitants impoverished, but it was allied with Rome. An incident induced Philip to march against Athens. The Athenians implored the protection of Rome.

Lex Cincia Muneralis, A.U.C. 550 (B.C. 204).—This law was carried by the tribune M. Cincius Alimentus; its object was to suppress the practice of bribing judges with presents.

Second Macedonian War.—In B.C. 200 the second Macedonian war was commenced.

[1] 173. [2] 158. [3] 159.

CHAPTER V.

THE REPUBLIC—*continued.*

THE SECOND CENTURY B.C.

i.e., A.U.C. 555 till A.U.C. 654;—B.C. 199 till B.C. 100.

The Orators, Historians, Philosophers, Poets, &c., of the Period.

CATO, orator and prose writer, born B.C. 232, died B.C. 148.

TERENCE or TERENTIUS (PUBLIUS ACER), a pleasing play-writer, born about B.C. 194.

SULPICIUS GALLUS, astronomer, flourished about B.C. 168.

PACUVIUS (MARCUS), tragic poet, flourished about B.C. 154.

ALBINUS, author of a history of Rome written in Greek, flourished about B.C. 157.

LUCILIUS (CAIUS ENNIUS), called the father of Roman satire, born B.C. 149, died [?].

VARRO (MARCUS TERENTIUS), prose writer, born B.C. 118, died B.C. 29.

THE second Macedonian war, which, as already stated, had commenced in the last year of the preceding century, endured till B.C. 197, when the power of the Macedonians was broken, and they were driven out of Greece.

At the Isthmian games, in B.C. 196, the consul Flaminius proclaimed the freedom and independence of all the Greek cities and islands which had been under the dominion of Macedonia.[1]

In B.C. 193, all Greece was divided into two parties, the one

[1] 173.

being in favour of the Romans. The Ætolians, who were antagonistic to the Romans, invited Antiochus, styled the Great, king of Syria, with whom Hannibal then was, to come over into Greece and help them. He did so. He was defeated by the Romans, and retired to Asia, where he thought himself safe. The Romans, however, destroyed one of his fleets, and acquired several important positions. In B.C. 190 L. Cornelius Scipio, afterwards styled *Asiaticus*, arrived in Asia with an army of about 20,000 men. Antiochus had 70,000. At Magnesia,[1] at the foot of Mount Sipylus, Antiochus was defeated. He sued for peace. It was granted to him B.C. 188 on the condition of his surrendering to Rome all his dominions in Asia Minor west of Mount Taurus,[2] all his ships of war, making certain heavy payments, and delivering up Hannibal. Hannibal escaped. The power of the Syrian empire was broken for ever.

Meanwhile the Roman arms were no less active elsewhere, *e.g.*, among the Spaniards, the Ligurians,[3] the Insubrians,[4] and the Boians.[4] The Ligurians kept them employed till B.C. 181; the Spaniards till B.C. 179.

In B.C. 183, finding escape from the Romans, who were treacherously permitted to surround his house, impossible, Hannibal took poison and died. Scipio Africanus (the elder), his conqueror and admirer, died about the same time.

For generations the people believed that the spirit of Scipio had soared up to the abode of the gods, and that a serpent of supernatural size guarded the access to his tomb.

Lex Orchiana, A.U.C. 573 (B.C. 181).—This was a sumptuary law. It limited the number of persons who were allowed to meet at repasts.

Lex Æbutia—Ordinary or formulary procedure (*Ordinaria judicia vel per formulas*), **A.U.C. 577 (B.C. 177).**—The date of this important change is unfortunately very uncertain. It, however, by common consent is placed between B.C. 234 and B.C. 171. Ortolan fixes it at the date here given as the most probable, regard being had to other legislation.

[1] 174. [2] 220. [3] 112. [4] 111.

To the *lex Æbutia* is ascribed the introduction, or, perhaps more correctly, the sanction of the *formula* system. As theretofore, the parties went before the *magister*, to whom they stated their case, whereupon he nominated the *judex* and defined his duty, not, however, as formerly by word of mouth, but by filling up and handing to him a species of interpleader issue. The following is a copy of one:—"Let N—— be the judge. Whereas A. B. has sold a slave to C. D., if it appears that C. D. ought to pay to A. B. ten thousand *sesterces*, condemn C. D., judge, to pay the ten thousand to A. B. If it does not so appear, acquit him."

When a suit was brought for the partition of an *hæreditas* (*familiæ erciscundæ*), or the division of a thing held jointly (*communi dividundo*), or for the fixing and settling of boundaries of contiguous landowners (*finium regundorum*), the final clause ran—"as much as ought to be adjudged, judge, adjudge to A. B." (*quantum adjudicare oportet, judex, A. B. adjudicato*).

The selection of the form applicable to the plaintiff's case appears to have been left to the *magister*. In order that the *formulæ* should concisely and, at the same time, accurately define the question or questions to be determined, great labour was bestowed upon the construction of the *formulæ*, and it was not uncommon for the *magister* and the litigants to consult the most learned jurists and to secure their aid in the construction of a particular *formula*. It is the opinion of M. Ortolan that the *formula* system was first adopted in the case of disputes between the *peregrini*, subsequently between Romans and *peregrini*, in which case the *jus gentium* was the law applicable to the case, and that, working well in those cases, it was ultimately adopted in suits between Roman and Roman. When the case was tried by the *magister* himself, the procedure was styled *extra ordinem cognoscere*, or *extraordinaria judicia*.

The Third Macedonian War.—In B.C. 171, Perseus, king of Macedonia, irritated by the conduct of the Romans, declared war against them. At first he gained some important advantages, but, on the 23rd June, B.C. 168, he was defeated by the aged L. Æmilius Paulus near Pydna[1] in a battle that only

[1] 174.

lasted one hour. The Macedonian infantry were cut to pieces and the cavalry dispersed. The kingdom of Macedonia was no more. The country was divided into four districts. The inhabitants of one were forbidden to intermarry with those of another.

The enormous wealth now in the Roman treasury enabled the state to remit the poll tax. In the same year (B.C. 168) the third and last of the little Illyrian[1] wars was terminated. The country in this instance was divided into three districts. It is said that L. Æmilius Paulus caused no fewer than 70 towns to be destroyed, and 15,000 Epirots to be either massacred or sold into slavery.

At this period the bulk of the wealthy Romans had become brutalized; the poor miserably poor; the middle class almost extinct. The treasury, however, was full.

Incessant wars of extermination on the one hand, wholesale plunder on the other, can scarcely fail to destroy all that is noble in man—everything yields to the sensual gratification of the moment. The orgies of Bacchus, introduced into Rome from Southern Italy, were celebrated at night with the grossest violations of decorum and morality. A slave who happened to be a good cook fetched a higher price in the market than any other. Luxury, gluttony, debauchery, and licentiousness were the order of the day. In vain did the stern old Cato denounce effeminate luxury and prophesy its necessary consequence. To him the philosophy of the Athenian ambassadors, Carneades,[2] Diogenes, and Critolaus, who visited Rome B.C. 155, was as hateful as was the existence of Carthage or effeminacy itself. He secured the removal of the ambassadors; but he could not efface their teachings. The people became divided between the doctrines of the Stoics and those of the Epicureans.

Lex Fanniana, A.U.C. 593 (B.C. 161).—This law limited the expenditure to be incurred at great banquets. It was subse-

[1] 157.

[2] It is said that Carneades on one occasion maintained the existence of justice as a fact, and on the following day undertook to prove that it was nothing but a word; and that his conduct so affected Cato that he demanded that such ambassadors should be immediately dismissed.

quently re-enacted and more strictly defined by the Didian and Lucinian laws.

Lex Calpurnia Repetundarum, A.U.C. 605 (B.C. 149).—The origin of *quæstiones perpetuæ* requires somewhat careful consideration. The reader will remember that—1st the king, 2nd the comitia (first *curiata*, then *centuriata*, and finally *tributa*), and 3rd the senate, were those in whose hands criminal jurisdiction was lodged; that these bodies respectively might either themselves investigate a criminal charge, or might delegate the investigation (the *quæstio*); that the person or persons to whom the investigation was delegated were styled a *quæstor* or *quæstores;* and that in all cases the delegation had reference solely to a particular case or charge. That question disposed of, the delegate was *functus officio.* In its etymological meaning, therefore, the expression *quæstiones perpetuæ* would simply suggest that a *quæstor*, instead of being appointed for one case, and for that only, received a permanent appointment; that, however, is but a part, and a minor part, of what must be understood by the expression. The expression must be understood as conveying the facts—I. That at the time of the institution of *quæstores perpetuæ* all the various kinds of delicts were more or less carefully and accurately defined; II. That a given number of individuals were appointed for one year, each to act in a given class of cases only, as president of the tribunal; III. That the verdict was that of the jury or citizen judges, selected for the particular occasion, sometimes numbering as many as 100 persons—the number was determined by the law that regulated the particular *quæstio perpetua;* IV. That the jury pronounced its verdict according to the law of the case,—condemnation, acquittal, or insufficient evidence—*condemno, absolvo, non liquet;* V. That each crime had its penalty, its tribunal, and its procedure.

The institution of *quæstiones perpetuæ* was thus, obviously, not merely a strong check upon the arbitrary exercise of power, but a distinct advance in scientific procedure. There were crimes and cases, however, for which no *quæstio perpetua* had been provided. In such cases the uncertain and arbitrary decision of the *comitia*, the senate, the prætor, or the special delegates, as the case might be, existed as theretofore. The procedure in such cases was termed *cognitiones extraordinariæ,—extra ordinem cognoscere.*

The Third Punic War (B.C. 149 to 146).—Masinissa, king of Numidia,[1] was a source of annoyance to Carthage. Rome secretly sided with Masinissa. Cato never lost an opportunity when addressing the Senate of saying, "*Delenda est Carthago*" (Carthage must fall).

Masinissa fought and defeated the Carthaginians. It was alleged at Rome that the Carthaginians had broken the peace. P. Cornelius Scipio Nasica argued in favour of Carthage, Cato against it. Scipio saw in the existence of an honourable rival—and such Carthage was—advantage to Rome. The counsel of Cato prevailed. A large army was sent to Carthage. The consuls demanded that Carthage should deliver up her arms and military engines. She did so. The consuls then demanded that the city should be razed to the ground. The Carthaginians, exasperated to madness, closed all the city gates, and slew all the Romans and Italians who were within the walls. The 70,000 inhabitants resolved, though unarmed, to defend their city or to die. It is not easy to realize, it is impossible to describe, the horrors of this conflict, the heroism of the Carthaginians, or the brutality of the Romans. Suffice it to say, Scipio set fire to the city at three different points, and when the whole city was in a blaze promised to spare the lives of those who should come forth and surrender: 50,000 men and women bearing olive branches in their hands came forth. Scipio kept the letter of his word. The Carthaginians were sold as slaves. Carthage, the city, was reduced to ashes. Carthage became a Roman province under the name of Africa, B.C. 146.

Greece a Roman Province.—In the same year, viz., B.C. 146, Greece lost the last remnant of independent existence, and was made a Roman province.

[1] 101.

War in Spain.—Between B.C. 153 and B.C. 133 Rome carried on war against the tribes of Spain. For eight years Variathus, a Lusitanian,[1] bade the Romans defiance. In B.C. 141 the consul Servilianus concluded a peace with Variathus as the friend and ally of Rome. The next year Q. Servilius Caspio procured his assassination. In B.C. 138 Lusitania was subdued. At Numantia[2] the Romans fared badly. The consul was obliged to conclude a peace. In B.C. 137 the consul, C. Hostilius Mancinus, renewed the war, and was compelled to accept humiliating conditions. The Romans were permitted to depart in safety. Numantia was to be treated as a friend of Rome. The senate declared the treaty void. Scipio Africanus (the younger), the destroyer of Carthage, was sent to Numantia. He resolved to do by starvation what the Roman sword had failed to accomplish. He constructed a fourfold line of fortifications round the city. A brave little band of Numantians[2] broke through and reached Lutia[2] in quest of provisions. Lutia rendered assistance. Scipio, who had followed the Numantians, ordered the hands of 400 citizens of Lutia to be cut off. When the sufferings of the besieged became intolerable they begged for a truce of three days. The request was granted. When the gates were opened on the third day a small number came out and surrendered. The rest were dead. Rather than trust to Roman humanity the three days had been spent in destroying wives, children, each other, and themselves. The city was destroyed B.C. 133.

The First Servile War, A.U.C. 620 (B.C. 134).—The number of slaves throughout the empire was enormous. Slaves were buyable in the market for a mere trifle. Eunus, a Syrian slave, by reason of his piety acquired considerable influence among his fellows in Sicily. He was ill-treated by his master. He associated himself with Cleon. At a given signal 70,000 slaves rose in arms. Eunus assumed the diadem, and called himself King Antiochus. All the freemen who could not make their escape were massacred. Several Roman armies were defeated. In B.C. 132 the slaves were overcome; 20,000 of them were put to the sword; many were nailed on crosses along the high road.

[1] 23. [2] 52.

Lex Sempronia Agraria, A.U.C. 621 (B.C. 133).—By this law no citizen was allowed to possess more than 500 jugera of *ager publicus*, with an addition of 250 for each child. Those who had more were to be deprived of the surplus, but were to be indemnified by the public treasury for all outlays incurred by them for the benefit of the property. The lands thus recovered were to be distributed among the poorer citizens, and to be held by them at an annual rental payable to the state.

In B.C. 133, Attalus Philometer, king of Pergamus,[1] died. He had bequeathed his kingdom and treasures to the Roman people. They were enormous. His natural son Aristonicus refused to recognise the will. He was defeated, B.C. 129. Some of the vices of Asia now found their way to Rome.

Tiberius Gracchus, Tribune, B.C. 133.—The power of the senate was now everything; that of the assemblies of the people next to nothing. The illustrious families were in the exclusive possession of the most important and lucrative offices. Those *optimates* accumulated their wealth in the provinces. At home they amused and corrupted the people by distributions of money or food, by games, spectacles, and bribes. The brothers Tiberius and Caius Sempronius Gracchus essayed reform. Tiberius determined to renew the Licinian law. His object was to take from those who had more than their due portion of land the surplus, and to distribute it among the poor. He sought and obtained the tribuneship for B.C. 133. Appius Claudius, his father-in-law, P. Mucius Scævola, the great jurist, and other just and noble-minded men encouraged him. He succeeded in passing several important measures. P. Scipio Nasica charged him with aiming at kingly power, and called upon the senators to save the republic. Tiberius and some 300 others were murdered and thrown into the Tiber, B.C. 132. Caius Sempronius Gracchus was elected tribune, and was re-elected in B.C. 122. He was made consul, B.C. 121. He also carried several laws in the interests of the people.

Lex Sempronia, Frumentaria, A.U.C. 631 (B.C. 123).—This was the first of a series of laws, enacted from time to time,

[1] 204.

regulating the distribution of wheat among the poorer classes, sometimes at reduced prices, at others gratuitously.

Lex Sempronia, Judiciaria, A.U.C. 632 (B.C. 122).—By this plebiscitum the theretofore exclusive right of the senators to act as judges in the case of Romans was transferred to the knights. This is the first of a series of laws abrogating or modifying one another as the senators or knights happened to be in the ascendency, and ultimately admitting to the judicial office citizens lower in rank than the knights. The total number of these *judices* inscribed on the annual list was gradually raised from 300, till in the reign of the emperor Augustus it reached about 4,000. L. Opimius (the prætor) assembled the people with a view to abolish the laws of C. Sempronius Gracchus. A tumult arose; 3,000 perished in the affray. To avoid civil bloodshed Sempronius escaped to the other side of the Tiber. It is said that he, at his own request, fell by the hand of a faithful slave. The blessings striven for by the Gracchi were realized but in part.

The Jugurthine War, A.U.C. 643—648 (B.C. 111—106).—The war against Jugurtha, king of Numidia, commonly called the usurper, cannot be passed over without mention, though its incidents are unworthy of detail. It is another instance of Roman intrigue. It is memorable for the fact that Jugurtha, before quitting Rome, where he had been to negotiate, exclaimed, "Oh, the venal city! It will perish as soon as it can find a purchaser." It was during that war that Marius and Sylla became for the first time conspicuous in Roman history.

C. Marius was a man of humble origin, but of strong, energetic, and ambitious temperament. He was a native of Arpinum.[1] He had the rustic severity of the early Romans, and despised the fashions of his time. He was unequalled as a commander and tactician. L. Cornelius Sylla, who accompanied Marius to Numidia[2] in B.C. 106, had nothing in common with Marius save ambition and ability. He was a patrician, a man of fashion, talented and refined. Jugurtha, defeated, was carried to Rome a prisoner, and there starved to death in a dungeon.

[1] 128. [2] 101.

Lex Thoria, Agraria, A.U.C. 647 (B.C. 107).—This reactionary law guaranteed to the holders of public lands their possession free from incumbrance. It was followed by seven agrarian laws within fifty-two years, the tendency of which was to nullify the effect of the *lex Thoria*. All but the last were practically inoperative. The last was the *lex Julia agraria*.

The Cimbri and Teutons, B.C. 107 to B.C. 101.—About B.C. 113 the Cimbri, supposed to be a Celtic tribe, appeared in Noricum,[1] then inhabited by Celts under the protection of Rome, where they were joined by the Teutons, undoubtedly Germans. They promised not to molest the friends of Rome. A Roman consul thought fit treacherously to attack them. He was defeated. The Cimbri reappeared near Gaul in B.C. 109. They prayed the Roman consul to assign them a country to live in, promising to support the Roman arms when called upon. Their petition was rejected. They attacked and defeated the consul. In B.C. 107 the consul, L. Cassius Longinus, was defeated and slain near the Lake of Geneva.[2] Not long after two consular armies were completely annihilated: 80,000 soldiers and 40,000 camp followers are said to have been slain. The Romans, in dismay, turned to Marius as the only man in whom they had confidence. Unsolicited, and in his absence, he was raised to the consulship B.C. 104. He created and trained an entirely new army, which for the most part consisted of the *populus* and the veterans who returned with him from Africa. He met the enemy in the neighbourhood of Aquæ Sextiæ (Aix).[3] The battle lasted for two days. The Teutons were utterly defeated; in short, annihilated, for many who had survived the battle destroyed themselves. This was in B.C. 101, in which year Marius was, for the fifth time, elected consul.

Marius next joined his army to that of Catulus, and diverted the approach of the Cimbri, who had spread over the plains of Lombardy. He drew up his forces at Campi Raudii, near Verona.[4] The battle was fought on the 30th July, B.C. 101: 14,000 of the Cimbri were left on the battlefield, and 60,000

[1] 125. [2] 96. [3] 97. [4] 126.

captured were sold as slaves. Marius was appointed consul for the sixth time, an event unprecedented in Roman history.

The Second Servile War, B.C. 102 to B.C. 99.—In B.C. 102 the prætor L. Licinius Nerva manumitted all the slaves in Sicily who were natives of a Roman province. The remaining slaves resolved to free themselves. The war lasted four years. Marius took no part in it. The slaves were defeated.

CHAPTER VI.

THE REPUBLIC—*continued.*

THE FIRST CENTURY B.C.

i.e., A.U.C. 655 to A.U.C. 753-4;—B.C. 99 to A.D.

The Orators, Historians, Philosophers, Poets, &c., of the Period.

LICINIUS (LUCIUS CRASSUS), orator, flourished about B.C. 96.

CÆSAR (CAIUS JULIUS), orator, historian, jurist, born B.C. 99, died B.C. 43.

ANTONIUS (MARCUS), orator, born B.C. [?], died B.C. 67.

CICERO (MARCUS TULLIUS), the prince of Roman orators, born B.C. 106, died B.C. 43.

CATULLUS (CAIUS VALERIUS), poet, born B.C. 86, died B.C. 57?

HORTENSIUS (QUINTUS), orator, born B.C. [?], died B.C. 49.

SALLUST—CAIUS CRISPUS SALLUSTIUS, historian, born B.C. 83, died B.C. 35.

POLLIO (CAIUS ASINIUS), historian, orator, and writer of tragedies, born B.C. 84, died B.C. 4.

VIRGIL—PUBLICIUS VIRGILIUS MARO—the most distinguished epic, didactic, and pastoral poet of Rome, born B.C. 70, died B.C. 19.

GALLUS (CORNELIUS), poet, born B.C. 70, died B.C. 28.

PROPERTIUS (SEXTUS AURELIUS), elegiac poet, born B.C. [?], died about B.C. 12.

HORATIUS FLACCUS (QUINTUS), lyric poet and satirist, born B.C. 65, died B.C. 9.

VARIUS, poet, temp. VIRGIL and HORACE.

LIVY or LIVIUS (TITUS), historian, born B.C. 59, died A.D. 16.

TIBULLUS (ALBIUS), poet, born B.C. 43? died B.C. 19?

OVID—OVIDIUS PUBLIUS, surnamed NASO—poet, born B.C. 43, died A.D. 18.

GRATIUS (FALISEUS), poet, believed to be contemporary with OVID.

NEPOS (CORNELIUS), historian, temp. JULIUS CÆSAR and AUGUSTUS.

TROGUS POMPEIUS, historian, temp. AUGUSTUS, B.C. 31 to A.D. 14.

SENECA (MARCUS ANNÆUS), rhetorician, temp. AUGUSTUS.

MANLIUS (MARCUS), poet, temp. AUGUSTUS.

ALBINOVANUS (C. PEDO), poet, temp. AUGUSTUS.

SEVERUS (CORNELIUS), poet, temp. AUGUSTUS.

LUCRETIUS (TITUS CARUS), philosopher and poet, born B.C. 29, died B.C. 48.

IN B.C. 91 the tribune, M. Livius Drusus, who was bent on reforming abuses, proposed, among other things, that the franchise should be given to the Italians.

The senate refused the franchise to the Italians. Drusus was murdered. It so happened that many Italians who lived in Rome, though not legally qualified to vote as Roman citizens, had long been allowed to live and act as if Roman citizens. In B.C. 95, however, the consul, L. Licinius Crassus, and the pontifex maximus, Mucius Scævola, one of the great Roman jurists, carried a law which forbade the exercise of citizen rights by any but citizens. This enactment, in conjunction with the murder of Drusus, threw the Italians throughout Italy into a state of the greatest excitement.

The senate favoured the claim of the Italians, but the equites and the rabble, with whom the equites made common cause, rejected it. The Italians determined to appeal to the sword. The various Italian nations formed themselves into a confederacy. Their alternative was the franchise or the destruction of Rome. Fortunately for Rome, the Latins, the Etruscans, the Umbrians, and the Campanians, held aloof. For the purposes of the war the Italian nations may be divided into three groups, inasmuch as three Roman armies took the field against them, viz., 1. Picenum;[1]

[1] 127.

2. Vestini,[1] Marrucini,[1] Marsi,[1] Frentani,[1] and Samnium;[2] 3. Hirpini,[2] Apulia,[2] and Lucania.[2]

The Roman army in central Italy was under the command of Marius and Sylla. That in the south was commanded by L. Julius Cæsar. That between the two was under the command of the consul Cn. Pompeius Strabo. In B.C. 90, L. Julius Cæsar and P. Rutilius Lupus were unsuccessful against the Italians. The legates, Sylla and Marius, however, were more fortunate. In B.C. 89, the consul C. P. Strabo defeated the Marsians and Vestinians with 70,000 near Asculum.[1] The town was taken by storm. The fate of its inhabitants was dreadful. It is said that 300,000 fell in this war. Rome promised the franchise to all who laid down their arms. The war was thus brought to an end except as to Samnium,[2] which held out till B.C. 88.

Lex Julia, A.U.C. 664 (B.C. 90).—By this law, which was carried by the consul L. Julius Cæsar, the franchise was granted to all the Latins both in Latium and the Latin colonies, in consideration of their not having taken up arms against Rome in common with the Italians.

Lex Plautia, A.U.C. 665 (B.C. 89).—In this year the consul, M. Plautius Silvanus, carried a law which in effect gave the franchise to all the Italians. The Umbrians and Etruscans, either in this or the previous year, had received the franchise. It is said that Pompeius Strabo carried a law granting the Latin franchise to all the inhabitants of the country between the Alps and the Po.

Roman Citizenship.—The rights of Roman citizenship were now enjoyed by nearly the whole of Italy, the only condition imposed being a declaration by the new citizens that they would adopt the civil law of Rome. The Roman civil law thus became the law of all Italy.

[1] 128. [2] 143.

As the whole of the new citizens were placed in eight tribes, whereas Rome itself had thirty-five, the then political influence of the new commoners may be approximately estimated.

Civil War—Marius and Sylla, B.C. 87 to B.C. 81.—When we are told that Sylla, who ultimately triumphed over Marius and his party, in doing so caused the destruction of 46 persons of consular, prætorian, or ædile dignity, 200 senators, 1,600 equites, 8,000 Samnite captives, and 15,000 citizens, it is not difficult to sympathize with Montesquieu when he prays to be permitted to turn away his eyes from the wars of Marius and Sylla. Those who can find pleasure in gladiatorial exhibitions may have stomachs strong enough to read the detailed account of this wading through human blood to power, but even they, so one would think, must mentally ask, how could such things be? Marius and Sylla were rivals as individuals, but perhaps not so much as individuals as representative men. Each regarded the other as the embodiment and exponent of principles, theories, or prejudices to be detested: hence the following of each, hence their fury. Each being resolved to gain the ascendency regarded no means as too base or brutal. The advantage gained by either was used in butchering and blotting out the friends and supporters of his adversary. Marius made himself consul for the seventh time B.C. 86, in the 70th year of his age.

In B.C. 81, Sylla, at his own instance, was appointed dictator for an indefinite period. He assigned colonies in Italy to twenty-three legions. The places thus made over to the soldiers as a reward for past services were called military colonies. He conferred the Roman franchise on 10,000 emancipated slaves, who received from him the name of Cornelii; they constituted his body guard, and were distributed among the thirty-five old tribes. He filled up the vacancies in the senate with *equites* and centurions. He deprived the tribunes of the right of proposing legislative measures and of holding any other magistracy after the expiration of their term of office. He restored to the senators the right to try cases of a public character. He increased the number of the prætors to eight, the quæstors to twenty, the augurs and pontiffs to fifteen each. He placed the criminal law on a solid foundation. He made other alterations, and, to the astonishment of all, voluntarily laid down the dictatorship in B.C. 79 and retired to Puteoli,[1] where he died in the following year of disease. He had ordered it to be inscribed on his tomb, that "no man had ever equalled him in doing evil to his enemies, nor in doing good to his friends."

The wars of Marius and Sylla gave the deathblow to the Roman republic. Between B.C. 81, when Sylla made himself perpetual dictator, and B.C. 31, when Octavius Augustus laid the foundation of monarchy (Empire), the Roman world witnessed the spectacle of wars waged for the sole purpose of individual aggrandizement.

In B.C. 78, Lepidus and Catullus were the consuls; the senate made them promise on oath not to take up arms against each other. Lepidus raised an army, marched to the gates of Rome, but was repulsed by Catullus. In B.C. 70, the power of the tribunes was restored, and most of Sylla's laws as to the administration of justice were repealed. In B.C. 82, the prætor Q. Sertorius, who had joined the Marian party on account of his detestation of aristocratic intrigues, was sent to Spain, there to maintain his party's interests. His object was to blend Spaniards and Romans into one people, and to establish a new Roman republic in Spain. He there formed a senate of 300, consisting in part of proscribed Romans, and in part of illustrious Spaniards. He appointed republican magistrates in imitation of those of Rome. He founded a great school at Osca[2] for the education of the sons of distinguished Spaniards. In B.C. 79, Q. C. Pius was sent against him. Sertorius became suspicious of the Spaniards. He caused all the boys at Osca to be put to death. He was murdered at the instance of Perpenna, B.C. 72. Perpenna put himself at the head of the Marian army: he was defeated by Pompey, and put to death. The last then remnant of the Marian party was annihilated.

In B.C. 74, the third Mithridatic war broke out.

In B.C. 73, some gladiators, headed by Spartacus, made their

[1] 112. [2] 67.

escape from Capua.[1] Spartacus soon found himself at the head of 10,000 slaves. Time after time, he, in B.C. 72, defeated the consuls and laid waste a large part of southern Italy. In B.C. 71, he was defeated by M. Licinius Crassus. 5,000 of the slaves who had escaped to the north of Italy were defeated and cut to pieces by Pompey.

In B.C. 70, Pompey and Crassus were the consuls. Early in B.C. 67, Pompey was invested for three years with supreme command over all ports and coasts of the Mediterranean, then infested by pirates. Before the middle of the summer the whole of the Mediterranean was cleared. The strongholds of the pirates were destroyed.

In B.C. 66, it was proposed that the command of Pompey should be extended to Bithynia,[2] Pontus,[3] and Armenia,[4] in order that he might cope with Mithridates, who had thus far proved victorious in the war. C. Julius Cæsar and Cicero supported the proposition. It was carried. Mithridates was defeated. His son Pharnaces headed a rebellion against him. The king caused his slave to kill him. Pharnaces sent his corpse to Pompey.

Pompey made Judæa[5] and Cilicia[6] Roman provinces.

The Catiline Conspiracy.—In B.C. 66, C. Sergius Catilina, a noble who had squandered all his property, leagued himself with profligates of all parties, as also with many of the dregs of the populace. He offered himself as a candidate for the consulship in B.C. 65: failing, he plotted the murder of the consuls. His scheme was frustrated. In B.C. 64, he again stood for the consulship. Cicero was elected in his stead. He resolved to destroy the city by fire and to massacre all the leading men. His plans were ripe for execution. Curio, one of the conspirators, divulged the scheme to his mistress, Fulvia; Fulvia reported it to Cicero, who revealed it in the senate on the 8th November. Catiline, who was declared a public enemy, made his escape. Documents that fell into the hands of Cicero proved that Lentulus the prætor, Cethegus, Statilius, and

[1] 128. [2] 218. [3] 248. [4] 263. [5] 252. [6] 235.

Cæparius were among the conspirators. Cicero delivered his fourth speech against Catiline on the 5th December. Those conspirators were arrested and strangled in prison on the same day by order of the senate. In B.C. 62, Catiline, with 3,000 of his co-conspirators, fell in battle, sword in hand.

The First Triumvirate.—C. Julius Cæsar's aunt, Julia, his father's sister, the widow of the elder Marius, died in B.C. 67. Cæsar delivered the funeral oration. Two years later, he (Cæsar), during the night, replaced the statues of Marius in the Capitol. They had been removed by the order of Sylla. The senate was filled with alarm, the people with delight. Cæsar was recognised as the avowed head of the remnants of the Marian party. In B.C. 62, he was made prætor. Spain was assigned to him as his province. In Spain, Cæsar collected enough for himself during his year of office to enable him to pay off his debts (1,000,000*l.*). He, Pompey, and Crassus, then (B.C. 60) agreed together that no political measure should be taken that was displeasing to either of the three. The three were all-powerful. It was agreed between them that Pompey should have Spain; Crassus, Syria; and Cæsar, Gaul. Cæsar was consul in B.C. 59.

Lex Julia, Agraria, A.U.C. 695 (B.C. 59).—By this law, passed at the instance of Julius Cæsar, the public lands of Campania[1] were distributed among the poor citizens who had three or more children. It is said that the distribution benefited more than 20,000 heads of families.

In B.C. 61, P. Clodius had had an intrigue with Cæsar's wife. Cicero not merely refused to defend Clodius, but testified against him. Clodius was elected tribune for the year B.C. 58. He carried a law enacting that whosover had put to death a Roman citizen without a formal trial should be outlawed. The law was aimed at Cicero. Neglected by Pompey, Crassus, and Cæsar, Cicero went into exile. In B.C. 57, Cicero was recalled. In B.C. 53, Clodius was killed in one of his feuds with Milo. Pompey was sole consul. Milo was accused and condemned.

[1] 143.

Pompey had surrounded the forum with armed soldiers. Cicero, for the first time, was unnerved. He could not plead for Milo. His oration for Milo was written afterwards. He sent a copy of it to Milo. Milo replied saying, "If you had delivered that speech at my trial, I should not now be eating the fine fish of Marseilles."

Cæsar's campaigns in Gaul, where he is said to have subdued 300 tribes, and his invasions of Britain in the years B.C. 55 and 54, created in the then Roman world the same feeling of wonder and admiration that they still inspire in the bosoms of those who delight in chivalry and adventure.

In B.C. 55, Crassus went to Syria.[1] From the temple of Jerusalem he took 2,000 talents. In B.C. 54, he went into Mesopotamia.[2] He was unsuccessful, and in the following year was defeated; 10,000 Romans with their camp fell into the hands of the Parthian conquerors. While attempting escape Crassus was struck down by an unknown hand.

In B.C. 54, Julia, the daughter of Cæsar and wife of Pompey, died. The bond of union between Cæsar and Pompey was severed. Cæsar and Pompey were now rivals. Pompey administered Spain through his legates, and spent most of his time at Rome. His princely mode of living suggested to many the idea that he aimed at absolutism. Cato publicly denounced some of his doings: Pompey, on the other hand, laid that charge to Cæsar. Each bribed heavily to secure friends at Rome.

Cæsar wrote to the senate expressing his readiness to disband his army if Pompey would disband his. On the motion of Scipio, Pompey's father-in-law, the senate ordered Cæsar to disband his army at a given date. It was evident that Pompey had resolved to crush Cæsar if he could. M. Antonius and Q. Cassius, two tribunes who had opposed the motion, fled in disguise to Cæsar, and called upon him to protect the inviolable persons of the tribunes.

Everything at Rome was in confusion. Pompey was entrusted by the senate with the conduct of the war, if war there should be. He and the aristocracy believed that Cæsar dared not march against them.

[1] 251. [2] 265.

No sooner did Cæsar hear of the decree than he assembled his soldiers and told them all that had taken place. The soldiers promised to follow wherever Cæsar should lead. Cæsar marched to the little river Rubicon,[1] the line which no general was permitted to pass with an army without the permission of the senate. Arrived, he halted for a moment; he wavered, then exclaimed, "The die is cast." Cæsar crossed the Rubicon with one legion in the middle of January B.C. 49. So great was Cæsar's popularity that town after town threw open its gates as he approached. Pompey, bewildered, quitted the city at dusk. Consuls, senators, and others followed him, leaving behind them all the money in the public treasury. At first they went to Capua,[2] then to Brundusium,[3] intending, if possible, to make their escape to Greece.

The soldiers of L. Domitius deserted in a body to Cæsar. Cæsar followed Pompey as far as Brundusium; but, not having ships, he could not then go further. Pompey gone, all Italy declared for Cæsar. Arrived at Rome, Cæsar acted with mildness, but as sovereign. He took what money he wanted from the public treasury. After a short stay he left his friends in charge of Rome and Italy.

It is said that in forty days Cæsar overcame his enemies in Spain and returned to Rome. In December, B.C. 49, Cæsar left Rome in pursuit of Pompey. He laid siege to Dyrrhachium,[4] but was obliged to raise it; disease had broken out among his soldiers, and his provisions were falling short. From Dyrrhachium he went towards Thessaly.[5] Pompey, elated, followed him. On the 9th of August, B.C. 48, they fought in the plain of Pharsalus;[5] Pompey's army was routed and his camp taken. On the 28th September Pompey was murdered by an emissary of Ptolemy. Cæsar landed in Egypt a few days later. In Egypt Cæsar became involved both in love and war. The fascinations of the lovely and licentious Cleopatra overcame him. Cleopatra was reseated by Cæsar on the throne of her fathers. Cæsar was enslaved by Cleopatra. Pharnaces the son of Mithridates had defeated one of Cæsar's legates. Cæsar heard of it, tore himself

[1] 127 [2] 128. [3] 143. [4] 158. [5] 174.

from his mistress, and went to meet Pharnaces. It was concerning the result of that meeting that Cæsar wrote to the senate, saying, "I have come, I have seen, I have conquered" (*Veni, vidi, vici*). In September, B.C. 48, Cæsar, having returned to Rome, entered on his dictatorship. He made M. Antony his master of the horse. Cæsar was invested for life with the rights and privileges of a tribune. The senate and the people vied with each other to do him honour. His unexpected and unexampled mildness seemed to fill all with admiration. The partisans of Pompey, however, were plotting. In B.C. 46, Cæsar went to Africa and triumphed. Cato, unable to hold Utica[1] against Cæsar, advised the inhabitants to surrender to Cæsar. That done, Cato put an end to his own existence. If Cato was not the last, he was at least the best of the party of Pompey. Cæsar, sole master of the Roman world, returned to Rome at the end of July, and there proclaimed a general amnesty. The dictatorship was conferred on him for ten years. Cæsar commenced reforms. He added ninety days to the calendar of the year B.C. 46, and decreed that confusion should be avoided in the future by strict adherence to the solar motions. He conferred the Roman franchise on all Cisalpine Gaul,[2] thenceforth styled *Gallia Togata*. In imitation of Sylla, he established colonies in Gaul, Italy, and Africa. He endeavoured to reform the law and to curtail the duration of administration in the provinces. While thus engaged, the Pompeian party again broke out in Spain. Cæsar left Rome B.C. 46. On the 17th March, B.C. 45, he defeated the Pompeians at Munda,[3] and, as the detachments of the defeated army would not accept his pardon, Cæsar destroyed them. It is said that shortly before this victory Cæsar was so dejected that he contemplated suicide. Returned to Rome, Cæsar received the titles of *imperator*, *dictator*, and *præfectus morum* for life, and was appointed consul for the next ten years. He adopted M. Octavius as his son. He hoped that he might be his successor in dignity. M. Antony, on the 15th February, B.C. 44, offered to Cæsar the diadem; Cæsar declined the honour. Antony caused the statue of Cæsar to be crowned. Two tribunes ordered the

[1] 115. [2] 111. [3] 39.

crown to be removed. A conspiracy was formed against Cæsar's life; it was joined by Brutus, a nephew of Cato, a man for whom Cæsar had great respect. Cæsar was warned of the plot, but disregarded the warning. He was assassinated in the senate house on the 15th March, B.C. 44, in the fifty-sixth year of his age, stabbed, it is said, in thirty-three places. Brutus was one of those who slew him. Was there ever a more senseless murder?

By his will, Cæsar appointed his great-nephew, C. Julius Octavius, the heir of three-fourths of his private property. At the date of Cæsar's death Octavius was nineteen years of age, and by that event his name became C. Julius Cæsar Octavianus. He, Antony, M. Lepidus, Brutus, Cassius, and Cicero are the individuals who stand out conspicuously in the history of Rome of the period immediately following the death of Cæsar. Antony was one of the consuls of the year. There are but few who have not heard of Antony's funeral oration over the dead body of Cæsar, of his attempts to defraud Octavius of his inheritance, of his intrigue to make himself absolute, and of his having been declared by the senate a public enemy.

The Second Triumvirate.—In November, B.C. 43, on a small island in the river Rhenus,[1] Octavianus, Antony, and Lepidus met and entered into an alliance. They assumed the title of "The three constituents of the republic"—*triumviri rei publicæ constituendæ*—which position they agreed to hold for five years. Africa, Sicily, and Sardinia were, by their common consent, assigned to Octavianus, Gaul to Antony, and Spain to Lepidus. Each drew up a list of those whom he, or the others, wished proscribed, and their property confiscated. Octavianus, to please Antony, entered the name of Cicero; Antony put down the name of his own uncle, L. Cæsar; Lepidus inscribed that of his own brother Paulus. The *triumviri* went to Rome. Every part of the city was occupied by soldiers. A tribune asked the people to sanction without investigation certain arrangements made by the *triumviri*. The sanction was obtained. The lists

[1] 109.

were distributed among the commanders of the forces. Three hundred senators and two thousand *equites* were massacred. Cicero was murdered by Antony's emissaries on the 7th December, B.C. 43.

Octavianus and Antony went to Greece to carry on war against Brutus and Cassius. The fortunes of war favoured Octavianus and Antony. Cassius bade one of his servants take his life. Brutus put an end to the war by destroying himself, B.C. 42. Antony went to Asia. Octavianus returned to Italy. Fulvia, the wife of Antony, excited the consul Antonius against Octavianus. Antonius took up his quarters at Perusia[1] in Etruria; he was defeated by Octavianus early in B.C. 40, and turned traitor to his party. Antony meanwhile was first in Asia, and then in Egypt, with Cleopatra, indulging in wild excesses. Fulvia died at Sicyon.[2] Antony and Cn. Domitius Ahenobarbus, the republican admiral, sailed to Brundusium.[3] Octavianus shut the gates of the city against them. A reconciliation was effected. A general amnesty was declared, and a new distribution of the provinces agreed to. Antony was to have all the provinces east of the Adriatic; Octavianus, all the western provinces; Lepidus, Africa; Italy was to belong to the three in common. Antony, to seal this *fœdus Brundusinum*, married Octavia, the sister of Octavianus. Sextus Pompeius was to be regarded by all as the common enemy. Lepidus laid down his state, returned to Rome, and became pontifex maximus, which office he retained till death, B.C. 12. Octavianus joined the province and army of Lepidus to his own. Pompeius was defeated, and subsequently put to death, B.C. 35.

In B.C. 36, Antony went on an expedition against the Parthians:[4] he had with him sixteen legions. He was defeated, and returned to Alexandria and to sensual pleasure with his mistress Cleopatra. Octavia had gone to Greece with reinforcements, money, and clothing for his army. Antony wrote telling Octavia not to follow him about. He openly divorced her. Octavianus and his sister were now regarded as the injured parties. War was declared B.C. 32. In the spring of B.C. 31,

[1] 127. [2] 175. [3] 143. [4] 293.

Octavianus set sail. The fleets met at Actium[1] on the 2nd September, B.C. 31. Octavianus was victorious; Antony and Cleopatra made their escape. In B.C. 30 Antony, having abandoned hope, threw himself upon his own sword. Cleopatra, to avoid being carried prisoner to Rome, placed a viper to her breast and died. Egypt became a Roman province.

[1] 159.

THE ROMAN EMPIRE.

A.U.C. 723 till A.U.C. 753-4;—B.C. 31 till A.D.

The battle of Actium, in effect if not in name, made Octavianus sole master of the Roman world, on the 2nd of September, B.C. 31. That is the date commonly accepted as that of the foundation of the Roman empire as distinguished from the Roman republic. In the spring of B.C. 29 the temple of Janus was closed. There was peace throughout the Roman dominions. The senate conferred on Octavianus the title of *imperator* for life. In B.C. 27 the senate decorated Octavianus "FATHER OF HIS COUNTRY" and "AUGUSTUS." It vested in him the supreme power for ten years.

In B.C. 27 an arrangement was concluded by which the provinces were divided between the senate and Augustus. Those assigned to the senate were styled *provinciæ senatoriæ* or *populi*, and were governed by persons appointed annually by the senate, who, however, had not the *imperium.*

The provinces assigned to Augustus, by far the most important, were styled *provinciæ Cæsareæ*, and were governed by his nominees, styled *legati Cæsaris* or *Augusti.* The income derived from the provinces of the senate went into the public treasury, *ærarium*, out of which the expense of the civil government was defrayed. The revenue derived from Cæsar's provinces, styled *tributum*, went into his treasury, the *fiscus*, which had to bear the cost of the army. The *fiscus* was not the emperor's private purse. In B.C. 23 the senate conferred on Octavianus the tribunician power for life. In B.C. 19 consular power was conceded to him in perpetuity. In B.C. 17 the ten years' term of absolute power was renewed, and the power of a censor was granted to him; and in B.C. 12, on the death of Lepidus, he was made *pontifex maximus*. He ostentatiously, but prudently, refused the title of dictator. Power he loved, and contrived not merely to get but to hold. The history of the past had possibly taught him that the substance might be enjoyed by one willing to forego the shadow—the name.

Consuls, proconsuls, prætors, tribunes, and the rest were appointed as before; but now as the colleagues of Augustus, to whom all were in fact subordinate. Those nominated by him were certain of election. It is said that his nephews, sons-in-law, and even his grandsons, when little better than boys, were placed in offices of trust.

In order to avoid exciting alarm he lived with the simplicity of a private citizen. He established, however, a guard—the prætorian guard—a body of from 8,000 to 10,000 men, who were in effect, though not in name, his body guard.[1]

He exerted himself in correcting abuses, both public and private. He paid special attention to the due worship of the gods, which for some time past had been neglected. He cleared the streets of the banditti and assassins that had long infested them both by night and day; he brought every part of the city under direct and efficient police, *i. e.* prætorian supervision.

He gave a new form to the senate; he enacted laws for the improvement of the law and the morality of the people; he introduced discipline into the army, which consisted of about 450,000 men, and order into the games of the circus; he so greatly improved the city that it was said that "he found it of brick and left it of marble." He protected and favoured the learned; he travelled largely. Villeius says—"He made journeys everywhere in increase of the blessings of peace."

With the exception of the reverses of Varus, who was defeated by the Germans A.D. 9, his arms were uniformly successful; and in B.C. 10, for the third time in the history of Rome, the temple of Janus was closed.

[1] Gibbon says, "That crafty tyrant, sensible that laws might colour, but that arms alone could maintain, his usurped dominion, had gradually formed this powerful body of guards in constant readiness to protect his person, awe the senate, and either to prevent or to crush the first motions of rebellion." (Vol. I. 163.)

Chapter VII.

THE ROMAN EMPIRE—*continued.*

THE FIRST CENTURY OF THE CHRISTIAN ERA.

i. e., A.U.C. 753-4 till A.U.C. 852;—A.D. till A.D. 99.

Emperors of Rome.

A.D.
1 to 14. OCTAVIANUS AUGUSTUS—*continued.* His reign commenced B.C. 27.

14—37. TIBERIUS.

37—41. CALIGULA.

41—54. CLAUDIUS.

54—68. NERO.

68. GALBA.

69. OTHO.

69. VITELLIUS.

69—79. VESPASIAN.

79—81. TITUS.

81—96. DOMITIAN.

96—98. NERVA.

98— . TRAJAN.

Jurists.

Temp. Augustus—M. ANTISTIUS LABEO, C. ATEIUS, CAPITO.

Temp. Tiberius—MASURIUS SABINUS, M. COCCEIUS NERVA, SEMPRONIUS PROCULUS, C. CASSIUS.

Temp. Trajan—P. JUVENTIUS CELSUS, NERALIUS PRISCUS, PRISCUS JAVOLENUS.

Orators, Historians, Philosophers, Poets, &c.

PHÆDRUS, a fabulist in iambic verse, temp. AUGUSTUS and TIBERIUS.

VALERIUS MAXIMUS, historian, &c., temp. TIBERIUS, i.e. A.D. 14 to A.D. 37.

SENECA (LUCIUS ANNÆUS), philosopher, poet, and prose writer, born A.D. [?], died A.D. 65.

MARTIAL or MARCUS VALERIUS MARTIALIS, poet, epigrammatist, born A.D. [?], died A.D. 164.

VALERIUS MAXIMUS, historian, temp. TIBERIUS.

SILIUS ITALICUS (CAIUS), poet, born A.D. 15, died A.D. 90.

PLINY—CAIUS PLINIUS SECUNDUS—the elder, a prolific and learned historian, &c., born A.D. 22, died A.D. 79.

PERSIUS (AULUS FLACCUS), satirical poet, born A.D. 34, died A.D. 62.

LUCAN—MARCUS ANNÆUS LUCANUS—poet, born A.D. 37, died A.D. 65.

STATIUS (PUBLIUS PAPINIUS), poet, born A.D. 61, died A.D. 96.

PLINY—CAIUS PLINIUS CÆCILIUS SECUNDUS—the younger, philosopher, historian, and orator, born A.D. 62, died A.D. [?].

FRONTO (MARCUS CORNELIUS), orator and teacher of oratory, temp. MARCUS AURELIUS and LUCIUS VERUS (A.D. 161 to 199).

SULPICIA, poetess, flourished about A.D. 90.

QUINTILIAN or QUINTILIANUS (MARCUS FABIUS), advocate, rhetorician, and critic, flourished during this century.

TACITUS (CAIUS CORNELIUS), poet, philosopher, and historian, born about A.D. 56, died about A.D. 135.

FLACCUS (CAIUS VALERIUS), poet, flourished during this century.

JUVENAL—DECIMUS JUNIUS JUVENALIS—satirist, flourished during the second half of this century.

Special attention must now be directed to the "*Leges Julia et Papia*," the *lex Ælia Sentia* and the *lex Furia Caninia*, to *fidei commissa* and *codicilli*, to the *responsa prudentum*, and to the *constitutiones principum*.

Leges Julia et Papia (Lex Julia, B.C. 18—Lex Papia, A.D. 9).—Foreign and domestic war, wholesale proscriptions and suicides, inordinate luxury coupled with absolute insecurity, had toward the close of the republic necessarily made libertinism and celibacy characteristic features of the period. The old race was fast becoming extinct: a race of freedmen, foreigners, and slaves threatened to take their place. Legislation was resorted to. The two laws above mentioned, and commonly by subsequent Roman writers referred to under the title "*Leges Julia et Papia,*" or "*Novæ leges,*" or simply as "*Leges,*" they being regarded as *laws par excellence*, in short, divided the whole Roman society into—1, the married and unmarried (*cœlibes*); 2, into parents (*patres* or *matres*) and the childless (*orbi*).

The fundamental object of the two laws was Roman procreation, legitimate marriage, or, failing that, citizen cohabitation. Fecundity on the part of the female Roman citizen, whether her children were legitimate or not, was rewarded. Three confinements, she being *ingenua*, or four, she being an enfranchised, gave her the *jus liberorum*. Rewards were offered to the fruitful, while the childless were punished.

By the old law, unaltered by the new, any Roman citizen might by testament be appointed heir or legatee. The Roman citizen had the *testamenti factio*. The *leges Julia et Papia* took from them, however, the right to receive the inheritance or legacy under the will (*jus capiendi ex testamento*) unless they had previously, or within a given period after the reading of the will, complied with the provisions of the new laws. The unmarried could not take any part of what had been left them by will. The *orbi* could only take one-half; neither husband nor wife could effectually bequeath a legacy to the other, unless they had a common child. The property thus lost to the person named in the will was styled *caduca*. The *lex Papia* determined its devolution, and the order in which the *patres* mentioned in the will should, as the reward for their paternity, be allowed to claim the *caduca* (*jus caduca vindicandi*). The fruitful, therefore, succeeded, *ex lege*, to the *caduca*, and not by virtue of the terms of the will. Should it happen that no heir or legatee had children, the *caduca* were swept into the *ærarium* or treasury of the people, in order, says Tacitus, that, failing the rights of paternity, the people, as being the common father, should realize the forfeited gifts. In the course of time, forfeitures arising from other causes incident to a will were described as *in causâ caduci*.

Lex Ælia Sentia, A.D. 4—Lex Fusia (or Furia) Caninia, A.D. 8.

Enfranchisement.—Marius and Sylla, Pompey and Cæsar, having armed thousands of slaves, threw into Rome legions of freedmen. Added to this, citizens had of late enfranchised their slaves in order to increase the number of their clients—sometimes, in order that the slaves, having become citizens, should receive their share in the gratuitous distributions, but still more frequently, at the moment of death, in order that a long retinue of freedmen, with the cap of liberty on their heads, might follow the funeral car of their former master. To check these revolutionary practices, the *lex Ælia Sentia* enacted that slaves who, by way of punishment, had been placed in irons by their master, or who had been branded with a hot iron, or who had been accused and found guilty of a crime, or who had been delivered over to combat with either man or beast, or had been thrown into a gladiatorial school or prison, and afterwards enfranchised, could thereby only acquire the right of *peregrini dediticii*. Slaves, who had not suffered either of the before-mentioned indignities, by enfranchisement became either *Latini Juniani*, or Roman citizens. The *Latini Juniani* were so styled because they acquired the privileges of *Latins* by virtue of the *lex Junia*. If the slave was, firstly, more than thirty years of age; secondly, in the quiritarian ownership of the master; and, thirdly, enfranchised "for just cause," either by *vindicta*, *census*, or *testament*, he became a Roman citizen. If either of those three essentials was wanting, he became merely a Latin. The instances given by Gaius of "*justæ causæ*" are the enfranchisement of a son or daughter, of a natural brother or sister, of a nurse or teacher, of a slave for the purpose of making him an agent (*procurator*), or of a female slave for the purpose of marrying her.

A slave under thirty years of age would, however, by enfranchisement, become a Roman citizen if his master, being insolvent, instituted him heir in his testament. The *lex Ælia Sentia* also provided that any one who, by reason of being under thirty when enfranchised, became a Latin merely, might subsequently acquire the Roman citizenship by marriage with a Roman, or a Latin, and the possession of a son by that marriage of one year of age, upon proof of those facts by seven Roman citizens of full age before the competent authority. No provision was made by which the *dediticii* could become Roman citizens. They were forbidden to live within one hundred miles of Rome. If the enfranchisement was in fraud of creditors, or of a patron, it was void. If the master was under twenty years of age, he could only enfranchise by *vindicta* before the council after having shown just cause.

The Lex Fusia Caninia forbade the enfranchisement by testament of more than a given proportion of the testator's slaves. The owner of two might enfranchise both; of from two to ten, one-half; of from ten to thirty, one-third; of from thirty to one hundred, one-fourth; of more than one hundred, one-fifth. In no case could more than one hundred be enfranchised by testament.

Fidei commissa—Codicilli.—By the then law, precise legal expression, accompanied by the strict observance of certain formalities, was necessary to the due execution of a will. Certain testamentary dispositions, if made, could not be enforced by the aid of the civil law. The testator in such cases had to trust to the honour of his heirs (*fidei committere*). Such dispositions were styled *fidei commissa*. Written without the solemnities of a will, the documents containing them were called *codicilli*. Augustus was several times instituted heir. In each case he made it a point of duty faithfully to execute the trust. He ordered the consuls to exert their authority to the like effect. The practice gained general favour and was made law. Trusts and codicils became general.

Licensed Jurists—Responsa prudentum.—Augustus, wishing, so he said, to give to the *responsa prudentum* more authority than they theretofore enjoyed (*ut major juris auctoritas haberetur*), created a class of privileged jurists, who thus became officials invested by him with the right of responding under imperial sanction. The opinions (*responsa*) of these jurists were given under the sanction of their seals (*responsa signata*). It does not, however, appear that the creation of this privileged class of jurists took from other jurists the right of giving opinions: it merely gave to the *responsa prudentum* of the privileged a value they otherwise would not possess. At this period *responsa prudentum* had not the force of law which they afterwards obtained (*legis vicem obtinent*). Augustus, so far as we know, merely introduced the thin edge of a wedge destined to play a mighty part in the moulding of Roman law.

Augustus appears personally to have consulted these jurists in matters of legal doubt. Thus, when he had to determine a point regarding codicils, he convoked the jurists and submitted the matter to them.

Pomponius says:—"Before the time of Augustus, the right to give opinions publicly concerning the law had not been conceded by the chiefs of the republic. All who considered themselves sufficiently learned were at liberty to give their opinion to those who thought fit to consult them. These opinions were not given under the seal of the jurists who delivered them, but, in many cases, the jurists themselves wrote to the judge; in other cases, the parties who went to consult them took with them witnesses, who testified before the judge as to the opinion given. Augustus, whose object it was to give additional authority to the law, was the first, as already stated, who gave to the jurists the right to express their opinion by virtue of imperial authority; and this authorization being once established, it was supplicated as a favour."

Constitutiones Principum.—The generic term "*Constitutiones*" embraces all imperial acts. Those acts are divisible into three distinct classes, viz.: (1) *Edicta, i. e.*, general ordinances; (2) *Decreta, i. e.*, judgments delivered by the emperor personally in his tribunal; (3) *Mandata, epistolæ, rescripta, i. e.*, orders issued to individual lieutenants, magistrates, &c., or to private individuals who petitioned him.

When those *constitutiones* were first introduced is matter of discussion. Some writers date their rise from the reign of Hadrian (A.D. 117—138). Ortolan makes them commence with Augustus. His reason appears to be almost conclusive. We know that Augustus, who never shirked labour, transacted judicial business even at night, altogether regardless of the *sol occasus* of the Twelve Tables. Augustus, however, and his immediate successors always took care to obtain the sanction of the people, or of the senate, never allowing it to appear that they issued edicts or decrees except in virtue of the functions conferred upon them.

Lex de Imperio—Lex Curiata—Lex Regia.—Vast discussion concerning these three terms has practically ended in this—the act styled in the case of the king *lex regia* or *lex curiata;* in that of the republic, *lex curiata;* and lastly, in the case of the emperors, *lex regia* or *lex de imperio*, means, wherever either term is met with in Roman law, but one and the same thing, *i. e.*, the investiture of the supreme power—the *imperium.*

The system of the imperial government as it was instituted by Augustus, and maintained by those princes who understood their own interests and those of the people, may be defined to have been an absolute monarchy disguised by the forms of a commonwealth. The masters of the Roman world surrounded their thrones with darkness, concealed their irresistible strength, and humbly professed themselves the accountable ministers of the senate, whose supreme decrees they dictated and obeyed.

The face of the court corresponded with the forms of the administration. The emperors, if we except those tyrants whose capricious folly violated every law of nature and decency, disdained that pomp and ceremony which might offend their countrymen, but could add nothing to their real power. In all the offices of life they affected to confound themselves with their subjects, and maintained with them an equal intercourse of visits and entertainments. Their habits, their palace, their table, were suited only to the rank of an opulent senator. Their family, however numerous or splendid, was composed entirely of their domestic slaves and freedmen. Augustus or Trajan would have blushed at employing the meanest of the Romans in their menial affairs, which, in the household bedchamber of a limited monarch, are so eagerly solicited by the proudest nobles of Britain. (Gibbon, I. 109.)

The domestic relations of Augustus were not satisfactory; the debauchery of his daughter Julia was to him a source of great grief. It is said that when he felt death approaching, he called for a mirror, arranged his hair, and said to the bystanders: "Have I played my part well?" Being answered in the affirmative, he added, "*Valete et plaudite*"—farewell, and grant me your applause. He died on the 19th August, A.D. 14, æt. 79.

His testament was publicly read in the senate. He bequeathed as a valuable legacy to his successors the advice to confine the empire within those limits which nature seemed to have placed as its permanent bulwarks and boundaries. On the west, the Atlantic Ocean, the Rhine, and Danube. On the north, the Euphrates. On the east and towards the south, the sandy deserts of Arabia and Africa.

The people erected altars to him, and, by a decree of the senate, the month *Sextilis* was thenceforth called "*August.*"

The reign of Augustus has necessarily occupied considerable space. It is a point of departure in Roman history. Tacitus says that at this period consuls, senators, and knights were rapidly degenerating into a state of abject servitude, and that the higher the dignity of the individual, the lower was his probity (Ann. 1. 7). He gives a graphic account of the contemptible conduct both of the senate and Tiberius—who had been appointed by Augustus heir to two-thirds of his estate—when the time came to determine the position Tiberius should occupy in the state. He describes how, by feigned humility and reluctance to assume so important a position, Tiberius contrived to make himself the successor of Augustus. Tiberius,—who assembled the prætorian guards at Rome, and lodged them in a fortified camp under the pretext of relieving Italy,—was intentionally suffocated.

Caligula, whose favourite companions were actors, gladiators, and prostitutes, was murdered in his own palace. Claudius, at the instance of Agrippina, his wife, was poisoned. The monster Nero, who is said, among his other villainies, to have fired Rome that he might enjoy the spectacle of a city in flames, put an end to his own existence in order to escape the fury of Galba. It was about this time that the prætorian guard assumed the right of electing the emperors. The sanction of the senate became an empty form. Not long after, the legions in the provinces claimed to exercise the like privilege. Galba was assassinated in the forum. Otho, fearing Vitellius, committed suicide. Vitellius was murdered. The death of Titus was commonly laid to the charge of his brother Domitian. Domitian —who concluded peace with Decebulus, the king of the Dacians, undertaking that the Romans should pay him tribute—was assassinated by, or at the instance of, his wife. In short, out of the eleven emperors who reigned between Augustus and Trajan, two only, *i.e.*, Vespasian and Nerva, died natural deaths.

"During fourscore years—excepting only the short and doubtful respite of Vespasian's reign—Rome groaned beneath an unremitting tyranny which exterminated the ancient families of the republic, and was fatal to almost every virtue and every talent that arose in that unhappy period." (Gibbon, I. 129.)

These facts give some idea of the state of things among what are termed the upper classes; but to the student of Roman civil law, there is another and more pleasing phase of the then existing Roman life.

Ortolan says:—"The period of the [early ?] emperors was that in which the civil law made the greatest stride: jurists were multiplied, and numerous works on law made their appearance. All the principles of law were developed and connected together, and jurisprudence became a general science closely studied in every branch. Political rights, however, did not undergo much change, for despotism is not an innovator. Augustus had laid down all the fundamental bases of absolute power, and his successors had only to allow them to be consolidated by time. New institutions are rarely met with, even at long intervals."

The Two Schools—The Sabinians or Cassians, and the Proculeians or Pegasians.—During the reign of Augustus there were two representative men, Labeo and Capito. Labeo, the prætor, independent and incorruptible, was learned, not merely in the law, but in science in general, and was gifted with originality. He did not hesitate to suggest, and at times to make, innovations in the existing law. The consul, Capito, a favourite of his imperial master, was also learned in the existing law, but he loved wealth and power, and hated change; he continued to present things as they had been presented to him. To these jurists Pomponius refers the origin of the two famous Roman schools of law, respectively known by the names of the Sabinians or Cassians, and the Proculeians or Pegasians. It was from Proculus and Pegasus, two of the most illustrious of the pupils of Labeo, and from Sabinius and Cassius, pupils of Capito, that the respective schools took their names, for it was not till the disciples had succeeded to their masters that the two schools were in fact founded as rival teachers. The difference between the two schools was rather matter of tendency to change or retain than anything else. There was no inflexible line of demarcation. On more than one occasion the followers of one system abandoned the doctrines of their own school and adopted those of the other. New cases gave rise to fresh controversies. The result was that for nearly two centuries—the life of the schools—every legal proposition that admitted of fair discussion was thoroughly sifted by each. With the exception of the *lex Junia Norbana*, this period furnishes no new law worthy of record. Private law, however, became a science.

Lex Junia Norbana, A.U.C. 772 (A.D. 19).—By this law all freedmen were divided into two classes depending on the mode of enfranchisement, viz:—enfranchised citizens or enfranchised Latins, styled *Latini Juniani.* The former enjoyed full liberty and all citizen rights; the latter had only the rights of Latin colonists. They had not the *testamenti factio,* but they might be provided for in a codicil.

Gibbon sums up the history of Rome during this century thus:—"Happily for the repose of mankind, the moderate system recommended by the wisdom of Augustus was adopted by the fears and vices of his immediate successors. Engaged in the pursuit of pleasure, or in the exercise of tyranny, the first Cæsars seldom showed themselves to the armies, or to the provinces; nor were they disposed to suffer that those triumphs which their indolence neglected should be usurped by the conduct and valour of their lieutenants. The military fame of a subject was considered as an insolent invasion of the imperial prerogative, and it became the duty as well as interest of every Roman general to guard the frontiers entrusted to his care, without aspiring to conquests which might have proved no less fatal to himself than to the vanquished barbarians. The only accession which the Roman empire received during the first century of the Christian era was the province of Britain. In this single instance, the successors of Cæsar and Augustus were persuaded to follow the example of the former, rather than the precept of the latter. The proximity of its situation to the coast of Gaul seemed to invite their arms; the pleasing though doubtful intelligence of a pearl fishery attracted their avarice; and as Britain was viewed in the light of a distinct and insulated world, the conquest scarcely formed any exception to the general system of continental measures. After a war of about forty years, undertaken by the most stupid (Claudius), maintained by the most dissolute (Nero), and terminated by the most timid (Domitian), of all the emperors, the far greater part of the island submitted to the Roman yoke." "Such was the state of the Roman frontiers, and such the maxims of imperial policy from the death of Augustus to the accession of Trajan." (Cap. 1.)

CHAPTER VIII.

THE EMPIRE—*continued.*

THE SECOND CENTURY.

i. e., A.U.C. 853 till 952;—A.D. 100 till A.D. 199.

Emperors of Rome.

A.D.

to 117. TRAJAN (his reign commenced A.D. 98).

117—138. HADRIAN.

138—161. ANTONINUS PIUS.

161—180. MARCUS AURELIUS ANTONINUS.

180—193. M. COMMODUS ANTONINUS.

193. { PERTINAX.
DIDIUS JULIANUS.
SEPTIMIUS SEVERUS (LUCIUS).

Jurists.

Temp. TRAJAN—P. JUVENTIUS CELSUS, NERATIUS PRISCUS, PRISCUS JAVOLENUS.

Temp. HADRIAN—ALBURNUS VALENS, SALVIUS JULIANUS, SEXTUS CÆCILIUS AFRICANUS.

Temp. ANTONINUS PIUS—TERENTIUS CLEMENS, SEXTUS POMPONIUS.

Temp. MARCUS AURELIUS—PAPIRIUS JUSTUS, TARRANTENUS PATERNUS, Q. CERVIDIUS SCÆVOLA, ULPIUS MARCELLUS, GAIUS.

Temp. SEPTIMIUS SEVERUS—ÆMILIUS PAPINIANUS, CLAUDIUS TRYPHONIUS.

The Orators, Historians, Philosophers, Poets, &c., of the Period.

SUETONIUS (CAIUS TRANQUILLUS), historian, flourished about A.D. 100.

FLORIS (LUCIUS ANNÆUS), historian, temp. TRAJAN and HADRIAN.

GELLIUS (AULUS), prose writer, author of *Noctes Atticæ*, born about A.D. 130, died [?].

Trajan.—Trajan was born at the town of Italica[1] in Spain. He was the first Roman emperor who was not a native of Italy. He was one of the most noble and able rulers that Rome ever had. One of his first acts was the establishment of a system of national education for the sons and daughters of the poorer classes of citizens. He founded the Ulpian Library (*Bibliotheca Ulpia*) at Rome. The virtue and example of his wife and sister materially influenced the conduct of the Roman ladies. The notion of paying tribute to the Dacians[2] was to him intolerable. He fought and conquered them, first in A.D. 101, and again in A.D. 105, when Dacia (modern Moldavia, Wallachia, and Transylvania), was made a new Roman province. The Columna Trajana, in commemoration of this conquest, was erected A.D. 114.[3]

Hadrian.—With the exception of the last three years of his reign, in which he was guilty of many acts of cruelty and injustice, attributed by his adopted son and successor to a mental disease, Hadrian was a good ruler of his people. He surrendered the eastern conquests of his warlike predecessor. He restored to the Parthians[4] the election of an independent sovereign, and withdrew the Roman garrison from Armenia,[5] Mesopotamia,[6] and Assyria.[7] For the purpose of better jurisdiction, he divided Italy into four regions, and placed a consul at the head of each.

1 39. 2 171.

3 He subdued the whole of Arabia Petræa [253]. Mesopotamia [265] recognised the supremacy of Rome. Every day the astonished senate received, so we are told, the intelligence of new names and new nations that acknowledged his sway. "About 250 years after his death, the senate, in pouring out the customary acclamations on the accession of a new emperor, wished that he might surpass the felicity of Augustus and the virtue of Trajan." (Gibbon I. 121.)

4 293. 5 263. 6 265. 7 251.

He made journeys, largely, it is said, on foot, throughout the empire, correcting abuses and making improvements. He decreed that the child born of a female Roman citizen married to a Latin should be a Roman citizen. The most senseless act of his life was an edict forbidding the Jews to practise the rite of circumcision. The Jews rose in arms under Barcochab. It is said that 580,000 Jews were slain by the Romans. Those that survived and were not sold as slaves were forbidden to live in or near Jerusalem—a sad fate, but not worse than that to which the Old Testament tells us the Jews in the time of their prosperity and in the name of God had subjected not a few other nations. The Jews thus dispersed in time became the pioneers of commerce throughout the globe. The Jews have never since had a territory of their own, but may it not be said that no nation has given them shelter without thereby deriving benefit to itself?

Lex de Responsis Prudentum—Sententiæ et Opiniones made part of the Lex Scripta.—By a rescript of the Emperor Hadrian the *responsa prudentum* of the official jurists acquired the force of written law, but only in cases where the jurists were unanimous (*quibus permissum est jura condere*)—(*quæ legis vicem obtinent*). From this period the *responsa prudentum*, when unanimous, must be taken as part of the *lex scripta*.

Edictum Perpetuum, A.D. 131.—The work of the illustrious jurist, the prætor Salvius Julianus, that bore this title, appears to have been a code, or digest of the then prætorian law, to which imperial authority was given, and to which all prætors were obliged to conform. It appears, however, that subsequent prætors had the right of adding such accessory rules and forms as altered circumstances necessitated or suggested.

Aulus Ofilius, an intimate friend of Cæsar, is believed to have been the first to make and publish a digest of the edicts of the prætors. He is mentioned by Pomponius.[1]

[1] Of Hadrian, Gibbon says:—"He encouraged the arts, reformed the laws, asserted military discipline, and visited all his provinces in person. His vast and active genius was equally suited to the most enlarged views, and the minute details of civil policy. But the ruling passions of his soul were curiosity and vanity. As they prevailed and as they were attracted by

Antoninus Pius.—It is said of this man that he was the most virtuous of all the Roman emperors, and one of the noblest beings that ever lived. He lived as a private citizen accessible to all. He granted toleration to the Christians and protected them. By two constitutions in favour of slaves he enacted (1) That any one who killed his slave without just cause should be dealt with as if he had killed the slave of another; (2) That any master proved to have rendered the condition of his slave intolerable should be compelled to sell him. Owing to the almost total suspension of wars, the absence of violence and public crime, his reign of twenty-two years is historically a blank. During his reign and that of his predecessor, it is estimated that the standing military force of Rome amounted to 375,000 men, whose valour and discipline were well maintained, notwithstanding the leniency of the period. What finer monument to emperor or people?

It was in this reign and in that of Marcus Aurelius that the jurist Gaius, now so famous for his Institutes, lived. Till the year 1816 Gaius or Caius was unknown to the modern world except by name. In that year Niebuhr, when at Verona, discovered a copy of his Institutes written on a parchment that had previously borne other writing (a palimpsest). Who Gaius was we do not know. It has been conjectured that he professed law in one of the minor towns of the empire, possibly in Asia Minor, but why I confess myself unable to say. He belonged to the school of the Sabinians. That he and his Institutes were well known in the time of Justinian appears to me obvious, unless there were many works similar to his, of which there is no evidence, and which is highly improbable. I say that in my opinion his Institutes were well known in the time of Justinian, for it appears to me that the author of the Institutes of Justinian, though not sufficiently candid to admit it, simply brought

different objects, Hadrian was by turns an excellent prince, a ridiculous sophist, and a zealous tyrant. The general tenor of his conduct deserved praise for its equity and moderation. Yet in the first days of his reign, he put to death four consular senators, his personal enemies, and men who had been judged worthy of empire; and the tediousness of a painful illness rendered him at last peevish and cruel. The senate doubted whether they should pronounce him a god or a tyrant; and the honours decreed to his memory were granted to the prayers of the pious Antoninus." (I. 122.)

Gaius down to date, and wherein he otherwise deviated from his model did so to the no small disadvantage of the legal student.

Marcus Aurelius Antoninus.—It is said of this prince, who became emperor in his fortieth year, that at the age of twelve he embraced Stoicism, that he was severe to himself, indulgent as to the imperfection of others, just and beneficent to all mankind. War he detested as the disgrace and calamity of human nature, but when the necessity of a just defence called upon him to take up arms, he readily exposed himself to eight winter campaigns on the frozen banks of the Danube, the severity of which was at last fatal to the weakness of his constitution. It is said, however, that he ordered or sanctioned a cruel persecution of the Christians in Gaul in A.D. 177. Of him and his predecessor, who are referred to in history as "The two Antonines," Gibbon says, "Their united reigns are possibly the only period of history in which the happiness of a great people was the sole object of government." (I. 124.)

M. Commodus Antoninus.—Not long after the death of Aurelius, his son Commodus, then about nineteen years of age, concluded peace with the Marcomani[1] and Quadi,[2] and returned to Rome, where the love and veneration entertained for his father secured for him a welcome reception. Though nothing had been neglected by the anxious father, or by the men of virtue and learning by whom he had been surrounded, to fit him for his exalted position, there are few characters in history which inspire so unmingled a feeling of disgust and detestation as does his. During the first two years of his reign he wavered between the counsels of his father's friends and the temptation of his youthful associates, and contented himself with extravagances and pleasures which were more or less excused by reason of his years. In A.D. 182, however, the discovery by him of a conspiracy plotted against him determined his future career.

One evening, as he was returning through a dark and narrow

[1] 124. [2] 139.

portico in the amphitheatre to his palace, an assassin rushed upon him with a drawn sword, exclaiming, "The senate send you this!" Though the deed was not executed, and though it was discovered that the author of the plot was his licentious and jealous sister Lucilla, and not the senate, yet the words of the would-be assassin produced in Commodus an indelible impression of fear and hatred against the whole body of the senate. Nearly all the friends of his father and those who had risen to eminence under him were put to death. The remainder of his life was an uninterrupted series of sanguinary and disgusting excesses. He gratified his lusts in a harem which, it is said, contained 300 concubines. He fought as a gladiator in the circus more than 700 times, where he slew wild beasts and human beings, for which he demanded worship, as a second Hercules. Finally, having resolved to put the consuls for A.D. 193 to death, together with a number of others, on the 1st January of that year, he drew up the list of those whose fate he had sealed. The list fell into the hands of his mistress Marcia, who to her astonishment found her own name at its head, together with those of the præfect Lætus and the chamberlain Eclectus, who all three had endeavoured to dissuade him from the execution of his plan. The fact was communicated by Marcia to Lætus and Eclectus. Commodus was poisoned that evening; as the poison operated, however, but slowly, he died strangled by a celebrated athlete during the night of the 31st December, A.D. 192. The news of the death of Commodus was glad tidings to all but the prætorian guard.

Pertinax, the immediate successor of Commodus, reigned for eighty-six days. His virtues, his moderation, his expressed and obvious determination to repair the damage done to the state and to private individuals by Commodus, so far as in him lay, once more made life tolerable to all but the prætorian guards, the household dependents, and the debauched associates of the late emperor. To them virtue was a hateful thing. The prætorian guards dreaded a return to discipline and order. Lætus, the præfect of the prætorian guard, awoke to the fact that the new emperor would reward a servant, but would not be ruled by a favourite. Two attempts to place others in the emperor's stead having failed, a general sedition broke out in the camp. Some two or three hundred soldiers marched at noonday to the palace; the gates were thrown open to them by the soldiers on guard. Pertinax disdained either to conceal himself or to fly; he fell pierced with many wounds on the 28th March, A.D. 193. From that date the Roman republic was a military despotism.

Didius Julianus.—From the ramparts the prætorians proclaimed that the Roman world was to be disposed of to the highest bidder. Salpicianus, the father-in-law of the late emperor, offered 5,000 drachms (above £160) to each soldier; Didius Julianus, a wealthy senator, bid 6,250 drachms. The camp gates were thrown open to him. He was declared emperor. The prætorian guard, after taking the oath of allegiance to Didius Julianus, led him to the senate, who obsequiously conferred on him every branch of imperial power. The armies of Britain, of Syria,[1] and of Pannonia[2] refused to ratify the ignominious bargain of the prætorians. Septimius Severus, who was at the head of the army of Pannonia,[2] crossed the Alps, and hastened with his legions towards Rome. Arrived at Interamna,[3] about seventy miles from Rome, Septimius Severus despatched his emissaries to the Capitol to assure the guards that on condition of their abandoning Julianus and the perpetrators of the murder of Pertinax to the justice of the conquerors, he would not treat the murder as an act of the whole body of the prætorians. The prætorians, fearing the Pannonian legions, seized the greater part of the assassins, and signified to the senate that they no longer defended the cause of Julianus. Severus was acknowledged emperor, and divine honours were decreed to Pertinax. Julianus was deposed, condemned to death, and beheaded as a common criminal on the 2nd June, 193.

[1] 251 [2] 141. [3] 128.

It is at this stage that the student of Roman history is permitted to turn from excitement, at times pleasing, at others revolting, to the calm study of Roman private law. It is there and there alone that the principles of Roman social life can be found. He cannot, therefore, do better at this point than to read the Institutes of Gaius (see *post*, pp. 200 *et seq.*).

CHAPTER IX.

THE EMPIRE—*continued.*

THE THIRD CENTURY.

i. e., A.U.C. 953 till A.U.C. 1052;—A.D. 200 to A.D. 299.

Emperors of Rome.

A.D.	
to 211.	SEPTIMIUS SEVERUS.
211—217.	CARACALLA.
211—212.	GETA.
217—218.	MACRINUS.
218—222.	ELAGABALUS.
222—235.	ALEXANDER SEVERUS.
235—238.	MAXIMIN.
238.	GORDIANUS I. GORDIANUS II.
238.	PUPIENUS MAXIMUS. BALBINUS.
238—244.	GORDIANUS III.
244—249.	PHILIPPUS.
249—251.	DECIUS.
251—254.	HOSTILIANUS. TREBONIANUS GALLUS.
253.	ÆMILIANUS.
253—260.	VALERIAN.
260—268.	GALLIENUS.
268—270.	CLAUDIUS II.
270—275.	AURELIAN.
275—276.	TACITUS.

A.D.	
276.	FLORIANUS.
276--282.	PROBUS.
282—283.	CARUS.
283—284.	CARINUS. NUMERIANUS.
284—305.	DIOCLETIAN.
286—305.	MAXIMIAN.

Jurists.

Fragments preserved by the Digest of Justinian.

PAPINIAN	596
ULPIAN	2462
PAUL	2083
CALLISTRATUS	99
ÆLIUS MARCIANUS	2757
FLORENTINUS	427
ÆMILIUS MACER	62
HERRENIUS MODESTINUS	345

The Orators, Historians, Philosophers, Poets, &c., of the Period.

CLAUDIANUS (CLAUDIUS), poet, flourished about A.D. 275 to A.D. 299.

CALPURNIUS (TITUS), poet, flourished during this period.

Septimius Severus.—After a stay of thirty days in Rome, Severus started with his legions first against Pescennius Niger, who was at the head of the army in Syria, and afterwards against Clodius Albinus, at the head of the army in Britain, each of whom contested his right to the throne, hence once more civil war. Severus was ultimately successful. His triumph was marked by many acts of cruelty. Large numbers of the senators who had belonged to the party of his unfortunate competitors were put to death, and the noblest provincials of Spain and Gaul were involved in the like ruin. Byzantium,[1] the strongest bulwark of the Romans against the barbarians of Pontus[2] and Asia, adhered to the cause of Niger, even after his death. For three years it withstood the siege of Severus, but ultimately succumbed to famine, when, to the discredit of Severus, its magistrates and soldiers were put to the sword, and, to the peril of the state, its fortifications were razed to the ground. When Severus had secured his position, however, it must be said to his credit that he governed with wisdom and justice. Salutary laws, enforced with inflexible firmness, corrected most of the abuses that succeeded the death of Marcus. He secured peace and property at home, and revived abroad the ancient respect for the Roman name. He disbanded the prætorian guard, but substituted for it a military guard drawn from the legions of the frontier, into which were drafted from time to time the soldiers most distinguished for strength, valour, and fidelity. By this act he at once diverted the Italian youth from the exercise of arms, and overawed the senate and citizens of Rome by the presence of 50,000 armed men, mostly barbarians. He disdained the show of subservience to the senate, and where his predecessors had requested, he ordered. The command of his favourite troops became the first office of the state. Theretofore the prætorian præfect had been a simple captain of the guard; he was placed by Severus at the head of the army, the finances, and the law. Plautianus was the first; Papinian, the most famous of Roman jurists, was his immediate successor. Alas! lawyers and historians taught that the emperor was freed from the restraint of civil laws; they unblushingly said that he could command by his arbitrary will the lives and fortunes of his subjects, and was at liberty to dispose of the empire as of his private patrimony. He conferred on his two sons, Caracalla and Geta, the rank of augustus and the revered name of Antoninus. When more than sixty years of age, he went to Britain, where he subdued the barbarians of the north. He died at York in the sixty-fifth year of his age, in A.D. 211. The peace and glory of his reign made his contemporaries forget the

[1] 203. [2] 248.

cruelties of its inauguration; but posterity has ascribed to his military system the main cause of the decline and fall of the Roman empire. It was during his reign that Roman jurisprudence is regarded as having attained its full maturity and perfection. It was then that Papinian, Paulus, and Ulpian, the most celebrated of the Roman jurists, flourished.

Caracalla and Geta.—Severus, in his last moments, commended his two sons, Caracalla and Geta, to the army as his joint successors: he recommended concord to his sons. On the death of their father the two were proclaimed emperors. They both returned to Rome on the 27th February, A.D. 212. Geta was assassinated in his mother's chamber when she was endeavouring to reconcile the brothers. In her presence, and in the presence and at the instance of Caracalla, 20,000 persons of both sexes, alleged to be the friends of Geta, were put to death, and among them Papinian, who, being commanded by Caracalla to make a studied apology for the assassination of Geta, replied:—"It is easier to commit than to justify a parricide." When an attempt was made to convince him that Geta had merited his death, he said:—"To accuse a person who has been assassinated unjustly is to be guilty of a second assassination." Caracalla, never to return, left the capital about a year after the death of Geta. He visited province after province, particularly those of the east: rapine and barbarity attended him. From a secure spot in the temple of Serapis at Alexandria[1] he viewed and directed the slaughter of many thousands of citizens and strangers. In March, A.D. 217, he was assassinated by a centurion named Martialis, at the instance of Macrinus, the prætorian præfect, who entertained, and not without reason, fears concerning his own safety.

Two important matters in the legal history of the Romans mark this reign. Execrated by the virtuous and those who had anything to lose, Caracalla secured the support of the soldiery by the most extravagant liberality. To enable him to provide the necessary funds he had to resort to two expedients.

[1] 223.

All Subjects Citizens, A.D. 212 (A.U.C. 965).—By an enactment of the emperor Caracalla, all Roman subjects were made Roman citizens, "*In orbe Romano qui sunt, ex constitutione imperatoris Antonini cives Romani effecti sunt.*" The real object of this apparent act of grace was, according to Dion Cassius, to swell the revenue. Caracalla first increased the amount of the taxes payable by citizens, and then increased the number of citizens. Caracalla placed all on a level, but that level was subjection to the imperial will. The boast, "*I* am a Roman citizen," had long been a thing of the past.

There is considerable doubt as to the true meaning and effect of this enactment, but there is no doubt that after, as well as before it, *dedititii* and *Latini Juniani* were well known in Rome and its provinces. From this period *peregrini* were those who were in fact strangers to Rome, barbarians, mercenaries in the pay of the emperor. The idea attached to the word *peregrinus* was thus changed a second time.

Roman slaves thenceforth had to be obtained from beyond the frontiers of the Rhine, the Danube, of Asia Minor, or of Roman Africa.

This constitution, which gave to all subjects the rights of Roman citizenship, did not give to all Roman territory the status of *ager romanus.*

Leges Julia et Papia Poppæa Modified.—Caracalla, who had doubled the impost upon inheritances, legacies, *donationes mortis causâ*, and enfranchisements, before he made all Roman subjects Roman citizens, also abrogated that portion of the *leges Julia et Papia Poppæa* that gave the *caduca* to those named in the will who had children, and swept the whole *caduca* into the *fiscus. Hodie ex constitutione imperatoris Antonini omnia caduca fisco vindicantur.*

Macrinus, A.D. 217—218.—Three days after the assassination of Caracalla, the troops, with some reluctance, proclaimed Macrinus emperor. They despised his military talent, and suspected his personal valour. The senate ratified the choice, as matter of course, though indignant that a man of equestrian rank should dare to don the purple. The prodigality of Caracalla had left the exchequer low. Macrinus, to meet the exigency, essayed the rôle of reformer. He tried economy in the army. A general rebellion was the result. Bassianus, who was falsely, but in his supposed interest, alleged to be the natural son of Caracalla, was high priest of the sun at Emesa[1] in Syria, where a large number of the troops were then stationed. Bought over by the grandmother of Bassianus, the troops at Emesa declared Bassianus emperor, May 16th, A.D. 218. Macrinus marched to meet him, but in the heat of the battle made a shameful and precipitate flight. He died a few days later.

Elagabalus (or Heliogabalus).—The sun was worshipped at Emesa under the name of Heliogabalus. As pontiff, Bassianus presumed to adopt the sacred name. His sole serious object in life, if serious it can be called, appeared to be the triumph of the worship of the god of Emesa, to whom he attributed his elevation. That end he endeavoured to secure by costly and showy processions through the streets of Rome, and by sacrifices celebrated in the temple with every circumstance of pomp. Such was the grossness of his sensuality that it is said even the licentious soldiery blushed at the object of their choice. Mesa, his grandmother, by whose instrumentality he had been placed on the throne, feeling that his glaring vices must ere long destroy him, persuaded him (A.D. 221) to adopt his cousin Alexander, and to invest him with the title of Cæsar, "that his own divine occupations might be no longer interrupted by the cares of earth." Alexander became popular; Elagabalus grew jealous. Report said that Alexander was dead. The troops refused to be pacified. Elagabalus, mortified at the attachment shown to Alexander, punished the leaders of the mutiny. Elagabalus was massacred by the enraged prætorians. His corpse was dragged through the streets, and thrown into the Tiber, March 10th, A.D. 222.

Alexander Severus (A.D. 222—235).—Alexander, born at Acre, in Phœnicia, was elevated to the throne when in his seventeenth

[1] 250.

year. He was a virtuous youth, endowed with excellent understanding, fond of study and the society of the learned. Ulpian, the great jurist, was his chief adviser and a frequent guest at his table, which was served with the most frugal simplicity. With the approbation of the senate, his mother, Mammæa, chose sixteen of the wisest and most virtuous senators as a perpetual council of state. On his accession the reins of government were in the hands of his mother, and Mæsa, his grandmother. Mæsa died shortly after. Mammæa continued her influence over her son and the affairs of state during the whole of Alexander's reign. She, her son, and the council devoted their energies to the redress of the damage done to the state by Alexander's immediate predecessors, the consequence being that his thirteen years' reign secured the love and gratitude of the people as distinguished from the army. The dignity, the freedom, and the authority of the senate were restored, and every virtuous senator knew and felt that he could approach the person of the emperor without fear and without a blush. Mammæa, though wishing well to the empire and her son, through jealousy was guilty of gross cruelty to her son's first wife and her father. She secured the banishment of the former and the death of the latter.

By the most gentle arts Alexander laboured to inspire the fierce and lawless soldiery with a sense of duty, and endeavoured to restore the semblance, at least, of that discipline for which the Roman legions had been so famous, and to which Rome was mainly indebted for its greatness. His attempt, however, proved fatal, not merely to Ulpian and others who co-operated with him, but eventually to himself.

The attachment of the guards to their youthful prince induced them at first to think that the attempted reform was the work of Alexander's advisers. Their anger centred itself on their præfect, Ulpian, who fell a victim to their fury, being assassinated at the feet of the emperor, who vainly strove to cover him with the purple. The historian Dion Cassius, who had commanded the Pannonian legions, escaped their fury by retreat at the emperor's entreaty to his villa in Campania. Alexander was murdered in Gaul, together with his mother, during an insurrection of the legions, headed by Maximin.

It is reported that when at Antioch[1] during his Persian expedition, which, if not a failure, could hardly be called a success, he ordered the punishment of some soldiers who had been discovered in the baths of women. That act excited sedition in the legion to which the men belonged. Hearing of it, Alexander ascended his tribunal, and in a modest but firm manner declared it to be his intention to correct the vices introduced by his predecessors, and to maintain the discipline which could not be relaxed without the ruin of the Roman name and empire. Being interrupted by the clamour of the soldiers, he said, "Reserve your shouts till you take the field against the Persians, the Germans, and the Sarmatians. Be silent in the presence of your sovereign and benefactor, who bestows upon you the corn, the clothing, and the money of the provinces. Be silent, or I shall no longer style you soldiers, but *quirites* (simple citizens), if those, indeed, who disclaim the laws of Rome deserve to be ranked among even the meanest of the people." Being then threatened by their brandished arms, he added, "Your courage would be more nobly displayed in the field of battle. You can destroy me, but you cannot intimidate me. The justice of the republic would punish your crime and would revenge my death." The legion still retaining their threatening bearing, he cried out with a loud voice, "Citizens! lay down your arms and depart in peace to your respective habitations." The tempest was instantly appeased; grief and shame took the place of defiance. The men laid down their arms and retired, not to their camp, but to the inns of the city. After thirty days, and after the execution of the tribunes, whose connivance had occasioned the mutiny, Alexander restored the men to their places in the legion, which gratefully served him while living, and revenged him when dead.

We are told that no sooner had Alexander returned from Persia than he marched against the Germans; that he was at the head of a large army on the borders of the Rhine, when Maximin, a soldier of fortune who had risen from the condition of a Thracian peasant to high command, stimulated the discontent of the soldiers, and incited his emissaries to ask the men

[1] 250.

how long they intended to submit to a man who was no general but the timid slave of his mother and the senate, and to ask them why they did not select as their prince and general a real soldier educated in camps and exercised in wars, who would assert the glory and distribute among his companions the treasure of the empire. It is said that shortly after, when Maximin went on the parade ground, the troops saluted him emperor, after which they hastened to the murder of Alexander; that Alexander, perceiving their intention, withdrew to his tent; that he was followed by a tribune and some centurions; that instead of receiving them with manly resolution, he, with unavailing cries, entreated them to spare his life. The reader may find it difficult to reconcile these two alleged incidents, though it is easy to reconcile the former with conscious virtue, and to suppose the latter to be the lying version of the scoundrel who caused the death of a noble man.

For a long time after the death of Alexander Severus history is silent as to jurisprudence. It is occupied solely with military seditions, emperors reigning for a few months, armies fighting in support of their respective candidates, and the mention of the numerous pretenders to imperial rank.

Maximin (A.D. 235—238).—During the three years of this man's reign he neither visited Rome nor Italy. He trampled on every principle of law and justice. Noble birth, accomplishments, or knowledge excluded the possessor of either from the imperial presence. The aristocracy were plundered and murdered; the treasure of every city reserved for the purchase of corn, or the cost of the public games, was confiscated; the temples were stripped of their ornaments of gold and silver; a universal cry of execration and prayer for vengeance went up. Gordianus, the proconsul of the African province, was compelled by the African legions to accept the imperial purple in his eightieth year. His son was declared his colleague in the imperial dignity. The Roman senate unanimously and gladly ratified the choice and appointments. Maximin, his son and adherents were pronounced common enemies. The senate in the meantime assumed the reins of government, and made arrangements to meet Maximin in the field. Unhappily the younger Gordian, who went out to meet the enemy, was killed. He died honourably, sword in hand. The news of his death paralyzed the old man, his father. He put an end to his life, after a reign of thirty-six days, in March A.D. 238.

Maximus and Balbinus.—The Roman senate, on the news of the fate of the Gordians, conferred the imperial dignity on Maximus and Balbinus, two distinguished senators, the latter a polished orator and poet, the former a rougher but able statesman. The multitude, jealous of the senate, demanded the elevation of the younger Gordian, a lad of thirteen, to the imperial rank, in token of their gratitude to his predecessors for the sacrifice of their lives in the national cause. The senate conferred on him the title of Cæsar. Meantime, Maximin had crossed the Alps on his way to Rome. In April, A.D. 238, he appeared before Aquileia.[1] The city was ready for him, and the generals had rendered the surrounding country an undesirable camping ground. Want bred disaffection in his legions. A band from the prætorian guard of Alba,[2] entrusted with the execution of the sentence of the senate, met with no resistance. The ponderous monster and his son were slain in the imperial tent. His legions swore allegiance to the senate, to Maximus and Balbinus.

That Maximus and Balbinus proved themselves all that was expected was freely admitted by the senate and the people. Neither the senate nor the people were, however, the soldiery. The whole city a few days after unsuspectingly gave itself up to the Capitoline games. While aristocracy and commonalty were so engaged, a band of assassins from the prætorian guard entered the palace, seized the emperors, and finally, to prevent their rescue, mangled them with a thousand wounds.

Gordianus III.—After the murder of Maximus and Balbinus the soldiers carried the boy Gordian to the camp, where they saluted him Augustus and emperor. Possibly the recollection

[1] 126. [2] 111.

of the reign of Septimius Severus gilded the pill with many. Misitheus, a learned man of the time and a master of rhetoric, had a daughter. The young emperor fell in love with and married the daughter, and appointed his father-in-law prætorian præfect. About this time the Persians threatened Antioch.[1] Misitheus advised Gordianus to take the field against them. He did so, and so far as history records opened for the last time the temple of Janus. He was successful, and had the pleasure of announcing the fact to the senate, though modestly, and possibly deservedly, ascribing his good fortune to Misitheus. Be that as it may, the prosperity of Gordianus ended with Misitheus. The death of Misitheus was followed by suggestions of poison. His successor as prætorian præfect, Philip, was by birth an Arab. It is hinted that he created an artificial scarcity in the camp, and then ascribed the distress of the army to the incapacity of the prince. We know this—The emperor was murdered March, A.D. 244, and Philippus was proclaimed emperor by the soldiery.

Philippus (A.D. 244—249).—In order to captivate the people, Philippus solemnized the secular games which, since their institution or revival by Augustus, had only been celebrated by Claudius, Domitian, and Severus. The mystic sacrifices were performed during three nights. Slaves and strangers were excluded. Five years after the accession of Philippus the legions of Mœsia revolted in favour of one Marinus. Philippus sent the senator Decius to quell the insurrection. The legions of Mœsia[2] gave Decius the choice between the purple and death. He elected the former. Somehow or the other, Philippus met his death a few days after at Verona[3] (A.D. 249). His son and associate in the empire was assassinated at Rome by the prætorian guard.

Decius (A.D. 249—251).—Decius was universally acknowledged by the senate and the provinces. This reign is primarily memorable as being the time when the Goths, who at a later

[1] 250. [2] 172. [3] 126.

date sacked the Roman Capitol, and reigned in Gaul, Spain, and Italy, first made a perceptible impression on the Roman power. The inhabitants of Marcianopolis[1] bought off the invaders by the payment of a considerable sum of money. Not long after the Goths returned, and crossed the Danube a second time, under the leadership of Cniva, their king. The troops of Decius, who was defeated, fled in disorder. Philippopolis[2] succumbed to the barbarians; 100,000 persons are said to have been massacred. Decius, having at length restored discipline and recruited his numbers, again met the enemy, when, being confident of victory, he refused to listen to any terms of accommodation. The Goths fought, resolved on death rather than slavery. The Romans were defeated, and perished in a morass, A.D. 251. The body of the emperor was never found.

Gallus and Hostilianus.—Hostilianus, the only surviving son of Decius, was created emperor from a just regard for the memory of his father. Gallus was associated with him on account of his experience and ability. Gallus bought off the Goths from the Illyrian provinces, and promised to pay them an annual tribute. Hostilianus perished during a pestilence. Some said that Gallus had more than the pestilence to do with his death. The bribes of Gallus encouraged the Goths to fresh attempts. Æmilianus, governor of Pannonia and Mœsia, encountered, defeated, and pursued the enemy beyond the Danube. He distributed among his soldiers as a donation the money collected for the tribute. Gallus went out to meet his aspiring lieutenant. When the armies were in sight of each other, the soldiers of Gallus murdered him and his son, and thus put an end to the projected civil war in May, A.D. 253.

Æmilianus, A.D. 253.—Æmilianus reigned four months. He was slain by his troops on the approach of Valerian, bent on revenging the murder of his master Gallus, August, A.D. 253.

Valerian (A.D. 253—260) and Gallienus (A.D. 253—268).—Valerian, who was about sixty years of age when made emperor.

[1] 187. [2] 188.

by the unanimous voice of the Roman world on account of his noble birth, his unblemished manners, learning, prudence, and experience, united with himself his son Gallienus, a youth who did not reflect the image of his father. The whole period of these reigns was one uninterrupted series of confusion and calamity. The Franks, the Alemanni, the Goths, and the Persians attacked Rome from without. Nineteen pretenders to the throne attacked the empire from within. The Franks carried their devastations to the foot of the Pyrenees, and, having crossed those mountains, devastated Spain during twelve years, after which they seized the vessels in the Spanish ports, and transported themselves to Mauritania.[1] The Alemanni passed through the Rhætian Alps, advanced as far as Ravenna,[2] and there displayed their victorious banners in sight of Rome, A.D. 259. Valerian was then in the east, and Gallienus on the Rhine. The senators called out the prætorian guard, left to garrison the Capitol, and filled up their numbers by enlisting into their ranks the stoutest and most willing of the plebeians. The Alemanni, astonished at their numbers, retreated, but returned to Germany laden with spoil. In A.D. 258—259, the Goths, sailing round the eastern extremity of the Euxine Sea,[3] arrived at Trebizond,[4] a large and populous city, fortified by a double line of walls, and garrisoned by 10,000 men. While the garrison was occupied in riot and luxury, the Goths were diligently erecting a lofty pile of fascines. In the silence of the night the Goths, sword in hand, ascended the walls, entered the city, massacred the inhabitants, and stripped the temples and other buildings. They then ravaged the province of Pontus,[5] and sailed off to their new establishments in the kingdom of Bosporus,[6] for the time being content with their acquisitions. Thus ended the first of the naval expeditions of the Goths.

The second naval expedition of the Goths soon followed. The cities of Nicomedia,[7] Nice,[7] Prusa,[7] Agamea,[7] and Cius[7] were devastated, Nice and Nicomedia being left in flames.

In A.D. 262 the Goths made a third naval expedition. Cyzicus was sacked, Athens was seized. There the Goths abandoned

[1] 56. [2] 126. [3] 232. [4] 247. [5] 248. [6] 231. [7] 203.

themselves not merely to plunder, but to intemperance. While so occupied, the brave Dexippus, with a band of volunteers, successfully attacked their fleet. Greece for the moment showed signs of its ancient heroic greatness. Gallienus at length appeared in arms. The ardour of the Goths was checked, and their strength divided. Naulobatus, a chief of the Heruli, accepted an honourable capitulation, and with a large body of his countrymen entered the Roman service. He was the first barbarian invested with the ornaments of consular dignity.

Sapor, king of Persia,[1] first seized Armenia,[2] then the strong garrisons of Carrha and Nisibus, and subsequently devastated both sides alike of the Euphrates.[3] Valerian resolved to march in person to the defence of the east. He encountered the Persian monarch near the walls of Edessa.[4] He was vanquished and taken prisoner. He and his troops laid down their arms A.D. 260. Valerian died the captive of Sapor, by whom it is reported he was treated with the greatest indignities.

The news of his father's death is said to have rather gratified than displeased Gallienus. He made no attempt whatever to revenge. The news of invasions, defeats, and rebellions was received by him with a careless smile. Taking one day with affected contempt a particular product of a lost province, he carelessly asked, "Must Rome be ruined if it is not supplied with linen from Egypt or arras from Gaul?"

It is needless to give the names of the nineteen pretenders to the throne, not one of whom enjoyed a life of peace, or died a natural death. In justice to many of them it may be said that they were rather driven to rebellion by fear as to their personal safety than urged to it by ambition. Several of them were men of virtue, and almost all were possessed of vigour and ability.

It may be said of Gallienus that though not destitute of courage, he was void of patriotism, and that he attempted everything but the arts of war and good government. Gibbon says:—"He was a master of several curious but useless sciences, a ready orator, an elegant poet, a skilful gardener, an excellent cook, and a most contemptible prince." In addition to its

[1] 32° N., 60° E. [2] 263. [3] 280. [4] 264.

other ills, the Roman world had to bear between A.D. 250 and A.D. 265 the ravages of a frightful plague. It is said that at one time during that period 5,000 died daily in Rome alone, that many towns were absolutely depopulated, and that one-half of the population of Alexandria[1] perished.

The army that was stationed on the Upper Danube invested their leader Aureolus with the purple. He passed the Alps, and occupied Milan (*Midiolanum*).[2] He there challenged Gallienus to contest with him in the field the sovereignty of Italy. Gallienus, provoked by the insult, took arms against him. Aureolus was defeated, and, being wounded, retired to Milan. Gallienus immediately laid siege to the place. Aureolus corrupted the besieging soldiery. Late one night, being informed that Aureolus had made a desperate sally from the town, Gallienus mounted his horse and rode at full speed to the supposed place of the attack. By an unseen hand he was mortally wounded on the 20th March, A.D. 268.

Claudius II. (A.D. 268—270).—Claudius, a man of humble origin, but whose abilities had raised him to high offices under Decius, Valerian, and Gallienus, ascended the throne when about fifty-four years of age. Aureolus attempted to negotiate with him a treaty of alliance and partition. "Tell him," said Claudius, "that such proposals should have been made to Gallienus; he, perhaps, might have listened to them with patience and accepted a colleague as despicable as himself." Aureolus was obliged to yield at discretion; he was condemned and put to death. Claudius was resolved, so far as in him lay, to restore the empire to its ancient splendour. With the authority of a veteran commander he insisted on the advantage of discipline and pointed to the consequence of laxity in the army. His teaching was not unheeded. The German nations, with a fleet far superior to any they had previously possessed, anchored near the foot of Mount Athos,[3] and assaulted Thessalonica.[4] Claudius went to its relief. The Germans left the city and hastened to meet him in the field. They met in the neighbourhood of Naissus,[5] a city

[1] 223. [2] 111. [3] 190 [4] 174. [5] 172.

of Dardania. The barbarian host, defeated with a loss of 50,000 men, was weakened, but not crushed. The Goths fought in Mœsia,[1] Thrace,[2] and Macedonia,[3] and at length, driven into the most inaccessible parts of the mountains of Hæmus,[4] there found shelter, such as it was, for the time being. During a rigorous winter the troops of Claudius besieged them. Famine and pestilence had frightfully supplemented the devastation of the sword. When spring came it was but a small, though a hardy and desperate band that made its appearance in arms. Claudius succumbed to the pestilence. He died in A.D. 270. During his last illness Claudius recommended Aurelian, one of his generals, to the principal officers of state as the man most deserving of the throne.

Aurelian (A.D. 270—275).—The death of Claudius gave fresh courage to the Goths. The Goths and the Vandals in vast numbers threatened Rome. Aurelian met them on the field. The approach of night ended a bloody and doubtful conflict. After twenty years of perpetual fighting the Goths and Romans consented to a lasting peace. The Goths engaged to supply the armies of Rome with a body of 2,000 auxiliaries—cavalry, in return for an undisturbed retreat. Aurelian withdrew the Roman forces from Dacia,[5] and tacitly relinquished that great province to the Goths and Vandals.

In A.D. 270, Aurelian defeated the Alemanni in three great battles. They were almost exterminated.

The seven hills of Rome had been surrounded by Servius Tullius by a wall seven miles in length. Rome had overgrown the enclosure. The suburbs were unprotected. Aurelian commenced, and Probus finished, the erection of an outflanking wall between eleven and twelve miles in length. Between the building of the first and second of these walls, Rome for centuries had trusted, and with reason, to the valour of her legions.

The Goths, the Vandals, and the Alemanni disposed of, Aurelian turned his attention to Gaul, Spain, and Britain on

[1] 172. [2] 188. [3] 173. [4] 187. [5] 171.

the one hand, Egypt, Syria, and Asia Minor on the other. Owing to the imbecility of recent emperors these Roman provinces had been seized and long enjoyed by usurpers.

Tetricus—the Gaul—the slave and sovereign of a licentious army, whom he dreaded and by whom he was despised, desired to escape unhurt from his unenviable position. He colluded with Aurelian. War was declared. Tetricus took the field against Aurelian, posted his men in the most disadvantageous manner, revealed his position to Aurelian, and, with a few chosen friends, deserted in the beginning of the action, A.D. 271.

Zenobia was the then mistress of the east. Aurelian went to contest her pretensions. She was a charming, high-spirited, and accomplished woman, fond of the chase, and no less fond of Homer and Plato. The forces of Zenobia were defeated first at Antioch[1] and again at Emesa.[1] Unable to collect a third army, Zenobia retired to Palmyra,[2] which she stoutly defended till famine made her position no longer tenable, when she resolved on flight. She reached the banks of the Euphrates, sixty miles from Palmyra, where she was overtaken by Aurelian's light horse and carried back. On his way to Rome, Aurelian heard that the Palmyrans had massacred the governor and garrison he had left among them. He hastened back and slaughtered the inhabitants without distinction of age or sex.

One Firmus had dared to assume the imperial purple at Alexandria. He raised an army. It was routed. He was captured, tortured, and put to death. It is said that no previous triumph had excelled in magnificence that of Aurelian on this occasion (A.D. 274).

Tetricus and Zenobia were permitted to spend the remainder of their lives in affluence and repose. Not long after his triumph an insurrection broke out at Rome; its cause and object are uncertain. Aurelian lost 7,000 of his veteran soldiers in its suppression. History does not say the number of thousands slain by him, but the blood of rich and poor seems to have flowed like water. The most illustrious of the senate were either killed or disappeared. Aurelian disdained to hold power otherwise than by the sword.

[1] 250. [2] 266.

While on his way to punish the Persian monarch, and when between Byzantium and Heracles, Aurelian was murdered in March, A.D. 275.

Tacitus, A.D. 275—276.—The army requested the senate to nominate an emperor; the senate declined, and requested the army to nominate one. The counter-propositions were thrice repeated and rejected. Six months after the assassination of Aurelian the senate raised the aged and virtuous Tacitus, then in his seventy-fifth year, to the imperial dignity. The army confirmed the election. Tacitus marched in person against the Alani, a Scythian[1] people. They were defeated, and the province of Asia was delivered from their yoke. Exhausted by fatigues to which he was not accustomed, and mortified by the insolence of the soldiery, Tacitus, after a reign of six months and about twenty days, expired at Tyana in Cappadocia,[2] on the 12th April, A.D. 276.

Florianus, A.D. 276.—Florianus, the brother of Tacitus, unasked, assumed the purple. Probus, the general of the east, declared himself the avenger of the senate. Florianus prepared to meet Probus, but his own soldiers settled the matter by assassinating him after a reign of about three months.

Probus, A.D. 276—282.—Probus, a native of Illyricum,[3] the man to whom Aurelian was indebted for the conquest of Egypt, was unanimously declared emperor by the army in the east, whereupon he immediately submitted his claims to the senate who joyfully ratified the choice on the 3rd August, A.D. 276. Incredible as it may appear, almost all of the districts crushed by Aurelian had again, and with more fury than before, risen in defiance of Roman supremacy. To meet the occasion, Probus, incapable of attending to all, selected as his lieutenants Carus, Diocletian, Maximian, Constantius, Galerius, and others who afterwards either ascended or supported the throne. In a short reign of about six years Probus broke the power of the wandering

[1] 273. [2] 234. [3] 142.

Sarmatian[1] tribes, attacked and subdued the Isaurians[2] in their mountain fastnesses, chastised the cities of Ptolemais[3] and Coptos[4] that still adhered to the fortunes of Firmus in Upper Egypt, and delivered Gaul and about seventy flourishing cities from the barbarous oppression of the Germans. He compelled the Germans to restore the effects and captives they had carried away from the provinces, and concluded peace with them on the condition of their supplying the Roman army with 16,000 recruits,—the bravest and most robust of their youth. Saturninus, who revolted in the east in A.D. 279, and Bobosus and Proculus, who revolted in Gaul in A.D. 280, were successively suppressed.

Foreign and civil war ended, Probus returned to Rome, and commemorated his victories by a splendid triumph.

As to the 16,000 German recruits, Probus dispersed them throughout the provinces in bands of from fifty to sixty among the national troops, saying that "the aid which the republic derived from the barbarians should be felt, but not seen." It may be asked—Was this a long or a short sighted policy? It is a fact that the state of things for a long time previously had checked marriage and discouraged agriculture. The then generation of adult Roman citizens in Italy was rapidly dwindling; the rising population was not, or was but barely, sufficient to take their place. Probus bestowed land, cattle, instruments of husbandry, and every encouragement upon fugitive and captive barbarians, to induce them to settle on the exhausted frontiers, hoping thus to breed and educate a race of soldiers for the Roman service.

Probus did much for Egypt; he improved the navigation of the Nile; he erected and repaired public buildings. His military discipline, though less cruel than that of Aurelian, was yet severe. On one of the hottest days of summer he is said to have unduly pressed on the unwholesome labour of draining the marshes of Sirmium.[5] Impatient with fatigue, the soldiers threw down their tools and seized their arms. The emperor took refuge in a lofty tower: it was forced, he fell pierced by

[1] 197. 220. [3] 239. [4] 253. [5] 157.

many wounds. With him the authority of the senate expired, August, A.D. 282.

Carus (A.D. 282—283).—Carus was elected by the army. The senate was not consulted. Carus simply informed the senate that he had ascended the vacant throne. He conferred on his sons, Carinus and Numerianus, the title of Cæsar. Leaving Carinus in command of the western provinces, he started with his younger son for the east, bent on the subjugation of the Persians.[1] Varanes, or Bahram, sent ambassadors to Carus to negotiate for peace. The ambassadors reached the Roman camp at the hour of the evening meal. Having desired to be introduced to the emperor, they were conducted to a soldier seated on the grass with a piece of salt bacon and a few hard beans before him as his supper; a coarse woollen garment of purple was the only circumstance that announced his dignity. The conference was conducted with equal simplicity. Carus, taking off his cap, which concealed his baldness, assured the ambassadors that unless their master acknowledged the supremacy of Rome he would speedily render Persia[1] as naked of trees as his own head was destitute of hair. The ambassadors retired. It is said that they trembled. The threats of Carus were not idle threats. He ravaged Mesopotamia,[2] seized the cities of Seleucia and Ctesiphon, and carried his victories beyond the Tigris. In the midst of his victories he perished in a storm. It was reported that he had been killed by lightning 25th December, A.D. 283.

Carinus and Numerianus (A.D. 283—284).—Carinus and his absent brother were at once proclaimed emperors. It was expected that the sons would follow up the advantage gained by their father, but they were helpless. The legions, though strong in number and discipline, were superstitious. Death by lightning was an evil omen. It was regarded as the act of the wrathful hand of heaven. An oracle, it was remembered, had marked the river Tigris as the fatal boundary of the Roman arms. The troops called on the youthful Numerianus to obey the will of the gods and lead them back.

[1] 32° N., 60° E. [2] 280.

Carinus, released from his father's control, let loose his passion for vulgar pleasures and show. The oldest citizens said that the triumphal pomp of Probus, or Aurelian, and the secular games of Philip, were surpassed in magnificence by the exhibitions of Carinus. It has been said of the two brothers that Carinus was not worthy to live in the most corrupt of times; whereas Numerianus deserved to live in better times than his. Though physically, and by his previous training, unfit to command those by whom he was surrounded, Numerianus was a gentle, affable, virtuous, and contemplative youth. The hardships of the Persian war and the heat of the climate had so affected his sight as to make him a close prisoner in his tent. He entrusted the administration of affairs and himself to Arrius Aper, the prætorian præfect, who was at the same time his father-in-law.

About eight months after the death of Carus the army by slow marches reached the Thracian Bosporus.[1] A report was circulated through the camp that the emperor was dead. The soldiers broke into the imperial tent, and discovered the corpse of Numerianus. Aper, suspected of foul play, was seized. A general assembly of the army was appointed to be held at Chalcidor, whither Aper was transported in chains. A vacant tribunal was erected. The generals and tribunes formed a military council; they announced that their choice had fallen on Diocletian, commander of the domestic and body guards, as the person most capable of succeeding and revenging their beloved emperor (17th September, A.D. 294). Diocletian ascended the tribunal, raised his eyes towards the sun, made a solemn profession of his own innocence. Assuming the tone of sovereign and judge, he commanded Aper to be brought before him. When Aper reached the foot of the tribunal, Diocletian, saying, "This man is the murderer of Numerianus," drew his sword, and without giving Aper the opportunity to speak, plunged it into his breast. In the spring of A.D. 285, the forces of the east and the west met in the plains of Margus, near the Danube.[2] A tribune, whose wife had been seduced by Carinus, seized the opportunity

[1] 203 [2] 125.

for revenge, stabbed Carinus, and put an end to the civil war, A.D. 285.

Diocletian, A.D. 284—305.—Diocletian was one of the most remarkable men that ever lived. His parents had been slaves in the house of a Roman senator. He was great as a warrior, greater as a statesman, and greatest as a true philosopher.

In A.D. 286, he made Maximian, born a peasant, a soldier of fortune, a man insensible to pity and fearless of consequences, his colleague and *augustus*. For some reason not easy to divine, Diocletian assumed the title of Jovius, while Maximian assumed that of Herculius.

Diocletian and Maximian, A.D. 286—305.—In the year A.D. 292, Diocletian, sensible of the necessity of maintaining large armies on the frontiers, and the danger of entrusting them to the charge of mere lieutenants, elevated, with the approval of his colleague, Galerius (Armentarius) and Constantius (Chlorus)—the former of humble, the latter of noble birth, soldiers of distinction—to the rank of Cæsars; and further to cement the union, he adopted Galerius as his son-in-law; while Maximian, in like manner, adopted Constantius: each—obliging the adopted to repudiate his then wife—bestowed his daughter in marriage on his adopted son.

These four princes divided the Roman empire between them. Diocletian retained for himself Thrace, Egypt, and the rich countries of Asia. Maximian took Italy and Africa. Constantius had assigned to him Gaul, Spain, and Britain. Galerius was stationed on the banks of the Danube as the safeguard of the Illyrian provinces. Each was sovereign within his own jurisdiction. All were united as to the common weal. Diocletian was by all regarded as the common parent. This division was resolved on by Diocletian as the result of what he had seen, or supposed that he had seen, during the arduous campaigns of the first few years of his reign, which, though attended with success, had satisfied him that the ever-increasing hostility to the Roman sway could no longer be resisted by any emperor seconded only by mere lieutenants. It will be remembered, that in the beginning of the empire the emperors derived position and power from the senate; that on the death of Pertinax the prætorian guard claimed the right to nominate the emperor, and sold the dignity to Didius Julianus on the 28th March, A.D. 193; that the legions in the provinces subsequently claimed that right; and that finally, in A.D. 282, the authority of the senate expired, and the army became all-powerful.

Diocletian, by instituting two Augusti and two Cæsars, made the succession devolve on the Cæsars, who were appointed by the existing Augusti, without consulting or even reference to either the senate or the army.

In the year A.D. 287, Caransius, who had been entrusted by Diocletian with a Roman fleet, and stationed at Boulogne to watch and chastise the German pirates, seized the booty that he connived at the Germans taking, and appropriated it to his own use. Maximian ordered his death. Caransius, who had attached the fleet to him, sailed for Britain, and persuaded the legions there to confer on him the title of Augustus. His fleets rode the seas triumphant, ravaging the coasts beyond the Columns of Hercules.[1] Diocletian and his colleague, dreading his enterprising spirit, resigned to him the sovereignty of Britain, and reluctantly permitted him participation in the imperial honours.

The adoption of two Cæsars imparted new military vigour. Constantius raised a stupendous mole across the entrance to the harbour of Boulogne. The town ultimately surrendered. A large portion of the fleet of Caransius fell into the hands of Constantius. Caransius was murdered by Allectus, his first minister, A.D. 293. Allectus seized the government, and held it for three years. Asclepidotus, an officer of Constantius, landed in Britain, defeated and slew Alectus, A.D. 296. Britain was restored to the imperial sway. After a siege of eight months, Diocletian took Alexandria, A.D. 297. The city was treated with the utmost severity. It was said that the Egyptians, though insensible to kindness, were extremely susceptible of fear. Few persons in Egypt obnoxious to the emperor escaped

[1] 40.

death or exile. Thousands of Alexandrians perished in a promiscuous slaughter. In A.D. 297, Diocletian, in support of the cause of the Armenian king, went to war with the Persians. He took up his station in the city of Antioch, whence he directed the military operations, the execution of which he entrusted to Galerius. The armies met in the plains of Mesopotamia. Two battles were fought with doubtful issue; in the third the Roman army was totally defeated on the same ground where Crassus and the legions had fallen in the year B.C. 53. Diocletian received Galerius on his return with the indignation of an offended sovereign, and compelled him to follow the emperor's chariot for more than a mile on foot, thus exhibiting before the whole court the spectacle of his disgrace. A second campaign was undertaken, A.D. 298. Galerius fell upon the Persian camp during the night, and put them to flight with dreadful carnage. The Persian Narses sued for and obtained a treaty of peace, by which, *inter alia*, five provinces were ceded to the Romans, and peace secured in the east for forty years.

CHAPTER X.

THE EMPIRE—*continued.*

THE FOURTH CENTURY.

i.e., A. U. C. 1053 till A. U. C. 1152;—A.D. 300 to A.D. 399.

Emperors of Rome.

A.D.	
to 305.	DIOCLETIAN. MAXIMIAN.
305—306.	CONSTANTIUS I. (Chlorus).
305—311.	GALERIUS.
306—337.	CONSTANTINE I. (the Great).
306—312.	MAXENTIUS.
306—310.	MAXIMIAN (returned).
306—307.	SEVERUS.
307—313.	MAXIMIN.
307—323.	LICINIUS.
337—340.	CONSTANTINE II.
337—350.	CONSTANS I.
337—361.	CONSTANTIUS II.
361—363.	JULIAN.
363—364.	JOVIAN.
364—375.	VALENTINIAN (West).
364—378.	VALENS (East).
367—383.	GRATIAN (West).
383—388.	MAXIMUS (West).
375—392.	VALENTINIAN (West).
392—395.	THEODOSIUS I. (West and East).

DIVISION OF THE EMPIRE.

West.	East.
395—423. HONORIUS.	395—408. ARCADIUS.

The Orators, Historians, Philosophers, Poets, &c., of the Period.

EUTROPIUS (FLAVIUS), historian, temp. CONSTANTINE and JULIAN.

AMMIANUS (MARCELLINUS), historian, born A.D. [?], died A.D. 390.

AUSONIUS (DECIUS MAGNUS), poet of this period.

LAMPRIDUS (ÆLIUS), historian, temp. DIOCLETIAN and CONSTANTINE

Diocletian, *continued.*—In A.D. 303, Diocletian entered on the twentieth year of his reign, and, as the empire was then entirely relieved from the tyrants and barbarians that had troubled it, he resolved on a Roman triumph. Maximian was his only companion in the glory of that day. Africa and Britain, the Rhine, the Danube, and the Nile furnished their respective trophies, but the Persian victory and conquest was the most important feature. This triumph is remarkable as being the last ever beheld in Rome. Diocletian entertained a deeply rooted aversion to, and contempt for, Rome and its senate, possibly the not unnatural consequence of early associations. When he seized the imperial sway, he simply informed the senate of the fact, disdaining to ask for their recognition. When he divided the empire and took the East as his portion, he made Nicomedia [1] his capital. It is doubtful whether Diocletian had ever visited Rome from the date of his elevation till he went there to celebrate his triumph, and then he only stayed there for about two months. He, his colleague, and successors enacted what laws they thought fit, regardless of the senate. It was his intention to make Nicomedia [1] rival Rome. Maximian made Milan [2] his capital of the West, and concerning it he had a like ambition. Both spent their leisure and resources in the embellishment of these new capitals. No emperor, prior to Diocletian, had been distinguished in his dress from other citizens save in the use of the purple. Diocletian, conscious of

[1] 203. [2] 111.

the effect on the eastern mind of personal splendour, adopted the stately magnificence of the court of Persia. He did not hesitate to adopt the ornament the most detested by the Romans, the diadem. His robes were of silk and gold. New forms and ceremonies made access to the sacred persons of the two Augusti daily more difficult. Prostration and adoration after the manner of the East were best suited to the easterns, and were accordingly adopted.

No stronger proof of his unceasing activity in matters legal could be furnished than the fact that his name appears no fewer than 1,200 times in the code of Justinian. He definitively and generally substituted the *extraordinarium judicium* for the *formula* system. He created, or, perhaps more correctly, greatly increased, a class of inferior judges styled *judices pedanei*.

Ortolan says:—"Just as the *formula* system of procedure was gradually substituted for the *actiones legis*, so in its turn was the *formula* gradually superseded and finally displaced by the *extraordinaria judicia*, or extraordinary procedure.

"The principle of the *cognitio extraordinaria* consisted in the fact that the magistrate heard the case and decided it himself. This principle was already recognised in the system of the *actiones legis* as well as in that of the *formulæ*. In those two systems of the Roman procedure, however, and especially in that of the *formulæ*, it only existed as an exception. The procedure by *formula*, which involved the separation of the *jus* and the *judicium*, the guarantee of the *juge-jurés* chosen or accepted by the parties, and the technical regulation of that or those judges' commission, was the established form of procedure. The magistrate himself only heard and decided the case as an extraordinary measure (*extra ordinem*) in cases where his *juris dictio* could end the matter: when he wanted to make use of his *imperium:* when there was no given action according to civil law nor according to the edict, and when extraordinary recourse was had to the power itself of the magistrate (*cognitio extraordinaria persecutio*, and not *actio*). But under the imperial government, when the arbitrary power of the emperor was every day increasing, when his will and his decisions had acquired superior authority, when the number of suits called or brought before him multiplied, when his officers, his *prætorian* præfects, and his lieutenants participated, through delegation, in the powers of their master, the practice of using the *cognitiones extraordinariæ* became very much more frequent. . . . It was in this state of things that Diocletian, through a constitution that we find inserted in the code of Justinian (A.D. 294), ordered the presidents of the provinces to themselves hear and decide all cases, even those which it was formerly the practice to send before judges. This rule, which seems to apply—in the terms of the constitution—only to the provinces, was made general for the whole empire. Diocletian, it is true, reserved to the presidents the right of giving to the parties subordinate judges, when their public occupations, or the multiplicity of the suits, prevented them from hearing them themselves; but in such cases the suits were no longer sent before the judges in accordance with the formulary system: the distinction between the *jus* and *judicium*, the regulation of the judges' commission by the terms of the *formula*, was gone: the whole case was transmitted bodily. The formulary procedure had completely fallen through, and what was formerly the exception had become the rule; all procedure was *extra ordinem.* The *jus* and the *judicium*, the office of the magistrate and that of the judge, were confounded, and the name *judex*, *judices majores*, is now applied to the magistrate.

"From that time, the word *actio* a second time completely changed its meaning; and the *exceptiones*, and the interdicts, institutions of the formulary system, lost their true character. . ." [1]

During the first nineteen years of the reign of Diocletian the Christians continued to enjoy the free exercise of their religion without molestation. But notwithstanding this seeming security, indications were not wanting of coming trouble. The policy of Diocletian and the humanity of Constantius, which inclined them to preserve inviolate the maxims of toleration, succumbed to the aversion of Maximian and Galerius for the name and religion of the Christians. Diocletian, long importuned by Galerius, issued an edict for the general persecution of the Christians on the 24th February, A.D. 303. Some account

[1] Pritchard and Nasmith's translation, pp. 361 *et seq.*

of the horrors of that persecution will be found in Gibbon's "History of the Decline and Fall of the Roman Empire" (vol. 2, pp. 456 *et seq.*). No sooner had Diocletian published his edicts against the Christians—for the consequences of the first led to others—than, as if desirous of committing to other hands the work of persecution, he divested himself of the imperial purple.

Diocletian, however, had for some time meditated abdicating. He discussed and at length agreed with his colleague, that both should do so on the same day. On the 1st May, A.D. 305, Diocletian ascended a lofty throne, erected for the occasion in a plain about three miles from Nicomedia,[1] and in a speech, full of reason and dignity, declared his intention both to the people and to the soldiers there assembled. He then divested himself of his imperial robes, and in a covered chariot drove to his favourite retirement in his native country of Dalmatia. Maximian on the same day resigned his imperial dignity at Milan.[2]

Maximian grew weary of private life, and sent soliciting Diocletian to resume the reins of government. Diocletian, with a smile of pity, calmly said: "If I could show Maximian the cabbages I have planted with my own hand at Salona,[3] I should no longer be urged to relinquish the enjoyment of happiness for the pursuit of power."

Vopiscus tells us that Diocletian, in conversation with a friend, said: "How often is it the interest of four or five ministers to combine together to deceive their sovereign! secluded from mankind by his exalted dignity, the truth is concealed from his knowledge: he can see only with their eyes, he hears nothing but their representations. He confers the most important offices upon vice and weakness, and disgraces the most virtuous and deserving among his subjects. By such infamous arts, the best and wisest princes are sold to the venal corruption of their courtiers."

Diocletian lived for eleven years in the enjoyment of private life, and died A.D. 313.

Constantius I., A.D. 305—306; Galerius, A.D. 305—311.—The abdication of Diocletian and Maximian was followed by eighteen

[1] 203. [2] 111. [3] 142.

years of discord and confusion. Five civil wars distract attention from all else. Daza—afterwards called Maximin—and Severus were appointed Cæsars. Constantius and Galerius retained their former provinces, Egypt and Syria were allotted to Daza, Italy and Africa to Severus. The British expedition, in which Constantius was accompanied by his son Constantine, and in which he had an easy victory over the Caledonians, was the last exploit of Constantius, who died in the imperial palace at York, July 25, A.D. 306. Galerius had hoped that on the death of Constantius he would become sole master of the Roman world, but. it was otherwise. The troops in Britain, on the death of Constantius, saluted Constantine emperor and Augustus. Galerius dissembled his rage, conferred on Constantine the title of Cæsar, and at the same time conferred the title of Augustus on Severus. Galerius introduced into Italy the same system of taxation that prevailed in the provinces. The Romans, unaccustomed to taxation, resented the innovation. The senate, chafed by the treatment they had received from their absent emperors, fanned the flame of discontent, and excited the feeble remnant of the prætorian guards to revolt. Maxentius, the vicious, and at the same time incapable, son of Maximian, was proclaimed emperor at Rome. Maxentius invited his father to re-assume the purple. He did so, A.D. 309. Severus hastened to Rome to chastise the (to him) usurpers. The gates were closed against him, his own soldiers deserted him, he capitulated, and not long after was compelled to put an end to his own life, February, A.D. 307. A common interest against Galerius united two dissimilars—Constantine and Maxentius.

Maximian married his daughter Fausta to Constantine, upon whom he, at the same time, conferred the dignity of Augustus. Appearances led the Romans to conclude that Constantine had adopted their cause. Galerius appeared in arms in Italy, resolved to avenge the death of Severus. He found the gates of every town shut against him, and, though he marched to within sixty miles of Rome, he deemed it prudent to retreat, leaving Maximian and Maxentius in the undisputed possession of Italy.

In November, A.D. 307, Galerius raised Licinius to the rank of Augustus. Maximin forced from Galerius the same honour for himself. For the first and last time the Roman world was administered by six emperors, A.D. 308. Maxentius resented the attempted control of his father. The prætorian guards gave to the dispute between father and son their careful consideration. The cause was solemnly pleaded before them. The life of Maximian was spared, but he was required to leave Italy. He went into Illyricum.[1] Galerius obliged him to leave that place. He took refuge in the court of his son-in-law, Constantine. When, shortly after, Constantine was compelled to go to the Rhine, Maximian seized the vacant throne. Constantine returned, Maximian fled, but was captured and surrendered to Constantine, who compelled him to take his own life, February, A.D. 310. Galerius died after a lingering and painful illness, A.D. 311. Maximin and Licinius divided his dominions between them. Licinius concerted with Constantine. Maximin formed a secret alliance with Maxentius. Maxentius filled Rome and Italy with troops, connived at their tumults, and suffered the plunder and even the massacre of the defenceless people. He publicly insulted the name of Constantine, and ordered statutes erected to him to be thrown down. At the head of 40,000 men Constantine marched into Italy. The last of three battles between them was fought at Saxa Rubia, about nine miles from Rome. Maxentius was defeated and driven into the Tiber, where he was drowned, October 28th, A.D. 312. Constantine abolished the prætorian guard. This was the final blow to the dignity of the Roman senate. The city was left defenceless.

In A.D. 313, Maximin marched against Licinius; the two armies met near Heraclea;[2] Maximin was defeated and fled. Three or four months later he died at Tarsus. The immediate cause of his death is not known.

In A.D. 314, Constantine and Licinius turned their victorious arms against each other. Licinius, who was defeated in two battles, sued for peace; Constantine deemed it prudent to grant it; Licinius was left in possession of Thrace, Asia Minor, Syria, and Egypt. Constantine annexed Pannonia,[3] Dalmatia,[4] Dacia,[5]

[1] 142. [2] 144. [3] 141. [4] 142. [5] 171.

Macedonia,[1] and Greece.[2] The peace endured for about eight years, during which period Constantine was largely occupied with the Goths, who ultimately contracted to supply his armies with 40,000 men, whenever required to do so. Constantine resolved on the ruin of Licinius. Their first battle was fought near Adrianople,[3] July 3rd, 323. Each brought more than 100,000 men into the field. Licinius was defeated. He was again defeated at Chrysopolis,[3] he surrendered and laid down the purple at the feet of his conqueror, who promised him life. He was sent to Thessalonica,[4] where, not long after, he was executed, A.D. 324. Constantine reigned alone.

Constantine Sole Emperor, A.D. 323—337.—Of remarkable historical characters, Constantine is perhaps the most remarkable. We have already traced his career up to the point where he commenced to reign alone. We have now to regard him as the founder of a new capital, the author of the reorganization of the administration of the Roman empire, of a new nobility, of a new state religion, and of important changes in the private law.

The New Capital.—We have already seen that for some time past Rome had been distasteful to the emperors. Diocletian had established his court at Nicomedia,[5] his colleague his at Milan.[6] Constantine, born in the neighbourhood of the Danube, and whose travels had made him familiar with much of the territory of the then Roman empire, selected Byzantium[6] as the site of the new imperial capital. The prospect of beauty, of safety, and of wealth, united in a single spot was sufficient to justify the choice. With his own hand, he marked with a lance, in imitation possibly of Romulus, the boundary of the projected new city. It being suggested to him at a particular stage of his progress that he had already exceeded the most ample measure of a great city, he said, "I shall still advance till He, the invisible guide who marches before me, thinks proper to stop." All that money and art could do was done to render the new capital attrac-

[1] 158. [2] 175. [3] 188. [4] 174. [5] 203. [6] 111.

tive. Thither the nobility, the dignitaries, and the wealthy flocked. The city was dedicated on the 11th May, A.D. 330.

Reorganization of the Administration.—Constantine divided the empire into four great prætorian præfectorates—the East, Illyria, Italy, and Gaul. He divided each præfectorate into dioceses, each diocese into provinces. At the head of each præfectorate he placed a *prætorian præfect*, at that of each diocese a *vicar*, at that of each province a *rector provinciæ*.

Rank.—He selected as his intimate counsellors and private advisers a few of the most eminent of those who had filled high magistracies, and conferred upon them for life the title of *patricii*. They had no jurisdiction or *imperium*, but enjoyed the highest rank (*qui cæteris omnibus anteponitur*).

He increased the number of the council styled *comites consistoriani*, and, in addition to the council, established a senate like that at Rome. His high chancellor was styled *quæstor sacri palatii*. The princes of the imperial family were styled *nobilissimi*. The prætorian præfects, the præfects of the city, the quæstors of the sacred palace, and certain classes of comites, were styled *illustres*. After these followed the *spectabiles*, the *clarissimi*, the *perfectissimi*, and, lastly, as men of rank, the *egregii*.

Christianity the State Religion.—Though not himself baptized, Constantine declared Christianity to be the religion of the State. He professed himself to belong to, and to have adopted, the new faith. Most of his nobles, and many of his subjects, followed his example. The whole system of the *jus sacrum*, including the *jus publicum* connected with it, fell to pieces. The pontiffs, the flamens, the vestals, and others disappeared from the temple and the court. *Episcopi* (bishops) and others took their places. We are told that Saint Paul had advised the Christians to keep away from the civil tribunals, and to settle their differences like brethren through the ministry of the elders of the church. Constantine made it a legislative institution, and invested the bishops with certain jurisdiction. To them, as to the consuls, the pro-consuls, and the prætors, was given the power of enfranchising slaves. They were permitted to act for certain magistrates during their absence, and thus, pressing nearer to the throne, they not infrequently advised the emperor in the affairs of state.

Changes in the Private Law.—Constantine reduced the power of the father to dispose, by sale, of his child, to the period of the earliest infancy, and then only permitted its exercise in the case of extreme poverty. He removed the testamentary incapacity of the *cœlibes* and the *orbi*, and, by allowing parents to succeed *ab intestato* to their children, he abolished a portion of the *jus liberorum*. He originated *peculium quasi castrans* (*castrense*), *i.e.*, he declared all property acquired by a son in the service of the court to be free from the father's control. He originated *peculium adventitium*, *i.e.*, he declared all property derived by a son from his mother to belong to the son absolutely, subject only to the life usufruct of the father.

Legal Text Books—Authorities and Opinions.—We have seen that Pomponius, Scævola, Gaius, Papinian, Ulpian, Paul, Marcian, and Modestinus, the most illustrious jurists ever produced by the Roman nation, flourished between the time of Hadrian and Alexander Severus. Not satisfied with writing independent treatises of their own, however, Ulpian, Paul, and Marcian took upon themselves to write commentaries on the works of Papinian. It is, perhaps, unnecessary to remind the reader that long before the reign of Constantine the Romans had ceased to produce jurists in the proper sense of the term. The judges and advocates of his time perplexed themselves and others with extracts and quotations; they avoided dealing with principles, the delight of the Roman jurists. To meet the then deplorable state of the legal profession, and to put a stop to wrangling about trifles (*perpetuas prudentium contentiones eruere cupientes*), Constantine prohibited the use of the commentaries on Papinian of Ulpian and Paul, A.D. 321. When those by Marcian were treated in like manner is not known. In A.D. 327 the emperor, however, declared that the independent works of

Paul, and particularly his *sententiæ*, were worthy of being confirmed and quoted as authority before the judge.

Constantine was twice married. By Minervina, his first wife, he had one son, Crispus. By Fausta, his second wife, he had three daughters, and three sons, Constantine, Constantius, and Constans. Crispus deserved the esteem, and he engaged the affection of the court, the army, and the people. It is said that Constantine became jealous of his son's popularity, and kept him practically a prisoner at his court. Fausta accused the youthful Crispus of an attempt on her chastity: he was sentenced to death by his father. His grandmother, Helena, revenged the youth's death. Fausta was accused of adultery with a slave: she was condemned, and suffocated. Constantine died near Nicomedia,[1] where he had gone for the benefit of his health, in his sixty-fourth year, and in the thirtieth year of his reign, 22nd May, A.D. 337.

Constantine II., A.D. 337—340; Constans I., A.D. 337—350; Constantius II., A.D. 337—361.—From A.D. 337 to 361 the Roman Empire was in the hands, first of the three sons of Constantine, then of two, and during the last eleven years Constantius reigned alone. Constantine had raised each of his sons, and his nephew Dalmatius, to the dignity of Cæsar, and had conferred on his nephew Hannibalianus the new title of *nobilissimus*, reserving to himself the title of Augustus. To each of these princes he had entrusted the government of certain provinces. On the death of Constantine, the troops, no doubt thereunto duly stimulated, declared that none but the sons of Constantine should reign. Upon the arrival of Constantius in the capital, he sanctioned a promiscuous massacre; and among many others of high birth, Dalmatius and Hannibalianus fell victims. Constantine, then twenty-one years of age, took the new capital and its dependencies; Constans, then twenty, took Italy, Africa, and the western Illyricum; Constantius, then seventeen, took Thrace and the countries of the East.

Constantius had to sustain the weight of the Persian war

[1] 203.

against Sapor, who was bent on recovering the five provinces that had been torn from his ancestor. In nine bloody battles on the field, victory attended the Persians; but so long as the fortified towns of Mesopotamia,[1] and particularly Nisibis,[1] remained in the hands of the Romans, Sapor's dream could not be realized. Each of his efforts to reduce those strongholds failed, which, coupled with the invasion of the Massagetæ on his eastern provinces, induced him to conclude a truce with Constantius, to whom it was not unwelcome, he having then lost his two brothers and become involved in a civil contest in the west.

While Constantius was engaged as already stated, Constantine, not long after his accession, complained that he had not his full share of the spoils of their murdered kinsman. He invaded the territory of Constans, but was betrayed into an ambush, surrounded, and slain, A.D. 340.

Suppression of the Formulæ—De Formulis Sublatis, A.D. 342.—By this constitution of the Emperor Constantius, the then existing remnants of the formula system were abolished. Its technicalities, troublesome to the ignorant, had long been distasteful to them. Legal learning was now rendered unnecessary. The use of any language was permitted that was deemed sufficient to convey and express the ideas and intentions of the parties.

Eight years later, Constans was slain at the instance of Magnentius, an ambitious soldier, who had induced the troops to salute him Augustus, A.D. 350.

Constantius hastened to Europe. He met Magnentius near Mursa,[2] or Eszek. 54,000 fell in the battle. Magnentius was defeated, and fled on the 28th September, A.D. 351. The assumptions of Vetranio and Nepotian are mentioned merely that they may be passed over. The Roman empire was once more in the hands of one—that one a man destitute of all personal merit, the mere slave of his eunuchs, who appealed alternately to his fears, his indolence, and his vanity.

[1] 265. [2] 141.

Constantine had left two nephews, Gallus and Julian. Though carefully educated, they were nothing more nor less than state prisoners in the castle of Macellum. Restraint developed in Gallus the worst features of his nature. Julian, similarly situated, found solace in literature, and conceived a passion for Greece and the Greeks. In A.D. 351 Gallus was made Cæsar. He was married to Constantina, one of those infernal furies in human form who gloat over mortal sufferings. He settled in Antioch,[1] where with delegated authority he administered the five great dioceses of the eastern præfecture. Suffice it to say that he and his wife so ruled that Constantius or his eunuchs decoyed him to Petavia, in Pannonia,[2] made him captive, went through the form of an investigation into his government, and beheaded him in prison like a common malefactor, in December, A.D. 354.

Julian, the sole survivor of the numerous posterity of Constantius Chlorus, had, through the influence of the empress Eusebia, been suffered to take honourable exile at Athens.[3] He had been there, however, scarcely six months when Constantius, oppressed with the burden of sole rule, and troubled both in the west and in the east, summoned him to Milan,[4] where he was declared Cæsar on the 6th November, A.D. 355, and given jurisdiction over the countries beyond the Alps. Though young and inexperienced, the philosophy of Plato had animated him with the love of virtue, the desire of fame, and the contempt of death. Sallust, an officer of rank and experience, soon conceived for him a sincere attachment, and aided him in his study of the arts of war and government. In the course of four campaigns (A.D. 356—359) he not only drove the Franks and the Alemanni out of Gaul, but made three expeditions beyond the Rhine, and carried the terror of the Roman arms into the very heart of Germany. He gave to Gaul a new constitution. He settled the finances, reduced the taxes, personally administered justice in important cases, and laid the foundation of various cities and castles. Constantius and his entourage, the only persons in the Roman empire who were not proud of the

[1] 250. [2] 141. [3] 175. [4] 111.

youthful hero and delighted with his success, resolved to undo him. Constantius sent positive orders to Julian to despatch four entire legions and 300 of the bravest youths of each of his remaining legions to aid him—Constantius—in his Persian war. Julian issued the necessary orders. His legions refused obedience. They encompassed the palace and proclaimed Julian Augustus, telling him that if he wished to live he must consent to reign. He reluctantly consented, and wrote to Constantius narrating what had taken place, and requesting him to ratify the appointment, at the same time expressing his and his legions' willingness to content themselves with the Gallic provinces.

Constantius rejected the proposal with scorn. Julian resolved to try the fortune of civil war. His legions, in three divisions and by different routes, started for Sirmium,[1] which he reached in an incredibly short space of time. Civil war was averted by the death of Constantius, who succumbed to a fever on the 3rd November, A.D. 361.

Julian, A.D. 361—363.—Julian, who reigned for a period of about one year and eight months, has been branded by some Christian writers with the epithet "The Apostate." It is true that he had been brought up in the Christian religion; but it is no less true that he and his brother Gallus had been forced to enter the Christian priesthood, and had been appointed readers in their church, for the sole purpose of excluding them from the throne. There is no evidence that Julian ever otherwise embraced Christianity. There is strong evidence that he was always attached to the old Roman faith. Personal safety seems to have prevented his publicly avowing his disbelief in the new religion prior to his being made emperor. From the moment that he declared himself he encouraged the revival of the old faith; and though he decreed toleration to the believers in the new, the professed Christians were carefully excluded from places of trust and profit. That he was no ordinary man is beyond dispute. He began his reign by putting a stop to many abuses. He substituted for the splendour and luxury of his imperial

[1] 141.

predecessors the habits of a frugal citizen, and thereby was enabled to reduce the taxes by one-fifth. He devoted the whole of his time and energies to public duties, private study, and devotion. He was a philosopher and a writer. The two schemes the most dear to his heart were the restoration of the ancient faith and the long-cherished Persian conquest. His campaign against the Persians, though well designed and at first promising, proved a failure. He was misled; his provisions failed him; he was obliged to retreat. The Persians followed. By his personal valour they were driven off, but, fleeing, discharged a parting volley of arrows at the Romans. Julian received one in his side. His dying moments were not unlike those of Socrates. He reproved the immoderate grief of some of those who surrounded him, and bade them not to disgrace by unmanly tears the fate of a prince who, in a few moments, would be united with heaven and with the stars.

Jovian.—Jovian reigned from the 28th June, 363, till the 17th February, 364 A.D. Being a professed Christian, he restored that religion to state favour. The venerable Athanasius emerged from his seclusion, and resumed the ecclesiastical government of Alexandria[1] at the age of seventy. Jovian, however, published an edict of toleration, giving to his subjects the right to exercise with freedom and safety the ceremonies of the ancient worship. He, at the same time, declared it to be his intention to suppress the rites of magic, which he denounced as sacrilegious. One night he supped heartily, and on the following morning was found dead in his bed.

Valentinian I. and Valens.—The crown was for a second time offered to the venerable præfect Sallust, and was a second time refused by him. With his hearty approval, it was conferred on Valentinian, the son of Count Gratian, a native of Cibalis in Pannonia.[2] Valentinian, who had greatly distinguished himself in the army, was a warm supporter of the Christian religion, in which he had been educated. He was proclaimed emperor on

[1] 222. [2] 141.

the 26th February, A.D. 364; and thirty days after, he bestowed the title of Augustus on his brother Valens. Shortly after, these two brothers solemnly divided the Roman empire between them. Valentinian reserved to himself Illyricum, Italy, and Gaul, from the extremity of Greece to the Caledonian ramparts, and from the ramparts of Caledonia to the foot of Mount Atlas.[1] The rest he assigned to his brother Valens.

Though it was not till A.D. 395 that the empire was finally severed, it is advisable, as far as possible, to keep the histories of the west and east henceforth distinct.

In the West.—Valentinian condemned the exposure of new-born infants, and appointed fourteen skilled physicians, one in each of the fourteen quarters of Rome. He caused rhetoric and grammar to be taught in the metropolis of every province. The finances were carefully administered, and frugality marked the palace. Under Julian, he had been zealous in the cause of Christianity. During his own reign, the believers in the ancient faith, as also the Jews and all the various sects of Christians, were protected from arbitrary power and popular insult. But he was hasty in the extreme, and was cursed with an ungovernable temper. "Strike off his head," "Burn him alive," "Let him be beaten to death," were expressions not infrequently used by him on the slightest provocation. They were orders duly executed. In A.D. 365, and again in A.D. 366, the Alemanni[2] crossed the Rhine, laid waste the villages of the Gauls, and, with their spoils, returned to their German forests. When they renewed their incursion, A.D. 368, they were defeated by Valentinian with great slaughter. By subsequently fomenting their intestine disputes, in imitation of Diocletian, Valentinian for a time freed the empire from further molestation. In A.D. 368, Theodosius, a distinguished Roman general, drove back the Picts and Scots, who had overrun Britain; and in A.D. 374, he quelled the insurrection of Mauritania[3] and Numidia.[4] In A.D. 374, the Quadi,[4] enraged at the treacherous murder of their king by one of the Roman governors, invaded the

[1] 12. [2] 124. [3] 41. [4] 101.

province of Pannonia,[1] and laid it waste with fire and sword. In A.D. 375, Valentinian, at the head of a large force, carried the extreme devastation and promiscuous massacre of savage warfare into the midst of the unhappy Quadi, without, it is said, the loss of a single man on his side. To avert the completion of their destruction in the following year, as threatened by Valentinian, their ambassadors prostrated themselves before the emperor. Incapable of governing his passion, Valentinian reviled, in the most intemperate language, their baseness, their ingratitude, and their insolence. Such was the violence of his fury, that he burst a large blood-vessel, and fell speechless into the arms of his attendants, on the 17th November, A.D. 375.

In the East.—The first difficulty of Valens was the insurrection, not without some justification, of Procopius, a relative of Julian. Procopius was captured and executed in May, A.D. 366, when 30,000 Goths had crossed the Danube on their way to help him. In A.D. 370, Valens concluded a treaty with the Goths.

In the west the Arians were not numerous. In the east, the two Christian factions—the Arians and the Trinitarians—were more evenly balanced. Athanasius still reigned at Alexandria. The ecclesiastical thrones of Constantinople and Antioch were occupied by Arian bishops. Every episcopal vacancy was the occasion of a popular tumult. The death of Athanasius, on the 2nd May, A.D. 373, was followed by religious persecution at Alexandria. Christians sought the blood of Christians.

The fall of the Roman empire has been dated from the reign of Valens.

The nomadic Scythians[2]—Tartars—had long since driven the Huns[3] southward. The Huns, in their turn, descended on the Goths. The Visigoths implored Valens to let them settle on the south bank of the Danube, and cultivate the waste lands of Thrace.[4] He complied, on condition of their delivering up their arms, and suffering their children to be dispersed through the provinces of Asia. The lust or avarice of the imperial

[1] 141. [2] 273. [3] 96, 111, 126. [4] 188.

officers induced them to accept the price offered by the Visigoths for permission to retain their weapons, their ensigns of honour, and pledges of safety. It is said that 100,000 armed fighting men were allowed to spread themselves over the plains and hills of Lower Mœsia[1] in A.D. 376.

The imperial officials, contrary to their instructions, imposed on the new comers and drove them to desperation. Starvation was in their midst, abundance within their reach, weapons were in their hands. They advanced against Marcianopolis,[2] defeated Lupicinus at the head of a Roman army, and laid waste Thrace[3] with fire and sword. Valens, at the head of a large army, came up with them near Adrianople.[3] They had previously engaged his generals. They were then joined by Huns and Alani. The Roman cavalry fled; the infantry, abandoned, were surrounded and cut to pieces. Valens, wounded, was conveyed to a cottage. The cottage was fired; Valens perished in the flames on the 9th August, A.D. 378.

In the West—Gratian, A.D. 367; Valentinian II., A.D. 375.—Gratian, who had received the title of Augustus during the life of his father Valentinian, was seventeen years of age at the date of his father's death. Valentinian II., the son of Valentinian by his second wife, Justina, was four years of age. The infant was proclaimed emperor by the troops. Gratian cheerfully accepted the choice of the army, and said that he should always regard the son of Justina as a brother and not as a rival. He advised Justina to settle with her son at Milan, and himself assumed the more arduous command of the countries beyond the Alps. He was far advanced on his march towards the plains of Adrianople[3] when news reached him of the death of Valens. Too late to assist, and too weak to revenge, his wisdom suggested the necessity of appointing a successor to Valens able to cope with the difficulties of the situation. He suggested Theodosius, who was sent for to Sirmium,[4] and there, amidst the general acclamation, was compelled to accept the title of Augustus on the 19th January, A.D. 379. The province

[1] 172. [2] 187. [3] 188. [4] 157.

over which Valens had reigned was entrusted to Theodosius. As willingly as Gratian had accepted the baby Valentinian as his colleague, so willingly did he abandon the reins of government to those about him who desired to hold them. His heart was in the hunting field. So enraptured did he become with the skill in the chase of a body of the Alani, whom he received into the military and domestic service of the palace, that he did not hesitate, to the great disgust of the Romans, to show himself in the dress and with the arms of a Scythian warrior.

The legions of Britain compelled Maximus to assume the imperial title, A.D. 383. He invaded Gaul with a powerful fleet and army. The soldiers of Gratian received him with joyful acclamations. Gratian fled, was captured and assassinated, A.D. 383.

In the West—Maximus, A.D. 383—388.—Immediately on the death of Gratian, Maximus sent his ambassador to Theodosius with the alternative of peace or war. Rightly or wrongly, Theodosius chose the former, and entered into a treaty with Maximus, by which the countries beyond the Alps were to belong to him. Italy, Africa, and Western Illyricum were reserved to Valentinian II. It was not long, however, before Maximus aspired to the conquest of Italy. He was almost under the walls of Milan[1] when Justina first heard of his designs. Flight being her only hope, she, the young emperor, and his lovely sister Galla made their escape to Thessalonica.[2] Their flight left Maximus, for the moment, master of the whole of the western empire, A.D. 387.

Theodosius, for a second time, wavered between war and peace with his now undoubted rival. He referred the question to his council. He listened to the soft entreaties of Galla on the behalf of her brother, and, touched by her charms, took her to wife. He reflected on the fact that war would, at the same time, occupy his newly acquired legions abroad, and somewhat thin their numbers. War was declared. One battle on the banks of the Save[3] almost annihilated the army of Maximus. He fled, was captured and beheaded, A.D. 388.

[1] 111. [2] 173. [3] 141.

In the East—Theodosius I., A.D. 379—395.—On the 19th January, A.D. 379, Theodosius, the son of the celebrated Roman general who, a few years before, had been executed for no cause other than jealousy of his fame, assumed, at the instance of Gratian, the government of Thrace, Asia, and Egypt; but, as he was specially entrusted with the conduct of the Gothic war, the Illyrian præfecture was dismembered, and the two great dioceses of Dacia[1] and Macedonia[2] were added to the dominion of the eastern empire. Theodosius fixed his headquarters at Thessalonica,[3] whence he could watch the irregular movements of the invaders, and direct the operations of his lieutenants from the gates of Constantinople[4] to the shores of the Adriatic.[5] Little by little he restored discipline and confidence to the Roman troops. Sallies, rarely hazarded without almost certainty of success, gradually engendered the belief that the apparently invincible foe might be overcome. At this juncture, fortunately for the Romans, Fritigern, the leader of the barbarians, whose genius had kept them together, died. Intestine dissensions induced tribe after tribe to secure treaties with the Romans. The final capitulation of the Goths, who did not depart, took place on the 3rd October, A.D. 382.

In A.D. 386, the Gruthungi, or Ostrogoths, who had departed in A.D. 382, returned in increased numbers to the banks of the Lower Danube. They were defeated. The survivors formed a treaty with the emperor, who fixed their settlements in Phrygia[6] and Lydia.[7] Though the royal dignity was abolished among them, their hereditary chiefs were permitted to command their followers in peace and war. Their generals, however, were subject to removal at the pleasure of the emperor. An army of 40,000 Goths was maintained for the perpetual service of the empire of the east. They assumed the title of *Fœderati*, and were distinguished by their gold collars, liberal pay, and licentious privileges. The natural effect of this more than doubtful expedient on the part of Theodosius was to extinguish in the Romans the last spark of military ardour.

In A.D. 380, Theodosius was baptized by the Trinitarian bishop

[1] 171. [2] 173. [3] 174. [4] 203. [5] 143. [6] 219 [7] 204.

Acholius of Thessalonica, shortly after which he dictated a solemn edict which proclaimed the Athanasian doctrine of the Trinity, and branded all who would not accept it heretics. He declared it to be his intention to expel from all the churches of his dominions the bishops and their clergy who should obstinately refuse to believe the doctrine of the council at Nice (*Nicæa*).[1] In May, A.D. 381, he convened at Constantinople a synod of 150 bishops. That council completed the theological system which had been established in the council of Nice, and declared, by a unanimous sentence, the equal deity of the Holy Ghost. In the course of fifteen years Theodosius promulgated as many edicts against those who rejected the doctrine of the Trinity.

In A.D. 388, Theodosius, in aid of Justina and Valentinian II., as already stated, fought and conquered Maximus.

In A.D. 390, some of the inhabitants of Thessalonica murdered Botheric, the general in charge of the garrison, together with some of his principal officers, for imprisoning one of the favourite charioteers, and refusing to allow him to take part in the festival on the day of the public games. Instead of seeking out, trying, and punishing the malefactors, Theodosius resolved to wreak his vengeance on the entire community. He entrusted the work to his barbarians. The people of Thessalonica were invited in the name of their sovereign to the games of the circus. Thousands flocked to the spectacle. The signal was given. The soldiers, who had been kept in ambush, rushed on the defenceless crowd. Natives, strangers, young and old, guilty and innocent, were slaughtered. Some say that 7,000, others that 15,000 perished. We are told that shortly after, when the emperor proceeded in his accustomed manner to perform his devotions in the great church at Milan,[1] he was stopped at the porch by archbishop Ambrose, who declared that private contrition was not sufficient to atone for a public fault, or to appease offended Deity, whereupon Theodosius replied, that if he had contracted the guilt of homicide, David, the man after God's own heart, had been guilty, not only of murder, but of adultery; to which Ambrose replied, "You have imitated David in his crime, imitate his

[1] 111.

repentance." It is further said that, stripped of the ensigns of royalty, and in the midst of the church of Milan, the emperor humbly solicited, with sighs and tears, the pardon of his sins; and that after a delay of about eight months he was restored to the communion of the faithful.

From A.D. 388 till A.D. 391 Theodosius resided in Italy. When he departed, he left Valentinian in possession, not merely of Italy, but of the dominions beyond the Alps. Theodosius, before his departure, appointed Arbogastes master-general of the armies in Gaul. Arbogastes, it is said, resolved either to rule or to ruin the empire of the west. Justina did not long survive the restoration of her son. Arbogastes undermined his power, and insulted him to his face. Valentinian was found strangled in his apartment, A.D. 392. Arbogastes bestowed the purple on a Roman—one of his tools—the rhetorician Eugenius.

The ambassadors of the new emperor were sent to Theodosius. He dismissed them with splendid presents and an ambiguous answer. He spent two years in his preparation for the overthrow and chastisement of Arbogastes. Late in the summer of A.D. 394, Theodosius met Arbogastes in the north of Italy, on the banks of the Frigidus;[1] a desperate battle was fought during the whole day, in which the advantage was with Arbogastes. Night came to the relief of Theodosius. When day broke, Theodosius found that during the night Arbogastes had surrounded him. He realized the extremity of his danger. At that moment a friendly message from the leaders of the forces in his rear dispelled his apprehension. Theodosius was victorious. Eugenius was beheaded, Arbogastes died by his own hand.

The Severance of the Eastern from the Western Empire.—About four months after, feeling that, though only fifty, he had not long to live, Theodosius solemnly divided the empire, nominated his son Arcadius emperor of the east, and his son Honorius emperor of the west. He died of dropsy on the 17th January, A.D. 395. Theodosius has by some been styled "the Great."

[1] 126.

The Western Empire, A.D. 395—399; Honorius, A.D. 395—423.—On the 17th January, A.D. 395, Honorius was saluted emperor, he then being eleven years of age. Stilicho, the uncle of the young emperors, and who regarded himself as their natural guardian, had been made by Theodosius master-general of the Roman forces in the west. He now became actual ruler of the west. In the summer of A.D. 395, Alaric, the bold and able leader of the Goths, entered Macedonia,[1] and during that and the following year ravaged almost the whole of Greece. In A.D. 396, Stilicho resolved to chastise the invader, and for that purpose marched into Peloponnesus;[2] but the ministers of Arcadius, more jealous of Stilicho than fearful of the Goths, promoted their leader to the rank of master-general of the eastern Illyricum,[3] whereupon Stilicho retired. The talent and successes of Alaric induced the Visigoths to proclaim him their king. He resolved on the invasion of Italy. His ambition was to plant the Gothic standard on the walls of Rome.

The Eastern Empire, A.D. 395—399; Arcadius, A.D. 395—408.—On the 17th January, A.D. 395, Arcadius was saluted emperor of the east, when eighteen years of age. Rufinus, the præfect of the east, conspired to become its actual ruler; but at the instance of Stilicho, he was assassinated by the soldiers of Gainas the Goth on the 27th November, A.D. 395. From A.D. 395, Eutropius, the eunuch, was the actual governor of the east till A.D. 399, when he fell a victim to the intrigues of Gainas, and was put to death.

[1] 173. [2] 175. [3] 142.

Chapter XI.

THE EMPIRE—*continued.*

THE FIFTH CENTURY.

i. e., A.U.C. 1153 till A.U.C. 1252;—A.D. 400 to A.D. 499.

The West.

A.D.

395 to 423. HONORIUS.

423—425. THEODOSIUS II. (West and East).

423—455. VALENTINIAN III.

455. PETRONIUS MAXIMUS.

455—456. AVITUS.

457—461. MAJORIAN.

461—467. LIBIUS SEVERUS.

467—472. ANTHEMIUS.

472. OLYBRIUS.

473—474. GLYCERIUS.

474—475. JULIUS NEPOS.

475—476. ROMULUS AUGUSTULUS.

THE EAST.

395—408. ARCADIUS.
408—450. THEODOSIUS II.
450—453. PULCHERIA (Empress).
450—457. MARCIAN.
457—474. LEO I.
474. LEO II.
474—491. ZENO.
491—518. ANASTASIUS I.

Jurists.

(*Not One.*)

Orators, Historians, Philosophers, Poets, &c.

MACROBIUS (AURELIUS AMBROSIUS THEODOSIUS), prose writer, died about A.D. 420.

THE WESTERN EMPIRE.

Honorius, A.D. 395—423.—In A.D. 402, and toward the end of the year, Alaric appeared under the walls of Milan before Stilicho had had time to prepare for his reception. Honorius fled to Ravenna.[1] By the spring of A.D. 403, Stilicho had collected troops from Gaul, Germany, and Britain. At Easter he attacked Alaric near Pallentia,[2] and practically annihilated the Gothic infantry. Alaric escaped, however, with the larger part of his cavalry. He resolved to conquer or to die before the gates of Rome.

For reasons best known to himself, Stilicho resolved, if possible, to buy off the Goths. Alaric hesitated. His chieftains urged him to accept the bribe. A treaty was concluded. The Goths repassed the Po (*Padus*)[3] with the remnant of their army and a pension. In A.D. 404, Honorius celebrated the event by a

[1] 127. [2] 52. [3] 127.

triumphal procession, and the usual games, the last at which a Roman assembly witnessed a gladiatorial combat. Honorius fixed his residence in the inaccessible fortress of Ravenna upon the Adriatic.

In A.D. 405, a large force composed of Vandals (Slavonians), of Suevi (Germans), of Burgundians (Germans), and of Alani (Scythians), under their leader Radegast (Radagasius), passed the Alps, the Po, and the Apennines.

Many Italian cities were pillaged, some destroyed. Stilicho at length succeeded in so surrounding them that famine, rather than the sword, wrought their destruction. Radegast was beheaded. Two parts of his army, estimated at not less than 100,000, made their way into Gaul, of which they made themselves the masters, A.D. 406.

On the 23rd August, A.D. 408, Stilicho fell a victim to the suspicions of Honorius and the intrigues of Olympius, and was beheaded.

In A.D. 408, Alaric appeared before the walls of Rome. He starved the city into submission. The price of his departure, which took place in December, was 5,000 pounds of gold, 30,000 pounds of silver, 4,000 robes of silk, 3,000 pieces of fine scarlet cloth, and 3,000 pounds weight of pepper. He settled in the fair and fruitful province of Tuscany.[1] In A.D. 409, Honorius refused to appoint Alaric master-general of the armies of the west. Alaric laid siege to Ostia,[1] the granary of Rome.

The præfect Attalus, proclaimed emperor at the instance of Alaric, acknowledged Alaric master-general of the armies of the west.

Alaric again made overtures to Honorius, and undid Attalus to forward his projects, but, being unsuccessful, again visited Rome. At midnight the Salarian gate was silently opened to him. The inhabitants were awakened by the sound of the Gothic trumpets. It is said that Alaric bade his followers to help themselves freely, but to respect the churches of Saint

[1] 128.

Peter and Saint Paul, and not to shed innocent blood. Be that as it may, the streets were filled with dead bodies. The 40,000 Roman slaves may have taken some part in the slaughter. After a pillage of six days, the Goths retired. Articles of value and small compass not satisfying their cupidity, sideboards of massy plate, splendid and costly furniture, works of art, vases, and, indeed, everything fancied by them, was tumbled into their waggons. Alaric, after a short illness, died in A.D. 410. He was succeeded by his brother-in-law, Adolphus.

Adolphus offered himself, and was accepted, as an ally of Honorius, and in the character of a Roman general entered Gaul, A.D. 412. In A.D. 414, he, much to the distaste of Honorius and his ministers, but not to that of the lady herself, married Placidia, the daughter of Theodosius. In the same year it was his good fortune to restore Gaul to the rule of his brother-in-law, Honorius. In the same year Adolphus marched into Spain for the purpose of recovering that also; but, being assassinated there in A.D. 415, the task devolved on his successor, Wallia, who, in the course of three campaigns, conquered the Vandals, and again annexed Spain to the empire of Honorius.

On their return to Gaul in A.D. 418, Honorius bestowed on the Goths the maritime province between the Garonne and the Loire. The royal residence of the Goths was fixed at Toulouse.[1]

In A.D. 409 Britain and Armorica[2] were released by Honorius from allegiance to the Roman empire. From that year till A.D. 449, the date of the first Saxon invasion, Britain was governed by the nobles, the clergy, and the municipal authorities. Honorius died A.D. 423.

Valentinian III. (A.D. 423—455).—After the death of her affectionate husband, Adolphus, and after some sad experiences, Placidia, the widow of Adolphus, the daughter of Honorius, the captive and the queen of the Goths, married the general Constantius in A.D. 417, subsequently emperor for seven months, by whom she had two children, Honoria and Valentinian.

[1] 82. [2] 64.

Valentinian III. was declared emperor in the sixth year of his age, A.D. 423. The reins of government were in the hands of Placidia.

The western empire had at that time two generals of no ordinary ability, Ætius and Boniface. What the two, if united, might have done for the empire, is not easy to say. Their disunion cost it the loss of Africa. Ætius, who was near Placidia, for purposes of his own persuaded her to recall Boniface from the government of Africa, and, at the same time, secretly advised Boniface to disobey the imperial summons, assuring him that his life was in danger. So situated, Boniface invited the Vandal Genseric, then in Spain, to his aid. The invitation was accepted. When too late, the fraud of Ætius was discovered. Its consequence was equally lamented by Placidia and Boniface. Boniface, with the aid of the eastern empire, endeavoured in vain to dislodge Genseric. Leaving Africa in the hands of Genseric, Boniface returned to Placidia, by whom he was made master-general of the Roman armies of the west.

In A.D. 432 Boniface died of a mortal wound, received in combat with Ætius. Ætius was proclaimed a rebel by Placidia, and thus the west, by the fraud of Ætius, lost Africa and its two, then, most competent soldiers. Ætius retired for a time to the tents of the Huns, to whom he was indebted for his safety and subsequent restoration to power.

At the head of 60,000 Huns, Ætius presented himself before Placidia, not to supplicate pardon, but to demand restoration to power. He left Valentinian in the possession of the purple, and permitted him to enjoy in indolence the luxury of Italy.

Master of the whole military power of the west, Ætius cultivated the alliance of the Huns, concluded a treaty with Genseric, restored the imperial authority in Gaul and Spain, aided the Britons, made the Franks and Suevi his confederates, and concluded a peace with Theodoric, king of the Visigoths, in conjunction with whom he met Attila in the plains of Chalons.[1]

[1] 94.

Some say that 162,000, others that 300,000, fell in that memorable encounter. Theodoric was slain, but Torismond, his son, forced Attila to give way. Approaching night prevented the total defeat of Attila, whose retreat beyond the Rhine confessed the last victory achieved in the name of the western empire, A.D. 461.

The avowed object of the invasion of Attila had been to claim the hand of Honoria, the daughter of Placidia, and with her a share of the imperial patrimony.

In the spring of A.D. 462, Attila renewed his demand. It was again rejected. Attila crossed the Alps; Acquilia, Altinum, Concordia, and Padua were reduced to heaps of ruins; Vicenza, Verona, and Bergamo were sacked; the inhabitants of Milan and Pavia delivered up their wealth and applauded the Hun clemency which spared them their lives. Avienus and Leo, bishop of Rome, headed an embassy to Attila. The deliverance of Italy was purchased by the promised surrender of Honoria and her dower. Attila had numerous wives. While waiting for his Honoria, he took to himself another, the young and beautiful Ildico. Before the arrival of Honoria, Attila ruptured an artery and died, A.D. 453.

Ætius demanded Eudoxia, the emperor's daughter, in marriage for his son Gaudentius. Pressing his suit, apparently too warmly, Valentinian drew his sword, the first sword he had ever drawn, and plunged it into the breast of Ætius, the general who had saved his empire, A.D. 454.

By a base artifice, the chaste and beautiful wife of Petronius Maximus, a wealthy senator, was decoyed into a remote and silent bedchamber of the palace, where she was violated by Valentinian. Maximus incited two of the followers of Ætius to avenge their master's death. Valentinian was stabbed to the heart on the 14th March, A.D. 455.

Ortolan says:—"Valentinian III., the emperor of the west, also published it [The Theodosian Code, see *post*, p. 152] in the same year, and the discovery made by M. Clossius in our own time, together with other interesting documents, presents us with the verbal process employed for the reception of this code by the Roman senate, and the acclamations to which it gave rise: '*Augusti Augustorum, Maximi Augustorum,*' eight times repeated; 'God has given thee to us, may He preserve thee to us' (*Deus vos nobis dedit, Deus vos nobis servet*), repeated twenty-seven times; 'Hope lives in thee, safety depends upon thee' (*Spes in vobis, salus in vobis*), repeated twenty-six times; 'Dearer than our children, dearer than our fathers' (*Liberis cariores, parentibus cariores*), repeated sixteen times; 'Honours spring from thee, patrimonies are derived from thee, all things flow from thee' (*Per vos honores, per vos patrimonia, per vos omnia*), repeated twenty-eight times."[1]

Between the death of Valentinian and the fall of the western empire (A.D. 476), no fewer than nine emperors in succession occupied the throne. Their names appear in chronological order at the head of this chapter.

For fourteen days and nights, *i. e.*, from June 15th to the 29th, A.D. 455, Rome was pillaged by Genseric, who returned to Africa, his vessels laden with its spoil, taking with him as his prisoners Eudoxia, the widow of Valentinian, and her two daughters.

Eudoxia, the elder daughter of Valentinian, having reluctantly become the wife of Hanneric, the eldest son of Genseric, gave to Genseric a pretext for demanding, on the behalf of his daughter-in-law, an adequate portion of the imperial patrimony. The emperor of the east purchased his peace with Genseric.

We pass over the acts of Ricimer, the actual, though not the nominal, ruler of the west; the murder of three, if not of four of its emperors; the fact of the practical division of Italy into two hostile kingdoms; but pause to note the epistle addressed by the unanimous decree of the Roman senate to Zeno, the emperor of the east. In that epistle the Roman senate solemnly disclaimed the necessity and even the wish to continue any longer the imperial succession in Italy, since, in their opinion, the majesty of a sole monarch was sufficient to pervade and protect both the east and the west. They begged that Zeno would invest Odoacer with the title of patrician and the administration

[1] Prichard and Nasmith's Translation, p. 418.

of the diocese of Italy. The imperial ensigns, the sacred ornaments of the throne and palace, were forwarded to and accepted by Zeno.

Odoacer, the son of Orestes, the subject of Attila the Hun, became the ruler of Italy, A.D. 476.

THE EASTERN EMPIRE.

Arcadius, A.D. 395—408.—The reign of Arcadius is marked by the rebellion of the Goths, already mentioned in connection with the history of the west; the conspiracy of Gainas against Eutropius, one of the principal eunuchs of the palace of Constantinople, and the actual ruler of the east from A.D. 395 till 399; the revolt of Gainas, and his execution in January, A.D. 401; the expulsion of St. John Chrysostom, the archbishop of Constantinople, whose pastoral labours provoked and gradually united against him two sorts of enemies—the aspiring clergy, who envied his success, and the ministers and ladies of the court, who were offended by his orations, in which he declaimed with peculiar asperity against female vices, not hesitating, in the exordium of one of his sermons, to exclaim, alluding to the empress Eudoxia, "Herodias is again furious; Herodias again dances; she once more requires the head of John," an insolent allusion, which, as Gibbon says, "a woman and a sovereign, it was impossible for her to forgive." He was banished, and expired in the sixtieth year of his age, A.D. 407.

Theodosius II., A.D. 408—450.—At the date of his accession Theodosius was seven years of age. The præfect Anthemius assumed the government. When sixteen years of age, Pulcheria, the eldest sister of Theodosius, received the title of augusta. It was she who, in fact, governed during the whole of her brother's reign. She and her sisters, Arcadia and Marnia, in the presence of the clergy and the people, dedicated their virginity to God. The palace was, in effect, converted into a nunnery. The sisters renounced the vanities of life, and spent much time in religious exercises. Pulcheria, however, never suffered her attention to be diverted from the affairs of state. Her deliberations were matured; her actions prompt and decisive. She selected a wife for her brother, the celebrated Athenais, educated in the religion and sciences of the Greeks, who received at her baptism the christian name of Eudocia; and when that lady's ambition subsequently induced her to aspire to the government of the east, Pulcheria prevailed, and Eudocia was banished. During the reign of Theodosius, the kingdom of Armenia was finally divided between the Persians and the Romans.

Between A.D. 441 and 450, Attila ravaged the eastern empire between the Euxine and the Adriatic, but nothing could induce Theodosius to appear in person at the head of his legions. In three successive engagements his forces were vanquished. Thrace and Macedonia were ravaged without resistance and without mercy. The walls of Constantinople protected Theodosius, his court, and his unwarlike people, while seventy of the cities of the empire were being successfully erased from the face of the earth, and their inhabitants slaughtered.

Theodosius sued for peace. Attila granted it on terms, viz:—(1) The cession to Attila of the extensive and important territory on the southern banks of the Danube, between Singidunum or Belgrade and Novæ in the diocese of Thrace. (2) An annual tribute of 2,100 pounds of gold. (3) The payment down of 6,000 pounds of gold. (4) The unconditional surrender of all Huns taken prisoners by the Romans. (5) The ransom of all Roman prisoners at twelve pieces of gold per head. Theodosius had yet one degree lower to fall. He became party to the proposed assassination of Attila.

Thrown from his horse, Theodosius was seriously injured, and expired some days later, on the 28th July, 450.

Contemptible as was the man, the period of his reign is of considerable interest to the jurist.

The Gregorian and the Hermogenian Codes.—Between A.D. 312 and A.D. 429, but when, exactly, is not known, two works were published under the respective titles of "*Gregorianus Codex*" and "*Hermogenianus Codex.*" Neither of these codes has descended to us in a complete form. Our knowledge of them is limited to extracts from them, found in more recent works, and to statements in those works concerning them. We are told that they contained a collection of the imperial rescripts down to the time of Constantine (A.D. 306—337). We are told that Theodosius ordered the code that bears his name, and which was published A.D. 438, to be constructed on the model of these codes, and that his example was subsequently followed by Justinian, in the case of the code published by him A.D. 529. If this be so, these codes were collections of imperial rescripts, or rather parts of the imperial rescripts, under titles indicative of the subject dealt with; the rescripts, or parts of rescripts, on a given subject being arranged in their chronological order.

Lex de Responsis Prudentum, A.D. 426.—By this constitution bearing the name of Theodosius, the works of Papinian, Paul, Gaius, Ulpian, and Modestinus were confirmed, as also those passages from other jurists quoted by them. The previous enactment as to the notes of Paul and Ulpian on Papinian was affirmed. When those authorities differed, the majority determined the point; when equally divided, the opinion supported by Papinian was to prevail; if Papinian was silent, the judge was free to take which he pleased. By this enactment the labour of judges and the legal profession was reduced to the level of the living jurisprudence of the period. The seed, long before sown—when authority was substituted for argument, and legal practitioners were converted from reasoning beings into mere quoting and counting machines—had taken root, had grown apace, and had choked all true science. A matter of peculiar interest in connection with this *lex* is the fact that Gaius is ranked with Papinian, Paul, Ulpian, and Modestinus.

Theodosian Code, A.D. 438.—This code or collection of rescripts was prepared by the order, or perhaps, more correctly, with the sanction of the emperor whose name it bears, on the model of the Gregorian and Hermogenian codes (*ad similitudinem Gregoriani atque Hermogeniani codicis*). It brought the collection down to date. For the preparation of this code the emperor appointed two successive commissions—the first in A.D. 429, in which were eight members of the rank of *illustres* or *spectabiles*, and a jurist styled *vir disertissimus et scolasticus;* the second in A.D. 435, in which were sixteen members *illustres*, or *spectabiles*. At the head of each was Antiochus, a man of consular and præfectorial dignity. The preparation of this work involved, so we are told, the labour of nine years; and when published it was declared to be the sole source of imperial law (*jus principale*). Valentinian III., the emperor of the west, also published it in the same year as the imperial law of his people.

Among the many acclamations in the Roman senate to which the publication gave rise was this, "Let it be forbidden to add notes."[1]

The Novellæ.—All constitutions that were enacted subsequently to the publication of the Theodosian code were styled *novellæ*. As the code was made law both in the east and the west, it was agreed that *novellæ* should not have the force of law, till having been initiated in one empire they had been also published in the other. The *novellæ* that appear in the code of Justinian are those of the east only.

Ortolan, alluding to this period, says:—"We have now reached the last regulation of the lower empire, concerning the authority of the jurists. The first step which bound the judges in this respect was made by Adrian when he ordered them rather to count than to weigh the *responsa prudentum*. This direction was, however, well fenced, and the judges were only bound where there was unanimity of opinion; where this did not exist they were free to elect. Constantine, when he invalidated the notes of Ulpian and Paul upon Papinian, did not change the rule: he only desired, by a legislative act, to disentangle Papinian from the controversy which had tended to obscure him, and he in this way aided the tendency which in fact then existed to give to the dicta of Papinian authority in all cases where there was a difference of opinion. Such was the condition of things

[1] It is reported that Napoleon I., on seeing the first commentary on his Civil Code, exclaimed, "My code is lost!"

till the period at which we have arrived, that is to say, for more than a century after Constantine: but this rule requiring unanimity in so great a number of opinions, collected from different and remote periods, and in default of unanimity leaving the judge free to act, was altogether behind the then state of legal knowledge. The science had decayed step by step, and the ancient jurists were rapidly becoming obsolete. It became necessary to concentrate and reduce. It was clearly necessary with regard to the imperial constitutions, and it soon became equally evident that it was as necessary with regard to the works of the jurists. There was a desire to meet this want, and to facilitate the task which fell upon judges, suitors, and advocates, by limiting the collective body of legal opinions to the works of a comparatively small number of authors, who were the best known, and were designated by name: on the other hand, it made them mere machines. These were the final results of a vicious principle which attributed to the opinions of certain accredited jurists the force of laws, instead of allowing those opinions to rest upon their legitimate basis—the force of reason and intellect. These were the last fruits developed in the course of time from the seeds which the despotism of Augustus had first sown when he instituted a class of official jurists. It ended in their becoming *conditores legum*. This new rule is contained in a constitution which it is customary to call the *loi des citations*, or *lex de responsis prudentum*, and which has been preserved in the ancient fragments of the Theodosian code, inserted in the Breviarium Alaricianum, which emanated in fact from Theodosius II., A.D. 426. It was, however, first published for the western empire in the name of Valentinian, then an infant, and was subsequently enforced both in the east and in the west."

"This constitution mentions by name five of the most celebrated modern jurists—Papinian, Paul, Gaius, Ulpian, and Modestinus: it declares that it confirms all their writings, so that Gaius has the same authority as either of the others. This principle is, as it were, the pivot upon which judges, litigants, advocates, and the public had to turn.

"As to the other jurists, the constitution confirms them, but only in those cases where the five jurists just mentioned had introduced passages from them into their own works, such as Scævola, Sabinus, Julian, Marcellus, and others, provided that the correctness of the quotation was ascertained by a comparison of manuscripts. This proviso was rendered necessary by the possibility of errors creeping into the old MSS. The works of these jurists and of those whose decisions they quoted, the accuracy having been secured by comparison of different MSS., were the authorities to which it was permitted to refer, to determine and solve all legal difficulties.

"The constitution adds that the notes of Paul and Ulpian upon Papinian should continue to be held invalid, as they had been declared to be by Constantine, and it was necessary, inasmuch as the term *scripta universa*, which is general, had been employed, that the restriction also should be specified. As to the notes of Marcian, from the simple fact that nothing was said as to them, they remained under the proscription, with which we know they had been branded by an enactment, the text of which we do not however possess.

"The jurists whose works it was permitted to quote, and whose opinions were thus supposed to be settled, having been fixed by law, the judge and the parties interested were bound by them, provided that if these authorities differed the majority determined the point; if they were equally divided, the opinion supported by Papinian was to prevail, and if the opinion of Papinian was not expressed, the judge was at liberty to follow whichever he pleased.

"We may well ask what the magistrates, judges, and lawyers of that period were like, when we find the duties of their respective offices reduced to mere compilation or comparison and numerical calculation of legal opinions. Was this a legitimate application of the powers of reason and of learning? Assuredly the science of jurisprudence could not sink to lower depths of degradation. . . ."

"In addition to the enactments of Theodosius upon the works of the jurists, to which we have just alluded, we have others, enacted three years later, on the imperial constitutions. He took as a model (*ad similitudinem Gregoriani atque*

Hormogeniani Codicis) the collection of rescripts methodically arranged and published under the title of codes, but without legislative authority, by Gregorianus and Hermogenianus, and which did not go below the time of Constantine, and he directed a similar collection of all the constitutions of Constantine and the succeeding emperors, including himself, commencing from the period when the other collection left off, to be drawn up by two successive commissions under the superintendence of Antiochus, ex-consul and ex-prætorian præfect (*cunctas colligi constitutiones decernimus, quas Constantinus inclytus, et post eum divi Principes Nosque tulimus*). In the title of this collection, we find set down the composition of the first commission, which was appointed A.D. 429, in which there were eight members of the rank of *illustres* or *spectabiles*, and a jurist styled *vir disertissimus et scolasticus*, and the appointment for the same object of a second commission, A.D. 435, in which were sixteen members, *illustres* or *spectabiles*. In both cases, at the head of these commissions, we find the name of Antiochus, a personage of consular and præfectorial dignity. The principal object assigned by Theodosius for this undertaking was the astonishing paucity of persons familiar with the civil law (*tam pauci raroque extiterint, qui plena juris civilis scientia ditarentur*). After all their labours, scarcely two were to be found who had anything like a perfect acquaintance with the law (*in tanto lucubrationum tristi pallore vix unus aut alter receperit soliditatem perfectæ doctrinæ*). This is a result which must be attributed to the immense accumulation of books (*copia immensa librorum*), and to the pile of imperial constitutions (*moles Constitutionum divalium*), which involved the human mind in a maze of inextricable confusion (*quæ velut sub crassæ demersa caliginis et obscuritatis vallo sui, notitiam humanis ingeniis interclusit*)."

"This work, which was completed after nine years' labour, received the imperial sanction, and was published in the east in the February of A.D. 438, under the name of the Theodosian Code, with the injunction that from the calends of January, A.D. 439, it was to be the sole source of imperial law (*jus principale*)." [1]

[1] Prichard and Nasmith's translation, pp. 412 *et seq.*

Pulcheria and Marcian.—On the death of Theodosius, his sister Pulcheria was unanimously proclaimed empress of the east. She was the first female sovereign of the empire. She chose as her associate Marcian, a senator about sixty years of age, who became her nominal husband and was solemnly invested with the imperial purple. Pulcheria died A.D. 453, Marcian A.D. 457.

Leo I. (A.D. 457—474).—During three generations the armies of the east were successively commanded by one Aspar, his father, and his son. Such was the power and popularity of Aspar, who was an Arian, when the throne became vacant by the death of Marcian, that it is said he might have placed the diadem on his own head if he would have subscribed to the Nicene creed. He recommended Leo of Thrace, a military tribune, the principal steward of his own household. His nomination was ratified by the senate. Leo was the first emperor who received the imperial crown from the hands of a bishop. Aspar, knowing that he had placed Leo on the throne, assumed a dictatorial rôle, and, when he found that he could not appoint a præfect of Constantinople, presumed to reproach his sovereign with a breach of promise, and insolently shaking his purple, said, "It is not proper that the man who is invested with this garment should be guilty of lying!" to which Leo replied, "Nor is it proper that a prince should be compelled to resign his own judgment and the public interest to the will of a subject." After the fall of Aspar, who had favoured the cause of Genseric, to whom he is said to have been indebted, Leo listened to the entreaties of Ricimer, nominated Anthemius emperor of the west, and resolved to put an end to the tyranny of the Vandals. He prepared a fleet of 1,113 ships, at a cost of about 5,200,000*l.*, which, with 100,000 soldiers and mariners, was entrusted to Basilicus, the brother of the empress Verina. The troops were landed at about forty miles from Carthage. The efforts of the Vandals, both by sea and land, to oppose his progress were abortive; and had he pushed on to Carthage, the downfall of the Vandal kingdom seemed assured. He consented, however, it is suggested, induced by private interest, to a truce for five days, during which Genseric, seizing his opportunity, destroyed the larger part of the Roman fleet by means of fire ships. Basilicus returned to Constantinople, having lost one-half of his ships and men, A.D. 468. Genseric once more ruled the seas, and ravaged the coasts of Italy, Greece, and Asia. He lived to see the final extinction of the empire of the west. He died A.D. 477.

The remaining years of this century may be passed over in silence.

Chapter XII.

THE EMPIRE—*continued.*

THE SIXTH CENTURY.

i. e., A.U.C. 1253 till A.U.C. 1352;—A.D. 500 till A.D. 599.

The East.

491—518. ANASTASIUS I.
518—527. JUSTIN I.
527—565. JUSTINIAN.

Anastasius I., A.D. 491—518.—The chief characteristic of the twenty-seven years' reign of Anastasius is the fact that he not only delivered his people from the most odious and oppressive taxes, but saved from his annual revenue the enormous sum of 13,000,000*l.* or 320,000 pounds of gold.

In A.D. 505, his general, Sabinian, with 100,000 men, was defeated by the numerically inferior force of Theodoric in the the fields of Margus,[1] when the flower of his army, and even the hope of the eastern empire, was irretrievably destroyed. To avenge this ignominious defeat, 200 ships, manned by 8,000 men, were despatched by the Byzantine Court to plunder the sea coast of Calabria[2] and Apulia.[2] The fleet assaulted the ancient city of Tarentum,[3] interrupted the trade and agriculture of a happy country, and sailed back to the Hellespont,[4] proud of piratical victory over a people whom the Romans still professed to consider their brethren, A.D. 509.

The long wall of sixty miles, built by Anastasius, from the Propontis[5] to the Euxine,[5] proclaimed the impotence of his arms.

[1] 39° N., 54° E. [2] 143. [3] 144. [4] 189. [5] 203.

If Anastasius had no soldiers, he had at least monks in plenty, whose characteristics, however, do not seem to have been loyalty, charity, and brotherly love. The Antioch addition of the now-familiar words, "Who was crucified for us," to the trisagion (thrice holy)—"Holy, holy, holy, Lord God of Hosts"—nearly cost the emperor his throne and his life. It was his lot to be anathematised as the Manichæan tyrant, and to witness the first war waged in the name of Christ. Vitalian, a Gothic chief, with an army of Huns and Bulgarians, declared himself the champion of the catholic faith, and in the execution of his pious enterprise depopulated Thrace,[1] besieged Constantinople,[2] and exterminated, it is said, 65,000 of his fellow Christians, A.D. 514.

Justin I., A.D. 518—527.—Justin and two other peasants of his native village in Bulgaria (Dardania or Dacia),[3] when youths, made their way to Constantinople, where their strength and stature secured them admission among the guards of Leo. Justin gradually accumulated wealth and honours, and on the death of Anastasius was invested with the purple in his sixty-eighth year. About four months before his death, he caused the diadem to be placed on the head of his nephew, Justinian, whom he had brought up and educated, and who, from that moment, was regarded as the emperor.

Justinian I., A.D. 527—565.—On the 1st April, A.D. 527, Justinian commenced his reign of 38 years, 7 months, and 13 days.

The object of the thin line of general history hitherto traced being to lead the reader gradually down to this period when the history of Roman law is for all practical purposes completed, attention will now be strictly confined to the consideration of Roman law during this reign. What part the emperor took in the legislation that bears his name it is not easy to say. That he did take personal interest in what he intended and supposed to be legal reform cannot reasonably be doubted, any more than that the burden of the labour nominally fell upon Tribonian,

[1] 188 [2] 203. [3] 171.

who was possibly also the prime mover in the matter, and who, as it will appear, was in fact made the legislator.

Tribonian, who was a native of Sido in Pamphylia,[1] is said to have been distinguished for the diversity of his mental attainments. His actual or reputed acquaintance with jurisprudence secured for him the favour of Justinian, who raised him to the rank of quæstor of the palace and consul. He has been compared to our Bacon, whether justly or otherwise may be matter of doubt. The two, it is said, combined great and diversified learning with the vice of avarice. Each, as matter of history, was dismissed from high judicial office for corruption. The similarity between their respective sovereigns is somewhat striking. Inórdinate conceit was their common characteristic. Each sovereign made a parade of attachment to the religion in fashion at his time, while secretly destitute of any sympathy with it. Justinian married a public prostitute. The morality of James was not above suspicion. The flagrant injustice of Justinian to Belisarius was matched by the treatment by James of Raleigh. The meanness of the one was equalled by that of the other. Neither enjoyed either the affection or respect of his subjects. Both died unlamented.

Facts are superior to all criticism. The reader can better judge of Justinian from his writings and the books published in his name than from anything it would be possible for another to say concerning him. He addressed himself to the senate thus:—

"To the Senate of Constantinople.

"To diminish the length of lawsuits, and to do away with the confused mass of constitutions contained in the Gregorian, Hermogenian, and Theodosian codes, published by Theodosius, by his successors, and by ourselves, we wish to put them all together in a single code, under our own auspicious name." (Theodosius had merely said, "*nostro nomine nuncupatus*"; with Justinian it is, "*sub felici*," and later, "*divino nostri nominis vocabulo*.") "Efficiently to perform so great a work, we choose . . . ." (Here follow the names of ten personages whom Justinian distinguishes respectively with one of these

[1] 220.

epithets, excellentissimus, eminentissimus, magnificus, disertissimus, &c. At their head can be remarked John, ex-quæstor of the sacred palace, ex-consul and patrician; among them, Tribonian or Tribunian, who was soon to assume the first place, and Theophilus, count of the consistory, professor of law at Constantinople.)

"We permit them, suppressing preambles, repetitions, contradictory or disused clauses, to collect and classify the laws under proper titles, adding, cutting down, modifying, compressing, if need be, several constitutions into a single enactment, so as to render the sense more clear, and yet preserve in each title the chronological order, so that their order may be noted by position in the code as well as by date. Ides of February (13 Feb.), A. D. 528."

(The work was entrusted to six individuals, and was divided into twelve books. The code, manufactured in the space of one year, was published on the Ides of April (13th April), A. D. 529, and came into force from the 16th of the Kalends of May in the same year.)

On its publication, Justinian decreed as follows:—

"We forbid all pleaders and advocates to quote, under the penalty of making themselves guilty of fraud, any other constitutions than those which are inserted in our code, or to quote otherwise than is written there; for these constitutions, together with the works of the ancient interpreters of the law, must suffice to decide all suits. No difficulty must be raised on account of some of them being without date, or of their having been originally only private rescripts."

Codex repetitæ prælectiones (A.D. 534).—This work was a second edition of the Code of Justinian embodying fifty decisions and certain constitutions of later date than A.D. 529. It is this edition which we possess.

The following table shows its construction and titles:—

THE TITLES AND SUB-TITLES OF THE CODE.

Liber 1.—Tit. 1. De summa trinitate et de fide catholica. 2. De sacrosanctis ecclesiis et de rebus et privilegiis earum. 3. De episcopis et clericis et Orphanotrophis et Brephotrophis et Xenodochis et Ptochotrophis et Asceteriis et Monachis et privilegio eorum et castrensi peculio et de redimendis captivis, et de nuptiis clericorum vetitis seu permissis. 4. De episcopali audientia et de diversis capitulis, quæ ad jus curamque et reverentiam pontificalem pertinent. 5. De hæreticis et Manichæis et Samaritis. 6. Ne sanctum baptisma iteretur. 7. De apostatis. 8. Nemini licere signum salvatoris Christi vel in silice, vel in marmore aut sculpere aut pingere. 9. De Judæis et cœlicolis. 10. Ne Christianum mancipium hæreticus, vel paganus, vel Judæus habeat, vel possideat, vel circumcidat. 11. De paganis sacrificiis et templis. 12. De his qui ad ecclesias confugiunt, vel ibi exclamant. 13. De his qui in ecclesiis manumittuntur. 14. De legibus et constitutionibus principum et edictis. 15. De mandatis principum. 16. De senatus consultis. 17. De vetere jure enucleando et de auctoritate juris prudentium qui in Digestis referuntur. 18. De juris et facti ignorantia. 19. De precibus imperatori offerendis et de quibus rebus supplicare liceat vel non. 20. Quando libellus principi datus litis contestationem facit. 21. Ut lite pendente, vel post provocationem, aut definitivam sententiam, nulli liceat imperatori supplicare. 22. Si contra jus vel utilitatem publicam, per vel mendacium fuerit aliquid postulatum vel impetratum. 23. De diversis rescriptis et pragmaticis sanctionibus. 24. De statuis et imaginibus. 25. De his qui ad statuas confugiunt. 26. De officio præfectorum prætorio orientis et Illyrici. 27. De officio præfecti prætorio Africæ et de omni ejusdem diœceseos statu. 28. De officio præfecti urbi. 29. De officio magistri militum. 30. De officio quæstoris. 31. De officio magistri officiorum. 32. De officio comitis sacrarum largitionum. 33. De officio comitis rerum privatarum. 34. De officio comitis sacri palatii. (34 bis.) De officio comitis sacri patrimonii. 35. De officio proconsulis et legati. 36. De officio comitis orientis. 37. De officio præfecti Augustalis. 38. De officio vicarii. 39. De officio prætorum. 40. De officio rectoris provinciæ. 41. Ut nulli patriæ suæ administratio sine speciali permissu principis permittatur. 42. De quadrimenstruis tam civilibus quam militaribus brevibus. 43. De officio præfecti vigilum. 44. De officio præfecti annonæ. 45. De officio civilium judicum. 46. De officio militarium judicum. 47. Ne comitibus rei militaris, vel tribunis lavacra præstentur. 48. De officio diversorum judicum. 49. Ut omnes tam civiles, quam militares, judices post administrationem depositam per quinquaginta dies in civitatibus vel certis locis permaneant. 50. De officio ejus qui vicem alicujus judicis vel præsidis obtinet. 51. De adsessoribus et domesticis et cancellariis judicum. 52. De annonis et capitu administrantium, vel adsessorum aliorumve publicas sollicitudines gerentium, vel eorum qui aliquas consecuti sunt dignitates. 53. De contractibus judicum, vel eorum qui sunt circa eos, et inhibendis donationibus in eos faciendis et ne administrationis tempore proprias ædes ædificent sine sanctione pragmatica. 54. De modo multarum quæ ab judicibus infliguntur. 55. De defensoribus civitatum. 56. De magistratibus municipalibus. 57. De officio juridici Alexandriæ.

Liber 2.—Tit. 1. De edendo. 2. De in jus vocando. 3. De pactis. 4. De transactionibus. 5. De calculi errore. 6. De postulando. 7. De advocatis diversorum judiciorum. 8. De advocatis diversorum judicum.[1] 9. De advocatis fisci. 10. De errore advocatorum vel libellos seu preces concipientium. 11. Ut quæ desunt advocatis partium judex suppleat. 12. Ex quibus causis infamia inrogatur. 13. De procuratoribus. 14. Ne liceat potentioribus patrocinium litigantibus præstare, vel actiones in se transferre. 15. De his qui potentiorum nomine titulos prædiis adfigunt, vel eorum nomina in lite prætendunt. 16. Ut nemo privatus titulos prædiis suis, vel alienis imponat, vel vela regalia suspendat. 17. Ut nemini liceat sine judicis auctoritate signa imprimere rebus, quas alius tenet. 18. Ne fiscus vel respublica procurationem alicui patrocinii causa in lite præstet. 19. De negotiis gestis. 20. De his quæ vi metusve causa gesta sunt. 21. De dolo malo. 22. De in integrum restitutione minorum viginti quinque annis. 23. De filio familias minore. 24. De fidejussoribus minorum. 25. Si tutor, vel curator intervenerit. 26. Si in communi eademque causa in integrum restitutio postuletur. 27. Si adversus rem judicatam. 28. Si adversus venditionem. 29. Si adversus venditionem pignoris. 30. Si adversus donationem.

[1] N.B.—§§ 7 and 8 commonly form one title, § 8 being in fact a continuation of § 7.

31. Si adversus libertatem. 32. Si adversus transactionem vel divisionem minor restitui velit. 33. Si adversus solutionem a debitore vel a se factam. 34. Si adversus dotem. 35. Si adversus delictum suum. 36. Si adversus usucapionem. 37. Si adversus fiscum. 38. Si adversus creditorem. 39. Si ut se hereditate abstineat. 40. Si ut omissam hereditatem vel bonorum possessionem, vel quid aliud adquirat. 41. In quibus causis in integrum restitutio necessaria non est. 42. Qui, et adversus quos, in integrum restitui non possunt. 43. Si minor se majorem dixerit vel probatus fuerit. 44. Si sæpius in integrum restitutio postuletur. 45. De his qui veniam ætatis impetraverunt. 46. Si major factus ratum habuerit. 47. Ubi, et apud quem, cognitio in integrum restitutionis agitanda sit. 48. De reputationibus quæ fiunt in judicio in integrum restitutionis. 49. Etiam per procuratorem causam in integrum restitutionis agi posse. 50. In integrum restitutione postulata ne quid novi fiat. 51. De restitutione militum et eorum qui reipublicæ causa afuerunt. 52. De uxoribus militum, vel eorum, qui reipublicæ causa absunt. 53. De temporibus in integrum restitutionis tam minorum, et aliarum personarum, quæ restitui possunt, quam etiam heredum eorum. 54. Quibus ex causis majores in integrum restituuntur. 55. De alienatione judicii mutandi causa facta. 56. De receptis. 57. De satisdando. 58. De formulis et impetratione actionum sublatis. 59. De jurejurando propter calumniam dando.

Liber 3.—Tit. 1. De judiciis. 2. De sportulis et sumptibus in diversis judiciis faciendis et de exsecutoribus litium. 3. De pedaneis judicibus. 4. Qui pro sua jurisdictione judices dare darive possunt. 5. Ne quis in sua causa judicet vel sibi jus dicat. 6. Qui legitimam personam in judiciis habent vel non. 7. Ut nemo invitus agere vel accusare cogatur. 8. De ordine judiciorum. 9. De litis contestatione. 10. De plus petitionibus. 11. De dilationibus. 12. De feriis. 13. De jurisdictione omnium judicum et de foro competenti. 14. Quando imperator inter pupillos vel viduas vel miserabiles personas cognoscat et ne exhibeantur. 15. Ubi de criminibus agi oportet. 16. Ubi de possessione agi oportet. 17. Ubi fidei-commissum peti oportet. 18. Ubi conveniatur qui certo loco dare promisit. 19. Ubi in rem actio exerceri debet. 20. Ubi de hereditate agatur et ubi scripti heredes in possessionem mitti postulare debent. 21. Ubi de ratiociniis tam publicis quam privatis agi oportet. 22. Ubi causa status agi debeat. 23. Ubi quis de curiali vel cohortali aliave condicione conveniatur. 24. Ubi senatores vel clarissimi civiliter vel criminaliter conveniantur. 25. In quibus causis militantes fori præscriptione uti non possunt. 26. Ubi causæ fiscales vel divinæ domus hominumque ejus agantur. 27. Quando liceat unicuique sine judice vindicare se vel publicam devotionem. 28. De inofficioso testamento. 29. De inofficiosis donationibus. 30. De inofficiosis dotibus. 31. De petitione hereditatis. 32. De rei vindicatione. 33. De usufructu et habitatione et ministerio servorum. 34. De servitutibus et de aqua. 35. De lege Aquilia. 36. Familiæ erciscundæ. 37. Communi dividundo. 38. Communia utriusque judicii tam familiæ erciscundæ quam communi dividundo. 39. Finium regundorum. 40. De consortibus ejusdem litis. 41. De noxalibus actionibus. 42. Ad exhibendum. 43. De aleatoribus et alearum lusu. 44. De religiosis et sumptibus funerum.

Liber 4.—Tit. 1. De rebus creditis et jurejurando. 2. Si certum petatur. 3. De suffragio. 4. De prohibita sequestratione pecuniæ. 5. De condictione indebiti. 6. De condictione ob causam datorum. 7. De condictione ob turpem causam. 8. De condictione furtiva. 9. De condictione ex lege et sine causa vel injusta causa. 10. De obligationibus et actionibus. 11. Ut actiones et ab herede et contra heredem incipiant. 12. Ne uxor pro marito vel maritus pro uxore vel mater pro filio conveniatur. 13. Ne filius pro patre vel pater pro filio emancipato, vel libertus pro patrono conveniatur. 14. An servus ex suo facto post manumissionem teneatur. 15. Quando fiscus vel privatus debitoris sui debitores exigere potest. 16. De actionibus hereditariis. 17. Ex delictis defunctorum in quantum heredes conveniantur. 18. De constituta pecunia. 19. De probationibus. 20. De testibus. 21. De fide instrumentorum et amissione eorum et antapochis faciendis et de his quæ sine scriptura fieri possunt. 22. Plus valere quod agitur quam quod simulate concipitur. 23. De commodato. 24. De pigneraticia actione. 25. De exercitoria et institoria actione. 26. Quod cum eo qui in aliena est potestate negotium gestum esse dicitur, vel de peculio seu quod jussu aut de in rem verso. 27. Per quas personas nobis adquiritur. 28. Ad senatusconsultum Macedonianum. 29. Ad senatusconsultum Velleianum. 30. De non numerata pecunia. 31. De compensationibus. 32. De usuris. 33. De nautico fœnore. 34. Depositi. 35. Mandati. 36. Si servus se emi mandaverit. 37. Pro socio. 38. De contrahenda emtione et venditione. 39. De hereditate vel actione vendita. 40. Quæ res venire non possunt, et qui vendere vel emere vetantur. 41. Quæ res exportari non debeant. 42. De eunuchis. 43. De patribus qui filios distraxerunt. 44. De rescindenda venditione. 45. Quando liceat ab emtione discedere. 46. Si propter publicas pensitationes venditio fuerit celebrata. 47. Sine sensu vel reliquis fundum comparari non posse. 48. De periculo et commodo rei venditæ. 49. De actionibus empti et venditi. 50. Si quis alteri vel sibi sub alterius nomine vel aliena pecunia emerit. 51. De rebus alienis non alienandis et de prohibita rerum alienatione vel hypotheca. 52. De communium rerum alienatione. 53. Rem alienam gerentibus non interdici rerum suarum alienatione. 54. De pactis inter emptorem et venditorem compositis. 55. Si servus exportandus veneat. 56. Si mancipium ita venierit ne prostituatur. 57. Si mancipium ita fuerit alienatum, ut manumittatur vel contra. 58. De ædiliciis actionibus. 59. De monopoliis et de conventu negotiatorum illicito vel artificum ergolaborumque nec non balneatorum prohibitis illicitisque negotiationibus. 60. De nundinis. 61. De vectigalibus et commissis. 62. Vectigalia nova institui non posse. 63. De commerciis et mercatoribus. 64. De rerum permutatione et de præscriptis verbis actione. 65. De locato et conducto. 66. De emphyteutico jure.

Liber 5.—Tit. 1. De sponsalibus et arris sponsaliciis et proxeneticis. 2. Si rector provinciæ vel ad eum pertinentes sponsalia dederint. 3. De donationibus ante nuptias vel propter nuptias et sponsaliciis. 4. De nuptiis. 5. De incestis et inutilibus nuptiis. 6. De interdicto matrimonio inter pupillam et tutorem seu curatorem liberosque eorum. 7. Si quacumque præditus potestate vel ad eum pertinentes ad suppositarum jurisdictioni suæ adspirare temptaverint nuptias. 8. Si nuptiæ ex rescripto petantur. 9. De secundis nuptiis. 10. Si secundo nupserit mulier, cui maritus usum fructum reliquerit. 11. De dotis promissione vel nuda pollicitatione. 12. De jure dotium. 13. De rei uxoriæ actione in ex stipulatu actionem transfusa et de natura dotibus præstita. 14. De pactis conventis tam super dote quam super donatione ante nuptias et paraphernis. 15. De dote cauta et non numerata. 16. De donationibus inter virum et uxorem et a parentibus in liberos factis et de ratihabitione. 17. De repudiis et judicio de moribus sublato. 18. Soluto matrimonio dos quemadmodum petatur. 19. Si dos constante matrimonio soluta fuerit. 20. Ne fidejussores vel mandatores dotium dentur. 21. Rerum amotarum. 22. Ne pro dote mulieri bona mariti addicantur. 23. De fundo dotali. 24. Divortio facto apud quem liberi morari vel educari debent. 25. De alendis liberis ac parentibus. 26. De concubinis. 27. De naturalibus liberis et matribus eorum et ex quibus casibus justi efficiuntur. 28. De tutela testamentaria. 29. De confirmando tutore. 30. De legitima tutela. 31. Qui petant tutores vel curatores. 32. Ubi petantur tutores vel curatores. 33. De tutoribus et curatoribus illustrium vel clarissimarum personarum. 34. Qui dare tutores vel curatores et qui dari possunt. 35. Quando mulier tutelæ officio fungi potest. 36. In quibus causis tutorem habenti tutor vel curator dari potest. 37. De administratione tutorum et curatorum et de pecunia pupillari feneranda vel deponenda. 38. De periculo tutorum et curatorum. 39. Quando ex facto tutoris vel curatoris minores agere vel conveniri possunt. 40. Si ex pluribus tutoribus vel curatoribus omnes vel unus agere pro minore vel conveniri possunt. 41. Ne tutor vel curator vectigal conducat. 42. De tutore vel curatore qui satis non dedit. 43. De suspectis. 44. De in litem dando tutore vel curatore. 45. De eo qui pro tutore negotia gessit. 46. Si mater indemnitatem promiserit. 47. Si contra matris voluntatem tutor datus sit. 48. Ut causæ post pubertatem adsit tutor. 49. Ubi pupilli educentur. 50. De alimentis pupillo præstandis.

51. Arbitrium tutelæ. 52. De dividenda tutela et pro qua parte quisque tutorum conveniatur. 53. De in litem jurando. 54. De heredibus tutorum. 55. Si tutor non gesserit. 56. De usuris pupillaribus. 57. De fidejussoribus tutorum seu curatorum. 58. De contrario judicio. 59 De auctoritate præstanda. 60. Quando curatores vel tutores esse desinant. 61. De actore a tutore seu curatore dando. 62. De excusationibus et temporibus earum. 63. Si falsis adlegationibus excusatus est. 64. Si tutor rei publicæ causa aberit. 65. De excusatione veteranorum. 66. Qui numero liberorum se excusant. 67. Qui ætate. 68. Qui morbo. 69. Qui numero tutelarum. 70. De curatore furiosi vel prodigi. 71. De prædiis vel aliis rebus minorum sine decreto non alienandis vel obligandis. 72. Quando decreto opus non est. 73. Si quis ignorans rem minoris esse sine decreto comparavit. 74. Si major factus sine decreto factam alienationem ratam habuerit. 75. De magistratibus conveniendis.

Liber 6.—Tit. 1. De fugitivis servis et libertis mancipiisque civitatum artificibus et ad diversa opera deputatis et ad rem privatam vel dominicam pertinentibus. 2. De furtis et de servo corrupto. 3. De operis libertorum. 4. De bonis libertorum et de jure patronatus. 5. Si in fraudem patroni alienatio facta est. 6. De obsequiis patronis præstandis. 7. De libertis et eorum liberis. 8. De jure aureorum anulorum et de natalibus restituendis. 9. Qui admitti ad bonorum possessionem possunt, et intra quod tempus. 10. Quando non petentium partes petentibus adcrescunt. 11. De bonorum possessione secundum tabulas. 12. De bonorum possessione contra tabulas, quam prætor liberis pollicetur. 13. De bonorum possessione contra tabulas liberti, quæ patronis vel liberis eorum datur. 14. Unde liberi. 15. Unde legitimi et unde cognati. 16. De edicto successorio. 17. De Carboniano edicto. 18. Unde vir et uxor. 19. De repudianda bonorum possessione. 20. De collationibus. 21. De testamento militis. 22. Qui facere testamentum possunt vel non possunt. 23. De testamentis: quemadmodum testamenta ordinantur. 24. De heredibus instituendis et quæ personæ heredes institui non possunt. 25. De institutionibus et substitutionibus seu restitutionibus sub condicione factis. 26. De impuberum et de aliis substitutionibus. 27. De necessariis et servis heredibus instituendis vel substituendis. 28. De liberis præteritis vel exheredatis. 29. De postumis heredibus instituendis vel exheredandis vel præteritis. 30. De jure deliberandi et de adeunda vel adquirenda hereditate. 31. De repudianda vel abstinenda hereditate. 32. Quemadmodum aperiantur testamenta et inspiciantur et describantur. 33. De edicto divi Hadriani tollendo et quemadmodum scriptus heres in possessionem mittatur. 34. Si quis aliquem testari prohibuerit vel coegerit. 35. De his quibus ut indignis auferuntur et ad senatusconsultum Silanianum. 36. De codicillis. 37. De legatis. 38. De verborum et rerum significatione. 39. Si omissa sit causa testamenti. 40. De indicta viduitate et de lege Julia miscella tollendo. 41. De his quæ pœnæ nomine in testamento vel codicillis relinquuntur. 42. De fideicommissis. 43. Communia de legatis et fideicommissis et de in rem missione tollenda. 44. De falsa causa adjecta legato vel fideicommisso. 45. De his quæ sub modo legata vel fideicommissa relinquuntur. 46. De condicionibus insertis tam legatis quam fideicommissis et libertatibus. 47. De usuris et fructibus legatorum vel fideicommissorum. 48. De incertis personis. 49. Ad senatusconsultum Trebellianum. 50. Ad legem Falcidiam. 51. De caducis tollendis. 52. De his qui ante apertas tabulas hereditates transmittunt. 53. Quando dies legati vel fideicommissi cedit. 54. Ut in possessionem legatorum vel fideicommissorum servandorum causa mittatur et quando satisdari debet. 55. De suis et legitimis liberis et ex filia nepotibus ab intestato venientibus. 56. Ad senatusconsultum Tertullianum. 57. Ad senatusconsultum Orfitianum. 58. De legitimis heredibus. 59. Communia de successionibus. 60. De bonis maternis et materni generis. 61. De bonis, quæ liberis in potestate constitutis ex matrimonio vel aliter adquiruntur et eorum administratione. 62. De hereditatibus decurionum naviculariorum cohortalium militum et fabricensium.

Liber 7.—Tit. 1. De vindicta libertate et apud consilium manumissione. 2. De testamentaria manumissione. 3. De lege Fusia Caninia tollenda. 4. De fideicommissariis libertatibus. 5. De deditticia libertate tollenda. 6. De Latina libertate tollenda et per certos modos in civitatem Romanam transfusa. 7. De servo communi manumisso. 8. De servo pignori dato manumisso. 9. De servis reipublicæ manumittendis. 10. De his qui a non domino manumissi sunt. 11. Qui manumittere non possunt et ne in fraudem creditorum manumittatur. 12. Qui non possunt ad libertatem pervenire. 13. Pro quibus causis servi præmium accipiunt libertatem. 14. De ingenuis manumissis. 15. Communia de manumissionibus. 16. De liberali causa. 17. De adsertione tollenda. 18. Quibus ad libertatem proclamare non licet, et de rebus eorum, qui ad libertatem proclamare non prohibentur. 19. De ordine cognitionum. 20. De collusione detegenda. 21. Ne de statu defunctorum post quinquennium quæratur. 22. De longi temporis præscriptione, quæ pro libertate et non adversus libertatem opponitur. 23. De peculio ejus qui libertatem meruit. 24. De senatusconsulto Claudiano tollendo. 25. De nudo ex jure Quiritium tollendo. 26. De usucapione pro emptore vel transactione. 27. De usucapione pro donato. 28. De usucapione pro dote. 29. De usucapione pro herede. 30. Communia de usucapionibus. 31. De usucapione transformanda et de sublata differentia rerum mancipi et nec mancipi. 32. De adquirenda et retinenda possessione. 33. De præscriptione longi temporis decem vel viginti annorum. 34. In quibus causis cessat longi temporis præscriptio. 35. Quibus non obiciatur longi temporis præscriptio. 36. Adversus creditorem. 37. De quadriennii præscriptione. 38. Ne rei dominicæ vel templorum vindicatio temporis exceptione submoveatur. 39. De præscriptione 30 vel 40 annorum. 40. De annali exceptione Italici contractus tollenda et de diversis temporibus et exceptionibus et præscriptionibus et interruptionibus earum. 41. De adluvionibus et paludibus et de pascuis ad alium statum translatis. 42. De sententiis præfectorum prætorio. 43. Quomodo et quando judex sententiam proferre debet præsentibus partibus vel una absente. 44. De sententiis ex periculo recitandis. 45. De sententiis et interlocutionibus omnium judicum. 46. De sententia, quæ sine certa quantitate prolata est. 47. De sententiis, quæ pro eo quod interest proferuntur. 48. Si non a competenti judice judicatum esse dicatur. 49. De pœna judicis, qui male judicavit, vel ejus, qui judicem vel adversarium corrumpere curavit. 50. Sententiam rescindi non posse. 51. De fructibus et litis expensis. 52. De re judicata. 53. De executione rei judicatæ. 54. De usuris rei judicatæ. 55. Si plures una sententia condemnati sunt. 56. Quibus res judicata non nocet. 57. Comminationes epistulas programmata subscriptiones auctoritatem rei judicatæ non habere. 58. Si ex falsis instrumentis vel testimoniis judicatum erit. 59. De confessis. 60. Inter alios acta vel judicata aliis non nocere. 61. De relationibus. 62. De appellationibus et consultationibus. 63. De temporibus et reparationibus appellationum seu consultationum. 64. Quando provocare necesse non est. 65. Quorum appellationes non recipiantur. 66. Si pendente appellatione mors intervenerit. 67. De his qui per metum judicis non appellaverunt. 68. Si unus ex pluribus appellaverit. 69. Si de momentaria possessione fuerit appellatum. 70. Ne liceat in una eademque causa tertio provocare vel post duas sententias judicum, quas definitio præfectorum roboraverit, eas retractare. 71. Qui bonis cedere possunt. 72. De bonis auctoritate judicis possidendis seu venumdandis et de separationibus. 73. De privilegio fisci. 74. De privilegio dotis. 75. De revocandis his quæ per fraudem alienata sunt.

Liber 8.—Tit. 1. De interdictis. 2. Quorum bonorum. 3. Quod legatorum. 4. Unde vi. 5. Si per vim vel alio modo absentis perturbata sit possessio. 6. Uti possidetis. 7. De tabulis exhibendis. 8. De liberis exhibendis seu de ducendis et de homine libero exhibendo. 9. De precario et de Salviano interdicto. 10. De ædificiis privatis. 11. De operibus publicis. 12. De ratiociniis operum publicorum et de patribus civitatum. 13. De pignoribus. 14. In quibus causis pignus tacite contrahitur. 15. Si aliena res pignori data sit. 16. Quæ res pignori obligari possunt vel non et qualiter pignus contrahatur. 17. Qui potiores in pignore habeantur. 18. De his qui in priorum creditorum locum succedunt. 19. Si antiquior creditor pignus vendiderit. 20. Si communis res pignorata sit. 21. De prætorio pignore et ut in actionibus etiam debitorum missio prætorii pignoris procedat. 22. Si in causa judicati pignus captum sit. 23. Si pignus pignori datum sit. 24. De partu pignoris et omni causa. 25. De remissione pignoris. 26. Etiam ob chirographariam pecuniam pignus teneri. 27. De distractione pignorum. 28. Debitorem venditionem pignorum impedire non posse. 29. Si vendito pignore agatur. 30. De luitione pignoris. 31. Si unus ex pluribus heredibus creditoris vel debitoris partem suam debiti solverit vel acceperit. 32. Si pignoris conventionem numeratio secuta non sit. 33. De jure dominii impetrando. 34. De factis pignorum et de commissoria lege in pignoribus rescindenda. 35. De exceptionibus sive præscriptionibus. 36. De litigiosis. 37. De contrahenda et committenda stipulatione. 38. De inutilibus stipulationibus. 39. De duobus reis stipulandi et duobus reis promittendi. 40. De fidejussoribus et mandatoribus. 41. De novationibus et delegationibus. 42. De solutionibus et liberationibus. 43. De acceptilationibus. 44. De evictionibus. 45. Creditorem evictionem non debere. 46. De patria potestate. 47. De adoptionibus. 48. De emancipationibus liberorum. 49. De ingratis liberis. 50. De postliminio et de redemptis ab hostibus. 51. De infantibus expositis liberis et servis et de his qui sanguinolentos emptos vel nutriendos acceperunt. 52. Quæ sit longa consuetudo. 53. De donationibus. 54. De donationibus quæ sub modo vel condicione vel ex certo tempore conficiuntur. 55. De revocandis donationibus. 56. De mortis causa donationibus. 57. De infirmandis pœnis cœlibatus et orbitatis et decimariis sublatis. 58. De jure liberorum.

Liber 9.—Tit. 1. Qui accusare non possunt. 2. De accusationibus et inscriptionibus. 3. De exhibendis vel transmittendis reis. 4. De custodia reorum. 5. De privatis carceribus inhibendis. 6. Si reus vel accusator mortuus fuerit. 7. Si quis imperatori maledixerit. 8. Ad legem Juliam majestatis. 9. Ad legem Juliam de adulteriis et de stupro. 10. Si quis eam cujus tutor fuerit corruperit. 11. De mulieribus quæ servis propriis se junxerunt. 12. Ad legem Juliam de vi publica seu privata. 13. De raptu virginum seu viduarum nec non sanctimonialium. 14. De emendatione servorum.

15. De emendatione propinquorum. 16. Ad legem Corneliam de sicariis. 17. De his qui parentes vel liberos occiderunt. 18. De maleficis et mathematicis et ceteris similibus. 19. De sepulchro violato. 20. Ad legem Fabiam. 21. Ad legem Visselliam. 22. Ad legem Corneliam de falsis. 23. De his qui sibi adscribunt in testamento. 24. De falsa moneta. 25. De mutatione nominis. 26. Ad legem Juliam de ambitu. 27. Ad legem Juliam repetundarum. 28. De crimine peculatus. 29. De crimine sacrilegii. 30. De seditiosis et his qui plebem audent contra publicam quietem colligere. 31. Quando civilis actio criminali præjudicet et an utraque ab eodem exerceri potest. 32. De crimine expilatæ hereditatis. 33. Vi bonorum raptorum. 34. De crimine stellionatus. 35. De injuriis. 36. De famosis libellis. 37. De abigeis. 38. De nili aggeribus non rumpendis. 39. De his qui latrones vel in aliis criminibus reos occultaverint. 40. De requirendis. 41. De quæstionibus. 42. De abolitionibus. 43. De generali abolitione. 44. Ut intra certum tempus criminalis quæstio terminetur. 45. Ad senatusconsultum Turpillianum. 46. De calumniatoribus. 47. De pœnis. 48. Ne sine jussu principis certis judicibus liceat confiscare. 49. De bonis proscriptorum seu damnatorum. 50. De bonis mortem sibi consciscentium. 51. De sententiam passis et restitutis.

Liber 10.—Tit. 1. De jure fisci. 2. De conveniendis fisci debitoribus. 3. De fide et jure hastæ fiscalis et de adjectionibus. 4. De venditione rerum fiscalium cum privatis communium. 5. Ne fiscus rem quam vendidit evincat. 6. De his qui ex publicis rationibus mutuam pecuniam acceperunt. 7. Pœnis fiscalibus creditores præferri. 8. De fiscalibus usuris. 9. De sententiis adversus fiscum latis retractandis. 10. De bonis vacantibus et de incorporatione. 11. De delatoribus. 12. De petitionibus bonorum sublatis. 13. De his qui se deferunt. 14. Si liberalitatis imperialis socius sine herede defecerit. 15. De thesauris. 16. De annona et tributis. 17. De indictionibus. 18. De superindicto. 19. De exactionibus tributorum. 20. De superexactionibus. 21. De capiendis et distrahendis pignoribus tributorum causa. 22. De apochis publicis et descriptionibus curialium. 23. De canone largitionalium titulorum. 24. Ne operæ a collatoribus exigantur. 25. De immunitate nemini concedenda. 26. De conditis in publicis horreis. 27. Ut nemini liceat in coemptione specierum se excusare et de munere sitoniæ. 28. De collatione donatorum vel relevatorum aut translatorum seu adæratorum. 29. De collatione æris. 30. De discussoribus. 31. . . . . 32. De decurionibus et filiis eorum et qui decuriones habentur quibus modis a fortuna curiæ liberentur. 33. Si libertus aut servus ad decurionatum adspiraverit. 34. De prædiis curialium sine decreto non alienandis. 35. Quando et quibus debetur quarta pars ex bonis decurionum et de modo distributionis eorum. 36. De imponenda lucrativus descriptione. 37. De præbendo salario. 38. Si curialis relicta civitate rus habitare maluerit. 39. De municipibus et originariis. 40. De incolis et ubi quis domicilium habere videtur et de his qui studiorum causa in alia civitate degunt. 41. De honoribus et muneribus non continuandis inter patrem et filium et de intervallis. 42. De muneribus patrimoniorum. 43. Quemadmodum civilia munera indicuntur. 44. De his qui sponte munera susceperunt. 45. De his qui a principe vacationem acceperunt. 46. De vacatione muneris. 47. De decretis decurionum super immunitate quibusdam concedenda. 48. De excusationibus munerum. 49. De quibus muneribus et præstationibus nemini liceat se excusare. 50. Qui ætate se excusant. 51. Qui morbo. 52. De his qui numero liberorum vel paupertate excusationem meruerunt. 53. De professoribus et medicis. 54. De athletis. 55. De his qui non impletis stipendiis sacramento soluti sunt. 56. Quibus muneribus excusantur ii, qui post impletam militiam vel advocationem per provincias suis commodis vacantes commorantur, et de privilegiis eorum. 57. De conductoribus vectigalium fisci. 58. De libertinis. 59. De infamibus. 60. De reis postulatis. 61. De his qui in exsilium dati vel ordine moti sunt. 62. De filiis familias et quemadmodum pater pro his teneatur. 63. De periculo successorum parentis. 64. De mulieribus in quo loco munera sexui congruentia et honores agnoscant. 65. De legationibus. 66. De excusationibus artificum. 67. De potioribus ad munera nominandis. 68. Si propter inimicitias creatio facta sit. 69. De sumptuum recuperatione. 70. Si post creationem quis decesserit. 71. De tabulariis scribis logographis et censualibus. 72. De susceptoribus præpositis et arcariis. 73. De ponderatoribus et auri illatione. 74. De auri publici prosecutoribus. 75. De his quæ ex publica collatione illata sunt non usurpandis. 76. De auro coronario. 77. De irenarchis. 78. De argenti pretio quod thesauris infertur.

Liber 11.—Tit. 1. De tollenda lustralis auri collatione. 2. De naviculariis seu naucleris publicas species transportantibus. 3. De prædiis naviculariorum. 4. De navibus non excusandis. 5. Ne quid oneri publico imponatur. 6. De naufragiis. 7. De metallariis et metallis et procuratoribus metallorum. 8. De murilegulis et gynæciariis et procuratoribus gynæcii et de monetariis et bastagariis. 9. De vestibus holoveris et auratis et de intinctione sacri muricis. 10. De fabricensibus. 11. De veteris numismatis potestate. 12. Nulli licere in frenis et equestribus sellis et in balteis margaritas et smaragdos et hyacinthos aptare, et de artificibus palatinis. 13. De classicis. 14. De decuriis urbis Romæ. 15. De privilegiis corporatorum urbis Romæ. 16. De pistoribus. 17. De suariis et susceptoribus vini et ceteris corporatis. 18. De collegiatis et chartopratis et nummulariis. 19. De studiis liberalibus urbis Romæ et Constantinopolitanæ. 20. De honoratorum vehiculis. 21. De privilegiis urbis Constantinopolitanæ. 22. De metropoli Beryto. 23. De canone frumentario urbis Romæ. 24. De frumento urbis Constantinopolitanæ. 25. De annonis civilibus. 26. De mendicantibus validis. 27. De nautis Tiberinis. 28. De frumento Alexandrino. 29. De Alexandriæ primatibus. 30. De jure rei publicæ. 31. De administratione rerum publicarum. 32. De vendendis rebus civitatis. 33. De debitoribus civitatum. 34. De periculo nominatorum. 35. De periculo eorum qui pro magistratibus intervenerunt. 36. Quo quisque ordine conveniatur. 37. Ne quis liber invitus actum rei publicæ gerere cogatur. 38. Injuncti muneris sumptus ad omnes collegas pertinere. 39. De his qui ex officio quod administraverunt conveniuntur. 40. De solutionibus et liberationibus debitorum civitatis. 41. De spectaculis et scænicis et lenonibus. 42. De expensis publicorum ludorum. 43. De aquæductu. 44. De gladiatoribus penitus tollendis. 45. De venatione ferarum. 46. De maiuma. 47. Ut armorum usus inscio principe interdictus sit. 48. De agricolis censitis vel colonis. 49. De capitatione civium censibus eximenda. 50. In quibus causis coloni censiti dominos accusare possunt. 51. De colonis Palæstinis. 52. De colonis Thracensibus. 53. De colonis Illyricianis. 54. Ut nemo ad suum patrocinium suscipiat vicos vel rusticanos eorum. 55. Ut rusticani ad nullum obsequium devocentur. 56. Non licere metrocomiæ hābitatoribus loca sua ad extraneum transferre. 57. Ut nullus ex vicanis pro alienis debitis vicanorum teneatur. 58. De censibus et censitoribus et peræquatoribus et inspectoribus. 59. De omni agro deserto et quando steriles fertilibus imponuntur. 60. De fundis limitrophis et terris et paludibus et pascuis limitaneis vel castellorum. 61. De pascuis publicis et privatis. 62. De fundis patrimonialibus et saltuensibus et emphyteuticis et eorum conductoribus. 63. De mancipiis et colonis patrimonialium et salsuensium et emphyteuticariorum fundorum. 64. De fugitivis colonis patrimonialibus et emphyteuticis et saltuensibus. 65. De collatione fundorum patrimonialium et emphyteuticorum. 66. De fundis rei privatæ et saltibus divinæ domus. 67. De fundis et saltibus rei dominicæ. 68. De agricolis et mancipiis dominicis vel fiscalibus sive rei privatæ. 69. De prædiis Tamiacis et de his qui ex colonis dominicis aliisque liberæ condicionis procreantur. 70. De diversis prædiis urbanis et rusticis templorum et civitatum et omni reditu civili. 71. De locatione prædiorum civilium vel fiscalium sive templorum sive rei privatæ vel dominicæ. 72. De conductoribus et procuratoribus sive actoribus prædiorum fiscalium et domus Augustæ. 73. Quibus ad conductionem prædiorum fiscalium accedere non licet. 74. De collatione fundorum fiscalium vel rei privatæ vel dominicæ vel civitatum vel templorum. 75. De privilegiis domus Augustæ vel rei privatæ et quarum collationum excusationem habent. 76. De grege dominico. 77. De palatiis et domibus dominicis. 78. De cupressis ex luco Daphnensi vel Perseis per Ægyptum non excidendis vel vendendis.

Liber 12.—Tit. 1. De dignitatibus. 2. De prætoribus et honore præturæ et gleba et folli et septem solidorum functione sublata. 3. De consulibus et non spargendis ab his pecuniis et de præfectis et magistris militum et patriciis. 4. De præfectis prætorio sive urbis et magistris militum in dignitatibus exæquandis. 5. De præpositis sacri cubiculi et de omnibus cubiculariis et privilegiis eorum. 6. De quæstoribus magistris officiorum comitibus sacrarum largitionum et rei privatæ. 7. De primicerio et secundocerio et notariis. 8. Ut dignitatum ordo servetur. 9. De magistris scriniorum. 10. De comitibus consistorianis. 11. De comitibus et tribunis scholarum. 12. De comitibus rei militaris. 13. De comitibus et archiatris sacri palatii. 14. De comitibus qui provincias regunt. 15. De professoribus qui in urbe Constantinopolitana docentes ex lege meruerint comitivam. 16. De decurionibus et silentiariis. 17. De domesticis et protectoribus. 18. De præpositis labaru. 19. De proximis sacrorum scriniorum ceterisque qui in sacris scriniis militant. 20. De agentibus in rebus. 21. De principibus agentum in rebus. 22. De curiosis. 23. De palatinis sacrarum largitionum et rerum privatarum. 24. De stratoribus. 25. De castrensianis et ministerianis. 26. De canis. 27. De mensoribus. 28. De privilegiis eorum qui in sacro palatio militant. 29. De privilegiis scholarum. 30. De castrensi omnium palatinorum peculio. 31. De equestri dignitate. 32. De perfectissimatus dignitate. 33. Qui militare possunt vel non et de servis ad militiam vel dignitatem adspirantibus, et ut nemo duplici militia vel dignitate et militia simul utatur. 34. Negotiatores ne militent. 35. De re militari. 36. De castrensi peculio militum et præfectianorum. 37. De erogatione militaris annonæ. 38. De excoctione et translatione militarium annonarum. 39. De militari veste. 40. De metatis et epidemeticis. 41. De salgamo hospitibus non præbendo. 42. De commeatu. 43. De tironibus. 44. De litorum et itinerum custodia. 45. De desertoribus et occultatoribus eorum. 46. De veteranis. 47. De filiis officialium militarium qui in bello moriuntur. 48 De oblatione votorum. 49. De numerariis actuariis et chartulariis et adjutoribus scriniariis et exceptoribus sedis excelsæ ceterorumque judicum tam civilium quam militarium. 50. De cursu publico angariis et parangariis. 51. De tractoriis et stativis. 52. De apparitoribus præfectorum prætorio et privilegiis eorum. 53. De apparitoribus præfecti urbis. 54. De apparitoribus magistrorum militum et privilegiis eorum. 55. De apparitoribus proconsulis et legati. 56. De apparitoribus comitis orientis. 57. De cohortalibus principibus cornicularii et primipilaribus. 58. De apparitoribus præfecti annonæ. 59. De diversis officiis et apparitoribus judicum et probatoriis eorum. 60. De exsecutoribus et exactoribus. 61. De lucris advocatorum et concussionibus officiorum sive apparitorum. 62. De primipilo. 63. Publicæ lætitiæ vel consulum nuntiatores vel insinuatores constitutionum et aliarum sacrarum vel judicialium litterarum ex descriptione vel ab invitis ne quid accipiant immodicum.

"To Tribonian.

"After the code of the imperial constitutions which we have published in our name, we have resolved to make a complete revision of the whole civil law, and of all Roman jurisprudence, by collecting together in a single code the dispersed volumes of so many jurists."

"§ 3. We have entrusted you with the office of choosing for this work the most skilful professors, the greatest advocates; and accepting those you have presented to us, we order them to perform that work, but under your direction.

"§ 4. Choose and correct all that has been written by the jurists whom the emperors authorized to interpret the laws (*conscribendarum interpretandarumque legum*). But, as others have also written books of law, which have neither been recognised as texts nor in practice, we do not desire to have them incorporated in your collection.

"§ 5. From this collection we have determined to draw up a work of the utmost perfection to be sacred as a temple of justice, to be in fifty books, divided by titles according to the order observed in our code, or in imitation of the *edictum perpetuum*, as you may think best. In these fifty books let all the ancient laws, thrown into confusion during the course of nearly fourteen hundred years, be expurgated, and surrounded, as it were, by a rampart, beyond which there shall be nothing more: equal authority being given to all jurists, and no preference observed for one above another." (This is supposed to be an allusion to the preponderance which the *lex de responsis prudentum* gave Papinian in case of difference.)

"§ 6. Do not set down one opinion as the best because a majority has adopted it; one alone, and the least, might by chance, on a certain point, surpass all the others. Do not absolutely reject the notes of Ulpian, of Paul, and of Marcian, on Papinian, which were formerly denuded of all authority on account of the honour paid to the most illustrious Papinian" (this is an allusion to the constitution of Constantine, and to the *lex de responsis*, which had proscribed these notes); "but do not hesitate to take and lay down as law whatever you shall think fit. The decisions of all the authors you quote will have authority just as if they emanated from the imperial constitutions, and were given forth by our divine breath (*et nostro divino fuerant ore profusa*).

"§ 7. Eliminate everything which may appear to you out of place, superfluous, or bad; the corrections you make, even contrary to the ancient laws, will have legal force; and let no one dare, by making comparisons of ancient manuscripts, to impute any imperfection to anything which you shall have written." (This is an allusion to the same enactment, which required a collation of quoted passages with the old manuscripts.) "The sanction which we give it is not divided between these or those fragments of the founders of the laws, but comes entirely from us, entirely from the choice we make. How should antiquity abrogate any of our laws?

"§§ 8, 9, and 10. Do not leave any *antinomy*" (the name in Greek for a contradiction between two laws) "or any repetitions; avoid as much as possible inserting anew the imperial constitutions contained in our code; put aside all things that have fallen into disuse.

"§ 11. Everything will be ruled by these two codes—the code of the constitutions, and that, to be drawn up, of the revised laws; and if we promulgate a third, in the shape of Institutes, by that code also, in order that learners, after being grounded in principles, may proceed to higher and more abstruse studies.

"§ 12. This work will bear the name of '*Digest*' or '*Pandects.*' We forbid jurists to add commentaries, and to obscure it with their prolix observations, as was done in the case of the ancient laws. It will only be allowed to add under each article a summary indicating its contents, which is called *παράτιτλα*, without interpretation.

"§ 13. We forbid, in writing this code, the use of signs or abbreviations, confusing enigmas, sources of numerous *antinomies*. The succession of letters must be used everywhere, even to indicate the numbers of the articles, or what not." (This injunction was addressed to the copyists, who were much given to the use of signs or abbreviations; it is repeated in other constitutions, with penalties attached.)

"Given the 18th of the Kal. of January, A.D. 531" (15th December, A.D. 530).

THE TITLES AND SUB-TITLES OF THE DIGEST OR PANDECTS.

Liber 1.—Tit. 1. De justitia et jure. 2. De origine juris et omnium magistratuum et successione prudentum. 3. De legibus senatusque consultis et longa consuetudine. 4. De constitutionibus principum. 5. De statu hominum. 6. De his, qui sui vel alieni juris sunt. 7. De adoptionibus et emancipationibus et aliis modis, quibus potestas solvitur. 8. De divisione rerum et qualitate. 9. De senatoribus. 10. De officio consulis. 11. De officio præfecti prætorio. 12. De officio præfecti urbi. 13. De officio quæstoris. 14. De officio prætorum. 15. De officio præfecti vigilum. 16. De officio proconsulis et legati. 17. De officio præfecti Augustalis. 18. De officio præsidis. 19. De officio procuratoris Cæsaris vel rationalis. 20. De officio juridici. 21. De officio ejus, cui mandata est jurisdictio. 22. De officio assessorum.

Liber 2.—Tit. 1. De jurisdictione. 2. Quod quisque juris in alterum statuerit, ut ipse eodem jure utatur. 3. Si quis jus dicenti non obtemperaverit. 4. De in jus vocando. 5. Si quis in jus vocatus non ierit, sive quis eum vocaverit, quem ex edicto non debuerit. 6. In jus vocati ut eant, aut satis vel cautum dent. 7. Ne quis eum, qui in jus vocabitur, vi eximat. 8. Qui satisdare cogantur, vel jurato promittant, vel suæ promissioni committantur. 9. Si ex noxali causa agatur, quemadmodum cavetur. 10. De eo, per quem factum erit, quo minus quis in judicio sistat. 11. Si quis cautionibus in judicio sistendi causa factis non obtemperaverit. 12. De feriis et dilationibus et diversis temporibus. 13. De edendo. 14. De pactis. 15. De transactionibus.

Liber 3.—Tit. 1. De postulando. 2. De his, qui notantur infamia. 3. De procuratoribus et defensoribus. 4. Quod cujuscumque universitatis nomine, vel contra eam agatur. 5. De negotiis gestis. 6. De calumniatoribus.

Liber 4.—Tit. 1. De in integrum restitutionibus. 2. Quod metus causa gestum erit. 3. De dolo malo. 4. De minoribus viginti quinque annis. 5. De capite minutis. 6. Ex quibus causis majores viginti quinque annis in integrum restituuntur. 7. De alienatione judicii mutandi causa facta. 8. De receptis, qui arbitrium receperint, ut sententiam dicant. 9. Nautæ, caupones, stabularii ut recepta restituant.

Liber 5.—Tit. 1. De judiciis et ubi quisque agere vel conveniri debeat. 2. De inofficioso testamento. 3. De hereditatis petitione. 4. Si pars hereditatis petatur. 5. De possessoria hereditatis petitione. 6. De fideicommissaria hereditatis petitione.

Liber 6.—Tit. 1. De rei vindicatione. 2. De publiciana in rem actione. 3. Si ager vectigalis, id est emphyteuticarius, petatur.

Liber 7.—Tit. 1. De usu fructu et quemadmodum quis utatur fruatur. 2. De usu fructu adcrescendo. 3. Quando dies usus fructus legati cedat. 4. Quibus modis ususfructus vel usus amittitur. 5. De usu fructu earum rerum, quæ usu consumuntur vel minuuntur. 6. Si ususfructus petatur, vel ad alium pertinere negetur. 7. De operis servorum. 8. De usu et habitatione. 9. Usufructuarius quemadmodum caveat.

Liber 8.—Tit. 1. De servitutibus. 2. De servitutibus prædiorum urbanorum. 3. De servitutibus prædiorum rusticorum. 4. Communia prædiorum tam urbanorum quam rusticorum. 5. Si servitus vindicetur, vel ad alium pertinere negetur. 6. Quemadmodum servitutes amittuntur.

Liber 9.—Tit. 1. Si quadrupes pauperiem fecisse dicatur. 2. Ad legem Aquiliam. 3. De his, qui effuderint vel dejecerint. 4. De noxalibus actionibus.

Liber 10.—Tit. 1. Finium regundorum. 2. Familiæ erciscundæ. 3. Communi dividundo. 4. Ad exhibendum.

Liber 11.—Tit. 1. De interrogationibus in jure faciendis et interrogatoriis actionibus. 2. De quibus rebus ad eundem judicem eatur. 3. De servo corrupto. 4. De fugitivis. 5. De aleatoribus. 6. Si mensor falsum modum dixerit. 7. De religiosis et sumptibus funerum, et ut funus ducere liceat. 8. De mortuo inferendo et sepulcro ædificando.

Liber 12.—Tit. 1. De rebus creditis, si certum petetur et de condictione. 2. De jurejurando sive voluntario, sive necessario, sive judiciali. 3. De in litem jurando. 4. De condictione causa data causa non secuta. 5. De condictione ob turpem vel injustam causam. 6. De condictione indebiti. 7. De condictione sine causa.

Liber 13.—Tit. 1. De condictione furtiva. 2. De condictione ex lege. 3. De condictione triticiaria. 4. De eo, quod certo loco dari oportet. 5. De pecunia constituta. 6. Commodati, vel contra. 7. De pigneraticia actione, vel contra.

Liber 14.—Tit. 1. De exercitoria actione. 2. De lege Rhodia de jactu. 3. De institoria actione. 4. De tributoria actione. 5. Quod cum eo, qui in aliena potestate est, negotium gestum esse dicetur. 6. De senatusconsulto Macedoniano.

Liber 15.—Tit. 1. De peculio. 2. Quando de peculio actio annalis est. 3. De in rem verso. 4. Quod jussu.

Liber 16.—Tit. 1. Ad senatusconsultum Velleianum. 2. De compensationibus. 3. Depositi vel contra.

Liber 17.—Tit. 1. Mandati vel contra. 2. Pro socio.

Liber 18.—Tit. 1. De contrahenda emtione, et de pactis inter emtorem et venditorem compositis, et quæ res venire non possunt. 2. De in diem addictione. 3. De lege commissoria. 4. De hereditate vel actione vendita. 5. De rescindenda venditione, et quando licet ab emtione discedere. 6. De periculo et commodo rei venditæ. 7. De servis exportandis, vel si ita mancipium venierit, ut manumittatur, vel contra.

Liber 19.—Tit. 1. De actionibus emti et venditi. 2. Locati, conducti. 3. De æstimatoria. 4. De rerum permutatione. 5. De præscriptis verbis et in factum actionibus.

Liber 20.—Tit. 1. De pignoribus et hypothecis, et qualiter ea contrahantur, et de pactis eorum. 2. In quibus causis pignus, vel hypotheca tacite contrahitur. 3. Quæ res pignori vel hypothecæ datæ obligari non possunt. 4. Qui potiores in pignore, vel hypotheca habeantur, et de his, qui in priorum creditorum locum succedunt. 5. De distractione pignorum et hypothecarum. 6. Quibus modis pignus vel hypotheca solvitur.

Liber 21.—Tit. 1. De ædilicio edicto et redhibitione, et quanti minoris. 2. De evictionibus et duplæ stipulatione. 3. De exceptione rei venditæ et traditæ.

Liber 22.—Tit. 1. De usuris, et fructibus, et causis, et omnibus accessionibus, et mora. 2. De nautico fœnore. 3. De probationibus et præsumptionibus. 4. De fide instrumentorum et amissione eorum. 5. De testibus. 6. De juris et facti ignorantia.

Liber 23.—Tit. 1. De sponsalibus. 2. De ritu nuptiarum. 3. De jure dotium. 4. De pactis dotalibus. 5. De fundo dotali.

Liber 24.—Tit. 1. De donationibus inter virum et uxorem. 2. De divortiis et repudiis. 3. Soluto matrimonio dos quemadmodum petatur.

Liber 25.—Tit. 1. De impensis in res dotales factis. 2. De actione rerum amotarum. 3. De agnoscendis et alendis liberis, vel parentibus, vel patronis, vel libertis. 4. De inspiciendo ventre custodiendoque partu. 5. Si ventris nomine muliere in possessionem missa eadem possessio dolo malo ad alium translata esse dicatur. 6. Si mulier ventris nomine in possessione calumniæ causa esse dicetur. 7. De concubinis.

Liber 26.—Tit. 1. De tutelis. 2. De testamentaria tutela. 3. De confirmando tutore vel curatore. 4. De legitimis tutoribus. 5. De tutoribus et curatoribus datis ab his, qui jus dandi habent, et qui, et in quibus causis, specialiter dari possunt. 6. Qui petant tutores vel curatores, et ubi petantur. 7. De administratione et periculo tutorum et curatorum, qui gesserint, vel non, et de agentibus, vel conveniendis uno vel pluribus. 8. De auctoritate et consensu tutorum et curatorum. 9. Quando ex facto tutoris vel curatoris minores agere vel conveniri possunt. 10. De suspectis tutoribus et curatoribus.

Liber 27.—Tit. 1. De excusationibus. 2. Ubi pupillus educari vel morari debeat, et de alimentis et præstandis. 3. De tutelæ et rationibus distrahendis, et utili curationis causa actione. 4. De contraria tutelæ et utili actione. 5. De eo, qui pro tutore prove curatore negotia gessit. 6. Quod falso tutore auctore gestum esse dicatur. 7. De fidejussoribus, et nominatoribus, et heredibus tutorum et curatorum. 8. De magistratibus conveniendis. 9. De rebus eorum, qui sub tutela vel cura sunt, sine decreto non alienandis vel supponendis. 10. De curatoribus furioso et aliis extra minores dandis.

Liber 28.—Tit. 1. Qui testamenta facere possunt, et quemadmodum testamenta fiant. 2. De liberis et postumis heredibus instituendis vel exheredandis. 3. De injusto, rupto, irrito facto testamento. 4. De his, quæ in testamento delentur, inducuntur, vel inscribuntur. 5. De heredibus instituendis. 6. De vulgari et pupillari substitutione. 7. De conditionibus institutionum. 8. De jure deliberandi.

Liber 29.—Tit. 1. De testamento militis. 2. De acquirenda vel amittenda hereditate. 3. Testamenta quemadmodum aperiantur, inspiciantur et describantur. 4. Si quis omissa causa testamenti ab intestato, vel alio modo possideat hereditatem. 5. De senatusconsulto Silaniano et Claudiano, quorum testamenta ne aperiantur. 6. Si quis aliquem testari prohibuerit vel coegerit. 7. De jure codicillorum.

Liber 30.—De legatis et fideicommissis.

Liber 31.—De legatis et fideicommissis.

Liber 32.—De legatis et fideicommissis.

Liber 33.—Tit. 1. De annuis legatis, et fideicommissis. 2. De usu, et usufructu, et reditu, et habitatione, et operis per legatum vel fideicommissum datis. 3. De servitute legata. 4. De dote prælegata. 5. De optione vel electione legata. 6. De tritico, vino, vel oleo legato. 7. De instructo vel instrumento legato. 8. De peculio legato. 9. De penu legata. 10. De supellectile legata.

Liber 34.—Tit. 1. De alimentis vel cibariis legatis. 2. De auro, argento, mundo, ornamentis, unguentis, veste vel vestimentis, et statuis legatis. 3. De libertatione legata. 4. De adimendis vel transferendis legatis vel fideicommissis. 5. De rebus dubiis. 6. De his quæ pœnæ causa relinquuntur. 7. De regula Catoniana. 8. De his quæ pro non scriptis habentur. 9. De his, quæ ut indignis auferuntur.

Liber 35.—Tit. 1. De conditionibus, et demonstrationibus, et causis, et modis eorum, quæ in testamento scribuntur. 2. Ad legem Falcidiam.

Liber 36.—Tit. 1.—Ad senatusconsultum Trebellianum. 2. Quando dies legatorum vel fideicommissorum cedat. 3. Ut legatorum seu fideicommissorum servandorum causa caveatur. 4. Ut in possessione legatorum vel fideicommissorum servandorum causa esse liceat.

Liber 37.—Tit. 1. De bonorum possessionibus. 2. Si tabulæ testamenti extabunt. 3. De bonorum possessione furioso, infanti, muto, surdo, cæco competente. 4. De bonorum possessione contra tabulas. 5. De legatis præstandis contra tabulas bonorum possessione petita. 6. De collatione. 7. De dotis collatione. 8. De conjungendis cum emancipato liberis ejus. 9. De ventre in possessionem mittendo et curatore ejus. 10. De Carboniano edicto. 11. De bonorum possessionibus secundum tabulas. 12. Si a parente quis manumissus sit. 13. De bonorum possessione ex testamento militis. 14. De jure patronatus. 15. De obsequiis parentibus et patronis præstandis.

Liber 38.—Tit. 1. De operis libertorum. 2. De bonis libertorum. 3. De libertis universitatum. 4. De assignandis libertis. 5. Si quid in fraudem patroni factum sit. 6. Si tabulæ testamenti nullæ extabunt, unde liberi. 7. Unde legitimi. 8. Unde cognati. 9. De successorio edicto. 10. De gradibus, et affinibus, et nominibus eorum. 11. Unde vir et uxor. 12. De veteranorum et militum successione. 13. Quibus non competit bonorum possessio. 14. Ut ex legibus senatusve consultis bonorum possessio detur. 15. Quis ordo in possessionibus servetur. 16. De suis et legitimis heredibus. 17. Ad senatusconsultum Tertullianum et Orphitianum.

Liber 39.—Tit. 1. De operis novi nuntiatione. 2. De damno infecto et de sugrundis et protectionibus. 3. De aqua, et aquæ pluviæ arcendæ. 4. De publicanis et vectigalibus et commissis. 5. De donationibus. 6. De mortis causa donationibus, et capionibus.

Liber 40.—Tit. 1. De manumissionibus. 2. De manumissis vindicta. 3. De manumissionibus, quæ servis ad universitatem pertinentibus imponuntur. 4. De manumissis testamento. 5. De fideicommissariis libertatibus. 6. De ademptione libertatis. 7. De statuliberis. 8. Qui sine manumissione ad libertatem perveniunt. 9. Qui et a quibus manumissi liberi non fiunt, et ad legem Æliam Sentiam. 10. De jure aureorum annulorum. 11. De natalibus restituendis. 12. De liberali causa. 13. Quibus ad libertatem proclamare non licet. 14. Si ingenuus esse dicetur. 15. Ne de statu defunctorum post quinquennium quæratur. 16. De collusione detegenda.

Liber 41.—Tit. 1. De acquirendo rerum dominio. 2. De acquirenda, vel amittenda possessione. 3. De usurpationibus et usucapionibus. 4. Pro emtore. 5. Pro herede, vel pro possessore. 6. Pro donato. 7. Pro derelicto. 8. Pro legato. 9. Pro dote. 10. Pro suo.

Liber 42.—Tit. 1. De re judicata, et de effectu sententiarum, et de interlocutionibus. 2. De confessis. 3. De cessione bonorum. 4. Quibus ex causis in possessionem eatur. 5. De rebus auctoritate judicis possidendis seu vendundis. 6. De separationibus. 7. De curatore bonis dando. 8. Quæ in fraudem creditorum facta sunt ut restituantur.

Liber 43.—Tit. 1. De interdictis sive extraordinariis actionibus, quæ pro his competunt. 2. Quorum bonorum. 3. Quod legatorum. 4. Ne vis fiat ei, qui in possessionem missus erit. 5. De tabulis exhibendis. 6. Ne quid in loco sacro fiat. 7. De locis et itineribus publicis. 8. Ne quid in loco publico vel itinere fiat. 9. De loco publico fruendo. 10. De via publica, et si quid in ea factum esse dicatur. 11. De via publica, et itinere publico reficiendo. 12. De fluminibus, ne quid in flumine publico ripave ejus fiat, quo pejus navigetur. 13. Ne quid in flumine publico fiat, quo aliter aqua fluat, atque uti priore æstate fluxit. 14. Ut in flumine publico navigare liceat. 15. De ripa munienda. 16. De vi, et de vi armata. 17. Uti possidetis. 18. De superficiebus. 19. De itinere actuque privato. 20. De aqua quotidiana et æstiva. 21. De rivis. 22. De fonte. 23. De cloacis. 24. Quod vi aut clam. 25. De remissionibus. 26. De precario. 27. De arboribus cædendis. 28. De glande legenda. 29. De homine libero exhibendo. 30. De liberis exhibendis, item ducendis. 31. De utrubi. 32. De migrando. 33. De Salviano interdicto.

Liber 44.—Tit. 1. De exceptionibus, præscriptionibus et præjudiciis. 2. De exceptione rei judicatæ. 3. De diversis temporalibus præscriptionibus, et de accessionibus possessionum. 4. De doli mali et metus exceptione. 5. Quarum rerum actio non datur. 6. De litigiosis. 7. De obligationibus et actionibus.

Liber 45.—Tit. 1. De verborum obligationibus. 2. De duobus reis constituendis. 3. De stipulatione servorum.

Liber 46.—Tit. 1. De fidejussoribus et mandatoribus. 2. De novationibus et delegationibus. 3. De solutionibus et liberationibus. 4. De acceptilatione. 5. De stipulationibus prætoriis. 6. Rem pupilli vel adolescentis salvam fore. 7. Judicatum solvi. 8. Ratam rem haberi et de ratihabitione.

Liber 47.—Tit. 1. De privatis delictis. 2. De furtis. 3. De tigno juncto. 4. Si is, qui testamento liber esse jussus erit, post mortem domini ante aditam hereditatem surripuisse, aut corrupisse quid dicetur. 5. Furti adversus nautas, caupones, stabularios. 6. Si familia furtum fecisse dicetur. 7. Arborum furtim cæsarum. 8. Vi bonorum raptorum, et de turba. 9. De incendio, ruina, naufragio, rate nave expugnata. 10. De injuriis et famosis libellis. 11. De extraordinariis criminibus. 12. De sepulcro violato. 13. De concussione. 14. De abigeis. 15. De prævaricatione. 16. De receptatoribus. 17. De furibus balneariis. 18. De effractoribus et expilatoribus. 19. Expilatæ hereditatis. 20. Stellionatus. 21. De termino moto. 22. De collegiis et corporibus. 23. De popularibus actionibus.

Liber 48.—Tit. 1. De publicis judiciis. 2. De accusationibus et inscriptionibus. 3. De custodia et exhibitione reorum. 4. Ad legem Juliam majestatis. 5. Ad legem Juliam de adulteriis coercendis. 6. Ad legem Juliam de vi publica. 7. Ad legem Juliam de vi privata. 8. Ad legem Corneliam de sicariis et veneficis. 9. De lege Pompeia de parricidiis. 10. De lege Cornelia de falcis, et de senatusconsulto Liboniano. 11. De lege Julia repetundarum. 12. De lege Julia de annona. 13. Ad legem Juliam peculatus, et de sacrilegis, et de residuis. 14. De lege Julia ambitus. 15. De lege Favia de plagiariis. 16. Ad senatusconsultum Turpillianum, et de abolitionibus criminum. 17. De requirendis vel absentibus damnandis. 18. De quæstionibus. 19. De pœnis. 20. De bonis damnatorum. 21. De bonis eorum, qui ante sententiam vel mortem sibi conscierunt, vel accusatorem corruperunt. 22. De interdictis, et relegatis, et deportatis. 23. De sententiam passis, et restitutis. 24. De cadaveribus punitorum.

Liber 49.—Tit. 1. De appellationibus et relationibus. 2. A quibus appellari non licet. 3. Quis a quo appelletur. 4. Quando appellandum sit, et intra quæ tempora. 5. De appellationibus recipiendis vel non. 6. De libellis dimissoriis, qui apostoli dicuntur. 7. Nihil innovari appellatione interposita. 8. Quæ sententiæ sine appellatione rescindantur. 9. An per alium causæ appellationum reddi possunt. 10. Si tutor, vel curator, magistratus creatus appellaverit. 11. Eum, qui appellaverit, in provincia defendi. 12. Apud eum, a quo appellatur, aliam causam agere compellendum. 13. Si pendente appellatione mors intervenerit. 14. De jure fisci. 15. De captivis, et de postliminio, et redemtis ab hostibus. 16. De re militari. 17. De castrensi peculio. 18. De veteranis.

Liber 50.—Tit. 1. Ad municipalem et de incolis. 2. De decurionibus et filiis eorum. 3. De albo scribendo. 4. De muneribus et honoribus. 5. De vacatione et excusatione munerum. 6. De jure immunitatis. 7. De legationibus. 8. De administratione rerum ad civitates pertinentium. 9. De decretis ab ordine faciendis. 10. De operibus publicis. 11. De nundinis. 12. De pollicitationibus. 13. De extraordinariis cognitionibus, et si judex litem suam fecisse dicetur. 14. De proxeneticis. 15. De censibus. 16. De verborum significatione. 17. De diversis regulis juris antiqui.

THE INTRODUCTION TO THE INSTITUTES.

In Nomine Domini Nostri Jesu Christi.

Imperator, Cæsar Flavius Justinianus, Almanicus, Gothicus, Francicus, Germanicus, Anticus, Alanicus, Vandalicus, Africanus, Pius, Felix, Melytus Victor ac Triumphator, semper Augustus, cupidæ legum juventuti. S.

The Imperial dignity should not be merely decorated by arms, but should be guarded by laws, that the people, in time of peace as well as war, may be secured from dangers and rightly governed: for a Roman emperor ought not only to be victorious over his enemies in the field, but should also take every legal means to clear the state from all those members whose crafts and iniquities are subversive of the law. Be it the care, therefore, of him upon whom government devolves, to be renowned for a most religious observance of law and justice, as well as for his triumphs.

1. By our incessant labours, and the assistance of Divine Providence, we have acquired the double fame of a lawgiver and a conqueror, for the barbarian nations have proved us in battle, and submitted to our yoke: even Africa and many other provinces, after so long an interval, are again added to the

Roman empire; and yet this vast people, and our whole dominions, are governed either by laws enacted by ourselves, or laws which, though framed by others, have by our sovereign authority been better regulated.

2. When we had ranged the Imperial Constitutions in a regular order, and made those, which were before confused and contradictory, to agree perfectly and with each other, we then extended our care to the numerous volumes of the ancient law, and have now completed, through the favour of heaven, a work which exceeded even our hope, and was attended with the greatest difficulties.

3. As soon as this our undertaking was accomplished, we summoned Tribonian, our chancellor, with Theophilus and Dorotheus, men of known learning and tried fidelity, whom we enjoined by our authority to compose the following Institutions, to the intent that the rudiments of law might be more effectually learned by the sole means of our imperial authority, and that your minds for the future should not be burdened with obsolete and unprofitable doctrines, but instructed only in those laws, which are allowed of and practised: and whereas it was formerly necessary that all students should go through a course of study, at least for the space of four years, preparatory to their reading the Constitutions, they may now (having been thought worthy of our princely care, to which they are indebted for the beginning and end of their studies) apply themselves immediately to the Imperial ordinances.

4. When, therefore, by the assistance of Tribonian and other illustrious persons, we had digested the whole ancient law into fifty books, called Digests or Pandects, it was our pleasure, that the Institutions should be divided into four books, which might serve as the first elements introductory to the science of the law.

5. In these Institutes we have briefly set forth the old laws, which formerly obtained, and those also which for a time have lain dormant, but are now revived by our princely care.

6. The four books of our Institutes were compiled by Tribonian, Theophilus, and Dorotheus, from all the Institutes of the ancient law, but chiefly from the commentaries, institutes,

and other writings of Caius (Gaius). As soon as these our Institutes were finished and presented to us, we read and diligently examined their contents; and, in testimony of our approbation, we have now given them a constitutional authority.

7. Receive therefore our laws, and so profit by them that when the course of your studies is completely finished, you may with reason expect to bear a part in the government, and be able to discharge the duties allotted to you.

Given at Constantinople on the eleventh day before the Kalends of December (*i.e.*, the 21st November), A. D. 533, in the third consulate of the Emperor Justinian, always August.

The following are the titles of the Institutes:—

THE TITLES AND SUB-TITLES OF THE INSTITUTES.

Liber 1.—Tit. 1. De justitia et jure. 2. De jure naturali, gentium et civili. 3. De jure personarum. 4. De ingenuis. 5. De libertinis. 6. Qui et quibus ex causis manumittere non possunt. 7. De lege Furia Caninia sublata. 8. De iis qui sui, vel alieni juris sunt. 9. De patria potestate. 10. De nuptiis. 11. De adoptionibus. 12. Quibus modis jus potestatis solvitur. 13. De tutelis. 14. Qui testamento tutores dari possunt. 15. De legitima agnatorum tutela. 16. De capitis deminutione. 17. De legitima patronorum tutela. 18. De legitima parentum tutela. 19. De fiduciaria tutela. 20. De Atiliano tutore et eo, qui ex lege Julia et Titia dabatur. 21. De auctoritate tutorum. 22. Quibus modis tutela finitur. 23. De curatoribus. 24. De satisdatione tutorum et curatorum. 25. De excusationibus tutorum et curatorum. 26. De suspectis tutoribus et curatoribus.

Liber 2.—Tit. 1. De rerum divisione. 2. De rebus incorporalibus. 3. De servitutibus. 4. De usufructu. 5. De usu et habitatione. 6. De usucapionibus et longi temporis possessionibus. 7. De donationibus. 8. Quibus alienare licet vel non. 9. Per quas personas nobis acquiritur. 10. De testamentis ordinandis. 11. De militari testamento. 12. Quibus non est permissum facere testamentum. 13. De exheredatione liberorum. 14. De heredibus instituendis. 15. De vulgari substitutione. 16. De pupillari substitutione. 17. Quibus modis testamenta infirmantur. 18. De inofficioso testamento. 19. De heredum qualitate et differentia. 20. De legatis. 21. De ademtione et translatione legatorum. 22. De lege Falcidia. 23. De fideicommissariis hereditatibus. 24. De singulis rebus per fideicommissum relictis. 25. De codicillis.

Liber 3.—Tit. 1. De hereditatibus, quæ ab intestato deferuntur. 2. De legitima agnatorum successione. 3. De senatusconsulto Tertulliano. 4. De senatusconsulto Orphitiano. 5. De successione cognatorum. 6. De gradibus cognationis. 7. De successione libertorum. 8. De assignatione libertorum. 9. De bonorum possessionibus. 10. De acquisitione per arrogationem. 11. De eo cui libertatis causa bona addicuntur. 12. De successionibus sublatis, quæ fiebant per bonorum venditionem et ex senatusconsulto Claudiano. 13. De obligationibus. 14. Quibus modis re contrahitur obligatio. 15. De verborum obligatione. 16. De duobus reis stipulandi et promittendi. 17. De stipulatione servorum. 18. De divisione stipulationum. 19. De inutilibus stipulationibus. 20. De fidejussoribus. 21. De literarum obligatione. 22. De consensu obligatione. 23. De emtione et venditione. 24. De locatione et conductione. 25. De societate. 26. De mandato. 27. De obligationibus quasi ex contractu. 28. Per quas personas nobis obligatio acquiritur. 29. Quibus modis obligatio tollitur.

Liber 4.—Tit. 1. De obligationibus, quæ ex delicto nascuntur. 2. De vi bonorum raptorum. 3. De lege Aquilia. 4. De injuriis. 5. De obligationibus, quæ quasi ex delicto nascuntur. 6. De actionibus. 7. Quod cum eo, qui in aliena potestate est, negotium gestum esse dicatur. 8. De noxalibus actionibus. 9. Si quadrupes pauperiem fecisse dicatur. 10. De iis, per quos agere possumus. 11. De satisdationibus. 12. De perpetuis et temporalibus actionibus, et quæ ad heredes et in heredes transeunt. 13. De exceptionibus. 14. De replicationibus.

15. De interdictis. 16. De pœna temere litigantium. 17. De officio judicis. 18. De publicis judiciis.

"To the senante and to all the peoples:

"It were a marvellous thing to reduce into one uniform shape all the laws of Rome, from the foundation of the city down to our own time, a period of nearly fourteen hundred years. After having invoked the aid of God, we have commissioned Tribonian, a high personage, with other very illustrious and very learned men, to carry out our design; all the results of their labour being first submitted to our royal investigation and scrutiny.

"1. After arranging the Imperial constitutions in twelve books in the code which is adorned with our name, we have entered on a more considerable work, the revision and the arrangement of the whole of the ancient jurisprudence, comprising nearly two thousand volumes, and more than three million lines, which we have undertaken to read and examine in order to make the best selections; and we have collected the whole into fifty books, under the name of Digest or Pandects, reducing it to about one hundred and fifty thousand lines (that is to say, about a twentieth), and dividing it into seven parts, not promiscuously, but in order of numbers (*sed in numerorum naturam et artem respicientes*).

"2 to 8. The first part contains what the Greeks call '*premises*,' divided into four books; the second into seven; the third into eight; the fourth, which is, as it were, the pith of the whole composition (*qui totius compositionis quasi quoddam invenitur umbilicum*), into eight books; the fifth into nine books; the sixth into eight; and the seventh into six." (The text, in mentioning each part summarily, indicates the different subjects which are therein treated. This division of the Digest into seven parts is no longer, in the work of Justinian, of any practical utility.)

"9. All these things have been brought to an end by . . . ." (Here follows the designation of the seventeen commissioners. Tribonian, who directed it; Constantine, *comes sacrarum largitionum;* two professors of law at Constantinople, Theophilus and Cratinus; two at Berytus, Dorotheus and Anatolius; besides eleven lawyers of renown occupying a superior position in Constantinople, whose names the constitution gives individually.)

"10. Our respect for antiquity is so great that we have in nowise suffered the names of the jurists to be passed over in silence; each of them who was the author of a law (*qui auctor legis fuit*) is inscribed in our Digest. All the modifications made in their laws (*in legibus eorum*), or even in the Imperial Constitutions quoted by them, are sanctioned by us, as if the whole had been written by ourselves, no one having authority to compare the text as it formerly stood with that which we have declared authorized.

"11. But in order to afford beginners the opportunity of commencing their primary studies, so as to facilitate their subsequent progress to deeper subjects, we have charged Tribonian, and, under his direction, Theophilus and Dorotheus, to collect the divers works of the ancients, which contained the elementary exposition of the laws, and which were called *Institutiones*, to extract the passages which might be most useful and best adapted to the present time, and to form them into four books, with authority to exercise the same power of revision as in our other compilations. This work, when completed and laid before us, will be re-read by us (*nobis oblatum et relectum*), and will have the force of a constitution emanating from us.

"12. The whole of this compilation of the Roman law in three volumes, the Institutes, the Digest or Pandects, and the Code, has been completed, by the favour of Almighty God, in three years—a work which, when it was begun, we scarcely hoped to accomplish in ten.

"13. We notify this act of legislation to all. It is a collation of direct concise laws, placed within the reach of everybody, the text of which can be obtained by the poor as well as by the rich, for a small sum instead of the expense which would have been entailed in procuring a large and superfluous mass of volumes.

"14, 15, and 16. Should there be any repetitions or any apparent discordance—for there is no real discordance and no omission—it must be excused on the score of the imperfection of human nature; for it is Deity alone which fails in nothing.

"17. These laws have been collected from so many volumes that the most aged men not only were ignorant of their names, but had never heard them mentioned. These volumes of ancient lore have been furnished for the most part by Tribonian, a most excellent personage, many of them being unknown even to the most learned. The collectors of our work have read not only all the books from which our laws have been extracted, but also a great number of others, in which they have found nothing either useful or new, fit to be incorporated into our Digest.

"18. But as even divine works are susceptible of improvement, and as there is nothing which can perpetually remain in the same condition, if there should arise any reason to add to or to modify the Code, wisdom and imperial power will minister to that want.

"19. Conscript fathers, and all inhabitants of the terrestrial globe, render ye therefore thanks to the supreme Divinity, which has reserved for your age so salutary a work! Venerate and observe these laws (*et adorate, et observate*). Let no one attempt either before the judge or in any other discussion where the law should intervene, to quote, or to point out any passage whatever of other books than our Institutes, our Digest, and our Constitutions, arranged and promulgated by us, under the penalty due to the crime of fraud to the fool capable of such a deed, and to the judge who shall have suffered it in his hearing.

"20. In order that it may be manifest from what legislators (*ex quibus legislatoribus*), from which of their works (*quibusque libris eorum*), and from what thousands of materials this temple of Roman law has been constructed, we have ordered the list of them to be placed at the beginning of our Digest. We have chosen the legislators or commentators (*legislatores autem vel commentatores*) who were worthy of so great a work, whose ability the princes, our predecessors, condescended to recognise, and we have invested them with an equal authority, no superiority of one over the other being recognised; for, all the provisions adopted by us having the force of a constitution promulgated by us, there can be no distinction.

"21. Let no jurist, at the present time or in the future, dare to annex commentaries to these laws: we only permit translations from Latin into Greek, and the summaries called *paratitla*, intended to describe the articles; but not *interpretationes* or rather *perversiones*."

(Penalties due to the crime of fraud are threatened on those who shall contravene this prohibition, and the destruction of their works.)

"22. The same penalties are applicable to those who shall in future write our laws in signs or abbreviations; everything, including the names of the jurists, the articles, the numbers of the articles, must be expressed, not by signs, but by letters. Let those who buy books written with signs in any portion whatever know, that they will have a useless property, as they will not be allowed to quote them before a court of justice. As to the writer, over and above the penalty of fraud, he will be bound to restore double the estimated value of the book to him who shall have bought, or caused it to be bought, in good faith.

"23. The laws of these codes, namely, the Institutes or Elements, and the Digest or Pandects, will be in force from our third and blessed consulate, the third of the Kalends of January (30th December, A.D. 533), over all future or still pending suits before the judges, but not those settled by final judgment or by amicable arrangement, which we would not in any way disturb.

"24. Let all our judges adopt these laws within their jurisdiction; and especially let the præfect of Constantinople, and the three prætorian præfects of the east, of Illyria, and of Libya, have them published and made known to all within their respective jurisdiction.

"Given the 17th of the Kalends of January, under the third consulate of Justinian (16th December, A.D. 533)."[1]

Novellæ Constitutiones, afterwards Authenticæ, Corpus Authenticorum.—Between A.D. 534, the date of the second edition of the Code, and A.D. 565, the date of his death, Justinian published no fewer than 146 *Novellæ* modifying the Code, the Digest, and the Institutes: 108 of these were enacted during

[1] Extracted from Prichard and Nasmith's translation of Ortolan's History of Roman Law, pp. 447 *et seq.*

the five years immediately following the publication of the second edition of the Code. What a comment on hasty legislation and Justinian's boastful finality!

So great was the decline of the Roman language at Constantinople within forty years after the death of this emperor, that his laws in general were not otherwise intelligible to the major part of the people than by the assistance of a Greek version; but, notwithstanding this disadvantage, they still subsisted entire, till the promulgation of the Basilicæ (A.D. 906 to 911) by which the east was governed, till the dissolution of the empire, 1453.

The laws published by Justinian were still less successful in the west; where, even in the lifetime of the emperor, they were not received universally; and after the Lombard invasion (A. D. 568) they became so totally neglected, that both the Code and the Pandects were lost, till the twelfth century; when it is said that the Pandects were accidentally recovered at Amalphi, and the Code at Ravenna.

Corpus Juris Civilis.—The whole collection of the Institutes, the Digest, the Code, and the Novellæ is called the *corpus juris;* or, more commonly, the *corpus juris civilis*, by way of antithesis to *corpus juris canonici.*

THE INSTITUTES OF GAIUS.

FIRST COMMENTARY.

PERSONS.

I. *De Jure Gentium et Civili.*

§ 1. Every human community that is regulated by laws and customs, observes a rule of conduct which in part is peculiar to itself, and in part is common to mankind in general. The rule of conduct which a people has settled for its own observance, and which is peculiar to that people, is termed the *jus civile.* Those principles which natural reason has taught to all mankind, are equally observed by all, and collectively are termed the *jus gentium.* The Roman law is consequently in part peculiar to the Romans, and in part common to all mankind. We will note the distinction when the occasion arises.

§ 2. The law of Rome consists of *leges*, *plebiscita*, *senatus-consulta*, *constitutiones principum*, *edicta*, and *responsa prudentum.*

§ 3. A *lex* is that which is ordained and established by the *populus*, a *plebiscitum* is that which is ordained and established by the *plebs.* The word *plebs* differs from the word *populus* in this, that, whereas the word *populus* designates all citizens, including the patricians, the word *plebs* designates all citizens other than patricians. Consequently, in former times, the patricians contended that the *plebiscita* had no binding force on them: however, when the *lex Hortensia* enacted that the *plebiscita* should be binding on all equally, *plebiscita* became equivalent to *leges.*

§ 4. A *senatusconsultum* (S. C.) is a decree of the senate, and has the force of a *lex*, though that, at one time, was questioned.

§ 5. A *constitutio principis* is a decree, edict, or rescript of the emperor; the fact that a *constitutio principis* has the force of a *lex* has never been doubted, it being by virtue of a *lex* that the emperor has his *imperium*.

§ 6. All Roman magistrates have the right of issuing edicts; those, however, of the *prætor urbanus* and the *prætor peregrinus* constitute the most important part of this branch of law, as their jurisdiction extends to the provinces, it being there exercised by the presidents. The jurisdiction of the *curule ædiles* extends to the quæstors in the provinces of the Roman people. Quæstors are not sent into the provinces of the emperor, and consequently such edicts are not published in those provinces.

§ 7. The *responsa prudentum* are the decisions and opinions of those to whom permission has been given to expound the law. When they are all agreed, their joint opinion has the force of law; when they differ, the judge is free to act on the opinion that commends itself the most to him: the late Emperor Hadrian said so in one of his rescripts.

II. *De Juris Divisione.*

§ 8. Law deals either with persons, or with things, or with actions. We will, in the first place, treat of persons.

III. *De Condicione Hominum.*

§ 9. The principal division relative to the rights of persons is this: Every one is either free or slave.

§ 10. Freemen are subdivided into *ingenui* and *libertini*.

§ 11. The *ingenui* are those who were born free; the *libertini* are those who by mancipation have been delivered from lawful servitude.

§ 12. There are three classes of *libertini*—they are either *cives Romani*, or *Latini*, or *dediticii*. We will consider them separately, and will commence with the *dediticii*.

IV. *De Dediticiis vel lege Æliâ Sentiâ.*

§ 13. The *lex Ælia Sentia* provides that slaves, who by way of punishment have been placed in chains by their masters, or have been branded, or submitted to torture and convicted of crime, or who have been delivered over to fight with swords, or against wild beasts, or who have been cast into a gladiatorial school, or into prison, and subsequently manumitted, whether by the same or any other master, acquire, when free, the status of *peregrini dediticii.*

V. *De Peregrinis Dediticiis.*

§ 14. *Peregrini dediticii* are those who, having taken arms against the Romans, and being defeated, have surrendered at discretion.

§ 15. We say then, that slaves thus disgraced, no matter how or at what age they may have been enfranchised, even assuming them to have been the absolute property of their masters, never become Roman citizens, or Latins, but for ever remain *dediticii.*

§ 16. But when a slave has not been thus disgraced, he becomes, when manumitted, in some cases a Roman citizen, in others a Latin.

§ 17. When three things concur—*i. e.*, when the individual is (1) above thirty years of age; (2) is the property of his master *ex jure Quiritium;* and (3) is manumitted legally and formally, *i. e.*, by *vindicta*, census, or testament—he becomes a Roman citizen. Either of these requisites being wanting, he becomes a Latin.

VI. *De Manumissione et Causæ Probatione.*

§ 18. The provision as to age was introduced by the *lex Ælia Sentia.* That law prohibited slaves manumitted under thirty years of age from becoming Roman citizens, unless, after *justa causa* proved, they had been manumitted by *vindicta* before a consul.

§ 19. *Justa causa* exists, for example, when before the consul one manumits his son, or his daughter, or his natural brother or sister, or his foster-child, or teacher, or a slave for the purpose of making him his procurator, or a female slave for the purpose of marrying her.

VII. *De Recuperatoribus.*

§ 20. At Rome the council consists of five senators and five adult Roman knights; in the provinces of twenty *recuperatores*—Roman citizens. These manumissions take place in the provinces on the last day of the meeting of the council, and in Rome on certain fixed days. The manumission of slaves more than thirty years of age can be effected at any time and at any place, *e. g.*, by the prætor, or proconsul, on his way to the bath or the theatre.

§ 21. A slave under thirty years of age, by manumission, becomes a Roman citizen when his master, who is not solvent, declares him, in his will, free, and at the same time appoints him his heir. . . .

§ 22. Those thus enfranchised are styled *Latini Juniani: Latini* because they are ranked with the Latin colonists: *Juniani* because their liberty is acquired by virtue of the *lex Junia*. Prior to that enactment they were regarded as slaves.

§ 23. However, the *lex Junia* neither enables them to make a will nor to take anything under the will of another, nor by will to be appointed tutors.

§ 24. When we say that they cannot take under a will, it must be understood that they cannot take directly, *i. e.*, as heir or legatee; they can take by *fidei commissum*.

§ 25. Those who rank as *dediticii* cannot, in any way, take under a will, any more than can a free foreigner; nor according to the opinion of the majority of our authorities can they make a will.

§ 26. The liberty, therefore, of those who rank as *dediticii* is the most circumscribed, as no *lex*, no *senatusconsultum*, no imperial constitution opens for them the road to Roman citizenship.

§ 27. Worse than that, they are forbidden to live in or within 100 miles of Rome on pain of being sold, together with their property, for the benefit of the public treasury, and on the condition that even as slaves they cannot serve in or within 100 miles of Rome, and if manumitted that they become slaves of the Romans. Such are the provisions of the *lex Ælia Sentia*.

VIII. *Quibus Modis Latini ad Civitum Romanum perveniant.*

§ 28. Latins may acquire Roman citizenship in several ways.

§ 29. The *lex Ælia Sentia* expressly provides that a slave manumitted when not thirty years of age, and who thereby becomes a Latin, may—provided he has married a Roman citizen or a Latin colonist, or one of his own condition, by whom he has a son one year old—by attesting to those facts in the presence of not fewer than seven witnesses, adult Roman citizens, apply to the prætor, or, if in a province, to the governor, for a declaration that he, his wife, and son, provided all are of the same condition, are Roman citizens.

§ 30. We add in the case of the son, "if he is in the same condition," because, if the wife of a Latin is a Roman citizen, her child was born a Roman citizen by virtue of a recent *senatusconsultum*, enacted at the instance of the late Emperor Hadrian.

§ 31. Though the *lex Ælia Sentia* only provides for the case of slaves manumitted when under thirty years of age, and who thereby become Latins, yet, by a *senatusconsultum* subsequently enacted during the consulship of Pegasus and Pusio, the privilege was extended to those over thirty years of age when manumitted.

§ 32. Furthermore the Latin mother, in the event of her husband's death before proof made by him, can make it herself, and thus acquire Roman citizenship for herself and son.

§ 33. . . . § 34. . . . .

§ 35. If a slave is both *in bonis*, and in the Quiritarian ownership of the person by whom he is manumitted, he can both become a Latin and obtain the *jus Quiritium* . . .

IX. *Qui et ex quibus Causis manumittere non possunt.*

§ 36. But one cannot enfranchise just as he may think fit.

§ 37. Thus, an enfranchisement made in fraud of creditors or of a patron is a nullity, by reason of the *lex Ælia Sentia.*

§ 38. So the same law prohibits any one under twenty years of age to enfranchise otherwise than by *vindicta* before the council, and then only on *justa causa* shown.

§ 39. The enfranchisement of a father, a mother, a teacher, or a foster-brother are instances of enfranchisement *justâ causâ.*

The causes instanced in reference to the slave under thirty years of age equally apply in this case. The *causæ* specified in the case of the master under twenty years of age are equally applicable to the case of a slave under thirty years of age.

§ 40. The *lex Ælia Sentia* having regulated the mode of enfranchisement that must be adopted by the master who is under twenty years of age, it follows that, though one who is fourteen years of age may make a will, and in it institute an heir and grant legacies, yet, if he is not twenty years of age, he cannot give liberty to a single slave.

§ 41. What is more, though the master who is under twenty years of age may only wish to make a Latin, he must nevertheless prove *justa causa* before the council, and subsequently manumit *inter amicos* (privately) . . .

X. *De lege Furiâ Caniniâ.*

§ 42. The *lex Furia Caninia* has further limited the power of manumitting by will.

§ 43. By that law, the owner of more than two, and fewer than ten, slaves, is permitted to manumit any not exceeding one-half; he that has more than ten, but not more than thirty, may manumit one-third; he who has more than thirty, but not more than 100, may manumit one-quarter; and finally, he who has more than 100, but not more than 500, may not manumit more than one-fifth . . . That law forbids any one to manumit more than 100 slaves . . . One who has only one or two slaves is not affected by the law, and consequently he may manumit both or either at his pleasure.

§ 44. This law does not affect manumissions otherwise than by will. Consequently, by *vindicta*, *censu*, or *inter amicos*, one may manumit all his slaves, there being no other reason to the contrary.

§ 45. What has been said as to the number of slaves that may be manumitted by testament must be understood in this sense:—when it is said that of a given number, the half, the third, the fourth, or the fifth may be manumitted, it must be understood that it is always lawful to manumit as many as might be manumitted under the regulation affecting the preceding and lower number, for it would be absurd to give the owner of ten slaves the right to free five, he being permitted to manumit one-half of his slaves, whereas he who has twelve slaves could not manumit more than four; and that those who have more than ten . . .

§ 46. When the testator writes in a circle the names of his slaves that he desires to manumit, no one of them is enfranchised, as there is no order of manumission, and the *lex Furia* declares every act done in fraud of its provisions to be void. Furthermore, there are *senatusconsulta* which declare everything done for the purpose of evading the provisions of the *lex Furia* to be null and void.

§ 47. Lastly, it must be borne in mind that the provisions of the *lex Ælia Sentia*, which declare that slaves manumitted in fraud of creditors are not in fact manumitted, apply equally to *peregrini;* for, at the instance of Hadrian, a *senatusconsultum* issued to that effect. The other provisions, however, of the *lex Ælia Sentia* do not apply to *peregrini.*

XI. *De his qui Sui vel Alieni Juris sint.*

§ 48. We have now come to another division of persons: some are *sui juris*, others *alieno juri sunt subjectæ.*

§ 49. Of those who *alieno juri sunt subjectæ*, some are *in potestate*, others *in manu*, and others *in mancipio.*

§ 50. We will consider those who are *alieno juri subjectæ*, for if we learn who those are, we know that all others are *sui juris.*

§ 51. First then, let us consider those who are *in alienâ potestate.*

§ 52. Slaves are *in potestate* of their masters by virtue of the *jus gentium*, for we find that in all nations the life or death of the slave is in the hand of the master, nor can a slave acquire otherwise than as agent of his master.

§ 53. Now, however, it is unlawful for a Roman citizen or any one else who is subject to the Romans to inflict severe and unmerited chastisement on his slave. For since a constitution of the most pious Antoninus, he who without just cause kills his own slave is subject to the same penalties as he who kills the slave of another. Excessive severity on the part of masters is also repressed by a constitution of the same prince; in short, being consulted by certain presidents of provinces on the subject of slaves who sought refuge in the temples of the gods or by the statues of the princes, he ordered that masters whose severity should be proved to be insupportable, should be compelled to sell their slaves. These two provisions are just, for no one is justified in abusing his rights; it is on this principle that prodigals are denied the management of their own affairs.

§ 54. Besides, as in the case of Roman citizens *dominium* is duplex, being *in bonis* or *ex jure Quiritium,* the master may own his slave by either of these titles. When the slave is his *ex jure Quiritium* merely, he is not in his *potestas:* to be in his *potestas* the master's title must be *in bonis.*

XII. *De Patriâ Potestate.*

§ 55. Our children begotten by us in lawful wedlock are in our *potestas.* This right is peculiar to Roman citizens; for, possibly, no other nation gives to the father like powers over his son. This fact was noted by the late Emperor Hadrian in an edict published by him with regard to those who asked him for Roman citizenship for themselves and their children. I do not forget that the Galatians believe their children to be in their *potestas.* . . . .

XIII. *De Nuptiis.*

§ 56. Roman citizens have their children in their *potestas* if they have married Roman citizens, or Latins, or even foreigners, provided they have with them the *connubium;* for as the effect of *connubium* is to make the children follow the condition of the father, the consequence is that they are not merely Roman citizens, but are also under their father's *potestas.*

§ 57. Hence the imperial constitutions not unfrequently grant to certain veterans the *connubium* with such *Latinæ* or *peregrinæ* as they take to wife after their discharge from service; and the offspring of such marriages become both Roman citizens and in the *potestas* of their father. . . .

§ 58. It must be remembered that we cannot take to wife any woman at pleasure, for there are some from marriage with whom we must abstain.

§ 59. In short, marriage cannot be contracted between persons who occupy relatively to each other the position of ascendant and descendant, for example, father and daughter, mother and son, grandfather and granddaughter; the *connubium* does not exist between them, and if such persons cohabit they are said to have contracted a nefarious and incestuous marriage. This prohibition is so rigid that it applies even in the case where the relationship is the mere result of adoption; and even after the adoption has been dissolved it equally subsists; thus we cannot marry a woman who, by adoption, has once acquired the status of our daughter or granddaughter, though we may have emancipated her.

§ 60. Between collaterals there is a like, but not so strict a rule.

§ 61. Marriage is strictly prohibited between brother and sister, whether both are by the same parents, or one by one and the other by the other. If a woman has become my sister by adoption, though marriage cannot take place between us so long as the adoption subsists, when the adoption has been dissolved by emancipation I can take her to wife; so in the event of my being emancipated, the prohibition of marriage no longer continues.

§ 62. It is lawful to marry a brother's daughter; that practice was introduced when the pious Claudius married Agrippina, his brother's daughter. But it is unlawful to marry a sister's daughter; that has been decreed by the imperial constitutions. It is also unlawful to marry a paternal or a maternal aunt.

§ 63. The prohibition extends to a woman who has formerly been our mother-in-law or daughter-in-law, or step-daughter or step-mother. We say "has formerly been," because if the marriage which established that relationship still subsists there is another bar to marriage between us, that is, that a woman cannot have two husbands at one and the same time, nor can a man have two wives.

§ 64. If then any one contracts a nefarious or incestuous alliance, he is regarded as having neither wife nor child; for the offspring of such a union are reputed as having a mother but no father; consequently they are not in *potestas*, but are like children conceived by a woman from intercourse with the first comer; such children are regarded as having no father because of the uncertainty of their parentage. It is for that reason that they are commonly styled *spurii*, whether by derivation from the Greek word *σποράδην* as children conceived haphazard, or as fatherless children. . . .

XIV. *De Erroris Causæ Probatione.*

§ 65. It sometimes happens that children, who at the moment of their birth were not in *patria potestas*, subsequently become so.

§ 66. Thus, when a Latin, being married conformably to the *lex Ælia Sentia*, has begotten a son, who is Latin the mother being a Latin, or a Roman citizen the mother being a Roman citizen, the son will not be in his *potestas;* whereas upon proof of the facts he and his son attain to Roman citizenship, and the son by that fact becomes in his father's *potestas.*

§ 67. So, if a Roman citizen has taken to wife a Latin or a *peregrina*, in ignorance of the fact, he believing her to be a Roman citizen, and by her has a son, that son is not in his *potestas*, he not being even a Roman citizen, but a Latin or *peregrinus*, that is to say, of the same condition as his mother; for the son only follows his father's condition when there is *connubium* between his father and mother; but by virtue of a *senatusconsultum* the father is permitted to prove his error; and on doing so both mother and son acquire the status of Roman citizens, and from that moment the son is subject to the *potestas* of his father. It is the same when a Roman citizen in error marries one of the *dediticii*, except that in this case the wife does not become a Roman citizen.

§ 68. In like manner, if a female Roman citizen in error marries a *peregrinus* whom she believed to be a Roman citizen, it is competent for her to prove her error; and by so doing both her son and her husband acquire Roman citizenship, and at the same time the son is subjected to the *potestas* of his father. It is the same if she has married a *peregrinus*, believing that she was marrying a Latin, conformably to the *lex Ælia Sentia;* for the *senatusconsultum* has a special provision on the point. To a certain extent it is the same when she has married one of the *dediticii*, believing that she was marrying a Roman citizen, or a Latin in conformity with the provisions of the *lex Ælia Sentia;* for in this case the *dediticius* remains in his condition, and consequently his son, though becoming a Roman citizen, does not pass into the *potestas* of his father.

§ 69. So, if a Latin woman marries a *peregrinus*, believing him to be a Latin, she may, by virtue of the *senatusconsultum*, so soon as a son is born to them, prove her error; whereupon the father, mother, and son become Roman citizens, and the son passes into the *potestas* of his father.

§ 70. It is absolutely the same when a Latin in error marries a *peregrina*, believing that he is marrying a woman who is a Latin or a Roman citizen in pursuance of the *lex Ælia Sentia.*

§ 71. In addition, if a Roman citizen, who regarded himself as a Latin, married a Latin woman, it is lawful for him, upon the birth of a son, to prove his error, as if he had married conformably to the provisions of the *lex Ælia Sentia.* So those who, notwithstanding the fact of their being Roman citizens, believed themselves to be *peregrini* and married *peregrinæ*, have, according to the *senatusconsultum*, after the birth of a son, the right to produce proof of their error; which done, the *peregrina* becomes a Roman citizen, and the son . . . . not merely acquires the right of Roman citizenship, but at the same time passes under the *potestas* of his father.

§ 72. All that we have said concerning a son applies equally to a daughter.

§ 73. The age of the son or daughter is immaterial as to the proofs of the cause of error. . . . A Latin man . . . . if the son or daughter is under one year of age, the proof of the conditions being satisfied cannot be made. I do not overlook the fact that a rescript of the divine Hadrian grants a hearing for the purpose of proving the cause of error. . . .

§ 74. So, in the case of a *peregrinus* who had married, and who, after the birth of a son, had otherwise obtained the right of Roman citizenship; when it was subsequently asked whether he could make the requisite proof, the Emperor Antoninus by a rescript decided that he could prove in the same way that he could have done had he remained a *peregrinus;* whence we conclude that a *peregrinus* can also prove.

§ 75. From what we have said it results that . . . .

XV. *De Statu Liberorum.*

§ 76. . . . has taken to wife . . . . as we have said a lawful marriage is thus contracted, and the child born of it is a Roman citizen and subjected to the *potestas* of his father.

§ 77. Consequently, if a female Roman citizen marries a *peregrinus* . . . . the condition of her son is the same as if his father had begotten him of a *peregrina.* Now, by virtue of a *senatusconsultum* promulgated at the instance of the divine Hadrian, though the *connubium* does not exist between a female Roman citizen and a *peregrinus*, the child born of their union is *justus patris filius.*

§ 78. When we said that the son of a union between a female Roman citizen and a *peregrinus* is a *peregrinus* . . . .

§ 79. It is equally true that . . . . but also those who are styled Latins; but it applies to those other Latins who constitute particular communities having their own cities, and who are regarded as *peregrini.*

§ 80. . . . On the contrary, the offspring of a Latin man and a female Roman citizen is born a Roman citizen. There have been jurists, however, who were of opinion that the marriage having been contracted in conformity with the *lex Ælia Sentia*, the child was born a Latin, because it appeared that in this case the *connubium* is established between them by the *leges Ælia Sentia et Junia*, and that the *connubium* always produces this effect, that the child follows the condition of the father, whereas, the marriage being otherwise contracted, the child, by the *jus gentium*, follows the condition of the mother. However, it is now of little moment; for according to the law now in vogue, as the result of the *senatusconsultum* enacted on the suggestion of the divine Hadrian, the child born of a Latin and a female Roman citizen is born a Roman citizen.

§ 81. In conformity with this principle the *senatusconsultum* passed during the reign of the divine Hadrian added that the child born of a Latin and a *peregrina*, or reciprocally of a *peregrinus* and a female Latin, follows the condition of the mother.

§ 82. Another consequence of the same principle is, that the child of a female slave and a free man is born a slave by the *jus gentium*, and that the issue of a free woman by a slave is born free.

§ 83. We must, however, inquire whether the rule of the *jus gentium* has not been modified in certain cases by some law or by some act having the force of law.

§ 84. For example, by a *senatusconsultum* in the reign of Claudius, a female Roman citizen, who cohabited with another person's slave with the consent of his master, might herself by agreement, she remaining free, yet bear a slave; for whatever was agreed between her and the master of the slave was confirmed by the *senatusconsultum*. Subsequently, however, the late Emperor Hadrian, struck by the want of equity in the matter and the anomalous character of the rule, re-established the rule of the *jus gentium* by which the mother, remaining free, gives birth to a freeborn child.

§ 85. By the *lex* . . . free children may be born of a female slave and a free man, for the *lex* enacts that, if any one cohabits with a female slave belonging to another, he believing her to be free, the male offspring will be free, whereas the female offspring will belong to the master of the slave. However, in this instance also, the late Emperor Vespasian, struck by the anomalous character of the rule, restored the regulation of the *jus gentium*, that the children, whether male or female, the offspring of a union between a free man and a female slave, supposed to be free, belong to the owner of the slave.

§ 86. But the provision of that *lex* which enacts that the offspring of a free woman by another man's slave, whom she knew to be a slave, are born slaves, still remains in force. Among nations, therefore, who have no such law, the child, by the *jus gentium*, follows the mother's condition, and is consequently free.

§ 87. Whenever the child follows the condition of the mother and not that of the father, it is evident that he is not in the *potestas* of his father, even though he be a Roman citizen. In some cases, however, as I have already said, when the flaw in the marriage was the result of mistake, the senate interferes, repairs the defect, and by so doing, in the majority of cases, subjects the son to his father's *potestas*.

§ 88. But when a female slave has conceived by a Roman citizen, and, being subsequently enfranchised, she gives birth to the child, though the father and child are Roman citizens, the child is not in the *potestas* of the father, he not having been conceived of valid marriage; and no *senatusconsultum* has placed such cohabitation on the footing of lawful marriage.

§ 89. The rule that, when a female slave conceives of a Roman citizen and subsequently, after being enfranchised, gives birth to the child, the child is born free, is a dictate of natural reason, for the status of those whose conception is illegitimate is determined by the status of the mother at the date of the child's birth. Therefore, those born of a free woman are free, and it matters little by whom she conceived when she was a slave. On the other hand, the status of the children legitimately conceived follows the status at the time of conception.

§ 90. Consequently, if a female Roman citizen, whilst pregnant, be interdicted fire and water, and she, thus becoming a *peregrina*, then gives birth to a child, many jurists distinguish the two cases, and are of opinion that if she conceived in lawful wedlock her child is born a Roman citizen, whereas if she conceived out of lawful wedlock the child is born a *peregrinus*.

§ 91. So, if a female Roman citizen, being pregnant, be reduced to slavery by virtue of the *senatusconsultum Claudianum* for having in opposition to the will of a master cohabited with his slave, many jurists hold that if she conceived *ex justis nuptiis* her child was born a Roman citizen, but if she conceived of promiscuous intercourse the child was born the slave of the person to whom the mother had become the slave.

§ 92. So a *peregrina*, who, having conceived by promiscuous intercourse, afterwards becomes a Roman citizen and is confined, gives birth to a Roman citizen; but if she has conceived of a *peregrinus*, to whom she has been united conformably to the laws of the *peregrini*, the child is reputed a *peregrinus* by virtue of a *senatusconsultum* of Hadrian, unless Roman citizenship has been acquired by the father.

§ 93. When a *peregrinus* has received, together with his children, the right of Roman citizenship, the children do not pass into the father's *potestas* unless the emperor expressly subjects them to it, which is never done except for the benefit of the children. When the child is under age, or absent, the matter must be most carefully investigated. Such are the provisions of an edict of the late Emperor Hadrian.

§ 94. So, if Roman citizenship is conferred on a man and his wife, pregnant at the time, though the child is born a Roman citizen, it is not in its father's *potestas*. This is determined by a rescript of the late Emperor Hadrian. Therefore, when a man applies to the emperor for Roman citizenship for himself and wife, if to his knowledge she is pregnant at the time, he should also ask that the child to be born may be in his *potestas*.

§ 95. It is otherwise with Latins who acquire Roman citizenship together with their children, for their children pass *in potestatem*. This right is accorded to certain *peregrini*. . . .

§ 96. Greater Latinity is the right whereby the magistrates of certain towns acquire Roman citizenship along with their wives and children: lesser Latinity is the right whereby the magistrates themselves acquire the Roman citizenship, but not their wives and children, a distinction intimated in several imperial rescripts.

XVI. *De Adoptionibus.*

§ 97. In addition to our children as above explained, our adopted children are in our *potestas*.

§ 98. **Adoptio.**—*Adoptio* is effected in two ways, viz. (1) by the authority of the *populus*; (2) under the jurisdiction of the magistrate, *e.g.*, the prætor.

§ 99. **Adrogatio.**—We adopt by the authority of the *populus* those who are *sui juris*. This species of adoption is styled *adrogatio*, because the parties are interrogated (*rogatio, i.e. interrogatio*). The adopter is asked whether he wishes to take the other to him as a legitimate son or not. The other is asked if he is willing to be so adopted, and the *populus* are asked if they ordain that it shall be so. Under the jurisdiction of a magistrate we adopt those who are in the *potestas* of their ascendants, whether a descendant is in the first degree as a son or daughter, or in a more remote degree as a grandson or granddaughter, great-grandson or great-granddaughter.

§ 100. The adoption which is made by the *populus* can only take place at Rome, whereas the other may take place in the provinces before the president.

§ 101. Females cannot be adopted by the authority of the *populus;* at least, such is the general opinion. But they may be adopted before the prætor, or in the provinces before the proconsul or the legate.

§ 102. At times it has been lawful, at others not, to adopt a minor by the authority of the *populus*. Now, by an epistle of Antoninus, addressed to the pontiffs, it is lawful, provided good cause be shown. Before the prætor at Rome, however, and in the provinces before the proconsul or legate, a person of any age may be adopted.

§ 103. There is one matter common to both modes of adoption, viz. the impotent may adopt.

§ 104. Women cannot adopt by either method, because they have no *potestas* even in the case of their own children.

§ 105. An adopted person may be given in adoption to another.

§ 106. It is not clear whether one can adopt another older than himself.

§ 107. It is peculiar to *adrogatio* that the children, if any, of the adopted pass to the adopter in the relationship of grandchildren.

XVII. *De Manu.*

§ 108. This right is also peculiar to Roman citizens.

§ 109. Males and females may be *in potestate.* Females only can be *in manu.*

§ 110. Formerly there were three ways by which a female might become *in manu*, viz., *usu*, *farreo*, *coemptione.*

§ 111. A female became *in manu* by *usu* by cohabitation with her husband throughout one whole year, for his enjoyment of her for that period gave him a certain possessory right as by *usucapio*, and ranked her in his family as a daughter. That was why the law of the Twelve Tables enacted that a woman who did not wish to pass *in manum* of her husband should absent herself each year for three nights, and thus prevent the right by *usucapio* from accruing in any one year. But this law has been abrogated in part by legislation and in part by desuetude.

§ 112. By *farreo* women pass *in manum*. It is a species of sacrifice . . . . in which a meal cake is employed, hence the name *confarreatio*. This legal ceremony involves various formalities and rites, accompanied by the use, in the presence of ten witnesses, of a prescribed and solemn form of words. This ceremony is still in vogue, for the *flamines majores*, *i.e.*, those of Jupiter, Mars, and Quirinus. . . . .

§ 113. By *coemptione*, women become *in manu* by *mancipatio*, *i.e.*, a symbolical sale of the woman to the man for an *as*. The ceremony must be performed in the presence of a *libripens*, and at least five witnesses, who must be adult Roman citizens. The ceremony completed, the woman is said to be *in manu*.

§ 114. A woman can go through the ceremony of *coemptio* not merely with her husband, but with a stranger. Hence it is said that *coemptio* is either for the purpose of marriage or trust. A woman who goes through the ceremony of *coemptio* with her husband in order to assume in relation to him the position of a daughter, is said to have gone through the ceremony as a marriage ceremony. But she who has performed it for another object, whether with her husband, or with another, *e.g.*, to avoid *tutelage*, is said to have performed it *fiduciæ causâ*.

§ 115. This is accomplished thus: If a woman wishes to replace her present tutor by another, she, with the authorization of the existing tutor, sells herself, after which she is emancipated by the buyer to the person indicated by her, and, being enfranchised by him by means of the *vindicta*, she has thenceforth as tutor him who has enfranchised her, and who is styled her *tutor fiduciarius*, as will hereafter appear.

§ 115a. Formerly, females, certain persons excepted, could only make a will by means of *coemptio fiduciaria*—*i.e.*, they made *coemptio*, were remancipated, and subsequently manumitted; but by a S. C. at the instance of Hadrian this necessity was removed.

§ 115b. Though the woman may have performed the ceremony of *coemptio* with her husband solely *causâ fiduciariâ*, she nevertheless takes the place of daughter; for, for whatever motive she becomes *in manu* of her husband, it has been decided that she takes the place and rights of a daughter.

XVIII. *De Mancipio.*

§ 116. It remains to show who may be *in mancipio.*

§ 117. All children, whether male or female, who are *in potestate parentis*, may be mancipated by the parent in the same manner as slaves.

§ 118. So with females who are *in manu*, for a woman may be mancipated by her *coemptionator* in the same way as children are mancipated by a parent; and although she only acquires the relation of daughter when the *coemptionator* is her husband, nevertheless, even when he is not the husband, and consequently does not thereby acquire the status of father, she may be mancipated by him.

§ 118a. Persons are rarely mancipated unless their parents or *coemptionatores* desire to liberate them from their dependence, as we shall hereafter see.

§ 119. As we have already said, *mancipatio* is a species of fictitious sale, and is an institution peculiar to Roman citizens. The ceremony is performed thus:—In the presence of at least five witnesses, adult Roman citizens, and a Roman *libripens*, he who receives the other *in mancipium*, holding the *æs*, says: "I declare that this man is mine by Quiritarian law; I have bought him with this metal and these metal scales": after which he strikes the scales with the piece of metal, and gives it as the price to him from whom he receives the person *in mancipium.*

§ 120. In this way slaves and free persons are mancipated, as also are all animals that are *mancipi*, such as oxen, horses, mules, asses; so also lands, whether urban or rural, that are *mancipi*, for example, Italian lands.

§ 121. The only difference between the mancipation of land

and of other subjects of mancipation is, that persons, whether slave or free, as also animals that are *mancipi*, must be present to be mancipated, so that he who accepts *mancipio* may physically take that which is given him *mancipio*: hence the term *mancipatio*, because the thing is seized by the hand (*manu capitur*). *Prædia*, though absent, may be mancipated.

§ 122. Brass and the scales (*æs et libra*) are used because in ancient times there was no money but brass. They had *asses*, *dupondii*, *semisses*, and *quadrantes*, but neither gold nor silver coins, as may be gathered from the Twelve Tables. The value of the pieces of metal was determined, not by number but by weight. For instance, the *asses* weighed a pound each, and the *dupondii* two; whence the name *dupondius*, as being *duo pondo*; a name which is still employed. The *semisses* (half *asses*) and *quadrantes* (quarter *asses*) have also a definite weight according to their fractional part of the pound of copper. As money was weighed and not counted, the slaves to whom the administration of money was entrusted were and are styled *dispensatores* (weighers out).

§ 123. Should any one ask in what respect *coemptio* differs from *mancipatio*, it is this:—In the case of *coemptio* the woman is not reduced to a servile condition, whereas *mancipatio* by ascendants and *coemptionatores* reduces the mancipated to so servile a condition that they can neither inherit to, nor receive a legacy from, the person in whose *mancipium* they are, unless they are declared free in the same testament according to the rule of law in force in the case of slaves. The reason of this difference is manifest, for parents and *coemptionatores* mancipate by the use of the very words employed in the mancipation of slaves, which is not the case in a *coemptio*.

XIX. *Quibus Modis Jus Potestatis solvatur.*

§ 124. We will now consider how those who are *alieni juris* are liberated.

§ 125. And first, of those who are *in potestate*.

§ 126. As to slaves it is only necessary to refer to what has already been said concerning their manumission.

§ 127. Those who are in the *potestas* of their ascendants,

become *sui juris* by the death of the ascendants. It must, however, be observed that, though in all cases the death of the parent makes the child, whether male or female, *sui juris*, the death of the grandfather does not in all cases render the grandchild *sui juris*, but only in the case where by the death of the grandfather the grandchild does not pass into the *potestas* of the father. If, therefore, at the time of the grandfather's decease the father is living, and himself in the *potestas* of the grandfather, the death of the grandfather does not render the grandchildren *sui juris*, for they thereby pass into the *potestas* of their father. If, on the contrary, the father is either dead or had ceased to be in the *potestas* of the grandfather prior to the death of the grandfather, his children by the death of the grandfather become *sui juris*, for in that case they cannot fall under the *potestas* of their father.

§ 128. As one to whom water and fire are interdicted by a penal law, in consequence of crime, loses his citizenship, his children cease to be his in *potestas* as if he were dead, for reason forbids that a person in the condition of a *peregrinus* should have a Roman citizen subject to him. For the like reason, if water and fire have been interdicted to one who is *in potestate*, he immediately ceases to be so, for by parity of reasoning a *peregrinus* cannot be in the *potestas* of a Roman citizen.

§ 129. If a parent has been made captive by the enemy, though, for the moment, he is their slave and as such has lost his citizen rights, the condition of his descendants is in suspense by reason of the doctrine of *postliminium*, by which all prisoners of war who return recover their former rights. Therefore, on his return, his descendants will be in his *potestas*. Should he die in captivity, his descendants become *sui juris*. Whether they become so at the moment of his captivity or death is matter of discussion. A like effect results from the captivity of the child.

§ 130. Males become *sui juris* when inaugurated *flamens* of Jupiter, females when made vestal virgins.

§ 131. Formerly also, when the Romans founded colonies in Latium, the son who by the order of his father settled in one of those colonies was held to be liberated from the *patria potestas*, inasmuch as his settlement there made him a citizen of another state.

§ 132. Descendants also cease to be *in potestate* by emancipation. Three emancipations are necessary to release the son; one is sufficient for other children, or grandchildren, whether male or female, for the laws of the Twelve Tables only mention three mancipations in the case of a son. It enacts, "If a father sell a son three times, let the son be free from the father." The ceremony is as follows:—The father mancipates his son to some one who manumits him by *vindicta;* that done, the son returns *in potestatem.* The father mancipates a second time, usually, but not necessarily, to the same person, who manumits by *vindicta;* in like manner the son again returns *in potestatem.* Then the father a third time mancipates, either to the same or to another person, when the son ceases to be *in potestate*, though he has not been manumitted. He is in the condition called *mancipium.* . . .

§ 133. It is lawful for one who has a son and his son's son in his *potestas* to release both, or to retain either while releasing the other. The same may be said as to the great-grandfather. . . .

§ 134. Further, ascendants cease to have their descendants in their *potestas* when they are given in adoption; and in the case of a son, if he be given in adoption, three mancipations and two intervening manumissions take place, in like manner as when the father liberates him from his *potestas* in order that he may become *sui juris.* He is then either remancipated to his father, from whom the adopter claims him before the prætor as his son, whereupon, the father not alleging any claim on his part, the prætor assigns the son to the adopter,—or the son is mancipated in court to the adopter, who claims him as son from the person with whom he is left after the third mancipation. The more convenient form is for the son to be remancipated to his father. In the case of other descendants, whether male or female, one mancipation alone is sufficient, and they are either remancipated to their ascendants, or mancipated in court to some other person. In the provinces a like ceremony may take place before the president.

§ 135. A child conceived from a son once or twice manumitted, although born after the third mancipation of his father, is nevertheless in the *potestas* of his grandfather, and therefore may be either emancipated or given in adoption by him. But a child conceived from a son who has gone through the third mancipation is not born in the *potestas* of his grandfather. Labeo, however, thinks he is in the *mancipium* of the man to whom his father is mancipated. The rule, however, that has obtained acceptance is, that so long as the father is in *mancipium*, the status of the child is in suspense; and if the father is manumitted after the mancipation, he falls into his *potestas;* whilst if the father dies in *mancipium*, he becomes *sui juris.*

§ 135a. . . . As we have said above, what three mancipations effect in the case of a son, one mancipation effects in the case of a grandson.

§ 136. Women are not freed from the *potestas* of their ascendants, although *in manu*, unless they have made a *coemptio;* and this rule is confirmed in the case of the wife of a *flamen Dialis* by a *senatusconsultum*, published at the instance of the consuls Maximus and Tubero, which provides that such an one is to be regarded as *in manu* only so far as relates to sacred matters, but in respect of other matters to be as though not *in manu.* Women who have made a *coemptio* are freed from the *potestas* of their ascendants by *mancipation:* nor is it material whether they be *in manu* of their husband or of a stranger; although the status of quasi-daughter only belongs to a woman who is *in manu* of a husband.

§ 137. A woman who by *coemptio* becomes *in manu* is released therefrom by *remancipation*, and becomes *sui juris.* A wife who is *in manu* of her husband can no more compel him to release her without dissolution of the marriage than a daughter can her father. A daughter, even though such by adoption, has no means of compelling her father, whereas a wife, by sending a message of divorce, can compel her husband to release her, as though she had never been married to him (*i. e.*, as if he were a mere *coemptionator*).

§ 138. Those who are in the condition called *mancipium*, being regarded as in the position of slaves, become *sui juris* when manumitted either by *vindicta*, *census*, or *testament*.

§ 139. To them, however, the *lex Ælia Sentia* has no application. The question of age, whether on the part of the manumitter or the manumitted, does not arise. The fact of patron or creditor is also immaterial. The *lex Furia Caninia* is inapplicable.

§ 140. Moreover, one can obtain his liberty by *census*, even in opposition to the will of the person in whose *mancipium* he is. To this rule, however, there are exceptions. A son who has been given *in mancipium* by his father on condition that he shall be *remancipated* cannot, because in that case the father, in a certain sense, has retained him in his *potestas*. So in the case of a son given by his father *in mancipium ex noxali causâ*, *e. g.*, where the father condemned for a theft committed by the son has given his son *in mancipium* to the plaintiff, for, in that case, the plaintiff has him in lieu of the money due to him.

§ 141. It must be observed that an *actio injuriarum* lies for treating one in *mancipium* contumeliously. Men never remain long in *mancipium;* ordinarily they pass into it by way of form for the moment. To this, however, must be excepted the case of mancipium *ex noxali causâ*.

XX. *De Tutelis*.

§ 142. Let us now pass to another division of those who are neither in *potestas*, *manus*, nor *mancipium*. Some are in *tutela*, some in *curatio*, and others not in either. Let us therefore consider who are in *tutela* or *curatio:* for thus we shall ascertain those who are not in either.

§ 143. First, then, let us consider who are in *tutela*.

§ 144. The law allows ascendants to appoint by will *tutores* (guardians?) to descendants whom they have in their *potestas*, to males when below the age of puberty, to females even if above that period; for, according to our ancestors, women who have attained their majority require, by reason of their levity of soul, to be kept under tutelage.

§ 145. Accordingly, when a brother and sister have a testamentary *tutor*, on attaining the age of puberty the son ceases to be a ward, but the sister continues in tutelage, unless, indeed, she is a vestal virgin, till she has given birth to a certain number of children, when, by virtue of the *leges Julia et Papia Poppæa*, she is freed. Vestal virgins were exempted by the ancients in honour of the priesthood. They are so, also, by a provision of the Twelve Tables.

§ 146. One cannot by testament appoint a *tutor* to his grandchildren who are in his *potestas*, if, by the fact of his death, those children pass into the *potestas* of their father. If, therefore, at the moment of my death, my son is in my *potestas*, my grandchildren by him cannot have a *tutor* by virtue of my testament, though they are in my *potestas*, because, on my death, they pass into the *potestas* of their father.

§ 147. As in many other cases, posthumous children are regarded as already born. It has been decided that *tutores* may be given to them by testament, provided that, if born during the life of the testator they would be in his *potestas*. They may also be appointed heirs. The posthumous children of strangers cannot be appointed heirs.

§ 148. A man may appoint a *tutor* to his wife who is *in manu* in the same way as to his daughter, as also to his daughter-in-law *in manu* of his son, and to his granddaughter.

§ 149. Strictly speaking, a *tutor* should be appointed in these terms: "I give Lucius Titius as *tutor* to my descendants" (*Lucium Titium liberis meis tutorem do*). But if written, "Titius be *tutor* to my descendants or to my wife" (*Liberis meis vel uxori meæ Titius tutor esto*), it is sufficient.

§ 150. In the case of a wife *in manu*, it is lawful to give her the privilege of nominating her *tutor*, thus: "I give to my wife Titia the option of a *tutor*" (*Titiæ uxori meæ tutoris optionem do*). In such case it is lawful for her to appoint a *tutor* either in respect of her entire affairs, or to manage one or more matters.

§ 151. The option given is at times unlimited, at others limited.

§ 152. Unlimited option is commonly given in the form above mentioned; limited option is conferred thus: "I give to Titia, my wife, the selection of a *tutor* once only"; or "I give it twice only" (*Titiæ uxori meæ duntaxat tutoris optionem semel do, aut duntaxat bis do*).

§ 153. The effect of these forms is very different. A woman who has unlimited option may change her tutor two, three, or even more times, whereas one who has limited option only is restricted to the number of times specified.

§ 154. *Tutores* who are specifically named in the testament are styled *dativi;* those who are elected by the wife are named *optivi.*

XXI. *De Legitimâ Agnatorum Tutelâ.*

§ 155. Those to whom *tutores* are not given by testament, have, by the Twelve Tables, their *agnati* as *tutores*, who are styled *tutores legitimi.*

§ 156. The *agnati* are those who are united by *cognation* of the male line of the father, *e. g.*, a brother by the same father, the son of that brother, or his grandson. Those who are related to us through the female line are not *agnati*, but merely *cognati ; i. e.*, relations by the law of nature. Thus, between our maternal uncle and our sister's son there is no agnation, though there is cognation. So between the son of my aunt, whether paternal or maternal, and myself, there is not *agnation*, but simply *cognation*, because children follow the family of their father, and not that of their mother.

§ 157. Formerly, by the provisions of the Twelve Tables, the *agnati* were the *tutores legitimi* of females as well as of males, but by a law of Claudius so much of that law as related to the *tutores legitimi* of females was repealed. Thus, a male under age has his adult brother or paternal uncle as his *tutor*, whereas the female has no such *tutor*.

§ 158. The rights of agnation are extinguished by a *capitis diminutio ;* those of cognation are not affected by it, for, as civil rights are creatures of civil law, one civil law may nullify another, but no civil law can abrogate a natural law.

XXII. *De Capitis Diminutione.*

§ 159. *Capitis diminutio* is the deterioration of the original *caput* (status). It occurs in three ways, styled respectively *maxima, minor* (sometimes called *media*), and *minima.*

§ 160. *Capitis diminutio maxima* occurs when the individual loses at the same time citizenship and liberty, *e. g.*, when one is exiled. In the same way a free woman, by virtue of a S. C. of Claudius, becomes the slave of the master of a slave with whom she cohabits in opposition to the master's will and prohibition.

§ 161. *Capitis diminutio minor* occurs where citizenship, but not liberty, is lost. This happens where an individual is interdicted fire and water.

§ 162. *Capitis diminutio minima* occurs when, though citizenship and liberty are preserved, the status is changed, *e. g.*, where a person is adopted; so in the case of *coemptio*, and those who are given *in mancipio* and afterwards enfranchised. Each time that one is mancipated or remancipated he suffers a *capitis diminutio.*

§ 163. The right of agnation is destroyed by either *capitis diminutio.* If, therefore, the father of two children emancipates one, neither, after the death of the father, can be *tutor* of the other by the right of *agnatio.*

§ 164. When the tutorship devolves on the *agnati*, the nearest agnate takes it. . . .

XXIII. *De Legitimâ Patronorum Tutelâ.*

§ 165. By the Twelve Tables, the tutorship of the enfranchised of either sex belongs to the patron and his children. This tutorship is also styled *legitima*, but not because the Twelve Tables contain any express provision as to it. The rule is one of implication, not one of express enactment; for as the Twelve Tables enact that the inheritance of the enfranchised of either sex who dies intestate belongs to the patron and his children, the ancients considered that the intention of the law was that the tutorship should belong to them also, inasmuch as it enacted that when the inheritance devolved on the *agnati*, the tutorship did so also.

XXIV. *De Fiduciariâ Tutelâ.*

§ 166. The tutorship of the patron being thus established, *fiduciariæ tutelæ* subsequently followed. They are appropriately so styled, because we have in their case manumitted a free person who has been mancipated to us either by a parent or by a *coemptionator.*

§ 167. The tutorship of Latin minors of either sex does not necessarily belong to the manumitter. It belongs to him to whom the manumitted belonged by Quiritarian law before manumission. Consequently, if a female slave is yours by Quiritarian law, but is mine *in bonis*, and by me alone is manumitted—*i. e.*, not by you also—she can become a Latin, in which case her property belongs to me, but her tutorship devolves on you by the *lex Junia.* If she was made a Latin by one to whom she belonged both *in bonis* and *ex jure Quiritium*, both her property and her tutorship would devolve on him.

XXV. *De Cessiciâ Tutelâ.*

§ 168. It is lawful for *agnati* who are *legitimi tutores* and also for manumitters, formally—by *cessio in jure*—to transfer the tutorship of females, but not that of males, because, in the case of males, the tutorship is not considered onerous, inasmuch as it ceases when the pupil comes of age.

§ 169. The person to whom a tutorship is transferred is styled *cessicius tutor*.

§ 170. Upon the death or *capitis diminutio* of the transferee, the tutorship reverts to the transferor. Should he have died or suffered a *capitis diminutio*, the tutorship passes to the person next in succession to the transferor (the original tutor).

§ 171. As the *lex Claudia* abolished the tutorship of the *agnati* in the case of females, the question of "*cessicia tutela*" has ceased to be of importance.

§ 172. Some jurists have been of opinion that *tutores fiduciarii* cannot delegate their duty, inasmuch as the office has been voluntarily undertaken by them. In adopting this opinion we must not confound *tutores fiduciarii* with an ascendant who has mancipated a daughter, a granddaughter, or a great-granddaughter to another on the condition that she should be remancipated to him, and who has manumitted her after the remancipation, for such are also *tutores legitimi*, and as such are no less worthy of respect than patrons.

XXVI. *De petendo alio Tutore.*

§ 173. Besides, by a S. C., females are authorized when their tutor is absent to demand that he shall be replaced by another.

After demand granted, the first ceases to be tutor. The distance at which the original tutor may be (how long he may have been absent?) is of little moment.

§ 174. A freed woman, however, has no right to the substitution of a *tutor* in place of an absent patron.

§ 175. The ascendant who, by mancipation, remancipation, and manumission of his daughter, granddaughter, or great-granddaughter, obtains over her the *tutela legitima*, is regarded for this purpose in the same light as a patron. In fact the children of such ascendants are reckoned among the *tutores fiduciarii*, whereas the children of a patron have the same tutelage as their father had.

§ 176. There are, however, purposes for which a female can demand a *tutor* even to replace an absent patron, *e.g.*, to authorize the acceptance of an inheritance.

§ 177. The senate adopted the same rule where the son of the patron was a minor.

§ 178. In like manner the *lex Julia de maritandis ordinibus* permits a female, who is under the *tutela legitima* of a pupil, to demand a *tutor* from the *prætor urbanus* for the purpose of arranging her marriage settlement.

§ 179. The son of the patron, though a minor, becomes the *tutor* of a freed woman, though he cannot authorize any act, inasmuch as he cannot himself act without the authorization of his *tutor*.

§ 180. So if a female is in *tutela legitima* of an insane or dumb person she can by the terms of the *senatusconsultum* demand a tutor for the purpose of arranging her marriage settlement.

§ 181. In all these cases it is evident that the tutorship is vested in the patron and his son.

§ 182. It has been decided by the senate that where a *tutor* is dismissed from the tutorship on the ground of unworthiness, or is excused for sufficient reason, another *tutor* must be appointed, and upon his nomination the functions of the former cease.

§ 183. These provisions hold equally in Rome and in the provinces. . . .

§ 184. Formerly, when the *legis actiones* were in force, a *tutor* was granted whenever there was a *legis actio* between the *tutor* and a female or ward; for, as the *tutor* could not be *auctor* in his own matter, another was appointed, with whose authorization the *legis actio* was prosecuted: that *tutor* was styled *prætorius tutor*, because he was appointed by the *prætor urbanus*. Since the abolition of the *legis actiones*, some think that this species of *tutor* is unnecessary: however, it is still resorted to in the case of legal as distinguished from prætorian actions.

XXVII. *De Atiliano Tutore et eo qui ex lege Juliâ et Titiâ datur.*

§ 185. If any one is absolutely without a *tutor*, one is given to him at Rome, in virtue of the *lex Atilia*, by the *prætor urbanus* and the major part of the plebeian tribunes. Such tutor is styled "*Atilianus tutor*"; in the provinces the tutor is appointed by the governors under the *lex Julia et Titia.*

§ 186. Consequently, if by testament a *tutor* has been appointed upon a specified condition, or from a given date, till the condition has been fulfilled, or the time has arrived, a *tutor* may be appointed; so, if the testamentary *tutor* has been appointed, without condition, no one, for the time being, being heir, a *tutor* should, by the provisions of this law, be demanded. Such *tutor* ceases to act the moment that a *tutor* comes into existence by virtue of the testament.

§ 187. When the *tutor* has been made captive by the enemy, another *tutor* is appointed conformably to these laws, who ceases to act on the return of the former, who thereby regains his original position *ex jure postliminii.*

§ 188. From what has been said, we see how many different species of *tutores* there are. But should we endeavour to determine the number of classes among which these species are properly distributable, the discussion would be long, for the ancients were greatly divided upon the point. We have treated the question with care, both in the interpretation of the Edict and in the commentaries that we have based on the works of Quintus Mucius. Suffice it here to say that some have held that there are five classes, as Quintus Mucius; others three, as Servius

Sulpicius; others two, as Labeo; and others, again, that there are as many classes as there are species.

XXVIII. *De Mulierum Tutelâ.*

§ 189. The doctrine that minors should be in tutelage is common to all nations, for natural reason teaches us that persons of immature age should be under the direction of another, and there is scarcely any community that does not permit ascendants to appoint by testament a *tutor* to their children who are under age, although the Romans only, as we have said, seem to have their children *in potestate.*

§ 190. But that adult women should be in tutelage does not appear to be based on any solid ground: the reason commonly assigned, viz., that as owing to their weakness of judgment, they are apt to be made the dupes of the unscrupulous, and therefore they should be under the control of others, appears rather specious than sound. The fact is that adult women do manage their own affairs, and it is only in certain cases and as a matter of form that the *tutor* interposes his assent. When the *tutor* declines voluntarily to give the necessary authorization, he is not unfrequently compelled to do so by the prætor.

§ 191. By reason of the doctrine of perpetual tutelage of females, they have no right of action against their *tutores;* but where the *tutores* manage the affairs of their pupils of either sex, they are bound by an *actio tutelæ* to render them an account when they come of age.

§ 192. However, the *legitima tutela* of the patrons and ascendants is not a mere nominal power, inasmuch as the *tutores* cannot be compelled to authorize the woman either to make a testament, to alienate *res mancipi*, or to contract an obligation unless, indeed, there be some weighty reason why she should alienate the *res mancipi*, or contract the particular obligation. These provisions have been imposed in the interest of the patrons and ascendants, in order that, as the inheritance of women dying intestate belongs to them, they should not be deprived of it by a testament, or the value of the inheritance be lessened by the alienation of the most valuable portion of it, or by its being encumbered with debts.

§ 193. Among the *peregrini* women are not in tutelage as they are with us; they are, however, generally subjected to a species of tutelage, *e.g.*, by the law of the Bithynians the contracts of a woman must be authorized by her husband, or an adult son.

XXIX. *Quibus Modis Tutela finiatur.*

§ 194. Women who are *ingenuæ* are freed from tutelage when they have three children; the *libertinæ* when they have four, *i.e.*, if they are in *tutela legitima* of a patron or his children; those who have any other species of tutor, *e.g.*, *Atilianos* or *fiduciarios*, are liberated by the possession of three.

§ 195. There are various ways in which an enfranchised woman may have a tutor of a different kind, *e.g.*, if she has been manumitted by a woman; in which case she must apply for a *tutor* under the *lex Atilia*, or, in the provinces, under the *lex Julia et Titia* . . . . So when she has been manumitted by a man, if she with his authority has made a *coemptio* and afterwards has been remancipated and manumitted, her patron ceases to be her *tutor*, and he by whom she has been manumitted becomes her *tutor* and is styled *fiduciarius:* so if her patron or his son has given himself in adoption, she ought to apply for a *tutor* under the *lex Atilia* or the *lex Titia:* so if her patron dies leaving no male representative she ought to apply for a *tutor* under the same laws.

§ 196. Males are freed from tutelage upon attaining puberty. Sabinus, Cassius, and our other masters are of opinion that a male attains the age of puberty so soon as his body attests that fact, *i.e.*, so soon as he can generate, but that, in the case of the impotent, the age at which males in general can generate must be adopted. The authors of the other school are of opinion that puberty ought to be regulated by age simply, *i.e.*, that those who have completed their fourteenth year should be reputed of age. . . .

XXX. *De Curatoribus.*

§ 197. . . . so soon as he has attained the age when he can attend to his own affairs. We have already indicated that the same rule prevails in other nations.

§ 198. It has been ordained that curators should be given in the provinces for the same cause.

XXXI. *De Satisdatione Tutorum vel Curatorum.*

§ 199. In order that the property of pupils and of those who have curators may not be wasted or diminished by their tutors or curators, the prætor insists on sufficient security being given.

§ 200. This, however, is not always the case, for on the one hand testamentary tutors are not bound to furnish sureties, their trustworthiness and ability having been approved by the testator; so curators who do not become such simply by virtue of the law, but who have been appointed by a consul, a prætor, or a governor of a province, are for the most part exempt from giving security, inasmuch as the magistrate, before appointing, satisfies himself as to their fitness.

SECOND COMMENTARY.

DE REBUS SINGULIS ET DE RERUM UNIVERSITATIBUS.

I. *De Rerum Divisione.*

§ 1. In the preceding commentary we expounded the law of persons: we will now consider things. Things are either in our *patrimonio* or they are not.

§ 2. The primary division of things is into two classes: they are either *divini juris* or *humani juris.*

§ 3. Things *divini juris* are either *res sacræ* or *res religiosæ.*

§ 4. *Res sacræ* are things consecrated to the gods above. *Res religiosæ* are things abandoned (*relictæ*) to the gods below (*diis manibus*).

§ 5. Land never becomes *sacra* without the authority of the Roman people; for it must be expressly consecrated by a *lex* or S. C.

§ 6. Whereas any one may render a particular portion of his own land *religiosus* by interring the dead in it, provided it is his right or duty to bury that person.

§ 7. The majority, however, of our authorities are of opinion that a private individual cannot, by burying in provincial land, make it *religiosus*, inasmuch as such land belongs either to the Roman people or to the emperor, and that private individuals can only have possessory and usufructuary rights in respect of it: however, though this provincial land is not strictly speaking *religiosus*, it is regarded as such, just as land in the provinces which is consecrated, though without the authority of the Roman people, is regarded as *sacra.*

§ 8. Things *sanctæ*, such as city walls and gates, are, in a certain sense, regarded as *divini juris.*

§ 9. Nothing that is *divini juris* is *in bonis;* whereas whatever is *humani juris* is ordinarily *in bonis* of some one, but is not necessarily so, for an inheritance before it vests in the heir is not *in bonis* of any one.

§ 10. Things *humani juris* are either *publicæ* or *privatæ.*

§ 11. Those that are *publicæ* are not *in bonis* of any individual. They are regarded as the property of all (*universitatis*). Things *privatæ* belong to the individual person or persons.

II. *De Rebus Incorporalibus.*

§ 12. Some things are *corporeal*, others *incorporeal.*

§ 13. Things corporeal are such as are capable of being touched, *e.g.*, land, a man, a garment, gold, silver, and the like.

§ 14. Things *incorporeal* are such as are incapable of being appreciated by the sense of touch, such as things having no existence except in contemplation of law (they are creations of the law), *e.g.*, an inheritance, a usufruct, or obligations however contracted. The fact that the inheritance consists of or contains corporeal things is immaterial, for the fruits of an estate in land are also corporeal; so that which is due to us by virtue of an obligation is ordinarily corporeal, *e.g.*, land, a man, money; whereas the right to inherit, or to use and enjoy, or rights created by contract, *e.g.*, to do, or to abstain from doing, are incorporeal. So the rights attached to landed property, whether urban or rural, styled *servitutes*, are likewise incorporeal. . . . So, . . .

III. *Rerum Corporalium Adquisitiones Civiles.*

§ 15. All things are either *mancipi* or *nec mancipi. Res mancipi* are estates in Italian soil, whether rustic, as a field, or urban, as a house; likewise rights over rustic estates, as *via*, *iter*, *actus*, *aquæ ductus;* likewise slaves, and quadrupeds which are tamed by yoke and saddle (*lit.* by neck and back), as oxen, mules, horses, asses. These animals our authorities hold to be *mancipi* the moment they are born; but Nerva and Proculus, and other authors of the opposite school, consider that they are not *mancipi* unless they be broken in, and if, through their excessive fierceness, they cannot be broken in, they are regarded as being *mancipi* on arriving at the age at which animals are usually broken in.

§ 16. Wild beasts, on the other hand, such as bears and lions, are *nec mancipi;* so are those animals which are usually in the category of wild beasts, as elephants and camels, and therefore it is not material that such animals are (sometimes) tamed by yoke and saddle. . . .[1]

§ 17. Nearly all things that are incorporeal are *nec mancipi.* Rural servitudes on Italian soil are *mancipi.*

§ 18. There is a great difference between *res mancipi* and *res nec mancipi.*

§ 19. *Res nec mancipi* may be alienated by simple tradition (delivery), provided they are corporeal and consequently susceptible of being handed over.

§ 20. If, therefore, I hand to you a garment, gold, or silver, whether by way of sale, gift, or for any other cause, the property in it passes to you without any legal formality.

§ 21. It is the same in the case of provincial lands, some of which we call *stipendiaria*, others *tributaria.* The *stipendiaria* lands are those situated in the provinces which are considered the property of the Roman people; the *tributaria* are those in the provinces reputedly belonging to the emperor.

§ 22. *Res mancipi* are such as are alienated by *mancipatio. Mancipatio* produces the same effect as *in jure cessio*, hence the name.

§ 23. We explained the ceremony of *mancipatio* in the previous commentary.

§ 24. *In jure cessio* is effected thus:—The person to whom the thing is ceded, taking hold of it in the presence of a magistrate, *e.g.*, the *prætor*, or in the provinces the president,

[1] This passage is taken verbatim from Dr. Abdy's Gaius. He says, "The first six lines are supplied from Ulpian, xix. 1."

says, "I declare this man to be mine by Quiritarian law," after which the magistrate before whom the ceremony is being performed asks the transferor if he claims it. If he answers in the negative, or does not speak, the magistrate adjudges the thing to the claimant. That ceremony is styled a *legis actio.* It may be performed in the provinces before a governor.

§ 25. However, *mancipatio* is far more frequently resorted to than *in jure cessio,* for that which, in the presence of our friends and with their assistance, can be easily done, it is needless, with greater difficulty, to do it before the prætor or governor.

§ 26. But if a *res mancipi* has been delivered otherwise than by *mancipatio* or *in jure cessio* . . . .

§ 27. It must be remembered that conveyance by *nexum* is peculiar to Italian land (*Italicum solum*); there is no *nexum* of provincial land: it only applies to *res mancipi,* and, as provincial land is *nec mancipi,* there is no *nexum* of such land. . . .

IV. *Rerum Incorporalium Adquisitiones Civiles.*

§ 28. That things incorporeal cannot be physically delivered is manifest.

§ 29. Interests in urban land must be conveyed by *cessio in jure.* Interests in rustic land may also be conveyed by *mancipatio.*

§ 30. The right to a usufruct can only be granted by *cessio in jure.* The owner of land by *cessio in jure* can alienate the *usufruct* of his land, while retaining the bare ownership. The usufructuary may by *cessio in jure* re-transfer the usufructuary right to the owner of the soil, in which case the soil and the right to the fruits of the soil once more become vested in one and the same individual. The usufructuary cannot by *cessio in jure* assign his usufructuary right to any person other than the owner of the soil, for a *cessio in jure* purporting to do so is a nullity.

§ 31. These rules only apply to *Italicum solum,* which must be alienated either by *mancipatio* or *cessio in jure.* In the case of lands in the provinces, neither *mancipatio* nor *cessio in jure* is necessary: indeed, either would be inapplicable, as the lands do not admit of *mancipatio* or *cessio in jure;* but by pacts and stipulations servitudes or easements may be created, *e. g.*, *jus eundi*, *agendi*, *aquam ducendi*, *altius tollendi*, or *non tollendi*.

§ 32. As the usufruct of slaves and other animals may be created, it is not difficult to understand that it may be created in the provinces by *cessio in jure*.

§ 33. When we said that a *usufruct* can only be vested by *cessio in jure*, we spoke advisedly. The same practical result however may be brought about by *mancipatio*, for, when mancipating the soil, the usufruct may be retained, in which case, though the usufruct is not manumitted, it is separated from the bare ownership of the land, and therefore the naked possession may vest in one, while the beneficial ownership is vested in another. . . . .

§ 34. So an *hereditas* can only be conveyed by *cessio in jure*.

§ 35. He to whom an *hereditas* legally belongs *ab intestato*, may, by *cessio in jure*, convey his rights to another, either before or after entering on the inheritance. The difference, however, is this:—If, by *cessio in jure*, he conveys the right of inheritance to another before entering upon the inheritance, his rights and obligations in respect of the inheritance pass to his alienee; whereas, if by *cessio in jure* he conveys the inheritance to another after he has once entered on it, he remains liable to the creditors, whereas the debtors are not liable to him, and, not being liable to his alienee, their debts are extinguished, and they thereby benefited. Those portions of the inheritance which consist of things corporeal pass, however, to the alienee, as if each had been separately conveyed to him by *cessio in jure*.

§ 36. If a testamentary heir by *cessio in jure* purports to convey the inheritance to another before he has entered upon it, his act is null and void; but if, after having entered upon it, he conveys it by *cessio in jure* to another, the same consequence follows as in the previous case, where the heir *ab intestato* makes a *cessio in jure* after having accepted the obligation.

§ 37. Writers of the other school (Proculians) hold that the same applies in the case of *heredes necessarii*, because to them it appears immaterial whether one becomes heir involuntarily or voluntarily by entering on the inheritance. The meaning of this will appear hereafter. Our masters, however (*i, e.*, the

Sabinians) are of opinion that *cessio in jure* of the inheritance by a *heres necessarius* is a void act.

§ 38. Obligations, however contracted, are inalienable by either of these methods, for if I desire to transfer to you a debt due from X. to me, I cannot effect the transfer by either of the methods by which I might transfer *res corporales*. To effect the transfer, you, by my order, must stipulate with X., by which act he becomes released as to me, and bound to you. That is what is termed *novatio obligationis*.

§ 39. In the absence of this *novatio*, you cannot proceed against X. in your own name, but must sue in my name as being my *cognitor* or *procurator*.

V. *De Usucapionibus.*

§ 40. We must here observe that the *peregrini* have but one species of ownership. A person is either the absolute owner or he is not regarded as being an owner at all. Formerly, it was the same with the Romans, for a Roman either had Quiritarian dominion over a given thing, or he had no dominion over it. When, however, *dominium* was divided into two classes, one person might be the owner *ex jure Quiritium* of a thing, and another have it *in bonis*.

§ 41. For if I simply deliver to you a *res mancipi*, and do not convey it to you either by *mancipatio* or *cessio in jure*, though it becomes as to you *in bonis*, I retain the Quiritarian ownership until by effluxion of time you acquire Quiritarian *dominium* by *usucapio*, when both rights become consolidated and vested in you.

§ 42. *Quiritarian* ownership by *usucapio* is acquired, in the case of movables, by possession for one year; in the case of immovable property, land or houses, by possession for two years. Such is a provision of the Twelve Tables.

§ 43. It is also to be observed that we may, by *usucapio*, acquire a thing that has been delivered to us by one who was not the owner, and that whether it is *res mancipi* or *res nec mancipi*, provided always that we received it in good faith from the person, believing him to be the owner.

§ 44. This principle was established to avoid uncertainty as to the ownership of property, the space of one year or of two years, as the case may be, in which property may be acquired by *usucapio* being deemed sufficient for the owner to discover and recover his property.

§ 45. There are cases, however, in which the property of another cannot be acquired by *usucapio*, even where there is the greatest good faith on the part of the possessor, *e.g.*, in the case of stolen property or things acquired by violence, for the Twelve Tables enact that property in stolen goods cannot be acquired by *usucapio*, and the *lex Julia et Plautia* contains a similar provision as to things obtained by violence.

§ 46. Provincial land is also incapable of acquisition by *usucapio*.

§ 47. So, formerly, the *res mancipi* of a woman who was in the tutelage of her agnates could not be acquired by *usucapio*, unless indeed they had been delivered to the possessor by her and with the sanction of her *tutor*. This, also, was a provision of the Twelve Tables.

§ 48. That freemen, *res sacræ* and *res religiosæ*, cannot be acquired by *usucapio* is manifest.

§ 49. When it is said that stolen goods and things obtained by violence cannot be acquired by *usucapio*, it is not intended that the thief or the perpetrator of the violence cannot himself acquire by *usucapio*, for it is evident that neither could, inasmuch as each has possessed himself of the property *malâ fide*. What is meant is that no one else, even the *bonâ fide* purchaser of such property, can acquire it by *usucapio*.

§ 50. Hence, as to things movable, acquisition by *usucapio* on the part of a *bonâ fide* possessor is not easy, since he who has sold and delivered the property of another has thereby committed a theft: so if the property sold has been delivered to the vendor by its owner for another purpose. However, this is not always the case, for should an heir sell or give an article lent, let to, or deposited with the deceased, believing it to be the property of the deceased and therefore to be a portion of the inheritance, he would not commit a theft, because there can be no theft where there is no intention to steal. Therefore the same may be said of one who, having the usufruct of a female slave, sells or gives her offspring, believing them to be his property. Other instances may present themselves, in which, owing to the absence of fraudulent intent on the part of the transferor, the transferee may by *usucapio* acquire the property in an article transferred to him by some person other than the owner.

§ 51. The land of another may also be acquired without violence; *e.g.*, if the owner negligently vacates it, or dies without a successor, or for a long time is absent from it, though a squatter, by reason of his knowledge that the land is not his own, cannot by *usucapio* acquire a title to it, yet a *bonâ fide* purchaser from him of the land may acquire a valid title to it by *usucapio.* The doctrine of those who were of opinion that land might be the subject of theft has been exploded.

§ 52. Again, there is the converse case, viz., that a person by *usucapio* may acquire the property of another, knowing the fact; *e.g.*, the possessor of an article forming part of an inheritance, upon which inheritance the heir has not entered, may acquire it by *usucapio*, provided always that the article is one to which title can be acquired by *usucapio.* This species of possession and *usucapio* is styled *pro herede.*

§ 53. Title by *usucapio* in such case has been so greatly favoured, that even in the case of things pertaining to the land possession for one year is held sufficient.

§ 54. The reason why occupation of land for one year only should, in this case, give title by *usucapio* is this:—Formerly it was held that possession for one year of the property appertaining to an inheritance constituted possession of the inheritance. Now as the law of the Twelve Tables enacts that land can only be acquired by *usucapio* in two years, whereas all "other things" capable of being acquired by *usucapio* may be acquired in that manner by possession of one year, an inheritance was held to be one of the "other things," inasmuch as it is not land, for indeed it is not even corporeal; and though it was subsequently thought that an inheritance could not be *acquired* by *usucapio*, yet it was held that all the components of the inheritance, *i.e.*, the property belonging to the inheritance, including the land, might by possession for one year be acquired by *usucapio.*

§ 55. The reason why this very questionable rule was adopted was two-fold. The ancients, above all things, desired that the heir should enter upon the inheritance at the earliest possible moment; first, that the necessary religious rites, which in those times were strictly observed, might be duly performed; and secondly, that the creditors might know to whom to address themselves.

§ 56. This species of possession and *usucapio* was styled *lucrativa*, because knowingly one profited by taking possession of the property of another.

§ 57. *Lucrativa* no longer exists; for, by a S. C. passed at the instance of Hadrian, it is enacted that such *usucapiones* are revocable, and that the heir may, when he has entered on the inheritance, sue for and recover any portion of the inheritance from one to whom it would otherwise belong by *usucapio.*

§ 58. However, in the case of *heredes necessarii*, who become such by operation of law merely, *usucapio pro herede* is possible.

§ 59. There are other circumstances under which one may, by *usucapio*, knowingly acquire the property of another; *e.g.*, he who has alienated anything *fiduciæ causâ*, whether by *mancipatio* or *in jure cessio*, may, should the thing return into his possession, acquire title to it by *usucapio* in the space of one year, even should the thing savour of the realty. This species of *usucapio* is styled *usureceptio*, inasmuch as the thing which was formerly his has been re-acquired by him by *usucapio.*

§ 60. The fiduciary alienee is usually either a creditor who has the right of pawnee, or a friend to whom property has been handed as depositee, for the purpose of securing it in his custody. If it is with a friend, *usus receptio* is in all cases allowable. If, however, it is with a creditor, payment is a condition precedent to the right of *usucaptio lucrativa* arising. Before payment *usucaptio lucrativa* is only allowed when the possession was acquired otherwise than by hire, or *precarium* (loan at will).

§ 61. So the owner of a thing pledged to the *populus*, which has been sold by the *populus* for non-payment of the debt, the owner being allowed to retain the possession, may acquire title to it by *usureceptio:* in this instance, however, land (*prædium*) can only be so acquired by possession for two years. This species of acquisition of land is commonly styled *ex prædiaturâ possessionem usu recipi*, because one who buys from the *populus* is termed a *prædiator*.

VI. *Quibus alienare liceat vel non.*

§ 62. It sometimes happens that one who is the owner (*dominus*) of property has not the faculty to alienate it, or that he who is not the owner of property has the faculty to alienate.

§ 63. The *lex Julia* forbids a husband to alienate, without the consent of his wife, his wife's realty, whether acquired by him by *mancipatio, dotis causa, in jure cessio*, or *usucapio*. Whether this restriction is limited to Italian land (*Italica prædia*), or extends to provincial land, is matter of doubt.

§ 64. On the other hand, the *agnatus curator* of a madman (*furiosus*) may by the Twelve Tables alienate his property: so a *procurator*, . . . so also a creditor with whom a pledge has been deposited may, by agreement, alienate the pledge though it is not his property. In this latter case, however, it is possible that the right to sell the pledge has, properly speaking, been conferred by the debtor, the contract between them being that, on default of payment, the creditor should be at liberty to dispose of the pledge.

VII. *Adquisitiones Dominii Naturales.*

§ 65. From what we have said it appears that certain things are alienable by the *jus naturale, i. e.*, those that are alienable by mere delivery; while others are only alienable by compliance with the provisions of the civil law, *i. e.*, the law peculiar to the Romans, *e. g.*, by *mancipatio, in jure cessio*, and *usucapio*.

§ 66. We may acquire, however, by natural modes other than mere delivery (*traditio*), for by the law of nature we acquire by the mere fact of possession (*occupando*) . . . . of that which did not belong to any other, *e. g.*, all things that we capture, whether on land, in the sea, or in the air (*cœlo*).

§ 67. Thus when a wild beast, or bird, or fish is captured . . . . it is understood to belong to the captor, so long as it remains in his custody. When, however, it makes its escape and recovers its natural liberty, it becomes the property of its next captor, inasmuch as by its escape it has ceased to be the property of its first captor. It is said to have recovered its natural liberty, when it has either escaped out of our sight, or being still in sight its recapture has become difficult.

§ 68. As to those animals which are in the habit of going away and returning, *e. g.*, pigeons and bees, as also deer, which, though they wander into the woods, yet return, our traditionary rule is that so soon as they cease to have the *animus revertendi*, they cease to be ours, and become the property of the first captor. The *animus revertendi* is held to be non-existent when the creatures have lost the habit of returning.

§ 69. Those things also that are captured by us from the enemy are ours by the law of nature (*naturali ratione*).

§ 70. So alluvial deposits are ours by the same law. By *alluvio* is intended that which the stream adds to our land so slowly that we are unable to appreciate each addition, the process being perpetual though imperceptible. Hence it is commonly said that by *alluvio* we see that something is added without being able to see it being added.

§ 71. If, however, the stream detaches a portion of your land and annexes it to mine, it still remains yours.

§ 72. Should an island arise in the middle of a stream, it becomes the common property of the riparian owners on either side. Should it not be in the middle, it becomes the common property of the riparian owners to whom it is nearest.

§ 73. So whatever is erected on my land, though erected in the name and for the use of the builder, belongs to me by the law of nature (*jure naturali*), because whatever is attached to the land belongs to the owner of the land (*quia superficies solo cedit*).

§ 74. *A fortiori* is this so in the case of trees planted by another in our land, so soon as they have taken root.

§ 75. The same may be said of corn sown in our land by another.

§ 76. But should we claim the fruit or the building, and refuse to pay the cost of construction, planting, or sowing, as the case may be, the builder, planter, or sower may resist the claim by an *exceptio doli*, provided always he was *bonæ fidei* possessor.

§ 77. For the same reason it has been decided that if any one writes on my paper or parchment, even in letters of gold, the letters become mine, inasmuch as they cede to the paper or parchment. If, therefore, I claim the paper or parchment, and refuse to defray the cost of writing, the writer may avail himself of the *exceptio doli mali*.

§ 78. But if any one has painted on my tablet, for example, a likeness, the contrary has been held, for it is said that in that case the tablet cedes to the picture. It is not easy to explain the rationale of this distinction. However, such is the rule; if, therefore, the picture being yours, and the tablet mine and in my possession, you claim the picture and refuse to pay for the tablet, I can defeat your claim by an *exceptio doli mali*. But if, on the other hand, the tablet with the picture on it is in your custody, I am entitled to a *utilis actio* against you, in which case, unless I pay the price of the picture, you may defeat me by an *exceptio doli mali*, always assuming that you are a *bonâ fide* possessor. It is clear that if either you or any one else stole the tablet from me, I could maintain an *actio furti*.

§ 79. There are other instances in which recourse is had to natural reason. Thus, if from or with my grapes, olives, or corn, you have made wine, oil, or flour, the question is:—To whom does the wine, the oil, or the flour belong?—you or me? So if you have made a vase out of my gold or silver, or a ship, chest, or seat out of my timber, or if you have made a garment out of my wool, or mead with my wine and honey, or a plaster or eye-salve with my drugs, to whom does either belong? Is that which you have made, the material being mine, yours or mine? Some are of opinion that the material and the substance should be looked to, *i.e.*, that the thing fabricated belongs to the owner of the material. This view is favoured by Sabinus and Cassius. Others contend that the thing fabricated is the property of the fabricator. This is the view generally adopted by the opposite school, but even they admit that an *actio furti* would lie at the suit of the owner of the material against a thief of the fabricated article. They also admit that though he could not maintain *vindicatio*, the original material being extinct in form, if not otherwise, yet that he might maintain *condictio* against the thief and certain other possessors.

VIII. *De Pupillis, an aliquid a se alienare possunt.*

§ 80. We must observe that no female or pupil can alienate *res mancipi* without the authority of the *tutor*. Things *nec mancipi* may be alienated by a female, but cannot be by a pupil.

§ 81. Consequently, if a woman, without the authority of her *tutor*, lends money which is *res nec mancipi* to another, she conveys the property in the money to the borrower, and he contracts a legal obligation to repay it.

§ 82. A pupil cannot by tradition pass the property in money to the recipient. No obligation is created by the transfer. The pupil is, therefore, at liberty to bring *vindicatio* for the recovery of the actual coins wherever they may be. . . .

§ 83. Females and pupils may, however, receive *res* whether *mancipi* or *nec mancipi* without the authority of the *tutor*, for the authorization of the *tutor* is unnecessary for acts that improve the condition of the female or pupil.

§ 84. So if the debtor of a pupil pays the debt to the pupil, though he transfers the property in the money to the pupil, he does not discharge his own liability, because no obligation to the pupil can be dissolved without the sanction of the *tutor*, for nothing belonging to him can be alienated without the authority of the *tutor*. However, having received the money and benefited thereby, should he demand its repayment, he would be met with an *exceptio doli mali*.

§ 85. A female may accept payment of a debt due to her without the sanction of her *tutor*, and by so doing discharge her debtor from all obligation, inasmuch as the money is *res nec mancipi* as already stated. In order, however, to discharge her debtor, she must be actually paid the money; she cannot forego the debt or liberate her debtor by *acceptilatio*, except with the authority of her *tutor*.

IX. *Per quas Personas nobis adquiratur.*

§ 86. Acquisition of property may be made by us personally or by the agency of those who are in our *potestas*, *manus*, or *mancipium*, as also by slaves of whom we have the usufruct, or by freemen, and the slaves of others, of whom we have the *bonâ fide* possession: we will deal with each of these separately.

§ 87. First, then, as to freemen whom we have *in potestate* and our slaves:—That which either of these receives by *mancipatio* or *traditio*, or by *stipulatio*, or by any method whatsoever, is ours. He who is in our *potestas* cannot have anything of his own. That being so, if he is instituted heir otherwise than by our command, he cannot enter upon the inheritance; and when he enters upon an inheritance in obedience to our command, he acquires simply as our agent, the result being the same as if we personally had been instituted heir. Hence a legacy given to him is acquired by us.

§ 88. We must not forget that if a slave is *in bonis* of one, whereas he belongs to another *ex jure Quiritium*, all acquisitions made by him belong to the person who has him *in bonis*.

§ 89. It is not *proprietas* alone that we acquire through those whom we have *in potestate*, for through them we also acquire *possessio*, for whatever is in their possession is considered as being in ours, and consequently through them we may acquire Quiritarian title to property by *usucapio*.

§ 90. Concerning those whom we have *in manu* or *in mancipio*, it may be said, that we can, through them, acquire the *proprietas* in the same way as through those whom we have *in potestate;* but whether we can acquire *possessio* through them is doubtful, inasmuch as they themselves are not in our *possessio*.

§ 91. Concerning those slaves of whom we have merely the usufruct, it has been decided that the fruits of their labour, or of our own property in their charge, is ours, whereas anything of which they may become otherwise possessed belongs to their owners; hence, if such a slave is instituted heir, or if a legacy be left him, the succession or legacy belongs to his owner.

§ 92. Again, concerning those who are *bonâ fide* in our possession, whether they be freemen or the slaves of another, the same may be said as has been said concerning the usufructuary.

Anything acquired independently of us, or ours, belongs in the one case, *i.e.*, when the man is free, to the man himself,—and in the other, to his master.

§ 93. But if the *bonâ fide* possessor of a slave has, by *usucapio*, acquired Quiritarian ownership of him, he may through him acquire in any way. A *usufructuarius* cannot acquire by *usucapio*, first, because he does not in fact possess, but merely has the right to use and enjoy; secondly, because he knows that the slave is not his, but belongs to another.

§ 94. It is a matter of question whether we can possess and thus acquire by *usucapio* through a slave of whom we have merely the usufruct, inasmuch as we do not possess him. There is no doubt as to our being able to possess and thus acquire by *usucapio* through a slave who is *bonâ fide* in our possession. In both cases, we bear in mind the distinction we have already made, viz., between property acquired as the fruit of our own property, or the result of the slave's labour which belongs to us, and that acquired from any other source which does not.

§ 95. It appears that it is impossible for us to acquire anything either through freemen who are neither subject to us nor *bonâ fide* in our possession, or through the slave of another of whom we have neither the usufruct nor the legal possession; hence the maxim, "No one can acquire anything but possession through a stranger. . . ."

§ 96. In conclusion, it is to be observed that nothing can be conveyed by *cessio in jure* to any one who is *in potestate*, *in manu*, or *in mancipio*, inasmuch as such persons cannot acquire to their own use, a necessary consequence being that they cannot recover anything by *vindicatio*.

X. *Quibus Modis per Universitatem res adquirantur.*

§ 97. What we have said as to the acquisition of individual things in general is sufficient for the moment. The discussion of legacies will be deferred to a more convenient place. We will now consider the methods by which we may acquire *per universitatem*.

§ 98. When we become the heir of any one, or obtain possession of the goods of a deceased by *petitio hereditatis*, or purchase the estate of an insolvent, or adrogate a person, or take a woman *in manu* as wife, the entire property of the individual becomes ours.

§ 99. First, then, of inheritance, of which there are two kinds, viz., *ex testamento* and *ab intestato.*

§ 100. Concerning, then, inheritance *ex testamento.*

XI. *De Testamentis ordinandis.*

§ 101. There were originally two kinds of testaments, viz., those made in the *comitia* convoked for that purpose, which were styled *calatis comitiis*—the *comitia* used to be convoked twice each year for the purpose of making testaments—and secondly, testaments made when an army was going into action, styled *in procinctu.* The word *procinctus* signifies an army under arms and ready for battle. The former, therefore, were made during peace and repose, the latter on the eve of battle.

§ 102. Subsequently, a third species of testament was introduced, styled *per æs et libram, i. e.*, when one had not made a testament either *calatis comitiis* or *in procinctu*, but, apprehending sudden death, gave his *familia, i. e.*, his patrimony, *in mancipio* to a friend, praying him after his decease to distribute it in the manner indicated by him: that species of testament was styled *per æs et libram*, because it was effected by *mancipatio.*

§ 103. The two former methods have fallen into disuse; the last, *i. e.*, *per æs et libram*, is that now in use. There is, however, some difference between the old and the present practice *per æs et libram.* Formerly, the person styled the *familiæ emptor*, *i. e.*, he to whom the testator manumitted, took the place of heir, and received from the testator his instructions as to the disposition of his estate; now one person is appointed the testamentary heir, whose business it is to distribute the legacies, and another is made *familiæ emptor*, simply for the sake of form in imitation of the earlier practice.

§ 104. The ceremony is as follows:—The testator, as any other manumitter, secures the attendance of five witnesses—adult Roman citizens—and a *libripens.* He then, having already written his testament on tablets, mancipates his patrimony for the sake of form to one, the *familiæ emptor*, who says, "That you may make a testament valid by the public law, I declare to be in my mandate, tutelage, and custody, your entire patrimony and fortune with this brass," and some add, "and with these scales." "I buy them." Then, striking the scales with the brass, he hands it to the testator as the purchase-money. The testator then, taking the tablets on which his testament is written, says, "As it is written on these tablets and in this wax, so do I give, bequeath, and testify, and so do you *Quirites* bear me witness." This is what is styled *nuncupatio*, the meaning of *nuncupare* being to proclaim aloud, the testator by these general words being considered as having published the provisions of his testament.

§ 105. No one can be a witness who is in the *potestas* of either the *familiæ emptor* or the testator, for, as in imitation of the old law, the transaction takes place between the testator and the *familiæ emptor*, who, as we have said, acquires the status of heir when he receives the estate of the testator *in mancipio*, the evidence of any member of the family (*domesticum testimonium*) is inadmissible, it not being disinterested testimony.

§ 106. Consequently, if any one who is in his father's *potestas* is selected as the *familiæ emptor*, his father cannot be a witness; nor can any one who is in the same *potestas*, *e. g.*, his brother. When a *filiusfamilias* makes a testament disposing of his *castrense peculium*, after having obtained his discharge from service, he cannot rightly have either his father, or any one in the *potestas* of his father, as a witness.

§ 107. What we have said concerning the witness applies equally to the *libripens*, for he is also a witness.

§ 108. He, however, who is in the *potestas* of the heir or of a legatee, or the person in whose *potestas* the heir or legatee is, or he who is in the same *potestas* as either of them, may be the *libripens*, or other witness, inasmuch as the heir himself or a legatee may be. It is, however, advisable that the heir, or one in his *potestas*, or he in whose *potestas* the heir is, should not exercise this right when it can be avoided.

XII. *De Testamentis Militum.*

§ 109. Owing to the great inexperience of the military in

testamentary matters, they have been exempted from the ordinary formalities by several imperial constitutions. Their testaments have been held valid where there has not been the requisite number of witnesses, where there has not been a sale of the patrimony, and where nuncupation has been omitted.

§ 110. Furthermore, they are permitted to make *peregrini* or *Latini* their heirs or legatees, whereas otherwise the *peregrini*, by a rule of the civil law, are incapable of inheriting or receiving a legacy, as are the *Latini* by the *lex Junia.*

§ 111. In like manner *cœlibes*, who by the *lex Julia* are deprived of the right of accepting an inheritance or a legacy, and the *orbi*, *i. e.*, those who have no children, whom the *lex Papia* prohibits from taking more than the half . . . .

XIII. *Testamenti Factio.*

§ 112. But the senate, at the instance of the late Emperor Hadrian, as we stated above, also allowed women to make a testament, even though they had not entered into a *coemptio*, provided only they were above twelve years of age, and made it with the authorization of their *tutor;* that is, the senate ruled that women not freed from *tutela* should so make their testaments.

§ 113. It therefore appears that for testamentary purposes females are in a better position than males, for a male under fourteen years of age cannot make a testament, even with the sanction of his *tutor*, whereas a female who is twelve years of age may.

§ 114. When, therefore, the question arises as to whether a particular testament is valid, we first inquire whether the testator had the *testamenti factio;* if he had, then, whether he has conformed to the rules of the civil law, always excepting soldiers, who, as we have said, on account of their great inexperience, are allowed to make their testaments as they wish and as best they can.

XIV. *Bonorum Possessio secundum Tabulas.*

§ 115. In order, however, that a testament may be valid by the civil law, it is not sufficient that there should be the sale of the patrimony, the requisite number of witnesses, and the *nuncupatio* to which we have already alluded.

§ 116. Above all things it is necessary that the heir be instituted in solemn form, for otherwise the sale of the patrimony, the assembling of witnesses, and the *nuncupatio* of the testament are worthless.

§ 117. The following is the solemn form of institution: "*Titius heres esto*" (Let Titius be heir). At the present time the following is also held valid: "*Titium heredem esse jubeo*" (I order that Titius be heir). The following has been disapproved of by the authorities: "*Titium heredem esse volo*" (I wish Titius to be heir). The following have been rejected by the great majority: "*heredem instituo*" (I institute heir) and "*heredem facio*" (I make heir).

§ 118. Furthermore it must be observed that if a female, who is in tutelage, makes a testament, she must do so with the authority of her *tutor*, otherwise by the civil law her act is a nullity.

§ 119. The prætor, however, has promised that when a testament is sealed with the seals of seven witnesses, the *bonorum possessio* shall pass by the terms of the testament, provided always that there is no person to whom the inheritance would legally belong *ab intestato*, *e.g.*, a brother by the same father, a father's brother, or a brother's son. The same rule prevails if for any other cause the testament is invalid, *e.g.*, if the *familia* has not been sold, or the testator has not pronounced the words of nuncupation.

§ 120. Assuming that there is a brother or paternal uncle, we have to inquire whether either is preferred to a testamentary heir. By a rescript of the Emperor Antoninus those who claim the goods of a deceased under a testament which is informal are permitted to avail themselves of the *exceptio doli mali* should *vindicatio* be brought by a person entitled *ab intestato*.

§ 121. There is no doubt that this provision applies to the testaments of males, equally with those of females, that are invalid by reason of want of sale of the *familia* or utterance of the *nuncupative* words; but does it apply also to testaments made by females without the authorization of their *tutors?* Let us see.

§ 122. It is understood that we are not speaking of females who are in the *tutela legitima* of ascendants or patrons, but of those who have some other species of *tutor*, one who is compellable to grant his authorization. It is evident that an ascendant or patron cannot be ousted by a testament made without his authority.

XV. *De Exheredatione Liberorum.*

§ 123. He who has a son in his *potestas* should take care either to nominate him heir or in terms to disinherit him, because if he passes him over in silence his testament is void. Our masters (*i.e.*, the Sabinians) are indeed of opinion that when the son has pre-deceased his father no one can take the inheritance by virtue of such a testament, inasmuch as the testament was inoperative *ab initio.* Those of the other school admit that if the son is living at the date of the death of his father, he succeeds *ab intestato* and excludes the person named as heir in the testament; but they maintain that where the son pre-deceases his father the testamentary heir may take the inheritance, inasmuch as the son does not claim it as against him, they being of opinion that the mere fact of passing over the son does not make the testament void *ab initio.*

§ 124. The fact of passing over any of the other children does not invalidate the testament. Those passed over are in fact regarded as accretions to those named. When *sui heredes* have been appointed, those passed over take equally with them; if strangers have been appointed, they take one-half: *i.e.*, if any one has by name appointed three sons heirs, and has not mentioned his daughter, she takes one-fourth of the inheritance by the right of accretion, that being the portion she would have been entitled to *ab intestato;* but if the testator has appointed as his heirs persons strangers to him, and has passed over a daughter, she by accretion succeeds to one-half of the inheritance. What has been said concerning a daughter applies equally to a grandson, and all other descendants, male or female.

§ 125. But what is the actual position? Although according

to what we have said the heirs nominated in the testament are only deprived of one moiety of the inheritance when a daughter has been passed over, yet as the prætor secures to the descendants the *bonorum possessio* of the deceased, notwithstanding the terms of the testament, the *extranei heredes* (stranger heirs) are in fact excluded from the inheritance.

§ 126. The effect, therefore, of this doctrine of *bonorum possessio* would be to place male and female children on an equality. The Emperor Antoninus, however, not long since, by a rescript decided that females who are *suæ heredes* shall not take more by *bonorum possessio* than they would be entitled to *jure adcrescendi.* The same principle applies to females who have been emancipated, *i.e.*, they are entitled by *bonorum possessio* to the share to which they would have been entitled *jure adcrescendi*, had they been *suæ heredes.*

§ 127. When a son is disinherited by his father, he must be disinherited *nominatim* (by name), for he cannot otherwise be disinherited. One is considered to be disinherited *nominatim* when he is disinherited as follows:—"*Titius filius meus exheres esto*" (let my son Titius be disinherited); or "*Filius meus exheres esto*" (let my son be disinherited), without adding his proper name.

§ 128. Other males or any females may be disinherited either by name or collectively, *e.g.*, thus:—"*Ceteri exheredes sunto*" (let the others be disinherited). These words are commonly added after the institution of heirs: these, however, are only rules of the civil law.

§ 129. For the prætor requires all descendants of the male sex, whether sons, grandsons, or great-grandsons, to be disinherited by name, and females to be disinherited collectively; and if they are not so disinherited, he has promised them the *bonorum possessio*, notwithstanding the testament.

§ 130. Posthumous children must either be instituted heirs, or be disinherited.

§ 131. In one respect the condition of all is the same, viz., when mention of a posthumous child of either sex has been omitted, the testament is valid *ab initio*, but by the agnation (conception, birth, or adoption) of a posthumous child it becomes void. If then the woman who is to give birth to the expected posthumous child miscarries, the heirs named take.

§ 132. Posthumous female children may be disinherited either by name or collectively. If, however, they are disinherited collectively, something should be left them by way of legacy, in order that it may appear that they have not been unintentionally overlooked. It has been decided that to properly disinherit posthumous male children, *e.g.*, a son, grandson, and so on, the following form should be adopted:—"*Quicumque mihi filius genitus fuerit exheres esto*" (whatever son may be born to me let him be disinherited).

§ 133. He who by taking the place of a *suus heres* becomes heir to his ascendants by quasi-agnation, is regarded as a posthumous child: *e.g.*, if I have in my *potestas* a son, and a grandson or granddaughter by him, inasmuch as the son is nearest to me in degree he only has the right of *suus heres*, though the grandson and granddaughter are in the same *potestas;* but if my son dies during my life, or in any other way is released from my *potestas*, the grandson or the granddaughter takes his place, and in this way acquires the right of *suus heres* by quasi-agnation.

§ 134. In order, then, that my testament may not become inoperative in this manner, it is not sufficient that I appoint my son heir or disinherit him by name: I must in like manner institute or disinherit the grandson or granddaughter by him, in order that, should my son pre-decease me, either, taking his place, should not by quasi-agnation vitiate my will. The *lex Junia Velleia* expressly provides that such male children must be disinherited by name, and that such female children may be disinherited either by name or collectively, provided that, if disinherited collectively, some legacy be left them.

§ 135. By the civil law it is not necessary either to institute or to disinherit emancipated children, inasmuch as they are not *sui heredes;* but the prætor requires all children, whether male or female, either to be instituted or disinherited, males of whatever degree by name, females collectively. He has promised to all not so dealt with the *bonorum possessio*, be the provisions of the testament what they may.

§ 136. Adopted children, so long as they remain such, occupy the same position as natural children; but when once emancipated by the adopter, they are no longer regarded as children by the civil law, nor do they come within the provisions of the prætor's edict.

§ 137. The consequence is that an adopted child, so long as the adoption subsists, is, relatively to the natural father, a mere stranger, but when emancipated by the adopter acquires the position he or she would have held had the emancipation been made by the actual father.

XVI. *Quibus Modis Testamenta infirmentur.*

§ 138. If any man, after making a testament, adopts a son, whether one who is *sui juris* by authority of the *populus*, or one who is in the *potestas* of an ascendant by authority of the prætor, his testament is invalidated by this *quasi-agnation* of a *suus heres.*

§ 139. The like result after the making of a will attends the placing of a wife *in manu*, or the marriage of a woman already *in manu*, as she thereby assumes the condition of a daughter and becomes *quasi sua heres.*

§ 140. The fact that the female or the adopted has been instituted heir in the testament is immaterial. It is needless to discuss the question of their being disinherited, for at the time of the making of the testament they were not among the number of the *sui heredes.*

§ 141. As enfranchisement after a first or second mancipation replaces a son in his father's *potestas;* it invalidates his father's previous testament; and it is immaterial whether he was therein instituted heir or disinherited.

§ 142. The rule was formerly the same, in the case of one to whom the *senatusconsultum* applied, respecting marriages with a foreigner or a Latin made in error, supposing the woman to be a Roman citizen. In short, whether the child had been instituted heir by his father or had been disinherited by him, and whether the fact of the error had been established during the life of the father, or after his death, the proof of the fact in either case nullified the testament by *quasi-agnatio.*

§ 143. Now, however, by a recent *senatusconsultum*, passed at the instance of the late Emperor Hadrian, when the error is established during the life of the father, the child invalidates the testament, as before; but if the error is proved after the father's death, the son who has been passed over invalidates the testament, whereas, if he has either been instituted heir or expressly disinherited, he does not; the desire being not to undo that which has been solemnly done when it is too late for it to be done afresh.

§ 144. A prior testament is revoked by the execution of a valid subsequent one. It is immaterial whether the testator has instituted any one heir in the last testament or not; the only question is whether any one could have become heir. If, then, he who has been appointed heir in the last testament, duly executed, has either declined the inheritance, or has died, whether during the life of the testator or after his death, before entering on the inheritance, or has been excluded by *cretio*, or has not complied with the condition upon which he was made heir, or on the ground of celibacy has been excluded by the *lex Julia*, in either case the father has died intestate, for his former testament was revoked by the latter, and the latter is equally inoperative when no one becomes heir by virtue of it.

§ 145. There is yet another way in which a testament properly made and executed may become a nullity, *i.e.*, by a *capitis deminutio* of the testator, which, as we have related in the first commentary, occurs in several ways.

§ 146. But in this case we say that the testament is *irritum*, *i.e.*, it has become inoperative. No doubt those testaments that are invalidated are *irrita*, as are those also that at the first were not duly executed, while, on the other hand, those that were originally made in due form, but have subsequently become *irrita* by "*capitis deminutio*," may none the less be said to be inoperative. But as it is obviously convenient to distinguish particular cases by particular names, we say of some testaments that they were not legally executed (*non jure fieri*); of others, that, though duly executed, they have been invalidated (*rumpi*), or have become *irrita*.

XVII. *Bonorum Possessio secundum Tabulas.*

§ 147. Testaments are not absolutely useless, even when defective *ab initio*, or when, though perfect at their inception, they have become *inrita*, or *rupta;* for if a testament is sealed with the seals of seven witnesses, the heir therein named may demand the *bonorum possessio* according to its tenor, provided that the testator was, at the time of his death, a Roman citizen and *sui juris.* If, however, the testament has become *inritum* by reason of the testator having subsequently lost his citizenship, or even his liberty, or if he gave himself in adoption and died while in the *potestas* of the adopter, the heir named in the testament cannot claim the *bonorum possessio.*

§ 148. Those who acquire the *bonorum possessio* under testaments invalid *ab initio*, or under those which, though valid at inception, have become *rupta* or *inrita*, retain the beneficial possession (*possessionem cum re*), provided they can retain the inheritance. If, however, they are deprived of that, they have merely the naked possession (*possessionem sine re*).

§ 149. For if any one has been instituted heir according to the civil law, either by the original or subsequent testament, or has become entitled *ab intestato*, he may wrest the inheritance from them. But if there is no one who is entitled by the civil law, the person named who has obtained the *bonorum possessio* has the right to retain it as beneficial owner, or to an interdict *Quorum bonorum* against those who hold them for the purpose of acquiring possession; and this is so even when either of those persons exists, in cases where the defect consists in not having manumitted the inheritance, or in not having pronounced the *nuncupationis verba.*

§ 150. Those who, failing all successors *ab intestato*, took possession of a heritage without any title of their own, were formerly unmolested; but by the *lex Julia caducaria*, such property becomes *caduca*, and is ordered to be delivered over to the *populus*, if no one becomes successor to the deceased.

§ 151. . . . .

XVIII. *De Heredum Qualitate et Differentiâ.*

§ 152. Heirs are styled either *necessarii*, or *sui et necessarii*, or *extranei.*

§ 153. The *necessarius heres* is a slave who has been granted his liberty, and at the same time has been instituted heir. He is so called because, at the death of the testator, he becomes, whether he wills it or not, both free and the heir.

§ 154. One who is uncertain as to his solvency commonly institutes his slave free and heir in the first, or second, or even in an inferior degree, in order that, should his estate prove insufficient to pay his creditors in full, his effects may be sold as the estate of his heir, instead of as his own, and his memory be thereby relieved from the ignominy of the sale of his effects. Fufidius says that Sabinus was of opinion that no ignominy should attach to the slave, inasmuch as it is no fault of his, the sale of his effects being brought about by operation of law; but we adhere to the contrary rule.

§ 155. However, by way of compensation, the *heres necessarius* is allowed this advantage, that anything acquired by him after the death of the testator is his own property, whether acquired before or after the sale. Though the sale may only realize sufficient to pay the creditors in part, he is not liable to a second sale on account of the inheritance, unless, indeed, subsequently to the sale, other portions of the inheritance come into his hands, *e.g.*, the estate of a deceased Latin who was a freed man of the testator, by which he has been enriched. It is different with other insolvents; for if the sale of their effects proves insufficient to pay all their creditors in full, their after-acquired property may, from time to time, be sold.

§ 156. *Sui et necessarii heredes* are, for example, the son or the daughter, the grandson or the granddaughter by the son, and the other descendants in succession, provided always that they were in the *potestas* of the deceased at the date of his death. In order that the grandson or granddaughter may be *suus heres*, it is not sufficient for him or her to have been in the *potestas* of the grandfather at the date of his death. It is necessary that the father should, during the life of the grandfather, have ceased to be his *suus heres*, he having been released from his father's *potestas*, whether by death, or one of the other modes, for it is then, and then only, that the grandson, or granddaughter, takes the place of the father.

§ 157. *Sui heredes* are so called because they are the domestic heirs, and, as such, are regarded even during the life of the ancestor in a certain sense as proprietors. Therefore, when one dies intestate, the children rank first in the succession. They are styled *necessarii* because, whether they become such by the testament or *ab intestato*, they are heirs whether they will it or no.

§ 158. However, when the ancestor dies insolvent, the prætor permits them to decline the inheritance, in order that the estate of the deceased may be sold rather than theirs.

§ 159. The same privilege is extended to a wife *in manu*, as she occupies the position of daughter, and to the daughter in law *in manu* of her husband, as she occupies that of a granddaughter.

§ 160. Furthermore, the prætor extends the like privilege to a mancipated son, that is, to one who is *in causâ mancipii*, when made free and at the same time appointed heir; for though, like a slave, he is *heres necessarius*, he is not *suus*.

§ 161. Other heirs, who were not subject to the testator, are styled *extranei heredes*. Thus, even our own children who, having ceased to be in our *potestas*, have been instituted heirs by us, are regarded as *extranei heredes*. For this reason, those who have been instituted heirs by their mother are ranked in the same class, inasmuch as women have not their children in their *potestas*. So also slaves instituted heirs, and at the same time declared free, who, after the making of the testament, have been manumitted by the testator, their master, rank in the same class.

§ 162. *Extranei heredes* have the right to determine whether they will accept the inheritance or not.

§ 163. But if he who has the right to refuse the inheritance, or to decide whether he will or will not accept it, once intermeddles with it, he cannot afterwards retire from it, unless, indeed, he is under twenty-five years of age. If, being under that age, he has imprudently taken upon himself an onerous inheritance, the prætor will relieve him as he does others of the same age who have been deceived. I do not forget that the late Emperor Hadrian relieved one who had taken upon himself an inheritance in ignorance of serious liabilities, which subsequently were revealed, even though he was more than twenty-five years of age.

§ 164. *Extranei heredes* have ordinarily a fixed period, styled *cretio*, within which they must make their election. It is called *cretio* because *cernere* signifies as it were "to look into" and "to determine" (*constituere*).

§ 165. Therefore, after having written, "Let Titius be heir," we ought to add, "and within the first 100 days after knowledge of the appointment and ability to accept it, let him make *cretio* or be disinherited."

§ 166. Any one so instituted must make his *cretio* within the time limited, *i. e.*, if he desires to be heir, in which case he must make the following declaration:—"Inasmuch as Publius Mevius has made me his heir in his testament, I hereby accept the inheritance and make my election to be his heir." One who does not so make his *cretio* within the time limited is excluded. Whether he has or has not meddled with the inheritance is immaterial.

§ 167. He, on the other hand, who has been instituted heir without *cretio*, or who is heir *ab intestato*, may acquire all the rights and become liable to all the duties and obligations of an heir, either by making the declaration necessary in *cretio*, or by assuming the character of heir, or by an informal declaration of willingness to take the inheritance upon himself; in either case he may enter upon the inheritance whenever he thinks fit. At the instance of the creditors, however, the prætor usually fixes a period within which the nominated must take upon himself the inheritance, or in default the creditors be at liberty to sell the estate of the deceased.

§ 168. As he who is instituted heir with *cretio* cannot become heir without making *cretio*, so till the time has elapsed within which he may do so, he cannot be excluded from the inheritance; therefore, should he before the expiration of the time express his determination not to become heir, and subsequently change his mind, he may by *cretio* become heir at any time within the prescribed period.

§ 169. He who has been instituted heir without *cretio* becomes heir by his mere volition. He who has been called to the inheritance by the law, *i.e.*, *ab intestato*, and declines it, is, in like manner, excluded from it by his mere volition.

§ 170. The period of *cretio* has a certain limit. One hundred days is considered a reasonable time. By the civil law it may be made more or less; but if more than 100 days are given, the prætor sometimes abridges the period.

§ 171. Though every *cretio* is limited to a fixed number of days, yet there are two kinds of *cretio*, *i. e.*, *cretio vulgaris* (ordinary *cretio*) and *cretio certorum dierum* (*cretio* of fixed days). *Cretio vulgaris* is that which we have explained, *i.e.*, that in which the words "after knowledge and ability" appear. Those words are omitted in the *cretio certorum dierum*.

§ 172. There is a marked difference between these two kinds of *cretio*. In the case of *cretio vulgaris* time does not run in the absence of knowledge and ability, whereas in *cretio certorum dierum* time runs even against one who does not know that he has been instituted heir, or who, from any other cause, has been prevented from making *cretio*, as also against one instituted heir on condition. It is obvious therefore that *cretio vulgaris* is the preferable form.

§ 173. *Cretio certorum dierum* is styled *continua* on account of time running under all circumstances; but as this form is oppressive, the other is mostly used, hence its name *vulgaris* (common).

XIX. *De Vulgari Substitutione.*

§ 174. Sometimes two or even more degrees of heirs are instituted thus:—"Let Lucius Titius be my heir, and make *cretio* within the first 100 days after knowledge and ability, or in default of his making *cretio* let him be disinherited. Then let Mevius be heir and make *cretio* within 100 days, &c." In this way we may make as many substitutions as we may think fit.

§ 175. One, or several, may be substituted for one, or for several.

§ 176. Thus, then, the first-mentioned heir, by making *cretio*, becomes heir, and the substitute is excluded. By omitting to make *cretio* the nominated heir is dislodged, even though he may have acted as heir, and is superseded by the substitute. So if there are several degrees of substitution, the prior failing, the next in order may make *cretio*.

§ 177. If *cretio* is given, and nothing said about the appointed heir being disinherited should he fail to make *cretio*, *e. g.*, should the appointment run thus—" If he does not make *cretio*, then let Publius Mevius be heir"—the result is this: If the first omits to make *cretio*, yet acts as heir, the substitute is admitted as to part, and the two take the inheritance between them in equal shares; whereas, if the first neither makes *cretio* nor acts as heir, he is excluded, and the substitute takes the entire inheritance.

§ 178. It was long since decided that though the first instituted may have acted as heir without making *cretio*, yet that till the time for making *cretio* expired he did not thereby let in the substitute, but having so acted, if he allowed the time to expire without making *cretio*, he then let in the substitute as co-heir. Previous to that decision it was held that the mere fact of acting as heir before making *cretio* let in the substitute as to part, and the first could not by subsequently making *cretio* exclude the substitute.

XX. *De Pupillari Substitutione.*

§ 179. We can substitute to our infant children in our *potestas* not only in the manner already described, *i.e.*, in the sense that if they do not become our heirs, another may, but in the case where they have in fact become our heirs, but have died before attaining puberty, we may nominate another as heir thus:—" Let Titius, my son, be my heir. If my son shall not become my heir, or should he be my heir but die before attaining puberty, let Seius be heir."

§ 180. In this case, if the son is not the heir, the substitute becomes the heir of the father; but if the son is heir of his father, and dies before attaining puberty, the substitute becomes the heir of the son. In one sense, therefore, in this case there are practically two testaments, the one of the father, the other of the son, as if the son had himself instituted his heir; or at all events, there is one testament that disposes of two inheritances.

§ 181. In order that after the death of the father the pupil may not be subjected to foul play, it is usual to make the ordinary substitution openly, *i.e.*, in the clause where we institute the pupil heir, as the ordinary substitution clause does not call the substituted to the inheritance except in default of the pupil becoming heir, as when he dies during the father's life, in which case no danger is to be apprehended from the substitute, for during the father's life the contents of his testament are unknown. But the substitution by which provision is made for the event of the pupil heir dying before he attains his majority is written separately on other tablets carefully tied together and sealed, and in the first tablet it is expressly forbidden to open them during the life of the son and while he is under age. It is, however, safer to place both substitutions together in the latter tablets and separately by themselves, because, if they are sealed separately as we have described, it is easy from the perusal of the former to conjecture the contents of the latter, and to conclude that the same person is substituted in the second.

§ 182. It is not merely when instituting our children who are under age heirs, that we can appoint substitutes in the event of their death before puberty, for we can also do so when we disinherit them, in which case all that the pupil may have acquired, whether by inheritance, legacy, or donation from relations, goes to the substitute.

§ 183. All that has been said respecting substitution in the case of children under age, whether instituted heirs or disinherited, is equally applicable to the case of posthumous children.

§ 184. When we institute one who is a stranger heir, we cannot provide that, in the event of his becoming heir and dying within a given period, a given person shall be his heir. All that we can do is to bind him by *fideicommissum* to transfer our estate either in whole or in part. In its proper place we will explain the nature of this right.

XXI. *De Heredibus instituendis.*

§ 185. Slaves, whether our own, or the property of another, may equally with freemen be instituted heirs.

§ 186. If, however, the slave belongs to us, he must be declared to be free and heir, thus:—"Let Stichus my slave be free and heir," or "Let him be heir and free."

§ 187. Because if he is instituted heir without at the same time being made free, even should he afterwards be manumitted by his master, he could not become the heir, inasmuch as the institution was bad; consequently, even if he had been alienated, he could not make *cretio* for the inheritance by the order of his master.

§ 188. When, however, he is instituted heir with his liberty, if he remains with the testator he becomes by virtue of the testament free and *necessarius heres;* if he is manumitted by the testator it is competent for him to take the inheritance at his pleasure: if he has been alienated he must take the inheritance if commanded to do so by his new master, in which case his new master becomes the heir by his agency, because having been alienated he cannot himself be either heir or free.

§ 189. So the slave of another instituted heir, if he retains his position, must take the inheritance, if at all, by the order of his master; but if he has been alienated by him, whether during the life of the testator or after his death, he must first make *cretio* by the order of his then master before he can enter on the inheritance; if he has been enfranchised before entering on the inheritance, he is at liberty to accept it or not, as he may think fit.

§ 190. But if the slave of another has been instituted with *cretio vulgaris*, time does not commence to run against him till he is made aware of the fact that he has been instituted heir, and there is nothing to prevent his informing his master of the fact in order that he may be able to make *cretio* by his order.

XXII. *De Legatis.*

§ 191. We will now consider legacies. This branch of the law seems to be foreign to our present discussion, which is an inquiry into the various legal methods by which we acquire *per universitatem*, but having explained testaments, and heirs who are instituted by testament, there is in fact reason for our immediately discussing the subject of legacies.

§ 192. There are four species of legacies, *i.e.*, we grant legacies either by *vindicatio*, by *damnatio*, *sinendi modo*, or by *præceptio*.

§ 193. By *vindicatio* we bequeath thus:—"I give and bequeath say, for example, the man Stichus;" but if one has only employed one of the two verbs, *e.g.*, "I give the man Stichus," or other terms such as "Let him take," "Let him have," "Let him seize," a legacy by *vindicatio* is equally conferred.

§ 194. Such legacies are styled legacies by *vindicatio* because the moment any one has entered on the inheritance, whether as heir or otherwise, the thing becomes the property of the legatee *ex jure Quiritium*, and he has the right of *vindicatio* respecting it, *i.e.*, he has the right to claim the things as his by Quiritarian law.

§ 195. However, the jurists are divided in opinion as to this. Sabinus and Cassius and the rest of our authorities maintain that the legacy vests in the legatee the moment the inheritance has been accepted, though the legatee be ignorant of the fact of the bequest, but that, if after the knowledge of the fact he declines the legacy, it is as if no legacy had been left him. On the other hand, Nerva and Proculus, together with the other authors of that school, contend that the legacy does not vest in the legatee till he has accepted it. Now, however, since a constitution of the late Emperor Antoninus Pius, we in practice follow the rule of Proculus, for in the case of a Latin having been bequeathed by *vindicatio* to a colony, that emperor said, "Let the *decuriones* consider whether they will, or will not, accept the legacy as if the bequest had been made to a private individual."

§ 196. Nothing can be bequeathed legally by *vindicatio* except things of which the testator has Quiritarian ownership. As to things capable of being weighed, or counted, or measured, it has been decided that it is sufficient that the testator should have the Quiritarian ownership at the time of the death, *e.g.*, such things as wine, oil, wheat, cash. As to other things, it has been decided that the testator must have Quiritarian *dominium* over them at two periods, *i.e.*, at the time of the making of the testament and at the date of death, otherwise the legacy is void.

§ 197. Such is doubtless the civil law. However, on the proposition of the Emperor Nero, it was enacted by a *senatusconsultum* that if any one bequeathed anything to another, although it did not belong to him, yet the legacy should be held as valid as if the legacy had been granted in the form most favourable to the legatee, *i.e.*, by *damnatio*, by which, as we shall see hereafter, one may even bequeath the property of another.

§ 198. But if any one bequeaths that which is his own, and after the making of the testament alienates it, the majority are of opinion not merely that the bequest is void by the civil law, but that it is not made operative by the *senatusconsultum*, the reason being, that, had one by *damnatio* bequeathed property of his own which he afterwards alienated, though by the strict letter of the law the legatee would be entitled to it, yet in the opinion of the majority of the jurists, should the legatee demand it, he might successfully be met with the plea of *doli mali* on the ground that he was demanding property of the deceased contrary to the intention of the deceased.

§ 199. In all cases where one by *vindicatio* has granted a legacy to two or more whether jointly or severally, if all the legatees claim, each takes his fractional part; if one, or more, do not claim, the unclaimed portion is divided equally among the claimants as *accretio*. A joint bequest is made in the following form:—"I give and bequeath the man Stichus to Titius and Seius." A several bequest thus:—"I give and bequeath the man Stichus to Lucius Titius; I give and bequeath the same man to Seius."

§ 200. When a thing has been bequeathed by *vindicatio* on condition, the question is:—To whom does the thing belong before the happening or performance of the condition? Our masters, the Sabinians, contend that it belongs to the heir, from analogy to the case of the *statuliber*, *i.e.*, the slave to whom liberty has been granted by the testament on a certain condition, for it is clear that, in that case, till the condition has been satisfied, the slave is the property of the heir. However, the authorities of the other school—the Proculians—are of opinion that during the interval the thing does not belong to any one, and they insist still more strongly that it is so in the case of an unconditional legacy, before the legatee accepts.

§ 201. We bequeath by *damnatio* thus:—"Let my heir be condemned to give Stichus my slave." So if the words are "Let him give" it is equally a legacy by *damnatio*.

§ 202. By this species of legacy it is possible to bequeath the property of another, for the heir is bound either to buy the thing bequeathed and transfer it to the legatee, or to give to the legatee its value.

§ 203. One may also by *damnatio* bequeath that which does not exist, provided it will come into existence, *e.g.*, the fruit that shall grow in a certain field, or the child that shall be born of a certain female slave.

§ 204. A bequest made by *damnatio*, though absolute, does not vest the property in the bequest in the legatee by the heir's acceptance of the inheritance, as it does in the case of *vindicatio*. The property in the subject of the bequest by acceptance of the inheritance vests in the heir. Consequently, the legatee must sue the heir if at all *in personam*, *i. e.*, he must allege that the heir is bound to give him, &c. If the thing is *res mancipi*, the heir must convey it to the legatee by *mancipium*, or by *cessio in jure* and transfer of the possession. If it is *res nec mancipi*, delivery of possession is sufficient. If the heir delivers possession merely of a *res mancipi* it is only by *usucapio* that full proprietary rights in the thing vest in the legatee. As we have already said, title by *usucapio* is acquired by possession for one year in the case of movables, by two years' possession in the case of immovables.

§ 205. There is yet another difference between these two species of legacies—it is this: When the same thing has been bequeathed by *damnatio* to two or more persons, if the bequest is joint, one share is due to each. . . . If it is several the entire thing belongs to each, and the heir is bound to give the thing itself to one and its value to the other. Where the bequest is joint, should one fail to take his portion, that portion does not go to his co-legatee, but remains in the inheritance.

§ 206. When we say that the portion of the one failing to take in the case of a legacy by *damnatio* remains in the inheritance, whereas in the case of a legacy by *vindicatio* it goes to the co-legatee, we must be understood to say that such was the law before the *lex Papia.* Since the *lex Papia* the lapsed share becomes *caduca* and the property of those named in the testament who have children.

§ 207. And although in the *vindicatio* of things *caduca* heirs who have children rank first, and if the legatees have none, then legatees who have, yet the *lex Papia* provides that in a joint bequest the co-legatee who has children shall be preferred to heirs, even though they may have children.

§ 208. The majority are of opinion that this provision of the *lex Papia* in favour of the co-legatee equally applies whether the legacy is by *vindicatio* or *damnatio.*

§ 209. *Sinendi modo* (*Permissive legacies*). We bequeath by way of permission thus:—"Let my heir be compelled to permit Lucius Titius to take and keep as his own the man Stichus."

§ 210. By this method the testator has greater latitude than in *vindicatio*, but less than in *damnatio*, for by this method the testator may make a valid bequest, not merely of his own property, but of that of his heir, whereas by *vindicatio* he can only bequeath his own property, and by *damnatio* he can bequeath the property of any one.

§ 211. If at the time of the death of the testator the thing bequeathed belonged either to the testator or to the heir, the legacy is without doubt valid, even though at the time of the making of the testament it did not belong to either.

§ 212. It is asked:—In the event of the thing not becoming the property of the heir till after the death of the testator, whether the bequest would be valid or not. The majority are of opinion that it would not. What follows? Though a testator may have bequeathed something which was never his and which never becomes the property of his heir, yet by a *senatusconsultum* of Nero, the legacy is regarded as having been made by *damnatio*.

§ 213. We have already seen that a bequest made by *damnatio* does not transfer the property in the subject of the legacy to the legatee, by the entrance of the heir on the inheritance, and that it remains vested in the heir till by *traditio*, *mancipatio*, or *cessio in jure* he has transferred it to the legatee. It is precisely the same in the case of *sinendi modo*. A legacy so made gives to the legatee an action *in personam* by which the legatee claims that the heir shall be adjudged "to give, or do, all that he ought to give, or do, according to the terms of the testament."

§ 214. Some authors are, however, of opinion that in this case the heir is not bound to vest the property in the legatee, whether by *mancipatio*, *cessio in jure*, or *traditio*, but that it suffices if he permits the legatee to take the thing, inasmuch as the testator has only directed him to permit, *i.e.*, to suffer the legatee to take the thing bequeathed as his own.

§ 215. A more serious dispute has arisen in respect of this mode of bequest in the case where one and the same thing has been bequeathed severally to two or more persons. Some are of opinion that each is entitled to the entire thing, as in the case of a legacy by *damnatio;* others contend that the position of the first claimant is the best, because, as the heir in this species of legacy is directed to allow the legatee to take the thing, it follows that if he has allowed the first claimant to take it, he will be safe as against either of the others who may demand it, inasmuch as he has not the thing for them to take, and it is no fault of his that he has not.

§ 216. We bequeath *per præceptionem* thus:—"Let Lucius Titius first take the man Stichus."

§ 217. Our masters (the Sabinians) are of opinion that a bequest cannot be made in this form to any one who has not been instituted heir as to part of the inheritance, for the word *præcipere* signifies to take in advance, which can only apply to one who has been instituted heir as to a portion of the inheritance; and therefore that the intention is that one so situated should be at liberty in the first place to take his legacy, and afterwards his full share of the remaining inheritance.

§ 218. Consequently, if such a legacy be bequeathed to a stranger, the legacy is void. Sabinus, indeed, is of opinion that it could not be rendered valid by the operation of the *senatusconsultum* of Nero, for, said he, that *senatusconsultum* only validates legacies invalid by the civil law by reason of the language used, and not those inoperative by reason of the person of the legatee. Julianus, however, according to Sextus, was of opinion that the bequest was perfected by the *senatusconsultum*, for even in this case, it is by reason, said he, of the language used that the bequest is bad by the civil law; for he argued, "It is clear that the same result might be attained in another way by other language, *e.g.*, by *vindicatio*, by *damnatio*, or *sinendi modo*, whereas, when the bequest is bad by reason of the person, it is because a legacy has been left to one who, by law, cannot take it; *e.g.*, a legacy to a *peregrinus*, with whom a Roman has no *testamenti factio*, in which case it is clear that the *senatusconsultum* could not apply."

§ 219. Our authorities also contend that one to whom such a legacy has been left can only recover it by an *actio familiæ erciscundæ*, which is employed in the case of disputes between heirs as to the division of the inheritance, it being one of the duties of the judge in such an action to adjudge what has been left by *præceptio*.

§ 220. The result of the opinion of our authorities is that the testator by *præceptio* can only bequeath that which actually belongs to him, no other property being the subject of the action. If, therefore, a testator by this form bequeaths anything that is not his, the bequest is void by the civil law, but it will be enforced by the *senatusconsultum*. There is one case, they say, however, in which the property of another may be bequeathed by *præceptio*, *i.e.*, when a thing mancipated to a creditor *fiduciæ causâ* is bequeathed to the creditor, for they hold that the heirs may be compelled by the judge to free the article by paying the money due, in order that the legatee may take it in advance.

§ 221. The authorities of the opposite school are of opinion that property may be bequeathed by *præceptio* even to a stranger, as if the language used was "Let Titius take the man Stichus," the syllable *præ* in the word *præceptio* being regarded by them as superfluous, the consequence being that the thing bequeathed is, in fact, bequeathed as by *vindicatio*. It is said that this opinion has been confirmed by a constitution of the late Emperor Hadrian.

§ 222. Consequently, according to this doctrine, if the article belonged to the deceased *ex jure Quiritium*, the legatee might recover it by *vindicatio*, whether he be an heir or a stranger. If it was only *in bonis* of the testator, the legacy would be valid in the case of its being left to a stranger by virtue of the *senatusconsultum*, and it might be recovered in the case of its being left to the heir by the executive authority of the *judex* in the *actio familiæ erciscundæ;* and if the testator had no title to the article, the legacy would, by the *senatusconsultum*, be equally available to the heir and a stranger.

§ 223. When the same thing is bequeathed jointly, or severally, to two or more legatees, whether according to our authorities they be heirs, or according to our opponents they be even strangers, all take equal shares.

XXIII. *Ad Legem Falcidiam.*

§ 224. At one time it was lawful for the testator to exhaust his entire patrimony in legacies and enfranchisements, leaving to his instituted heir nothing beyond the bare title. Such appears to be the law of the Twelve Tables, which enacts that testamentary dispositions shall be valid; note the text, "*Uti legassit suæ rei, ita jus esto*" (Let the testamentary dispositions of the testator concerning his property be law); consequently, many who were instituted heirs declined the inheritance, the result being that many died intestate.

§ 225. To meet this state of things, the *lex Furia* enacted that no one, certain specified persons excepted, should take either as a legacy or as a *donatio mortis causâ* more than 1,000 *asses*. That law, however, failed to accomplish the object in view, for he who, for example, had a patrimony of 5,000 brass *asses*, might, by bequeathing to five persons 1,000 *asses* each, exhaust the whole of his patrimony.

§ 226. Hence the *lex Voconia*, which forbade any one to take, whether as a legacy or as a *donatio mortis causâ*, more than the heirs. By this, doubtless, the heirs appeared to be secured as to something; however, it created an almost equal disadvantage, for testators, when distributing their estate between a large number of legatees, might leave so little to the heir that it would not be worth his while, for so small an amount, to take upon himself the burden of the entire inheritance.

§ 227. Consequently the *lex Falcidia* was passed, which enacted that it was unlawful for any one to bequeath more than three-fourths in legacies, the consequence being that one-fourth of the inheritance is necessarily secured to the heir. Such is the law at present in force.

§ 228. The *lex Furia Caninia*, as already explained in the first commentary, in like manner limited the power of enfranchising.

XXIV. *De inutiliter relictis Legatis.*

§ 229. A bequest appearing before the institution of the heir is void, inasmuch as testaments derive their force from the institution of the heir: consequently, the institution of the heir is regarded as the head and foundation of the entire testament.

§ 230. For the same reason, liberty cannot be granted before the institution of the heir.

§ 231. Our authorities also hold that a tutor cannot be appointed in that part of a testament. Labeo and Proculus, however, think that one may be, because, say they, in the appointment of a tutor no portion of the inheritance is disposed of.

§ 232. A bequest made to take effect after the death of the heir is also void, *e. g.*, "After the death of my heir, I give and bequeath," or "let him give." A bequest, however, is valid if made thus: "when my heir is dying": because the disposition is not, in that case, to take effect after the death of the heir, but is only postponed to the end of his life. Again, a bequest in the following terms is also void: "the day before my heir shall die." For this rule there does not appear to be any valid reason.

§ 233. What we have said is equally applicable to enfranchisements.

§ 234. Whether the appointment of a tutor can be made to take effect after the death of the heir or not possibly admits of the same divergence of opinion as whether he can be appointed before the institution of the heir.

XXV. *De Pœnæ causâ relictis Legatis.*

§ 235. A bequest by way of penalty is also void. A bequest is considered as made by way of penalty when it is so made as to constrain the heir to do, or to omit to do, *e.g.*, "If my heir gives his daughter in marriage to Titius, let him give ten thousand (sesterces) to Seius," or "If you do not give your daughter in marriage to Titius, give ten thousand (sesterces) to him." So if the testator has directed that if within two years the heir does not, *e.g.*, erect a monument to his memory, then that he shall give 10,000 sesterces to Titius, the bequest is regarded as a penal legacy. In short the definition is in itself sufficient to enable us to suggest numerous cases.

§ 236. A grant of liberty cannot be made by way of penalty: this proposition, however, has been questioned.

§ 237. We cannot raise the same question in the case of a tutor, because the heir cannot be constrained by the appointment of a tutor to do, or to abstain from doing, a given thing; and therefore no tutor is given by way of penalty, and if one were so appointed he would be considered as appointed conditionally rather than by way of penalty.

§ 238. A legacy to an uncertain person is void. One is regarded as uncertain of whom the testator has no certain conception, *e.g.*, should the testator say, "Let my heir give 10,000 (sesterces) to the first comer to my funeral." It is the same if he used general terms, *e.g.*, "to all who shall attend my funeral." We may place in the same category a bequest made thus:—"Let my heir give 10,000 (sesterces) to him who shall give his daughter in marriage to my son:" so, "to those who are the first consuls designate after the execution of my testament," for such a legacy is equally regarded as being bequeathed to uncertain persons. Many other similar instances might be given. However, a valid bequest may be made to an uncertain member of a certain class, *e.g.*, "Let 10,000 (sesterces) be given to him of my now existing cognates who shall first come to my funeral."

§ 239. In like manner liberty cannot be given to an uncertain person, for the *lex Furia Caninia* requires slaves to be enfranchised by name.

§ 240. The appointed tutor must in like manner be a person certain.

§ 241. A bequest to a posthumous stranger is void. A posthumous stranger is one who at his birth would not be a *suus heres* of the testator: thus, the child conceived of an emancipated son is, as to his grandfather, a posthumous stranger; so, the child in the womb of the woman whom the *jus civile* does not recognise as a wife for the want of *connubium* is held to be a posthumous stranger in regard to his father.

§ 242. A posthumous stranger cannot be instituted heir, for he is an uncertain person.

§ 243. As to the other observations that we have made concerning penal dispositions, it may be said that properly speaking they relate solely to legacies. However, certain authors maintain, and not without reason, that an heir cannot be instituted by way of penalty, for it matters little whether the heir is directed to pay a legacy in the event of his doing or not doing a given something, or in that event to have a co-heir tacked on to him, because, alike by the addition of a co-heir and by the giving of a legacy, he is compelled to do or to forbear, be his inclination what it may.

§ 244. Can a valid bequest be made to one who is in the *potestas* of the person whom we institute heir? Servius maintains that the bequest is valid, but that it becomes void if at the time the legacy would otherwise vest the legatee is still in *potestas*; consequently, if the bequest is unconditional, and during the lifetime of the testator the legatee has ceased to be in the *potestas* of the instituted heir, or if it be conditional and he has ceased to be in the *potestas* before the happening of the condition, then in either case the legatee is entitled. Sabinus and Cassius are of opinion that the conditional bequest is good, but that the unconditional one is not; for, say they, though the legatee may cease during the lifetime of the testator to be in the *potestas* of the instituted heir, the bequest ought to be regarded as void, as it would be absurd to hold that that which could have no force should the testator die immediately after the execution of his testament, would acquire force by the mere fact that the testator happened to live for some time longer. The authorities of the opposite school hold that conditional bequests are also void, because we cannot be indebted to those in our *potestas* conditionally, any more than we can be unconditionally.

§ 245. On the other hand, it is clear that any one who institutes as his heir one who is in your *potestas* may make a valid bequest to you. If, however, you become the heir through him, the legacy lapses, for you cannot be debtor to yourself; whereas, if the instituted heir, being your son, is emancipated, or being your slave, is manumitted or alienated, and thus himself becomes the heir, or makes another the heir, the legacy is yours.

XXVI. *De Fideicommissariis Hereditatibus.*

§ 246. Let us now pass on to *fideicommissa.*

§ 247. We will first consider inheritance.

§ 248. The first thing to be observed is that it is absolutely necessary that an heir should be formally instituted, and that the inheritance should be entrusted to him to be transferred by him to another, for a testament in which no heir has been instituted with due legal formality is invalid.

§ 249. The technical terms and those most in use for the creation of *fideicommissa* are "*Peto, rogo, volo, fideicommitto,*" (*I beg, I request, I desire, I commit to your good faith.*) Each has the same force as all would have if combined.

§ 250. Thus after having written, "Let Lucius Titius be heir," we may add, "I ask you, Lucius Titius, and beg of you that so soon as you can enter on my inheritance you will deliver it over to Gaius Seius." We may also request him to transfer a part. We are at liberty to leave *fideicommissa* either conditionally or unconditionally, or from a specified date.

§ 251. After the transfer the transferor remains heir notwithstanding. The transferee at times assumes the place of heir, at others that of legatee.

§ 252. Formerly, he had neither the status of heir nor legatee, but rather that of purchaser, for it was customary, for the sake of form, to sell the inheritance to him for a single coin, with the stipulations commonly made between vendor and purchaser of an inheritance, thus: The heir stipulated with the transferee that he should be indemnified by him against all losses he might sustain by reason of his being heir, or for anything he may have parted with *bonâ fide*, and, generally, that should any one take proceedings against him as heir, he should be properly defended. On the other hand, he to whom the inheritance was transferred stipulated that the heir should deliver to him any portion of the inheritance that might thereafter get into the possession of the heir, and that he should also allow him to institute suits concerning the inheritance as *procurator* or *cognitor*.

§ 253. Subsequently, however, that is to say, during the consulate of Trebellius Maximus and Annæus Seneca, it was enacted by a *senatusconsultum* that, when an inheritance has been transferred by the heir to another by way of *fideicommissum*, all actions given to or against the heir by the civil law should lie by or against the transferee by virtue of the trust. Since that *senatusconsultum*, the stipulations of which we have spoken have fallen into disuse, for the prætor began to grant *utiles actiones* to and against the transferee, treating him as if he were heir: these actions are set forth in the edict.

§ 254. As the instituted heir, being ordinarily requested to transfer either the whole or nearly all of the inheritance, refused to enter upon it, there being little or nothing for him, *fideicommissa* came to nought, whereupon the senate, during the consulship of Pegasus and Pusio, decreed that the instituted heir, who was requested to transfer the inheritance, should be allowed to retain one-fourth, as in the case of legacies under the *lex Falcidia*, and gave a similar right of retaining the fourth of any specific thing left in trust. By virtue of this *senatusconsultum*, the heir bears the expenses of the inheritance, while he who takes the rest of the inheritance by virtue of the *fideicommissum* takes the place of a partiary legatee, *i. e.*, of a legatee to whom a portion of the goods is left. This species of legacy is styled *partitio*, because the legatee divides (*partitur*) the inheritance with the heir; consequently, the same stipulations that are commonly made between the heir and the partiary legatee are made between the transferee of the inheritance, by way of *fideicommissum*, and the heir, in order to secure to each a share proportioned to his interest of the profits and losses of the inheritance.

§ 255. Thus, then, when the instituted heir is not required to transfer more than three-quarters of the inheritance, the transfer is made under the *senatusconsultum Trebellianum*, and the *actiones hereditariæ* are given to each in respect of his part against the heir according to the civil law, and against the receiver of the inheritance by virtue of the *S. C. Trebellianum*. In all cases the heir remains heir even as to that which he has transferred, and actions as to the whole lie in principle by and against him, but in practice the charges do not fall on him, nor are actions given to him, beyond the extent of his remaining interest in the inheritance.

§ 256. But when the heir is required to deliver over the whole or more than three-fourths of the inheritance, the *senatusconsultum Pegasianum* applies.

§ 257. But he who has once entered on the inheritance, provided he has done so voluntarily, whether he retains, or does not wish to retain, the fourth, bears personally all the burden of the inheritance; when he retains the fourth, stipulations should be employed resembling those used between a partiary legatee and an heir, styled *partis et pro parte;* and if he delivers over the whole inheritance, he should use stipulations similar to those used in the case of the sale and purchase of an inheritance.

§ 258. But should the appointed heir decline to enter upon the inheritance, alleging that he believes it to be insolvent, then by the provisions of the *S. C. Pegasianum* he ought, on the demand of him to whom he is directed to transfer it, to obtain the order of the prætor for him to enter and transfer, in which case, stipulations are unnecessary, as the heir is secured and the actions are given to and against the person to whom the inheritance is transferred, as in the case of the *S. C. Trebellianum*.

§ 259. Whether the heir is instituted to the whole inheritance and directed to transfer the whole or only a part, or whether he is instituted to a part only of the inheritance and directed to transfer the whole or only a part of that part, is of little moment, for in either case the fourth is retained by virtue of the *S. C. Pegasianum*.

XXVII. *De Singulis Rebus per Fideicommissum relictis.*

§ 260. It is also competent by *fideicommissum* to leave individual things, *e.g.*, a field, a slave, a garment, plate, money, and to direct the heir or a legatee to deliver it to some third person, notwithstanding the fact that a legacy cannot be charged on a legatee.

§ 261. A testator may, by *fideicommissum* leave not merely his own property, but that of the heir or legatee, or in short of any person. Thus a legatee may be requested to transfer to some third person, not merely the thing bequeathed to him, but some other object belonging either to himself or another. The only limit to be observed is that he must not be charged to transfer more than he receives under the testament, for as to the surplus the direction is futile.

§ 262. When one by *fideicommissum* leaves the property of another, it is incumbent on the person charged, either to deliver it, or its value: he must either purchase the thing and hand it over, or pay its value, as in the case of the property of another bequeathed by *damnatio*. Some authors, however, are of opinion that if the owner of the thing bequeathed by *fideicommissum* refuses to sell it, the trust is extinguished, but that it is otherwise in the case of a legacy by *damnatio*.

§ 263. Liberty may be given to a slave by *fideicommissum* by praying either the heir or the legatee to manumit him.

§ 264. It is immaterial whether the testator makes the request in respect of a slave of his own, of the heir, of a legatee, or of a stranger.

§ 265. Thus the slave of another ought to be purchased and enfranchised. If, however, the master of the slave refuses to sell him, there is no doubt in that case that the *fideicommissum* of liberty is extinguished, because the value of liberty cannot be computed.

§ 266. The person enfranchised as the result of a *fideicommissum* does not become the freed man of the testator, even though he may have been his slave, but he becomes the freed man of his manumitter.

§ 267. It is otherwise when liberty has been granted directly by the testament, for example, in these terms, "Let my slave Stichus be free," or "I direct that Stichus my slave be freed," in which case the emancipated slave is the freed man of the testator himself. No one can derive liberty directly by virtue of a testament unless he has been the slave of the testator by Quiritarian law both at the date of the execution of the testament and of the death of the testator.

§ 268. There is a great difference between things left by *fideicommissum* and legacies left directly.

§ 269. Thus by *fideicommissum* one can leave . . . . (by a mere nod of the head) whereas a legacy . . . . (must be granted by testament).

§ 270. So one about to die intestate may by *fideicommissum* charge his successor with a trust, but cannot charge him with a legacy.

§ 270a. So a legacy left by a codicil is invalid unless the codicil has been confirmed by testament, that is to say, unless the testator has in his testament declared that what he shall direct in his codicils must be observed: a *fideicommissum*, on the contrary, may be left even in codicils not ratified.

§ 271. So a legatee cannot be charged with a legacy, but may be with a *fideicommissum*: nay more, it is competent to charge one to whom something is left by *fideicommissum* with a *fideicommissum* in favour of another.

§ 272. Though liberty cannot be given directly to the slave of another it may be secured to him by *fideicommissum*.

§ 273. So, no one can be instituted heir or disinherited by codicil, even if confirmed by testament; but he who has been instituted heir by testament can, by codicil, be charged to transfer the inheritance to another whether in whole or in part, though such codicil may not have been previously ratified by testament.

§ 274. So a woman, who by the provisions of the *lex Voconia* cannot be instituted heir by any one registered as worth more than 100,000 asses, may, however, receive from him an inheritance by *fideicommissum*.

§ 275. So Latins, who by the *lex Junia* are debarred from taking inheritances and legacies directly, may acquire them by *fideicommissum*.

§ 276. So, notwithstanding that a *senatusconsultum* has forbidden the freeing of a slave under thirty years of age, and at the same time appointing him heir, it is the prevalent opinion that we can direct that he shall be made free when he is thirty years of age, and the heir may be bound by a declaration of trust to convey the inheritance to him.

§ 277. So, though one cannot institute an heir to our heir, we can desire our heir, when apprehensive of death, to transfer the inheritance to another, whether in whole or in part, and, inasmuch as a trust may be limited to take effect after the death of the trustee, the same end may be attained by the use of these words :—" When Titius my heir shall be dead, I desire that my inheritance shall belong to Publius Mevius." In either case Titius leaves his heir bound to convey the inheritance to the person designated.

§ 278. Besides, we sue for legacies by means of a *formula;* whereas trusts are enforced by the extraordinary jurisdiction of the consul or *prætor fideicommissarius* at Rome, and in the provinces before the president of the province.

§ 279. Again, at Rome cases of *fideicommissa* will be heard at any time, whereas legacy cases are only taken during the sittings.

§ 280. The interest and profits in the case of *fideicommissa* are due and payable by the person charged, when found guilty of delay in making the transfer; whereas, by reason of a rescript of Hadrian, interest is not payable in the case of legacies. I do not forget that Julian was of opinion that on legacies *sinendi modo* the same rule should be adopted as in the case of *fidei-*

commissa, and I observe that that opinion is now gaining ground.

§ 281. It is to be observed that legacies written in Greek are void, whereas *fideicommissa* written in that language are valid.

§ 282. So if the heir disputes a legacy left *per damnationem* an action lies against him to recover the double value, whereas in the case of *fideicommissa* the actual value only is recoverable.

§ 283. So anything paid in error in excess of the amount due in the case of *fideicommissa* is recoverable, whereas anything paid in error over and above the amount due in the case of a legacy *per damnationem* cannot be recovered. The same undoubtedly is the law as to a legacy which, though not due, has for some cause or other been paid by mistake.

§ 284. There were other differences which, however, no longer exist.

§ 285. For example, *peregrini* could receive *fideicommissa:* in fact, we may even say that this was the origin of *fideicommissa.* But that was subsequently prohibited, and now, by a *senatusconsultum* passed at the instance of Hadrian, *fideicommissa* made in favour of *peregrini* are forfeited to the *fiscus.*

§ 286. At one time *cœlibes*, who by the *lex Julia* are prohibited from taking a legacy, were held capable of taking *fideicommissa.* So the *orbi*, who by the terms of the *lex Papia* lose the half of inheritances or legacies left to them by reason of their being childless, were nevertheless, in former times, held capable of receiving the whole of the property left to them by *fideicommissa.* In the course of time, however, by the *senatusconsultum Pegasianum* they were forbidden to take *fideicommissa* as well as legacies and inheritances. The *senatusconsultum* at the same time transferred the caducal portion to those named in the testament who had children, and, in the event of there not being any, to the *populus*, as in the case of legacies and inheritances.

§ 287. For the same or a similar reason one could formerly, by *fideicommissum* leave property to an uncertain person, or to a posthumous stranger, though such person could neither be instituted heir nor made a legatee; but a *senatusconsultum* published at the instance of Hadrian applied to *fideicommissa* the rule applicable to inheritances and legacies.

§ 288. It is unquestionable that a bequest by way of penalty cannot now be made, even by *fideicommissum*.

§ 289. Though in many respects *fideicommissa* admit of greater latitude than direct dispositions, and in others the two are equal, yet a tutor cannot be given by testament otherwise than directly, *e. g.*, thus :—" Let Titius be tutor to my children," or " I appoint Titius tutor to my children." A tutor cannot be given by *fideicommissum*.

THIRD COMMENTARY.

DE RERUM UNIVERSITATIBUS ET DE OBLIGATIONIBUS.

I. *De Hereditatibus quæ ab Intestato deferuntur.*

§ 1. By the law of the Twelve Tables the estates of those who die intestate belong in the first instance to the *sui heredes.*

§ 2. By the expression *sui heredes* is intended the children who were in the *potestas* of the deceased at the time of his death, *e.g.*, the son or daughter, the grandson or granddaughter by a son, the great-grandson or great-granddaughter, issue of a grandson born of a son, whether actual or adopted is immaterial. The grandson and the granddaughter, the great-grandson and the great-granddaughter, are not however *sui heredes*, unless their immediate male ancestor has ceased to be in the *potestas* of his ascendant, whether by reason of his death or any other cause, *e.g.*, emancipation; for if at the time of death the son is in the *potestas* of his father, the son of that son cannot be *suus heres* of his grandfather. The same may be said of the other descendants.

§ 3. The wife *in manu* is also a *sua heres*, inasmuch as she occupies the place of a daughter. It is the same in the case of the daughter-in-law *in manu* of a son, for she occupies the place of granddaughter; but she is not *sua heres* if at the time of the death of the father the son to whom she is *in manu* was in the *potestas* of his father. The same may be said of the woman who is *in manu* of the grandson *matrimonii causâ*, because she ranks as a great-granddaughter.

§ 4. Posthumous children also, who, had they been born during the life of their ascendant, would have been in his *potestas* are *sui heredes.*

§ 5. It is the same as to those concerning whom conformably to the *lex Ælia Sentia*, or the *senatusconsultum*, cause is shown after the death of the father, because such children would have been in the *potestas* of their father if the proof of cause had been made during his life.

§ 6. The son, who has been manumitted from a first or second mancipation, after the death of his father, must also be included.

§ 7. Thus, then, when there is a son or a daughter, and grandsons or granddaughters by another son, they are called together to the inheritance, for he who is the nearest in degree does not exclude the more remote, it having been considered equitable that grandsons and granddaughters should take the place and portion of their father; for the same reason, if there is a grandson or a granddaughter of a son, and a great-grandson or great-granddaughter of a grandson, they also are called simultaneously to the inheritance.

§ 8. As it had been decided that the grandsons or granddaughters, as also the great-grandsons or great-granddaughters, should take the place of their ascendant, it appeared as a consequence that the estate should be divided not *per capita* but *per stirpes*, so that the son may take one-half of the inheritance, and the grandsons born of another son, whatever may be their number, the other moiety, and so that should there exist grandsons, issue of two sons—one or two, for example by the one, three or four by the other—one moiety would belong to the one or two children of the one son, and the other moiety to the three or four children of the other.

II. *De Legitimâ Agnatorum Successione.*

§ 9. If there is no *suus heres*, the inheritance, by the Twelve Tables, belongs to the agnates.

§ 10. *Agnati* are those who are united by *legitima cognatio. Legitima cognatio* is descent traced through persons of the male sex. Thus, the brothers born of the same father are *agnati* the one to the other, they are also called *consanguinei;* it is immaterial whether or not they had the same mother. So the paternal uncle is the *agnatus* of the brother's son, and reciprocally *fratres patrueles* (cousins-german) are, each, relatively to the other, *agnati*, *i.e.*, those who are born of two brothers and commonly called *consobrini*. By continuing in this manner, we should arrive at various other degrees of agnation.

§ 11. The law of the Twelve Tables does not, however, give the inheritance to all the *agnati* simultaneously, but to those who are of nearest degree at the time when it has become certain that the deceased died intestate.

§ 12. In this case there are no successive devolutions. If, therefore, the nearest *agnatus* will not take the inheritance, or, should he happen to die before entering on the inheritance, the *agnati* more remote than he have no title in law.

§ 13. The reason for ascertaining the nearest *agnatus* at the time when it has been ascertained that the deceased has died intestate, and not at the time of the death, is, that it is possible that the deceased has left a testament, appointing some one else heir.

§ 14. In matters concerning females, different principles prevail, depending upon the question, whether it is a case of succession to a woman's inheritance, or by her to the goods (*in ceterorum bonis*) of another. In short, the estates of females descend to the *agnati* in the same manner as the estates of males, whereas the estates of males do not go to females who are beyond the degree of *consanguineæ*. Thus, the sister is legitimate heir of her brother, or of her sister; whereas the paternal aunt, or the daughter of a brother, cannot be the *legitima heres*. The mother or step-mother *in manum conventionem* occupies the position of daughter to her husband, and therefore of sister to his children, whether hers or not.

§ 15. If the deceased leaves a brother, and a nephew by another brother, it is easy to see from what has been already said, that the brother is preferred, because he is nearer in degree; but the law has been otherwise interpreted in the case of *sui heredes*.

§ 16. Thus, if the deceased has left no brother, but has left nephews by his brothers, the inheritance belongs to all: when the numbers are unequal, *e.g.*, where there is one, or there are two nephews by one brother, and three or four by another, the question arose whether the inheritance should be divided *per stirpes*, as in the case of *sui heredes*, or *per capita*. It has now been long settled that the inheritance ought to be divided *per capita*. Whatever, therefore, may be the number of persons in each branch, the inheritance being divided by the collective number, each individual gets his equal share.

§ 17. Should there be no *agnati*, the law of the Twelve Tables then calls the *gentiles* to the inheritance. In our first commentary, we explained what is intended by the term "*gentiles*"; and as we there said that the law of the Twelve Tables respecting the *gentiles* had fallen into disuse, it would be superfluous to treat of the matter here in detail.

III. *Bonorum Possessio Intestati.*

§ 18. These are all the rules contained in the Twelve Tables as to succession *ab intestato:* how narrow (*strictum*) the then law was may readily be seen.

§ 19. In the first place, by that law, emancipated descendants had no rights as to the estate of their ancestor, they having ceased to be *sui heredes.*

§ 20. So if the children were not in the *potestas* of their father, by reason of Roman citizenship having been conferred on them when it was conferred on their father, without the emperor at the same time placing them in his *potestas.*

§ 21. So *agnati* who have suffered *capitis diminutio* are excluded according to that law from the inheritance, for by *capitis diminutio* title by *agnatio* is destroyed.

§ 22. Again, the fact of the nearest *agnatus* declining the inheritance was of no advantage to the remaining *agnati.*

§ 23. In like manner female *agnati*, who were not at the same time *consanguineæ*, had no title by that law.

§ 24. So *cognati* having a common female ancestry were excluded, the effect being that, even between mother and her son or daughter, the right to inherit the one to the other did not exist, unless indeed by *conventio in manum* the rights of consanguinity were created between them.

§ 25. But these inequitable rules of the law have been corrected by the prætor's edict.

§ 26. By him all descendants, who have no title by the Twelve Tables, are called to the inheritance as if they had been in the *potestas* of the ascendant at the time of his death, and that whether they are the sole claimants, or whether they claim jointly with *sui heredes*, *i. e.*, with children who were actually in the *potestas* of their parent.

§ 27. As to the *agnati* who have suffered *capitis diminutio*, the prætor calls them, but not to the same degree, *i. e.*, next to the *sui heredes*, where they are placed by the law when they have not suffered *capitis diminutio;* but in the third degree by reason of blood relationship; for though they have lost the legal title by reason of the *capitis diminutio*, they at least retain the rights of cognation. Consequently, when there is another who has preserved his right of agnation, he will be preferred, though he may be of a degree more remote.

§ 28. According to some authors, the rule is the same in the case of an *agnatus*, who, notwithstanding the refusal of the inheritance by the nearest *agnatus*, was not thereby admitted by the law; others, however, are of opinion that he is called by the prætor in the same order as that in which the inheritance is given by the law to the *agnati*.

§ 29. One thing is certain, viz., that female *agnatæ* who are beyond the degree of *consanguineæ* are called in the third degree, that is to say, if there is neither *suus heres*, nor male *agnatus*.

§ 30. Relations through the female line are called in the same degree.

§ 31. Children who have been adopted are in like manner called in the third degree to the inheritance of their actual ascendants.

§ 32. Those called by the prætor to the inheritance do not, it is true, become legal heirs, because the prætor cannot make heirs; the rank of heir can only be conferred by a *lex* or by a decree of like force, *e. g.*, a *senatusconsultum*, or a *constitutio principalis* (an imperial constitution); but when the prætor gives them the *bonorum possessio* they enjoy the position of heir.

§ 33. So in the case of *bonorum possessio* itself, the prætor has adopted various degrees, his primary object being to secure that no one shall die without a successor. Having treated of this subject in detail in a work devoted to it, it is sufficient here to say . . . .

§ 34. . . . . . So in the case of intestacy, he calls the *heredes suos*, and *agnatos* to the *bonorum possessio*. In this case, the sole advantage accruing from the grant of the prætor appears to be, that the grantee suing for the *bonorum possessio* may use the interdict that commences "*Quorum bonorum.*" In its proper place we will explain the use of this interdict. Whether they have the *bonorum possessio* or not, the inheritance is theirs by the civil law.

§ 35. It must further be observed that the *bonorum possessio* is frequently given so as not to carry with it the inheritance, in which case it is called *bonorum possessio sine re.*

§ 36. For example, if the instituted heir has made *cretio* for the inheritance, but has not chosen to sue for the *bonorum possessio* according to the testament, being satisfied with his position as heir by the civil law, those, who in the absence of a testament are called to the succession, may demand the *bonorum possessio*, but take it *sine re*, inasmuch as the heir named in the testament can deprive them of the inheritance.

§ 37. So in the case of one dying intestate, should his *suus heres* be unwilling to demand the *bonorum possessio*, contenting himself with his legal right, in which case the *bonorum possessio* belongs to the agnate, but *sine re* because the inheritance can be wrested from him by the *suus heres.* Take another case—that of an inheritance belonging to an agnate by the civil law :—If he enters upon it, but does not care to sue for the *bonorum possessio*, the nearest cognate who sues for it will be entitled to it, but for the same reason will take it *sine re.*

§ 38. There are other similar cases, some of which have been dealt with in the previous commentary.

IV. *De Successione Libertorum Civium Romanorum.*

§ 39. We will now consider the goods of freedmen.

§ 40. It was formerly lawful for a freedman to omit mention of his patron in his testament, for by the law of the Twelve Tables, the patron did not succeed to the inheritance of his freedman unless he died intestate, leaving no *suus heres*. Thus, when the freedman died intestate, but left a *suus heres*, the patron had no right to his estate. Doubtless, when the freedman left as his *suus heres* a legitimate child of his own, the patron had no cause of complaint; but when the *suus heres* was an adopted son, or daughter, or a wife he had *in manu*, it appeared inequitable that the patron should be without any right.

§ 41. Consequently, in the course of time, this defect in the old law was cured by the edict of the prætor. When, then, a freedman makes a testament, it is incumbent upon him to leave one-half of his property to his patron. Should he not leave him anything, or leave him less than one-half, the patron may recover possession of the moiety of the property of his freedman, be the provisions of the testament what they may. If, on the other hand, the freedman dies intestate, leaving as his *suus heres* an adopted son, or a wife who was *in manu*, or a daughter-in-law who was *in manu* of his son, the patron is equally entitled as against those *sui heredes* to the possession of the moiety of the freedman's property. Natural (legitimate) children, whether in the *potestas* of the freedman at the time of his death, or then emancipated, or given in adoption, avail him against the claim of the patron, provided that they have been instituted heirs for some part of the estate, or, being passed over in silence, they have by virtue of the edict demanded the *bonorum possessio contra tabulas*. Those who have been disinherited have no title as against the patron.

§ 42. At a still later date the *lex Papia* increased the rights of the patron in the case of wealthy freedmen. That law enacts that when a freedman leaves an estate of 100,000 *sesterces*, or more, and fewer than three children, whether he dies testate or intestate, the patron shall be entitled to a share equal to that of each of the other beneficiaries. Thus, when the freedman leaves as his heir one son or one daughter, the patron takes half; it would be the same if he died leaving neither son nor daughter; when he leaves two heirs of either sex, the patron takes one-third; when he leaves three, the patron is excluded.

§ 43. In the case of the property of freedwomen, the old law did not prejudice the patron, for, as freedwomen were in the *legitima tutela* of the patron, they could not make a testament without his authorization: consequently, if the patron authorized the testament of his freedwoman, he had no ground of complaint if she left him less than he was in law entitled to. If she made her testament without his authority, his position was improved, for a freedwoman could not leave a *suus heres* to defeat the rights of her patron.

§ 44. But when at a later date the *lex Papia* liberated freedwomen who had four children from the *tutela* of their patrons, and consequently empowered them to make testaments without the authorization of the patron, it provided in favour of the patron, that he should receive out of the estate of the freedwoman a share proportioned to the number of children she left her surviving. . . .

§ 45. What has been said concerning the patron applies equally to the son of the patron, his grandson by his son, and to his great-grandson by his grandson born of his son.

§ 46. Though, by the Twelve Tables, the daughter of the patron, his granddaughter by his son, and his great-granddaughter by the grandson of his son, have the same right as the patron, yet the prætor only calls the male issue of the patron to the succession. By the *lex Papia*, however, the daughter who has three children is entitled to demand one-half of the property of the enfranchised *contra tubulas*, or in a case of intestacy as against an adopted son, the wife, or the daughter-in-law, but in no other case has she any title.

§ 47. The right to a portion of a child of the estate of a freedwoman who has had four children, does not always accrue to the daughter of the patron as a privilege attached to the number (three) of her children, as has been supposed by some. However, if the freedwoman has died intestate, the daughter of the patron does, by the *lex Papia*, become entitled to a proportionate share. If, on the contrary, the freedwoman has died testate, the daughter of the patron has the same right as that accorded to a female patron having three children, *i. e.*, the right enjoyed by the patron and his descendants to have *bonorum possessio contra tabulas* (possession of the goods notwithstanding the provisions of the will) of the freedman. This portion of the law, however, is not carefully worded.

§ 48. From what has been said, it follows that the *extranei heredes* of a patron are absolutely deprived of the rights which belong to the patron, in respect of the property of the enfranchised, whether he died testate or intestate.

§ 49. Formerly, *i. e.*, before the *lex Papia*, female patrons had, in respect of the property of their enfranchised, those rights merely that were given to them in common with male patrons by the Twelve Tables; for the prætor did not grant to them, as he did to the patron and his children, the right to demand the possession of one-half of the property *contra tabulas*, in cases where they had not been mentioned in the testament, or in the case of intestacy as against the adopted son, the wife, or the daughter-in-law.

§ 50. But afterwards the *lex Papia* conferred on the free-born female patron having two children, and on the enfranchised female patron having three children, almost the same rights as those given to the patron by the prætor's edict; while to the free-born female patron having three children it gave the same rights as by that law are given to a patron: it did not confer like rights on the enfranchised female patron.

§ 51. Concerning the property of enfranchised females who die intestate, the *lex Papia* makes no new concessions to the female patron having children. If, then, neither the female patron nor the enfranchised female has suffered *capitis diminutio*, the inheritance belongs by virtue of the Twelve Tables to the female patron, and the children of the freedwoman are excluded: this rule equally applies when the female patron has no children, for, as we have already said, a woman cannot have a *suus heres*. But if either has suffered *capitis diminutio*, the children of the freedwoman exclude the female patron, because, by the *capitis diminutio*, the civil bond being severed, the children of the freedwoman have the preference by law of cognation.

§ 52. When, on the other hand, the freedwoman dies testate, the female patron who has not the requisite number of children has no right as against the testament of the enfranchised, whereas she who has the requisite number of children obtains, by virtue of the *lex Papia*, the same right as a patron under the edict has, as against the testament of a freedman.

§ 53. The same *lex* awards to the daughter of the female patron, when a mother, the rights of a patron; it suffices if she has but one son or daughter.

§ 54. As in our commentaries, specially devoted to this subject, we have dealt with this matter in detail, what is here said must suffice for our present purpose.

V. *De Bonis Libertorum Latinorum.*

§ 55. We now come to consider the law as to the property of enfranchised Latins.

§ 56. To render this branch of the law more clear we must repeat what has already been said, viz., that those who are now styled *Latini Juniani*, were formerly slaves *ex jure Quiritium*, though by the aid of the prætors they acquired the semblance of freedom; hence property acquired by them belonged to their patrons by the title of *peculium*. In the course of time, however, and by virtue of the *lex Junia*, all those whose presumed liberty had been maintained by the prætor became free in fact, and were styled *Latini Juniani*. They were styled *Latini* because the law assimilated their freedom to that of free-born citizens of Rome, who, on quitting Rome for a Latin colony, became Latin colonists. They were styled *Juniani* because it was by the *lex Junia* that they were made free, though not made Roman citizens. The author of that law saw that by this fiction the property of deceased Latins would cease to belong to their patrons, for on the one hand they no longer died as slaves, so as to vest their *peculium* in their patrons, and on the other the property of an enfranchised Latin could not belong to the patrons by the right of manumission; he therefore judged it necessary, in order to prevent the advantages secured to the enfranchised from working damage to the patrons, to provide that the property of the enfranchised should revert to their manumitters just as if the law had never passed. In a certain sense therefore, the property of Latins belongs to their manumitters as *peculium*.

§ 57. Hence there is considerable difference between the rules applied to the goods of Latins by virtue of the *lex Junia* and those observed as to the inheritance of freedmen who are Roman citizens.

§ 58. In fact the inheritance of a freedman who is a Roman citizen never belongs to the *extranei heredes* of the patron, but always to the son of the patron, to his grandsons by his son, and to his great-grandsons by his grandsons born of his son, even when they have been disinherited; whereas the property of Latini belongs, as do the *peculia* of slaves, even to the *extranei heredes*, and does not belong to the disinherited descendants of the manumitter.

§ 59. So the inheritance of a freedman who became a Roman citizen belongs equally to two or more patrons, although they had unequal shares of property in him as a slave; whereas the inheritance of a freedman who became a Latin belongs to each patron in proportion to his actual share in the slave.

§ 60. So, in the case of the inheritance of a freedman who became a Roman citizen, one patron excludes the son of another patron, and the son of one patron excludes the grandson of another patron; whereas the property of a freedman who became a Latin is the property of one patron and the heirs of another patron, jointly, according to the proportion in which they would have belonged to the deceased manumitter himself.

§ 61. So, if, for example, there are three children of one patron, and one of another, the inheritance of the freedman who is a Roman citizen is divided *per capita*, that is to say, the three brothers take one-fourth each, and the sole son the remaining fourth; whereas the property of the freedman who is a Latin belongs to the successors in the same proportion as that in which it would have belonged to the manumitter himself.

§ 62. So, if one of the patrons renounces his share of the inheritance of a freedman who is a Roman citizen, or dies before having made *cretio*, the entire inheritance belongs to the other; whereas, under like circumstances, the property of a freedman who is a Latin becomes *caduca* as to that part of the inheritance not taken by the patron, and goes *ad populum*.

§ 63. At a later date, viz., during the consulship of Lupus

and Largus (A.D. 41), the senate decreed that the property of Latins should devolve in the first instance on the manumitter, and, failing him, on such of his children as had not been expressly disinherited, in the order of their proximity, and in default of any such, then, in conformity with the old law, to the heirs of those by whom they had been made free.

§ 64. Some are of opinion that the result of this *senatusconsultum* is to make the rules concerning the inheritances of freedmen who become Roman citizens applicable to those freedmen who become Latins; such was particularly the opinion of Pegasus. That opinion, however, is evidently erroneous: for the inheritance of a freedman who is a Roman citizen never devolves on the *extranei heredes* of the patron; whereas the property of Latins, even by this *senatusconsultum*, belongs to the *extranei heredes* as well, provided no children of the manumitter prove a bar. So, in the case of the freedman who is a Roman citizen, the fact that the children of the manumitter have been disinherited does not defeat their right; whereas, in that of Latins, the *senatusconsultum* expressly provides that the children, disinherited by name, lose their right. The truth is, the only effect of this *senatusconsultum* is, that the children of the manumitter who have not been disinherited by name are preferred to the *extranei heredes*.

§ 65. Consequently, in the case of Latins, the emancipated son of the patron passed over in silence, though he may not have demanded the *bonorum possessio* contrary to the terms of his father's testament, is preferred to the *extranei heredes*.

§ 66. So the daughter and the other descendants, who by the civil law may be disinherited collectively, and which is sufficient to exclude them from the inheritance of their ancestors, will, however, as to the estate of a Latin, be preferred to the *extranei heredes*, provided they have not been disinherited by name by their ancestor.

§ 67. So descendants who have declined the inheritance of their father do not thereby forfeit their right to the estate of a Latin; for, though their declining to enter on the estate of their ancestor destroys their right to it, it cannot be said that they have been disinherited any more than those who have been passed over in silence.

§ 68. It is sufficiently evident from what has been said, that, if he who has made a man a Latin . . . .

§ 69. So . . . . because no extraneous heir is concerned, the *senatusconsultum* does not apply.

§ 70. But if the patron, in addition to children, has left an extraneous heir, Cælius Sabinus says that all the property (of the Latin) will belong to the children of the deceased, in equal shares, because, when an extraneous heir intervenes, it is not the *lex Junia*, but the *senatusconsultum* that applies. Javolenus, however, contends that the children of the patron will only take in equal shares by the *senatusconsultum* that portion which the extraneous heirs would have had by the *lex Junia* before the *senatusconsultum;* but that the remainder belongs to them in the ratio of their interest as heirs.

§ 71. It is also matter of discussion whether this *senatusconsultum* applies to the descendants of the patron, the issue of his daughter, or granddaughter, *i.e.*, would a grandson by a daughter be preferred in the case of the estate of a Latin to the extraneous heir? Again, it is asked, Does this *senatusconsultum* apply to Latins belonging to a mother, so that the son of the female patron would be preferred to her extraneous heir, in the case of succession to the property of a Latin? Cassius held that the *senatusconsultum* applied in each case; but the majority of the authorities maintain the contrary, alleging that the senate did not contemplate the children of the female patron, inasmuch as they are members of another family. This appears also from the fact that they exclude children who have been disinherited by name. The attention of the senate therefore appears to have been occupied with those who are disinherited by an ascendant by reason of their not being instituted heirs; now there is no necessity, either for a mother to disinherit her son or daughter, or for a maternal grandfather to disinherit his grandson or granddaughter, if they do not institute them heirs; and this is so, whether it is a question of the civil law or of the edict of the prætor, who promises the *bonorum possessio contra tabulas* to children who have been passed over in silence in the testament.

§ 72. It sometimes happens that a freedman who is a Roman citizen dies in a certain sense a Latin; *e.g.*, when a Latin has obtained from the emperor the *jus Quiritium*, with a reservation of the rights of the patron; for the late Emperor Trajan made a constitution to this effect, to meet the case of a Latin who should obtain the *jus Quiritium* contrary to the will, or without the knowledge of his patron. In such cases, so long as the freedman lives, he is on the same footing with other Roman citizens, and begets legitimate children, but he dies as a Latin, and his children cannot be his heirs; his *testamenti factio* is limited to the institution of his patron as his heir, and in the event of his patron declining to act to the appointment of another in his stead.

§ 73. The effect of this constitution being, apparently, that such men could never die Roman citizens, although they subsequently resorted to the means whereby, either according to the *lex Ælia Sentia* or the *senatusconsultum*, Latins could become Roman citizens; the late Emperor Hadrian, impressed by the want of equity in the matter, secured the passing of a *senatusconsultum* enacting that those who unknown to, or in opposition to the will of their patrons, should obtain from the emperor the *jus Quiritium*, and afterwards avail themselves of the means whereby, had they remained Latins, they might have obtained Roman citizenship, either by virtue of the *lex Ælia Sentia*, or the *senatusconsultum*, should be regarded in the same light as if they had acquired Roman citizenship under the *lex Ælia Sentia* or the *senatusconsultum*.

VI. *De Bonis Libertorum Dediticiorum.*

§ 74. The property of those whom the *lex Ælia Sentia* ranks as *dediticii* devolves on their patrons, at times, like that of freedmen who are Roman citizens; at others, like that of Latins.

§ 75. The property of whose who, if being without taint, would, on their manumission, have become Roman citizens, goes by law to the patron, like that of freedmen who are Roman citizens. They have not, however, the *testamenti factio*; at least, so think the majority of the authorities, and with reason, as it is incredible that the legislature should have intended to give the *testamenti factio* to persons of the most abject order of freedmen.

§ 76. The property of those who, on manumission, would have become Latins, had there been no taint, goes to their patrons as if they had died Latins. I am aware, however, that the legislator has not expressed his intention in this matter in terms as unequivocal as might be desired.

VII. *Successio per Bonorum Venditionem.*

§ 77. We will now consider succession in the case of *emptio bonorum.*

§ 78. The estates (*bona*) of the living as well as those of the deceased are at times sold. For example, the estates of the living, who fraudulently conceal themselves, or, being absent, are unrepresented, are sold; as are also those of persons who, in pursuance of the *lex Julia*, make a *cessio bonorum;* so, those of judgment debtors after the expiration of the time given them in part by the law of the Twelve Tables, and in part by the edict of the prætor for the purpose of raising the money to satisfy the debt. The estates of the deceased are sold; for example, where it has become certain that there are neither *heredes* nor *bonorum possessores* nor other *justus successor*.

§ 79. When the estate to be sold is that of a living person, the prætor requires possession of it to be kept, and the sale to be advertised for thirty days. When the estate is that of a deceased, the possession and advertisement are limited to fifteen days. At the expiration of the prescribed period, the prætor orders the creditors to be assembled in order for them to elect one of their body as *magister*, that is to say, the person to be charged with the sale. So, when the sale is of the estate of a living person, the date of delivery is later than when the sale is of the effects of a person deceased, for he orders that the property of a living person shall be assigned (*addici*) to the purchaser after thirty days, and that of a deceased person after twenty days. The reason why more time is allowed in the case of the living is, that care should be taken that they should not lightly be subjected to a forced sale of their property.

§ 80. The absolute property in goods is not acquired, either by their possessor or purchaser, by reason of possession or purchase; he simply holds *in bonis*. Absolute property (*ex jure Quiritium*) is, however, acquired by *usucapio*. Sometimes, indeed, the title of *bonorum emptores* is regarded as practically equivalent to that of *mancipes*, *i. e.*, when the property is transferred to those who sell *sub hastâ* (by auction).

§ 81. Neither the debts due to, nor the liabilities of, the original owner pass to the purchaser of his property (by legal, as distinguished from equitable, title). . . .

VIII. *De Acquisitione per Arrogationem et per in Manum Conventionem.*

§ 82. There are also successions of another kind, which neither owe their origin to the Twelve Tables nor to the edict of the prætor, but to custom, *i.e.*, the law introduced by common consent.

§ 83. Thus, for example, when a *paterfamilias* gives himself in adoption, or when a female has made *conventio in manum*, all the property of either, whether corporeal or incorporeal, including *choses in action* (*quæque ei debitæ sunt*), passes to the adopter or *coemptionator*, those rights alone excepted which are extinguished by reason of the *capitis diminutio*, *e. g.*, usufructs, obligations to serve contracted by *jus jurandum*, and matter *sub judice* (*et quæ continentur legitimo judicio*).

§ 84. On the other hand, the debts of the male, who has given himself in adoption, or of a woman, who has made *conventio in manum*, devolve upon the *coemptionator*, or the adoptive father, provided they be inheritable debts; and, as the adoptive father, or the *coemptionator*, as the case may be, becomes himself heir in his own name, he, and not the person given in adoption, or the woman who has made *conventio in manum*, is held immediately liable, because, by the civil law, such son and wife, respectively, cease to be heirs. As to the personal obligations, however, of such persons contracted before the adoption or *conventio in manum*, neither the adoptive father nor the *coemptionator* is bound. As, however, the person given in adoption, or the woman who made the *conventio*, is by reason of the *capitis diminutio* freed from legal obligation in respect of those debts, an *actio utilis* lies against either; the *capitis diminutio* being treated as non-existent; in which case, if the action is not defended (by the *coemptionator*, or adoptive father), the prætor permits the creditor to sell all the property which would have belonged to him or her, were it not for the said subjection.

IX. *De Hereditatis in Jure Cessione.*

§ 85. So if he to whom an inheritance belongs *ab intestato* by statute law, makes *cessio in jure* of it to another before making *cretio*, or acting as heir, he to whom the cession is made acquires the full title to it as if he himself had been called by the law to the inheritance; whereas, if he makes the cession after he has accepted the inheritance, he retains the character of heir, and consequently is personally liable to the creditors: *res corporales*, however, he will convey just as if he had made cession of each article separately; whereas debts due to the inheritance perish, and the debtors to the inheritance are thereby benefited.

§ 86. It is the same if the heir named in the testament, after having assumed the character of heir, makes a *cèssio in jure* of the inheritance; whereas, by making the *cessio in jure* before, his act would be a nullity.

§ 87. Does the *suus heres* or the *necessarius heres*, by making a *cessio in jure*, effect anything? That is a disputed point. Our authorities are of opinion that their act is a nullity. The authorities of the other school contend that it produces the same effect as a *cessio in jure* made by other heirs after entrance on the inheritance; for, say they, it is immaterial whether one becomes heir by making *cretio*, or by acting as heir, or by being compelled to enter on an inheritance by operation of law.

X. *De Obligationibus.*

§ 88. We will now pass to the consideration of obligations; their primary division is into two classes, for every obligation springs either from a contract, or from a delict.

§ 89. We will first consider those that spring from contract, of which there are four kinds; in short, an obligation is contracted either *re*, *verbis*, *litteris*, or *consensu*.

XI. *Quibus Modis Re contrahatur Obligatio.*

§ 90. An obligation is contracted *re*, for example, by the giving of a *mutuum*. Strictly speaking, the things the subjects of the contract *re* are such things as are capable of being weighed, counted, or measured, such as coin, wine, oil, corn, brass, silver, gold. We transfer those things by counting, measuring, or weighing them out to the persons who receive them with the intention that they should become the proprietors, and that they will at a future date return to us, not the same things, but others of the same nature, whence comes the denomination *mutuum*, because that which is thus transferred to you by me ceases to be mine, and becomes yours (*ex meo tuum*).

§ 91. He who receives anything by way of payment, which is not due to him, from one who delivers it to him in error, is also under an obligation *re*, for the *condictio*, "*Si paret eum dare oportere*" (should it appear that he ought to give), lies against him as if he had received a *mutuum*. Consequently, some are of opinion that the pupil, or the woman to whom a payment has been made in error, and without the authority of the tutor, is not liable to the *condictio*, any more than he or she would have been, had it been the case of a *mutuum*. This species of obligation, however, does not appear to be founded in contract, for he who hands over with the intention of paying desires rather to dissolve, than to contract an obligation.

XII. *De Verborum Obligatione.*

§ 92. The obligation *verbis* is created by question and answer, thus: "*Dari spondes?—Spondeo*" (Do you engage that it shall be given?—I do). "*Dabis?—Dabo*" (Will you give?—I will give). "*Promittis?—Promitto*" (Do you promise?—I do promise). "*Fide promittis?—Fide promitto*" (Do you pledge your honour?—I do pledge my honour). "*Fide jubes?—Fide jubeo*" (Do you guarantee on your honour?—I do guarantee on my honour). "*Facies?—Faciam*" (Will you do?—I will do).

§ 93. The obligation *verbis*, "*Dari spondes?—Spondeo*" (Do you undertake that it shall be given?—I do undertake), is peculiar to Roman citizens; whereas the others belong to the *jus gentium*, and consequently are available by all and are binding on all, whether Roman citizens or *peregrini*. They are equally valid if expressed in Greek, thus: δώσεις; δώσω· ὁμολογεῖς; ὁμολογῶ· πίστει κελεύεις; πίστει κελεύω· ποιήσεις; ποιήσω. They are valid when in Greek, even if made between Roman citizens, provided they understand Greek; and reciprocally, though they are in Latin, they are valid between *peregrini*, provided they understand the Latin language. But the obligation *verbis*, "*Dari spondes?—Spondeo*" (Do you undertake that it shall be given?—I do undertake), is so peculiar to Roman citizens that it cannot even be rendered accurately in Greek, though it is alleged that the Latin expression is derived from a Greek word (σπένδω).

§ 94. It is said, however, that there is one case in which a *peregrinus* can bind himself by the use of this expression; that is, where our emperor, when concluding a treaty of peace, interrogates the leader of the foreign power thus: "*Pacem futuram spondes?*" (Do you engage that there shall be peace?), or if he himself be interrogated in like manner. But this is far too subtle; for, should there be any contravention of the treaty, it would not be a case of action on the contract for its breach, but of war to vindicate the right.

§ 95. There is room for doubt if any one . . . .

§ 96. . . . . they are obliged, at any rate, when the question is as to Roman law. If any one desires to know the law in this respect adopted by the *peregrini*, he, by examining the law peculiar to each state, will find out that one has one law and another another.

XIII. *De Inutilibus Stipulationibus.*

§ 97. If we stipulate that one shall give us something that he cannot give, the stipulation is *inutilis* (void): *e.g.*, if one stipulates that another shall give him a freeman, he believing him to be a slave; or a dead man, he believing him to be alive; or a spot that is *sacra* or *religiosa*, he believing it to be *humani juris*.

§ 97a. So, if one stipulates for the gift of something which in nature cannot exist, *e.g.*, for a centaur, the stipulation is void.

§ 98. So if one stipulates under a condition which cannot be fulfilled, *e. g.*, "If he touch heaven with his finger," the stipulation is void. But, when a legacy is left with an impossible condition, our authorities hold that the legacy is as valid as if the condition had not been attached, whereas the authorities of the other school contend that it is as invalid as a stipulation with a like condition. It certainly is not easy to suggest a satisfactory reason for the difference.

§ 99. A stipulation by which one makes another promise to give him that which is his already is void, because you cannot give a person that which already belongs to him.

§ 100. In like manner the following stipulation is void: "*Post mortem meam dari spondes?*" (Do you engage that it shall be given after my death?) or "*Post mortem tuam dari spondes?*" (Do you undertake that it shall be given after your death?). The stipulation, however, is valid if made thus:—"*Cum moriar dari spondes*" (Do you undertake that it shall be given when I am dying?) or "*Cum morieris dari spondes?*" (Do you undertake that it shall be given when you are dying?) that is to say, the stipulation is valid when it relates to the last moment of the life of the *stipulator* or *promissor*. For it appeared inconsistent with the general tenor of the law that the obligation should commence in the person of the heir. Nor can we stipulate thus—"*Pridie quam moriar, aut, Pridie quam morieris dari spondes?*" (Do you undertake that it shall be given the day before I die, or the day before you die?)—because it is impossible to say which is the day before till after the death, and death having taken place the stipulation is remitted to an anterior date: it is practically the same as saying "Do you undertake that it shall be given to my heir?" which is unquestionably void.

§ 101. All that has been said concerning death must be understood to apply in the case of *capitis diminutio*.

§ 102. The stipulation is also void when the answer varies the terms of the question, *e. g.*, if I stipulate for ten *sestertia*, and you promise me five, or if I stipulate unconditionally, and you promise conditionally.

§ 103. A stipulation is also void if we stipulate that a thing shall be given to a person to whom we are not legally subject.

Hence a question :—If one stipulates for a thing to be given to himself and another to whom he is not subject, to what extent is the stipulation valid? Our authorities contend that the stipulation is valid in its integrity, and that the entire benefit belongs to the person who stipulates as if he had not added the name of the stranger. But the authors of the other school maintain that he is only entitled to the moiety. . . .

§ 104. So the stipulation is void if I stipulate with one in my power, or if he stipulates with me. It must be observed that slaves and persons in *mancipium* cannot contract a legal obligation, whether to those to whom they are subject, or to any one else.

§ 105. It is evident that a dumb person can neither stipulate nor promise; the deaf are held to be under the same disability, for the stipulator must be able to hear the words of the promissor, and he who promises, the words of the stipulator.

§ 106. A madman cannot be a party to any business transaction, inasmuch as he does not know what he does.

§ 107. A pupil may be a party to any transaction, provided his tutor intervenes in cases where his authorization is necessary, *e. g.*, when he contracts an obligation: another can contract an obligation to him without the sanction of his tutor.

§ 108. It is the same in the case of females who are in tutelage.

§ 109. What has been said concerning pupils is only true of those who possess the requisite intelligence, for infants, and those bordering on infancy, differ but little from the insane—they lack the necessary intelligence. In the case of such pupils, however, convenience has induced a lenient interpretation of this law.

XIV. *Adstipulatio et Intercessio.*

§ 110. When stipulating it is competent for me to get another to stipulate the same thing; such person is commonly called an *adstipulator*.

§ 111. In which case an action will lie at his suit against the promissor, and the promissor may discharge his obligation by payment to the *adstipulator;* however, by an *actio mandati* the *adstipulator* may be compelled to deliver to me what he has received from the *promissor*.

§ 112. It is not necessary that the *adstipulator* should use the identical language employed by the *stipulator*, for example, if I have stipulated thus: "Do you undertake that it shall be given?" he may stipulate thus: "Do you promise the same thing on your word of honour" (become *fidepromissor*)? or "Do you guarantee on your word of honour the same thing" (become *fidejussor*)? or *vice versâ*.

§ 113. Though the *adstipulator* may stipulate for less, he cannot stipulate for more: consequently, if I have stipulated for ten sesterces he may adstipulate for five, but he may not stipulate for more than ten; so if I have stipulated unconditionally he may adstipulate conditionally, but if I have stipulated conditionally he cannot adstipulate unconditionally. The greater and the less must be understood, not only as relating to quantity, but also to time, for to give at once is to give more, to give hereafter is to give less.

§ 114. In the law upon this subject some somewhat singular principles are observed:—The heir of the *adstipulator* has no right of action. A slave *adstipulating* performs a void act; whereas he may in all other cases acquire for his master by *stipulatio*. The same principle holds in the case of one who is in *mancipium*, for he is in a position similar to that of a slave. On the other hand *adstipulatio* made by one who is in the *potestas* of his father is valid; he does not, however, thereby acquire for his ascendant, though in all other cases he does acquire for him by *stipulatio;* furthermore, an action on the *adstipulatio* does not lie at his suit unless, indeed, he has ceased to be *in potestate* by some method which did not involve a *capitis diminutio; e.g.*, by the death of his father, or by having been instituted *flamen Dialis*. What has been said applies equally to a female in *potestas* or in *manus*.

§ 115. In like manner others may become bound for the *promissor*. Of such persons some are styled *sponsores*, others *fidepromissores*, and others *fidejussores*.

§ 116. The *sponsor* is interrogated thus:—"Do you undertake that the same thing shall be given?" (*Idem dari spondes?*) The *fidepromissor* thus :—"Do you promise on your word of honour the same thing ?" (*Idem fidepromittis ?*) The *fidejussor* thus :— "Do you guarantee on your word of honour the same ?" (*Idem fide tuâ esse jubes ?*) We will inquire by what name those can be appropriately styled who are interrogated thus :—"Will you give the same thing ?" (*Idem dabis ?*) "Do you promise the same thing" (*Idem promittis ?*) "Will you do the same thing ?" (*Idem facies ?*).

§ 117. We frequently take *sponsores*, *fidepromissores*, and *fidejussores* for the purpose of increasing our security, whereas we rarely join *adstipulatores* except when we stipulate that something shall be given after our death, the only use of which is that the *adstipulator* may act after our death : our stipulation for this is void. If the *adstipulator* recovers anything he is bound to hand it over to our heir, and the *actio mandati* will lie against him to compel him to do so.

§ 118. The condition of *sponsor* and *fidepromissor* is very much the same ; that of *fidejussor* is very different.

§ 119. In short, the first two cannot be party to any obligation otherwise than *verbis*, even where the promissor is not bound, for instance, where a pupil has made a promise without the authorization of the tutor, or where any one has promised that something shall be given after his death. It is not certain when a slave or a *peregrinus* has promised by using the expression "*spondeo*," whether the *sponsor* or *fidepromissor* is bound for him. The *fidejussor*, on the contrary, can bind himself by either form of contract, *i.e.*, whether it be *re*, *verbis*, *litteris*, or *consensu* ; and it is of little moment whether the obligation to which he is party is civil or natural. The *fidejussor* may even bind himself for a slave, and that, either to a stranger, or to the master of the slave, in respect of that which is due from the slave to his master.

§ 120. Besides the heir of a *sponsor* or *fidepromissor* is not bound by his act, unless the *fidepromissor* is a *peregrinus* the law of whose country holds him liable ; whereas the heir of the *fidejussor* is equally bound with himself.

§ 121. Again, after the lapse of two years, the *sponsor* or the *fidepromissor* is released by virtue of the *lex Furia ;* and whenever the money is payable, and may be sued for, the amount is divided into as many parts as there are *sponsores* or *fidepromissores*, and each is liable for his portion only; whereas *fidejussores* are never released, and, whatever may be their number, each is liable for the whole amount. Consequently the creditor may demand the entire debt from which of the *fidejussores* he thinks fit. By a rescript, however, of Hadrian, the creditor is bound to demand from each his share, provided that all are solvent. This rescript differs then from the *lex Furia* in this, that where any of the *sponsores* or *fidepromissores* are insolvent the liability for their respective shares does not fall on the others. But as the *lex Furia* applies only to Italy, it follows that in the provinces *sponsores* and *fidepromissores* are, as *fidejussores*, liable in perpetuity and each for the whole, unless, indeed, they also are entitled to claim the benefit of the rescript of Hadrian.

§ 122. What is more, the *lex Apuleia* introduced a species of partnership between the *sponsores* and the *fidepromissores.* In fact, if either of them has paid more than his share he may maintain an action against the others for contribution. The *lex Apuleia* was enacted before the *lex Furia*, at a time when each was liable for the whole amount, whence it is a question whether since the *lex Furia* advantage can be taken of the *lex Apuleia*: there is no doubt that it is in force outside Italy, because the *lex Furia* only applies to Italy, whereas the *lex Apuleia* extends to the whole empire. In the case of *fidejussores* the matter is different, for the *lex Apuleia* does not apply to them; consequently, when a creditor has obtained the whole of his debt from one of the *fidejussores*, that *fidejussor* must bear the entire loss, should the person he has guaranteed prove insolvent: it is his own fault if he pays in full, for, as already said, when the creditor demands from him the whole amount he may avail himself of the rescript of Hadrian, and require that the claim against him shall be limited to his share.

§ 123. Furthermore by the *lex* . . . . it is provided that the creditor who obtains *sponsores*, or *fidepromissores*, shall make a public declaration as to the nature of the matter for which he requires sureties, and shall state how many *sponsores* or *fidepromissores* he requires; and in default of such declaration, it is lawful for the *sponsores* or *fidepromissores* to require within thirty days a preliminary inquiry as to whether the requisite declaration has been made, and, upon proof that it has not, to be adjudged free from all liability. This law makes no mention of *fidejussores*; it is, however, usual to make the like declaration in their case.

§ 124. The benefit of the *lex Cornelia* extends to all sureties. This law forbids any one to become surety for the same debtor, to the same creditor, in the same year, for a loan (*pecunia credita*) exceeding 20,000 *sesterces*, and enacts that if the *sponsor*, or *fidepromissor*, does become surety for a larger sum, *e.g.*, 100,000 *sesterces*, he shall not be liable beyond 20,000. We understand by borrowed money (*pecunia credita*) not merely that which is actually lent, but the whole amount which at the date of the contract it is certain will become due, *i.e.*, everything included unconditionally. Thus, whatever we stipulate shall be paid on a given date is so regarded, because it is certain that it will then be due, though there may be no right to demand it before. The word "*pecunia*" in this law designates all things; consequently, when we stipulate concerning wine, or corn, or even land, or a slave, the requirements of this law must be observed.

§ 125. However, in certain cases, this law permits the taking of security for undefined amounts, *e.g.*, it is lawful to take security for dower, or for whatever may come to one by testament, or for whatever may be adjudged due by a judge; and further, it is provided by the *lex Julia* (A.D. 6), which imposes a duty of one-twentieth on testamentary successions, that the securities therein required shall be excepted from the scope of the *lex Cornelia*.

§ 126. *Sponsores*, *fidepromissores*, and *fidejussores* are also on an equality in this: they cannot make their obligation greater than that of the person for whom they have become surety, though they may make it less, as we have already explained is the case with *adstipulatores*, for their obligation, like that of *adstipulatores*, is accessory to the principal obligation, and the accessory cannot exceed the principal.

§ 127. They also resemble each other in this: if either satisfies the debt he may maintain an *actio mandati* against the debtor to recover the amount. By the *lex Publilia*, the *sponsores* have an action peculiar to themselves for double the amount, styled *actio dispensi.*

XV. *De Litterarum Obligatione.*

§ 128. The contract "*litteris*" arises in the case of *nomina transcripticia.* A *nomen transcripticium* is made in two ways, either from thing to person, or from person to person.

§ 129. It is made from thing to person when, for example, I have placed to your debit the amount you owe me for a sale, a letting, or a partnership.

§ 130. It is made from person to person when I place to your debit the amount owed to me by Titius; *i. e.*, when Titius has substituted you for himself as my debtor.

§ 131. It is otherwise in the case of those *nomina* termed *arcaria*, for in those the obligation springs *re*, not *litteris;* inasmuch as the obligation does not arise till the money has been paid, and the paying over of money constitutes an obligation *re*, not *litteris.* We may with reason say that the *arcaria nomina* do not create an obligation, but merely furnish evidence of an obligation previously created.

§ 132. Consequently it is correct to say that even the *peregrini* are bound by *nomina arcaria*, because they are bound, not by the entry (*nomen*), but by the payment, for this species of obligation belongs to the *jus gentium.*

§ 133. But are the *peregrini* bound by *nomina transcripticia?* It is doubted, and with reason, for such obligations are in a certain sense creatures of the civil law. That was the opinion of Nerva. Sabinus and Cassius, however, thought that when the entry was from *thing* to *person*, the *peregrini* were bound, whereas, when it was from *person to person*, they were not.

§ 134. Besides, an obligation *litteris* appears to be contracted when a document is signed by a debtor only (*chirograph*), or by both debtor and creditor (*syngraph*), that is to say, when any one states in writing that he owes, or that he will give, provided there be no stipulation made concerning the matter. This species of obligation is peculiar to the *peregrini.*

XVI. *De Consensu Obligatione.*

§ 135. In the case of purchase and sale, or letting and hiring, partnership, or mandate, the obligation is contracted by the mere agreement of the parties.

§ 136. It is said that in all these cases the obligation is contracted by consent, inasmuch as no particular form of words or writing is required, the consent of the parties to the transaction being sufficient. Such engagements may be contracted by persons living at a distance from each other, for example, by letter or messenger; whereas the obligation *verbis* cannot be contracted with the absent.

§ 137. So, in these contracts, each party is bound to do all that equity demands; whereas, in the obligation *verbis*, the one stipulates and the other promises; and in the obligation *litteris*, by entering a sum as due, the one obliges and the other is obliged.

§ 138. By placing an amount to the debit of a person not present, he may be bound *litteris;* whereas the obligation *verbis* cannot be contracted with one who is not present.

XVII. *De Emptione et Venditione.*

§ 139. The contract of purchase and sale is concluded as soon as the price is agreed on, though the amount be not paid, or even earnest money not paid. Anything given by way of earnest is only evidence of a contract of purchase and sale having been entered into.

§ 140. The price ought to be determined (*certum esse debet*). If, for instance, the parties agreed, the one to sell and the other to buy a given thing at the price Titius should fix on it, Labeo says that such agreement would have no legal force, and Cassius is of the same opinion. Ofilius, however, contends that such an agreement would be a contract of sale and purchase, and his opinion has been adopted by Proculus.

§ 141. Furthermore, the consideration or price must be money. Could it consist of anything else? Could, for example, a slave, a garment, or a plot of land be the price of any other object? That is a question that has been warmly debated. Our masters contend that the price need not necessarily be money. Hence the common notion that the contract of purchase and sale can be effected by exchange, and that this species of contract is the most ancient. They, indeed, quote in support of their contention a passage from the Greek poet Homer, who somewhere says:—

> "Here touched Achæan barks in quest of wine:
> They purchased it with copper and with steel,
> With hides, with hornèd cattle, and with slaves."

The authors of the other school entertain a different view, and contend that exchange is one thing, and purchase and sale another; otherwise, say they, it is impossible to determine between the things exchanged, which of them is to be considered sold, and which given as the price, and, on the other hand, that it would be absurd to consider each thing as being at the same time the thing sold and the price. Cælius Sabinus, however, says, "If Titius has a thing to sell, *e. g.*, a plot of land, and I take it from him and give him, *e. g.*, a slave as the price, the plot of land would be considered the thing sold, and the slave the price paid for the land."

XVIII. *De Locatione et Conductione.*

§ 142. The contract of letting and hiring is governed by similar principles, for unless the amount of the rent is determined there is no contract of letting and hiring.

§ 143. When one has agreed to let to another, and both have agreed that the amount of the rent shall be determined by, say, Titius, it is asked;—Can that agreement be called a contract of letting and hiring? Or if I give garments to a fuller to be smoothed and cleaned, or to a tailor to be repaired, the terms not being settled at the time, but it being my intention to pay him what we may hereafter agree on, is there a contract of letting and hiring?

§ 144. Or if I hand something to you to be used by you, and you at the same time hand something to me to be used by me, is that a contract of letting and hiring?

§ 145. The contracts of purchase and sale, and of letting and hiring, have so much in common, that in some cases it is doubtful whether the transaction amounts to a contract of purchase and sale, or to a contract of letting and hiring, *e.g.*, when a thing is let in perpetuity, as in the case of city corporation lands which are let with a clause in the agreement, that so long as the rent is paid the land shall not be taken from the tenant or his heir. The prevalent opinion is, that it is a letting and hiring.

§ 146. So, if I have handed over to you gladiators on the condition that for each of them that comes safely out of the combat you shall give me 20 *denarii* for his exertions, and for each that shall be killed or wounded you shall give me 1,000 *denarii*, is that a sale or letting? The opinion generally favoured is, that as to those who return intact it is a case of letting and hiring, whereas, as to those who are killed, or wounded, it is a case of purchase and sale: that, in short, it is the event that decides which it is in respect of each individual, as each has been let or sold on condition, for it is no longer disputed that a thing may be the subject either of sale, or hire, on condition.

§ 147. So when I agree with a goldsmith that he shall make me certain rings of a given weight and form with his own gold, and that he shall receive from me, say 200 *denarii*, is that, it is asked, purchase and sale, or letting and hiring? Cassius says that it is sale of the material and hire of the labour. But the majority maintain that it is purchase and sale. If I had supplied the gold to the goldsmith, it is admitted by all, that the agreement as to what he should be paid for his labour would be a contract of letting and hiring.

XIX. *De Societate.*

§ 148. We contract a partnership either as to our affairs in general, or as to one particular matter, *e.g.*, slave dealing.

§ 149. There was a grand discussion as to whether a partnership could be so contracted as to allow one of the partners to take a larger proportion of the gains than he bore of the losses. Quintus Mucius maintained that such a provision was opposed to the very nature of partnership. On the other hand, Servius Sulpicius, whose opinion has prevailed, was so satisfied that such a partnership could be contracted, that he said there was no reason why it should not be agreed that one of the partners should not bear any of the losses though he should participate in the profits, provided his personal services were of such value to the firm as to render such an agreement equitable. There can be no doubt that a partnership may be entered into on the terms that one shall find all the capital, but that the profits shall be equally divided between them, for it frequently happens that the services of the one are as valuable to the firm as is the money of the other.

§ 150. It is clear that, when no special arrangement has been made as to the division of profits and losses, they are divisible equally; and, when the share of each has been agreed on in the one case, *e.g.*, the profits, and no mention made as to losses, they will be borne in the like proportion.

§ 151. A partnership subsists so long as the partners agree to continue partners, but the resignation of one dissolves the partnership. But, should the retiring partner have retired for the express purpose of securing to himself alone some particular benefit, *e.g.*, assuming him to have entered into partnership with me as to our affairs in general, and finding that he was about to inherit a valuable estate, he dissolved partnership in order to get the whole estate to himself, he would be compelled to bring that estate into the partnership account; but should he receive a windfall that he had not anticipated, the benefit of it would be his alone. All that I acquire after his retirement belongs to me.

§ 152. Partnership is also dissolved by the death of one of the partners, because he who contracts a partnership selects as his associate a particular individual.

§ 153. It is also said that a partnership is dissolved by a *capitis diminutio* of either of the partners, because, as a principle of the civil law, *capitis diminutio* is held equivalent to death. If the partners consent to remain associated as partners, a new partnership is in effect created.

§ 154. So, if the property of one of the partners is sold, to satisfy public or private creditors, the partnership is thereby dissolved, but in this case also a new partnership may be entered into between the same persons, for partnership is contracted by consent; the relationship belongs to the *jus gentium*, and natural reason tells us that all men can consent.

XX. *De Mandato.*

§ 155. When we give instructions to another, whether as to our own affairs, or as to those of a third person, we enter into the contract styled *mandatum.* If then I direct you to attend to my affairs, or to the affairs of another, obligations are imposed on both of us, and we are bound the one to the other, to do, each for the other, all that good faith demands.

§ 156. But if I commission you to attend to your own interests, my mandate is superfluous, for what you do for yourself is the result of your own determination; it is not my mandate that you obey. If then you tell me that you have money at home lying idle, and I advise you to put it out at interest, though you may lend it to some one from whom you cannot recover it, you cannot maintain an action of mandate against me. So if I have advised you to buy a certain thing, though the purchase may not have proved to your advantage. This proposition is so incontestable, that it was questioned whether you could maintain an action of mandate against one who instructed you to lend money on interest to Titius; but the affirmative has prevailed, because it is held that you would not have lent the money to Titius if you had not received the mandate to do so.

§ 157. It is clear that a mandate to do an immoral act does not create an obligation, *e.g.*, if I order you to rob, or injure Titius.

§ 158. So a mandate, to do something after my death, is void, because it is generally admitted that a successor cannot be the original subject of an obligation.

§ 159. A valid mandate may be revoked before it has been acted on.

§ 160. So the death of either of the parties, prior to action taken on the mandate, revokes it; but convenience has introduced the rule that, if after the death of him who gave me a mandate, I, being ignorant of the fact of his death, execute the mandate, I can maintain an action of mandate; otherwise, my actual and excusable ignorance would damnify me. By parity of reasoning, it has been decided that if my debtor, in error, pays to my steward, after I have manumitted him, what he owed me, the debt is discharged, though, according to the strict letter of the law, it is not, the debtor not having paid the person he was bound to pay.

§ 161. When the person to whom I have given a valid mandate deviates from his authority, I can maintain against him an action of mandate for the damage sustained by me by reason of his deviation, provided always that it was possible for him to execute my mandate. He has no action against me. If, then, I have given you a mandate, *e.g.*, to buy a plot of land for me for 100,000 *sesterces*, and you have bought it for 150,000, you have no action against me, even if you are willing to let me have the land for the sum I authorized you to pay for it: this was the decided opinion of Sabinus and Cassius. But, if you have bought it for a less sum, you will doubtless have an action against me, because he who authorizes a purchase at 100,000 must be taken to have authorized a purchase at a less sum if possible.

§ 162. In conclusion, it must be observed that whenever I hand over anything to be worked on without discussing the question of remuneration—which act, had I agreed a price, would have constituted a contract of letting and hiring—an action for mandate lies, *e.g.*, if I give garments to a fuller to be smoothed and cleaned, or to a tailor to be repaired.

XXI. *Per quas Personas nobis Obligatio acquiratur.*

§ 163. Having expounded the different kinds of obligation that spring from contracts, we must here observe, that we acquire, not only by ourselves, but also by those whom we have *in potestate*, *in manu*, or *in mancipio*.

§ 164. We also acquire through the instrumentality of freemen, and the slaves of others whom we *bonâ fide* possess, but only in two cases, viz., when the acquisition is the result of their labour, or the fruit of our property.

§ 165. In those two cases, also, we acquire through the slave of another of whom we have but the bare usufruct.

§ 166. He who has simply the Quiritarian property in a slave, though he is his proprietor, is, however, deemed to have inferior rights to him who has the usufruct, or who is the *bonâ fide* possessor; for it has been held that the slave can in no case acquire for him; in short, some authors are of opinion that even should the slave have expressly stipulated for his Quiritarian owner by name that something should be given to him, or have received something in his name *in mancipium*, no acquisition would thereby be made by him.

§ 167. It is certain that a slave who is the property of more than one master acquires for his several masters in the proportion of their respective interests in him: however, when stipulating, or receiving *in mancipium* for one of them by name, he acquires for him alone, *e. g.*, when he stipulates thus: "Do you promise to give to Titius my master?" or, when he receives *in mancipium*, thus: "I declare that this thing belongs, *ex jure Quiritium*, to Lucius Titius my master; and be it bought for him by this brass and with these scales."

§ 167a. It is questionable, whether the fact of a command having been given by one particular master has the same effect as the mention by the slave of his name. The leaders of our school are of opinion that the acquisition is made for the master who gave the order, just as it would be if the slave had stipulated, or received *in mancipium*, in his name. The authorities of the other school contend that the acquisition is made for the benefit of all, just as if no order had been given by any one.

XXII. *Quibus Modis Obligatio tollatur.*

§ 168. An obligation is dissolved, primarily, by the payment of that which is due. It is matter of discussion whether a debtor, who, with the consent of his creditor, pays one thing instead of another, is discharged according to the strict letter of the law, as our masters contend; or whether he, in law, remains bound, though able to defend himself by an *exceptio doli*, as is contended by the authorities of the other school.

§ 169. An obligation may also be dissolved by *acceptilatio*. *Acceptilatio* is a species of imaginary payment. Thus, if you wish to remit what I owe you by a contract *verbis*, you can do so by permitting me to say, "Will you acknowledge as received what I promised to give you?" you replying, "I do."

§ 170. No contracts other than those contracted *verbis* can be dissolved in this manner. It appeared reasonable, that that which has been contracted by word of mouth, should be dissoluble by word of mouth. That, however, which is due from any other cause may become the subject of a stipulation and be dissolved by *acceptilatio.*

§ 171. Without the authorization of her tutor a woman cannot make an *acceptilatio,* though an actual payment may be made to her without his authorization.

§ 172. Part payment of a debt may be made, but whether there can be *acceptilatio* as to part is doubtful.

§ 173. There is another species of imaginary payment, viz., that made *per æs et libram.* It, like the other, is only valid in certain cases, *e. g.,* when the obligation has been contracted *per æs et libram,* or results from a judgment.

§ 174. In this case there must be at least five witnesses and a *libripens.* In addition to which the person to be released from his obligation must say, "Inasmuch as I am bound to you in so many thousand *sesterces* by reason of *nexum,* I now pay you and discharge myself by means of this coin and copper balance. I have struck the scales once for all, and my obligation is at an end." He then strikes the scales with the coin, after which he hands it to the person, by whom he is released, in token of payment.

§ 175. In this way a legatee releases the heir from payment of a legacy left him by *damnatio,* provided only that, in like manner as a judgment-debtor admits himself bound by the sentence of the court, so must the heir of the deceased admit himself bound by a judgment. This method of discharge only applies when the obligation is to deliver something that may be weighed or counted, and when the quantity is determined; some think that it is applicable in the case of things measurable, provided the thing be definite.

§ 176. An obligation may also be dissolved by *novatio, e.g.,* if I stipulate with Titius that he shall hand me the sum you owe me. For, by the intervention of another person, a new obligation is created, and, the first being merged in the second, it is extinguished. Sometimes, even though the second stipulation may be void, the first nevertheless perishes by the law of novation; *e.g.*, if I stipulate with Titius that after his death he shall pay me the amount you owe me, or with a female, or with a pupil without the authorization of the tutor: in either case I lose what is due to me, for the original debtor is discharged, and the second agreement is void. It is otherwise if I stipulate with a slave, for in that case the original debtor remains bound as completely as if I had not subsequently stipulated with another.

§ 177. If I stipulate with the person with whom I had originally contracted, there is no novation, unless something new is introduced into the second contract, *e.g.*, if I add or remove a condition, or a *sponsor*, or a term.

§ 178. However, what I have said as to the *sponsor* is not quite clear, for the authorities of the other school contend that the addition or removal of a *sponsor* does not create a novation.

§ 179. When it is said that the addition of a condition creates a novation, it must be understood that we intend that it does so when the condition is fulfilled; if it is not, the original obligation stands. But let us see whether, in the event of the stipulator suing on the obligation, he could be defeated by the *exceptio doli mali*, or *pacti conventi.* The agreement between the parties appears to be that the thing stipulated for should not be demanded till the happening of the condition mentioned in the second stipulation. However, Servius Sulpicius thought that the novation takes effect immediately, *i.e.*, the moment the second stipulation is made, while the condition is still in suspense, and consequently, should the condition never happen, no action could be taken on either stipulation, and that the debt was gone. Consistently with that theory, he held that if any one stipulates with a slave for that which Lucius Titius owes to him (the stipulator), the stipulation works a novation, and the debt is lost, for no action will lie against the slave. In each case, however, our authorities adopt a different view, and say that a novation no more takes place in either of those cases than it would should I, in stipulating with a *peregrinus*, employ the word "*spondes*," there being no *sponsi communio* between us.

§ 180. An obligation is also dissolved by the *litis contestatio*, provided always that the plaintiff has sued *legitimo judicio*, for in that case the original obligation is extinguished, and the defendant becomes bound by virtue of the *litis contestatio*, and, should he be condemned, the *litis contestatio* in its turn merges in the judgment by which he is bound. This is the meaning of our old authorities when they say, "Before the *litis contestatio*, the debtor ought to convey; after the *litis contestatio*, he ought to submit to award; after the *condemnatio*, he ought to do what he has been adjudged to do."

§ 181. Hence it follows, that if I sue for a debt *legitimo judicio*, I cannot afterwards, by the letter of the civil law, maintain another action for the same debt, for it would be idle for me to aver that "it ought to be given to me," inasmuch as, by the *litis contestatio*, the defendant has ceased to be bound to give. It is otherwise if I proceed by action founded on the *imperium*, for in that case the obligation still remains, and consequently, strictly speaking, I may maintain a second action; but then I should be met with the plea (*exceptio*) of *rei judicatæ*, or *in judicium deductæ*. In the next commentary, we will state what actions are *legitima judicia*, and what are founded on the *imperium*.

XXIII. *De Obligationibus quæ ex Delicto nascuntur.*

§ 182. We will now pass to obligations *ex delicto*, for instance, where a theft has been committed, or goods have been carried off by force, or damage inflicted, or an injury done. Each and all of these acts create but one species of obligation, whereas, as we have already explained, obligations *ex contractu* are divided into four classes.

XXIV. *De Furtis.*

§ 183. Servius Sulpicius and Masurius Sabinus maintain that there are four kinds of theft: viz., *manifestum*, *nec manifestum*, *conceptum*, and *oblatum*. Labeo contends that there are but two, viz., *manifestum* and *nec manifestum*, for he says that *conceptum* and *oblatum* are rather kinds of actions arising from theft; which certainly seems the better view, as will appear hereafter.

§ 184. According to some authors *furtum manifestum* is theft that is discovered at the time it is committed. Others have gone further, and held that it is theft that has been discovered in the place where it was committed, *e. g.*, if a theft of olives is committed and discovered in an olive grove, or of grapes in a vineyard, while the thief is there, it is *manifestum;* or if a theft be committed in a house, so long as the thief is in the house. Others go further, and say that it is *manifestum* till the thief has succeeded in depositing the thing stolen in the place where he intended to deposit it. Others go still further, and say that it is *manifestum* whenever the thief has been seen in the possession of the stolen property. But this last contention has been discarded. The opinion also that a theft is *manifestum*, provided it is discovered before the thief has succeeded in depositing the stolen property where he intended to deposit it, has also been rejected, because it gave rise to doubt as to whether in respect of time the discovery was limited to one day, or extended to several; for the thief, having committed the robbery in one city, may intend to convey the stolen property to another city, or to another province. We are therefore limited to the first two opinions. Each has its supporters; the majority, however, prefer the second.

§ 185. From what has been said concerning *furtum manifestum*, it is easy to conclude what is intended by the expression *furtum nec manifestum*, for theft that is not *manifestum* must be *nec manifestum*.

§ 186. Theft is styled *conceptum* when the stolen property has been sought for, and found in the presence of witnesses in any one's possession; in which case, though the person in whose possession the stolen property is found may not be the thief, yet a particular action lies against him, styled the *actio concepti*.

§ 187. Theft is called *oblatum* when stolen property has been transferred to you and has been found in your custody, provided it was transferred to you with the intention that it should be discovered in your possession rather than in the possession of the person who transferred it to you. In that case, as against the person who transferred the stolen property to you, though he may not be the thief, you have a particular action styled an *actio oblati*.

§ 188. The action styled *actio prohibiti furti* lies against any one who offers resistance to any one wishing to search for stolen property.

§ 189. By the Twelve Tables *furtum manifestum* entailed capital punishment. When the thief was a freeman, after having been scourged, he was adjudicated to the person he had robbed, but whether he thereby became his slave, or was merely *adjudicatus*, was not settled by the ancients. A slave found guilty of *furtum manifestum* was first scourged, and then hurled from a rock. At a later date the severity of the punishment was disapproved of, and, by an edict of the prætor, an action to recover four times the value of the stolen property was substituted, whether the thief was a freeman or a slave.

§ 190. In the case of *furtum nec manifestum*, the Twelve Tables enacted that the thief should forfeit a sum equal to double the value of the property stolen, and the prætor has adopted the rule.

§ 191. By the Twelve Tables, the penalty in the case of *conceptum* and *oblatum* was the treble value; this also has been retained by the prætor.

§ 192. The penalty in the case of the *actio prohibiti* has been fixed by a prætor's edict at quadruple the value. The law has not enacted any penalty in that case; it simply provided that he who desired to make the search should do so naked, girt with a *linteum*, and holding a dish in his hand, and that in the event of his thus discovering the stolen property, the theft should be declared *manifestum*.

§ 193. There has been considerable discussion as to what is to be understood by the term "*linteum*," but the better opinion is that it was a species of girdle with which the private parts were covered. The whole of this provision of the law is ridiculous, for he who would resist search being made by a man in his ordinary clothing would do so if he were naked, and especially if the discovery of the property under those circumstances would subject him to heavier penalty. When the law ordained that the searcher should hold a plate in his hand, whether to prevent his concealing anything in his hand, or that he might place the stolen article, if found, on the plate, neither reason could apply should the article sought be of such dimensions or nature that it could not be concealed in the hand or placed on the plate. One thing, however, is undisputed: the law was satisfied, whatever might be the material of which the plate was made.

§ 194. Inasmuch as the law says that under these circumstances the theft is *manifestum*, some writers have said that *furtum manifestum* is of two kinds, *i.e.*, *in law* and *in fact*. *Furtum manifestum* in law is that theft of which we have just been speaking. *Furtum manifestum* in fact is that of which we treated previously. It is, however, more accurate to say that *furtum manifestum* must exist, if at all, in fact, for the law cannot make that *manifestum* which is not *manifestum*, any more than it can make that theft which is not theft, or that adultery or homicide which is not adultery or homicide. But the law can do this: it may make a man liable to punishment as if he had committed a theft, or had been guilty of adultery or homicide, though he had not committed either of those wrongs.

§ 195. Theft is committed, not merely by the taking of the property of another with the intention to appropriate it to the use of the taker, but, in general, by the disposing of property contrary to the will of the proprietor.

§ 196. If, then, a person appropriates to his own use the property of another deposited with him for safe keeping, he commits a theft; so, if one has received an article to be used by himself in one manner, and he appropriates it to another use, the *actio furti* will lie against him; *e. g.*, if one borrows silver plate for the alleged purpose of entertaining guests, and carries it with him on a journey; or if he borrows a horse for a short ride, and takes it for a long one, or, as the ancients had it, takes it into battle, the action will lie against him.

§ 197. It has been decided, however, that one who converts property to a use different from that for which he received it, does not commit a theft, unless he does so knowing that he acts contrary to the will of the owner, and that, had the owner known it, he would not have permitted it. If, however, he was of opinion that the owner would have sanctioned the particular use, he is not guilty of the crime of theft. The distinction is just, for theft cannot be committed without fraudulent intent (*dolo malo*).

§ 198. When one uses the property of another in a manner which he supposes to be contrary to the will of the owner, but which in fact is not contrary to his will, it is said that no theft is committed. Here is a question:—Titius solicits my slave to steal from me a certain article, and to take it to him; my slave tells me of it, when, for the purpose of catching Titius *flagrante delicto*, I permit my slave to take the article to Titius,—Can I maintain against Titius either an action of theft, or for the corruption of my slave? It has been said that neither action can be maintained against him:—that theft will not lie, because he did not possess himself of my property contrary to my will; and that an action for corrupting my slave cannot be maintained, because the slave was not in fact corrupted.

§ 199. A theft may even be committed of free persons, for example, if one carries off children who are in my *potestas*, or my wife who is *in manu*, or my judgment debtor, or one who has engaged himself to me as gladiator.

§ 200. Sometimes a theft is committed by one of his own property, for example, if a debtor subtracts from his creditor that which he has deposited with him as security, or if I take my property from one who has the possession of it *bonâ fide;* whence it has been concluded that he who conceals his own slave, that was *bonâ fide* in the possession of him from whom he escaped, commits a theft.

§ 201. On the other hand, we may, under certain circumstances, take, and, by *usucapio*, acquire the property in the goods of another without being guilty of theft; for example, property belonging to an inheritance of which the *heres necessarius* has not taken possession, for where there is a *heres necessarius* it is admitted that property may be acquired *pro herede* by *usucapio*. In like manner the debtor who retains possession of the article that he has made over to his creditor as a pledge, whether by *mancipatio*, or *cessio in jure*, can, as has been stated in the previous commentary, without theft, acquire the property in the article by *usucapio*.

§ 202. A man may be liable to an action for theft without having himself committed a theft, when, by his assistance, or counsel, a theft has been committed; for example, the man who knocks your money out of your hand in order that another may pick it up, or he who places himself before you and prevents your passage while another robs you, or he who has frightened and started your sheep or your oxen in order that another may seize them; our ancient authors say, "or he who has scattered a herd of oxen with a red rag." But if these things are done wantonly, and not with the intention of facilitating a robbery, we must see whether an *actio utilis* would lie under the *lex Aquilia;* for the *lex Aquilia*, concerning damage, makes one liable for the consequences of neglect.

§ 203. An action for theft (*actio furti*) may be maintained by any one who has an interest in the preservation of the property, even though he may not be the owner, but it cannot be maintained by the owner, unless he at the same time is interested in the preservation of the thing.

§ 204. Hence, a creditor could maintain the action against the person who abstracted his pledge, even should that person be the owner, that is to say, the debtor.

§ 205. So, if a fuller has received a garment to press or clean, or a tailor one to repair, for a certain reward, and it has been stolen, it is he who has the right of action, and not the owner, because the owner has no interest that the thing should not perish, inasmuch as by the *actio locati* he can recover from the fuller, or tailor, an indemnity, assuming that the fuller, or tailor, is in a position to give it; if, however, he should be insolvent, then, as the owner could not recover the value from the fuller, or tailor, he would be entitled to maintain the action of theft against the thief, for he would in that case be interested in the preservation of the article.

§ 206. What we have said concerning the fuller and tailor applies equally to the borrower; for, as the former, by receiving hire, becomes responsible for the safe custody, the borrower, by enjoying the use of an article, becomes in like manner responsible.

§ 207. A mere bailee is only responsible for his own wrong. If, therefore, the article deposited with him is stolen, he is not liable for it in an action of deposit, consequently, he has no interest in the safety of it; he cannot therefore maintain an action of theft for its recovery, but the owner may.

§ 208. It has been asked whether an infant, who appropriates to himself the property of another, thereby commits a theft. The majority of our authors maintain, that as theft involves criminal intent, an infant does not incur the obligation, unless, by reason of the fact of his bordering on manhood, he comprehends that he is committing a criminal act.

XXV. *De Vi Bonorum Raptorum.*

§ 209. He who possesses himself by force of the property of another is liable to the *actio furti;* for, who can be said more obviously to possess himself of the property of another against his will than he who takes it by violence? In fact, it has been said, and with reason, that the only difference between him and an ordinary thief is, that he is the more criminal of the two; he has consequently been styled an *improbus fur*. However, the prætor has instituted a special action for this species of wrong, which is called the *actio vi bonorum raptorum*. If the action is brought within one year of the date of the forcible taking, the injured may recover four times the value of the property seized; if he allows a year to elapse before bringing his action, he can only recover the actual value of the property taken. This action lies when a single thing only has been seized, and even when the value of that thing may be but very little.

XXVI. *De Lege Aquiliâ.*

§ 210. The action *damni injuriæ* (unlawful damage) was established by the *lex Aquilia,* in the first clause of which it is provided that he who unlawfully kills the slave of another, or an animal included in the category of cattle, shall be condemned to pay the highest value that the slave or beast had during that year.

§ 211. The killing is considered unlawful when it is the consequence of *dolus* (malice) or *culpa* (negligence). The law does not give any redress for damage caused without *injuria;* therefore he who occasions a loss to another by accident, there being neither malice nor negligence on his part, goes unpunished.

§ 212. In the action derived from the *lex Aquilia*, the measure of damage is not the actual value merely of the slave or beast destroyed, but the loss sustained by the owner by reason of the death; for example, if my slave had been instituted heir by any one, and was killed before making, by my order, *cretio* of the inheritance; for not merely his value, but that of the inheritance lost, is taken into consideration. So if one of a pair of slaves, or one of a troupe of comedians or musicians, is killed, to his value must be added the depreciation of the value of the survivors by reason of his death. The same rule applies when one of a pair of mules or of a team of horses has been killed.

§ 213. The owner of the slave may either proceed against the murderer criminally, or may sue him for damages under this law.

§ 214. The insertion in the law of the words "*The highest value the thing has had within the year*" has this effect:—If a lame or one-eyed slave is killed, whose infirmity was not of a year's standing at the time of his death, the damages recoverable are not his value at the time of his death but his highest value during the year, the result being that one sometimes recovers more than he has lost.

§ 215. The second clause of the *lex Aquilia* gives a right of action against an *adstipulator* who has given *acceptilatio* in fraud of his *stipulator* for the value of the subject-matter.

§ 216. That this section of the *lex Aquilia* gave an action to recover compensation for damage done is evident; the provision, however, was unnecessary, inasmuch as the *actio mandati* sufficed for this purpose. By the *lex Aquilia*, however, the injured can recover the double value from any one who wrongfully denies liability.

§ 217. The third section of the *lex Aquilia* embraces all other kinds of damage, *e.g.*, the wounding of a slave, or quadruped included under the name of cattle, or a quadruped not included in that class, such as a dog, or a wild beast, bear, or lion. It not only includes actionable damage done to any other species of animal, but to inanimate things. If anything is burnt or broken (*ruptum*), or shattered (*fractum*), this third section provides an action for the wrong done. The word *ruptum* includes damage of every kind; it therefore includes burning, breaking, shattering, tearing, bruising, spilling, tearing down, destroying, or deteriorating.

§ 218. For damage falling under this third section, the wrong-doer is only liable to the extent of the highest value the thing had during the preceding thirty days, not the preceding year. In fact the word *plurimi* (the highest value) is not used, for which reason certain authorities of the opposite school have contended that it is competent for the prætor to insert in the *formula* any day he may think fit, provided it is one of the next preceding thirty. Sabinus, however, maintained that the clause must be read as if the word *plurimi* was repeated in it, as the use of that word in the first section was intended by the legislature to be made once for all.

§ 219. It is admitted that no action will lie under the *lex Aquilia* for damage other than that directly inflicted by the wrong-doer (*corpore suo*). When the damage has been caused in any other way, *utiles actiones* are given: *e.g.*, if one shut up the slave, or animal, of another, and left it to perish of hunger, or so overdrove a beast of burden as to cause its death; or if a man persuaded the slave of another to go up a tree, or down a well, who while ascending, or descending, fell and was killed, or hurt. If one has pushed the slave of another over a bridge, or bank, into a stream where he was drowned, it is clear that in such case the damage is direct, for he pushed the man in.

XXVII. *De Injuriis.*

§ 220. We do an illegal act not merely by striking another with the fist, or a stick, or lash, but in publicly using abusive language concerning him; in declaring that his estate is for sale as if he were our debtor when we know that he does not owe us anything; in publishing a defamatory tract or verses concerning him, or by following about a chaste woman, or lad; and, in fact, in many other ways.

§ 221. We may sustain injury not merely in our own person, but also through children in our *potestas*, or through a wife, though not *in manu*. If, therefore, you injure my daughter who is married to Titius, the action will lie against you at the suit of either my daughter, Titius, or myself.

§ 222. In the case of a slave it is otherwise; he is not considered capable of sustaining an injury; the wrong done is considered as done to his master in the person of his slave. We are not, however, supposed to receive injury through the person of a slave in every case in which, under similar circumstances, we should be regarded as receiving it through a child, or wife; but only in cases where from the nature of the act it is evident that the insult was intended for the master; for example, when the slave of another has been lashed. For that offence a *formula* has been expressly prepared. But, for the use of abusive language in public to the slave of another, or for the striking him with the fist, no *formula* has been prepared, nor can one be easily obtained.

§ 223. By the Twelve Tables, the penalty for injuries was, in the case of a limb destroyed, retaliation; for a bone broken or crushed, a fine of 300 *asses;* for other bodily injuries in the case of a free man, 150 *asses*, in the case of a slave, 25 *asses*. In those days of great poverty, such sums appeared sufficient.

§ 224. We have now a different rule: we are allowed by the prætor to estimate the damage we have sustained, and the *judex* condemns either at the sum claimed, or at such lower figure as to him may appear just. However, as it is customary for the prætor to determine whether the injury is, or is not, atrocious (*atrocem*), should he at the same time have settled the amount of the *vadimonium* (security for due appearance), we insert that amount in the *formula* as the claim; for though the *judex* may award a smaller sum, he seldom ventures to do so on account of the dignity of the prætor.

§ 225. An injury is deemed atrocious, either from the nature of the act itself, *e.g.*, if a man is wounded, flogged, or beaten with sticks by another; or from the circumstances attending it, *e.g.*, if the injury be inflicted in the theatre, or forum: so on account of the position in life of the person injured, *e.g.*, if it is a magistrate who has been injured, or a senator insulted, by a low-bred person.

FOURTH COMMENTARY.

DE ACTIONIBUS.

I. *Generally.*

§ 1. If it is asked—How many kinds (*genera*) of actions are there?—the proper answer appears to be:—Two, viz., actions *in rem* and actions *in personam*. Those who said that there are four, framed on the different classes of *sponsiones*, overlooked the fact that species form themselves into *genera*.

§ 2. An action is *in personam* whenever we sue any one who is bound to us, whether by virtue of a contract, or of a delict: that is to say, when we allege that he is bound to give (*dare*), to do (*facere*), or to guarantee (*præstare*).

§ 3. An action is *in rem* when we allege that a given corporeal thing is ours, or that we have a certain right; *e.g.*, the right of using, or the right of using and enjoying the fruits, or the right of going across a particular place, or the right of driving cattle across it, or the right of drawing water from it, or the right of building on it, or the right of light and prospect. In either of which cases the action brought by the opposite party to stop the exercise of our alleged right is also an action *in rem*, but is negative.

§ 4. The different classes of actions being thus distinguished, it is clear that we cannot sue another for the recovery of our own property in these terms:—"*If it appears that he ought to give*," for that which is ours cannot be given to us. That only is given or reputed to be given to us which by the act of tradition becomes ours, and that which is ours cannot become more ours. Nevertheless such is the detestation of thieves, that in order that they may be made liable to a greater number of actions, it has been held that in addition to the penalty of double, or quadruple, as the case may be, they, to enable the owner to recover his stolen property, shall be liable to an action in these terms, "If it appears that he ought to give," (*si paret eum dare oportere*), notwithstanding that an action lies against them by which we can lay claim to the thing stolen as being our own.

§ 5. Certain actions *in rem* are styled *vindicationes*, whereas actions *in personam* in which we assert that something ought to be given or done we style *condictiones.*

§ 6. We sometimes sue for the recovery merely of the given thing; at others, to recover the penalty; and again, at others, to recover both the thing and the penalty.

§ 7. We sue to recover the thing itself just as if our action were *ex contractu.*

§ 8. We sue to recover the penalty merely, *e. g.*, by the *actio furti*, or by the *actio injuriarum*, and, in the opinion of some, by the *actio vi bonorum raptorum;* for, as to the thing itself, we have our remedy by *vindicatio* and *condictio.*

§ 9. We sue for the thing itself and the penalty in cases where, *e. g.*, we claim the double value against one who denies our right, as in the actions *judicati*, *dispensi*, *damni injuriæ*, under the *lex Aquilia*, and in the case of legacies of specific things left *per damnationem.*

II. *Legis Actiones.*

§ 10. There are, moreover, some actions which are formed on the model of a *legis actio*, and others which have an independent existence and force. To make this clear we must in the first instance treat of the *legis actiones.*

§ 11. The actions in use in the time of the ancients were styled *legis actiones*, either because they were enacted by the *leges*, for, in those days, the edicts of the prætors to which many actions owe their origin were not in existence; or because they were adapted to the words of the *leges*, and their terms were adhered to as rigidly as those of the *leges* themselves. Hence, when in an action brought for cutting down vines, the plaintiff, in his plaint, used the word "*vites*" instead of "*arbores*," it was held that the action must be dismissed, as "*arbores*" is the word used in the law of the Twelve Tables concerning cutting down trees in general, and upon which the action was founded.

§ 12. There were five forms of the *legis actio*, viz., *sacramentum*, *judicis postulatio*, *condictio*, *manus injectio*, and *pignoris captio*.

III. *Sacramentum.*

§ 13. The *actio sacramenti* was general, and was used whenever the law had not expressly provided another form. This form of action was as perilous for the party in the wrong as is our present *actio certæ creditæ pecuniæ*, on account of the *sponsio*, the risk of which was run by the defendant who defended vexatiously, and on account of the *restipulatio*, the risk of which was run by the plaintiff who made an unfounded claim. The unsuccessful party forfeited the amount of the *sacramentum* to the public treasury by way of penalty, for the securing of which sureties were given to the prætor; whereas, now, the penalty of the *sponsio* and the *restipulatio* goes to the successful party.

§ 14. The amount of the *sacramentum* was either 500 or 50 *asses*—500 when the value of the subject-matter in dispute was 1,000 *asses*, or more; 50 when its value was below that amount. Such were the provisions of the Twelve Tables. But if the matter in question was the liberty of a man, though the man might be of the greatest value, yet it was provided by the same law that the *sacramentum* should be 50 *asses*. The object being that the *vindex* or asserter of liberty should not be fettered by the necessity to find security for a heavy amount . . . .

§ 15. . . . . to come and receive a *judex*. The litigants having presented themselves at the time stated, a *judex* was assigned to them, in compliance with their request, from the numbers of the decemvirs, to take the case thirty days after, according to the provisions of the *lex Pinaria*. Before the passing of that *lex* it was not the practice to assign a *judex*. We have already said that if the value of the matter in dispute was less than 1,000 *asses*, the *sacramentum* was 50 and not 500 *asses*. When, however, it became the practice to assign a *judex*, the parties gave each other notice to appear before him on the next day but one. When, then before him, each party stated the points of his case, this was termed the *causæ collectio*, *i.e.*, a short outline of the case of each.

§ 16. If the action was *in rem* for a movable or moving

thing that could be brought into court, the thing itself was brought before the *judex*, and was there claimed in the following manner:—The claimant, holding a wand, laid his hand on the thing claimed, for example, a slave, and said, "I declare this man to be my property *ex jure Quiritium* in accordance with his status (*secundum suam causam*) as I have declared it." Then, touching him with his wand, he said, "See, I lay my wand upon him." His adversary, in his turn, employed the same words and acts. Each having thus asserted his claim, the prætor said, "Let go the man, both of you (*Mittite ambo hominem*)." Whereupon each did so. He who had first asserted his claim then said to the other, "State the grounds of your claim." The other replied, "I have satisfied the law, having placed my rod upon him." Then the first claimant said, "Mark you, as you have made an unjust claim, I challenge you to deposit 500 *asses*." His adversary then said, "I too challenge you." The *asses* thus deposited were styled the *sacramentum*. The remaining formalities were the same as those used in an action *in personam;* the prætor then assigned the *vindiciæ* to one of the parties, *i.e.*, he gave to one of them the interim possession of the subject of the litigation, ordering him at the same time to give sureties *litis et vindiciarum*, *i.e.*, for the thing in dispute and the mesne profits, or the value of the interim possession, in the event of losing the case. The prætor also took other sureties for the *sacramentum* from each party, inasmuch as that went to the treasury. The wand was used instead of the spear—the emblem of legal title—for, in the estimation of the ancients, no title was more indefeasible than that of capture from the enemy. This is the reason why the spear is set up in front of the courts of the *centumviri*.

§ 17. If the nature of the object in dispute was such as to prevent its being brought into court without inconvenience—for instance, if it were a column, or a herd of cattle—some portion was taken into court, and the claim was made upon the part in the name of the whole. Thus, in the case of a herd, one sheep, or one goat, out of the flock, was led into court, or, perhaps, a lock of wool merely taken from one of the beasts; whilst, from a ship, or a column, a portion was broken off; so if the matter in dispute was a field, or a house, or even an inheritance, some part was taken therefrom and brought into court; and the claim was made on that part as if the whole had been present; *e.g.*, a clod was taken from the field, or a tile from the house; so if the dispute were about an inheritance. . . .

IV. *Condictio.*

§ 18. This action was rightly styled *condictio* (notice), inasmuch as the plaintiff summoned his opponent to appear in court on the thirtieth day for the purpose of taking a *judex.* The term *condictio* is now, properly speaking, no longer applicable to an action *in personam* in the *intentio* of which we declare that the defendant ought to give something to us, for now there is no *denuntiatio* for that purpose.

§ 19. This *legis actio* was introduced by the *lex Silia* and the *lex Calpurnia:* by the *lex Silia* for the recovery of any certain sum of money, by the *lex Calpurnia* for the recovery of any other ascertained thing.

§ 20. What then was the need of this action when anything that ought to be given to us might be recovered by the *sacramentum* or *per judicis postulationem?* That is a question that has been largely discussed.

V. *Manus Injectio.*

§ 21. The action *manus injectio* (arrest) lay in cases where it was prescribed in any *lex;* for instance, against a judgment debtor by the Twelve Tables. In that action the judgment creditor said: "Whereas you have been adjudged, or condemned, to pay me 10,000 *sesterces* and fraudulently (*dolo malo*) have omitted to do so, I arrest you for the 10,000 *sesterces*, the amount of the judgment debt," at the same time laying his hand upon the judgment debtor. It was unlawful for the judgment debtor to remove the hand of his creditor, nor could he take any legal proceedings on his own behalf, but he was at liberty to appoint a *vindex* (attorney) to act for him; in default of his so doing, his creditor led him to his own house, where he was imprisoned and placed in irons.

§ 22. In the course of time, various *leges* authorized the use of that action, in cases other than those of judgment debtors. Thus, the *lex Publilia* granted it against the principal whose *sponsor*, having satisfied his obligation, had not been reimbursed within six months; so the *lex Furia de sponsu* granted it where a surety (*sponsor*) had been compelled to pay more than his share; in short, by various *leges* the *actio per manus injectionem* was accorded in numerous cases.

§ 23. Other *leges*, again, in certain cases gave the *actio per manus injectionem*, not by way of execution, but as an original action: thus the *lex Furia testamentaria* made it lie against one who had received more than 1,000 *asses* by way of legacy, or as a *donatio mortis causâ*, he not being one who was exempted by that law from its provision in that respect: so the *lex Marcia* granted it against usurers for the purpose of recovering the excessive interest exacted.

§ 24. When proceedings were instituted by virtue of these and similar *leges*, it was lawful for the person arrested to remove the arrest, and to defend himself in person, because the plaintiff, in such cases, did not use the expression *pro judicato* (by virtue of a judgment), but, having stated his ground of complaint, merely added, "therefore I make the arrest by placing my hand upon you;" whereas those (judgment creditors) to whom this *legis actio* was given by way of execution, after having stated the cause of the arrest, added, "for that reason (*i. e.*, the judgment) I arrest you, by placing my hand upon you *pro judicato* (as a judgment debtor)." I do not forget that in the form given in the *lex Furia testamentaria* the words "*pro judicato*" appear, though they are not to be found in the text of the statute, but they appear to me to have been inserted without reason.

§ 25. Later on, however, permission was given by the *lex* (*Varia ?*) to all except judgment debtors, and those for whom money had been paid (by a *sponsor*), when proceeded against *per manus injectionem* to resist the arrest and litigate the matter in person. A judgment debtor, therefore, or one for whom money had been paid, was compelled, even after the passing of this *lex*, to nominate a *vindex*, or, in default, was liable to be carried off by the creditor to his house. Indeed, so long as the *legis actiones* remained in force this practice prevailed, and even in our own times he against whom an action is brought on a judgment, or by a surety not reimbursed, is compelled to find sureties to satisfy the judgment.

VI. *Pignoris Captio.*

§ 26. The *legis actio per pignoris captionem* (distress) in certain cases applied by virtue of custom, and in others by virtue of a particular *lex.*

§ 27. By custom it was introduced in the case of military matters. In fact, it was lawful for a soldier to seize a pledge for his pay from the paymaster who had omitted to hand him his pay. Money supplied to the paymaster for the pay of the soldiers was styled *æs militare.* So, it was lawful for a cavalry soldier to seize a pledge for the money necessary to buy his charger; that money was styled *æs equestre:* so, for the money provided for the purchase of provender, styled *æs hordearium.*

§ 28. The *pignoris captio* was introduced by a *lex, e.g.*, by the Twelve Tables against one who had purchased a sacrificial victim, but had not paid for it; so against one who had not paid for the hire of a beast of burden let in order that the hire money might be expended in a banquet, that is to say, on a sacrificial feast; so also the *lex censoria* gave the *pignoris captio* to the farmers of the public revenues of the Roman people against those who had not paid their taxes due by virtue of some particular *lex.*

§ 29. In all these cases the taking of the pledge was accompanied by the use of a set form of words, for which reason the majority of the jurists concluded that this also was a *legis actio.* Other jurists, however, were not of that opinion, first, because the *pignoris captio* was transacted out of court and most commonly in the absence of the adversary, whereas the other *legis actiones* must be executed before the prætor and in the presence of the adversary; and, lastly, because the pledge might be seized even on a *dies nefastus*, that is to say, at a time when proceedings in court were unlawful.

VII. *De Fictionibus.*

§ 30. All these *legis actiones*, however, became by degrees odious, for by their excessive refinements the authors of our law brought the matter to such a pitch that a suit was lost for the most trifling technical error. Hence the *lex Æbutia* and the two *leges Juliæ* suppressed the *legis actiones*, and substituted for them a system of written statements called *formulæ*.

§ 31. The *legis actiones* are now lawful in two cases only, *i.e.*, in a case of threatened damage, and in the case of an action that must be brought before the *centumviri*. All proceedings before the *centumviri* must be preceded by the *actio sacramenti* before the *prætor urbanus*, or the *prætor peregrinus*. As to the case of threatened damage, no one now thinks of resorting to the *legis actio*, it being far preferable to bind the adversary by the stipulation provided by the prætor in his edict; that process is at the same time more convenient and more complete. . . .

§ 32. In the case of the revenue collector the *formula* contains a species of fiction, inasmuch as it recites that the debtor is to be condemned in the amount that in former days, when pledges were taken, would have been payable by the person who redeemed the pledge.

§ 33. No *formula* has been framed on the fiction of a *condictio*, for when we sue either for a definite sum of money, or any other ascertained thing due to us, we allege in the *intentio* that such sum or thing "ought to be delivered to us," and do not add any fictitious *condictio*. It is therefore to be observed that the *formulæ* by which we claim money, or any ascertained thing, avail of their own special force. Actions in respect of loans, fiduciary obligations, gratuitous services, and an innumerable number of other matters are the same.

§ 34. We have also another species of fiction in certain *formulæ*, *e.g.*, when a claim is made of *bonorum possessio* in virtue of the edict, under the fiction of being heir. For, as the claimant succeeds to the position of the deceased by prætorian law, and not by the old civil law, he has no direct action; he cannot claim, as his, that which was the property of the deceased, or that that which was due to the deceased has, by reason of his death, become due to him; he is therefore compelled to feign being heir, and to formulate his claim thus:—"Let there be a *judex*.—If Aulus Agerius (*i.e.* the plaintiff himself) was the heir of Lucius Titius, then, should it appear that the estate in question is his *ex jure*

Quiritium, &c.;" or when the action is *in personam* after a similar fiction the *formula* runs thus:—"If it appear that Numerius Negidius ought to give to Aulus Agerius 10,000 *sesterces*, &c."

§ 35. In like manner the *bonorum emptor* sues in the fictitious character of heir. Sometimes, however, he sues in another way. He declares himself the principal of the man whose estate he has bought, and directs the *condemnatio* to himself, that is to say, he obtains judgment in his own favour against the former owner and the present possessor of the property, for the property belonging and due to the former owner. This species of *actio* is styled *Rutilian*, because it was framed by the prætor Rutilius, who is also credited with the invention of the proceeding known as *bonorum venditio*. The before-mentioned *actio* in which the purchaser feigned to be heir is styled *Servian*.

§ 36. The *actio* styled *Publiciana* is of the same genus. This action is given to one to whom something has been delivered *ex justâ causâ*, but who has been deprived of it before he has by *usucapio* acquired Quiritarian title to it, in order to enable him to recover it. As he cannot allege that the thing is his *ex jure Quiritium*, he is, by fiction, assumed to have completed his *usucapio*, and thus, as though he had become owner *ex jure Quiritium*, his *intentio* runs thus:—"Let there be a *judex*. If Aulus Agerius has possessed for a year the man that he bought, and who was delivered to him, if then it should appear that the man that he claims in this action is his *ex jure Quiritium*, &c."

§ 37. In like manner Roman citizenship is by a fiction imputed to a *peregrinus* when he is either plaintiff or defendant in a suit in cases where our law has furnished an *actio;* provided always, that it is but just to extend the *actio* to a *peregrinus*, *e. g.*, when the *peregrinus* is plaintiff or defendant in an action for theft. The formula against the *peregrinus* runs thus:—"Let there be a *judex*. If it appears that a theft of a golden goblet has been committed on Lucius Titius by the assistance or advice of Dio Hermæus, for which, were he a Roman citizen, he would have to make satisfaction as though he were the thief, &c." So, when a *peregrinus* is plaintiff in an action for a theft, by legal fiction he is, for the purposes of the action, held to be a Roman citizen. So, when a *peregrinus* is plaintiff or defendant in an action which lies by virtue of the *lex Aquilia* for damage unlawfully inflicted, the fiction that he is a Roman citizen prevails.

§ 38. Again, we sometimes feign that our adversary has not sustained a *capitis diminutio;* for, when one, whether male or female, being under an obligation to us by reason of a contract, suffers a *capitis diminutio, e. g.*, a woman by *coemptio* or a man by *adrogatio*, and thereby ceases, according to the civil law, to be bound by the contract, we consequently cannot allege that he or she "ought to give." To prevent, however, him or her from being able to defeat our just claim, the *actio utilis* was introduced, in which, by a fiction of law, it was held that neither, though having in fact sustained a *capitis diminutio*, had altered his or her legal status.

VIII. *De Partibus Formularum.*

§ 39. A *formula* consists of the following parts:—the *demonstratio*, the *intentio*, the *adjudicatio*, and the *condemnatio*.

§ 40. The *demonstratio* is that part of the *formula*, the chief object of which is to demonstrate the matter in question in the action; for example, "Whereas Aulus Agerius has sold a slave to Numerius Negidius," or "Whereas Aulus Agerius has deposited a slave with Numerius Negidius."

§ 41. The *intentio* is that part of the *formula* in which the plaintiff states his claim or the subject of the action; for example, "If it appears that Numerius Negidius ought to give to Aulus Agerius 10,000 sesterces"; or,—"Whatever it may appear that Numerius Negidius ought to give to, or do for, Aulus Agerius"; or,—"If it appears that this man belongs to Aulus Agerius according to Quiritarian law."

§ 42. The *adjudicatio* is that part of the *formula* by which the *judex* is empowered to adjudge the matter in question to the several parties as he may think fit, as in the case of a distribution of an inheritance between co-heirs, or the division of property held in common, or the settlement of boundaries, for in either of such cases the *formula* runs thus:—"Whatever is due to Titius, *judex*, adjudge to him."

§ 43. The *condemnatio* is that part of the *formula* which confers upon the *judex* the right to condemn or absolve; for example, "*Judex*, condemn Numerius Negidius to pay Aulus Agerius 10,000 sesterces, but if it appears that he should not do so absolve him"; or,—"*Judex*, condemn Numerius Negidius to pay to Aulus Agerius a sum not exceeding 10,000 sesterces, but if it does not appear that he should do so absolve him"; or,—"*Judex*, condemn Numerius Negidius to pay Aulus Agerius 10,000 sesterces," without adding more. . . .

§ 44. A particular *formula* does not necessarily contain all of these parts. Some may be found wanting. The *intentio* is sometimes met with alone, *e. g.*, *in præjudicialibus formulis*, where the question is whether a certain person has been enfranchised, or where the question is as to the amount of a marriage settlement, and other like cases. The *demonstratio*, the *adjudicatio*, or the *condemnatio* is never found alone, for the *demonstratio* has no force independently of the *intentio* or *condemnatio;* so, a *condemnatio* or *adjudicatio* is of no effect without a *demonstratio* or *intentio*, therefore these are never met with alone.

IX. *Conceptio Formularum.*

§ 45. Those *formulæ* which are constructed for the purpose of determining a right are styled *in jus conceptæ;* for example, those in which Quiritarian ownership is alleged, or where the expression "*nobis dare oportere*" is used, or where it is alleged that the defendant ought to be condemned, *pro fure* (as for a theft). In each of these cases the *intentio* embodies, or is based on, a proposition of the old civil law.

§ 46. All other *formulæ* we style *in factum conceptæ*, that is to say, those *formulæ* in which the *intentio* is not drawn up as above, but in which, immediately after the allegation of fact, are added the words by which the power is given to the judge to condemn or acquit. Take, for example, the *formula* employed by a patron against his freedman who has sued him in violation of some prætorian edict:—"Let their be *recuperatores.*—Should it appear that such and such a patron has been sued by such and such a freedman contrary to the edict of such and such a prætor, *recupatores*, condemn the said freedman to pay to the said patron 10,000 sesterces; should it not so appear, acquit him." The other *formulæ* set forth under the title "*de in jus vocando*" are *conceptæ in factum;* as, for instance, the *formula* against him who, being summoned into court, has neither appeared in person nor by deputy; or that against one who by force has prevented a person summoned into court from appearing. In short, there are innumerable other *formulæ* of a like description set forth in the *album.*

§ 47. In certain cases, however, the prætor has framed *formulæ in jus conceptæ,* as well as *formulæ in factum conceptæ,* for example, in the case of an action on a deposit or a loan. In which case the *formula* is framed thus:—"Let there be a *judex.* Whereas Aulus Agerius has deposited with Numerius Negidius a silver table the subject of this action, whatever good faith requires that Numerius Negidius should give to or do for Aulus Agerius, *judex,* adjudge Numerius Negidius liable to Aulus Agerius, should he fail to restore the table. If it does not so appear, acquit him." That *formula* is *in jus concepta.* The *formula* framed as follows—"Let there be a *judex.* If it appears that Aulus Agerius has deposited with Numerius Negidius a silver table, and that Numerius Negidius has unlawfully deprived Aulus Agerius of it, *judex,* condemn Numerius Negidius to pay to Aulus Agerius the value of the table. If it does not so appear, acquit him"—is *in factum concepta.* There are like *formulæ* in the case of loan.

§ 48. Whenever a *formula* contains a *condemnatio* it is a case for pecuniary compensation. Consequently, even when the action is brought in respect of a corporeal thing, such as a field, a slave, a garment, gold, or silver, the *judex* does not condemn the defendant, as formerly, to deliver the thing itself, but to pay its estimated value in money.

§ 49. The *condemnatio* inserted in the *formula* is either for an ascertained or an unascertained amount (*vel certæ pecuniæ, vel incertæ*).

§ 50. It is ascertained (*certæ*) when the claim is for a certain sum, in which case, in the latter part of the *formula* are found these or like words—"*Judex,* condemn Numerius Negidius to pay to Aulus Agerius 10,000 sesterces. If it does not so appear, acquit him."

§ 51. The expression "*incertæ condemnatio pecuniæ*" has two significations. In one case a certain maximum is fixed, this is commonly styled "*cum taxatione*"; for example, when the claim is for unliquidated damages, in which case we find, in the latter part of the *formula*—"*Judex*, condemn Numerius Negidius to pay to Aulus Agerius a sum not exceeding 10,000 sesterces. If it does not so appear, acquit him." In other cases there is no limit fixed, for example, when the action is brought to recover property wrongfully detained from us, *i.e.*, when we sue *in rem*, or *ad exhibendum* (to have something produced in court), for in such cases the *condemnatio* runs thus:—"*Judex*, condemn Numerius Negidius to pay to Aulus Agerius the full value of the thing claimed. If it does not so appear, acquit him."

§ 52. What then is the result? When the *judex* condemns the defendant he must condemn him to pay a certain sum, although no sum may have been inserted in the *condemnatio*. The *judex* must be careful when a certain sum is fixed in the *condemnatio* not to condemn for a larger or for a smaller amount than that sued for, otherwise he makes the cause his own (*alioquin litem suam facit*); so when the amount has been limited (*si taxatio posita sit*) he must not exceed the limit, otherwise he makes the cause his own; he may, however, in that case condemn in an amount less than the limit. . . .

X. *Plus Petitio.*

§ 53. If the plaintiff in his *intentio* claims more than is justly due to him, he fails in his suit, *i.e.*, he loses the thing he is suing for; nor can he be restored to his former position, except in certain cases, where the prætor comes, by his edict, to his relief, [*e. g.*, where he is excused by his youth, or where the error has arisen from circumstances that might have misled the most wary. Too much is sued for in one of four ways, viz.: *re*, *tempore*, *loco*, or *causâ*. It is said to be sued for *re* when the claim is for, say 20,000 sesterces, the debt being only 10,000; or where the plaintiff, having only a share in a particular thing, claims in his *intentio* the entire thing, or more than his just share. It is said to be sued for *tempore*, when the action is brought before the arrival of the time named, or the happening of an agreed condition. It is said to be sued for *loco*, when the agreement was to pay at a particular place, and the plaintiff sues at another place without stating in his *intentio* the fact of agreement as to place; for instance, suppose the stipulation had been in this form: "Do you engage to give me 10,000 sesterces at Capua?" "I do so engage": and the plaintiff, omitting all mention of the place fixed, were to commence his action in Rome in the general form, thus: "Should it appear that Numerius Negidius is bound to give to Aulus Agerius 10,000 sesterces." The plaintiff, in this case, is assumed to be suing for too large an amount, as, by this ordinary *intentio*, he deprives the promissor of the advantage he might have had by the payment being made at Capua. If, however, the plaintiff brings his action in the place where it was presumed that the money would be paid, it is not necessary for him to add the name of the place].[1] It is said to be sued for *causâ*, when, for example, a creditor in the *intentio* deprives his debtor of a right of election given to him by the contract; thus, if the stipulation was in these words, "Do you promise to give me 10,000 sesterces, or the slave Stichus?" and the plaintiff sued for one only of the two; indeed, even when his claim is for the one of the smaller value, he is regarded as having claimed more than his due, inasmuch as it might happen that the defendant could more easily have furnished the other. It is the same when one has stipulated for a *genus*, and afterwards claims a *species;* for example, if he had stipulated for purple cloth and subsequently sued for the purple of Tyre, though he may be suing for that which is of less value, yet, for the reason already stated, the rule is the same. The like must be said if the stipulation was for a slave, without naming one in particular, and afterwards the plaintiff sued for one by name, *e.g.*, Stichus, even though he might be of very little value. It is therefore clear that the *intentio* of the *formula* should exactly coincide with the terms of the *stipulatio*.

§ 54. It is evident that, in what are styled *incertæ formulæ*, more cannot be claimed than is due, because, inasmuch as the claim is not for a determinate quantity, but for all that the

[1] The portion in brackets is taken from the conjectural reading of Heffter, the text being wanting.

defendant ought to give or do, no one can be guilty of a *plus petitio*. The same may be said when the action is *in rem* for an undefined part; for example, if the heir sue for "such" part of the land about which the action is, as shall appear to belong to him; a species of action which only lies in a very limited number of cases.

§ 55. It is also clear that when a man, in his *intentio*, in error, claims one thing for another, he does not thereby incur any risk, and may sue again, ... for example, if he sues for the slave Eros when he should have sued for Stichus, or when, in his *intentio*, he alleges that his right to the thing sued for is derived from a testament, whereas it is derived from a *stipulatio;* or when a *cognitor* or *procurator* has so worded his *intentio* as to make it appear that he is suing as principal.

§ 56. Though, as we have said, it is dangerous to claim more than is our due, it is not dangerous to claim less; if, however, we do, we must not sue for the balance during the residue of the term of office of the same prætor, for if we do we may be met with the *exceptio* styled *litis dividuæ*.

§ 57. The plaintiff is not prejudiced by a larger amount being stated in the *condemnatio* than is due; for if he has received (from the prætor) an improperly drawn *formula*, he will be remitted to his original position in order that the *condemnatio* may be reduced. But if too small an amount is stated in the *condemnatio*, the plaintiff cannot recover more; for, though it is true that the whole matter is before the *judex*, yet he is bound by the *condemnatio*, and cannot exceed its limit. In such a case the prætor will not remit the plaintiff to his original position, as he is more ready to assist defendants than plaintiffs. These observations do not apply to infants under twenty-five years of age, for the prætor always intervenes on their behalf when they have been misled.

§ 58. When, by error, too much, or too little, has been inserted in the *demonstratio*, there is nothing for the *judex* to try, and the matter remains as it was; that is what is meant by the expression "a false *demonstratio* settles nothing."

§ 59. There are authors, however, who contend that the *demonstratio* is not bad by reason merely of less being stated than is legally due, for, they say, he who has bought Stichus and Eros can make a valid *demonstratio* by saying, "Whereas I bought the slave Eros from you," and, if he pleases, can maintain another action in similar form to recover Stichus, because it cannot be doubted that he, who has bought two slaves, has bought each of them. Labeo was strong on this point. If, however, he, who has bought but one slave, sues for two, he makes a false *demonstratio.* The same may be said concerning other actions, *e. g.*, *commodatum*, *depositum.*

§ 60. Some writers, however, contend that in the case of *depositum*, and, indeed, in that of any action where ignominy attaches to a judgment against the defendant, an excessive claim in the *demonstratio* is fatal to the plaintiff's action; thus, should the bailor of one article allege in his *demonstratio* that he had deposited two, or should one who has been struck in the face allege in his *demonstratio* that he had been struck in some other part of the body. Let us consider whether we can adopt this suggestion. Certainly, for, as already stated, there are in the case of *depositum* two *formulæ*, the one *in jus concepta*, at the commencement of which the subject of the action is stated and defined, after which the legal proposition is stated thus:—"Whatever the defendant is bound on that account to give to or do for me"; whereas, in the latter (*in factum concepta*) the matter in dispute is described in the *intentio* without any *demonstratio* thus:—"Should it appear that A. B. (the plaintiff) deposited such and such a thing with C. D. (the defendant)." It is obvious, that if, in the formula *in factum concepta* the plaintiff claims more than he has deposited, he must lose his action, inasmuch as he has claimed too much in the *intentio*. . . .

XI. *Compensatio et Deductio.*

§ 61. In actions *bonæ fidei*, full latitude being given to the *judex* to decide according to the principles of natural justice, questions of set-off are entertained and judgment given for the balance.

§ 62. The actions *bonæ fidei* are those arising from purchase, sale, letting, hiring, unsolicited or volunteer agency, mandate, deposit, fiduciary relationship, partnership, guardianship, gratuitous loan.

§ 63. Though by the terms of the *formula* no duty is imposed on the *judex* to take the question of compensation into his consideration, yet, as to disregard it would be inconsistent with the notion of an action *bonæ fidei*, it is considered part of his duty.

§ 64. It is otherwise in the case of a banker, for he must sue in the form of an account stated, that is to say, the debit and credit must appear in the *formula;* therefore, if he is indebted to Titius in the sum of 10,000 sesterces, whereas Titius is indebted to him in the sum of 20,000 sesterces, the *intentio* must be formulated thus:—"If it appears that Titius owes me 10,000 after giving him credit for what I owe him, &c."

§ 65. So, the *bonorum emptor* must sue (a debtor to a bankrupt estate) in the form of an account stated, so that, having shown the credit, the defendant may be condemned in the difference between the sum due from him to the bankrupt, and that due from the bankrupt to him.

§ 66. The set-off in the case of the banker differs from that in the case of the *bonorum emptor*. A balance can only be struck between things of the same genus and nature, money with money, wheat with wheat, wine with wine, and indeed, according to some, that cannot be effected in the case of wine with wine or wheat with wheat, unless the one parcel is of the same nature and quality as the other; whereas in *deductio, i. e.*, where the things are of different natures—for example, if the *bonorum emptor* claim a given sum of money while he owes wheat or wine—he must deduct the value and claim the difference.

§ 67. So, in the case of *deductio*, debts due *in futuro* are included, whereas in *compensatio* (set-off) those only are taken into consideration which are payable *in præsenti.*

§ 68. Again, the calculation in the case of *compensatio* is placed in the *intentio*, the consequence being, that, if the banker claims one single sesterce more than is due to him on the balance of account, he fails in his action, and thus loses the whole; whereas the *deductio* is placed in the *damnatio*, a part of the *formula* where an excessive demand does not involve any risk, especially when the action is brought by a *bonorum emptor*, who, though suing for a specified sum, formulates his *condemnatio* for an unliquidated amount.

XII. *De Actionibus ex Contractu Filiorum et Servorum.*

§ 69. Having already mentioned the action which lies against the father or master to recover the *peculium* of children *in potestate* and of slaves, we must now enter more into detail concerning that action and other like actions granted against fathers and masters.

§ 70. First, then, when the son or slave has acted in pursuance of instructions received from the father or master, the prætor has granted an action against the father or master, as the case may be, for the recovery of the whole debt, and rightly so, for those who contract with the son or slave under such circumstances, look to the father or master, rather than to the son or slave.

§ 71. For the same reason, the prætor has established two other actions, styled respectively *exercitoria* and *institoria*. The action *exercitoria* lies when a father or master has appointed his son or slave captain of a vessel, and some engagements have been entered into by the son or slave in connection with the enterprise; for, as this contract must be taken to have been made conformably to the wish of the father or master, it appeared to the prætor but equitable to give an action for the full amount. This prætorian action lies equally when the captain is a stranger, whether slave or free, against the person who appointed him. The action is styled *exercitoria* because the person who takes the daily profits of the working of a ship is called the *exercitor*. The *formula* styled *institoria* applies in the case of the management of a shop or business of any kind, entrusted whether to a son, a slave, or a stranger, whether bond or free, and lies in respect of all matters within the scope of the agency. This action is styled *institoria*, because the manager of a shop is called an *institor*. This formula is also for the full amount.

§ 72. The prætor has also granted another action against a father or master, styled the *actio tributoria*, in the case where the sons and daughters, or male and female slaves, with the knowledge of the father or master, trade with the goods in their *peculium*. When such trading has resulted in liabilities, the prætor's rule is, that all the stock comprised in the *peculium*, together with all profits arising therefrom, shall be divided between the father or master, if anything be due to him, and the other creditors in the ratio of their respective claims, and that the father or master, as the case may be, shall make the distribution. When, then, any one of the creditors complains that he has not had his just share assigned to him, the prætor gives him the *actio tributoria*.

§ 73. There is also another action relating to the *peculium*, and to moneys spent in the interest of the father or master. When the son or slave has contracted without the sanction of the father or master, in so far as the matter has resulted in profit to him, he is held liable to satisfy the obligation, but, where he has not been benefited, his liability is confined to the extent of the *peculium*. The father or master is considered as having derived profit from everything that the son or slave has necessarily expended in his interest; for example, if, with the money borrowed by the son or slave, he has satisfied the claims of the creditors of the father or master, or has propped up some ruinous building, or purchased corn for his household, or bought an estate, or any other necessary thing. If, then, out of the ten sesterces borrowed by your slave from Titius, he has paid five to your creditor, and has spent the other five in some way or other, you ought, as to the first five, to be condemned to pay in full, and, as to the remaining five, to the extent only of the *peculium*. If you have profited by the whole ten, Titius can recover the amount in full from you. Though in one and the same action the claim is made to the extent of the *peculium*, and to the extent of the profit, yet there are two *condemnationes*. Consequently, the *judex*, before whom the case comes, in the first instance inquires as to the profits, if any, to the father or master, and does not inquire into the extent of the *peculium* till satisfied that the father or master has not derived any profit, or only in part. In order to ascertain the amount of the *peculium*, deduction must first be made of whatever the son or slave is indebted to the father or master, as also to persons in the same *patria potestas;* anything over and above is reckoned as *peculium.* Sometimes, however, no deduction is made from the amount due by the son or slave to a person in the same *potestas*, for instance, when he owes it to a person in his own *peculium*, (*e. g.*, debts owing by a *servus ordinarius* to his *servus vicarius.*)

§ 74. There can be no doubt that he who has contracted with a son, or slave, as the agent of his father or master, and who is entitled either to the action *institoria*, or the action *exercitoria*, may also bring the action *de peculio aut de in rem verso.* No one, however, who could recover the full amount of his debt in either of the two former actions would be so foolish as to take upon himself the burden of proving that the father, or the master, had profited, or that the son, or slave, not merely had *peculium*, but sufficient to satisfy his debt. He who is entitled to an *actio tributoria* may also proceed by the *actio de peculio vel de in rem verso.* In his case, it is obvious that the latter is generally preferable to the former, for in the *actio tributoria* that portion only of the *peculium* is taken into consideration that is comprised in the stock in trade of the son, or slave, or that represents the profits of successful trading, whereas in the *actio de peculio* the whole is considered. It must be remembered that only a third, a fourth, or even a smaller portion of the *peculium* may be devoted to trading, the residue being invested in immovable, or other property. When it can be proved to the *judex* that the whole of the money has been devoted to the interests of the father, or master, this action should be adopted; for, as we have already said, the same *formula* includes both the *peculium* and money spent in the interest of the father or master.

XIII. *De Noxalibus Actionibus.*

§ 75. For the *delicts* of a son, or a slave, *e.g.*, a theft (*furtum*) committed, or damage (*injuria*) done by him, certain actions styled *noxales* were framed, in which the father, or master, had the option either to pay the damages assessed, or to abandon the delinquent as a *noxa;* for it was considered unjust that the father, or master, should forfeit more for the wrongful act of his son, or slave, than his body.

§ 76. *Noxales actiones* were established, in part by the *leges*, and in part by edict; *e.g.*, by the law of the Twelve Tables the action of theft (*actio furti*) was established, by the *lex Aquilia* the action for unlawful damage (*damni injuriæ*); by the edict of the prætor, *inter alia*, are the action for injury (*injuriarum*), and that for the forcible taking of goods (*vi bonorum raptorum*).

§ 77. All actions *noxales* follow the person of the delinquent: thus if your son, or slave, has committed a delict, so long as he remains in your *potestas*, the action lies against you; should he pass into the *potestas* of another, the action lies against that person; should he become independent, a direct action (*directa actio*) lies against him personally, in which case there is no *noxal* (abandonment). Conversely, a direct action may become *noxal;* for, if a *pater familias* has committed a *delict*, and then has given himself to you in *adrogatio*, or become your slave, as in the first commentary we have seen happens in certain cases, the action which previously was direct, against him, becomes *noxal* as against you.

§ 78. But if a son has committed a delict against his father, or a slave against his master, no action arises, because no obligation can exist between you and one who is in your *potestas;* consequently, even should he pass into the *potestas* of another, or become *sui juris*, no action will lie either against him or the person into whose *potestas* he has passed. Hence arises this question:—When the slave or the son of another has committed a delict against me, and subsequently becomes in my *potestas*, is the right of action gone, or is it merely in abeyance? Our masters contend that it is extinguished, because a relationship has been created between us in which it never could have come into existence; consequently, should the wrongdoer pass from my *potestas*, I could not maintain an action. The authorities of the other school contend that the action is in abeyance so long as the delinquent remains in my *potestas*, because I cannot sue myself; but that, so soon as he passes from my *potestas*, it revives.

§ 79. When a *filius familias* is given *in mancipio* by reason of a *noxal* act, the authorities of the other school contend that the ceremony should be repeated three times, inasmuch as the law of the Twelve Tables enacts, that, unless the son has been mancipated three times, he does not escape the *potestas* of his father. Sabinus and Cassius, as also the other writers of our school, contend that one mancipation is sufficient; they being of opinion, that the three mancipations required by the law of the Twelve Tables only relate to voluntary mancipations.

§ 80. Such are the rules applicable to those in *potestas* when the question of liability arises respecting their contracts or delicts. As to persons in *manus* or in *mancipium*, when the liability is *ex contractu*, unless they are defended as to the whole amount claimed by him to whose authority either is subject, the entire estate of the defendant, which would have been his had he not been subject to such authority, must be sold; but when the *capitis diminutio* is treated as non-existent in an action based on the *imperium* . . . .

§ 81. . . . . Although, as we have said, it was never permitted to a defendant to surrender dead slaves (instead of making compensation for the damage done by them while living), yet, if a man give up his slave, who has died a natural death, he is free from liability as in the other case.

XIV. *De his per quos agere possumus.*

§ 82. It must be remembered that a man may sue in his own name, or in the name of another, *e.g.*, when he sues as a *cognitor*, *procurator*, *tutor*, or *curator*. Formerly, however, in the time of the *legis actiones*, no one was permitted to sue in the name of another, except in two cases, *i.e.*, in an action brought *pro populo*, or *libertatis causâ*.

§ 83. A *cognitor* is appointed by the use, in the presence of the defendant, of a set form of words. In fact, by way of illustration, the plaintiff appoints a *cognitor* in these terms, "Inasmuch as I am suing you for an estate, I appoint Lucius Titius to be *cognitor* in the matter." The defendant appoints a *cognitor* thus:—"Since you demand an estate from me, I appoint Publius Mevius *cognitor* in the matter." The plaintiff may say, "Whereas I wish to commence an action against you, I appoint a *cognitor* in the matter;" and the defendant, "Since you wish to commence an action against me, I appoint a *cognitor* in the matter." It is immaterial whether the *cognitor* is present or not at the time of his appointment: however, if he is not then present, he does not in fact become *cognitor* till he is aware of the appointment and consents to act.

§ 84. A *procurator*, on the contrary, is appointed to an action by a simple mandate without the use of any given form of words, and that even in the absence, or without the knowledge, of the adversary; indeed, some writers hold that a man, who, without mandate, in good faith, undertakes the conduct of the affairs of another, may be regarded as a *procurator*, provided he gives sureties that what he does will be ratified by his principal. Therefore, even though the *procurator* produces no mandate, he may go on with the action, for it is a common thing not to produce a mandate at the commencement of an action, but to show it later on to the *judex*.

§ 85. We have already in the first commentary stated how tutors and curators are appointed.

§ 86. He who sues in the name of another inserts his principal's name in the *intentio*, but in the *condemnatio* he inserts his own; for example, if Lucius Titius sues for Publius Mevius, the formula runs thus:—"If it appears that Numerius Negidius ought to give 10,000 sesterces to Publius Mevius, *judex*, condemn Numerius Negidius to pay 10,000 sesterces to Lucius Titius; if it does not so appear, acquit him." In like manner, if the action is a real action, he alleges in the *intentio* that the thing belongs to Publius Mevius by Quiritarian law, and makes the *condemnatio* to himself.

§ 87. So, when an agent intervenes on behalf of the defendant, the allegation in the *intentio* is, that the defendant principal ought to give, &c., but the *condemnatio* is against the defendant agent. But, if the action is a real action, the name of the person against whom the action is brought, whether principal or agent, does not appear in the *intentio*, because the *intentio* simply alleges that the thing in question belongs to the plaintiff.

XV. *De Satisdationibus.*

§ 88. Let us now consider in what cases the defendant and plaintiff are respectively required to give security.

§ 89. If I bring a real action against you, you must give security, for it has appeared equitable that inasmuch as you are permitted to retain interim possession of a thing where your right to it is disputed, you should guarantee me by *satisdatio*, in order that, should you fail in the action, and neglect to deliver over the thing or its assessed value, I should be able to proceed against you or your sponsors.

§ 90. And still more ought you to give me security when you defend in the name of another person.

§ 91. Besides, as the action *in rem* may be brought in either of two forms, *i.e.*, by the *formula* styled *petitoria*, or by that styled *per sponsionem*, one of two forms of stipulation is open to the plaintiff. If the *formula petitoria* is adopted, the stipulation styled *judicatum solvi* (let the award of the *judex* be paid) is employed; whereas, if the *formula per sponsionem* is adopted, the stipulation styled *pro præde litis et vindiciarum* (see *post*, par. 94) is adopted.

§ 92. The *formula petitoria* is that in which the plaintiff claims the thing as his.

§ 93. We proceed *per sponsionem*, thus:—We challenge our adversary in a *sponsio* running as follows:—"If the slave, the subject of this action, is mine by Quiritarian law, do you undertake to give me 25 sesterces?" Then we cause him to be served with a *formula* in the *intentio* of which we allege that he is bound to pay us the amount of the *sponsio*. In which case we can only succeed by proving that the thing in question is ours.

§ 94. The amount, however, of the *sponsio* is never exacted; for the *sponsio* is not penal, but merely formal (*præjudicialis*)—an admittedly fictitious nominal amount—its sole object being to provide a means by which the question of title may be adjudicated upon. Therefore, the defendant does not re-stipulate. The stipulation *pro præde litis et vindiciarum* is so styled because it has taken the place of *prædes*, for formerly, when the proceeding was by *legis actio*, the person in possession gave to the plaintiff *prædes* (sureties) *pro lite et vindiciis*, that is to say, for the thing itself and its profits.

§ 95. When, however, the action is tried before the *centumviri*, we do not sue for the amount of the *sponsio* by a *formula*, but by a *legis actio*, for we challenge the defendant by a *sacramentum*, in which case the *sponsio* by the *lex* . . . . is 125 sesterces.

§ 96. When the plaintiff in a real action sues in his own name he does not give security.

§ 97. Even when he sues by a *cognitor* no sureties are demanded either from him or his *cognitor*, for as the *cognitor* is substituted for him by a formal, and in a certain sense solemn manner, he is considered, and with reason, as occupying the position of his principal.

§ 98. When, however, a *procurator* is the plaintiff, security must be given by him that his principal will ratify his acts; for in this case there is the risk that the principal may bring a second action for the same alleged cause of action, a risk which does not exist in the case of the *cognitor;* for when one has sued by a *cognitor*, he is equally estopped from suing again for the same cause of action as if he had sued in his own name in the first instance.

§ 99. According to the strict letter of the edict, tutors and curators are bound to give security, the same as *procuratores;* they are, however, sometimes excused.

§ 100. As to when, in the case of personal actions, security must be given by the plaintiff, we can only repeat what has been said as to real actions.

§ 101. As to security by the defendant:—When one defends in the name of another, sureties must always be furnished, for no one, without security given, is regarded as a sufficient substitute for the defendant. When the action is against a *cognitor*, his principal must provide the security; when it is brought against a *procurator*, the *procuratores* must provide it; so in the case of a tutor or curator.

§ 102. When, in a personal action, the defendant defends in his own name, security is, in certain cases, required by the prætor. There may be one or two reasons, namely, the nature of the action, or the character of the person. On account of the nature of the action may be instanced actions on a judgment, or for money paid by a *sponsor*, or the action *de moribus mulieris:* on account of the person, *e.g.*, when the defendant is one who has squandered his estate, or one whose goods have been seized, or advertised for sale by his creditors, or when the action has been brought against an heir whom the prætor has regarded with disfavour.

XVI. *De Judiciis Legitimis et quæ Imperio continentur.*

§ 103. Every action is either *legitimo jure* or *prætorian.*

§ 104. Actions *legitimo jure* are tried before a single judge in the city of Rome, or within one mile of the city, the *judex* and the parties being all Roman citizens; such actions by the *lex Julia judiciaria* (on *procedure*) expire, unless adjudicated upon within eighteen months from the date of the institution of the action. That is what is meant by the common saying:—"By the *lex Julia* an action dies in eighteen months."

§ 105. The other class (prætorian actions) comprises actions brought before *recuperatores* and those which are tried by a single *judex*, he, or either of the parties, being a *peregrinus.* In this category are also all actions tried beyond one mile from the city of Rome, whether the parties be citizens or *peregrini.* These actions are said to be based on, or contained within, the *imperium*, because they are valid only so long as the prætor who grants them remains in office, *i.e.*, retains his *imperium.*

§ 106. When the action is one of those limited by the term of the prætor's office, whether it be a real or personal action, whether the *intentio* of the *formula* be *in factum* or *in jus*, one can, notwithstanding, in strict law sue again for the same cause of action, in which case it is necessary to plead the *exceptio rei judicatæ*, or the *exceptio in judicium deductæ.*

§ 107. But when the action is *legitimo judicio* and *in personam*, the *intentio* in the *formula* being *juris civilis*, no subsequent action can be brought for the same cause of action, and therefore, in that case, the *exceptio* is superfluous. But when the plaintiff has sued *in rem* or *in factum*, in strict law he is not estopped from suing again on the same cause of action; but should he do so, the defendant can avail himself of the *exceptio rei judicatæ* or the *exceptio in judicium deductæ.*

§ 108. Formerly it was different in the case of *legis actiones*, for when a matter had once been litigated no second action could be maintained for the same cause of action, and in those days there was no such thing as an *exceptio*.

§ 109. Again, the right of action may be given by a *lex*, yet the action not be *legitimum;* and, conversely, the right of action may exist independently of any *lex*, and yet be *legitimum*. If, for example, an action is brought in the provinces by virtue of the *lex Aquilia*, or *Ovinia*, or *Furia*, it will be (prætorian) based on the *imperium;* so if it be brought in Rome before *recuperatores*, or before one *judex*, if either of the parties is a *peregrinus*. So, conversely, when the right of action is created by a prætorian edict the trial of which takes place at Rome before a single *judex*, all the parties being Roman citizens, the action is *legitimum*.

XVII. *De Perpetuis et Temporalibus Actionibus et quæ ad Heredes vel in Heredes transeunt.*

§ 110. It should here be observed that ordinarily the prætor grants either of those actions arising from a *lex* or *senatusconsultum* at any time, whereas he seldom grants either of the actions that spring from his own jurisdiction except within the year.

§ 111. Sometimes, however, the prætorian actions are framed on the model of the *jus legitimum*, *e.g.*, those that the prætor grants to *bonorum possessores*, and to others occupying the position of heir. The *actio furti manifesti*, though issuing from the jurisdiction of the prætor himself, is granted at any time, and rightly so, inasmuch as the capital penalty of the old law has been replaced by a pecuniary penalty.

§ 112. Actions maintainable by the civil law, or those which have been granted by the prætor, do not necessarily lie against the heir of the person against whom they might have been brought. In short, it is a well-established rule that penal actions originating in delicts do not lie . . . . against the heir, *e.g.*, the actions *furti*, *vi bonorum raptorum*, *injuriarum*, *damni injuriæ*, but actions of this kind do lie at the suit of the heir of the person injured, and, excepting the *actio injuriarum* and any other similar action, are never refused to him.

§ 113. Sometimes, indeed, actions *ex contractu* neither lie at the suit of, nor against the heir; in fact, a right of action never passes to the heir of the *adstipulator*, and the heir of the *sponsor* or of the *fidepromissor* is never actionable.

XVIII. *Si Reus ante rem judicatam satisfaciat Actori.*

§ 114. It now remains for us to inquire into the duty of the *judex*, when, after action brought but before judgment, the defendant satisfies the demand of the plaintiff:—Ought he to give judgment for the defendant, or ought he rather to give judgment against him on the ground that at the date of the commencement of the action judgment should under the then circumstances have been given against him? Our authorities hold that the *judex* ought to enter judgment for the defendant, and say that the nature of the action is immaterial. Hence comes the common saying that Sabinus and Cassius held that: "Every action admits of an acquittal." The authorities of the opposite school hold the same opinion in the case of actions *bonæ fidei*, because in them the discretion of the *judex* is unfettered. With regard to actions *in rem* they think it is so far . . . .

XIX. *De Exceptionibus.*

§ 115. We will now consider *exceptiones*.

§ 116. *Exceptiones* were introduced for the benefit of defendants. It frequently happens that a man is liable in law, and yet that it would be inequitable to decide against him in a particular action: for instance, if I stipulated with you for a certain sum of money on the pretext that I was about to lend you that sum, and then omitted to hand it over, it is clear that I can sue you for the amount, because you are bound by your stipulation; but as it would be inequitable for judgment to go against you in such an action, it has been provided that you may defend such an action by the *exceptio doli mali*. So if I have made a pact with you not to sue you for something you owe me, I can nevertheless sue you, alleging that you are bound to pay me, because the obligation is not extinguished by the pact; but it has been decided that my claim ought to be repelled by the *exceptio pacti conventi*.

§ 117. An *exceptio* may also be used in an action that is not *in personam*; *e.g.*, if by intimidation or by fraud you have compelled me to mancipate something to you, and you sue me for it, an *exceptio* is granted to me by which you will be defeated if I prove that you so acted as to frighten me, or that your conduct was fraudulent. So if you knowingly purchase an estate, the subject of litigation, from one not in possession, and you claim it from the possessor, you will be met with and absolutely defeated by an *exceptio*.

§ 118. Certain of the *exceptiones* are published by the prætor in his edict, the rest are granted by him to meet particular cases. All are founded either upon *leges*, or acts having the force of *leges*, or on the prætor's jurisdiction.

§ 119. All *exceptiones* are worded in the negative of the defendant's allegation. For example, if the defendant alleges that the plaintiff is acting fraudulently in claiming, say, money which he has never handed over, the *exceptio* runs thus:—"If in this matter there has not been nor is any fraud on the part of Aulus Agerius." So if the defendant says that the money is sued for in violation of an agreement, the *exceptio* runs thus:—"If it has not been agreed between Aulus Agerius and Numerius Negidius that this money should not be sued for." So in all other cases. Though every *exceptio* is interposed by the defendant, it is so inserted in the *formula* as to make the *condemnatio* conditional, *i.e.*, so that the *judex* is not to condemn the defendant if there has been any fraud in the transaction on the part of the plaintiff, or, in the other case, if there has been an agreement that the money should not be sued for.

§ 120. *Exceptiones* are said to be either *peremptoriæ* or *dilatoriæ*.

§ 121. Peremptory exceptions always avail, and cannot be evaded; *e.g.*, that styled "*metûs causâ*" or "*dolo malo*," or that something has been done in violation of a *lex* or *senatusconsultum*, or that a matter is *res judicata* or *sub judice*, or that it has been agreed that under no circumstances the money should be sued for.

§ 122. Dilatory exceptions are those that avail for a given time only; for example, all agreements that money should not be sued for, say, within five years, for when the five years have expired the *exceptio* is unavailing. Two *exceptiones* similar to that are the *exceptio litis dividuæ*, and the *exceptio rei residuæ*.

For if a person has brought an action for a part of a thing, and during the term of office of the same prætor sues for the remainder, he is met by the *exceptio litis dividuæ*. So, when one who has various causes of action against the same defendant sues on some only, and reserves the rest to try them before other *judices*, if, during the term of office of the prætor in power when the first action was commenced, he sues for the remaining causes of action, he is met by the *exceptio rei residuæ*.

§ 123. He, then, to whose suit a dilatory *exceptio* may be pleaded should take care to postpone his action, for if he goes on with it in the face of the *exceptio*, he loses not merely his case but his right, for when the time has arrived at which he might have sued, heedless of the *exceptio*, had matters remained in their original condition, he cannot maintain an action, the matter having been adjudicated on, and he defeated by the *exceptio*.

§ 124. *Exceptiones* are considered dilatory, not merely by reason of time, but by reason of the person, of which latter kind are the *exceptiones cognitoriæ;* for example, take the case of a person who, being incapacitated by the edict from nominating a *cognitor*, yet employs one to conduct an action; or that of one who, having the right to appoint a *cognitor*, appoints one who cannot legally act as *cognitor*. If the *exceptio cognitoria* is pleaded, should the plaintiff be one who cannot appoint a *cognitor*, he can carry on the suit himself; if, on the other hand, the person who has been nominated *cognitor* cannot fill that office, the plaintiff can appoint another *cognitor*, or can conduct the suit in his own name, and thus, in one way or the other, avoid the *exceptio;* whereas, should he, notwithstanding the *exceptio*, go on with the *cognitor* appointed by him, he loses his cause.

§ 125. When a defendant, in error, has omitted to avail himself of a peremptory *exceptio*, he is restored to his original position, *i. e.*, he is allowed to amend; but if he has omitted to avail himself of a dilatory *exceptio*, it is doubtful whether he can be so restored.

XX. *De Replicationibus.*

§ 126. *Replicatio.* It sometimes happens that an *exceptio* which, at first sight, appears just, does the plaintiff great injustice. In a case of this kind, a further addition must be made to the *formula* in the favour of the plaintiff. This addition is styled a *replicatio*, because by it the effect of the *exceptio* is repelled and destroyed. Suppose, for instance, that I had agreed with you not to sue you for certain money that you owe me, and that afterwards we made a fresh agreement, *i. e.*, one permitting me to sue you; if then I commence an action against you, and you cause an *exceptio* to be inserted to the effect that you ought to be condemned "unless it should appear that there has been an agreement between us that I should not sue you," this *exceptio* of *pacti conventi* would defeat me, because the fact that we subsequently entered into a further agreement does not render the fact of the former less true. But as it would be unjust for me to be defeated by this *exceptio*, I am, by virtue of the subsequent agreement, granted a *replicatio* in these terms: "If it has not subsequently been agreed that it shall be lawful for me to sue." So if, when a money dealer (*argentarius*) sues for the price of a thing sold by auction, he is met with the *exceptio* that the purchaser is to be condemned only if the thing has been delivered to him, which is a good *exceptio*, but if, at the auction and before the sale, it was announced that the thing would not be delivered to the purchaser before the price was paid, the money dealer might avail himself of the *replicatio*. So if, before the sale, it was publicly announced that the thing would not be delivered to the buyer before the price was paid.

§ 127. *Duplicatio*, *Triplicatio*, &c. It sometimes happens that the *replicatio*, though at first sight appearing just, in fact works an injustice to the defendant; in such case, in order to relieve the defendant, an addition is made, styled a "*duplicatio*."

§ 128. Should this, though at first sight appearing just, do in fact, owing to some circumstance, an injustice to the plaintiff, another addition must be made, styled a *triplicatio*.

§ 129. The variety of business matters has caused these additional clauses to be extended in certain cases even beyond those we have specified.

XXI. *De Præscriptionibus.*

§ 130. Let us now consider *præscriptiones*, which are employed for the benefit of the plaintiff.

§ 131. It frequently happens that by virtue of one and the

same contract, something becomes due at the moment, and something else at a future date: that happens, for example, when we have stipulated that a certain sum of money shall be paid each year, or each month. When a certain number of years, or months, have elapsed, the sums that correspond to the time ought to be paid; but, as to those that correspond to the periods to come, though it is true that the obligation is contracted, the time to demand payment has not come. If, then, we wish to sue for that which is actually due, and leave the obligation as to the future instalments still subsisting, it is necessary to include in our action this *præscriptio*, "Let the amount already due be the subject of the suit." Otherwise, if we sue without this *præscriptio*, using the *formula* for an unliquidated demand the *intentio* of which is in these terms: "Whatever it appears that Numerius Negidius ought to give and do to Aulus Agerius:" in which case we include in the submission to the *judex* the whole obligation, *i.e.*, that which is payable *in præsenti* and that which is payable *in futuro;* and as, whatever may be the total obligation, the *judex* can only adjudge that portion that was due at the commencement of the action (*litis contestatio*), we lose our remedy as to the rest, being estopped from bringing another action. So, if we sue *ex empto* (on a purchase) to secure the transfer to us by *mancipatio* of a field, the *præscriptio* must run thus: "Let the action be for the mancipation of the field:" so that, should we afterwards desire to have the possession vacated, and transferred to us, we may be able to sue for delivery either in virtue of the stipulation, or in virtue of the purchase. For, if we adopt the *formula* of the *incerta actio*:—"Whatever Numerius Negidius ought to give or do to Aulus Agerius:"—the whole obligation resulting from the contract is at once adjudicated on, and no action can afterwards be brought to recover the possession.

§ 132. That *præscriptiones* are so styled from the fact that they are written at the head of *formulæ* is more than obvious.

§ 133. In our days, as already stated, all the *præscriptiones* are introduced by the plaintiff; formerly, some were introduced by the defendant. Such was the *præscriptio*:—"Let the action on the question raised proceed, provided that it does not prejudice the question of inheritance." This *præscriptio* has now taken the form of an *exceptio*, and is used when a person claiming an inheritance brings an action to recover some particular portion of it, for it would be unjust to suffer the general question as to the inheritance to be prejudiced by a decision as to an individual article. . . . .

§ 134. . . . . The *intentio* of the *formula* determines the person to whom the subject of the action ought to be given; and obviously it is the master of the slave who stipulated; while the *præscriptio* inquires who, according to the true meaning of the contract, is to exercise the power.

§ 135. What we have said concerning slaves must be understood to apply to all others subject to our authority.

§ 136. In like manner we must observe that when we commence an action against any one who has promised us something *incertum*, the formula provided for such a claim is so constructed that the *præscriptio* takes the place of the *demonstratio*, thus :—"Let so and so be *judex*. Whereas Aulus Agerius has stipulated for something uncertain from Numerius Negidius, the day for the delivery of which is past, whatsoever on that account Numerius Negidius ought to give or to do to Aulus Agerius, &c."

§ 137. If the action is brought against a *sponsor*, or a *fidejussor*, the *præscriptio* runs in the case of a *sponsor* thus: "Let this be the subject of the action—Whereas Aulus Agerius has stipulated for something uncertain from Lucius Titius, in respect whereof Numerius Negidius was *sponsor*, whatever amount be now due, &c." In the case of a *fidejussor* it runs thus: "Let this be the subject of the action—Whereas Numerius Negidius became *fidejussor* for Lucius Titius, whatever amount be now due, &c.;" then follows the *formula*.

XXII. *De Interdictis.*

§ 138. It now remains for us to treat of interdicts.

§ 139. In certain cases the prætor or the proconsul interposes his authority directly, in order to put an end to litigation, especially in the case of disputes between persons as to possession or quasi-possession. In short, he commands the doing, or the abstaining from doing, of particular acts. The *formulæ* employed on these occasions are styled *interdicta*, or *decreta*.

§ 140. They are called *decreta* when the magistrate orders the doing of a given something; *e.g.*, when he orders the production, or restitution of a particular thing. They are called *interdicta* when he forbids the doing of a given act; *e.g.*, when he directs that no violence shall be done to one possessed innocently, or, that nothing shall be done on sacred ground (*loco sacro*). Hence all interdicts are said to be either *restitutoria* or *exhibitoria*, or *prohibitoria.*

§ 141. The matter, however, is not terminated by the command or prohibition, but the parties go before a *judex*, or *recuperatores*, and there, *formulæ* being issued, an investigation is made as to whether anything has been done in violation of the edict, or whether anything has been omitted to be done that was ordered to be done. At times a penalty accompanies the action, at others there is no penalty. A penalty is attached, for instance, when the proceedings are by *sponsio;* there is no penalty when an *arbiter* is demanded. In the case of prohibitory interdicts the proceeding is always by *sponsio*, in that of restitutory, or exhibitory, interdicts it is sometimes by *sponsio*, at others by the *formula* styled *arbitraria.*

§ 142. The principal division of interdicts is, then, into *prohibitoria, restitutoria*, and *exhibitoria.*

§ 143. Another division springs from their immediate object, *i. e.*, to acquire, to preserve, or to recover possession.

§ 144. An interdict, the object of which is to acquire possession, is given to the *bonorum possessor;* it begins with these words, "*Quorum bonorum;*" the object of this edict is to secure to the *bonorum possessor* restitution to him of any portion of the inheritance that may be in the custody of another claimed *pro herede*, or *pro possessore.* One is deemed to hold *pro herede* whether he is in fact the heir, or whether he only supposes himself to be the heir. One is deemed to hold *pro possessore* who has in his custody the inheritance or any part thereof without title, and knowing that it does not belong to him. This interdict is styled *adipiscendæ possessionis*, for it only avails one who is for the first time endeavouring to gain possession of the thing; consequently, if he has once had possession and lost it, this interdict is of no use to him.

§ 145. The *bonorum emptor* receives a similar edict, which is sometimes called *interdictum possessorium.*

§ 146. In like manner the purchaser of public property is provided with an edict styled *interdictum sectorium,* because those who buy property sold for the benefit of the state are called *sectores.*

§ 147. The interdict styled *sylvianum* has also been prepared for the acquisition of possession, and is resorted to by the owner of land to recover the property of his tenant pledged to him to secure the rent.

§ 148. An interdict for the purpose of retaining possession is granted when there is a dispute between two parties as to the property in a given thing; and the first question for decision is, which of them should have the custody, and which be plaintiff? For this purpose, two edicts have been provided, viz., *uti possidetis* (as you possess), and *utrubi* (he of you two who has it).

§ 149. The interdict *uti possidetis* is granted in the case of land, or a house; the interdict *utrubi* for the possession of movable property.

§ 150. When the interdict relates to land or a house, the prætor gives the preference to the person in possession at the time the edict issues, provided the possession has neither been acquired by violence, clandestine conduct, nor sufferance on the part of his opponent (*nec vi nec clam nec precario ab adversario possideat*). If the edict relates to movable property, the preference is given to him who has been in possession of the thing during the greater portion of the year, there not having been any violence, clandestine conduct, or sufferance (*i. e.*, no evidence that the possession was merely on sufferance). This is made clear by the terms of the edict.

§ 151. In the interdict *utrubi* each may avail himself, not merely of his own possession, but of that of any other person which lawfully accrues to him; for example, the possession of the person to whom he is heir, or that of the person from whom he has bought the thing, or that of the person from whom he has received it by way of . . . or as a gift. If, then, the lawful possession of another, added to our own, surpasses that of our opponent, we succeed on this interdict. But he who has no possession of his own does not and cannot acquire title by reason of the possession of another, for there can be no accession to that which does not exist. So he who has a tainted possession, *i. e.*, who has acquired possession from his opponent by violence, clandestinity, or by sufferance, cannot benefit by accession, for his own possession does not avail him.

§ 152. The year is reckoned backward. If, then, for example, you have been in possession during the first five months of the year, and I during the last seven months, I shall be in the better position by reason of the number of months of my possession, and you will not derive any advantage as regards this interdict from the fact that your possession was earlier in the year.

§ 153. We are deemed to be in possession, not merely when we are personally in possession, but also when any one is in possession in our name, though he may not be subject to our authority; for example, the tenants of our land or house. We are equally deemed to be in possession by the possession of those with whom we have deposited the thing, or to whom we have left it, or to whom we have given a right of habitation gratuitously, and this is the meaning of the popular saying, "Possession may be preserved by any one who holds in our name." Indeed, the majority contend that possession can be retained by the mere intention to retain it . . . In the second commentary we have indicated those through whom we may acquire possession. It is beyond doubt that we cannot acquire possession by the mere desire to possess.

§ 154. When any one has been ejected with violence, he may obtain an edict to recover the possession, for, to meet that case, a form of edict has been prepared which commences with these words—"*Unde tu illum vi dejecisti*" (whence thou hast expelled him by violence)—by means of which the person who has expelled the other is compelled to restore the possession; provided always that the person had not himself acquired the possession by violence, clandestinity, or by sufferance from his adversary; for if he had obtained possession by violence or clandestinity or by sufferance he may be ejected with impunity.

§ 155. Sometimes, however, the prætor would compel me to

restore the possession to one expelled by me by violence, though he had obtained it from me by force, clandestinity, or by sufferance; that is to say, if I had ejected him by force and with arms, for the prætor . . . without distinction . . .

§ 156. The third division of interdicts is into "simple" or "double."

§ 157. Those, for example, are simple, in which one party is plaintiff and the other defendant. All the *restitutoria* or *exhibitoria* edicts are edicts of this class. The plaintiff is the party who desires that the production or restoration should be made; the defendant is the party by whom it is decreed that the production or restoration should be made.

§ 158. Some of the *prohibitoria* edicts are double, others are simple.

§ 159. Those, for instance, by which the prætor enjoins the defendant not to do something in a sacred place, or in a public river, or on its banks, are simple, for the plaintiff is the person who desires that the act should not be done, and the defendant the person attempting or threatening to do it.

§ 160. The interdicts *uti possidetis* and *utrubi*, for example, are double. They are said to be double because the condition of the two parties is similar; neither is regarded as plaintiff or defendant, each in his turn taking the part of plaintiff and defendant. In short, the prætor addresses both in the same language, the terms of the edict in the former being, "I forbid violence to be employed to prevent you from possessing in the manner you now possess"; and in the latter, "I forbid force being used to prevent him of you two with whom the slave, the subject of this action, has been during the greater portion of the year from recovering possession."

§ 161. Having explained the different kinds of interdicts, we now come to the consideration of their process and results. We will begin with the simple interdicts.

§ 162. When an injunction *restitutoria* or *exhibitoria*, for example, is granted to secure the restitution of possession to one deprived by force, or for the production of a *libertus* to whom the patron wishes to allot services, the matter is conducted to its termination at times without, and at others with, risk.

§ 163. In short, if the defendant demands an *arbiter*, he receives a *formula* styled *arbitraria*, and then, if, by the award of the *judex*, he is ordered to restore or produce anything, and he does so, he does so without penalty, and is discharged; if he does not, he is condemned in the value of the subject-matter of the suit. So the plaintiff runs no risk in suing one who is under no obligation to restore or produce, unless an action for *calumnia* be commenced against him. The authorities of the opposite school contend, however, that a defendant who has demanded an *arbiter* is barred from instituting a suit for *calumnia*, since, by the mere fact of demanding an *arbiter*, he must be taken to have admitted that there is some reason for saying that he ought to restore or produce; but we contend otherwise, and with reason, for one may demand an *arbiter* without entertaining any doubt as to his being in the right, or as to the result of his case.

§ 164. One who wishes to have an *arbiter* ought to demand one at the time, before leaving the court, *i. e.*, before he leaves the prætor's presence; for if the demand is made afterwards, it will not be granted.

§ 165. When, then, an *arbiter* has not been demanded, and the defendant has left the court without saying anything, the matter proceeds at his risk, for the plaintiff challenges him with the *sponsio*, "Unless, contrary to the edict of the prætor, he should not produce or restore," whereupon the defendant makes a restipulation in the contrary sense. The plaintiff then presents to the defendant the *formula* of the *sponsio*, and the defendant hands to the plaintiff the *formula* of the *restipulatio;* the plaintiff, however, adds to the *formula* of the *sponsio* a claim for judgment on the alleged obligation to restore or produce, so that, should he succeed on the *sponsio*, and the defendant neglect to restore or produce . . . . (the defendant would be condemned in the value of the thing in dispute).

§ 166. When the prætor has granted an edict, he gives the *interim* possession of the thing in dispute to the party who makes the highest bid for the *usufructuary* right, provided that he gives security to his opponent by the *stipulatio* styled *fructuaria;* the consequence being that, should the case be decided against him, he has to pay double the value of the profits. Each then challenges the other by a *sponsio*, thus: "If, contrary to the edict of the prætor, force has been used against the person in possession." Each then restipulates against the *sponsio* . . . . the *judex* before whom the matter comes investigates the matter of the interdict, *i. e.*, ascertains which of the two possessed without force, or clandestine conduct, or by sufferance, the land or house at the time when the interdict was granted. When the *judex* has ascertained the facts and has decided in my favour, for example, he condemns my adversary to pay the amount of the *sponsio* and the *restipulatio* that I have made with him, and consequently acquits me from the *sponsio* and *restipulatio* that he has made with me; in addition to which, if my adversary has the *interim* possession, he having outbid me in the contest for the fruits, he is condemned in the action called *Cascellianum* or *secutorium*, unless he hands over the possession to me.

§ 167. If, then, he who has been successful in the bidding for the fruits does not succeed in showing that he was entitled to the possession, he has to pay, by way of penalty, the amount of the *sponsio*, that of the *restipulatio*, and that of the bid for the fruits, in addition to which he is ordered to deliver up possession, and what is more, he has to account for the profits he has reaped during his interim possession, for the amount of the bid for the fruits is not the value of the fruits, but a sum paid by way of penalty for having endeavoured to retain during that period possession of the property of another, and for having claimed the right to enjoy it.

§ 168. On the other hand, if he who has been defeated in the bidding for the fruits fails to prove his right to the possession, he has only to pay, by way of penalty, the amount of the *sponsio* and the *restipulatio*.

§ 169. It must be observed that he who is defeated in the bidding for the fruits is at liberty, even though no fructuary stipulations have been made, to proceed separately for the amount offered for the fruits, just as he can proceed separately for the recovery of the possession by the Cascellian or *secutorium* action; and for this purpose a special form of proceeding has been provided, called *judicium fructuarium*, by means of which the plaintiff can obtain security for the payment of the amount awarded by the *judex*. This action, like the other, is styled *secutorium*, because it follows success on the *sponsio*, but it is not properly called Cascellian also.

§ 170. Inasmuch as some persons after an edict had been granted, while adhering to the letter, refused to conform to the spirit of it, the proceeding became abortive, and the prætor . . . . provided (other) interdicts . . . .

XXIII. *De Pœnâ temere Litigantium.*

§ 171. In some cases an action for double the value of the matter in dispute is allowed against the defendant who denies his liability; for example, in the case of actions *judicati*, *depensi*, *damni injuriæ*, or for legacies left by *damnatio*. In some cases it is lawful to make a *sponsio;* for example, in the case of "*pecunia certa credita*" and "*pecunia constituta*"*:* in the case of "*pecunia certa credita*" for one-third, in that of "*pecunia constituta*" for one-half.

§ 172. When the defendant runs no risk, either of the *sponsio*, or action for the double, and the claim is confined to the simple principal, the prætor permits the plaintiff to require that the defendant shall state on oath that he does not defend vexatiously; hence, as heirs, and those in the position of heirs, are never liable to penalties, and as females and pupils are relieved from the penalty of the *sponsio*, such persons are only required to take the oath.

§ 173. As examples of actions in which from the outset the claim is for more than the simple value of the subject-matter of the action, may be mentioned the actions *furtum manifestum* for the four-fold value, *furtum nec manifestum* for the double value, and *furtum conceptum* and *furtum oblatum* for the three-fold value.

§ 174. Vexatious conduct (*calumnia*) on the part of the plaintiff is restrained either by the action *calumnia*, by a cross-action, by an oath, or by a *restipulatio*.

§ 175. The action "*calumnia*" may be brought (by way of cross-action) against any action, and lies to recover one-tenth of the value of the matter in dispute. In the case of an interdict it lies to recover one-fourth.

§ 176. The defendant is free either to reply by bringing the action *calumnia*, or to require the plaintiff to take the oath that his action is not brought vexatiously.

§ 177. The action *contrarium* lies in certain specified cases; for example, in that of the *actio injuriarum*, and the proceedings taken against a woman in which she is charged with having fraudulently transferred property to another, the possession of which she had acquired *ventris nomine;* and where it is alleged that having received the grant of possession from the prætor the plaintiff has been prevented from taking possession. When it is granted against the *actio injuriarum*, it lies to recover one-tenth; when against either of the other two, it lies to recover one-fifth.

§ 178. The penalty is the greater in the case of the *actio contrarium*, for in the *judicium calumniæ* the defendant is not condemned in the tenth unless it appears that he was aware of the injustice of his action, and that he brought it relying for success rather on the error or injustice of the *judex* than on the truth and merits of his own case; for *calumnia*, like *furtum*, is a question of intention. In the *actio contrarium*, on the contrary, the plaintiff is always condemned if he loses his case, even though, labouring under a misapprehension, he believed that his action was just.

§ 179. Whenever the *actio contrarium* may be brought, the *actio calumnia* also lies, but one only can be brought. For the same reason, whenever the oath has been demanded as to vexatiousness neither the *actio calumnia* nor the *actio contrarium* will lie.

§ 180. The penalty of the *restipulatio* also exists in certain cases only; and as in the cross-action the plaintiff is always condemned when he fails in the original suit—the question whether he knew or did not know that he was in the wrong not being inquired into—so the plaintiff is always condemned in the penalty of the *restipulatio*.

§ 181. . . . . If the penalty of the *restipulatio* is claimed from the plaintiff, the *actio calumnia* cannot be brought against him, nor can he be compelled to take the oath, for it is plain enough that there can be no *actio contrarium* (cross-action).

§ 182. In certain actions those against whom judgment is given are branded with infamy; such is the case in the *actio furti*, *vi bonorum raptorum*, *injuriarum*, so in *pro socio*, *fiduciæ*, *tutelæ*, *mandati*, and *depositi*. In the case of *furti*, *vi bonorum raptorum*, and *injuriarum*, not only is the condemned branded with infamy, but any one who has bought the plaintiff off is equally branded, and that rightly, for there is a vast difference between the debtor *ex delicto* and the debtor *ex contractu*. . . . .

§ 183. In conclusion, it must be borne in mind that . . . . he who sues and he who is sued . . . . patron and freedman . . . . and a penalty has been imposed on him who shall contravene.

§ 184. When any one is summoned into court by his adversary, and the matter is not settled on that day, he must enter into a *vadimonium*, *i.e.*, he must undertake to appear on the day fixed.

§ 185. In some cases the *vadimonia* are simple, *i.e.*, without sureties, in others they are with sureties; in some they are on oath, in others with *recuperatores*, that is to say, that should he fail to appear he will at once be condemned by the *recuperatores* in the sum of the *vadimonium*. All these matters are carefully set out in a prætor's edict.

§ 186. If the action is on a judgment, or for money paid, the amount of the *vadimonium* is equal to the amount for which the action is brought; in other cases the plaintiff fixes the amount himself, he at the same time swearing that he does not demand that sum vexatiously. The *vadimonium*, however, in such cases must never exceed the half of the value of the subject of the action, nor must it exceed 100,000 *sesterces*. If then the matter in dispute is worth 100,000 *sesterces*, and it is not an action on a judgment, or for money paid, the amount of the *vadimonium* must not exceed 50,000 *sesterces*.

§ 187. Lastly, those who cannot be sued without the permission of the prætor cannot be compelled to furnish *vadimonium* against their will without his sanction.

THE INSTITUTES OF JUSTINIAN.

BOOK I.

Tit. I. *De justitiâ et jure.*

JUSTICE is the constant and perpetual desire of giving to every man that which is due to him.

§ 1. Jurisprudence is the knowledge of things divine and human, and the exact discernment of what is just and unjust.

§ 2. These definitions being premised, we shall now proceed. But it seems right to begin our Institutions in the most plain and simple manner, although afterwards we intend to treat every particular with the utmost exactness: for, if at first we overload the mind of the student with a variety of things, we may cause him either wholly to abandon his studies, or bring him late, through a series of labours, to that knowledge which he might otherwise have attained with ease and expedition.

§ 3. The precepts of the law are these: to live honestly, not to hurt any man, and to give to every one that which is his due.

§ 4. The law is divided into public and private. Public law regards the state of the commonwealth; but private law, of which we shall here treat, concerns the interest of individuals, and is tripartite, being collected from natural precepts, from the law of nations, and from the civil law of any particular city or state.

Tit. II. *De Jure Naturali, Gentium, et Civili.*

The law of nature is not a law to man only, but likewise to all other animals, whether they are produced on the earth, in the air, or in the waters. From hence proceeds the conjunction of male and female, which we among our own species style matrimony; from hence arises the procreation of children, and our care in bringing them up. We perceive, also, that the rest of the animal creation are regarded as having a knowledge of this law, by which they are actuated.

§ 1. Civil law is distinguished from the law of nations because every community uses partly its own particular laws, and partly the general laws which are common to all mankind. That law which a people enacts for the government of itself is called the civil law of that people; but that law which natural reason appoints for all mankind is called the law of nations, because all nations make use of it. The people of Rome are governed partly by their own laws, and partly by the laws which are common to all men. But we propose to treat separately of these laws in their proper places.

§ 2. All civil laws take their denomination from that city in which they are established: it would, therefore, not be erroneous to call the laws of Solon or Draco the civil law of Athens; and thus the law which the Roman people make use of is styled the civil law of the Romans, or of the *Quirites*, for the Romans are also called *Quirites* from *Quirinus*. Whenever we mention the words "civil law" without addition we emphatically denote our own law. Thus, the Greeks, when they say the poet, mean Homer; and the Romans, Virgil. The law of nations is common to mankind in general, and all nations have framed laws through human necessity; for wars arose, and the consequences were captivity and servitude, both which are contrary to the law of nature, for by that law all men are free. But almost all contracts were at first introduced by the law of nations, as, for instance, buying, selling, letting, hiring, society, or deposit, or *mutuum*, and others without number.

§ 3. The Roman law is divided, like the Grecian, into written and unwritten. The written is six-fold, and comprehends the laws, the plebiscites, the decrees of the senate, the constitutions of princes, the edicts of magistrates, and the answers of the sages of the law.

§ 4. A law is what the Roman people enact at the request of a senatorial magistrate; as, for instance, at the request of a consul. A plebiscite is what the commonalty enact, when requested by a plebeian magistrate, as by a tribune. The word "commonalty" differs from "people," as a species from its genus; for all the citizens, including patricians and senators, are comprehended under the term "people." The term "commonalty" includes all the citizens, except patricians and senators. The plebiscites, by the Hortensian law, began to have the same force as the laws themselves.

§ 5. A senatorial decree is what the senate commands and appoints; for, when the people of Rome were increased to a degree which made it difficult for them to assemble for the enacting of laws, it seemed but right that the senate should be consulted instead of the whole body of the people.

§ 6. The constitution of the prince hath also the force of a law, for the people, by a law called *lex regia*, make a concession to him of their whole power. Therefore whatever the emperor ordains by rescript, decree, or edict, it is a law. These acts are called constitutions. Of these some are personal, and are not to be drawn into precedent; for, if the prince hath indulged any particular man on account of his merit, or inflicted any extraordinary punishment on a criminal, or granted him some unprecedented indulgence, these acts extend not to others in the like circumstances. But other constitutions are general, and undoubtedly bind all people.

§ 7. The edicts of the prætors are also of great authority. These edicts are called the honorary law, because those who bear honours in the state have given them their sanction. The curule ædiles also, upon certain occasions, published their edicts, which became a part of the *jus honorarium*.

8. The answers of the lawyers are the opinions of those who were authorized to give their answers concerning matters of law. For anciently they were persons who publicly interpreted the law, and to these the emperors gave a licence for that purpose. They were called *jurisconsulti*, and their opinions obtained so great an authority that it was not in the power of a judge to recede from them.

§ 9. The unwritten law is that which usage has approved, for all customs which are established by the consent of those who use them obtain the force of a law.

§ 10. The division of the law into written and unwritten seems to have taken rise from the peculiar customs of the Athenians and Lacedæmonians. For the Lacedæmonians trusted chiefly to memory for the preservation of their laws, but the laws of the Athenians were committed to writing.

§ 11. The laws of nature, which are observed by all nations, inasmuch as they are the appointment of divine Providence, remain constantly fixed and immutable. But those laws, which every city has enacted for the government of itself, suffer frequent changes, either by tacit consent or by some subsequent law repealing a former.

§ 12. The laws which we make use of have relation either to persons, things, or actions. We must, therefore, first treat of persons, for it would be to little purpose to aim at knowledge in the law while we are ignorant of persons on whose sole account the law was constituted.

Tit. III. *De Jure Personarum.*

The first general division of persons, in respect to their rights, is into freemen and slaves.

§ 1. Liberty or freedom, from which we are denominated free, is that natural power which we have of acting as we please, if not hindered by force or restrained by the law.

§ 2. Slavery is that by which one man is made subject to another, according to the law of nations, though contrary to natural right.

§ 3. Slaves are denominated *servi*, from the verb *servare*, to preserve: for it is the practice of our generals to sell their captives, being accustomed to preserve, and not to destroy them. Slaves are also called *mancipia* (*a manu capere*), in that they are taken by the hand of the enemy.

§ 4. Slaves are either born such, or become so. They are born slaves when they are the children of bond-women, and they become slaves either by the law of nations, that is, by captivity, or by the civil law, which happens when a free person, above the age of twenty, suffers himself to be sold for the sake of sharing the price given for him.

§ 5. In the condition of slaves there is no diversity, but among those who are free there are many: thus some are *ingenui*, others *libertini*.

Tit. IV. *De Ingenuis.*

The term "ingenuous" denotes a person who is free at the instant of his birth, by being born in matrimony of parents who are both ingenuous, or both libertines, or of parents who differ in condition, the one being ingenuous and the other a libertine. But when the mother is free, although the father is a slave, or even unknown, the child is ingenuous; and when the mother is free at the time of the birth of her infant, although she was a bond-woman when she conceived it, yet such infant will be ingenuous. Also if a woman, who was free at the time of conception, is afterwards reduced to slavery, and delivered of a child, her issue is, notwithstanding this, freeborn; for the misfortune of the mother ought by no means to prejudice her infant. It has been a question whether the child of a woman who is made free during pregnancy, but becomes bond before delivery, would be freeborn? Martianus proves that the child of such woman would be free, for, in his opinion, it is sufficient if the mother hath been free at any time between conception and delivery; and this opinion is strictly true.

§ 1. When any man is by birth ingenuous, it will not injure him to have been in servitude, and to have been afterwards manumitted; for there are diverse constitutions by which it is enacted that manumission shall not prejudice free birth.

Tit. V. *De Libertinis.*

"Libertines," or free men, are those who have been manumitted from just servitude. Manumission implies the giving of liberty: for whoever is in servitude is subject to the hand and power of another; but whoever is manumitted is free from both.

Manumission took its rise from the law of nations, for all men by the law of nature are born in freedom; nor was manumission heard of whilst servitude was unknown. But when servitude, under sanction of the law of nations, invaded liberty, the benefit of manumission became then a consequence. For all men were at first denominated by one common appellation, till by the law of nations they began to be divided into three classes, viz., into *liberi*, or those who are born free; into *servi*, or those who are in slavery; and into *libertini*, who are those who have ceased to be slaves by having freedom conferred upon them.

§ 1. Manumission is effected by various ways, either in the face of the church, according to the imperial constitutions, or by the *vindicta*, or in the presence of friends, or by letter, or by testament, or by any other last will. Liberty may also be properly conferred upon a slave by diverse other methods, some of which were introduced by the constitutions of former emperors, and others by our own.

§ 2. Slaves may be manumitted by their masters at any time, even whilst the prætor, the governor of a province, or the proconsul is going to the baths, or to the theatre.

§ 3. The *libertini* were formerly distinguished by a threefold division. Those who were manumitted sometimes obtained what was called "the greater liberty," and thus became Roman citizens; sometimes they obtained only "the lesser liberty," and became Latins, according to the law *Junia Norbana;* and sometimes they obtained only "the inferior liberty," and became *Dedititii*, by the law *Ælia Sentia.* But the condition of the *Dedititii* differing but little from slavery, the inferior liberty has been long since disused, neither has the name of Latins been frequent. It, therefore, being our ardent desire to extend our bounty, and to reduce all things into a better state, we have amended our laws by two constitutions, and re-established the ancient usage; for anciently liberty was simple and undivided, that is, it was conferred upon the slave as his manumitter possessed it; admitting this single difference, that the person manumitted became only a libertine, although his manumitter was ingenuous. We have entirely abolished the name of *Dedititii* by a constitution published among our decisions, by which, at the instance of Tribonian, our quæstor, we have suppressed all disputes concerning the ancient law. We have also, at the suggestion of the same illustrious person, altered the condition of the Latins, and corrected the laws which related to them by another constitution, which eminently distinguishes itself among the imperial sanctions, and we have made all the freed-men in general citizens of Rome, regarding neither the age of the person manumitted nor of the manumitter, nor any of the forms of manumission as they were anciently observed. We have also introduced many new methods by which slaves may become Roman citizens; and the liberty of becoming such is that alone which can now be conferred.

Tit. VI. *Qui et ex quibus causis manumittere non possunt.*

It is not in the power of every master to manumit at will, for whoever manumits with an intent to defraud his creditors may be said to commit a nullity, the law *Ælia Sentia* impeding all liberty thus granted.

§ 1. A master, who is insolvent, may appoint a slave to be his heir with liberty, that thus the slave may obtain his freedom, and become the only and necessary heir of the testator, on supposition that no other person is also heir by the same testament, and this may happen, either because no other person was instituted heir, or because the person so instituted is unwilling to act as such. This privilege of masters was, for wise and just reasons, established by the above-named law *Ælia Sentia;* for it claimed a special provision that indigent men, to whom no man would be a voluntary heir, might have a slave for a necessary heir to satisfy creditors; or otherwise, that the creditors themselves should make sale of the hereditary effects of the master in the name of the slave, lest the deceased should suffer ignominy.

§ 2. A slave also becomes free by being instituted an heir, although no mention was made of liberty in the testament; for our imperial constitution regards not only masters who are insolvent, but, by a new act of our humanity, it extends generally, so that the very institution of an heir implies the conferring of liberty. For it is highly improbable that a testator, although he hath omitted to mention liberty in his testament, would be willing that the person whom he hath instituted should remain in servitude, since a testator would thus defeat his own purpose and be destitute of an heir.

§ 3. A man may be said to manumit in order to defraud creditors if he is insolvent at the time when he manumits, or if he becomes insolvent by manumitting. It is, however, the prevailing opinion that liberty, when granted, is not impeached, unless the manumitter had an intent to defraud, although his goods are insufficient for the payment of his creditors, for men frequently imagine themselves to be in better circumstances than they really are. We therefore understand liberty to be then only impeded, when creditors are doubly defrauded—that is, both by the intention of the manumitter and in reality.

§ 4. By the before-named law *Ælia Sentia*, a master under the age of twenty years cannot manumit, unless a just cause is assigned, which must be approved of by a council appointed for that purpose, at whose command liberty is conferred by the *vindicta*.

§ 5. A minor is deemed to assign a just reason for manumission when he alleges any of the following, viz.: that the person to be manumitted is his father or mother, his son or daughter, his brother or sister, his preceptor, his nurse, his foster-child, or his foster-brother; or when he alleges that he would manumit his slave, in order to constitute him his proctor; or his bond-woman, with intent to marry her, on condition that the marriage is performed within six months. But a slave, who is to be constituted a proctor, cannot be manumitted for that purpose if he is under seventeen.

§ 6. A reason which has once been admitted in favour of liberty, whether true or false, cannot afterwards be disallowed.

§ 7. When certain bounds were prescribed by the law *Ælia Sentia* to all under twenty, with regard to manumission, it was observed that any person who was fourteen complete might make a testament, institute an heir, and bequeath legacies, and yet that no person under twenty could confer liberty; which was not longer to be tolerated: for can any just cause be assigned why a man, permitted to dispose of all his effects by testament, should be debarred from enfranchising his slaves? But liberty being of inestimable value, and our ancient laws prohibiting any person to make a grant of it who is under twenty years of age, we therefore make choice of a middle way, and permit all who are in their eighteenth year to confer liberty by testament. For since, by all former practice, persons at eighteen were permitted to plead for their clients, there is no reason why the same stability of judgment, which qualifies them to assist others, should not be of advantage to themselves, by enabling them to enfranchise their own slaves.

Tit. VII. *De lege Fusiâ Caniniâ tollendâ.*

By the law *Fusia Caninia*, all masters were restrained from manumitting more than a certain number by testament; but we have thought proper to abrogate this law, as odious and destructive of liberty; judging it inhuman, that persons in health should have power to manumit a whole family, if no just cause impedes the manumission, and that those who are dying should be prohibited from doing the same thing by testament.

Tit. VIII. *De his, qui sui vel alieni juris sunt.*

We now proceed to another division of persons; for some are independent, and some are subject to the power of others. Of those who are subject to others, some are in the power of parents, others in the power of their masters. Let us then inquire what persons are in subjection to others; for, when we apprehend who these persons are, we shall at the same time discover those who are independent. Our first inquiry shall be concerning those who are in the power of masters.

§ 1. All slaves are in the power of their masters, which power is derived from the law of nations: for it is equally observable among all nations, that masters have always had the power of life and death over their slaves, and that whatsoever is acquired by the slave is acquired for the master.

§ 2. All persons, under our imperial government, are now prohibited to inflict any extraordinary punishment upon their slaves without a legal cause. For, by a constitution of Antoninus, it is enacted, that whoever kills his own slave without a just cause, is not to be punished with less rigour than if he had killed a slave who was the property of another. The too great severity of masters is also restrained by another constitution made by the same prince: for Antoninus, being consulted by certain governors of provinces concerning those slaves who take sanctuary either in temples, or at the statues of emperors, ordained that, if the severity of masters should appear at any time excessive, they might be compelled to make sale of their slaves upon equitable terms, so that the full worth of such slaves might be given to their masters; and this constitution seems just and reasonable, inasmuch as it is a maxim expedient for the commonwealth, "that no one should be permitted to misuse even his own property."

Tit. IX. *De patriâ potestate.*

The children whom we have begotten in lawful wedlock are under our power.

§ 1. Matrimony is a social contract between a man and woman, obliging them to an inseparable cohabitation during life.

§ 2. The power which we have over our children is peculiar to the citizens of Rome; for there is no other people who have the same power over their children which we have over ours.

§ 3. The issue of yourself and your legal wife are immediately under your own power. Also issue of a son and son's wife, that is, either grandsons or granddaughters by them, are equally in your power; and the same may be said of great-grandchildren, &c. But children born of a daughter will not be in your power, but in the power of their own father or father's father, &c.

Tit. X. *De nuptiis.*

The citizens of Rome contract valid matrimony when they follow the precepts of the law, the males when they arrive at puberty, and the females when they attain to a marriageable

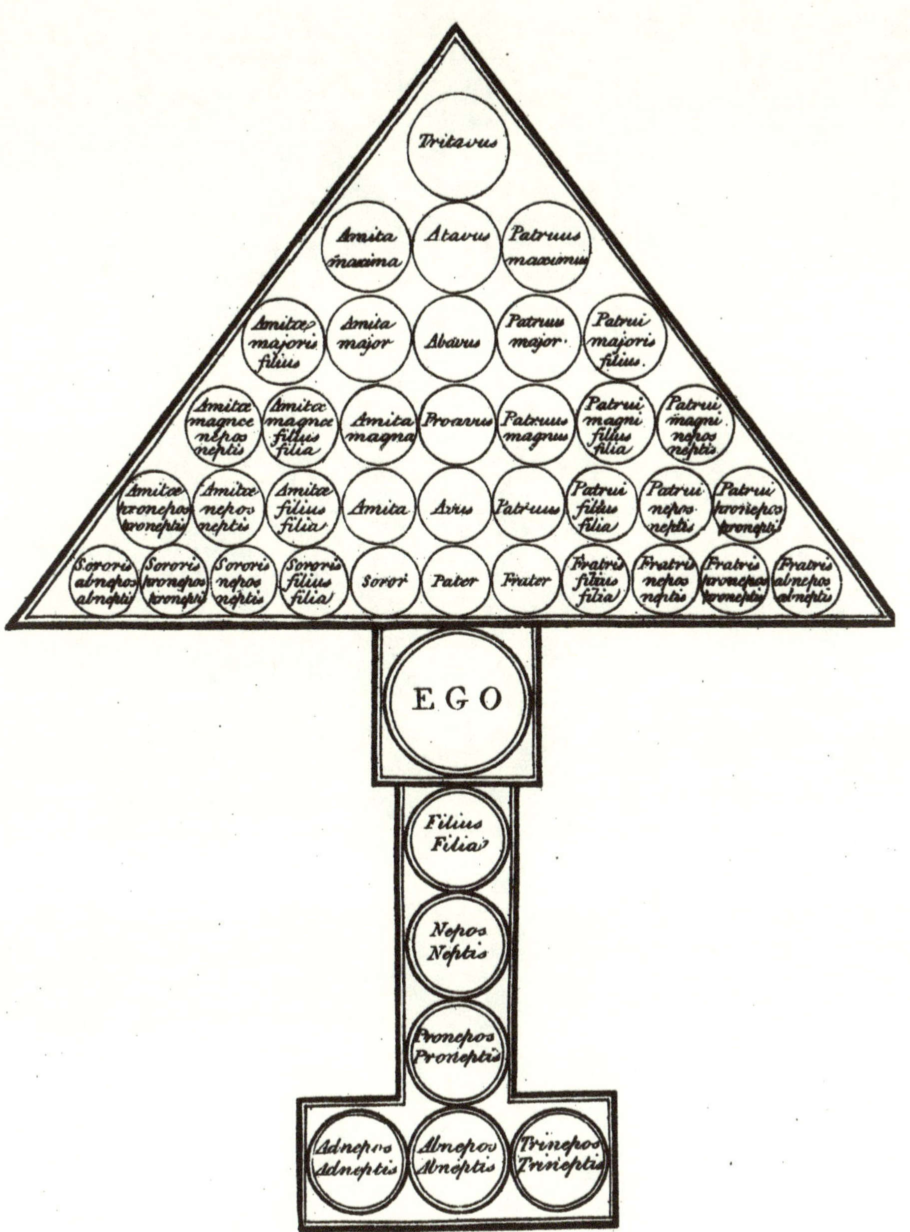

See p. 378, De Nuptii

age. The males, whether they are *patres familiarum*, fathers of a family, or *filii familiarum*, the sons of a family; but if they are the sons of a family they must first obtain the consent of the parents, under whose power they are. For reason, both natural and civil, convinces us that the consent of parents should precede marriage: and from hence it became a question whether the son of a madman could contract matrimony. But the opinions of lawyers being various, we published our decision, by which the son as well as the daughter of a madman is permitted to marry without the intervention of his father, provided always that the rules set forth in our constitution are observed.

§ 1. We are not permitted to marry all women without distinction; for there are some with whom marriage is forbidden. For matrimony must not be contracted between parents and their children, as between a father and daughter, a grandfather and his granddaughter, a mother and her son, a grandmother and her grandson; and the same prohibition extends with respect to all ascendants and descendants in a right line *in infinitum*. And if such persons cohabit together, they are said to have contracted a criminal and incestuous marriage; which is undoubtedly true, inasmuch as those who only hold the place of parents and children by adoption can by no means marry; and the same law remains in force, even after the adoption is dissolved. Whoever therefore hath once been either your adopted daughter or granddaughter, the same cannot afterwards be taken by you to wife, although she hath been emancipated.

§ 2. Matrimony is also prohibited between collaterals; but the prohibition is not of so great an extent as that which relates to parents and their children. A brother and sister are forbidden to marry, whether they are the children of the same father and mother, or of either. And if any person becomes your sister by adoption, as long as such adoption subsists a marriage contracted between her and you cannot be valid; but when the adoption is destroyed by emancipation, she may then be taken to wife. Also if you yourself are emancipated, there will not then remain any impediment, although your sister by adoption is not so. From hence it appears that if a man would adopt his son-in-law, he should first emancipate his daughter; and that whoever would adopt his daughter-in-law should previously emancipate his son.

§ 3. It is unlawful to marry the daughter of a brother or a sister; neither is it lawful to marry the granddaughter of a brother or sister, although they are in the fourth degree. For when we are prohibited to take the daughter of any person in marriage, we are also prohibited to take his granddaughter. But it appears not that there is any impediment against the marriage of a son with the daughter of her whom his father hath adopted, for they bear not to each other any relation either natural or civil.

§ 4. The children of two brothers or two sisters, or of a brother and sister, may legally be joined together in matrimony.

§ 5. A man is not permitted to marry his aunt on the father's side, although she is only so by adoption; neither can a man marry his aunt on the mother's side; because they are both esteemed to be the representatives of parents. And for the same reason no person can contract matrimony with his great-aunt, either on his father's or his mother's side.

§ 6. We are under a necessity of abstaining from certain marriages, through a veneration for affinity; for it is unlawful to marry a wife's daughter or a son's wife, in that both are in the place of daughters; and this rule must be understood to relate not only to those who actually are, but also to those who have been, our daughters-in-law at any time. For marriage with a son's wife, whilst she continues to be his wife, is prohibited on another account, viz., because the same woman cannot, at one and the same time, be the wife of two. And the marriage of a man with his wife's daughter whilst her mother continues to be his wife, is also prohibited, because it is unlawful for one man to have two wives at the same time.

§ 7. A man is forbidden to marry his wife's mother and his father's wife, because they both hold the place of mothers: and this injunction must be observed, although the affinity is dissolved: for, omitting our veneration for affinity, a father's wife, whilst she continues to be so, is prohibited to marry, because no woman can have two husbands at the same time. A man is also restrained from matrimony with his wife's mother, her daughter continuing to be his wife, because it is against the law to have two wives.

§ 8. The son of a husband by a former wife, and the daughter of a wife by a former husband, and *è contra*, the daughter of a husband by a former wife, and the son of a wife by a former husband, may lawfully contract matrimony, even though a brother or sister is born of such second marriage between their respective parents.

§ 9. If a wife, after divorce, brings forth a daughter by a second husband, such daughter is not to be reckoned a daughter-in-law to the first husband. It is, nevertheless, the opinion of Julian, that we ought to abstain from such nuptials. It is also evident that the espoused wife of a son is not a daughter-in-law to his father; and that the espoused wife of a father is not a step-mother to his son; yet those who abstain from such nuptials demean themselves rightly.

§ 10. It is not to be doubted, but that servile cognation is an impediment to matrimony, as when a father and daughter, or a brother and sister are manumitted.

§ 11. There are, besides these already mentioned, many other persons who, for diverse reasons, are prohibited to marry with each other; all whom we have caused to be enumerated in the Digests, collected from the old law.

§ 12. If any persons presume to cohabit together in contempt of the rules which we have here laid down, they shall not be deemed husband and wife, neither shall their marriage, or any portion given on account of such marriage, be valid; and the children born in such cohabitation shall not be under the power of their father. For, in respect to paternal power, they resemble the children of a common woman, who are looked upon as not having a father, because it is uncertain who he is. They are therefore called in Latin *spurii*, and in Greek *απατορες*, *i.e.*, without a father; and from hence it follows that, after the dissolution of any such marriage, no portion or gift, *propter nuptias*, can legally be obtained. But those who contract such prohibited matrimony must undergo the further punishments set forth in our constitutions.

§ 13. It sometimes happens, that the children who at the time of their birth were not under the power of their parents, are reduced under it afterwards. Thus, a natural son, who is made a decurion, becomes subject to his father's power; and he, also, who is born of a free woman, with whom marriage is not prohibited, will likewise become subject to the power of his father, as soon as the marriage instruments are drawn, as our constitution directs, which allows the same benefit to those who are born before marriage as to those who are born subsequent to it.

Tit. XI. *De adoptionibus.*

It appears from what has been already said, that all natural children are subject to paternal power. We must now add, that not only natural children are subject to it, but those also whom we adopt.

§ 1. Adoption is made two ways, either by a rescript from the emperor, or by the authority of the magistrate. The imperial rescript empowers us to adopt persons of either sex, who are *sui juris*, *i.e.*, independent, and not under the power of parents; and this species of adoption is called arrogation. But it is by the authority of the magistrate that we adopt persons actually under the power of their parents, whether they are in the first degree, as sons and daughters, or in an inferior degree, as grandchildren or great-grandchildren.

§ 2. But now, by our constitution, when the son of a family is given in adoption by his natural father to a stranger, the right of paternal power in the natural father is not dissolved, neither does anything pass to the adoptive father, neither is the adopted son in his power, although such son is by us allowed to have a right of succession to his adoptive father if he dies intestate. But if a natural father should give his son in adoption not to a stranger, but to the maternal grandfather of such son,—or if a natural father, who hath been emancipated, should give his son, begotten after emancipation, to his paternal or maternal grandfather or great-grandfather,—in this case, the rights of nature and adoption concurring, the power of the adoptive father is established both by natural ties and legal adoption, so that the adopted son would be both in the family and under the power of his adoptive father.

§ 3. When any person, not arrived at puberty, is arrogated by the imperial rescript, the cause is first inquired into, that it may be known whether the arrogation is justly founded and expedient for the pupil; for such arrogation is always made on certain conditions; and the arrogator is obliged to give caution before a public notary, thereby binding himself if the pupil should die within the age of puberty to restore all the goods and effects of such pupil to those who would have succeeded him if no arrogation had been made. The arrogator is also prohibited to emancipate, unless he has given legal proof that his arrogated son deserves emancipation; and even then he is bound to make full restitution of all things belonging to such son. Also, if a father upon his death-bed hath disinherited his arrogated son, or when in health hath emancipated him without a just cause, then the father is commanded to leave the fourth part of all his goods to his son, besides what such son brought to him at the time of arrogation, and acquired for him afterwards.

§ 4. A junior is not permitted to adopt a senior, for adoption imitates nature; and it seems unnatural that a son should be older than his father. He, therefore, who would either adopt or arrogate should be a senior to his adopted or arrogated son by full puberty—that is, by eighteen years.

§ 5. It is lawful to adopt a person, either as a grandson or granddaughter, great-grandson or great-granddaughter, or in a more distant degree, although the adopter hath no son.

§ 6. A man may adopt the son of another as his grandson, and the grandson of another as his son.

§ 7. If any man who has already either a natural or an adopted son is desirous to adopt another as his grandson, the consent of his son, whether natural or adopted, ought in this case to be first obtained, lest a *suus hæres*, or proper heir, should be intruded upon him. But, on the contrary, if a grandfather is willing to give his grandson in adoption, the consent of the son is not necessary.

§ 8. He who is either adopted or arrogated bears similitude in many things to a son born in lawful matrimony; and therefore whoever is adopted either by rescript, or before a prætor, or before the governor of a province, the same, if he is not a stranger, may be given in adoption to another.

§ 9. It is observed as a common rule, both in adoption and arrogation, that such who are impotent (whom we denominate *spadones*) may adopt children, but that those who are castrated cannot adopt.

§ 10. Women are also prohibited to adopt, for the law does not permit them to have even their own children under their power; but when death hath deprived them of their children they may, by the indulgence of the prince, adopt others, as a comfort and recompense for their loss.

§ 11. It is peculiar to that kind of adoption which is made by rescript that if a person, having children under his power, should give himself in arrogation, both he as a son and his children as grandchildren would become subject to the power of the arrogator. It was for this reason that Augustus did not adopt Tiberius till Tiberius had adopted Germanicus, so that Tiberius became the son and Germanicus the grandson of Augustus at the same instant by arrogation.

§ 12. The following answer of Cato was approved of by the ancient lawyers, viz., that slaves adopted by their masters obtain freedom by the adoption. And, from hence instructed, we have enacted by our constitution that a slave whom any master nominates to be his son in the presence of a magistrate becomes free by such nomination, although it does not convey to him any final right.

Tit. XII. *Quibus modis jus patriæ potestatis solvitur.*

Let us now inquire how those who are in subjection to others can be freed from that subjection. The means by which slaves obtain their liberty may be fully understood by what we have already said in treating of manumission; but those who are under the power of a parent become independent at his death; yet this rule admits of a distinction. When a father dies his sons and daughters are, without doubt, independent; but by the death of a grandfather, his grandchildren do not become independent, unless it happens that there is an impossibility of their ever falling under the power of their father. Therefore, if their father is alive at the death of their grandfather, and they are till then under his power, the grandchildren, in this case, become subject to the power of their father. But if their father is either dead or emancipated before the death of their grandfather, they then cannot fall under the power of their father, and therefore become independent.

§ 1. If a man, upon conviction of some crime, is deported into an island, he loses the rights of a Roman citizen, and it follows that the children of such a person cease to be under his power, as if he was naturally dead. And, by a parity of reasoning, if a son is deported, he ceases to be under the power of his father. But if, by the indulgence of the prince, a criminal is wholly restored, he regains instantly his former condition.

§ 2. A father who is relegated retains his paternal power, and a son who is relegated still remains under the power of his father.

§ 3. When a man is judicially pronounced to be the slave of punishment, he loses his paternal jurisdiction. The slaves of punishment are those who are condemned to the mines, or sentenced to be destroyed by wild beasts.

§ 4. If the son of a family becomes a soldier, a senator, or a consul, he still remains under the power of his father, from which neither the army, the senate, nor consular dignity can emancipate him. But it is enacted by our constitution that the patrician dignity, conferred by our special diploma, shall free every son from all paternal subjection. For it is absurd to think that a parent may emancipate his son, and that the power of an emperor should not be sufficient to make any person independent whom he hath chosen to be a father of the commonwealth, or, in other words, a senator.

§ 5. If a parent is taken prisoner by the enemy, although he thus becomes a slave, yet he loses not his paternal power, which remains in suspense by reason of a privilege granted to all prisoners, namely, the right of *postliminium:* for captives, when they obtain their liberty, are re-possessed of all their former rights, in which paternal power of course must be included; and at their return they are supposed, by a fiction of law, never to have been absent. If a prisoner dies in captivity, his son is deemed to have become independent, not from the time of the death of his father, but from the commencement of his captivity. Also if a son or grandson becomes a prisoner, the power of the parent is said, for the reason before assigned, to be only in suspense. The term *postliminium* is derived from *post* and *limen*. We therefore aptly use the expression *reversus postliminio*, when a person who was a captive returns within our own confines.

§ 6. Children also cease to be under the power of their parents by emancipation. Emancipation was effected, according to our ancient law, either by imaginary sales and intervening manumissions, or by the imperial rescript; but it has been our care to reform these ceremonies by an express constitution, so that parents may now have immediate recourse to the proper judge or magistrate, and emancipate their children, grandchildren, &c., of both sexes. And also, by a prætorian edict, the parent is allowed to have the same right in the goods of those whom he emancipates, as a patron has in the goods of his freedman. And further, if the children emancipated are within the age of puberty, the parent by whom they were emancipated obtains the right of wardship or tutelage by the emancipation.

§ 7. A parent having a son under his power, and by that son a grandson or granddaughter, may emancipate his son, and yet retain his grandson or granddaughter in subjection. He may also manumit his grandson or granddaughter, and still retain his son under his power; or, if he is so disposed, he may make them all independent. And the same may be said of a great-grandson or a great-granddaughter.

§ 8. If a father gives his son in adoption to the natural grandfather or great-grandfather of such son, strictly adhering to the rules laid down in our constitutions for that purpose enacted, which enjoin the parent to make his intention manifest before a competent judge, in the presence of the person to be adopted, in nowise contradicting, and also in the presence of the adopter, then does the right of paternal power pass wholly from the natural father to the adoptive, in whose person, as we have before observed, adoption has its fullest extent.

§ 9. It is necessary to be known, that if a son's wife hath conceived, and you afterwards emancipate that son, or give in adoption his wife being pregnant, the child which she brings forth will, notwithstanding this, be born under your paternal authority. But if the conception is subsequent to the emancipation or adoption, the child so conceived becomes subject at his birth either to his emancipated father, or his adoptive grandfather.

§ 10. Children, either natural or adopted, can rarely compel their parents by any method to dismiss them from subjection.

Tit. XIII. *De tutelis.*

Let us now proceed to another division of persons. Of those who are not in the power of their parents, some are under tutelage, some under curation, and some under neither. Let us then inquire what persons are under tutelage or curation, for thus we shall come to the knowledge of those who are not subject to either. We will first treat of those persons who are under tutelage.

§ 1. Tutelage, as Servius has defined it, is an authority and power given and permitted by the civil law, and exercised over such independent persons who are unable, by reason of their age, to protect themselves.

§ 2. Tutors are those who have the authority and power before mentioned, and they take their name from the nature of their office. For they are called tutors, *quasi tuitores;* as those who have the care of the sacred buildings are called *æditui, quod ædes tueantur.*

§ 3. Parents are permitted to assign tutors by testament to such of their children who are not arrived at puberty, and are under their power. And this privilege of parents extends without exception over sons and daughters. But grandfathers can only give tutors to their grandchildren when it is impossible that such grandchildren should ever fall under the power of their father after the death of their grandfather. And therefore, if your son is in your power at the time of your death, your grandchildren by that son cannot receive tutors by your testament, although they were actually in your power, because at your decease they will become subject to their father.

§ 4. As posthumous children are in many cases reputed to have been born before the death of their fathers, therefore tutors may be given by the testament of a parent as well to a posthumous child as to a child already born, if such posthumous child, had he been born in the lifetime of his father, would have been his proper heir and under his power.

§ 5. But if a father gives a tutor by testament to his emancipated son, such tutor must be confirmed by the sentence of the governor of the province without inquisition.

Tit. XIV. *Qui testamento tutores dari possunt.*

Not only the father of a family may be appointed by testament to be a tutor, but also the son of a family.

§ 1. A man may by testament assign his own slave to be a tutor with liberty. But note, that if a master by testament appoints his slave to be a tutor without mentioning liberty, such slave seems tacitly to have received immediate liberty, and is thus legally enabled to commence a tutor; yet if a testator through error, imagining his slave to be a free person, by testament appoint him as such to be a tutor, the appointment will not avail. Also the absolute appointment of another man's slave to be a tutor is altogether ineffectual; but if the appointment is upon condition that the person appointed obtains his freedom, then it is made profitably; but if a man by testament appoints his own slave to be a tutor when he shall obtain his liberty, the appointment will be void.

§ 2. If a madman or a minor is by testament appointed to be a tutor, the one shall begin to act when he becomes of sound mind, and the other when he has completed his twenty-fifth year.

§ 3. It is not doubted but that a testamentary tutor may be given either to a certain time, or from a certain time, or conditionally, or before the institution of an heir.

§ 4. A tutor cannot be assigned to any particular thing, or upon any certain account, but can only be given to persons.

§ 5. If a man by testament nominates a tutor for his sons or his daughters, the same person seems also to be appointed tutor to his posthumous issue; because under the appellation of son or daughter a posthumous child is comprehended. But should it be questioned whether grandchildren are denoted by the word sons, and can receive tutors by that denomination, we answer, that under the general term children grandchildren are undoubtedly included, but that the word sons does not comprehend them; for the words son and grandson widely differ in their signification. But if a testator assigns a tutor to his descendants, it is evident that not only his posthumous sons are comprehended, but all his other children.

Tit. XV. *De legitimâ agnatorum tutelâ.*

The *agnati* are by the law of the Twelve Tables appointed to be tutors to those to whom no testamentary tutor was given; and these tutors are called legitime.

§ 1. *Agnati* are those who are collaterally related to us by males, as a brother by the same father, or a son of a brother, or by him a grandson; also a father's brother, or the son of such brother, or by him a grandson. But those who are related to us by a female are not said to be agnate, but cognate, bearing only a natural relation to us. Thus the son of a father's sister is not related to you by agnation, but by cognation; and you are related to him in the same manner, that is, by cognation; for the children of a father's sister follow the family of their father, and not that of their mother.

§ 2. The law of the Twelve Tables, in calling the *agnati* to tutelage in case of intestacy, relates not solely to persons altogether intestate, in whose power it was to have appointed a tutor, but extends also to those who are intestate only in respect of tutelage; and this may happen if a tutor, nominated by testament, should die in the lifetime of the testator.

§ 3. The right of agnation is taken away by almost every diminution or change of status; for agnation is but a name given by the civil law; but the right of cognation is not thus altered; for although civil policy may extinguish civil rights, yet over our natural rights it has no such power.

Tit. XVI. *De capitis diminutione.*

Diminution is the change of man's former condition, which is effected three ways, according to the threefold division of diminution into the greater, the less, and the least.

§ 1. The greater diminution is when a man loses both the rights of a citizen and his liberty; which is the case of those who by the rigour of their sentence are pronounced to be the slaves of punishment,—and of freedmen who are condemned to slavery for ingratitude to their patrons,—and of all such who suffer themselves to be sold in order to become sharers of the price.

§ 2. The less or mesne diminution is when a man loses the rights of a citizen, but retains his liberty, which happens to him who is forbidden the use of fire and water, or to him who is transported into an island.

§ 3. The least diminution is said to have been suffered when the condition of a man is changed without the forfeiture either of his civil rights or his liberty, as when he who is independent becomes subject by adoption, or when the son of a family hath been emancipated by his father.

§ 4. The manumission of a slave works not any change of status in him, because he had before manumission no status or civil capacity.

§ 5. Those whose dignity is rather changed than their status are not said to have suffered diminution; and therefore it appears that they who are removed from the senatorial dignity do not suffer diminution.

§ 6. What has already been said in a section of the preceding title, to wit, that the right of cognation remains after diminution, relates only to the least diminution. For by the greater diminution, as, for instance, by servitude, the right of cognation is wholly destroyed, even so as not to be recovered by manumission. The right of cognation is also lost by the less or mesne diminution, as by deportation into an island.

§ 7. Although the right of tutelage belongs to the *agnati*, yet it belongs not to all the *agnati* in common, but to those only who are in the nearest degree. But if there are many in the same degree, the tutelage belongs to all of them, however numerous. For example, if there are several brothers, they are all called equally to tutelage.

Tit. XVII. *De legitimâ patronorum tutelâ.*

By the same law of the Twelve Tables, the tutelage of freedmen and freedwomen is adjudged to belong to their patrons, and to the children of such patrons; and this tutelage is called legitime, although it exists not nominally in the law, but it is as firmly established by interpretation as if it had been introduced by express words. For, inasmuch as the law commands that patrons and their children shall succeed to the inheritance of their freedmen or freedwomen who die intestate, it was the opinion of the ancient lawyers that tutelage also by implication should belong to patrons and their children. And the law which calls the *agnati* to the inheritance commands them to be tutors, because the advantage of succession ought to be attended in most cases with the burden of tutelage. We have said in most cases, because, when any person not arrived at puberty is manumitted by a female, such female is called to the inheritance, but not to the tutelage.

Tit. XVIII. *De legitimâ parentum tutelâ.*

In similitude of the tutelage of patrons another kind of tutelage is received, which is also called legitime; for if any parent emancipates a son or a daughter, or a grandson or a granddaughter who is the issue of that son, or any others descended from him by males in a right line and not arrived at puberty, then shall such parent be their legitime tutor.

Tit. XIX. *De fiduciariâ tutelâ.*

There is another kind of tutelage, called fiduciary; for if a parent emancipates a son or a daughter, a grandson or a granddaughter, or any other of his children not arrived at puberty, he is then their legitime tutor; but at his death his male children of age become the fiduciary tutors of their own sons, or of a brother, or sister, or of a brother's children emancipated by the deceased. But when a patron who is a legitime tutor dies, his children also become legitime tutors. The reason of which difference is this: a son, although he was never emancipated, becomes independent at the death of his father; and therefore, as he falls not under the power of his brothers, it follows that he cannot be under their legitime tutelage. But the condition of a slave is not altered at the death of his master, for he then becomes a slave to the children of the deceased. It must here be noted that the persons above mentioned cannot be called to tutelage unless they are of full age; and our constitution hath in general commanded this rule to be observed in all tutelage and curations.

Tit. XX. *De Atiliano tutore et eo, qui ex lege Juliâ et Titiâ dabatur.*

By virtue of the law Atilia, the prætor of the city, with a majority of the tribunes, had authority to assign tutors to all such who otherwise were not entitled to tutors, but in the provinces tutors were appointed by the respective governors of each province, in consequence of the law Julia and Titia.

§ 1. If a tutor had been given by testament conditionally, or from a certain day, another tutor might have been assigned by virtue of the above-named laws whilst the condition depended or till the day came. Also if a tutor had been given simply, *i. e.*, upon no condition, yet as long as the testamentary heir deferred taking upon him the inheritance, another tutor might have been appointed during the interval. But the office of such tutor ceased when the cause ceased for which he was appointed, as when the event of the condition happened, the day came, or the inheritance was entered upon.

§ 2. By the Atilian and Julio-Titian laws, if a tutor was taken by the enemy, another tutor was immediately requested, whose office ceased, of course, when the first tutor returned from captivity, for he then resumed the tutelage by his right of return.

§ 3. The Atilian and Julio-Titian laws concerning the appointment of tutors were first disused when the consuls began to give tutors to pupils of either sex with inquisition; and the prætors were afterwards invested with the same authority by the imperial constitutions. For, by the above-mentioned laws, no caution was required from the tutors for the security of their pupils, neither were these tutors compelled to act.

§ 4. But, by the later usage, at Rome the præfect of the city, or the prætor, according to his jurisdiction, and in the provinces the governors [each in his respective province], may assign tutors, after an inquiry into their morals and circumstances; and an inferior magistrate, at the command of a governor, may also appoint tutors, if the possessions of the pupil are not large.

§ 5. But we, for the ease of our subjects, have ordained by our constitution, that the judge of Alexandria, and the magistrates of every city, together with the chief ecclesiastic, may give tutors or curators to pupils or adults whose fortunes do not exceed five hundred *aurei*, without waiting for the command of the governor to whose province they belong. But all such magistrates must, at their peril, take from every tutor so appointed the caution required by our constitution.

§ 6. It is agreeable to the law of nature, that all such who are not arrived at puberty should be put under tutelage, to the intent that all who are not adults may be under the government of proper persons.

§ 7. Tutors, therefore, since they have the administration of the affairs of their pupils, may be compelled to render an account, by the action of tutelage, when their pupils arrive at puberty.

Tit. XXI. *De auctoritate tutorum.*

The authority or confirmation of a tutor is in some cases necessary, and in others not necessary. When a man stipulates to make a gift to a pupil, the authority of the tutor is not requisite; but if a pupil enters into a contract, there is a necessity for the tutor's authority; for it is an established rule, that pupils may better their condition, but not impair it, without the authority of their tutors. And therefore, in all cases where there are mutual obligations, as in buying, selling, letting, hiring, mandates, deposits, &c., he who contracts with a pupil is bound by the contract; but the pupil is not bound unless the tutor hath authorized it.

§ 1. But no pupil without the authority of his tutor can enter upon an inheritance, or take upon him the possession of goods, or an inheritance in trust; for, although there may be a probability of profit, there is a possibility of damage.

§ 2. If a tutor would authorize an act which he esteems advantageous to his pupil, such tutor ought to be present at the negotiation; for the authority of a tutor can have no effect when given by letter, by messenger, or after a contract is finished.

§ 3. When a suit is to be commenced between a tutor and his pupil, inasmuch as the tutor cannot exercise his authority as such against himself, a curator, and not a prætorian tutor (as it was formerly the custom), is appointed, by whose intervention the suit is carried on; and when it is determined the curatorship ceases.

Tit. XXII. *Quibus modis tutela finitur.*

Pupils, both male and female, are freed from tutelage when they arrive at puberty. The ancients judged of puberty in males not by years only, but also by the habit of their bodies. But our imperial majesty, regarding the purity of the present times, hath esteemed the inspection of males to be an immodest practice, and hath it proper, that the same decency which was ever observed in respect to females, should be also observed in respect to males; and therefore by our sacred constitution, we have enacted, that puberty in males should be reputed to commence immediately after the completion of their fourteenth year. But in relation to females, we leave that wholsesome and ancient rule of law unaltered, by which they are esteemed marriageable after the twelfth year of their age is completed.

§ 1. Tutelage is determined before puberty if the pupil is either arrogated, or suffers deportation; and it also determines if he is reduced to slavery, or becomes a captive.

§ 2. But if a testamentary tutor is given upon a certain condition, after that condition is fulfilled the tutelage ceases.

§ 3. Tutelage is also determined either by the death of the tutor or by the death of the pupil.

§ 4. When a tutor suffers the greater diminution of state, by which he at once loses his liberty and the privileges of a citizen, every kind of tutelage is then extinguished. But if the least diminution only is suffered, as when a tutor gives himself in arrogation, then no species of tutelage is extinguished except the legitime. But every diminution of state in pupils takes away all tutelage.

§ 5. Those who are by testament made tutors for a term only, are at the expiration of such term discharged from the tutelage.

§ 6. They also cease to be tutors who are either removed from their office upon suspicion or excuse, and exempt themselves from the burden of tutelage for just reasons, of which we shall treat hereafter.

Tit. XXIII. *De curatoribus.*

Males arrived at puberty and females marriageable do nevertheless receive curators till they have completed their twenty-fifth year; for, although they have attained to puberty, they are not as yet of an age to take a proper care of their own affairs.

§ 1. Curators are appointed by the same magistrates who appoint tutors. A curator cannot be absolutely given by testament, but a curator named in a testament must be confirmed such either by a prætor or the governor of a province.

§ 2. No adults can be obliged to receive curators unless *ad litem*, for a curator may be appointed to any special purpose, or to the management of any particular affair.

§ 3. By a law of the Twelve Tables, all madmen and prodigals, although of full age, must nevertheless be under the curation of their *agnati*. But if there are no *agnati*, or if such, who do exist, are unqualified, then curators are appointed at Rome by the præfect of the city, or the prætor, and in the provinces by the governors, after the requisite inquiry.

§ 4. Those who are deprived of their intellects, or deaf, or mute, or subject to any continual disorder, inasmuch as they are unable to take a proper care of their own affairs, must be placed under curators.

§ 5. Sometimes even pupils receive curators; for instance,

when the legal tutor is unqualified; for a tutor must not be given to him who already has a tutor. Also, if a testamentary tutor, or a tutor given by a prætor or the governor of a province, appear to be afterwards incapable of executing his trust, it is usual, although he is guilty of no fraud, to appoint a curator to be joined with him. It is also usual to assign curators in the place of such tutors who are not wholly excused, but excused for a time only.

§ 6. If a tutor, by illness or any other necessary impediment, should be hindered from the personal execution of his office, and his pupil should be absent, or an infant, then the prætor or the governor of the province shall decree any person whom the tutor approves of to be the pupil's agent, for whose conduct the tutor must be answerable.

Tit. XXIV. *De satisdatione tutorum vel curatorum.*

It is a branch of the prætor's office to see that tutors and curators give a sufficient caution for the safety and indemnification of their pupils. But this is not always necessary; for a testamentary tutor is not compelled to give caution, inasmuch as his fidelity and diligence seem sufficiently approved of by the testator. Also all tutors and curators, appointed to be such after inquiry, are supposed in every respect to be qualified, and are therefore not obliged to give security.

§ 1. If two or more are appointed by testament, or by a magistrate, after inquiry, to be tutors or curators, any one of them, by offering caution, may be preferred to the sole administration, or cause his co-tutor or co-curator to give caution in order to be admitted himself to the administration. Thus it appears that a man cannot demand security from his co-tutor or co-curator; but that, by offering caution himself, he may compel his co-tutor or co-curator to give or receive caution. But when no security is offered, if the testator hath appointed any particular person to act, such person must be preferred; but if no particular person is specified by the testator, then must the administration be committed to such person or persons whom a majority of the tutors shall elect, according to the prætorian edict; but if they disagree in their choice, the prætor may interpose his authority. The same rule is also to be observed when many, either tutors or curators, are nominated to the magistrate, viz., that a majority of them may appoint one of their number, to whom the administration shall be committed.

§ 2. It is necessary to be known that tutors and curators are not the only persons subject to an action on account of the administration of the affairs of pupils, minors, and others under their protection. For a subsidiary action, which is the last remedy to be used, will also lie against a magistrate either for entirely omitting to take sureties, or for taking such as are insufficient; and this action, according to the answers of the lawyers as well as by the imperial constitutions, is extended even against the heir of any such magistrate.

§ 3. And by the same constitution it is expressly enacted, that all tutors and curators who refuse to give caution may be compelled to it.

§ 4. Neither the præfect of the city, nor the prætor, nor the governor of a province, nor any other who has power to assign tutors, shall be subject to a subsidiary action; but those magistrates only are liable to it who exact the caution.

Tit. XXV. *De excusationibus tutorum vel curatorum.*

Persons who are nominated to be either tutors or curators may, upon diverse accounts, excuse themselves; but the most general plea offered is that of having children, whether they are subject or emancipated. For at Rome, if a man has three children living, in Italy four, or in the provinces five, he may therefore be excused from tutelage and curation, as well as from other employments of a public nature; for both tutelage and curation are esteemed public offices. But adopted children will not avail the adopter; they will nevertheless excuse their natural father who gave them in adoption. Also, grandchildren by a son, when they succeed in the place of their father, will excuse their grandfather; yet grandchildren by a daughter will not excuse him. But those children only who are living can excuse from tutelage and curation, for the deceased are of no service;

and should it now be demanded, whether a parent can avail himself of those sons whom war has destroyed, it must be answered, that he can avail himself of those only who have perished in battle; for those who have fallen for the republic are esteemed to live for ever in the immortality of their fame.

§ 1. The Emperor Marcus declared by rescript from his semestrial council, that whoever is engaged in the administration of affairs relating to the treasury may be excused from tutelage and curation whilst he is so employed.

§ 2. Those who are absent on the affairs of the republic are exempted from tutelage and curation; and if such who are already assigned to be either tutors or curators should afterwards be absent on the business of the republic, their absence is dispensed with whilst they continue in the public service, and curators must be appointed in their place; but when such tutors return, they must again take upon them the burden of tutelage. But they are not entitled (as Papinian asserts in the fifth book of his answers) to the privilege of a year's vacation, for that term is allowed to those only who are called at their return to a new tutelage.

§ 3. By a rescript of the Emperor Marcus all superior magistrates may, as such, excuse themselves; but they cannot desert a tutelage when once they have undertaken it.

§ 4. No man can excuse himself from taking the office of a tutor or curator by alleging a law suit with a pupil or minor, unless the suit is for all the goods or the whole inheritance of such pupil or minor.

§ 5. Three tutelages or curatorships, which are not acquired merely for advantage, will exempt a man during their continuance from the burden of a fourth. But the tutelage or curation of many pupils, as of three or more brothers under one patrimony, is reckoned only as a single tutelage or curation.

§ 6. The divine brothers (Marcus Aurelius and Ælius Verus?) have declared by their rescript, and the Emperor Marcus by his separate rescript, that poverty is a sufficient excuse, when it can be proved to be such as must render a man incapable of the burden imposed upon him.

§ 7. Illness, also, if it is so great as to hinder a man from transacting his own business, is a sufficient excuse.

§ 8. By the rescript of the Emperor Antoninus Pius, illiterate persons are to be excused; although, in some cases, an illiterate man may not be incapable of the administration.

§ 9. If a father, through enmity, appoints any particular person by testament to be tutor to his children, the motive of such an appointment will afford a sufficient excuse. But he who by promise hath engaged himself to a testator is not to be excused from the office of tutelage.

§ 10. The divine brothers have enacted, by their rescript, that the pretence of being unknown to the father of a pupil is not to be admitted solely as a sufficient excuse.

§ 11. A capital enmity against the father of a pupil or adult will sufficiently excuse any man, either from tutelage or curatorship, if no reconciliation hath intervened.

§ 12. Also he, whose condition hath been controverted at the instance of the father of the pupil, is upon that account excused from the tutelage.

§ 13. Any person who is above seventy years of age may be excused both from tutelage and curation. Also minors, as such, were formerly excusable; but by our constitution they are now prohibited from aspiring to these trusts, and, of course, all excuses are become unnecessary. It is also enacted by the same constitution that neither pupils nor adults shall be called even to a legitime tutelage. For it is absurd that persons who are themselves under governors, and known to want assistance in the administration of their own affairs, should, notwithstanding this, be admitted either as tutors or curators to have the management of the affairs of others.

§ 14. And we must also observe that no military person, although willing, can be admitted to become a tutor or curator.

§ 15. Both at Rome and in the provinces all grammarians, teachers of rhetoric, and physicians, who exercise their professions within their own country, and are within the number authorized, are exempted from tutelage and curation.

§ 16. He who can allege many excuses, and hath failed in his proof of those which he hath already given, is not prohibited from assigning others within the time prescribed. But tutors and curators, of whatever kind, whether legal, testamentary, or dative (if they are willing to excuse themselves), ought not to prefer an appeal merely on account of their appointment; but they should first exhibit their excuses before the proper magistrate, and this they ought to do within fifty days after they are certified of their nomination on supposition that they are within a hundred miles from the place where they were nominated. But if they are at the distance of more than a hundred miles they are allowed a day for every twenty miles, and thirty days besides, which taken together ought never, according to Scævola, to make a less number of days than fifty.

§ 17. When a tutor is appointed, he is reputed to have the care of the whole patrimony of his pupil.

§ 18. He who hath been the tutor of a minor cannot be compelled to become his curator: and, by the rescript of the Emperors Severus and Antoninus, although the father of a family should by testament appoint any person to be first the tutor of his children, and afterwards their curator, if the person so appointed is unwilling to take upon him the curation, he is by no means compellable.

§ 19. The same emperors have likewise by their rescript enacted that a husband may excuse himself from being a curator to his wife, even after he hath begun to act.

§ 20. If any man should by false allegations have appeared to merit a dismission from the office of tutelage, he is not therefore freed from the burden of this office.

Tit. XXVI. *De suspectis tutoribus vel curatoribus*

The accusation of a suspected tutor or curator is derived from the law of the Twelve Tables.

§ 1. At Rome the power of removing suspected tutors belongs to the prætor, and in the provinces to the governors, or to the legate of a proconsul.

§ 2. We have already showed what magistrates may take cognizance of suspected persons: let us now therefore inquire what persons may become suspected. And indeed all tutors may become so, whether they are testamentary, or of any other denomination. For even a legitime tutor may be accused; neither is a patron less subject to an accusation; but we must remember, that as such his reputation must be spared, although he is removed from his trust as a suspected person.

§ 3. It now remains as a consequence that we inquire by whom suspected persons may be accused. It must therefore be known, that an accusation of this sort is of a public nature, and open to all. For, by a rescript of the Emperors Severus and Antoninus, even women are admitted to be accusers; yet such only who are induced to it by their duty or by their relation to the minor: thus a mother, a nurse, or a grandmother may become accusers; and also a sister. But the prætor can at discretion admit any woman who, acting with a becoming modesty, but impatient of wrongs offered to pupils, appears to have no other motive than to relieve the injured.

§ 4. No pupil can bring an accusation of suspicion against his tutor; but adults, by the rescript of Severus and Antoninus, are permitted, when they act by advice of persons related to them, to accuse their curators.

§ 5. Any tutor who does not faithfully execute his trust, let his circumstances be ever so sufficient to answer damages, may, according to Julian, be pronounced suspected. And it is also the opinion of the same Julian (which opinion is adhered to in our constitutions) that a tutor may be removed from his office as suspected even before he has begun to execute it.

§ 6. When any person is removed upon suspicion, if it is of fraud, he is stigmatized with infamy; but if of neglect only, he does not become infamous.

§ 7. If any tutor is accused upon suspicion, his administration, according to Papinian, is suspended whilst the accusation is under cognizance.

§ 8. If a suspected tutor or curator should die pending the accusation, then the cognizance of it is extinguished.

§ 9. If a tutor fails to appear, with an intent to defer the appointment of an allowance for the maintenance of his pupil, it is provided by the constitution of Severus and Antoninus, that the pupil shall be put into the possession of his tutor's effects; and that a curator being appointed, those things which will be impaired by delay may be immediately put to sale: and therefore any tutor who, by absenting himself, impedes the grant of an allowance to his pupil, may be removed as suspected.

§ 10. But if a tutor makes a personal appearance, and falsely avers that the effects of his pupil are insufficient for an allowance, such tutor shall be remitted to the præfect of the city, and punished by him in the same manner as he who hath acquired a tutelage by bribery.

§ 11. Also a freedman, who is proved to have fraudulently administered the tutelage of the son or grandson of his patron, must be remitted to the præfect to be condignly punished.

§ 12. It is lastly to be observed, that they who unfaithfully administer their trust, must be immediately removed from it, although they tender a sufficient caution. For the act of giving caution alters not the malevolent purpose of the tutor, but procures him a longer time for the continuance of his depredations. We also deem every man suspected whose immoralities give cause for it: but a tutor or curator who, although poor, is yet faithful and diligent, can by no means be removed as a suspected person merely on account of poverty.

BOOK II.

Tit. I. *De rerum divisione, et acquirendo earum dominio.*

We have already treated of persons in the foregoing book; let us now, therefore, inquire concerning things, which may be divided into those which can and those which cannot come within our patrimony and be acquired; for some things are in common among mankind in general, some are public, some universal, and some are such to which no man can have a right. But most things are the private property of individuals, by whom they are variously acquired, as will appear hereafter.

§ 1. Those things which are given to mankind in common by the law of nature are the air, running water, the sea, and consequently the shores of the sea; no man, therefore, is prohibited from approaching any part of the sea-shore whilst he abstains from committing acts of violence in destroying farms, monuments, edifices, &c., which are not in common as the sea is.

§ 2. All rivers and ports are public; and, therefore, the right of fishing in a port or in rivers is in common.

§ 3. All that tract of land over which the greatest winter flood extends itself is the sea-shore.

§ 4. By the law of nations the use of the banks of rivers is also public, as the rivers themselves are; and therefore all persons have the same liberty to bring their vessels to the land to unload them, and to fasten ropes to trees upon the banks of a river, as they have to navigate upon the river itself; but, notwithstanding this, the banks of a river are the property of those who possess the land adjoining to such banks; and therefore the trees which grow upon them are also the property of the same persons.

§ 5. The use of the sea-shore is also public and common by the law of nations, as is the use of the sea; and therefore any person is permitted to erect a cottage upon it for his habitation, in which he may dry his nets and preserve them from the water; for the shores are not understood to be a property in any man, but are compared to the sea itself, and to the sand or ground which is under the sea.

§ 6. Theatres, ground appropriated for a race or public exercises, and things of the like nature which belong to a whole city, are universal, and not the property of any particular person.

§ 7. Things sacred, religious, and holy, cannot be vested in any person as his own; for that which is of divine right is *nullius in bonis*, and can be no man's property.

§ 8. Those things which have been consecrated by the pontiffs in due form are esteemed sacred; such are churches, chapels, and also all moveable things, if they have been properly dedicated to the service of God; and we have forbidden by our constitution that these things should be either aliened or obligated, unless for the redemption of captives. But if a man should consecrate a building merely by his own authority, it would not be rendered sacred by such a consecration; but the very ground upon which a sacred edifice hath once been erected will, according to Papinian, continue to be sacred, although the edifice is destroyed.

§ 9. Any man may, at his will, render any place which belongs solely to himself religious, by making it the repository of a dead body; yet when two are joint possessors of a place or spot of ground not before used for such a purpose, it is not in the power of the one without the consent of the other to cause it to become religious. But when there is a sepulchre in common among many it is in the power of any one joint possessor to make use of it, although the rest should dissent. And when there is a proprietor, and an usufructuary, of the same place, the proprietor, without the consent of the usufructuary, cannot render it religious. But it is lawful to lay the body of a dead person in a place belonging to any man who has given his consent to it; and although he should dissent after the burial, yet the place becomes religious.

§ 10. Holy things also, as the walls and gates of a city, are in some degree of divine right, and therefore the property of no man. The walls of a city are esteemed *sancti*, or holy, inasmuch as any offence against them is always punished capitally; and therefore all those parts of the laws by which punishments are inflicted upon transgressors we generally term sanctions.

§ 11. There are various means by which things become the property of private persons. Of some things we obtain dominion and property by the law of nature—which, as we have already observed, is also called the law of nations; and we acquire a property in other things by the civil law. But it will be most convenient to begin from the more ancient law: and that the law which nature established at the birth of mankind is the most ancient appears evident; for civil laws could then only commence to exist when cities began to be built, magistracies to be created, and laws to be written.

§ 12. Wild beasts, birds, fish, and all the animals which are bred either in the sea, the air, or upon the earth, do, as soon as they are taken, become instantly, by the law of nations, the property of the captor; for it is agreeable to natural reason that those things which have no owner should become the property of the first occupant; and it is not material whether they then are taken by a man upon his own ground or upon the ground of another; but yet it is certain, that whoever hath entered into the ground of another for the sake of hunting or fowling might have been prohibited from entering by the proprietor of the ground if he had foreseen the intent. But though wild beasts or fowl, when taken, are esteemed the property of the captor whilst they continue in his custody, yet when they have once escaped and recovered their natural liberty the right of the captor ceases, and they become the property of the first who seizes them. And they are understood to have recovered their natural liberty if they have run or flown out of sight; and even if they are not out of sight, when it so happens that they cannot without difficulty be pursued and retaken.

§ 13. It hath been a question, whether a wild beast is understood to belong to him by whom it hath been so wounded that it may easily be taken. And, in the opinion of some, it belongs to such person as long as he pursues it; but if he quits the pursuit, they say it ceases to be his, and again becomes the right of the first occupant. But others have thought that property in a wild beast cannot otherwise be obtained than by actually taking it. And we confirm this latter opinion, because many accidents frequently happen which prevent the capture.

§ 14. Bees also are wild by nature; and therefore, although they swarm upon a tree which is yours, they are not reputed until they are hived by you to be more your property than the birds which have nests there: and therefore, if any other person shall inclose them in an hive, he thus becomes their proprietor. Their honeycombs also become the property of him who takes them; but if you observe any person entering into your ground with that intent, you may justly hinder him. A swarm which hath flown from your hive is still reputed to continue yours as long as it remains in sight, and may easily be pursued; but in any other case it will become the property of the occupant.

§ 15. Peacocks and pigeons are also naturally wild; nor is it any objection to say, that after every flight it is their custom to return: for bees do the same thing; and that bees are naturally wild is evident. Some have been known to have trained deer to be so tame, that they would go into and return from the woods at regular periods; and yet no man denies but that deer are wild by nature. But with respect to these animals which go and return customarily, the rule to be observed is, that they are understood to be yours as long as they appear to retain an inclination to return; but if this inclination ceases, that they cease to be yours, and will again become the property of him who takes them. And these animals seem then to cease to have an inclination to return, when they disuse the custom of returning.

§ 16. But geese and fowls are not wild by nature; and this we are induced to observe, because there is a species of fowls and a species of geese which in contradistinction we term wild: and therefore if the geese or fowls of Titius, being disturbed and frightened, should take flight, they are nevertheless reckoned to belong to him, in whatever place they are found, although he shall have lost sight of them: and whoever detains such animals with a lucrative view, is understood to commit a theft.

§ 17. All those things which we take from our enemies in war become instantly our own by the law of nations: so that freemen may be brought into a state of servitude by capture; but if they afterwards escape, and shall have returned to their own people, they then obtain again their former state.

§ 18. Precious stones, pearls, and other things which are found upon the sea-shore, become instantly by the law of nations the property of the finder.

§ 19. The product of those animals of which we are the owners and masters is by the same law esteemed to be our own.

§ 20. And further, that ground which a river hath added to your estate by alluvion [*i.e.* by an imperceptible increase] is properly acquired by you according to the law of nations. And that is said to be added by alluvion which is added in a manner which renders it impossible to judge how much ground is added in the space of each moment of time.

§ 21. But if the impetuosity of a river should sever any part of your estate, and adjoin it to that of your neighbour, it is certain that such part would still continue yours; but if it should remain for a long time joined to the estate of your neighbour, and the trees which accompanied it shall have taken root in his ground, such trees seem, from the time of their taking root, to be gained and acquired to his estate.

§ 22. When an island rises in the sea—an event which rarely happens—the property of it is in the occupant, for the property before occupation is in no man. But if an island rises in a river—which frequently happens—and is placed exactly in the middle of it, such island shall be in common to them who possess the lands near the banks on each side of the river, according to the proportion of the extent and latitude of each man's estate adjoining to the banks. But if the island is nearer to one side than the other, it belongs to them only who possess lands next to the banks on that side to which the island is nearest. But if a river divides itself, and afterwards unites again, having reduced a tract of land into the form of an island, the land still continues to be the property of him to whom it before appertained.

§ 23. If a river, entirely forsaking its natural channel, hath began to flow elsewhere, the first channel appertains to those who possess the lands close to the banks of it, in proportion to the breadth of each man's estate next to such banks; and the new channel partakes of the nature of the river, and becomes public. And if after some time the river shall return to its former channel, the new channel commences to be the property of those who possess the lands contiguous to the banks of it.

§ 24. But it is otherwise in respect to lands which are overflowed only; for an inundation alters not the face and nature of the earth; and therefore, when the waters have receded, it is apparent that the property will be found still to remain in him in whom it was vested before the inundation.

§ 25. When a man hath made any species or kind of work with materials belonging to another, it is often demanded, which of them ought, in natural reason, to be deemed the master of it; whether he who made the species, or he who was the undoubted owner of the materials? as, for instance, if any person should make wine, oil, or flour, from the grapes, olives, or corn of another—should cast a vessel out of gold, silver, or brass belonging to another man—should make a liquor called mulse with the wine and honey of another—should compose a plaster or collyrium with another man's medicines—should make a garment with another's wool—or should fabricate with the timber of another a bench, a ship, or a chest? And, after much controversy concerning this question between the Sabinians and Proculians, the opinion of those who kept a mean between the two parties proved most satisfactory to us, and their opinion was this, that if the species can be reduced to its former rude materials, then the owner of such materials is also to be reckoned the owner of the new species; but if the species cannot be so reduced, then he who made it is understood to be the owner of it: for example, a vessel can easily be reduced to the rude mass of brass, silver, or gold, of which it was made; but wine, oil, or flour cannot be converted into grapes, olives, or corn; neither can mulse be resolved and separated into wine and honey. But if any man makes any species partly with his own materials and partly with the materials of another; as, for instance, if he should make mulse with his own wine and another's honey; or a plaster or eyewater partly with his own and partly with another man's medicines; or should make a garment with an intermixture of his own wool with the wool of another; it is not to be doubted in all such cases but that he who made the species is master of it, since he not only gave his labour, but furnished also a part of the materials.

§ 26. If any man shall have interwoven the purple of another into his own vestment, then the purple, although it may be more valuable, doth yield and appertain to the vestment by accession; and he who was the owner of the purple may have an action of theft, and a personal action, called a condiction, against the purloiner; nor is it of any consequence whether the vestment was made by him who committed the theft, or by another; for although things which become, as it were, extinct by the change of their form cannot be recovered identically, yet a condiction may be brought for the recovery of the value of them either against the thief or against any other possessor.

§ 27. If the materials of two persons are incorporated together, then the whole mass or composition is common to both the proprietors; for instance, if two owners shall have intermixed their wines, or shall have melted together their gold or their silver. The same rule is also observed if diverse substances are so incorporated as to become one species, as when mulse is made with wine and honey; or when an electrum is composed by an intermixture of gold and silver in different proportions; for in these cases it is not doubted but that the species becomes common. Neither is any other rule observed when either homogeneous or even different substances are confounded and incorporated together fortuitously, without the consent of their proprietors.

§ 28. If the corn of Titius hath been mixed with the corn of another by consent, then the whole is in common, because the single bodies or grains, which were the private property of each, are by mutual consent made common. But if the intermixture was accidental, or if Titius made it without consent, it then seems that the corn is not in common, because the single grains still remained ununited, and in their proper substance; for corn in such a case is no more understood to be in common than a flock would be if the sheep of Titius should accidentally intermix with the sheep of another. But if the whole quantity of corn should be retained by either of the parties, then an action *in rem* lies for the quantity of each man's corn; and it is the business and duty of the judge to make an exact estimate of the quality or value of the corn belonging to each party.

§ 29. When any man hath raised a building upon his own ground he is understood to be the proprietor of such building, although the materials used in it were the property of another, for every building is an accession to the ground upon which it stands. But notwithstanding this, he who was the owner of the materials does not cease to be the owner; yet he cannot demand his materials, or bring an action for the exhibition of them; for it is provided, by a law of the Twelve Tables, that a person whose house is built with the materials of another cannot be compelled to restore those materials; but by an action entitled *de tigno juncto* he may be obliged to pay double the value; and here note that all the materials for building are comprehended under the general term *tignum*. The above-cited provision, in the law of the Twelve Tables, was made to prevent the demolition of buildings. But if it happens that by any cause a building should be dissevered, or pulled down, then the owner of the materials, if he hath not already obtained double the value of them, is not prohibited to claim his identical materials, and to bring his action *ad exhibendum*.

§ 30. On the contrary, if a man shall have built an edifice with his own materials upon the ground of another, such edifice becomes the property of him to whom the ground appertains; for in this case the owner of the materials loses his property, because he is understood to have made a voluntary alienation of it: and this is the law if he was not ignorant that he was building upon another's land: and therefore, if the edifice should fall, or be pulled down, such person can even then have no claim to the materials. But it is apparent, if the proprietor of the ground, of which the builder was confirmed in possession, should plead that the edifice is his, and refuse to pay the price of the materials and the wages of the workmen, that then such proprietor may be repelled by an exception of fraud; and this may assuredly be done if the builder was the possessor of the ground *bonâ fide*. But it may be justly objected to any man, who understood that the land appertained to another, that he had built rashly upon that ground, which he knew to be the property of another.

§ 31. If Titius sets another man's plant in his own ground, the plant will become the property of Titius; and, on the contrary, if Titius shall have set his own plant in Mævius's ground, the plant will appertain to Mævius; on supposition in either case that it hath already taken root, for until then the property of the plant remains still in him by whom it was planted. But from the instant in which a plant hath taken root the property of it is changed: so that, if the tree of a neighbour borders so closely upon the ground of Titius as to take root in it, and be wholly nourished there, we may affirm that such tree is become the property of Titius; for reason doth not permit that a tree should be deemed the property of any other than of him in whose ground it hath cast its roots; and therefore, if a tree planted near the bounds of the lands of one person shall also extend its roots into the lands of another, such tree will become common to both the land proprietors.

§ 32. As all plants are esteemed to appertain to the soil in which they have rooted, so every kind of grain is also understood to follow the property of that ground in which it is sowed. But as he who hath built upon the ground of another may—according to what we have already said—be defended by an exception of fraud, if the proprietor of the ground should demand the edifice; so he who at his own expense and *bonâ fide* hath sowed in another man's land may also be benefited by the help of this exception.

§ 33. As whatever is built upon, or sowed in the ground, belongs to that ground by accession, so letters also, although written with gold, appertain to the paper or parchment upon which they are written. And therefore, if Titius shall have written a poem, a history, or an oration, upon the paper or parchment of Seius, then Titius will not be deemed the master of his own work, but the whole will be reputed to be Seius's property. But if Seius demands his books or parchments from Titius, and at the same time refuses to defray the expense of the writing, then Titius can defend himself by an exception of fraud; and this he may certainly do if he was in possession of such papers and parchments *bonâ fide*—that is, honestly, and believing them to be his own.

§ 34. If any man shall have painted upon the tablet of another, some think that the tablet should yield and accede to the picture; but it is the opinion of others that the picture—whatever the quality of it may be—should accede to the tablet. But it appears to us to be the better opinion that the tablet should accede to the picture; for it seems ridiculous that the painting of an Apelles or a Parrhasius should yield as an accession to a worthless tablet. But if he who hath painted upon a tablet demands it from the owner and possessor, and offers not the price of it, then such demandant may be defeated by an exception of fraud; but if the painter is in possession of the picture, the owner of the tablet is entitled to an action called *utilis, i. e.*, beneficial; in which case, if the owner of the tablet demands it, and does not tender the value of the picture, he may also be repelled by an exception of fraud, if he who painted upon the tablet was the possessor of it upon good faith. But if he who hath painted upon it, or any other, shall have taken away a tablet feloniously, it is evident that the owner of it may prosecute such persons by an action of theft.

§ 35. If any man shall have purchased lands from another, believing the seller to have been the true owner, when in fact he was not, or shall have obtained an estate *bonâ fide*, either by donation, or any other just means, it is agreeable to natural reason that the fruits which he shall have gathered shall be reckoned to have become his own, on account of his care in the culture and tillage; and therefore, if the true owner shall afterwards appear and claim his lands, he can have no action against the *bonâ fide* possessor for those fruits and that product which have been consumed. But this exemption from such an action is not granted to him who knowingly keeps possession of another's estate; and therefore, whenever there is a *mala fides*, the possessor is compellable to restore all the mesne profits together with the lands.

§ 36. He to whom the usufruct of lands belongs can gain no property in the fruits of such lands until he hath actually gathered them; and therefore, if the usufructuary should die whilst the fruits, although ripe, are yet ungathered, they could not be claimed by his heirs, but would be acquired by the proprietor of the lands; and the same may be said in general in relation to farmers.

§ 37. In estimating the product of animals, we not only reckon milk, skins, and wool, but also their young; and therefore lambs, kids, calves, colts, and pigs appertain by natural right to the usufructuary; but the offspring of a female slave is not to be included within this product, and can belong to him only in whom the property of such female slave is vested; for it seemed absurd to think that man, for whom nature hath framed all things, should be enumerated among the productions of the brute creation.

§ 38. He who has the usufruct of a flock ought, according to the opinion of Julian, to preserve the original number of his sheep entire, by supplying the place of those which die out of the produce of the flock; and the duty of a usufructuary is the same in regard to other things, for he ought to supply the place of dead vines, or trees, by substituting others in their stead, and to act in every respect like a good husbandman.

§ 39. It hath been allowed by the Emperor Adrian, in pursuance of natural equity, that any treasure which a man finds in his own lands shall become the property of the finder; and that whatever is casually found in a sacred or religious place shall also become the property of him who finds it. But if a person, not making it his business to search, should fortuitously find a treasure in the ground of another, the emperor hath granted the half of such treasure to the proprietor of the soil, and half to the finder. He hath in like manner ordained, that if anything is found within the imperial demesnes, half shall appertain to the finder and half to the emperor; and, similar to this, if a man finds any valuable thing in a place or district belonging to the treasury, the public, or the city, the same emperor hath decreed that half shall appertain to the finder, and half to the treasury, the public, or the city to which the place or district belongs.

§ 40. Things are also acquired, according to the law of nature, by tradition or livery; for nothing is more conformable to natural equity than to confirm the will of him who is desirous to transfer his property into the hands of another: and therefore corporal things, of whatever kind they are, may be delivered; and when delivered by the true owner, are absolutely aliened. Stipendiary and tributary possessions—and those which are situated in the provinces are so called—may also be aliened in the same manner; for between these and the Italian estates we have now taken away all distinction by our imperial ordinance: so that on account of a donation, a marriage portion, or any other just cause, stipendiary and tributary possessions may undoubtedly be transferred by livery.

§ 41. Things, although sold and delivered, are yet not acquired by the buyer until he hath either paid the seller for them, or satisfied him in some other manner, as by a bondsman or pledge. And although this is so ordained by a law of the Twelve Tables, yet the same rule of justice is rightly said to arise from the law of nations, that is, from the law of nature. But if the seller shall have given credit to the buyer, we must affirm that the things will then become instantly the property of the latter.

§ 42. It makes no difference whether the owner of a particular thing delivered it himself, or whether another, to whom the care and possession of it was entrusted, shall have delivered it with the owner's consent. And for this reason, if the free and universal administration of all business is committed by a proprietor to any certain person, and the committee, by virtue of his commission, shall sell and deliver any goods, then will such goods become the property of the receiver.

§ 43. In some cases, even without delivery, the mere consent of the proprietor is sufficient to transfer property; as when it happens that a person hath lent anything to you, hath let it, or deposited it in your possession, and hath afterwards sold it to you, made a donation of it, or given it to you as a marriage portion; for although he shall not have delivered it for any of these last-mentioned purposes, yet as soon as it is by consent reputed to be yours, you have instantly acquired the property of it; and that as fully as if it had actually been delivered to you as a thing sold, a donation, or a marriage portion.

§ 44. Also if a person hath sold any species of merchandise deposited in a storehouse, such person is understood to have transferred the property of his merchandise as soon as he hath delivered the keys of the storehouse to the buyer.

§ 45. It also sometimes happens that the property of a thing is transferred by the master of it to an uncertain person: thus, for instance, when the prætors and consuls cast their *missilia* or liberalities, among the people, they know not what any particular man will receive; and yet, because it is their will and desire that what every man then receives shall be his own, it therefore instantly becomes his property.

§ 46. By a parity of reason it appears true, that a thing which hath been made a derelict by the owner will become the property of the first occupant. And whatever hath either been thrown away or abandoned by the owner, to the intent that it might never more be reckoned among his possessions, is properly accounted a derelict, and therefore ceases to be his property.

§ 47. But the law is otherwise in respect to those things which are thrown overboard in a storm for the sake of lightening a ship; for such things remain the property of the owners, inasmuch as it is evident that they were not thrown away through dislike, but that each person in the ship might avoid the dangers of the sea. And upon this account whoever hath, with a lucrative intention, taken away such goods, although found even upon the high sea, he is guilty of theft. And with these those goods may be ranked which have dropped from a carriage in motion without the knowledge of the owner.

Tit. II. *De rebus corporalibus et incorporalibus.*

Things may also be further divided into corporeal and incorporeal. Things corporeal are those which may be touched; as, for example, land, slaves, vestments, gold, silver, and others innumerable. Things incorporeal are those which are not subject to the touch, but consist in rights and privileges; as inheritances, usufructs, uses, and all obligations, in what manner soever they are contracted. Nor is it an objection of any consequence to urge, that things corporeal are contained in an inheritance: for fruits gathered from the earth are corporeal; and that also is generally corporeal which is due to us upon an obligation, as a field, a slave, or money; but it must be observed that we here mean only the right to an inheritance, the right of using and enjoying any particular thing, and the right of an obligation; all which rights are undoubtedly incorporeal. And to these may be added the rights, or rather qualities, of rural and city estates, which are also termed services.

Tit. III. *De servitutibus rusticorum et urbanorum prædiorum.*

The rights or services of rural estates are these: a path, a road, a highway, and an aqueduct or free passage for water. A path denotes the right of passing and repassing on foot over another man's ground, but not of driving cattle or a carriage over it. A road implies the liberty of driving either cattle or carriages; and therefore he who hath a path hath not a road; but he who hath a road hath inclusively a path, for he may use such road when he doth not drive cattle. A highway is a service which imports the right of passing, driving cattle, &c., and includes in it both a path and a road; and an aqueduct is a service by which one man may have the right of a free passage or conduit for water through the grounds of another.

§ 1. The services of city estates and inheritances are those which appertain and adhere to buildings, and they are therefore called the services of city estates, because we call all edifices city estates, although they are built upon farms or in villages. It is required by city services that neighbours should bear the burdens of neighbours, and by such services one neighbour may be permitted to place a beam upon the wall of another;—may be compelled to receive the droppings and currents from the gutter-pipes of another man's house upon his own house, area, or sewer;

or may be exempted from receiving them;—or may be restrained from raising his house in height, lest he should darken the habitation of his neighbour.

§ 2. Some are with reason of opinion, that among rural services we ought to reckon those by which we obtain the right of drawing water, watering and feeding cattle, making lime, digging sand, &c. in the ground of another.

§ 3. All these services are called the services of estates or inheritances, because they cannot be constituted without an inheritance to support them, for no man can either owe or acquire a rural or city service if he possesses neither house nor lands.

§ 4. Whenever any one is willing to demise the right of a service to another, he may do it by contract and stipulation. A man may also by testament prohibit his heir from heightening his house, lest he should obstruct the view of his neighbour; or may oblige his heir to permit the rafter of another man's house to be laid upon his wall, or to receive upon his own house the droppings of another's, or to suffer any person to walk, drive cattle, or draw water in his grounds.

Tit. IV. *De usufructu.*

An usufruct is the right of using and enjoying, without diminution, the things which are the property of another. But although an usufruct is a right, and therefore incorporeal, yet as it appertains always to a substance, it necessarily follows that if the substance perishes the usufruct must cease.

§ 1. The usufruct of things is frequently separated from the property; and this happens by various means: it happens, for instance, when the usufruct is bequeathed by testament, for the heir hath then only the nude property vested in him, whilst the legatee possesses the usufruct; or, on the contrary, it happens when a testator hath bequeathed his lands without the usufruct, for then the legatary hath only the nude property, whilst the heir enjoys the profits; for the usufruct may be bequeathed to one man, and the lands, without the usufruct, to another. Yet if any man would constitute an usufruct otherwise than by testament, he must do it by paction and stipulation. But lest the property of lands should be rendered wholly unbeneficial by deducting the usufruct for ever, it was thought convenient that the usufruct should by certain means become extinguished, and revert to the property.

§ 2. The usufruct not only of lands and houses is grantable, but also the usufruct of slaves, cattle, and other things, except those of which the nature is such that they may be consumed by using, for the usufruct of such things is neither grantable by civil policy nor natural reason; and among these may be reckoned wine, oil, clothes, &c. And money also is almost of the same nature; for by constant use and the frequent change of owners it in a manner becomes extinguished. But the senate, through a motive of public utility, hath ordained that the usufruct of these things may be constituted if a sufficient caution is given upon this account to the heir; and therefore if the usufruct of money is bequeathed, the money is so given to the legatary as to make it instantly his own; but then the legatary, lest he should die or suffer diminution, is obliged to give security to the heir for the repayment of a like sum. Other things also, which are in their nature liable to consumption in using, when the usufruct of them is bequeathed, are so delivered to the legatary as to become wholly his property; but in this case, after an exact valuation hath been made, caution must be given to the heir for the payment of a sum equal to such valuation either at the death of the legatary, or if it happens that he should suffer diminution. It is not therefore to be understood that the senate hath created an usufruct of these things, which is impossible; but that the senate hath constituted a *quasi-usufruct* by means of a caution.

§ 3. The usufruct of a thing determines by the death of the usufructuary; and by two of the three diminutions, namely, the greatest and the middle diminution, or change of state; and also by not being used according to the manner and during the time prescribed: all which things are set forth in our constitution. The usufruct of a thing also determines if the usufructuary hath surrendered it to the lord of the property; but accession of it to a stranger does not work a surrender to the proprietor: or, on the contrary, an usufruct determines if the usufructuary hath acquired the property of it; and this is called consolidation. And it is certain, if a house hath been consumed by fire, or hath fallen by means of an earthquake, or through decay, that then the usufruct of such house is wholly destroyed, and that no usufruct of the area, or ground of it, can afterwards become due to the usufructuary.

§ 4. When the whole usufruct of a thing is determined it then reverts to the property; and from that instant of time the owner of the nude property commences to have a full and entire power over the thing.

Tit. V. *De usu et habitatione.*

The usufruct and the nude use of a thing are both of them constituted and both determined by the same means.

§ 1. There is less benefit and emolument in the use of a thing than in the usufruct; for he who hath but simply the use of lands is understood to have nothing more than the liberty of using such a quantity of herbs, fruit, flowers, hay, straw, and wood, which may be sufficient to supply his daily exigencies; and he is permitted only to be commorant upon the land on condition that he neither becomes troublesome to the owner, nor impedes the husbandmen in their country labours. And an usuary, having but a mere use, can neither let, sell, nor give away his right to another, although it is in the power of an usufructuary to convey his usufruct either by lease or donation.

§ 2. He who hath but the mere use of a house is understood to have a right in it so far only as to enable him to inhabit it himself; for he hath no power to transfer this right to another, and it is hardly thought allowable that he should receive a guest or a lodger. But the usuary, notwithstanding what has been said, hath a right to inhabit the house, together with his wife, his children, and his freedmen, and also with such other free persons who are in the quality of servants. And agreeably to this, if the use of a house appertains to a woman, she also hath the liberty of living in it with her husband and her dependents.

§ 3. He also who hath simply the use of a slave can benefit himself only by the labour and service of such slave; for it is by no means in the power of the usuary to transfer his right over to another. And the same law prevails in regard to beasts of burden.

§ 4. If the use of cattle is left by testament, as, for example, the use of sheep, yet the usuary can neither use the milk, the lambs, nor the wool; for these of right belong to the usufruct. But the usuary may undoubtedly employ the sheep in soiling and improving his lands.

§ 5. A habitation, whether given by testament or constituted by any other means, appears to be neither an use nor an usufruct, but seems to be rather a particular right. And for the public utility, and in conformity to the opinion of Marcellus, we have permitted by our decision that he who hath a habitation may not only live in it but also let it to another.

§ 6. What we have already delivered concerning real services, usufructs, uses, and habitations, may at this time be sufficient. Concerning inheritances and obligations, we will treat in their proper places. We have already explained summarily by what means things are acquired according to the law of nations; let us now, therefore, examine by what means they are acquired according to the civil law.

Tit. VI. *De usucapionibus et longi temporis præscriptionibus.*

It was anciently decreed by the civil law, that he who by means of purchase, donation, or any other just title, had obtained a thing from another whom he thought to be the true owner of it—although in reality he was not—and if it was moveable had possessed it *bonâ fide* for the space of one year, either in Italy or the provinces, or, if it was immoveable, had possessed it for the term of two years within the limits of Italy, should prescribe to such thing by use: and this was held to be law, lest the dominion or property of things should be uncertain. But although it was thought by the more ancient legislators that the above-mentioned terms were of sufficient length to enable every owner to search after his different kinds of property, yet a better determination hath suggested itself to our thoughts, lest the true owners should be defrauded, or too hastily excluded, by the circumscription of time and place, from the benefit of recovering their just due: and we have therefore promulged our ordinance, by which it is provided, that things moveable may be prescribed to after the expiration of three years, and that a possession during a long tract of time will also found a prescription to things immoveable: and note, that by a long tract of time we mean ten years if the parties are present—*i.e.* in the province—and twenty years if either of them is absent. By these means the property of things may be acquired, and this not only in Italy, but throughout our dominions in general, if the possession was justly founded.

§ 1. But it is certain in some cases, that although there hath been a possession incontestably *bonâ fide*, yet no length of time will be sufficient to found a prescription; and this happens when a man possesses as his property a free person, a thing sacred or religious, or a fugitive slave.

§ 2. It is also equally certain, that no prescription can be founded to things moveable which have been stolen, or to things immoveable seized by violence, although such things have been possessed *bonâ fide* during the length of time required by our constitution: for a prescription to things stolen is prohibited by a law of the Twelve Tables, and also by the law *Atilia;* and the laws *Julia* and *Plautia* forbid a prescription to things seized by violence. And it is not to be inferred from these laws that a thief or disseisor only is prohibited to take by prescription—for such are prohibited for another reason, namely, because they are fraudulent and dishonest possessors—but all other persons are also disabled from prescribing to things stolen or seized forcibly, although they shall have purchased such things *bonâ fide*, or otherwise received them upon a just account; and from hence it follows, that things moveable cannot easily be prescribed to even by honest possessors: for whoever hath either sold or delivered the goods of another knowingly, upon any consideration, he is guilty of theft. But this rule sometimes admits of exceptions: for in some cases a thing moveable may be prescribed to: thus if an heir, thinking a particular thing to be hereditary, which in reality had only been lent, let to, or deposited with the deceased, shall have sold, given it, or otherwise disposed of it to another, who received it *bonâ fide*, it is not to be doubted but that the receiver may prescribe: for such thing can never be reputed stolen, inasmuch as it was honestly possessed from the beginning; and the heir who hath aliened it, believing it to have been his own property, hath committed no theft. Also if he who hath the usufruct of a female slave either sells or gives away the child of such slave, believing it to be his own property, he does not commit theft; for theft cannot be constituted without an intention to commit it. It may also happen, by various means, that one man may transfer the property of another without theft, and give a right of prescription to the possessor. And in regard to things immoveable the law ordains, that if any man should take possession of an estate without force, by reason either of the absence or negligence of the owner, or because he died without heirs, and—although he hath thus possessed the land dishonestly—shall have made livery of it to another, who took it *bonâ fide*, the land by long possession may be acquired by such taker, who cannot be said to have received either a thing stolen, or possessed by violence: for the opinion of those ancient lawyers, who held that lands and things immoveable might be stolen, is now abolished: and it is therefore provided by the imperial constitutions, in favour of all such who possess an immoveable property, that a long and undoubted possession ought not to be taken away.

§ 3. A prescription may sometimes be founded even to things which have been stolen or possessed by violence; as, for instance, when such things shall have fallen again under the power of their true owner: for they are then reputed to be purged from the contamination of theft or violence, and may afterwards be claimed by prescription.

§ 4. The things which appertain to our treasury cannot be acquired by prescription. But when things escheatable have not been certified to the treasury, it is held by Papinian, that a purchaser *bonâ fide* may prescribe to any of them after delivery. And not only the Emperor Pius, but the Emperors Severus and Antoninus have also issued their rescripts conformable to this opinion.

§ 5. It is lastly to be observed, that if any man shall purchase a particular thing *bonâ fide*, or obtain the possession of it by any other just title, he can by no means prescribe to it unless the thing in itself is free from all manner of exception.

§ 6. A mistake of the cause of possession shall not give rise to a prescription: as when he who possesses a thing imagines that he hath purchased it, when he hath not purchased it; or that the thing was a gift, when in reality it was not given.

§ 7. If a thing immoveable is possessed by any man *bonâ fide*, so that the possession is justly commenced, then the heir of that man when deceased, or the possessor of his goods, may continue the possession so as to raise a prescription, although he is conscious that what he possesses is the property of another; but if the possession was commenced from the beginning *malâ fide*, or unjustly, then will the continuance of it avail neither the heir nor the possessor of the goods, although he was ignorant of any malfeasance. And we have enacted by our imperial constitution that the time of usucapion or prescription to things moveable shall be continued in the same manner from the deceased to his successor.

§ 8. And in regard to the computation of the years necessary to raise a prescription, the Emperors Severus and Antoninus have ordained by their rescript, that, between seller and buyer, the time of the continuance of the possession of the one shall be joined to the time of the continuance of the possession of the other.

§ 9. It is enacted by an edict of the Emperor Marcus, that when a thing is purchased from the treasury, the purchaser, after an uninterrupted possession of it for the space of five years subsequent to the sale, may repel the true owner by an exception of prescription. But the Emperor Zeno, of sacred memory, hath well provided by his constitution, that all those who by sale, donation, or any other title, have received things, either moveable or immoveable, from the public treasury, may instantly be secured in their possession, and made certain of success, whether they are plaintiffs or defendants; and that those who think that they are entitled to certain actions, either as proprietors or mortgagees of the things aliened, may commence their suits against the treasury at any time within the space of four years, but not afterwards. And in our own sacred ordinance, which we have lately promulged in favour of those who receive anything, whether moveable or immoveable, from the private possessions either of ourself or of the empress our consort, we have made the same regulations which are contained in the above-mentioned constitution of the Emperor Zeno concerning fiscal alienations.

Tit. VII. *De donationibus.*

There is another way by which property is acquired, namely, by donation, of which there are two kinds; the one, *mortis causâ, i.e.*, on account of death; the other, *non mortis causâ, i.e.*, not on account of death; and this takes effect during the life of the donor.

§ 1. A donation on account of death is that which is made under an apprehension or suspicion of death; as when anything is given upon condition that, if the donor dies, the donee shall possess it absolutely; or that the thing given shall be returned if the donor should survive the danger which he apprehends; or should repent that he hath made the gift; or if the donee should die before the donor. Donations *mortis causâ* are now reduced as far as possible to the similitude of legacies; for when it was much doubted by our lawyers, whether a donation *mortis causâ* ought to be reputed as a gift or as a legacy, inasmuch as in some things it partakes of the nature of both, we then constituted and ordained that every such donation should be considered as a legacy, and be made in the manner which our constitution directs. But in brief, a donation *mortis causâ* is then said to be made when a man so gives, as to demonstrate that he would rather possess the thing given himself than that the donee should possess it; and yet at the same time evinces that he is more willing that the donee should possess it than his own heir.

The donation which Telemachus makes to Piræus in Homer is of this species:—

He (when Piræus ask'd for slaves to bring
The gifts and treasures of the Spartan king)
Thus thoughtful answer'd: Those we shall not move,
Dark and unconscious of the will of Jove.
We know not yet the full event of all:
Stabb'd in his palace, if your prince must fall,

> Us and our house if treason must o'erthrow,
> Better a friend possess them than a foe.
> But on my foes should vengeance Heav'n decree,
> Riches are welcome then, not else to me;
> Till then retain the gifts.—*Pope's Odyss.* lib. 17.

§ 2. Donations made without any thought or apprehension of death we call donations *inter vivos;* and these admit of no comparison with legacies; for when once they are perfected, they cannot afterwards be revoked without cause; and donations are then esteemed perfect when the donor hath declared and manifested his will either in writing or otherwise. And it is appointed by our constitution, that a donation *inter vivos* shall, in imitation of a sale, necessarily enforce a delivery; for when things are given, they become fully and perfectly vested in the donee, and it is incumbent upon the donor to deliver them; and although it is enacted by the constitutions of our predecessors, that donations amounting to the value of two hundred *solidi* shall be publicly and formally enrolled and registered, we have yet thought it expedient to enlarge this sum to five hundred *solidi* by our ordinance, by which we permit all donations of less value to be firm and binding, without insinuation or enrolment; and there are likewise some donations which, although they exceed five hundred *solidi*, are yet of full force without insinuation. We have, also, for the enlargement of donations, enacted many other rules, all which may be collected by perusing our constitutions set forth for that purpose. It nevertheless remains to be observed, that when a donation is fully and validly made, the donor may revoke it on account of ingratitude in the donee in some particular cases; and this may be done lest he who hath been liberal and kind to another should in any of the instances enumerated in our constitution suffer either injury or damage from him upon whom a benefit was conferred.

§ 3. There is also another species of donations *inter vivos*, which was wholly unknown to the ancient lawyers, being introduced by later emperors. This species of donations *inter vivos* was called *ante nuptias*—*i. e.* before marriage—and contained in it the following tacit condition, namely, that it should then take effect when the marriage was performed; and these donations were properly called *ante nuptias*, because they could never be constituted after the celebration of matrimony. But inasmuch as it was permitted by the ancient law that portions might be augmented after marriage, the Emperor Justin, our father, hath enacted by his constitution that donations called *ante nuptias* might also be augmented at any time whilst the matrimony subsisted; and as it was improper that a donation should be still termed *ante nuptias* when it had received an augmentation *post nuptias*, *i. e.* after matrimony, we therefore being desirous that our sanctions might become as perfect as possible, and that names should be properly adapted to things, have ordained and constituted that the above-mentioned donations may be not only augmented, but may also receive their commencement at any time during matrimony; and that for the future they shall not be called donations *ante nuptias*, but donations *propter nuptias*, *i. e.* on account of marriage: and thus these donations are made equal with portions; for as portions may be augmented, and even made, when matrimony is subsisting, and persons are actually married, so donations, which are introduced on account of matrimony, may now not only precede marriage, but be augmented, or even constituted, after the celebration of it.

§ 4. There was formerly another manner of acquiring property by the civil law, namely, by accretion; as, for instance, if Primus had possessed a slave in common with Titius, and Primus had enfranchised that slave either by the *vindicta* or by testament, then would the share of Primus in that slave be lost, and accrue to Titius. But inasmuch as it affords a bad example that a man should be defrauded of his liberty, and that those masters who are most humane should suffer loss, whilst those who are most severe receive emolument, we have thought it necessary that a proper remedy should be applied to this grievance, and we have found a method by which the manumitter, his copartner, and the freed person may all partake of our beneficence; for we have decreed—and it is manifest that the ancient legislators have often transgressed the strict rules of law in favour of liberty—that freedom, although granted by one partner only, shall immediately take effect; so that the manumitter shall have reason to be pleased with the validity of his gift if his co-partner is indemnified by receiving his share of the worth of the slave.

Tit. VIII. *Quibus alienare licet, vel non licet.*

It sometimes happens that the proprietor of a thing cannot alien it, and on the contrary that he who is not the proprietor may alien it: for example, by the law *Julia* a husband is prohibited to make an alienation of lands which came to him in right of his wife, unless his wife consents to the alienation; and yet every man is deemed the proprietor of whatever is given to him as a marriage portion. But in this respect we have corrected the law *Julia*, and brought it into a better state: for having observed that this law regards only those immoveable possessions which are situated within the precincts of Italy, and that although it inhibits the husband to make a mortgage of such possessions, even with the consent of his wife, yet it permits him, with the consent of his wife, to make an alienation, we have therefore provided a remedy by our imperial authority, so that now no husband can either alien or mortgage, even with the consent of his wife, any immoveable possession, whether provincial or Italian, obtained with her as a marriage portion; and we have been induced to make these regulations, lest the frailty of women should occasion the ruin of their fortunes.

§ 1. But a creditor, by virtue of a compact, may sell or alien a pledge, although it is not his own property; yet this seems to be allowable for no other reason than because the pledge is understood to be aliened by the consent of the debtor, with whom it was covenanted from the commencement of the contract, that the creditor might be permitted to sell the pledge, if the money borrowed was not paid at the time stipulated. But, lest the creditors should be impeded from prosecuting what is justly due to them, and lest debtors, on the contrary, should lose the property of their possessions too soon, we have in our ordinance, promulged for this purpose, instituted certain methods, by which the sale of pledges may be warrantably made; and through the whole tenor of our constitution a sufficient caution hath been taken in regard to both creditors and debtors.

§ 2. It must now be observed that no pupil, whether male or

female, hath power to alien anything without the authority of a tutor: and therefore if a pupil, without the authority of his tutor, shall lend money to any man, such pupil contracts no obligation; for he is incapable of vesting the property of his money in the borrower; and therefore the money may be claimed by vindication—that is, by a real action—if it exists entire and unspent. But if money lent by a minor is consumed by the borrower *bonâ fide* (*i.e.*, believing that the lender was of full age), it may be recovered from such borrower by condiction: that is, by a personal action. And if such money is consumed by the borrower *malâ fide*, an action *ad exhibendum* will lie against him.

§ 3. But, on the contrary, the property of anything may be transferred to pupils, whether male or female, without the authority of their tutors: yet if a debtor makes a payment to a pupil, it is necessary that the debtor should be warranted by the authority of the pupil's tutor, otherwise he will not be acquitted of the debt; and this, for a most evident reason, was ordained by a constitution, which we promulged to the advocates of Cæsarea, at the suggestion of that most eminent man Tribonian, the quæstor of our sacred palace: and by this constitution it is enacted, that the debtor of a minor may lawfully pay any sum to his curator or tutor, if a judicial decree permitting the payment is previously obtained without expense to the minor; for when the payment of a debt is warranted by, and subsequent to, the decree of a judge, it is always attended with the fullest security. But although money hath been paid to a pupil otherwise than we have ordained, yet if he should afterwards require that the money should be paid him again, and demand it by action, he might be deprived of his plea by an exception of fraud, if it could be proved that he had become richer by the increase of this money, or even that he had preserved it safely. But if the pupil hath squandered and consumed the money paid to him, or lost it either by theft or violence, an exception of fraud will be of no benefit to the debtor, who will be compelled to make a second payment, because the first was made inconsiderately, without the authority of the tutor, and not according to our ordinance. Pupils are also incapacitated to pay money without the authority of their tutors; because money, when paid by a pupil without such authority, doth not become the property of him to whom it is paid: for the alienation of no one thing is granted to a pupil without the authority of his tutor.

Tit. IX. *Per quas personas cuique acquiritur.*

Things may be acquired not only by ourselves, but also by those who are under our power, and also by slaves of whom we have the usufruct only: acquisitions may also be made for us by freemen; and even by slaves whom we possess *bonâ fide*, although they are the property of another. Let us therefore inquire diligently concerning all these persons.

§ 1. It was anciently the law that whatever estate came to children, whether male or female, who were under the power of their parents, it was acquired for the parents of those children, without any diminution, if we except the *peculium castrense;* and these estates were so absolutely vested in the parents that what was acquired by one child they might have given to another child, or to a stranger, or might have sold it, or applied it in what manner and to what purpose they thought proper; but this seemed to be inhuman; and we have therefore, by a general constitution, mitigated the rigour of the law in regard to children, and have at the same time maintained that honour which is due to parents; having ordained that if anything accrues to the son by means of the father's fortune, the whole shall be acquired for the father, according to ancient practice;—for can it be unjust that the wealth which the son hath obtained by means of the father should revert to him?—but that the dominion and property of whatever the son of a family hath acquired by any other means shall remain in the son, and that the father shall be entitled only to the usufruct of such acquisition. And this we have thought proper to decree, lest that which hath accrued to a man from his labour or good fortune should be unjustly transferred to another.

§ 2. We have also regarded the interest of children in respect to emancipation; for a parent, when he emancipated his children, might, according to former constitutions, have taken to himself, if he was so inclined, the property of the third part of those things which were excepted from paternal acquisition, retaining it as the price of emancipation. But it appeared to be inhuman that the son should be thus defrauded of the third part of his property, and that the honour which he had obtained by becoming independent should be decreased by the diminution of his estate; and we have therefore decreed that the parent, instead of the third part of the property which he formerly might have retained, shall now be entitled to a half-share, not of the property, but of the usufruct; so that the property will for the future remain entire in the son, and the father will enjoy a greater share, namely half instead of a third part.

§ 3. Whatever our slaves have at any time acquired, whether by delivery, stipulation, donation, bequest, or any other means, the same is reputed to be acquired by ourselves; and we thus acquire things, although we are ignorant of, or even averse to, the acquisition, for he who is a slave can have no property. And if a slave is instituted an heir, he cannot otherwise take upon himself the inheritance than at the command of his master; but if the slave is commanded to do this, the inheritance is as fully acquired by the master as if he had been himself made the heir; and, consequently, a legacy left to a slave is acquired by his master. It is further to be observed, that masters acquire by their slaves not only the property of things, but also the possession; for whatever is possessed by a slave, the same is deemed to be possessed by his master, who may therefore found a prescription to it by means of his slave.

§ 4. In regard to those slaves of whom the possessor has the usufruct only, it is an established rule, that whatever they acquire by means of his goods, or by their own work and labour, it appertains to their usufructuary master; but whatever is obtained by a slave otherwise than by those means, it belongs to him who hath the property of the slave; and therefore, if a slave is instituted an heir, or hath received a legacy, or a gift, the inheritance, legacy, or gift, will not be acquired for the usufructuary master, but for the proprietor.

§ 5. The same rule is observed in regard to him who is possessed as a slave *bonâ fide*, whether he is a freeman, or the slave of another: for the law concerning an usufructuary master prevails equally in relation to a *bonâ fide* possessor; and therefore whatever is acquired otherwise than by the two causes above mentioned, it either belongs to the person possessed, if he is free, or to the proprietor, if the person possessed is the slave of another.

But a *bonâ fide* possessor, who hath gained a slave by usucapion or prescription, inasmuch as he thus becomes the absolute proprietor, can acquire by virtue of such slave by all manner of ways. But an usufructuary master cannot prescribe; first, because he can never be strictly said to possess, having only the power of using; and further, because he knows that the slave belongs to another. We nevertheless may acquire not only property, but also possession, by means of the slaves whom we possess *bonâ fide*, or of whom we have only the usufruct; and even by means of a free person, of whom we have a *bonâ fide* possession. But in saying this we adhere to the distinction which we have before explained, and speak of those things only of which a slave may acquire the possession either by means of the goods of his master, or by his own industry.

§ 6. It is apparent from what has been said that we can by no means make acquisitions by free persons who are not under our subjection, nor possessed by us *bonâ fide:* neither can we acquire property by another's slave, of whom we have neither the usufruct nor the just possession. And this is meant when it is said that nothing can be acquired by means of a stranger; which we must understand with an exception; for it hath been determined, according to the constitution of the Emperor Severus, that possession may be acquired for us by a free person, as, for instance, by a proctor, not only with, but even without, our knowledge; and by this possession the property may be gained, if the delivery was made by the proprietor; and an usucapion or prescription may be acquired, although the delivery was made by one who was not the proprietor.

§ 7. The observations which we have already made concerning the acquisition of particular things may suffice for the present; for we shall treat more opportunely hereafter in another place of the rights of legacies and trusts. We will now proceed to show how things may be acquired *per universitatem*, that is, wholly and in gross by one single acquisition: for example, if Titius is nominated an heir, or seeks the possession of the goods of another, or arrogates any one as his son, or if goods are adjudged to him for the sake of preserving the liberty of slaves; in all these cases the entire inheritance passes to Titius. Let us now therefore inquire into inheritances which are of a twofold nature; for they proceed either from a testacy or an intestacy. We will first treat of those which come to us by testament; and in doing this it will be necessary to begin by explaining the manner of making testaments.

Tit. X. *De testamentis ordinandis.*

A testament is so called from the Latin word *testatio*, because it bears witness or testimony to the determination of the mind.

§ 1. But, lest the ancient usage should be forgotten, it is necessary to observe that two kinds of testaments were formerly in use; the one was practised in times of peace, and named *calatis comitiis*, because it was made in the full assembly of the people; and the other was used when the people were going forth to battle, and was styled *procinctum testamentum.* But a third species was afterwards added, which was called *per æs et libram*, because it was effected by emancipation, which was an alienation made by an imaginary sale in the presence of five witnesses, and the *libripens*, or balance-holder, all citizens of Rome above the age of fourteen; and also in the presence of him who was called the *emptor familiæ*, or purchaser. The two former kinds of testaments have been disused for many ages; and that which was made *per æs et libram*, although it continued longer in practice, hath now ceased in part to be observed.

§ 2. The three kinds of testaments before mentioned all took their rise from the civil law; but afterwards another species was introduced by the edict of the prætor; for by the honorary or prætorian edict the signature of seven witnesses was decreed sufficient to establish a will without any emancipation or imaginary sale; but this signature of witnesses was not required by the civil law.

§ 3. When the civil and prætorian laws began to be blended together, partly by usage and partly by the emendation made by the imperial constitutions, it became an established rule that all testaments should be made at one and the same time, according to the civil law; that they should be sealed by seven witnesses, according to the prætorian law; and that they should also be subscribed by the witnesses, in obedience to the constitutions. Thus the law concerning testaments seems to be tripartite, for the civil law enforces the necessity of having witnesses to make a testament valid, who must all be present at one and the same time, without interval; the sacred constitutions ordain that every testament must be subscribed by the testator and the witnesses; and the prætorian edict requires sealing, and fixes the number of witnesses.

§ 4. To all these solemnities we have made an addition for the better security of testaments and the prevention of frauds, having enacted by our constitution that the name of the heir shall be expressed by the handwriting either of the testator or of the witnesses, and that everything shall be done in conformity to the tenor of our ordinance.

§ 5. Every witness to a testament, according to Papinian, may use the same signet; for otherwise what must be the consequence if seven seals should happen all to bear the same devices? It is also allowable to seal with the signet of another.

§ 6. Those persons are allowed to be good witnesses who are themselves legally capable of taking by testament; but yet no woman, slave, or interdicted prodigal, no person under puberty, mad, mute, or deaf, nor any one whom the laws have reprobated and rendered intestable, can be admitted a witness to a testament.

§ 7. If a witness, at the time of attesting, was reputed to have been a free person, but afterwards appeared to have been a slave at that time, the Emperor Adrian declared in his rescript to Cato, and afterwards the Emperors Severus and Antoninus by their rescript decreed in a similar case, that they would aid such a defect in a testament, and cause it to be accounted equally firm, as if it had been made as it ought, if the witness at the time of sealing was, in the estimation of all men, taken to be a free person, no one having made a question of his condition.

§ 8. A father and a son under his power, or two brothers under the power of the same father, may be made witnesses to a testament; for nothing hinders but that several persons may be admitted witnesses out of the same family to a business in which that family is not interested.

§ 9. No person can be a witness to a testament who is under the power of the testator. And if the son of a family gives away his military estate by testament after his dismission from the army, neither his father, nor any one under the power of his father, can be admitted a witness to it. For in this case the law does not allow of a domestic testimony.

§ 10. No heir can be admitted a witness to that testament by which he is appointed heir; neither can the testimony of any one be admitted who is in subjection to such heir; nor the testimony of his father, to whom he is himself under subjection; nor the testimony of his brothers, if they are under the power of the same father; for this whole business, which is performed for the sake of completing a testament, is now always transacted between the testator and the real or very heir. But formerly there was great confusion; for although the ancients would never admit the testimony of the *emptor familiæ*, or the supposed heir, nor of any one allied to him by subjection, yet they admitted that of the real heir, and of those who were connected with him by subjection; and the only precaution taken was to exhort and persuade those persons not to abuse their privilege. But we have corrected this practice, preventing by the coercion of law that which the ancient lawyers endeavoured to prevent by persuasion only; for we permit neither the real heir, who represents the *emptor familiæ* of the ancients, nor any person allied to such real heir, to be a witness to the testament by which he was nominated. And it is for this reason that we have not suffered the old constitutions to be inserted in our code.

§ 11. But we refuse not the testimony of legataries and trustees, and of those who are allied to them, because such persons are not universal heirs or successors; and, by virtue of our constitution, we have even specially granted to all legataries and trustees the liberty of bearing testimony; and therefore we grant this permission much more readily to those who are in subjection to them, and to those to whom they are subject.

§ 12. It is immaterial whether a testament is written upon a table of wax, upon paper, parchment, or any other substance.

§ 13. Any person may commit the same testament to diverse tablets, each of which will be an original, if the requisite forms are observed. And this sometimes is necessary; as when a man who is going a sea voyage is desirous to carry his will with him, and at the same time to leave a counterpart of it at home for his better security. Innumerable other reasons for doing this may arise, according to the various necessities of mankind.

§ 14. What we have already said concerning written testaments is sufficient. But if any man is willing to dispose of his effects by a nuncupative testament, *i.e.*, by a testament without writing, let him be assured, if in the presence of seven witnesses, he declares his will by word of mouth, that such verbal declaration will be a complete and valid testament according to the civil law.

Tit. XI. *De militari testamento.*

The before-mentioned strict observation of formalities, in the construction and formation of testaments, is dispensed with by the imperial constitutions in regard to all military persons, on account of their unskilfulness in these matters. For although they neither call the legal number of witnesses, nor observe any other solemnity, yet they may make a good testament if they are actually upon service against an enemy. This was introduced by our own ordinance with good reason; and thus in whatever manner the testament of a military person is conceived, whether in writing or not in writing, it prevails according to his intention: but when soldiers are not upon an expedition, and live in their own houses or elsewhere, they are by no means entitled to claim this privilege; but a soldier who is upon actual service against an enemy may make a testament, although he is the son of a family, and consequently under power; but, according to the common and general law, he must observe all the formalities which are required of others who are not soldiers when they make their testaments.

§ 1. The Emperor Trajan wrote as follows in his rescript to Catilius Severus concerning military testaments:—"The privilege which is given to military persons that their testaments, in whatever manner made, shall be valid, must be understood with this proviso, that it ought first to be apparent that a testament was made in some manner: and here observe, that a testament may be made without writing, even by a person who is not in the army. And therefore if it appears that the soldier, concerning whose goods question is now made before you, did, in the presence of witnesses purposely called, declare what person should be his heir, and upon what slave or slaves he would confer the benefit of liberty, he shall be reputed to have made his testament without writing, and his will shall be ratified. But if it is only proved that he said to some one, as it often happens in discourse, 'I appoint you my heir,' or 'I leave you all my estate,' such words do not amount to a testament. Nor are any persons more interested than the soldiery, that words so spoken should not amount to a will; for if this was once allowed, witnesses might without difficulty be produced after the death of any military man, who would affirm that they had heard him bequeath his estate to whomever they please; and thus the true intentions of many would be defeated."

§ 2. A soldier, though mute and deaf, may yet make a testament.

§ 3. The privilege of making testaments without the usual formalities was granted by the imperial constitutions to military men, to be enjoyed only during the time of actual service, and whilst they lived in their tents. For if veterans after dismission, or even soldiers, if not upon service against the enemy, would make their testaments, they must not omit the forms required to be observed in common by all the citizens of Rome. And if a testament is made by a soldier, even in his tent upon an expedition, yet if the solemnities of the law are not adhered to, such testament will continue valid only for one year after his dismission from the army. Suppose, therefore, that a soldier should die testate within a year after his dismission, and the event of the condition upon which his heir is instituted should not happen till after the expiration of the year, would the testament of such soldier be valid? We answer, that it would prevail as a military testament.

§ 4. If a man, before his entrance into the army, should make his testament, without observing the requisite formalities, and afterwards, when he became a soldier, and was upon an expedition, should open his testament for the sake of adding to it, or of subtracting something from it; or if he should cause it to appear manifestly by any other means that he was willing that his testament should be valid; we pronounce, that it would be valid, by virtue of this new act, amounting to a republication of his will.

§ 5. If a soldier is given in arrogation, or, being the son of a family, is emancipated, his testament is nevertheless good, having the same effect as if he had republished it by a new declaration: for it is by no means invalidated by his change of state.

§ 6. We must here make it known that since the ancient laws, as well as the later constitutions, have, in imitation of the *peculia castrensia*, or military estates, given to some persons *peculia quasi castrensia*, or quasi-military estates, and have indulged some of these in the liberty of making testaments whilst they were under power, we therefore, extending this privilege still further, have by our ordinance permitted all persons who possess these estates to make their testaments on condition that they observe the common solemnities of the law. But whoever thoroughly inspects our constitution will have an opportunity of informing himself of every point which relates to the before-mentioned privilege.

Tit. XII. *Quibus non est permissum facere testamentum.*

The right of making a testament with effect is not granted to all persons alike; for those who are under the power of others have not this right; insomuch that, although parents have given permission, their children will not be the more enabled by it to make a testament legally valid; if we except such whom we have already mentioned, and principally those who, on account of their being in the army, have permission by virtue of our constitutions to dispose by testament of whatever they have acquired by military service, although they are still under the power of their parents. This permission was at first granted by Augustus, Nerva, and that excellent prince Trajan, to actual soldiers only; but afterwards it was extended by the Emperor Adrian to the veterans, that is, to those who had received their dismission; and therefore, if the son of a family bequeaths his castrensian, or military estate, it will pass to him who is instituted the heir; but if such son dies intestate without children or brothers, his estate will then pass of common right to his father, or other paternal ascendants. We may from hence infer that whatever a soldier, although under power, hath acquired by military service, it cannot be taken from him, even by his father; and that the creditors of the father can neither sell it, nor otherwise disturb the son in his possession; and that what is thus acquired is not liable to be shared in common with brothers upon the demise of the father, but that it remains the sole property of him who acquired it; although by the civil law the *peculia*, or estates of those who are under power, are reckoned among the wealth of their parents, in the same manner as the *peculium* of a slave is esteemed the property of his master. But those estates must be excepted which, by the constitutions of the emperors, and chiefly by our own, are prohibited for diverse reasons to be acquired for parents. Upon the whole, if the son of a family, who is neither possessed of a military nor quasi-military estate, makes a testament, it will not be valid, even although he is afterwards emancipated, and becomes *sui juris* before his death.

§ 1. A person within the age of puberty can by no means make a good testament, because he is not supposed to possess that judgment of mind which is requisite; and the same holds true of a madman, inasmuch as he is deprived of his senses. And the testament of a minor under puberty will not become valid, although he arrives at puberty before his death; neither will the testament of a madman become valid, although he afterwards regains his senses, and then dies. But if he makes his testament during a lucid interval, he is a legal testator; since it is certain that the testament which a man hath made before the malady of madness has seized upon him is good: for a subsequent fit of frenzy can neither destroy the force of a regular testament, nor the validity of any other transaction, in which the rules of the law have been punctually observed.

§ 2. A prodigal also, who is under an interdiction, and prohibited from having the management of his own affairs, cannot make a testament; but if he has bequeathed his estate before interdiction, his testament will be valid.

§ 3. A man deaf and dumb is not always capable of making a testament: but we would be understood to mean this of him who is so deaf as to be unable to hear at all, and not of him who is afflicted only with a thickness of hearing; and of him who is so dumb as to be totally deprived of utterance, and not of him who only labours under a difficulty of speech: for it often happens that the most literate persons lose the faculty of hearing and speaking by various misfortunes; we have, therefore, published a constitution which aids all such persons; so that in certain cases they may make testaments, if they observe the rules of our ordinance, and may do many other acts which are there permitted. But if any man after making his testament becomes either deaf or mute by reason of ill-health or any other accident, his testament will notwithstanding this remain good.

§ 4. A blind man is not allowed to have the power of making a testament, unless he observes those rules which the law of the Emperor Justin, our father, has introduced.

§ 5. The testament of him who is in the hands of an enemy is not valid, if it was made during his captivity, even although he lives to return. But a testament made by a man in the city, or before captivity, is good, either by virtue of the *jus postliminii* if the prisoner returns; or by virtue of the law *Cornelia*, if he dies a captive.

Tit. XIII. *De exhæredatione liberorum.*

The solemnities of law, which we have before explained, are not alone sufficient to make a testament valid. For he who has a son under his power should take care either to institute him his heir, or to disinherit him nominally; for if a father in his testament pretermits or passes over his son in silence, the testament will have no effect. And even if the son dies, living the father, yet no one can take upon himself the heirship by virtue of that testament, inasmuch as it was null from the very beginning. But the ancients did not observe this rule in regard to daughters and grandchildren of either sex, though descended from the male line; for, although these were neither instituted heirs nor disinherited, yet the testament was not invalidated, because a right of accretion entitled them to a certain portion of the inheritance. Parents were, therefore, not necessitated to disinherit these children nominally, but might do it *inter cæteros.* A child is nominally disinherited if the words of the will are: "Let Titius my son be disinherited"; or even thus: "Let my son be disinherited," without the addition of any proper name, on supposition that the testator had no other son living.

§ 1. Also posthumous children should either be instituted heirs or disinherited; and in this the condition of all children is equal; but if a posthumous son, or any posthumous descendant in the right line, whether male or female, is pretermitted in a testament, such testament will nevertheless be valid at the time of making, but by the subsequent birth of a child of either sex it will be annulled. And therefore, if a matron, from whom there is reason to expect a posthumous child, should miscarry, nothing can prevent the written heirs from entering upon the inheritance. But female posthumous children may be either nominally disinherited, or *inter cæteros* by a general clause; yet, if they are disinherited *inter cæteros*, something must be left them to show that they were not omitted through forgetfulness. But male posthumous children—*i. e.*, sons and their descendants in the direct line—cannot be disinherited otherwise than nominally, in this form: " Whatever son is hereafter born to me, I disinherit him."

§ 2. Those also are reckoned in the place of posthumous children who, succeeding in the stead of proper heirs, become, by a quasi-birth, proper heirs to their parents. For example, if Titius has a son under his power, and by him a grandson or granddaughter, then would the son, because he is first in degree, have the sole right of a proper heir, although the grandson or granddaughter by that son is under the same parental power. But if the son of Titius should die in his father's lifetime, or should by any other means cease to be under his father's power, the grandson or granddaughter would succeed in his place, and would thus, by what may be called a quasi-birth, obtain the right of a proper heir. Therefore, as it behoves a testator for his own security either to institute or disinherit his son, lest his testament should be deemed not legal, so it is equally necessary for him either to institute or disinherit his grandson or granddaughter by that son, lest, if his son should die in his—the testator's—lifetime, his grandson or granddaughter, succeeding to the place of his son, should make void his testament by a quasi-agnation. And this has been introduced by the law *Julia Velleia*, in which is set forth a form of disinheriting quasi-posthumous children, similar to that of disinheriting posthumous children.

§ 3. In regard to emancipated children, the civil law does not make it necessary either to institute them heirs, or to disinherit them in a testament, inasmuch as they are not *sui hæredes*, *i.e.*, proper heirs. But the prætor commands, that all children in general, whether male or female, if they are not instituted heirs, shall be disinherited; the males nominally, the females *inter cæteros:* for if children have neither been instituted heirs, nor properly disinherited in the manner which we have mentioned, the prætor gives them the possession of the goods contrary to the disposition of the testament.

§ 4. Adopted children, as long as they continue under the power of their adoptive father, are entitled to the same rights as children born in lawful matrimony; and therefore they must either be instituted heirs, or disinherited, according to the rules laid down in regard to natural and lawful children. But it is neither enacted by the civil law, nor enjoined by prætorian equity, that children emancipated by an adoptive father should be numbered among his natural children, so as to partake of their rights: whence it happens, that adopted children, as long as they continue in adoption, are reputed strangers to their natural parents, who are not necessitated either to institute them heirs, or to disinherit them; but when they are emancipated by their adoptive father, they are then in the same state in which they would have been if they had been emancipated by their natural father.

§ 5. These were the rules which the ancient lawyers introduced. But we—not thinking that any distinction can reasonably be made between the two sexes, inasmuch as they both contribute alike to the procreation of the species, and because, by the ancient law of the Twelve Tables, all children, male as well as female, were equally called to the succession *ab intestato*, which law the prætors seem afterwards to have followed—have by our constitution introduced the same law in regard both to sons and daughters, and to all the other descendants in the male line, whether in being or posthumous: so that all children, whether they are proper heirs or emancipated, must either be instituted heirs, or nominally disinherited. And in regard to adopted children we have introduced certain regulations, which are contained in our constitution of adoptions.

§ 6. If a soldier makes his testament whilst he is upon a military expedition, and neither nominally disinherits his children already born, nor his posthumous children, but passes them over in silence, although it is known to him that he has such children, or that his wife was enceinte, it is provided by the constitutions of the emperors, that such silence shall be of equal force with a nominal disinherison.

§ 7. Neither a mother, nor a grandfather on the mother's side, is under any necessity of either instituting their children heirs or of disinheriting them, but may pass them by in silence; for the silence of a mother, a maternal grandfather, and of all other ascendants on the mother's side, works the same effect as an actual disinherison by a father. For a mother is not obliged to disinherit her children, if she does not think proper to institute them her heirs; neither is a maternal grandfather under a necessity either of instituting or disinheriting his grandson or granddaughter by a daughter, inasmuch as this is not required either by the civil law, or the edict of the prætor, which gives the possession of goods *contra tabulas*—*i.e.*, contrary to the disposition of the testament—to those children who have been passed over in silence. But children in this case are not without a remedy against the testament of their mother or maternal grandfather, which shall be showed hereafter.

Tit. XIV. *De hæredibus instituendis.*

A man may appoint slaves as well as freemen to be his heirs by testament, and may nominate the slaves of another as well as his own; yet, according to the opinion of many, no master could formerly institute his own slaves to be his heirs without giving them their liberty; but at present, by virtue of our constitution, masters may appoint their proper slaves to be their heirs without making even any mention of liberty: and this we have introduced, not for the sake of innovation, but because it seemed most just, and because Paulus, in his commentaries upon Sabinus and Plautius, affirms that this was also the opinion of Atilicinus. Here note, that we call a slave *proprius servus* if the testator had only a nude property in him, the usufruct being in another. But in a constitution of the Emperors Severus and Antoninus there is a case in which a slave was not permitted to be instituted an heir by his owner, although his liberty was expressly given to him. The words of the constitution are these:—"It is consonant to right reason that no slave, accused of adultery with his mistress, shall be allowed, before a sentence of acquittal, to be made free by that mistress, who is alleged to be a partner in the crime." It therefore follows, that if a mistress institutes such a slave to be her heir, the institution is of no avail. The expression *alienus servus*—*i.e.*, the slave of another—is also sometimes used to denote him of whom the testator had the usufruct, though not the property.

§ 1. When a slave hath been instituted by his master, and remains in the same state, he will obtain his freedom at the death of his master by virtue of the testament, and become his necessary heir. But if that slave is manumitted in the lifetime of his master, it is in his power either to accept or refuse the inheritance; for he will not become a necessary heir, as he cannot be said to have obtained both his liberty and the inheritance by virtue of the testament. But if such instituted heir should be aliened, he cannot then enter upon the inheritance but at the command of his new master, who, by means of his slave, may become the heir of the testator. For a slave who hath been aliened cannot afterwards obtain his liberty, or take an inheritance to his own use, by virtue of the testament of that master who made the alienation, although his freedom was expressly given by such testament, because a master who has aliened his slave seems to have departed from having any intention to enfranchise him. And when the slave of another is appointed an heir, but remains in the same condition, he cannot take the inheritance but by his master's order; and if the slave is aliened in the lifetime of the testator, or even after his death, at any time before he has actually taken the inheritance, he must then either accept or refuse it at the command of his new master. But if a slave is enfranchised, living the testator, or after his death before he has accepted the heirship, he either may or may not enter upon the inheritance at his own option.

§ 2. The slave of another may legally be instituted an heir after the death of his master; for the slaves of an inheritance not entered upon are entitled to the *factio passiva testamenti*, *i.e.*, are capable of taking though not of giving by testament; and the reason of this is, because an inheritance which is open, and not as yet entered upon, is supposed to represent the person of the deceased, and not the person of the future heir; and thus the slave, even of a child in the womb, may be constituted an heir.

§ 3. If the slave of many masters, who are all capable of taking by testament, is instituted an heir by a stranger, then that slave acquires a part of the inheritance for each master who commanded him to take it, according to their several proportions of property.

§ 4. A testator may appoint one heir, or as many heirs as he pleases *in infinitum*.

§ 5. An inheritance is generally divided into twelve *unciæ*, that is, parts or ounces, all which are comprehended under one total, termed an *as*: and each of these parts, from the *uncia* to the *as*, has its peculiar name, viz.:—

Sextans, a sixth part, or two ounces.

Quadrans, a fourth, or three ounces.

Triens, a third, or four ounces.

Quincunx, five ounces.

Semis, a moiety, or six ounces.

Septunx, seven ounces.

Bes, two-thirds, or eight ounces; *quasi, bis triens.*

Dodrans, nine ounces, or three-fourths; *quasi, dempto quadrante, as.*

Dextans, ten ounces; *quasi, dempto sextante, as.*

Deunx, eleven ounces out of twelve; *quasi, demptâ unciâ, as.*

But it is not necessary that an *as*, or total, should always be divided into twelve parts; for an *as* may consist of what parts the testator pleases; and if a man names but one heir, and appoints him *ex semisse, i.e.*, the heir of six parts, yet the whole *as* will be included; for no man can die partly testate and partly intestate, except a soldier, whose intention is solely to be regarded. And a testator may also divide his estate into as many parts as he thinks convenient.

§ 6. When a testator hath instituted many heirs, it is incumbent upon him to make a division of his effects if he does not intend that all his heirs should share his inheritance in equal portions: for if no distribution is made by the testator, it is evident that all his heirs must be equal sharers. But if the shares of some of the nominated heirs in a testament should be expressed, and the share or shares of one or more should be omitted, then he or they whose share or shares had not been specified would be entitled to the undisposed remainder of the inheritance. But if a whole *as*, or inheritance, is given among some of the nominated heirs, yet they whose shares are mentioned are entitled only to a moiety; and he or they whose shares are not mentioned are called to the succession of the other moiety. And when a whole inheritance is not given away, it is immaterial whether an heir whose share is not specified holds the first, middle, or last place in the nomination; for whatever place he holds in it, he is equally entitled to the part not bequeathed in the testament.

§ 7. Let us now inquire what the law would direct if a part of an inheritance should remain unbequeathed, and yet a certain portion of it should be given by testament to every nominated heir; as if three should be instituted, and a fourth given to each. It is clear in this case that the undisposed of part would vest in each of them in proportion to the share bequeathed to him, and that each would be reputed the written heir of a third. And, on the contrary, if many are nominated heirs in certain portions, so as to exceed the *as*, then each heir must suffer a defalcation *pro ratâ*: for example, if four are instituted, and a third is given to each, then this disposition would work the same effect as if each of the written heirs had been instituted to a fourth only.

§ 8. If more parts or ounces than twelve are bequeathed, then he who is instituted without any prescribed share shall be entitled to what remains of a *dupondius*, that is, of twenty-four parts; and if more than twenty-four parts are bequeathed, then the heir who is nominated without any determinate share is entitled to the remainder of a *tripondius*, *i. e.*, of thirty-six parts or ounces. But all these parts are afterwards reduced to twelve.

§ 9. An heir may be constituted simply or conditionally, but not from or to any certain period: as if a testator should say to Titius, "Be thou my heir after five years, to be computed from my death," or "from the calends of such a month," or "till the calends of such a month"; for time thus added is, in law, deemed superfluous, and such an institution takes place immediately, as if it was a simple appointment.

§ 10. An impossible condition in the institution of heirs, the disposition of legacies, the appointment of trusts, or the conferring of liberty, is treated as unwritten or void.

§ 11. If many conditions are jointly required in the institution of an heir; as thus, if this thing and that thing be done, then both must be complied with. But if the conditions are placed separately and in the disjunctive; as thus, if this or that be done, it will then be sufficient to obey either.

§ 12. A testator may appoint persons whom he hath never seen to be his heirs. He may, for example, institute his brother's sons, who are in a foreign country, although he does not know where they are; for the want of this knowledge in a testator will not vitiate the institution of an heir.

Tit. XV. *De vulgari substitutione.*

A man by testament may appoint many degrees of heirs; as thus: "If Titius will not be my heir, let Seius be my heir." And he may proceed in such a substitution as far as he shall think proper; and lastly, in default of all others, he may constitute a slave to be his necessary heir.

§ 1. A testator may substitute many in the place of one, or one in the place of many, or one in the place of each, or he may substitute even his instituted heirs reciprocally to one another.

§ 2. If a testator, having instituted several co-heirs in unequal portions, substitutes them reciprocally the one to the other, and makes no mention of their shares of the inheritance in the substitution, he seems to have given the same shares by the substitution which he gave by the institution; and this is agreeable to the rescript of the Emperor Antoninus.

§ 3. If a co-heir is substituted to an instituted heir, and a third person is substituted to that co-heir, the Emperors Severus and Antoninus have by rescript ordained that such substituted person shall be admitted to the portions of both the co-heirs without distinction.

§ 4. If a testator constitutes the slave of another to be his heir, supposing him to be free, and adds, "if he does not become my heir I substitute Mævius in his place," then, if that slave should afterwards enter upon the inheritance at the command of his master, Mævius the substitute would be admitted to a moiety. For the words, "if he does not become my heir," in regard to him whom the testator knew to be under the dominion of another are taken to mean, if he will neither become my heir himself, nor cause another to be my heir; but in regard to him whom the testator supposed to be free, they imply this condition, viz., if my heir will neither acquire the inheritance for himself, nor for him to whose dominion he may afterwards become subject. But it was determined by Tiberius, the emperor, in the case of his own slave Parthenius, that a substitute in such a case should be admitted to a moiety.

Tit. XVI. *De pupillari substitutione.*

A parent can substitute to his children, who are within puberty, and under his power, not only in the manner before mentioned, which is thus—"If my children will not be my heirs, let some other person be my heir;" but he may write, "If my children actually become my heirs, but die within puberty, let another become their heir;" for example: "let Titius, my son, be my heir; and if he either does not, or does, become my heir, and dies before he ceases to be under tutelage"—*i. e.*, before he arrives at the age of puberty—"let Seius be my heir." And in this case, if the son does not enter upon the inheritance, the substitute becomes heir to the father; and if the son takes the inheritance, and dies a pupil before the age of puberty, the substitute is then heir to the son. For custom has ordained that parents may make wills for their children when their children are not of age to make wills for themselves.

§ 1. Excited by humanity, and the reasonableness of the foregoing usage, we have inserted a constitution into our code by which it is provided that if a man has children, grandchildren, or great-grandchildren, who are mad or disordered in their senses, he may make a substitution of certain persons to such children in the manner of a pupillary substitution, although they are arrived at the age of full puberty. But we have decreed that this species of substitution shall be void as soon as they shall have recovered from their disorder; and this we have done in imitation of pupillary substitution, which ceases to be in force when the minor attains to puberty.

§ 2. In a pupillary substitution, made after the form before mentioned, there are in a manner two testaments, the one of the father, the other of the son; as if the son had instituted an heir for himself: at least there is in such a substitution one testament containing a disposition of two inheritances.

§ 3. If a testator is apprehensive lest, at the time of his death, his son, being as yet a pupil, should be liable to fraud and imposition if a substitute should be publicly given to him, he ought to insert a vulgar substitution in the first tablet of his testament, and to write that substitution, in which a substitute is named, if his son should die within puberty, in the lower tablet, which ought to be separately tied up and sealed; and it also behoves the testator to insert a clause in the first part of his testament, forbidding the lower part to be opened whilst his son is alive, and within the age of puberty. But although it is certain that a substitution to a son within puberty is not less valid because it is written on the same tablet in which the testator hath appointed him to be his heir, it is, however, unsafe and dangerous.

§ 4. Parents are not only allowed to give a substitute to their children within puberty if such children become their heirs, and die within puberty, but parents are also permitted to give a substitute to their disinherited children; and therefore whatever a disinherited child, within the age of puberty, may have acquired by inheritances, by legacies, or by the gift of relations and friends, the whole will become the property of the substitute. All which we have hitherto said concerning the substitution of pupils, whether they are instituted heirs or disinherited children, is understood to extend also to posthumous children.

§ 5. No parent can make a testament for his children unless he hath made a testament for himself, for the testament of a child within puberty is a part and consequence of the testament of the parent, insomuch that if the testament of the father is not valid the testament of the son will not take effect.

§ 6. A parent may make a pupillary substitution to each of his children, or to him who shall die the last within puberty. He may substitute to each of his children, if he is unwilling that any of them should die intestate; and he may substitute to the last who shall die within puberty if he is willing that they should preserve among themselves the entire right of succession.

§ 7. A substitution may be made to a child within puberty, either nominally, as, for example—"If my son becomes my heir and dies a pupil let Titius be my heir"; or generally thus —"Whoever shall be my heir, let the same person be a substitute to my son if he dies within puberty." And by these general words all who have been instituted, and have taken upon them the inheritance of the father, must be called, by virtue of the substitution, to the inheritance of the son if he dies within puberty, each being entitled to a part of the son's inheritance in proportion to the share which he had in the father's.

§ 8. A pupillary substitution may be made to males till they arrive at fourteen complete, and to females till they have completed their twelfth year; and when they exceed either of these ages the substitution becomes extinct.

§ 9. A pupillary substitution cannot be made with effect either to a stranger who is instituted, or even to a son who is instituted, if his age exceeds that of puberty. But a testator may oblige his heir to give to another either a part, or even the whole, of the inheritance, by virtue of a *fidei-commissum*, or gift in trust, which we will treat in its proper place.

Tit. XVII. *Quibus modis testamenta infirmantur.*

A testament legally made remains valid until it is either broken or rendered ineffectual.

§ 1. A testament is said to be broken or revoked when the force of it is destroyed, whilst the testator still remains in the same state. For if a testator, after making his testament, should arrogate an independent person, by licence from the emperor, or, in the presence of the prætor, should adopt a child under the power of his natural parent, by virtue of our constitution, then that testament would be broken by this quasi-birth of a proper heir.

§ 2. A former testament, although legally perfect, may be broken or revoked by a subsequent testament; nor is it material whether the heir nominated in the later testament can or will take the heirship at the death of the testator; for the only thing regarded is whether he might have been the heir; and therefore, if an instituted heir should refuse to take the heirship, or should die, living the testator, or after his death, and before he could enter upon the inheritance, or if he should die before the condition is accomplished upon which he was instituted, then in any of these cases the testator would die intestate; for the first testament would be invalid, being broken or revoked by the second, and the second would be of as little force for want of an heir.

§ 3. If a man who has already made a testament legally perfect, should make a subsequent testament equally good, and institute an heir in it to some particular things only, the Emperors Severus and Antoninus have by rescript declared, that in this case the first will shall be broken or revoked as a testament. But we have commanded the words of this constitution to be here inserted. "The Emperors Severus and Antoninus to Cocceius Campanus. We determine, that a second testament, although the heir named in it is not universal, but instituted to particular things only, shall be as good in law as if no mention had been made of particular things; yet it is not to be doubted but that the written heir shall be obliged to content himself either with the things given him, or with the fourth part, allowed by the Falcidian law, and shall be bound to restore the rest of the inheritance to the heirs instituted in the first testament, on account of the words, denoting a trust, inserted in the second testament, by which words it is expressly declared, that the first testament shall subsist." And in this manner a testament may be said to be broken or cancelled.

§ 4. Testaments legally made are also invalidated, if the testator suffers diminution, that is, changes his condition: and in the first book of our institutions we have showed by what means diminution, or a change of state, may happen.

§ 5. In the case of diminution testaments are said to become *irrita, i.e.*, ineffectual; although those which are broken or revoked, and those which from the beginning were not legal, do all equally become ineffectual—or *irrita*—in reality. We may also term those testaments broken which are at first legally made, but are afterwards rendered ineffectual by diminution, or change of state. But as it is proper that every particular defect should be distinguished by a particular appellation, those testaments which are illegal are termed null; those which were at first legal, but afterwards lose their force by some revocatory act of the testator, are said to be *rupta*, or broken; and those, since the making of which the testator hath suffered a change of state, are said to be *irrita*, or ineffectual.

§ 6. But a testament which was at first legally made, and hath afterwards been rendered void by diminution, is not always without effect; for the written heir is entitled to the possession of the goods by virtue of the testament, if it appear that it was sealed by seven witnesses, and that the testator was a Roman citizen, and not under power at the time of his death; but if a testament became void because the testator had lost the right of a citizen, or his liberty, or had given himself in adoption, and, at the time of his death, still continued under the power of his adopted father, then the written heir could not demand the possession of the goods in consequence of the testament.

§ 7. A testament cannot be invalidated solely because the testator was afterwards unwilling that it should subsist; so that if a man after making one testament should begin another, and by reason of death or change of mind should not proceed to perfect that testament, it is provided by the oration or ordinance of the Emperor Pertinax that the first testament shall not be revoked, unless the second is both legal and perfect; for an imperfect testament is undoubtedly null.

§ 8. The Emperor Pertinax hath declared by the same ordinance that he would not take the inheritance of any testator who left him his heir because a law suit was depending; that he would never establish a will deficient in point of form if he was upon that account instituted the heir; that he would by no means suffer himself to be nominated an heir by the mere word of mouth of a testator; and that he would never take any emolument by virtue of any writing whatever not authorized by the strict rules of law. The Emperors Severus and Antoninus have also often issued rescripts to the same purpose; "for although," say they, "we are certainly not subject to the laws, yet we live in obedience to them."

Tit. XVIII. *De inofficioso testamento.*

Inasmuch as parents often disinherit their children without cause, or omit to mention them in their testaments, it has therefore been introduced as law that children who have been unjustly disinherited, or unjustly omitted in the testaments of their parents, may complain that such testaments are inofficious, under colour that their parents were not of sane mind when they made them; but in these cases it is not averred to be strictly true that the testator was really mad or disordered in his senses, but it is urged as a mere fiction only; for the testament is acknowledged to have been well made, and the only exception to it is that the testament is not consistent with the duty of a parent. For if a testator was really not in his senses at the time of making his testament it is certainly null.

§ 1. Children are not the only persons allowed to complain that testaments are inofficious, for parents are in like manner permitted to make the same complaint. Also the brothers and sisters of a testator are, by virtue of the imperial constitutions, preferred to infamous persons, if any such have been instituted by the deceased to be his heirs; but brothers and sisters are not therefore allowed to make a complaint against any heir whom the testator shall have instituted. And collaterals, beyond brothers and sisters, can by no means complain of the undutifulness of a testament if their right to complain is opposed; but if their right of complaining is not disputed, and the testament is annulled, yet those only can be benefited who are the nearest in succession upon an intestacy.

§ 2. Adopted children, according to the distinction taken in our constitution, are admitted, as well as natural children, to complain against a testament as inofficious, if they can obtain the effects of the deceased no other way; but if they can get the whole or a part of the inheritance by any other means, they then cannot bring a complaint of undutifulness against the testament. Posthumous children also, who are unable to recover their inheritance by any other method are allowed to bring this complaint.

§ 3. What we have hitherto said must be understood to take place only when nothing has been left by the will of the deceased;—and this hath been introduced by our constitution out of reverence to parents and the ties of nature;—for if any single thing, or the least part of an inheritance, hath been bequeathed to those who have a right to a fourth part or legitime portion of the testator's estate, they are barred from bringing a querele or complaint against the testament as undutiful, but are entitled by action to recover whatever sum is wanting to complete their legitime, although it was not added by the testator, that their legitime portion should be completed according to the arbitration of some person of an approved character.

§ 4. If a tutor shall accept a legacy in the name of his pupil, in consequence of a bequest made in the testament of such tutor's father, who left nothing to his son, the tutor may nevertheless complain in his own name against the testament of his father as undutiful.

§ 5. And, on the contrary, if a tutor should bring a complaint of undutifulness in the name of his pupil against the testament of his pupil's father, who left nothing to his son, and this testament should be confirmed by sentence, yet the tutor would not afterwards be barred on account of this proceeding from taking whatever was left him in that testament, which he controverted only for the benefit of his pupil, and by virtue of his office.

§ 6. No person who hath right can be hindered from bringing a complaint of undutifulness, unless he hath in some manner received his fourth or legitime part, as by being appointed heir, by having a legacy, or by means of a trust for his use; or unless his legitime part hath been given him by donation *propter mortem*, or even *inter vivos*—in those cases of which our constitution makes mention—or by any other means set forth in our ordinances. What we have said of the fourth or legitime is to be so understood, that if there are more persons than one who have a right to bring a plaint of undutifulness against a testament, yet one-fourth will be sufficient, divided among them all in equal portions.

Tit. XIX. *De hæredum qualitate et differentiâ.*

Heirs are divided into three sorts, called proper, proper and necessary, and strangers.

§ 1. A slave instituted by his master is a necessary heir; and he is so called, because at the death of the testator he becomes instantly free, and is compellable to take the heirship; he therefore who suspects his circumstances, commonly institutes his slave to be his heir in the first, second, or some other place; so that if he does not leave a sum equal to his debts, the goods which are seized, sold, or divided among his creditors, may rather seem to be those of his heir than his own. But a slave, in recompense of this dishonour, is allowed to reserve to himself whatever he hath acquired after the death of his patron; for such acquisitions are not to be sold, although the goods of the deceased are ever so insufficient for the payment of his creditors.

§ 2. Proper and necessary heirs are sons, daughters, grandsons or granddaughters by a son, or any other descendants in the direct line, who were in the power of the deceased at the time of his death. But in order to constitute grandchildren proper or domestic heirs, it does not suffice that they were in the power of their grandfather at the time of his decease; but it is requisite that their father should have ceased to be a proper heir in the lifetime of his father, by having been freed, either by death or some other means, from paternal authority; for then it is that the grandson or granddaughter succeeds in the place of their father. And note, that heirs are called *sui*, or proper, because they are domestic, and in the very lifetime of their father are reputed masters or proprietors of the inheritance in a certain degree. Hence it is that if a man dies intestate, his children are preferred before all others to the succession, and are called necessary heirs, because, willing or unwilling, they become the heirs of their parent according to the law of the Twelve Tables, either by virtue of a testament, or in consequence of an intestacy. But when children request it, the prætor permits them to abstain from the inheritance, that the effects of their parents rather than their own may be seized by the creditors.

§ 3. But all other heirs, not subject to the power of the testator at the time of his death, are called strangers: thus, even children who are not under the power of their father, but yet are constituted his heirs, are reckoned strangers in a legal sense; and for the same reason children instituted heirs by their mother are also reputed strangers; for a woman is not allowed to have her children under her own power. A slave also whom his master hath instituted by testament, and afterwards manumitted, is numbered among those heirs who are called strangers.

§ 4. In regard to strangers, it is requisite that they should be capable of the faction of a testament, whether they are instituted heirs themselves, or whether those under their power are instituted. And this qualification is required at two several times; at the time of making the testament, that the institution may be valid; and at the time of the testator's death, that such institution may take effect: and further, whether an heir is appointed simply or conditionally, yet he ought to be capable of the faction of a testament at the time of entering upon the inheritance; for his right is principally regarded at the time of acquiring the possession. But in the intermediate time, between the making of the testament and the death of the testator, or the completion of the condition of the institution, the heir will not be prejudiced by incapacity or change of state; because the three particular times which we have mentioned are the times to be regarded. But a man capable of giving his effects by testament is not the only person who is said to have *testamenti factionem;* for whoever is capable of taking for the benefit of himself, or of acquiring by testament for the benefit of another, is also understood to have the faction of a testament; and therefore persons mad, mute, or posthumous, also infants, the sons of a family, or slaves not your own, may all be said to have the faction of a testament in its passive signification. For although such persons are incapable of making a testament, yet they are capable of acquiring by testament either for themselves or others.

§ 5. Strangers who are appointed heirs have the power of deliberating whether they will or will not enter upon an inheritance. But if even a proper or domestic heir, who has the liberty of abstaining, should intermeddle, or if a stranger who is permitted to deliberate should once take an inheritance, it will not afterwards be in his power to renounce it, unless he was under the age of twenty-five years; for the prætor, who in all other cases relieves minors who have been deceived, affords them also his assistance when they rashly take upon themselves an injurious inheritance. And here it must be noted, that the Emperor Adrian once gave permission to a major, or person of full age, to relinquish an inheritance, when it appeared to be encumbered with a great debt, which had been concealed till the heir had taken upon himself the administration. But this permission was granted as a very special instance of beneficence. The Emperor Gordian afterwards promulged a constitution for the indemnification of heirs, yet confined the force of it to those only who were of the soldiery. But our extended benevolence hath rendered this benefit common to all our subjects in general, having dictated a constitution both just and noble, which if heirs will strictly observe, they may enter upon their inheritance, and not be made further chargeable than the value of the estate will extend; so that they are under no necessity of praying a time for deliberation, unless they omit to observe the tenor of our ordinance, choosing rather to deliberate and submit themselves to the danger attending the acceptance of an inheritance according to the ancient law.

§ 6. A stranger who is instituted by testament, or called by law to take a succession in case of an intestacy, may make himself accountable as heir either by doing some act as such, or by barely signifying his acceptance of the heirship. And a man is deemed to act as the heir of an inheritance if he treats it as his own by selling any part of it, by cultivating the ground, or by tilling it; or even if he declares his consent to accept it in any manner, either by act or speech, when he knows at the same time that the person with whose estate he intermeddles is dead testate or intestate, and that he himself is the heir: for to act as heir is to act as proprietor; and the ancients frequently used the term heir when they would denote the proprietor of an estate. But as a stranger may become an heir by a bare consent only, so, on the contrary, by a mere dissent he may bar himself from an inheritance. And nothing prevents but that a person who was born deaf and dumb, or became so by accident, may, by acting as heir, either acquire the advantages or bring upon himself the disadvantages of an inheritance, if he was sensible of what he was doing, and that he was acting in the capacity of an heir.

Tit. XX. *De legatis.*

After what has been said we will make some observations upon the doctrine of legacies, although a discussion of this part of the law may not seem exactly to fall in with the subject proposed; for we are treating only of those legal methods by which things may be acquired universally; but as we have already spoken at large of testaments and testamentary heirs, it is not without reason that we intend to treat of legacies in the following paragraphs.

§ 1. A legacy is a species of donation which is left or ordered by the deceased, and, if possible, must be performed by his heir.

§ 2. Anciently there were four kinds of legacies in use, namely, *per vindicationem*, *per damnationem*, *sinendi modo*, and *per præ-*

ceptionem. And to each of these was assigned a certain form of words by which their different species were signified; but these fixed forms had been wholly taken away by the imperial ordinance of the later emperors, Constantinus, Constantius, and Constans. And we also, being desirous that the wills of deceased persons might be corroborated, and that their intentions should be more regarded than their words, have with great care and study composed a constitution, which enacts that the nature of all legacies shall be the same, and that legataries, by whatever words they are constituted, may sue for what is left them, not only by a personal but by a real or hypothecary action. But the reader may most perfectly comprehend the well-weighed matter of this constitution by perusing the tenor of it.

§ 3. But we have judged it expedient that our constitution should not rest here, but extend still further; for when we observed that the ancients confined legacies within very strict rules, and yet were extremely favourable to gifts in trust, it was thought necessary to make all legacies equal to gifts in trust, that no difference in effect should remain between them; so that whatever is deficient in the nature of legacies may be supplied by the nature of trusts, and whatever is abundant in the nature of legacies may become an accretion to the nature of trusts. But that we may not raise difficulties, and perplex the minds of young persons at their entrance upon the study of the law, by explaining these things promiscuously, we have esteemed it worth our pains to treat separately first of legacies, and afterwards of trusts, that, the nature of both being known, the student thus instructed may more easily understand their relation and intermixture.

§ 4. A testator may not only bequeath his own property, or that of his heir, but also the property of others; and if the thing bequeathed belongs to another, the heir can be obliged either to purchase and deliver it, or to render the value of it if it cannot be purchased. But if the thing bequeathed is not in commerce, and what the law will not permit to be purchased, the heir in this case can never be obliged to pay the value of it to the legatary; as if a man should bequeath to another the Campus Martius, the palaces of the prince, the temples, or any of those things which appertain to the public; for such legacies can be of no moment or efficacy. But when we said that a testator might bequeath the goods of another man, we would be understood to mean, that this can be done only if the deceased knew that what he bequeathed belonged to another, and not if he was ignorant of it; since if he had known it, he probably would not have left such a legacy: and to this purpose is the rescript of the Emperor Antoninus. And it is incumbent upon the party-agent or legatary to bring proof that the deceased knew that what he left belonged to another; for the heir is by no means obliged to prove that the deceased did not know it; because, by the general rule of law, the necessity of proving lies upon the complainant.

§ 5. If a man bequeaths a thing which he hath pledged to a creditor, the heir is under a necessity of redeeming it; but in this case, as in the former, concerning the goods of another, the heir cannot be obliged to redeem the thing bequeathed, unless the deceased knew that it was pledged; and this the Emperors Severus and Antoninus have declared by their rescript. But nevertheless, whenever it appears to have been the express will of the deceased that the legatary should himself redeem the thing left to him, then the heir is free from the obligation of doing it.

§ 6. If a thing bequeathed is the property of another, and the legatee becomes the proprietor of it in the lifetime of the testator, it is necessary to be known by what means the legatee became the proprietor; for if he bought it he may nevertheless recover the price given by an action in consequence of the testament; but if he obtained it as a gift, or by any such lucrative title, no action will lie; for it is a maxim, that two lucrative causes can never concur in the same person and thing. And therefore, if the same specific thing is left by two testaments to one and the same person, the question will be, when the legatary sues in virtue of one of the testaments, whether he hath obtained the thing itself, or the value of it, by virtue of the other? for if he is already possessed of the thing itself, the suit is at an end, because he hath received it on a lucrative account: but if he hath obtained the value of it only from the heir of one of the testators, he may bring an action for the thing itself against the heir of the other.

§ 7. Things which do not exist may be rightly bequeathed, if there is but a possibility that they may exist: thus, a man may devise the fruits which shall grow on such a spot of ground, or the offspring which shall be born of a particular slave.

§ 8. When the same specific legacy is left to two persons either conjunctively or disjunctively, if they are both willing to accept it, it must be divided between them. But if one of the legatees dies in the lifetime of the testator, dislikes his legacy, or is by any means prevented from taking it, the whole vests in his co-legatee. A legacy thus worded is in the conjunctive—"I give and bequeath my slave Stichus to Titius and Seius;" but a legacy worded as follows is in the disjunctive—"I give and bequeath my slave Stichus to Titius: I give and bequeath my slave Stichus to Seius." And although the testator should add, that he gives the "same slave Stichus to Seius," yet the legacy would nevertheless be understood to be left in the disjunctive.

§ 9. If a man hath bequeathed the ground of another, and the legatary hath purchased the property of that ground without the usufruct, which hath also afterwards accrued to him, it is said by Julianus, that the legatary may rightly bring an action by virtue of the testament, and demand the ground, because the usufruct is regarded as a service only. But it is the duty of a judge, in this case, to order the price of the property of the ground to be paid, the value of the usufruct being deducted.

§ 10. If a man bequeaths to another what already belongs to him, the legacy is ineffectual; for that which is already the property of a legatee can by no means become more so. And although the legatee should after the bequest alien the thing bequeathed, neither the thing itself, nor even the value of it, would become due to him from the heir of the testator.

§ 11. If a testator should bequeath what is his own, as if it was the property of another, the bequest would nevertheless be good; for truth is more prevalent than what is founded upon opinion only. But even suppose the testator to imagine that what he bequeaths belongs already to the legatary, yet if it does not, it is certain that such a legacy would also be valid, because the will of the deceased can thus take effect.

§ 12. But if a testator bequeaths what is his own property, and afterwards aliens it, it is the opinion of Celsus, that the thing bequeathed will nevertheless become due to the legatee if the testator did not dispose of it with an intention to oust him. The Emperors Severus and Antoninus have published their rescript to this effect; and they have also signified by another rescript, that whoever has bequeathed a legacy, and hath afterwards pawned or mortgaged it, shall not be deemed to have retracted it; and that the legatee may therefore of course bring an action against the heir, and oblige him to redeem. And if a testator shall have aliened but a part of the thing bequeathed, then all that part which remains unaliened is still due; and that which is aliened is only due, if it appears not to have been aliened by the testator with a design to retract the legacy.

§ 13. If a man by will bequeaths a discharge to his debtor, the bequest is effectual; and the heir can bring no suit against the debtor, or his heir, or any one who represents him; but, on the contrary, the heir of the testator may be convened by the debtor, and obliged to give him his discharge. A man may also by testament command his heir not to sue a debtor within a time limited.

§ 14. On the contrary, if a debtor bequeaths by testament to his creditor the money which he owes him, this legacy is ineffectual, if the value of the legacy amounts but merely to the value of the debt; for thus the creditor can receive no benefit from the legacy. But if a debtor bequeaths simply to his creditor a sum of money, which was to be paid at a day certain, or which he owed upon condition, the legacy will take effect on account of the representation, *i.e.*, on account of the immediate payment, the legacy becoming due before the debt. But according to Papinian, if the day of payment should come, or the event of the condition happen, in the lifetime of the testator, the legacy would nevertheless be effectual, because it was once good; which is true. For we are by no means satisfied with the opinion of those who imagine, that a legacy once good may afterwards become extinct, by falling into a state from which it could not have taken a legal commencement.

§ 15. If a man gives back to his wife by legacy her marriage portion, the legacy is valid; for such a legacy is more beneficial to her than the action which she might maintain for the recovery of her portion. But if a husband bequeaths to his wife her marriage portion, and hath never actually received it, the Emperors Severus and Antoninus have declared by their rescript, that if it is left simply without any specification of a sum certain, the legacy is void; but that if any certain sum or thing is specified, or if the instruments in which the exact value of the portion is mentioned are referred to, the legacy is valid.

§ 16. If a thing bequeathed should perish before delivery otherwise than by the act or fault of the heir, the loss must fall upon the legatary. And if the slave of another, who is bequeathed, should be manumitted, and the heir hath not been privy to the manumission, he can be subject to no action. But if a testator bequeaths the slave of his heir, who afterwards manumits that slave, it is the opinion of Julian that the heir is answerable; nor is it at all material whether he did or did not know of the legacy. And also if the heir hath made a present of a slave bequeathed, and the donee hath manumitted him, the heir is liable to an action, although he was ignorant of the bequest.

§ 17. If a testator gives by legacy his female slaves and their offspring, although the slaves die, yet their issue will become due to the legatary: and the same obtains if ordinary slaves are bequeathed together with vicarial; for although the ordinary slaves die, yet the vacarial slaves will pass by virtue of the bequest. But if a slave is bequeathed with his *peculium*, and afterwards dies, or is manumitted, or aliened, the legacy of the *peculium* becomes extinct. And the consequences will be the same, if a piece of ground is bequeathed with the instruments for improving it; for if the testator aliens the ground, the legacy of the instruments of husbandry is of course extinguished.

§ 18. If a flock is bequeathed, and afterwards reduced to a single sheep, that sheep is claimable; and if a flock receives an increase or addition after it hath been disposed of by testament, the increase or addition will also, according to Julian, become due to the legatary. For a flock is deemed one body, consisting of separate members, as a house is reckoned one body, composed of materials joined together and adhering.

§ 19. And lastly, when a house is bequeathed, the marble or pillars which are added after the bequest is made will pass under the general legacy.

§ 20. When the *peculium* of a slave is bequeathed, it is certain that the increase or decrease of it, in the life of the testator, becomes the loss or gain of the legatary. And if the *peculium* of a slave is left to him, together with his liberty, and such slave makes an acquisition to the *peculium* subsequent to the death of the testator, and before the inheritance is entered upon, it is the opinion of Julian, that whatever is acquired within that period will pass to him as the legatary; for such a legacy does not become due but from the day of the acceptance of the inheritance. But it is the opinion of the same Julian that if the *peculium* of a slave is bequeathed to a stranger, an increase acquired within the period above mentioned will not pass under the legacy, unless the acquisition was made by means of something appertaining to the *peculium;* for the *peculium* of a slave does not belong to him after he is manumitted by testament, unless it is expressly given; although, if a master in his lifetime manumits his slave, his *peculium* will pass to him of course, if not excepted: and thus the Emperors Severus and Antoninus have decreed by their rescript. And the same emperors have also declared, that when a *peculium* is bequeathed to a slave, it does not seem to be the intention of the testator that such slave should have the power of demanding what he may have expended for the use of his master. And the same princes have further declared that a slave seems to be entitled to his *peculium* if his liberty is left him on condition that he will bring in his accounts, and supply any deficiency out of the profits of his *peculium.*

§ 21. Things incorporeal may be bequeathed as well as things corporeal; and therefore a debt due to the testator may be left as a legacy, and the heir be obliged to transfer his right of action to the legatary, unless the testator in his lifetime received the money due to him; for in this case the legacy would become extinct. A legacy is also good if conceived in the terms following:—"I command my heir to rebuild the house of Titius;" or "to free him from his debts."

§ 22. If a testator bequeaths a slave, or any particular thing generally, the power of election is in the legatary, unless the testator hath declared otherwise.

§ 23. The legacy of an option is made when a testator commands his legatary to choose any slave whom he likes from among his slaves, or any one thing which he best approves of from any certain class of things; and such a legacy was formerly presumed to imply this condition, that if the legatee in his lifetime did not make his election, the legacy could not be transmitted to his heir. But by virtue of our constitution this presumed condition is now taken away, and the heir of the legatary is permitted to make his option, although the legatary in his lifetime hath neglected to do it. And, upon a more diligent inspection, we have further added to our constitution, that if there were several legataries to whom an option is left, and they differ in their choice, or if there are many heirs of one legatary who are of divers sentiments, then Fortune must be the judge; for lest the loss of the legacy should ensue—which loss the generality of the ancient lawyers, contrary to all benevolence, would have permitted—we have decreed that such dissensions between heirs or legataries should be decided by lot; so that the option of him to whom the lot falls shall be preferred.

§ 24. A legacy cannot be left but to those who have the capacity of taking by testament.

§ 25. It was not formerly permitted that either legacies or gifts in trust should be bequeathed to uncertain persons; for even a soldier was prohibited to bequeath to uncertain persons, as the Emperor Adrian hath declared by his rescript; and an uncertain person is reputed to be one whom the testator hath figured only in his imagination, without any determinate knowledge of him; as if a testator should thus express himself, "Whoever shall give his daughter in marriage to my son, to that person let my heir deliver up such a piece of ground." And if a testator had made a bequest to the first consuls designed after his testament was written, this also would have been esteemed a bequest to uncertain persons; and of the same kind there are diverse other examples. Freedom likewise could not be conferred upon an uncertain person, for it was necessary that all slaves should be nominally enfranchised; but a legacy might have been given to an uncertain person under a certain demonstration, or, in other words, to an uncertain person, if he was one of a number of persons certain; as, for instance, if a testator should bequeath in the manner following:—"I command Titius my heir to give such a particular thing to any one of my present collateral relations, who shall think proper to take my daughter in marriage." But if a legacy or fiduciary gift had been paid to uncertain persons by mistake, it was provided by the constitutions that such persons were not compellable to refund.

§ 26. Formerly a legacy could not have been profitably or legally given to a posthumous stranger; and a posthumous stranger is he who, if he had been born before the death of the testator, could not have been numbered among his proper heirs; and, of consequence, a posthumous grandson, by an emancipated son, was a posthumous stranger in regard to his grandfather.

§ 27. Such was the state of the ancient law, which hath not been left without a proper emendation; for we have promulged a constitution, by which we have altered the law concerning uncertain persons not only in respect to inheritances, but in regard also to legacies and fiduciary bequests. But this alteration will evidently appear from a perusal of the constitution itself; which nevertheless gives no authority to the nomination of an uncertain tutor; for it is incumbent upon every parent to take care of his posterity in this respect by a certain and determinate appointment.

§ 28. A posthumous stranger could formerly have been instituted, and may now be appointed, an heir, unless it appears that he was conceived by a woman who could not have been legally married to his father.

§ 29. Although a testator may happen to have mistaken the nomen, cognomen, prænomen, or agnomen of a legatary, yet if his person is certain the legacy is good. The same rule of law is also observed in regard to heirs, and with great reason; for the use of names is but to point out persons; and if persons can be denoted by any other method, it will make no difference.

§ 30. The rule of law which comes nearest to the foregoing is that a legacy is not rendered null by a false demonstration: suppose, for instance, that a bequest is thus worded—"I give and bequeath Stichus my slave, who was born in my family;" in this case, although Stichus was not born in the family of the testator, but bought, yet if there is a certainty of his person, the legacy is valid. And if a testator should write as follows: "I bequeath Stichus my slave, whom I bought of Seius;" yet, although he was bought of another, the legacy would be good, if there was no doubt as to the identity of the person of Stichus.

§ 31. *A fortiori* a legacy is not rendered the less valid, although a false reason is assigned for bequeathing it: as if a testator should thus express himself: "I give my slave Stichus to Titius, because he took care of my affairs in my absence;" or, "because I was acquitted upon an accusation of a capital offence by his care and protection." For although Titius had never taken care of the affairs of the deceased, and although the testator was never acquitted from any charge of a capital crime by means of Titius, the legacy will nevertheless be good. But if the bequest had been declared to be conditional; as, for example, if the testator had expressed himself as follows—"I give to Titius such a piece of ground, if it shall appear that he hath taken a proper care of my affairs;" then the law would be different.

§ 32. It hath been a question, whether a testator can legally give a legacy to the slave of his heir; and it is certain, that a legacy purely and simply given to such a slave can avail him nothing, although he should afterwards be freed from the power of the heir in the lifetime of the testator; for a bequest, which would have been null if the testator had expired immediately after he had made it, ought not to become valid merely because the testator happened to enjoy a longer life. But a testator may give a conditional legacy to the slave of his instituted heir, and such legacy will be good, if the slave is not under the power of the heir when the condition is fulfilled.

§ 33. On the contrary, it is not doubted but that a slave may be appointed an heir, and that his then master may take even a simple legacy by the same testament: for although the testator should die instantly after making his testament, yet the legacy is not understood to become immediately due from the slave, who is the heir; for the inheritance is here separate from the legacy, and another may become heir by means of the slave, if he should be transferred to a new master, before he hath entered upon the inheritance at the command of his master, who is the legatary; or the slave himself may become heir in his own right by manumission; and in these cases the legacy would be good. But if the slave should remain in the same state, and enter upon the inheritance by order of his master, who is the legatary, the legacy would, as such, become extinct.

§ 34. A legacy could not formerly have been given with effect till the heir was instituted, because a testament receives its whole force and efficacy from the institution of the heir, which is understood to be the basis and foundation of it: and, by a parity of reasoning, it was also necessary that the institution of an heir should always precede the grant of freedom in a testament. But we have thought it to be wrong and absurd that a strict regard should be paid to the mere order of writing, in direct opposition to the express intention of a testator; and the ancients themselves seem to have been of this opinion in general: we have therefore, by virtue of our constitution, amended the law in this point, so that a legacy may now be given, and, *à fortiori*, a grant of liberty, which is always favoured, may be bequeathed, before the institution of an heir, where there is but one; and either before or between the institutions of heirs, where there are several.

§ 35. A bequest made to take place after the death of an heir or legatary was also ineffectual: for if a testator had written, "When my heir is dead, I give and bequeath a hundred *aurei* to Titius;" or even thus, "I give and bequeath a hundred *aurei* to be paid on the day preceding the day of the death of my heir;" or, "on the day preceding the day of the death of my legatary;" the legacies in any of these cases would have been void. But we have corrected the ancient rule of law in this respect by giving all such legacies the same validity which is given to gifts in trust, lest trusts should be found to be more favoured than legacies.

§ 36. Also formerly, if a testator had given, revoked, or transferred a legacy *pœnæ nomine*, he would have acted ineffectually: and a legacy is reputed to be bequeathed *pœnæ nomine*, *i.e.*, as a punishment or penalty, when an heir is put under the necessity of doing or not doing something; as, for instance, if a testator had thus written; "If my heir gives his daughter in marriage to Titius;" or, "If he does not give her in marriage to Titius, let him pay ten *aurei* to Seius:" or thus, "If my heir shall alien my slave Stichus;" or, on the contrary, "If my heir shall not alien my slave Stichus, let him pay ten *aurei* to Titius." And this rule was so far observed, that it was expressly ordained by many constitutions, that even the emperor could not receive a legacy which was bequeathed *pœnæ nomine;* nor could a penal legacy be valid, even when it had been bequeathed by the testament of a soldier; although in every other respect the intention of a testator in a military testament was always scrupulously adhered to. And even freedom could not be bequeathed, nor, in the opinion of Sabinus, could an heir be added in a testament, *sub pœnæ nomine:* for if a testator had said, "Let Titius be my heir, but if he gives his daughter in marriage to Seius, let Seius also be my heir," the appointment of Seius would have been void; for the manner in which an heir was laid under coercion, whether it was by the gift of a legacy, or by the addition of another heir, worked no alteration in the general rule of law. But this scrupulosity hath been by no means agreeable to us; and we have therefore ordained, that in general the doctrine of the law in regard to anything left, revoked, or transferred, in punishment of an heir should not differ from the rules of law observed in relation to other legacies when the performance of the condition of obtaining them is neither impossible, prohibited by law, nor contrary to good manners: for the morality, religion, and justice of the present times will not suffer such testamentary dispositions to take place.

Tit. XXI. *De ademptione legatorum et translatione.*

A revocation of a legacy is valid, although it is inserted in the same testament or codicil in which the legacy was given. And it is immaterial whether the revocation is made in words contrary to the bequest; as when a testator gives a legacy in these terms, "I give and bequeath to Titius," and revokes it by adding, "I do not give and bequeath to Titius;" or whether the revocation is made by any other form of words.

A legacy may also be transferred from one person to another; as thus, "I give to Seius my slave Stichus, whom I have bequeathed to Titius." This may be done in the same testament or codicil in which the legacy was first given; and thus a legacy may be taken tacitly and by implication from Titius and transferred to Seius.

Tit. XXII. *De lege Falcidiâ.*

It remains to speak of the law *Falcidia*, by which legacies have received their latest regulation. By the law of the Twelve Tables, *uti quisque legassit suæ rei, ita jus esto*, a testator was permitted to dispose of his whole patrimony in legacies: but it was thought proper to restrain this licence even for the benefit of testators themselves, because they frequently died intestate, their heirs refusing to enter upon an inheritance from which they could receive no profit, or but very little. And this occasioned the introduction first of the law *Furia*, and afterwards of the law *Voconia:* but when neither of these was found adequate to the purpose intended, the Falcidian law was at length enacted, which prohibits a testator to give more in legacies than three-fourths of all his effects, so that whether there is one or more heirs, there must now remain to him or them an entire fourth part of the whole.

§ 1. When two heirs are instituted, for example, Titius and Seius, and Titius's moiety of the inheritance is wholly exhausted, or overcharged by legacies, which he is expressly ordered to pay; and on the other side Seius's moiety is either not encumbered, or is charged with legacies which amount only to a part of his share; it hath in this case been a question, whether, although Seius hath a fourth or more of the whole inheritance, it may not nevertheless be lawful for Titius to make a stoppage out of the legacies with which he is charged, so as to retain a fourth part out of his own moiety? and it hath been determined that Titius may make such stoppage; for the reason and equity of the law *Falcidia* extends to each heir in particular.

§ 2. But the law *Falcidia* hath regard only to the quantity of the estate at the time of the death of the testator; and therefore, if he who is worth but a hundred *aurei* at his decease bequeaths them all in legacies, the legatees must suffer a defalcation, for they will receive no manner of advantage, although the inheritance, after the death of the testator, and before it is entered upon, should so increase by the acquisitions of slaves, the children of female slaves, or the product of cattle, that, after a full payment of the hundred *aurei* in legaçies, an entire fourth of the whole estate might remain to the heir; for, notwithstanding the increase in the testator's estate subsequent to his death, a fourth part of the hundred *aurei* would still be due to the heir, and the legacies would remain subject to a defalcation upon that account. But, on the contrary, if a testator hath bequeathed seventy-five *aurei* in legacies, and was worth a hundred *aurei* at his death, then, although it should happen that, before the entrance of the heir, the estate should so decrease by fire, shipwreck, or the loss of slaves, that the whole value of it should not be more than seventy-five *aurei*, and perhaps less, yet the legacies would still be due without defalcation; nor is this law prejudicial to an heir, who is always at his election either to refuse or accept an inheritance; but it obliges legataries to come to an agreement with the heir to take a part, lest they should lose the whole of their legacies by his desertion of the testament.

§ 3. The Falcidian portion is not taken by the heir till the debts, funeral expenses, and the price of the manumission of slaves have all been previously deducted; and then the fourth part of the remainder appertains to the heir, and the other three parts are divided among the legataries in a rateable proportion. For example, let it be supposed that 400 *aurei* have been bequeathed in legacies, and that the estate from which these legacies are intended to issue is worth but exactly that sum. It follows that a fourth must be subtracted from the legacy of each legatary; but if the testator gave in legacies no more than 350 *aurei*, and there remained after debts paid 400, then an eighth only ought to be deducted from each legacy. And if a testator hath bequeathed 500 *aurei* in legacies, and there remain clear in the hands of the heir but 400, then a fifth must first be deducted from every legacy, and afterwards a fourth; but that which exceeds the real value of the goods of the deceased must first be subtracted, and then follows the deduction of what is due to the heir.

Tit. XXIII. *De fidei-commissariis hæreditatibus.*

Let us now proceed to trusts, in treating of which we will first speak of fiduciary inheritances.

§ 1. It must be observed, that in the first times all trusts were weak and precarious; for no man could be compelled to the performance of what he was only requested to perform. And yet, when testators were desirous of giving an inheritance or legacy to persons to whom they could directly bequeath neither, they then committed the inheritance or legacy in trust to those who were capable of taking; and such commitments were called fiduciary, because the performance of the trust could not be enforced by the law, but depended solely upon the honour of the trustee. But the Emperor Augustus, having been frequently moved with compassion on account of particular persons, and detesting the perjury and perfidiousness of trustees in general, commanded the consuls to interpose their authority; and this, being a just and popular command, gave them by degrees a continued jurisdiction; and in process of time trusts became so common, and were so highly favoured, that a prætor was purposely appointed to give judgment in these cases, and was therefore called the commissary of trusts.

§ 2. We must here observe that there is an absolute necessity of appointing an heir in direct terms to every testament; but he then may be requested to restore the inheritance to any other person; yet without an heir a testament is ineffectual. And therefore, when a testator says, "Let Lucius Titius be my heir," he may add, "and I request you, Lucius Titius, that as soon as you enter upon my inheritance you would restore it to Caius Seius." But a testator is at liberty to request his heir to restore a part of the inheritance only, and may make him a trustee upon condition, or from a day certain.

§ 3. After an heir hath restored an inheritance in obedience to the trust reposed in him, he nevertheless continues heir. But he who hath received the inheritance from such fiduciary heir is sometimes reputed to be in the place of the heir, and sometimes in the place of a legatary.

§ 4. In the reign of Nero the emperor, when Trebellius Maximus and Annæus Seneca were consuls, it was provided by a decree of the senate that, if an inheritance was restored by reason of a trust, all actions, which by the civil law might be brought by or against the heir, should be given to and against him to whom the inheritance was restored. And after this decree the prætor began to give equitable and beneficial actions to and against the receiver of an inheritance as if he was the heir.

§ 5. But when written heirs were requested to restore the whole, or almost the whole, of an inheritance, they often refused to accept it, since they could receive but little or no emolument; and thus it happened that trusts were frequently extinguished. But afterwards, in the consulate of Pegasus and Pugio, in the reign of the Emperor Vespasian, the senate ordained by their decree that an heir who was requested to restore an inheritance might retain a fourth, as in the case of legacies by the Falcidian law. And an heir is also allowed to make the same deduction from particular things which are left to him in trust for the benefit of another. For some time after this decree the heir alone bore the burden of the inheritance, *i. e.* all the charges and demands incident to it; but afterwards, whoever had received a share or part of an inheritance, by being benefited under a trust, was regarded as having a partial legacy; and this species of legacy was called partition, because the legatary took a part of the inheritance together with the heir; and thence it arose that the same stipulations which were formerly used between the heir and legatary in part were also interposed between the person benefited under the trust and the heir or trustee, to the intent that the profit and loss might be in common between them in due proportion.

§ 6. And therefore if a written heir, or heir in trust, had not been requested to surrender more than three-fourths of the inheritance, he was obliged to restore so much of it by virtue of the Trebellian *senatusconsultum;* and all actions, whether in favour of or against the inheritance, were brought or sustained by the heir and *fidei-commissary* according to their respective shares; and this obtains in regard to the heir by virtue of the civil law; and in regard to the *fidei-commissary* by virtue of the Trebellian decree. But if the written heir was requested by the testator to restore the whole inheritance, or more than three-fourths, then the Pegasian *senatusconsultum* took place; for if he had once taken upon himself the heirship voluntarily, he was obliged to sustain all charges, and this whether he did or did not retain the fourth to which he was entitled. But when an heir retained a fourth part the stipulations called *partis et pro parte* were entered into as between a legatary in part and an heir; and when the heir did not retain a fourth, then the stipulations called *emptæ et venditæ hæreditatis* were interposed. But if the written heir or heir in trust refused to accept the inheritance, on suspicion that there would not be assets, and that the acceptance would be detrimental to him, it was provided by the Pegasian decree that the prætor, at the instance of the *fidei-commissary*, might compel such heir to take upon himself the inheritance, and then restore it; and that afterwards all actions should be brought by or against the *fidei-commissary* only, as it is ordained by the Trebellian decree. And in this case stipulations are not necessary; for the heir who restores the inheritance is made effectually secure, and all hereditary actions are transferred to and against him by whom the inheritance is received, there being in this instance a concurrence of both decrees, the Pegasian and the Trebellian.

§ 7. But as the stipulations, which took their rise from the Pegasian decree, were displeasing even to the ancients themselves, insomuch that Papinian, a man of a true sublime genius, does not scruple to call them captious in some cases, and as simplicity is far more agreeable to us in all matters of law than unnecessary difficulties, it hath therefore pleased us, upon comparing the agreement and disagreement of each decree, to abrogate the Pegasian, which was subsequent to the Trebellian, and to transfer a greater authority to the Trebellian decree, by which all *fidei-commissary* inheritances shall be restored for the future, whether the testator hath given by his will a fourth part of his estate to his written heir, or more or less than a fourth, or even nothing; so that when either nothing is given to the heir, or less than a fourth part, he may be permitted to retain a fourth, or as much as will complete the deficiency, by virtue of our authority, or even to demand a repayment of what he hath paid in his own wrong, all actions being divided between the heir and the *fidei-commissary* in a just proportion, according to the Trebellian decree. But if the heir spontaneously restores the whole inheritance, all actions must be brought either by or against the *fidei-commissary*. And whereas it was the principal effect of the power of the Pegasian decree, that when a written heir had refused to accept an inheritance, he might be constrained to take it and restore it, at the instance of the *fidei-commissary*, to whom, and against whom, all actions passed, we have transferred that power to the Trebellian decree, so that this is now the only law by which a fiduciary heir can be compelled to enter upon the inheritance, when the *fidei-commissary* is desirous that it should be restored; and the heir in this case can neither receive profit nor suffer loss.

§ 8. But it makes no difference whether an heir, who is instituted to the whole of an inheritance, is requested by the testator to restore the whole or a part of it only; or whether an heir, who is nominated but to a part of an inheritance, is requested to restore that entire part, or only a portion of it; for we have ordained that the same rule of law shall be observed, whether an heir is requested to restore the whole or a part only of an inheritance.

§ 9. If an heir is requested by a testator to give up an inheritance, after deducting some specific thing, amounting to a fourth, as a piece of ground, &c., he may be compelled to give it up by the Trebellian decree, in the same manner as if he had been requested to restore the remainder of an inheritance, after reserving to himself a fourth. There is, however, this difference, that in the one case, when an heir is requested to give up an inheritance, after deducting a particular thing, then all actions, passive as well as active, are transferred by virtue of the decree to the *fidei-commissary*, and what remains with the heir is free of all incumbrance, as if acquired by legacy; and in the other case, when an heir is requested in general terms to give up an inheritance, after retaining a fourth to himself, all actions are proportionably divided; those which regard the three-fourths of the estate being transferred to the *fidei-commissary*, and those which regard the single fourth remaining for the benefit of the heir. And even if an heir is requested to give up an inheritance, after making a deduction of some particular thing, which amounts to the value of the greatest part of it, all actions, both active and passive, are nevertheless transferred to the *fidei-commissary*, who ought therefore always well to consider whether it will be expedient or not that the inheritance should be given up to him. And the law is the same, whether an heir is requested to give up an inheritance after a deduction of two or more specific things, or of a certain sum of money which exceeds in value the greatest part of the inheritance. Thus what we have said of an heir who is instituted to the whole of an inheritance, is equally true of him who is instituted only to a part.

§ 10. And further, even a man who is willing to die intestate may request the person who he thinks will succeed him, either by the civil or prætorian law, to give up the whole inheritance, or a part of it, or any particular thing, as a piece of ground, a slave, a sum of money, &c. But this liberty is granted to intestates in regard to trusts only; for legacies are not valid unless they are bequeathed by testament.

§ 11. A *fidei-commissary* may also himself be requested to pay over, or give up, to another either the whole or a part of what he receives; or even to give some other thing in lieu of it.

§ 12. All fiduciary gifts or bequests depended formerly in a precarious manner upon the sole faith of the heir; from which they took as well their name as their essence; and the Emperor Augustus was the first who thought it proper to reduce them under a judicial cognizance. But we have since endeavoured to exceed that prince; and, at the instance of that most excellent man Tribonian, the quæstor of our palace, we have enacted by our constitution, that if a testator hath trusted to the faith of his heir for the surrender of an inheritance, or any particular thing, and this trust cannot be made manifest by the depositions of five witnesses—which is known to be the legal number in such cases—there having been not so many, or perhaps no witnesses present, the heir at the same time perfidiously refusing to make any payment, and denying the whole transaction, then in this case the *fidei-commissary*, having previously taken the oath of calumny, may put the heir, although he is even the son of the testator, to his oath, and thus force him either to deny the trust upon oath, or comply with it, whether the trust is universal or particular; and this is allowed, lest the last will of a testator, committed to the faith of an heir, should be defeated. And we have thought it right that the same remedy should be taken against a legatary, or even a *fidei-commissary*, to whom a testator hath left anything with a request to give it up. And if any man, to whom something hath been left in trust to be given to another, should confess the trust after he hath denied it, but endeavour at the same time to shelter himself under the subtlety of the law, he may nevertheless be compelled to perform his duty.

Tit. XXIV. *De singulis rebus per fidei-commissum relictis.*

A man may also leave particular things in trust, as a field, silver, clothes, or a certain sum of money; and may request either his heir to restore them, or even a legatary, although a legatary cannot be made chargeable with a legacy.

§ 1. A testator may leave not only his own property in trust, but also the property of his heir, of a legatary, of a *fidei-commissary*, or of any other; so that a legatary or *fidei-commis-*

sary may not only be requested to give what hath been left to him, but what is his own, or even what is the property of another. And the only caution necessary to be observed by the testator is, that no man be requested to give more than he hath received by means of the testament; for the excess will be ineffectually bequeathed. And when the property of another is left in trust, the person requested to restore it is obliged either to obtain from the proprietor the very thing bequeathed, or to pay the value of it.

§ 2. Liberty may also be conferred upon a slave by virtue of a trust; for an heir, a legatary, or a *fidei-commissary*, may be requested to manumit: nor does it make any difference whether the testator requests the manumission of his own slave, of the slave of his heir, of the slave of a legatary, or of the slave of a stranger: and therefore, when a slave is not the testator's own property, he must be bought, if possible, and manumitted. But if the proprietor of the slave refuses to sell him—which refusal the proprietor may justify, if he hath taken nothing under the will of the testator—yet the fiduciary bequest is not extinguished, but deferred only till it can be conveniently performed. It is here to be observed, that he who is manumitted in consequence of a trust does not become the freedman of the testator, although he was the testator's own slave, but he becomes the freedman of the manumitter: but a slave to whom liberty is directly given by testament becomes the freedman of the testator, and is called *orcinus;* and no one can obtain liberty directly by testament, unless he was the slave of the testator, not only at the time of the testator's death, but also at the time of the making of his testament. And liberty is understood to be directly given, not when a testator requests that his slave shall be made free by another, but when he commands that the freedom of his slave shall commence instantly by virtue of his testament.

§ 3. The terms generally used in the commitment of trusts are the following: *peto, rogo, volo, mando, fidei tuæ committo:* any of which words singly taken is as firm and binding as if all were joined together.

Tit. XXV. *De codicillis.*

It is certain that codicils were not in frequent use before the reign of Augustus, for Lucius Lentulus, by whose means trusts became efficacious, was the first who caused authority to be given to codicils. When he was dying in Africa he wrote several codicils, which were confirmed by his testament, and in these he requested Augustus to perform some particular act in consequence of a trust. The emperor complied with the request; and many other persons afterwards, being influenced by the authority of the emperor's example, punctually performed trusts which had been committed to their charge; and the daughter of Lentulus paid debts, which in strictness of law were not due. But it is reported that Augustus, having convened upon this occasion the sages of the law, and also Trebatius, whose opinion was of the greatest authority, demanded whether codicils could be admitted to be of force, and whether they were not repugnant to the very reason of the law? To which Trebatius answered that codicils were not only most convenient but most necessary, on account of the great and long voyages which the Romans were frequently obliged to take, to the intent that where a man could not make a testament he might bequeath his effects by codicil. And afterwards, when Labeo, a lawyer of great eminence, disposed of his own property by codicil, it was no longer a doubt but that codicils might be legally allowed.

§ 1. Not only he who hath already made his testament is permitted to make a codicil, but even an intestate may commit a trust to others by codicil; yet when a codicil is antecedent to a testament, the codicil, according to Papinian, cannot otherwise take effect than by being confirmed by the subsequent testament. But the Emperors Severus and Antoninus have, by rescript, declared that a thing left in trust in a codicil preceding a testament may be demanded by the *fidei-commissary*, if it appears that the testator hath not receded from the intention which he at first expressed in his codicil.

§ 2. But an inheritance can neither be given nor taken away by codicil, lest the different operations of testaments and codicils should be confounded; and, of course, an heir cannot be disinherited by codicil. But although an inheritance can neither be given nor taken away by codicil in direct terms, yet it may be legally left from the heir in a codicil by means of a trust, or *fidei-commissum*. But no man is allowed to impose a condition upon his heir by codicil, nor to substitute directly.

§ 3. A man may make many codicils, and they require no solemnity.

BOOK III.

Tit. I. *De hæreditatibus, quæ ab intestato deferuntur.*

Every person is said to die intestate who hath either not made a testament, or, if he has made one, hath neglected to use the solemnities prescribed by law. A man is also said to die intestate if his testament, although rightly made, is either cancelled or rendered void, or if no one will take upon himself the heirship by virtue of the testament.

§ 1. The inheritances of intestates, according to the law of the Twelve Tables, belong primarily to the *sui hæredes*, *i.e.*, to the proper or domestic heirs of such intestates.

§ 2. And, as we have observed before, those are esteemed *sui hæredes*, or proper heirs, who at the time of the death of the deceased were under his power; as a son or a daughter, a grandson or a granddaughter by a son, a great-grandson or great-granddaughter by a grandson of a son, &c., neither is it material whether these children are natural or adopted. But in the number of natural children we must reckon those who, although they were not born in lawful wedlock, are nevertheless, according to the tenor of the imperial constitutions, entitled to the rights of proper heirs, by being admitted into the order of decurions. We must also add those persons who are comprised within our own constitutions, by which it is ordained, that if any person, without intending matrimony, shall keep a woman with whom he is not prohibited to marry, and have children by her, and shall afterwards, through the dictates of affection, marry that woman and have other children by her, sons or daughters, then not only these latter children, born after the celebration of marriage, shall be legitimate, and in the power of their father, but also the former, who gave occasion to the legitimacy of those who were born afterwards. And we have thought it expedient, that this law shall also obtain in regard to the children born before marriage, although the children born subsequent to it are dead, or even although there never were any children subsequent to the marriage. But a grandson or granddaughter, a great-grandson or great-granddaughter, is not reckoned in the number of proper heirs, unless the person preceding them in degree hath ceased to be under paternal power, either by death or some other means, as by emancipation: for if a son, when his father died, was under the power of his father, the grandson can by no means be the proper or domestic heir of his grandfather; and by a parity of reasoning, this rule is understood to take place in relation to all descendants in the right line. But all posthumous children, who would have been under the power of their father if they had been born in his lifetime, are esteemed *sui hæredes*, or proper heirs.

§ 3. Persons may become *sui hæredes*, or proper heirs, without their knowledge, and even although they are disordered in their senses: for as inheritances may be acquired without our knowledge, it is a consequence that they may also be acquired by persons deprived of their understanding. And here observe, that the dominion of an inheritance is continued in the heir from the very instant of the death of his ancestor; and that the authority of a tutor is not necessary to enable a pupil to inherit, because inheritances may be acquired by proper heirs without their knowledge: neither does a disordered person inherit by the assent of his curator, but by operation of law.

§ 4. But sometimes a child becomes a proper heir, although he was not under power at the time of the death of his parent; as when a person returns from captivity after the death of his father: and this is effected by the *jus postliminii*, or right of return.

§ 5. On the contrary, it may happen that a child, who at the time of the death of his parent was under his power, shall not be his proper heir; as when a parent, after his decease, is adjudged to have been guilty of lese-majesty, by which crime his memory is rendered infamous; for a criminal of this sort can have no proper heir, inasmuch as all his possessions are forfeited to the treasury. But a son in this case may strictly be said to have been the proper heir of his father, and afterwards to have ceased to be so.

§ 6. When there is a son or a daughter, and a grandson or granddaughter by another son, they are called equally to the inheritance of their parents; nor does the nearest exclude the more remote, for it appears just that grandsons and granddaughters should succeed in the place of their father. And by the same reasoning, if there is a grandson or granddaughter by a son, and a great-grandson or great-granddaughter by a grandson, they ought all to be called to the inheritance. And inasmuch as it hath been esteemed right that grandsons and granddaughters, great-grandsons and great-granddaughters should succeed in the place of their parent, it seemed convenient that inheritances should not be divided into *capita*, but into *stirpes;* so that where there is a son, and grandchildren by another son, the son possesses half the inheritance, and the grandchildren, however numerous, are entitled only to the other half as the representatives of their father. And, in like manner, where there are grandchildren by two sons, the one son leaving one or two children, and the other three or four, the inheritance must be equally divided, half belonging to the single grandchild or the two grandchildren by the one son, and half to the three or four grandchildren by the other son.

§ 7. Whenever it is demanded whether any person is a proper heir, we must inquire at what time it was certain that the deceased died without a testament; and a man is said to die without a testament if his testament is relinquished. Thus, if a son is disinherited and a stranger is instituted heir, and after the death of the son it becomes certain that the instituted heir was not in fact the heir, either because he was unwilling or unable to accept the inheritance, in this case the grandson of the deceased becomes the proper heir of his grandfather; for at the time when it was certain that the deceased died intestate there was no other heir but the grandchild; and this is evident.

§ 8. And although a child is born after the death of his grandfather, yet if he was conceived in the lifetime of his grandfather, he will, at the death of his father, and after his grandfather's testament is deserted by the instituted heir, become the proper heir of his grandfather. But if a child is both conceived and born after the death of his grandfather, such child, although his father should die, and the testament of his grandfather be deserted, could not become the proper heir of his grandfather, because he was never allied to his grandfather by any tie of cognation; neither is he whom an emancipated son hath adopted to be reckoned in any respect among the children of his adoptive father's father. So that the adopted children of an emancipated son can neither become the proper heirs of their father's father in regard to the inheritance, nor demand the possession of goods as next of kin. This is what we have thought it expedient to observe concerning proper heirs.

§ 9. Emancipated children by the civil law have no right to the inheritances of their parents; for those are not proper heirs who have ceased to be under the power of their parent deceased before his death, neither are they called to inherit by any other right according to the law of the Twelve Tables. But the prætor, induced by natural equity, grants them the possession of goods, by the edict beginning *unde liberi,* as fully as if they had been under power at the time of the death of their parent; and the prætor grants this whether they are sole, or mixed with others who are proper heirs. Therefore, when there are two sons, the one emancipated, and the other under power at the time of his father's death, the latter by the civil law is alone the heir, and alone the proper heir; but when the emancipated son by the indulgence of the prætor is admitted to his share, then the proper heir becomes the heir only of his own moiety.

§ 10. But those who after emancipation have given themselves in adoption are not admitted as children to the possession of the effects of their natural father, if at the time of his death they were in the adoptive family. But if in the lifetime of their natural father they were emancipated by their adoptive father, they are then admitted by the prætor to take the goods of their natural father, as if they had been emancipated by him, and had never entered into the family of their adopter; and consequently, in regard to their adoptive father, they are looked upon as mere strangers. But those who are emancipated by their adoptive father, after the death of their natural father, are nevertheless reputed strangers to their adoptive father; and in regard to the inheritance of their natural father they are not at all the more entitled to reassume the rank of children. These rules of law have been established, inasmuch as it was unjust that it should be in the power of an adopter to determine at his pleasure to whom the inheritance of a natural father should appertain, whether to his children or to his agnates.

§ 11. Adopted children have therefore fewer rights and privileges than natural children; for natural children, even after emancipation, retain the rank of children by the indulgence of the prætor, although they lose it by the civil law: but adopted children, when emancipated, lose the rank of children by the civil law, and are denied admittance into the rank of children by the prætor; and not without reason: for civil policy can by no means destroy natural rights, nor can natural children ever cease to be sons and daughters, grandsons and granddaughters, although they may cease to be proper heirs; but adopted children, when emancipated, commence instantly strangers; for the right and name of son or daughter, which were obtained by the civil right of adoption, may be destroyed by another civil right, namely, by emancipation.

§ 12. The same rules are observed in regard to that possession of goods which the prætor, contrary to the testament of the parent, grants to the children who are not mentioned in the testament, that is, to such who are neither instituted heirs, nor properly disinherited. For the prætor calls those who were under power at the time of the death of their parents, and those also who were emancipated, to the same possession of goods; but he repels those who were in an adoptive family at the time of the decease of their natural parents. And as the prætor admits not those adopted children who have been emancipated by their adoptive father to succeed him *ab intestato*, much less, therefore, does the prætor admit such children to possess the goods of their adoptive father contrary to his testament; for, by virtue of the emancipation, they cease to be in the number of his children.

§ 13. We must nevertheless observe, that although those who were in an adoptive family, but have been emancipated by their adoptive father, after the decease of their natural father, dying intestate, are not admitted by that part of the edict by which children are called to the possession of goods; yet they are admitted by another part, by which the cognates of the deceased are called to the possession of his effects. But, by this last-named part of the edict, the cognates are only called when there is no opposition from proper heirs, emancipated children, or agnates; for the prætor first calls the proper heirs with the emancipated children, then the agnates, and lastly the nearest cognates.

§ 14. These were the rules of law which formerly obtained; but they have received some emendation from the constitution which we promulged relating to those persons who are given in adoption by their natural parents; for we have found frequent instances of sons who by adoption have lost their succession to their natural parents, and who, by the ease with which adoption is dissolved by emancipation, have also lost the right of succeeding to their adoptive parents. We therefore, correcting as usual whatever is amiss, have enacted a constitution by which it is decreed, that when a natural father hath given his son in adoption, all the rights of such son shall nevertheless be preserved entire, in the same manner as if he had still remained under the power of his natural father, and there had been no adoption; except only, that the person adopted may succeed to his adopter if he dies intestate. And it is also enacted, that if the adopter makes a testament, and omits the name of his adopted son, such son can neither, by the civil nor the prætorian law, obtain any part of the inheritance, whether he demands the possession of the effects *contra tabulas testamenti*—contrary to the letter of the testament—or prefers a complaint, alleging that the testament is inofficious; for an adopter is under no obligation either to institute, or disinherit, his adopted son, inasmuch as there subsists not between them any natural tie or relation. And we have further decreed, that no adopted person shall receive any benefit from the Sabinian *senatusconsultum*, by being one of three sons; for in this case he shall neither obtain the fourth part of his adoptive father's effects, nor be entitled to any action upon that account. But all those who are adopted by their natural parents—*i. e.*, by a grandfather or great-grandfather, &c.—are excepted in our constitution; for, inasmuch as such persons are united together by the concurrence both of natural and civil rights, we have thought proper to retain the old law in relation to those adoptions, in the same manner as when the father of a family hath given himself in arrogation. But all which we have here observed may be collected from the tenor of the above-mentioned constitution.

§ 15. The ancient law, showing most favour to descendants from males, called those grandchildren only who were so descended to the succession as proper heirs, and preferred them by the right of agnation; for the old law, reputing the grandchildren born of daughters, and the great-grandchildren born of granddaughters, to be cognates, prohibited such children from succeeding to their grandfather and great-grandfather, maternal or paternal, till after the line of *agnati* was exhausted. But the Emperors Valentinian, Theodosius, and Arcadius would not suffer such a violence against nature to continue in practice; and inasmuch as the name of grandchild and great-grandchild is undoubtedly common as well to descendants by females as to descendants by males, they therefore granted an equal right of succession to descendants from males and descendants from females. But to the end that those persons, who have been favoured by nature as well as by the suffrage of antiquity, might enjoy some peculiar privileges, the same emperors have thought it right that the portions of grandchildren, great-grandchildren, and other lineal descendants of a female, should be somewhat diminished, and therefore they have not permitted such persons to receive so much by a third part as their mother or grandmother would have received, or their father or grandfather, paternal or maternal, at the decease of a female; for we now treat concerning inheritances derived from a female: and although there were only grandchildren by a female to take an inheritance, yet the emperors did not call the agnates to the succession. And as upon the decease of a son the law of the Twelve Tables calls the grandchildren and great-grandchildren, male and female, to represent their father in respect to the succession of their grandfather, so the imperial ordinance calls them to succession in the place of their mother or grandmother, with the before-regulated diminution of a third part of their share. But as there still remained matter of dispute between the *agnati* and the above-named grandchildren, the *agnati* claiming the fourth part of the estate of the deceased by virtue of a certain constitution, we have therefore not permitted it to be inserted into our code from that of Theodosius. And we have further taken care to alter the old law by our ordinance, having enacted that agnates shall not be entitled to any part of the goods of the deceased whilst grandchildren born of a daughter, or great-grandchildren born of a granddaughter, or any other descendants from a female in the right line are living, lest those who proceed from the transverse line should be preferred to lineal descendants. And we now decree that this our ordinance shall obtain according to its full tenor. But as the old law ordered that every inheritance should be divided into *stirpes* and not *in capita* between the sons of the deceased and his grandsons by a son, so we also ordain that distribution shall be made in the same manner between sons and grandsons by a daughter, and between all grandsons and granddaughters, great-grandsons and great-granddaughters, and all other descendants in a right line; so that the issue either of a mother or a father, or of a grandmother or a grandfather, may obtain their portions without any diminution; and if on the one part there should be only one or two claimants, and on the other part three or four, that the greater number shall be entitled only to one half, and the less number to the other half of the inheritance.

Tit. II. *De legitimâ agnatorum successione.*

When it happens that there are no proper heirs to succeed the deceased, nor any of those persons whom the prætor or the constitutions would call to inherit with proper heirs, then the inheritance, by a law of the Twelve Tables, appertains to the nearest agnate.

§ 1. Agnates, as we have observed in the first book, are those who are related or cognated by males—*quasi a patre cognati;*—and therefore brothers, who are the sons of the same father, are agnates in regard to each other; they are also called *consanguinei*, being of the same blood; but it is not required that they should have the same mother. An uncle is also agnated to his brother's son, and *vice versâ* the brother's son to his paternal uncle; and brothers *patruel*, that is, the children of brothers, who are also called *consobrini*, are likewise reckoned agnates. In this manner we may enumerate many degrees of agnation; and even those who are born after the decease of their parents obtain the rights of consanguinity: the law, nevertheless, does not grant the right of inheritance to all the *agnati*, but to those only who are in the nearest degree, when it becomes certain that the deceased hath died intestate.

§ 2. The right of agnation arises also through adoption; thus the natural and adopted sons of the same father are agnates; but such persons are without doubt improperly called *consanguinei*. Also if a brother, a paternal uncle, or any other who is agnated to you in a more remote degree, should adopt any person into his family, then such adopted person is undoubtedly to be reckoned in the number of your *agnati*.

§ 3. Succession among males proceeds according to the right of agnation, although they are in the most distant degree. But it hath pleased the ancient lawyers, that females should only inherit by consanguinity, if they are sisters, and not in a more remote degree; though males might be admitted in the most distant degree to inherit females: thus, in case of death, the inheritance of your brother's daughter, or of the daughter of your paternal uncle or aunt, would appertain to you, but your inheritance would not appertain to them. And this was so constituted, because it seemed expedient for the benefit of society that inheritances should for the most part fall into the possession of males. But, inasmuch as it was extremely unjust that females should be thus almost wholly excluded as strangers, the prætor admitted them to the possession of goods in that part of his edict, in which he gives the possession of goods on account of proximity; yet they are only admitted upon condition that there is no agnate, or nearer cognate. But the law of the Twelve Tables did not introduce these dispositions; for that law, according to the plainness and simplicity which are agreeable to all laws, called the agnates of either sex, or any degree, to succession, in the same manner as it admitted proper heirs. But the middle law, which was posterior to the law of the Twelve Tables, and prior to the imperial constitutions, subtilely introduced the before-mentioned distinction, and entirely repelled females from the succession of agnates, no other method of succession being known, till the prætors, correcting by degrees the asperity of the civil law, or supplying what was deficient, added in their edicts a new order of succession, being induced to it by a motive of humanity; and by introducing the line of cognation on account of proximity, they thus assisted the females, and gave them the possession of goods, which is called *unde cognati.* But we, although we have adhered to the law of the Twelve Tables, and strictly maintained it in regard to females, must yet commend the humanity of the prætors, though they have not afforded a full remedy in the present case. But since the same natural degree of relation, and the same title of agnation, appertains as well to females as to males, what reason can be assigned that males should be permitted to succeed all their *agnati*, and that no means of succession should be open to any female agnate except a sister? We therefore, reducing all things to an equality, and making our disposition conformable to the laws of the Twelve Tables, have by our constitution ordained, that all legitime persons, that is, descendants from males, whether male or female, shall be equally called to the rights of succession *ab intestato* according to the prerogative of their degree, and be by no means excluded, although they possess not the rights of consanguinity in so near a degree as sisters.

§ 4. We have further thought it necessary to add a clause to our constitution, by which one degree is transferred from the line of cognation to the line of legitime succession, *i.e.*, of agnation, so that not only the son and daughter of a brother—according to our former definition of agnates—shall be called to the succession of their paternal uncle, but the son or daughter of a sister, who is either by the same father or by the same mother, may also be admitted with agnates to the succession of their maternal uncle; but no one of the descendants of the son or daughter of a sister is by any means to be admitted. And when a person dies, who at his decease was both a paternal and maternal uncle, that is, who had nephews or nieces living, both by a brother and by a sister, then such children succeed in the same manner as if they were all descendants from males, when the deceased leaves no brother or sister, and they take the inheritance not *per stirpes*, or according to their respective stocks, but *per capita, i. e.*, by poll: but if there are brothers or sisters, and they accept the succession, all others of a more remote degree are excluded.

§ 5. When there are many degrees of agnates, the law of the Twelve Tables calls those who are in the nearest degree: if therefore, for example, there is a brother of the deceased, and a son of another brother, or a paternal uncle, the brother is preferred. But although the law of the Twelve Tables calls the nearest agnate in the singular number, yet it is not to be doubted but that, if there are many in the same degree, they ought all to be admitted. And although properly the nearest degree must be understood to denote the nearest degree of many, yet if there is but one degree of agnates, the inheritance must undoubtedly appertain to those who are in that degree.

§ 6. When a man dies and leaves no testament, then that person is esteemed his proximate kinsman who was the nearest of kin at the decease of the intestate. But when the deceased hath actually made a testament, then that person is esteemed his nearest of kin who was so at the time when it became certain that the testamentary heir had declined the inheritance; for till then a man who hath made a testament cannot be said to have died intestate: and thus an intestacy does not sometimes become evident till after a long time; in which space, the proximate kinsman being dead, it often happens that he becomes the nearest of kin who was not so at the death of the testator.

§ 7. But it hath obtained as law, that there should be no succession among agnates; so that if the nearest agnate is called to an inheritance, and hath either refused the heirship, or been prevented by death from entering upon it, his own legitime heir would not be admitted to succeed him. But this the prætors have in some measure corrected, and have not left the agnates of a deceased person wholly without assistance, but have ordered that they should be called to the inheritance as cognates, because they were debarred from the rights of agnation. But we, being earnestly desirous to render our law as perfect and complete as possible, have ordained by our constitution, which, induced by humanity, we published concerning the right of patronage, "that legitime succession should not be denied to agnates in the inheritances of agnates:" for it was sufficiently absurd that a right, which by means of the prætor was open to cognates, should be shut up and denied to agnates: but it was more abundantly absurd that, in tutelages, the second degree of agnates should succeed upon failure of the first; and that the same law which obtained in that which was onerous, should not also obtain in that which was lucrative.

§ 8. A parent who hath emancipated a son or a daughter, a grandson or a granddaughter, or any other of his lineal descendants under a fiduciary contract, is admitted to their legitime succession. But it is now effected by our constitution that every emancipation shall for the future be always regarded as if it had been made under such a contract; although among the ancients the parent was never called to the legitime succession of his children, unless he had actually emancipated them under a fiduciary contract.

Tit. III. *De senatusconsulto Tertylliano.*

Such was the rigour of the law of the Twelve Tables, that it preferred the issue by males, and excluded those who were related by the female line, so that the right of succession was not permitted to take place reciprocally between a mother and her son, or a mother and her daughter. But the prætors, on account of the proximity of cognation, admitted those who were related by the female line to the succession, giving them the possession of goods called *unde cognati.*

§ 1. But these narrow limits of the law were afterwards enlarged by the Emperor Claudius, who first gave the legitime inheritance of deceased children to their mothers, in assuasion of their grief for so great a loss.

§ 2. But afterwards, by the Tertyllian *senatusconsultum*, made in the reign of Adrian the emperor, the fullest care was taken that the succession of children should pass to their mother, though not to their grandmother: so that a mother who is born of free parents, and has the right of three children, and also a libertine or freedwoman who has the right of four children, may be admitted, although they are under the power of a parent, to the goods of their sons or daughters dying intestate. But when a mother is under power, it is required that she should not enter upon the inheritance of her children but at the command of him to whom she is subject.

§ 3. But when a deceased son leaves children who are proper heirs, or in the place of proper heirs, either in the first or an inferior degree, they are preferred to the mother of such deceased son. And the son or daughter of a deceased daughter is also preferred by the constitutions to the mother of the deceased daughter, *i.e.*, to their grandmother. Also the father of a son or daughter is preferred to the mother; but a grandfather or great-grandfather is not preferred to the mother when the inheritance is contended for by these only without the father. Also the consanguine brother either of a son or a daughter excluded the mother; but a consanguine sister was admitted equally with her mother. But if there had been both a brother and a sister of the same blood with the deceased, the brother of the deceased excluded his mother, although she was honoured with the privilege of those who have children: but the inheritance in this case was always divided in equal parts between brothers and sisters.

§ 4. But by a constitution, which we have inserted in the code and honoured with our name, we have thought proper that mothers should be favoured in regard to the law of nature on account of their pains in child-bearing, their great danger, and death itself, which they often suffer; we therefore have esteemed it to be highly unjust that the law should make that detrimental which is in its nature merely fortuitous; for if a married woman who is free born does not bring forth three children, or if a freedwoman does not become the mother of four children, can such persons, for that reason only, be with justice deprived of the succession of their children? for how can a failure of this nature be imputed to them as a crime? We therefore, not regarding any fixed number of children, have given a full right to every mother, whether ingenuous or a freedwoman, of being called to the legitime succession of her child or children deceased, whether male or female.

§ 5. But in examining the constitutions of former emperors relating to the right of succession, we observed that these constitutions were partly favourable to mothers and partly grievous, not always calling them to the entire inheritance of their children, but in some cases depriving them of a third, which was given to certain legitime persons, and in other cases doing the contrary, *i. e.*, allowing the mother a third only. It hath therefore seemed right to us that mothers should receive the succession of their children without any diminution, and that they should be exclusively preferred before all legitime persons, except the brothers and sisters of the deceased, whether they are consanguine or only cognate; but as we have preferred the mother to all other legitime persons, we are willing to call all brothers and sisters, legitime or otherwise, to the inheritance together with the mother; yet in such manner that if only the sisters, agnate or cognate, and the mother of the deceased, survive, the mother shall have one half of the effects and the sisters the other. But if a mother survives, and also a brother or brothers, or brothers and sisters, whether legitime or cognate, then the inheritance of the intestate son or daughter must be distributed *in capita*, *i. e.*, must be divided into equal shares.

§ 6. As we have taken a particular care of the interest of mothers, it behoves them in return to consult the welfare of their children. Be it known, therefore, that if a mother shall neglect, during the space of a whole year, to demand a tutor for her children, or shall neglect to require a new tutor in the place of a former, who hath either been removed or excused, she will be deservedly repelled from the succession of such children if they die within puberty.

§ 7. Although a son or a daughter is of spurious birth, yet the mother, by the Tertyllian *senatusconsultum*, may be admitted to succeed to the goods of either.

Tit. IV. *De senatusconsulto Orficiano.*

On the contrary, children are reciprocally admitted to the goods of their intestate mothers by the Orfician *senatusconsultum*, which was enacted in the consulate of Orficius and Rufus, in the reign of the Emperor Marcus Antoninus; and by this decree the legitime inheritance is given both to sons and daughters, although they are under power; and they are also preferred to the consanguine brothers, and to the agnates of their deceased mother.

§ 1. But since grandsons and granddaughters were not called by the *senatusconsultum* to the legitime succession of their grandmother, the omission was afterwards supplied by the imperial constitutions, so that grandsons and granddaughters were called to inherit as well as sons and daughters.

§ 2. But it must be observed that those successions which proceed from the Tertyllian and Orfician *senatusconsulta* are not extinguished by diminution; for it is an established rule that new legitime inheritances are not destroyed by diminution, but that it affects only those inheritances which proceed from the law of the Twelve Tables.

§ 3. It is lastly to be noted that even illegitimate children are admitted by the Orfician *senatusconsultum* to the inheritance of their mother.

§ 4. When there are many legitime heirs, and some renounce the inheritance, or are hindered from entering upon it by death or any other cause, then the shares or portions of such persons fall by the right of accretion to those who have accepted the inheritance; and although the acceptors happen to die even before the refusal or the failure of their co-heirs, yet the portions of such co-heirs will appertain to the heirs of the acceptors of the inheritance.

Tit. V. *De successione cognatorum.*

After the proper heirs, and those whom the prætor and the constitutions call to inherit with the proper heirs, and after the legitime heirs—among whom are the *agnati*, and those whom the above-mentioned *senatusconsulta* and our constitution have numbered with the *agnati*—the prætor calls the nearest cognates, observing the proximity of relation.

§ 1. By the law of the Twelve Tables, neither the agnates who have suffered diminution, nor their issue, are esteemed legitime heirs; but they are called by the prætor in the third order of succession: we must nevertheless except a brother and sister, although they are emancipated, but not their children; for the constitution of Anastasius calls an emancipated brother or sister to the succession of a brother or sister, together with those who have not been emancipated, and are therefore *integri juris;* but it does not call them to an equal share of the succession, as may easily be collected from the very words of the constitution. But this constitution prefers an emancipated brother or sister to other agnates of an inferior degree, although unemancipated; and consequently to all cognates in general.

§ 2. Those also who are collaterally related by the female line are called by the prætor in the third order of succession according to their proximity.

§ 3. Children who are in an adoptive family are likewise called in the third order of succession to the inheritance of their natural parents.

§ 4. It is manifest that baseborn children have no agnates, inasmuch as agnation proceeds from the father, cognation from the mother; and such children are looked upon as having no father. And, for the same reason, consanguinity cannot be said to subsist between the bastard children of the same woman, because consanguinity is a species of agnation. They can therefore only be allied to each other, as they are related to their mother, that is, by cognation; and it is for this reason that all such children are called to the possession of goods by that part of the prætorian edict by which cognates are called by the right of their proximity.

§ 5. In this place it will be necessary to observe that any person may by the right of agnation be admitted to inherit, although he is in the tenth degree; and this is allowed both by the law of the Twelve Tables, and the edict, by which the prætor promises that he will give the possession of goods to the legitime heirs. But the prætor promises the possession of goods to cognates only as far as the sixth degree of cognation, according to their right of proximity; and in the seventh degree to those cognates only who are the descendants of a cousin-german.

Tit. VI. *De gradibus cognationum.*

It is necessary in this place to show how the degrees of cognation are to be computed: and first we must observe that there is one species of cognation which relates to ascendants, another to descendants, and a third to collaterals. The first and superior cognation is that relation which a man bears to his parents; the second or inferior is that which he bears to his children; and the third is that relation which he bears to his brothers and sisters and their issue, and also to his uncles and aunts, whether paternal or maternal. The superior and inferior cognation commence at the first degree; but the transverse or collateral cognation commences at the second.

§ 1. A father or a mother is in the first degree in the right line ascending; and a son or a daughter is also in the first degree in the right line descending. A grandfather or a grandmother is in the second degree in the right line ascending; and a grandson or a granddaughter is in the second degree in the right line descending: and a brother or a sister is also in the second degree in the collateral line. A great-grandfather or a great-grandmother is in the third degree in the right line ascending; and a great-grandson or great-granddaughter is in the third degree in the right line descending: and the son or daughter of a brother or sister is also in the third degree in the collateral line; and, by a parity of reasoning, an uncle or an aunt, whether paternal or maternal, is also in the third degree. A paternal uncle, called *patruus*, is a father's brother; a maternal uncle, called *avunculus*, is a mother's brother; a paternal aunt, called *amita*, is a father's sister; and a maternal aunt, called *matertera*, is a mother's sister: and each of these persons is called in Greek θειος or θεια promiscuously.

§ 2. A great-great-grandfather or a great-great-grandmother is in the fourth degree in the right line ascending; and a great-

great-grandson or a great-great-granddaughter is in the fourth degree in the right line descending. Also in the transverse or collateral line the grandson or the granddaughter of a brother or a sister is in the fourth degree; and consequently a great-uncle or great-aunt, paternal or maternal, is in the fourth degree; and also cousins-german, who are called *consobrini*. But some have been rightly of opinion that the children of sisters are only properly called *consobrini, quasi consororini;* that the children of brothers are properly called *fratres patrueles*, or brothers *patruel*, if males, and *sorores patrueles*, or sisters *patruel*, if females; and that when there are children of a brother and children of a sister, they are properly called *amitini;* but the sons of your aunt by the father's side call you *consobrinus*, and you call them *amitini*.

§ 3. A great-grandfather's grandfather or a great-grandfather's grandmother is in the fifth degree in the line ascending, and a great-grandson or a great-granddaughter of a grandson or a granddaughter is the fifth degree in the line descending. And, in the transverse or collateral line, a great-grandson or great-granddaughter of a brother or sister is also in the fifth degree, and consequently a great-grandfather's brother or sister, or a great-grandmother's brother or sister, is in the fifth degree. The son or daughter also of a cousin-german is in the fifth degree; and so is the son or daughter of a great-uncle or great-aunt, paternal or maternal; and such son or daughter is called *propior sobrino* and *propior sobrinâ*.

§ 4. A great-grandfather's great-grandfather or a great-grandfather's great-grandmother is in the sixth degree in the line ascending, and the great-grandson or great-granddaughter of a great-grandson or a great-granddaughter is likewise in the sixth degree in the line descending. And, in the transverse or collateral line, a great-great-grandson or a great-great-granddaughter of a brother or sister is also in the sixth degree; and consequently a great-great-grandfather's brother or sister, and a great-great-grandmother's brother or sister, is in the sixth degree. And the son or daughter of a great-great-uncle or great-great-aunt, paternal or maternal, is also in the sixth degree; and so also is the son or daughter of a son or daughter of a great-uncle or great-aunt, paternal or maternal. The grandson also or the granddaughter of a cousin-german is in the sixth degree; and in the same degrees between themselves we reckon the *sobrini* and the *sobrinæ;* that is, the sons and daughters of cousins-german in general, whether such cousins-german are so related by two brothers, or by two sisters, or by a brother and a sister.

§ 5. It is sufficient to have showed thus far how the degrees of cognation are enumerated, and from the examples given it is evident in what manner we ought to compute the more remote degrees; for every person generated always adds one degree; so that it is much easier to determine in what degree any person is related to another than to denote such person by a proper term of cognation.

§ 6. The degrees of agnation are enumerated in the same manner as the degrees of cognation.

§ 7. But as truth is fixed in the mind much better by the eye than by the ear, we have therefore thought it necessary to subjoin to the account already given a tablet with the degrees of cognation inscribed upon it; that the student, both by hearing and seeing, may attain a most perfect knowledge of them. (*Vide* end of book.)

Tit. VII. *De servili cognatione.*

It is certain that the part of the edict in which the possession of goods is promised, according to the right of proximity, does not relate to servile cognation, neither hath such cognation been regarded by any ancient law. But by our own constitution concerning the right of patronage, which right was heretofore obscure and every way confused, we have ordained—humanity so suggesting—that if a slave shall have a child, or children, either by a freewoman or by a bondwoman, with whom he lives *in contubernio*, and on the contrary, that if a bondwoman shall have a child or children of either sex by a freeman, or by a slave with whom she lives *in contubernio*, and such father and mother are afterwards enfranchised, the children shall succeed to their father or mother, no regard being paid to the right of patronage.

And we have not only called these children to the succession of their parents, but also to succeed each other mutually, whether they are sole in succession, having all been born in servitude and afterwards manumitted, or whether they succeed with others who were conceived after the enfranchisement of their parents, and whether they are all by the same father and mother, or by a different father or a different mother. And, in brief, we have been willing that children born in slavery, and afterwards manumitted, should succeed in the same manner as those who are the issue of parents legally married.

§ 1. By what we have already said it appears, that those who are in an equal degree of cognation, are not always called equally to the succession; and further, that even he who is the nearest of kin is not constantly to be preferred. For, inasmuch as the first place is given to proper heirs, and to those who are numbered with proper heirs, it is apparent that the great-grandson or great-great-grandson is preferred to the brother, or even the father or mother, of the deceased; although a father and mother—as we have before observed—obtain the first degree of relation, a brother the second, a great-grandson the third, and a great-great-grandson the fourth: neither does it make any difference whether such grandchildren were under the power of the deceased at the time of his death, or out of his power, either by being emancipated, or by being the children of those who were emancipated; neither can it be objected that they are descended by the female line. But when there are no proper heirs, nor any of those who are permitted to rank with them, then an agnate, who hath the full right of agnation in him, although he is in the most distant degree, is generally preferred to a cognate, who is in the nearest degree; thus the grandson or great-grandson of a paternal uncle is preferred to an uncle or aunt who is maternal. We therefore observe, that when there are no proper heirs, nor any who are numbered with them, nor any who ought to be preferred by the right of agnation—as we have before noted—then he who is in the nearest degree of cognation is called to the succession; and that if there are many in the same degree, they are all called equally. But a brother and sister, although emancipated, are yet called to the succession of brothers and sisters; for although they have suffered diminution, they are nevertheless preferred to all agnates of a more remote degree.

Tit. VIII. *De successione libertorum.*

Let us now treat of the succession of freedmen. A freedman had it formerly in his power, without being subject to any penalty, wholly to omit in his testament any mention of his patron: for the law of the Twelve Tables called the patron to the inheritance only when the freedman died intestate, and without proper heirs; and therefore, though a freedman had died intestate, yet, if he had left a proper heir, the patron would have received no benefit; and indeed, when the natural and legitimate children of the deceased became his heirs, there seemed no cause of complaint; but when the freedman left only an adopted son, it was manifestly injurious that the patron should have no claim.

§ 1. The law was therefore afterwards amended by the edict of the prætor; for every freedman who made his testament was commanded so to dispose of his effects as to leave a moiety to his patron; or if the testator left nothing, or less than a moiety, then the possession of half was given to the patron *contra tabulas, i. e.*, contrary to the disposition of the testament. And if a freedman died intestate, leaving an adopted son his heir, the possession of a moiety of the effects was in this case also given to the patron, notwithstanding such heir; yet not only the natural and lawful children of a freedman, whom he had under his power at the time of his death, excluded the patron, but those children also who were emancipated, and given in adoption, if they were written heirs for any part, or even although they were omitted, if they had requested the possession *contra tabulas* by virtue of the prætorian edict. But disinherited children by no means repelled the patron.

§ 2. But afterwards the rights of those patrons who had wealthy freedmen were enlarged by the Papian law, by which it is provided, that an equal share shall be due to the patron out of the effects of his freedman, whether dying testate or intestate, who hath left a patrimony of a hundred thousand *sestertii*, and fewer than three children; so that when a freedman hath left only one son or daughter, then a moiety of the effects is due to the patron, as if the deceased had died testate without either son or daughter. But when there are two heirs, male or female, a third part only is due to the patron; and when there are three, the patron is wholly excluded.

§ 3. But by our imperial constitution—which we have caused to be promulged in the Greek language for the benefit of all nations—we have ordained that if a freedman or freedwoman dies possessed of less than a hundred *aurei*—for thus have we interpreted the sum mentioned in the Papian law, counting one *aureus* for a thousand *sestertii*—the patron shall not be entitled to any share in the succession where there is a will. But if either a freedman or a freedwoman dies intestate and without children, we have in this case reserved the right of patronage entire, as it formerly was, according to the law of the Twelve Tables. But if a freed person dies worth more than a hundred *aurei*, and leaves one child, or many, of either sex or any degree, as the heirs and possessors of his goods, we have permitted that such child or children shall succeed their parent to the entire exclusion of the patron and his heirs: and if any freed persons die without children and intestate, we have called their patrons or patronesses to their whole inheritances. And if any freed person worth more than a hundred *aurei* hath made a testament, omitted his patron, and left no children, or hath disinherited them; or if a mother or maternal grandfather, being freed persons, have omitted to mention their children in their wills, so that such wills cannot be proved to be inofficious, then, by virtue of our constitution, the patron shall succeed not to a moiety as formerly, but to the third part of the estate of the deceased, by the possession of the goods called *contra tabulas*: and when freed persons, men or women, leave less than the third part of their effects to their patrons, our constitution ordains, that the deficiency shall be supplied; and that this third part due to patrons shall not be subject to the burden of trusts or legacies, even for the benefit of the children of the deceased; for the coheirs only of the patron shall be loaded with this burden. In the before-mentioned constitution we have collected many more cases, which we have thought necessary in relation to the right of patronage, that patrons and patronesses, their children, and collateral relations, as far as the fifth degree, might be called to the succession of their freedmen and freedwomen, as will appear more fully from our ordinance itself. And if there are many children of one patron or patroness, or of two or more patrons or patronesses, he who is nearest in degree is called to the succession of his freedman or freedwoman; and when there are many in equal degree, the estate must be divided *in capita* and not *in stirpes;* and the same order is decreed to be observed among the collaterals of patrons and patronesses; for we have rendered the laws of succession almost the same in regard to the *ingenui* and *libertini*.

§ 4. But what we have said relates to the *libertini* of the present time, who are all citizens of Rome; for there is now no other species of freedmen, that of the *dedititii* and *Latini* being abolished; the latter of whom never enjoyed any right of succession; for although they led the lives of freedmen, yet with their last breath they lost both their lives and liberties: for their possessions, like the goods of slaves, were detained by their manumitter, who possessed them as a *peculium* by virtue of the law *Junia Norbana*. It was afterwards provided by the *senatus-consultum Largianum* that the children of a manumitter, who were not nominally disinherited, should be preferred to any strangers whom a manumitter might constitute his heirs. Then followed the edict of Trajan, which ordained that if a slave, either against the will or without the knowledge of his patron, should obtain the freedom of Rome by the favour of the emperor, such slave should continue free whilst living, but at his death should be regarded only as a Latin. But we, being averse to these changes of condition and dissatisfied with the difficulties attending them, have thought proper, by virtue of our constitution, for ever to abolish, together with the Latins, the law *Junia*, the *senatus-consultum Largianum*, and the edict of Trajan, to the intent that all freedmen may become freedmen of Rome. And we have happily contrived by some additions that the manner of conferring the freedom of Latins should now become the manner of conferring the freedom of Rome.

Tit. IX. *De assignatione libertorum.*

In regard to the possession of freedmen, it must be remembered that the senate hath decreed that although the goods of freedmen belong equally to all the children of the patron who are in the same degree, yet it is lawful for a parent to assign a freedman to any one of his children, so that after the death of the parent the child, to whom the freedman was assigned, is solely to be esteemed his patron; and the other children, who would have been equally admitted to a dividend of the goods of the freedman had he not been assigned, are wholly excluded; but if the assignee happens to die without issue the excluded children regain their former right.

§ 1. Every freed person is assignable, whether man or woman; and an assignment may be made not only to a son or grandson, but to a daughter or granddaughter.

§ 2. The power of assigning freed persons is given to him who hath two or more children unemancipated, so that a father may assign a freedman or freedwoman to those children whom he retains under his power; and hence it became a question if a father should assign a freedman to his son, and afterwards emancipate that son, whether the assignment would or would not be null? and the decision hath been in the affirmative; which hath been approved of by Julian and many others.

§ 3. But it makes no difference whether the assignment of a freedman is made by testament or not by testament; for patrons may assign even by word of mouth; which was permitted by the *senatusconsultum* made in the reign of Claudian, in the consulate of Sabellius Rufus and Asterius Scapula.

Tit. X. *De bonorum possessionibus.*

The right of succeeding by the possession of goods was introduced by the prætor in amendment of the ancient law, which he corrected, not only in regard to the inheritances of intestates—as we have before observed—but in regard also to the inheritances of those who die testate; for if a posthumous stranger was instituted an heir, although he could not enter upon the inheritance by the civil law, inasmuch as his institution as heir would not be valid, yet by the prætorian or honorary law he might be made the possessor of the goods when he had received the assistance of the prætor. But such stranger may at this time, by virtue of our constitution, be legally instituted an heir, being no longer regarded as a person unknown to the civil law. But the prætor sometimes bestows the possession of goods, intending neither to amend nor impugn the old law, but only to confirm it; for he gives the possession of goods *secundum tabulas* to those who are appointed the heirs of the deceased by a regular testament. He also calls proper heirs and agnates to the possession of the goods of intestates; and yet the inheritance would be their own by the civil law, although the prætor did not interpose his authority. But those whom the prætor calls to an inheritance merely by virtue of his office do not become legal heirs, inasmuch as the prætor cannot make an heir; for heirs are made only by a *lex*, or what has the effect of a *lex*, as a decree of the senate, or an imperial constitution. But when the prætor gives any persons the possession of goods, they stand in the place of heirs, and are called the possessors of the goods. But the prætor hath also devised many other orders of persons to whom the possession of goods can be granted, to the intent that no man may die without a successor; and by the rules of justice and equity, he hath greatly enlarged the right of taking inheritances, which was bounded within the most narrow limits by the laws of the Twelve Tables.

§ 1. The kinds or species of the possessions of goods or prætorian successions, when there is a testament, are the following. The first is that possession which is given to children of whom no mention is made in the testament, and this is called *possessio contra tabulas, i. e.*, a possession contrary to the testament. The second is that which the prætor promises to all written heirs, and it is therefore called *secundum tabulas, i. e.*, a possession according to the testament. These being fixed, the prætor proceeded to the possession of goods in regard to intestates: and first he gives the possession of goods called *unde liberi* to the proper heirs, or to those who by the prætorian edict are numbered among the proper heirs: secondly, to the legitime heirs: thirdly, to ten persons, in preference to a stranger, who was the manumitter, viz., to a father, a mother, or a grandfather or grandmother, paternal or maternal; to a son, a daughter, or to a grandson or granddaughter, as well by a daughter as by a son; to a brother or sister, either consanguine or uterine: fourthly, to the nearest cognates: fifthly, to those who are, as it were, of the family, *tanquam ex familiâ:* sixthly, to the patron or patroness, and to their children, and their parents: seventhly, to a husband and wife: eighthly, to the cognates of a manumitter or patron.

§ 2. The prætor's authority hath introduced these successions; but we, not suffering any useless institution to continue in the law, have nevertheless admitted by our constitutions the possession of goods *contra tabulas* and *secundum tabulas* as necessary, and also the possession of goods *ab intestato*, called *unde liberi* and *unde legitimi:* but we have briefly showed that the possession called *unde decem personæ*, which was ranked by the prætor's edict in the fifth order, was unnecessary: for, whereas that possession preferred ten kinds of persons to a stranger, who was the manumitter at emancipation, our constitution, which regards emancipation, hath permitted all parents to manumit their children, a fiduciary contract being presumed; so that the possession *unde decem personæ* is now useless. The afore-mentioned fifth possession being thus abrogated, we have now made that the fifth which was formerly the sixth, by which the prætor gives the succession to the nearest cognates. And whereas formerly the possession of goods called *tanquam ex famaliâ* was in the seventh place, and the possession of goods called *unde patroni patronæque, liberi et parentes eorum*, was in the eighth, we have now annulled them both by our ordinance concerning the right of patronage. And having brought the successions of the *libertini* to a similitude with those of the *ingenui*,—except that we have limited the former to the fifth degree, so that there may still remain some difference between them,—we think, that the possessions *contra tabulas, unde legitimi*, and *unde cognati*, may suffice, by which all persons may vindicate their rights, the niceties and inextricable errors of those two kinds of possessions, *tanquam ex familiâ* and *unde patroni* being removed. The other possession of goods called *vir et uxor*, which held the ninth place among the ancient possessions, we have preserved in full force, and have placed in a higher degree, namely, the sixth. The tenth of the ancient possessions, called *unde cognati manumissoris*, being deservedly abrogated for causes already enumerated, there now remain only in force six ordinary possessions of goods.

§ 3. But to these a seventh possession hath been added, which the prætors have introduced with the greatest reason: for by edict this possession of goods is promised to all those to whom it is appointed to be given by any law, *senatusconsultum*, or constitution: and the prætor hath not positively numbered this possession of goods either with the possessions of the goods of intestate or testate persons, but hath given it, according to the exigence of the case, as the last and extraordinary resource of those who are called to the successions of testates or intestates, by any particular law, any decree of the senate, or any new constitution.

§ 4. The prætor, having introduced many kinds of successions, and ranked them in order, hath thought proper, inasmuch as many persons of different degrees are often found in one species of succession, to limit a certain time for demanding the possession of goods, to the intent that the actions of creditors may not be delayed for want of a proper person against whom to bring them, and that the creditors themselves may not obtain the possession of the effects of the deceased too easily, and so consult solely their own advantage: therefore to parents and children, whether natural or adopted, the prætor hath given the space of one year, in which they may either accept or refuse the possession of goods. But to all other persons, agnates or cognates, he allows only a hundred days.

§ 5. And if any person entitled does not claim the possession of goods within the time limited, his right of possession accrues first to those in the same degree with himself; and in default of persons in the same degree, then the prætor by the successory edict bestows the possession of goods upon those in the next degree, as if he who preceded had no right. And if any man refuses the possession of goods when it is open to him, there is no necessity to wait till the time limited is expired, but those who are the next in succession may be instantly admitted by virtue of the before-mentioned edict.

§ 6. It is here to be observed, that, in regard to the time prescribed for demanding the possession of goods, we count all the days which are *utiles.*

§ 7. The emperors our predecessors have wisely provided in this case, that no person need be solicitous to demand the possession of goods in solemn form: for if by any act it manifestly appears that a man has in any manner consented to accept the prætorian succession within the prescribed time, he shall enjoy the full benefit of it.

Tit. XI. *De acquisitione per arrogationem.*

There is also an universal succession of another kind, which was introduced neither by the laws of the Twelve Tables, nor by the edict of the prætor, but by that law which takes its rise from general consent and usage.

§ 1. For example, if the father of a family gave himself in arrogation, all things which appertained to him, whether corporeal or incorporeal, and whatever was due to him, became anciently the property of the arrogator; those things only excepted which perished by diminution or change of state, as the duties of freedmen to their patrons and the rights of agnation. But although use and usufruct were heretofore numbered among those rights which perished by diminution, yet our constitution hath prohibited, that the use and usufruct of things should be taken away by the least diminution or change of state.

§ 2. But we have now limited the acquisitions obtained by arrogation, in similitude of what is gained by natural parents: for nothing is now acquired either by natural or adoptive parents but the bare usufruct of those things which their children possess adventitiously and extrinsically in their own right, the property still remaining entire in the adopted or natural child. But if an arrogated son dies under the power of his arrogator, then even the property of the effects of such son will pass to the arrogator in default of those persons, whom we have by our constitution preferred to the father in the succession of those things which could not be acquired for him.

§ 3. On the contrary, an arrogator is not bound at law to satisfy the debts of his adopted son in consequence of a direct action; but yet he may be convened in his son's name; and if he refuses to defend his son, then the creditors, by order of the proper magistrates, may seize upon and legally sell all those goods, of which the usufruct, as well as the property, would both have been in the debtor, if he had not made himself subject to the power of another.

Tit. XII. *De eo, cui libertatis causâ bona addicuntur.*

A new species of succession hath taken its rise from the constitution of Marcus Aurelius. For if those slaves, to whom freedom hath been bequeathed, are desirous, for the sake of obtaining it, that the inheritance, which hath not been accepted by the written heir, should be adjudged for their benefit, they shall obtain their request.

§ 1. And to the same effect is the rescript of the Emperor Marcus to Pompilius Rufus; the words of which are these: "If the estate of Virginius Valens, who by testament hath bequeathed to certain persons their freedom, must necessarily be sold, and there is no successor *ab intestato*, then the magistrate who has the cognizance of these affairs shall upon application hear the merits of your cause, that, for the sake of preserving the liberty of those to whom it was given, either directly or in trust, the estate of the deceased may be adjudged to you, on condition that you give good security to the creditors to pay them the whole of their just demands. And all those to whom freedom was directly given shall then become free, as if the inheritance had been entered upon by the written heir; but those whom the heir was ordered to manumit shall obtain their freedom from you only. And if you are not willing that the goods of the deceased should be adjudged to you on any other condition than that even they who received their liberty directly by testament shall also become your freedmen, we then order that your will shall be complied with, if the persons agree to it who are to receive their freedom. And, lest the use and emolument of this our rescript should be frustrated by any other means, be it known to the officers of our revenue, that whenever our exchequer lays claim to the estate of a deceased person, the cause of liberty is to be preferred to any pecuniary advantage; and that the estate shall be so seized as to preserve the freedom of those who could otherwise have obtained it; and this in as full a manner as if the inheritance had been entered upon by the testamentary heir."

§ 2. The contents of this rescript are calculated not only in favour of liberty, but also for the benefit of deceased persons, lest their effects should be seized and sold by their creditors; for it is certain that when goods are adjudged to a particular man for the preservation of liberty, a sale by creditors can never take effect: for he to whom the goods are adjudged is the protector of the deceased, and must always be a person who can give security for the full payment of creditors.

§ 3. This rescript takes place whenever freedom is conferred by testament. But when a master dies intestate, having bequeathed freedom to his slaves by codicil, and his inheritance is not entered upon, what will then be the consequence? We answer, that the favour of the rescript shall extend to this case; but it is most certainly not to be doubted that, if a master dies testate, and by codicil bequeaths freedom, the rescript shall be of full force.

§ 4. The words of the rescript show that it is then in force when there is absolutely no successor *ab intestato*. It therefore follows that as long as it remains doubtful whether there is or is not a successor, the constitution shall not take place; but when once it is certain that no one will enter upon the succession, the ordinance shall then have its effect.

§ 5. But if he who has a right to be restored *in integrum*—as a minor for example—should delay to take upon him the inheritance of his father, it may then be asked whether, notwithstanding this right of being restored, the constitution shall take place, and an adjudication of the goods pass to a stranger, or one of the slaves? And, again, it may be demanded what will be the consequence, if, after an adjudication has been made for the sake of liberty, the heir should be restored *in integrum?* We answer that freedom, when once obtained, shall not afterwards be revoked.

§ 6. This constitution was made for the protection of liberty; and therefore, when freedom is not given, the constitution has no effect. Suppose, then, that a master hath given freedom to his slaves, either *inter vivos* or *mortis causâ*, and that they, to prevent the creditors from complaining that this was done to defraud them, should petition that the estate of the deceased may be adjudged to them. Are these persons to be heard? We answer, that we incline to grant their request, although in this case the letter of the constitution is deficient.

§ 7. But perceiving that the rescript was deficient in many respects, we enacted a most express constitution containing many cases which explain the rights of succession in the fullest manner, of which every person who reads that condition will be sensible.

Tit. XIII. *De successionibus sublatis quæ fiebant per bonorum venditiones, et ex senatusconsulto Claudiano.*

There were many other kinds of universal successions before that which we treated of in the foregoing title; as the *bonorum emptio*, which was first introduced that the estates of debtors might be sold; but this was accompanied by many intricate and tedious proceedings. It continued, nevertheless, as long as the ordinary judgments were in practice; but as soon as the extraordinary judgments were made use of, the solemn *emptio bonorum* ceased at the same time with the ordinary judgments. And creditors can now possess themselves of the goods of their debtors, and dispose of them as they think most proper, by the decree of a judge. But these points are treated of more perfectly and at large in the books of our digests. There was also, by virtue of the Claudian decree, another universal acquisition, called *miserabilis;* for example, if a freewoman had debased herself by being enamoured of a slave she lost her freedom by the before-named decree, and, together with her freedom, her estate and substance. But it being our opinion that this part of the decree was unworthy of our reign, and ought therefore to be expunged from our laws, we have not permitted it to be inserted in the digests.

Tit. XIV. *De obligationibus.*

Let us now pass to obligations. An obligation is the chain of the law, by which we are necessarily bound to make some payment, according to the laws of our country.

§ 1. Obligations are primarily divided into two kinds, civil and prætorian. Civil obligations are those which are constituted by the laws, or by any species of the civil law. Prætorian obligations are those which the prætor hath appointed by his authority; and these are also called honorary.

§ 2. The second or subsequent division of obligations contains four species: for some obligations arise by contract, others by quasi-contract; some by malfeasance, and others by quasi-malfeasance. We must first treat of those obligations which arise from a contract; and of these there are also four kinds: for obligations are contracted by the thing itself, by word of mouth, by writing, or by the mere consent of parties. Let us now take a separate view of each of these methods of contracting.

Tit. XV. *Quibus modis re contrahitur obligatio.*

An obligation is contracted by the thing itself, that is, by the delivery of it, as a loan or *mutuum:* and any particular thing which consists of weight, number, or measure, as wine, oil, corn, coin, brass, silver, gold, may be delivered as a *mutuum;* and these substances, when so delivered, become in specie the absolute property of the receiver: and since the very identical things lent cannot be restored, but others of the same nature and quality must be paid in lieu of them, this loan is therefore called a *mutuum;* for in this case "I so give, that what is mine may become yours," *ut ex meo tuum fiat.* From this contract arises that action which is called *certi condictio.*

§ 1. He also who hath received what was not due to him, it being paid or delivered by mistake, is bound by the thing received, so that an action of *condictio* lies against him for the recovery of the thing at the suit of him who paid or delivered it erroneously. And this action may be brought against the receiver in these words, "*Si apparet, eum dare oportere,*" in the same manner as if he had accepted the thing delivered as a *mutuum.* And hence it is that a pupil, when a payment of anything not due hath been made to him without the authority of his tutor, is not subject to the action called *condictio indebiti,* because he is not subject to an action on account of the delivery of the thing, as a *mutuum.* And yet this species of obligation does not seem to proceed from a contract; since he who pays with an intention to satisfy his debts appears more willing to dissolve than to make a contract.

§ 2. He also to whom the use of any particular thing is granted or commodated is bound by the delivery of the thing, and is subject to an action called *commodataria.* But such person widely differs from him who hath received a *mutuum;* for a *commodatum,* or thing lent, is not delivered to the intent that it should become the property of the receiver; and therefore he is bound to restore the identical thing which he hath received. There is also another difference; for he who hath accepted a *mutuum* is not freed from his obligation if even by any accident, as by the fall of an edifice, fire, shipwreck, thieves, or the incursions of an enemy, he hath lost what he hath received; but he who hath received a *commodatum,* or a thing lent for his use only, is indeed commanded to employ his utmost diligence in keeping and preserving it,—and it will not suffice that he hath taken the same care of it which he was accustomed to take of his own property if it appears that a more diligent man might have preserved it;—yet if it is evident that the loss of it was occasioned by a superior force or some extraordinary accident, and not by any fault, he is then not obliged to make good the loss; but if a man by choice will travel with what he has received as a *commodatum* or loan, and should lose it by shipwreck, or by the incursion of enemies or robbers, it is not to be doubted but that he is bound to make restitution, or to pay an equivalent. A thing is properly said to be lent or commodated when one man permits another to enjoy the use of it, and receives nothing by way of hire; but if a price for hire is paid the thing is let, and not lent, for a *commodatum* or loan must be gratuitous.

§ 3. Any person who is entrusted with a deposit is bound by the delivery of the thing, and is subject to an action of deposit, because he is under an obligation of making restitution of that very thing which he received. But a depositary is only thus answerable on account of fraud; for where a fault only can be proved against him, such as negligence, he is under no obligation; and he is therefore secure if the thing deposited is stolen from him, even although it was carelessly kept. For he who commits his goods to the care of a negligent friend should impute the loss of them not to his friend, but to his own facility and want of caution.

§ 4. A creditor also, who hath received a pledge, is bound by the delivery of it; for he is obliged to restore the very thing which he hath received, by the action called *pigneratitia.* But inasmuch as a pledge is given for the mutual service of both debtor and creditor—of the debtor that he may obtain the money the more easily, and of the creditor that the repayment may be the better secured—it will suffice if the creditor shall appear to have used an exact diligence in keeping the thing pledged; for if such diligence appears to have been used, and the pledge was lost by mere accident, the law secures the creditor as to the loss of the thing pledged, and he is by no means impeded to sue his debt.

Tit. XVI. *De verborum obligationibus.*

An obligation in words is made by question and answer, when we stipulate that anything shall be given or done; and from hence arise two actions, viz., the action called *condictio certi,* when the stipulation is certain, and the action called *condictio ex stipulatu,* when the stipulation is uncertain. This obligation is called a stipulation because whatever was firm was termed *stipulum* by the ancients; the word *stipulum* being probably derived from *stipes,* denoting the trunk of a tree.

§ 1. The following words were probably used in all verbal obligations:—

Spondes? *Spondeo.*
Promittis? *Promitto.*
Fide-promittis? *Fide-promitto.*
Fide-jubes? *Fide-jubeo.*
Dabis? *Dabo.*
Facies? *Faciam.*

And it is not material whether the stipulation is conceived in Latin, Greek, or any other language, if the stipulating parties understand it: neither is it necessary that the same language should be used by each person, for it is sufficient if a congruent and pertinent answer is made to each question. It is, moreover, certain that two Greeks may contract in Latin. Anciently, indeed, it was necessary to use those solemn words before recited, but the constitution of the Emperor Leo was afterwards enacted, which takes away this verbal solemnity, and requires only the apprehension and consent of each party, expressed in any form of words.

§ 2. Every stipulation is made to be performed simply, or at a day certain, or conditionally. A stipulation is made to be performed simply, when a man says, "Do you promise to pay me five *aurei?*" and in this case the money may be instantly demanded. A stipulation is made to be performed at a day certain, when the day is added on which the money is to be paid, as when a man says, "Do you promise to pay me ten *aurei* on the 1st of March?" but note that what we stipulate to pay at a day certain, though it becomes immediately due, yet it cannot be demanded before the day comes; nor can it even then be sued for; for the whole day must be allowed for payment, because it can never be certain that there hath been a failure of payment on the day promised until that day is quite expired.

§ 3. But if a man thus stipulates, viz., "Do you promise to give me ten *aurei* annually as long as I live?" the obligation is understood to be made purely or simply, and becomes perpetual, so as to bind the heirs of the obliger; for an obligation cannot continue due for a time certain only; yet if the heir of the stipulator demands payment, he shall be barred by an exception of agreement.

§ 4. A stipulation is conditional, when an obligation is referred to an accident, and depends upon something to be done or not done, to happen or not to happen, before the stipulation can take effect; for instance, if a man stipulates thus, "Do you promise to pay me five *aurei* if Titius is made a consul?" or thus, "Do you promise to pay me five *aurei* if I do not ascend the Capitol?" which last stipulation is in effect the same as if he had stipulated that five *aurei* should be paid to him at the time of his death. It is to be observed that in every conditional stipulation there is only a hope that the thing stipulated will become due, and this hope a man transmits to his heirs if he dies before the event of the condition.

§ 5. Even places are often inserted in a stipulation, as, for example, "Do you promise to give me such a particular thing at Carthage?" and this stipulation, though it appears to be made simply, yet in reality carries with it a space of time, which the obliger may make use of to enable himself to pay the money promised at Carthage. And therefore, if a man at Rome should stipulate in these words, "Do you promise to pay me a sum of money this day at Carthage?" the stipulation would be null, because the performance of it would be impossible.

§ 6. Conditions which relate to the time present or past either instantly annul an obligation, or instantly enforce it; for example, if a man should thus stipulate, "Do you promise me the payment of a sum of money if Titius hath ever been a consul?" or thus, "If Mævius is now living?" If these things are not so, that is, if Titius hath never been a consul, and Mævius is not now living, the stipulation is void; and if they are so, that is, if Titius hath been a consul, and Mævius is actually living, then the stipulation is good, and may be enforced; for events which in themselves are certain delay not the performance of an obligation, although to us they are not certain.

§ 7. Not only things, as a field, a slave, or a book, but also acts, may be the subject of stipulations; as when we stipulate that something shall or shall not be done. And in these stipulations it will be right to subjoin a penalty, lest the value of the stipulation should be uncertain, and the demandant should therefore be forced to prove how far he is interested in it. And therefore, if a man stipulates that something shall be done, a penalty ought to be thus added, "Do you not promise to pay me ten *aurei* as a penalty if the act stipulated is not performed?" But if it is agreed in the same obligation that some things shall be done, and that others shall not be done, then ought some such clause as the following to be added: "Do you promise to pay me ten *aurei* as a penalty if anything is done contrary to agreement, or if anything is not done according to our agreement?"

Tit. XVII. *De duobus reis stipulandi et promittendi.*

Two or more persons may stipulate, and two or more may become obligers. The stipulating parties are bound, if, after all questions have been asked, the obliger answers, "I promise"; as when, for example, the obliger thus answers two persons separately stipulating, "I promise to pay each of you." For if he first promises Titius, and afterwards promises another who interrogates him, there will then be two obligations, and not two stipulators to one obligation. Two or more become obligers if, after they have been thus interrogated, "Mævius, do you promise to pay us ten *aurei?*" and "Seius, do you promise to pay us the same ten *aurei?*" they each of them answer separately, "I do promise."

§ 1. By these stipulations and obligations, the whole sum stipulated becomes due to every person stipulating, and every obliger is bound for the payment of the whole. But as one and the same thing is due by each obligation, therefore any one of the stipulators by receiving the debt, and any one of the obligers by paying it, discharges the obligation of the rest, and frees all parties.

§ 2. Where there are two obligers, the one may bind himself purely and simply, and the other may oblige himself only to make payment on a day certain, or upon condition: but neither the day certain nor the condition will secure the person, who is simply bound, from being sued for the payment of the whole.

Tit. XVIII. *De stipulationibus servorum.*

A slave obtains the liberty of stipulating from the person of his master; but in many instances the inheritance represents the person of a master deceased; and therefore, whatever an hereditary slave stipulates for before the inheritance is entered upon, he acquires it for the inheritance, and of course for him who afterwards becomes the heir.

§ 1. A slave, let him stipulate how he will, for his master, for himself, for a fellow-slave, or generally without naming any person, always acquires for his master. And the same obtains among children who are under the power of their father, in regard to those things which they can acquire for him.

§ 2. But when a fact or thing to be done is contained in a stipulation, the person of the stipulator is solely regarded; so that if even a slave stipulates that he shall be permitted to pass through a field, and to drive beasts or a carriage through it, it is not the master, but the slave only, who is to be permitted to pass.

§ 3. If a slave, who is in common to several masters, stipulates, he acquires a share for each master according to the proportion which each has in the property of him. But if such should stipulate at the command of any particular master, or in his name, the thing stipulated will be acquired solely for that master. And whatever a slave in common to two masters stipulates for, if part cannot be acquired for one master, the whole shall be acquired for the other; as when the thing stipulated already belongs to one of the two.

Tit. XIX. *De divisione stipulationum.*

Some stipulations are judicial, others prætorian, others conventional, and others common, that is, both prætorian and judicial.

§ 1. The judicial are those which proceed merely from the office of the judge; as when security is ordered to be given against fraud, or for pursuing a slave who hath fled, or for paying the price of him.

§ 2. The prætorian stipulations are those which proceed from the mere office of the prætor; as when security is ordered to be given *pro damno infecto*, that is, on account of damage not yet done, but likely to happen; and for the payment of legacies. And note, that under prætorian stipulations we comprehend the *Edilitian*, for these proceed from the jurisdiction of the prætor.

§ 3. Conventional stipulations are those which are made by the agreement of parties; that is, neither by order of a judge nor prætor, but by the consent of the persons contracting; and of these stipulations there are as many kinds, as of things to be contracted for.

§ 4. Common stipulations are those which are ordered for the security of the effects of a pupil,—for the prætor ordains a caution to be given on this account, and sometimes a judge decrees it, when there is an absolute necessity,—or for the ratification of a thing done in another's name.

Tit. XX. *De inutilibus stipulationibus.*

Everything of which we have the property may be brought into stipulation, whether it is moveable or immoveable.

§ 1. But if a man hath stipulated that a thing shall be given, which does not or cannot exist, as, for instance, that Stichus the slave, who is dead, but is thought to be living, or that a Centaur, who cannot exist, should be given to him, the stipulation is of no force.

§ 2. And the law is the same, if a thing sacred, which was thought to be not so, is brought into stipulation; or if a man stipulates for a thing of constant public use, as a forum or a theatre; or for a free person, who was thought to be bond; or for a thing which he cannot acquire; or for something which is already his own: nor shall any such stipulation continue in suspense, because a thing public may become private, a freeman may turn slave, a stipulator may become capable of acquiring, or because what now belongs to the stipulator may cease to be his; but every such stipulation shall be instantly void. And, on the contrary, although a thing may properly be brought into stipulation at first, yet, if it afterwards falls under the class of any of the things before mentioned without the fault of the obliger, the stipulation is extinguished. And such a stipulation as the following shall never be valid: for instance—"Do you promise to give me Lucius Titius when he shall become a slave?" for those things, which in their natures are exempt from our dominion, are by no means to be brought into obligation.

§ 3. If a man promises that another shall give or do something, such promissor shall not be bound; as if a man should promise that Titius shall pay five *aurei:* but if he promises that he will cause Titius to pay five *aurei*, his promise shall be binding.

§ 4. If a man stipulates for any other than for him to whom he is subject, such stipulation is a void act; but, nevertheless, a payment of a thing promised may be made to a stranger; as if a man should thus stipulate—"Do you promise to make payment to me, or to Seius?" for when the obligation is to the stipulator, the payment may well be made to Seius, though against his will; and this is allowed in favour of the debtor, that he may be legally freed from his debt; and the stipulator, if there is occasion, may have an action of mandate against Seius. And if a man should stipulate, that ten *aurei* shall be paid to him and to another not under his power, the stipulation would be good; yet it hath been a doubt, whether the whole sum due would be due to the stipulator, or only a moiety; and it hath been resolved, that the stipulator in this case acquires a moiety only. But if you stipulate for another who is subject to your power, you acquire for yourself; for your own words are reputed your son's, and your son's words are reputed yours, in regard to all those things which can possibly be acquired for you.

§ 5. A stipulation is void, if the party interrogated does not answer pertinently to the demand made; as when a person stipulates that ten *aurei* shall be paid him, and you answer five; or, *vice versâ*, if he stipulates for five, and you answer "I promise ten." A stipulation is also void if a man stipulates simply, and you promise conditionally; or, on the contrary, if he stipulates conditionally, and you answer purely, and in express terms; that is, if, when a man is stipulating conditionally or at a day certain, you answer him thus—"I promise you payment on this present day." But if you answer only, "I promise," you seem in brief speech to agree to his day or condition. For it is not necessary that in the answer every word should be repeated which the stipulator expressed.

§ 6. A stipulation is also void if you stipulate with him who is in subjection to your power, or if he stipulates with you. For a slave is not only incapable of entering into an obligation with his master, but is also incapable of binding himself to any other person. But the son of a family can enter into an obligation with any other person except his father.

§ 7. It is evident, that a dumb man can neither stipulate nor promise; and the same law is received in regard to deaf persons; for he who stipulates, ought to hear the words of the obliger; and he who promises, the words of the stipulator. But we speak not of him who hears with difficulty, but of him who has no hearing.

§ 8. A madman can transact no business, because he understands not what he does.

§ 9. A pupil is capable of transacting any business if his tutor consents, where his authority is necessary; as it certainly is, when the pupil would bind himself: but a pupil can stipulate, or cause others to be bound to him, without the authority of his tutor. What we have said of pupils must be understood of those who have some understanding; for an infant, or one next to an infant, differs but little from a person out of his senses; for pupils of such an age have no understanding; but a more favourable interpretation is given to the law in regard to those who are but little removed from infancy, whenever their own utility is concerned, so that they are then allowed the same rights as those who are near the age of puberty. But a son who is under the power of his father, and within the age of puberty, cannot bind himself, even although his father consents and authorizes the transaction.

§ 10. If an impossible condition is added to an obligation, the stipulation is null; and that condition is reckoned impossible of which nature forbids the event; as, for example, if a man should say, "Do you promise me ten *aurei* if I touch the heavens with my finger?" but suppose a stipulation to be thus made—"Do you promise me payment if I do not touch the sky with my finger?" such a stipulation would be understood to cause a simple obligation, the performance of which might be instantly demanded.

§ 11. A verbal obligation made between absent persons is also void. But when this doctrine afforded matter of strife to contentious men, alleging, after some time past, that either they or the other parties were not present, we issued our constitution addressed as a rescript to the advocates of Cæsarea, which effectually provided for the speedy determination of such suits: and by this we have ordained that full credit shall be given to those written acts or instruments which declare that the contracting parties were present, unless the party who alleges absence makes it evident by the most manifest proofs, either in writing or by witnesses, that either he or his adversary was in some other place during the whole day in which the instrument was made.

§ 12. A man could formerly no more stipulate that a thing should be given him after his own death than he could stipulate that a thing should be given him after the death of the obliger. Neither could any person under the power of another stipulate that anything should be given him after his death, because such person would appear to speak the words of his father or master. And if a man had stipulated in this manner—"Do you promise to give me five *aurei* the day before I die, or the day before you die?" the stipulation was also invalid. But since all stipulations, as we have already said, take their rise and force from the consent of the contracting parties, we have thought it proper to introduce a necessary emendation in this respect, so that whether it is stipulated that a thing shall be given after, or immediately before, the death either of the stipulator or the obliger, the stipulation shall be good.

§ 13. Also, if a man had stipulated in these words—"Do you promise me a sum of money to-day if a certain ship arrives to-morrow from Asia?" the stipulation would have been invalid because preposterously conceived. But since the Emperor Leo, of renowned memory, was of opinion that such stipulations ought not to be rejected in regard to marriage portions, it hath pleased us also to give a fuller force to this doctrine, by ordaining that every stipulation of like import shall hold good not only in marriage portions, but likewise in all other contracts.

§ 14. If a stipulation had been conceived in the following words—"Do you promise to give me ten *aurei* at the time when I shall die?" or thus, "at the time when you shall die?" it was good by the ancient law, and is now valid.

§ 15. We may also legally stipulate that a thing shall be given after the death of a third person.

§ 16. If it is written in an act or instrument properly attested that a man hath entered into an obligation by promise, it will be always presumed that the promise was in answer to a precedent interrogation, and that everything was done regularly.

§ 17. When many things are comprehended in one stipulation, a man binds himself to give them all if he answers simply, "I promise." But if he promises to give one or some of the things stipulated, an obligation is contracted only in respect to those things which he promised to give. For where there are many stipulations it may happen that only one or some of them may be made perfect by a separate answer; and strictly we ought to stipulate for everything severally, and to answer severally.

§ 18. No man can stipulate for another, as we have already observed; for stipulations and obligations have been invented, that every person may acquire for himself whatever may be of advantage to him; and if this is given to another, the stipulator has no interest. But if a man would effectually contract for another, he should stipulate, that unless the covenants of his stipulation are performed, the obliger shall be subject to a penalty, payable to him, who otherwise would receive no advantage from the obligation: for when a penalty is stipulated, the advantage or interest of the stipulator is not regarded, but the quantity of the penalty is the only thing considered. And therefore, if a man should stipulate, that a certain thing shall be given to Titius, it will not avail; but if to the stipulation he adds a penalty, as thus,—"Do you promise to give me ten *aurei*, if you do not give the thing stipulated to Titius?" the stipulation of the penalty will take place if the obligation is not performed.

§ 19. But if any man stipulates for the benefit of another, when he himself also receives an advantage from it, the stipulation is valid. Thus, if he who hath begun to administer the tutelage of a pupil, should afterwards cede or give up the administration to his co-tutor, and stipulate for the security of the estate of his pupil, in this case—inasmuch as such a stipulation is for the interest of the stipulator, who would be obliged to answer all damages to the pupil, if the co-tutor did not justly administer the pupillary trust—the obligation would bind. And upon the same principle, if a man stipulates that a thing shall be given to his proctor or attorney, the stipulation shall prevail. And a stipulation is also good which is made by a debtor for the use of his creditor, because it is the interest of the debtor either that the penalty, upon which he borrowed money of his creditor, should not be exacted from him, or that his goods, which are hypothecated with his creditor, should not be sold.

§ 20. On the contrary, he who promises that another, namely Titius, shall perform some particular act, is not bound by such promise, unless he makes himself subject to a penalty if the act is not performed by Titius.

§ 21. No man can legally stipulate that a thing shall be given him when it shall become his own.

§ 22. If the stipulator stipulates in regard to one thing, and the obliger promises in relation to another, no obligation is contracted; and the parties are as much at liberty as if no answer had been made to the interrogation: and this would be the case, if a man should stipulate that Stichus should be given to him; and the obliger should intend to give Pamphilus, upon a thorough persuasion that Pamphilus is called Stichus.

§ 23. A promise made for a dishonest purpose, as, for example, to commit homicide or sacrilege, is not binding.

§ 24. If a stipulation hath been entered into upon condition, and the stipulator should die pending the event of it, his heir will be entitled to an action against the obliger if the event afterwards happens. And if the obliger should die before the condition happens, his heir may be sued by the stipulator.

§ 25. Whoever stipulates that a thing shall be given to him this year or this month, cannot legally sue the obliger till the whole year or month is elapsed. And if a man stipulates, that a piece of ground or slave shall be given to him, he cannot instantly sue the obliger, but must wait till such a space of time hath passed in which a delivery might reasonably have been made.

Tit. XXI. *De fidejussoribus.*

It frequently happens, that others bind themselves for him who promises. These bondsmen or sureties are called *fide-jussors*, and are generally required by creditors for their greater security.

§ 1. *Fide-jussors* may be received in all obligations, whether contracted by the delivery of the thing itself, by words, by writing, or the mere consent of parties; nor is it material whether the obligation is civil or natural; for a man may intervene, and oblige himself as a *fide-jussor* or surety, even on the behalf of a slave; and this may be done, whether the person who accepts the *fide-jussor* is a stranger, or the master of the slave, when the thing due is a natural debt or obligation.

§ 2. A *fide-jussor* is not only bound himself, but by his death transmits the obligation to his heir.

§ 3. A *fide-jussor* may be accepted either before or after an obligation is entered into.

§ 4. Where there are *fide-jussors* or sureties, let them be ever so numerous, they are each bound by law *in solidum*, *i.e.*, for the whole debt; and the creditor is at liberty to choose from whom he will demand it. But, by a rescript of the Emperor Adrian, a creditor may be obliged to demand separately from every *fide-jussor*, who is solvent at the time of contestation of suit, his share of the debt *pro ratâ;* and if any of the *fide-jussors*, at the time of the contestation of the suit, is not solvent, the burden falls upon the rest. But if a creditor obtain his whole demand from one of the *fide-jussors*, the whole loss shall be his, if the party principal for whom he is bound is insolvent; for such *fide-jussor* can impute this loss only to himself, since he might have called to his aid the rescript of the Emperor Adrian, and have prayed that an action should not have been given against him, obliging him to the payment of more than his share of the debt, as a surety.

§ 5. *Fide-jussors* ought not to be bound in a greater sum than the debtor owes for whom they are bound; for their obligation is an accession to the principal obligation; and an accessory debt cannot be greater than the principal, though it may be less. Therefore, if the principal obliger promises ten *aurei*, the *fide-jussor* may be bound in five; but the *fide-jussor* cannot be bound in ten *aurei*, when the principal obliger is bound only in five. Also, when the obliger promises simply, the surety may promise conditionally; but if the surety is bound simply, when the principal debtor is bound only conditionally, the obligation is void. And the terms greater and less take place not only in quantity, but also in time; for an obligation to give or deliver a thing instantly is greater than an obligation to give or deliver it after a time.

§ 6. If a *fide-jussor* hath been obliged to pay money for the person for whom he was bound, the *fide-jussor* may have an action of mandate against him for the recovery of the sum paid.

§ 7. A *fide-jussor* may thus bind himself even in Greek: τῃ εμῃ πιστει κελευω, λεγω· that is, "I answer or speak solemnly upon my faith." But if a man should use the words θελω or βουλομαι, "I am willing," or φημι, "I promise," any of these would serve the same purpose as κελευω or λεγω.

§ 8. We must here observe, that it is a general rule in all fide-jussorial stipulations, that whatever is alleged in writing to have been done, is to be presumed to have been actually done: and therefore, if a man in writing confesses that he hath made himself a *fide-jussor*, it is also presumed, that all the necessary forms were observed.

Tit. XXII. *De literarum obligationibus.*

A species of written obligations anciently prevailed, which was effected by registering the names of the contractors; but these contracts, which were called *nomina*, are not now in use. But if a man confesses in writing, that he owes what in reality he never received, he cannot, when an action is brought against him for his confessed debt, oppose an exception to it, setting forth that the money was never paid, if much time has elapsed after the date of the obligation; and the limitation of this time has frequently been prescribed by the constitutions. Hence, it is, at this day, that a man must be bound by his written note, if he cannot legally bring an exception, and from this written contract arises an action called a *condiction*, when no stipulation or verbal obligation can be proved. And formerly the imperial constitutions gave a large space of time, not less than five years, in which any man was allowed to bring an exception *pecuniæ non numeratæ*, *i.e.*, an exception of money not paid. But we, for the safety of creditors in general, have greatly contracted this allowance of time by our imperial constitution, which ordains, that an exception shall not be brought after the expiration of two years.

Tit. XXIII. *De obligationibus ex consensu.*

Obligations are made by consent in buying, selling, letting, hiring, societies or partnerships, and mandates. And an obligation entered into by any of those means is said to be contracted by consent, because neither writing nor the presence of parties is absolutely requisite. Neither is it necessary that anything should be given or delivered, to the intent that the obligation should take effect; for it suffices that the contractors consent; and for this reason these contracts may be entered into by absent parties, either by letters or messengers. And note also, that in these contracts by consent, the parties are bound to each other mutually to do what is just and right; but in verbal obligations one party stipulates, and the other party promises.

Tit. XXIV. *De emptione et venditione.*

The contract of buying and selling is made perfect as soon as the price of the thing to be sold is agreed upon, although it is not paid, nor even an earnest of it given; for whatever is taken as earnest does not constitute a contract, but serves only for a proof of it. And this is the law with regard to those bargains and sales which are not in writing; for in such we have made no innovation. But where there is a written contract, we have ordained that a bargain and sale shall not become absolute unless the instruments of sale are written by the contracting parties, or at least signed by them if written by others. And when the instruments are drawn by a public notary, the contract is not binding if any formality hath been omitted, or if the instruments are not complete in all their parts; for if anything is omitted, either the buyer or seller may recede from his agreement without penalty, if nothing has been given in the name of earnest. But if earnest has once been given, then the buyer, whether the contract was written or unwritten, if he refuses to fulfil it, loses his earnest, and the seller, if he refuses, is compellable to restore double the value of the earnest, although no agreement of this kind was expressly made. But it is always necessary that the price of the thing to be sold should be fixed; for till then there can be no *emptio-venditio*, *i. e.*, buying and selling.

§ 1. The price, as we have before observed, ought to be certain. And formerly, when it was covenanted that a thing should be sold at whatever price Titius should value it, the ancient lawyers much doubted whether such a sale was good or not good. But we have ordained by our decision that as often as it is agreed that a thing shall be sold at a price to be fixed by a third person, such contract shall be valid under that condition; so that if the nominee or arbitrator determines the price, it ought instantly to be paid according to the determination, and the thing sold ought to be delivered, and the sale perfected; for otherwise the buyer may have an action *ex empto*, *i. e.*, on account of the thing bought, and the seller may have an action *ex vendito*, *i. e.*, on account of the thing sold. But if the arbitrator either refuses, or is unable, to determine the price, the sale is null. And as it hath been our pleasure that this shall be the law in relation to sales, it is but right that the same law should prevail in locations and conductions, *i. e.*, in letting and hiring.

§ 2. The price of anything bought should consist of cash or money told; for it hath been much doubted whether the price of goods can be said to be paid if any other thing is given for them than money; as, for instance, whether a slave, a piece of ground, or a robe, can be paid as the price of a thing. The lawyers Sabinus and Cassius thought that a price might consist of anything; and from hence it has been commonly said that *emptio-venditio*, or buying and selling, is contracted by commutation, and that this species of buying and selling is the most ancient. The advocates for this side of the question quote Homer, who relates in the following lines that a part of the Grecian army bought wine by giving other things in exchange for it.

> "Wine the rest purchas'd at their proper cost,
> And well the plenteous freight supplied the host:
> Each in exchange proportion'd treasures gave,
> Some brass or iron, some an ox or slave."—*Pope.*

But the lawyers of another sect maintained the contrary, and declared that commutation was one thing, and *emptio-venditio* another; for otherwise, said they, in the commutation of any two things, it can never appear which has been sold, and which has been given as the price of the thing sold; and it is contrary to reason that each should appear to have been sold, and that each also should appear to have been given as the price of the other. And the opinion of Proculus, who maintained that commutation is a species of contract separate from vendition, hath deservedly prevailed; for he is supported by other verses from Homer, and has enforced his opinion with the strongest arguments; and this is the doctrine which our predecessors, the Emperors Dioclesian and Maximian, have admitted, as it appears more at large in our digests.

§ 3. When emption and vendition are once contracted—and this, as we have observed, is effected as soon as the price is agreed upon, when there is no covenant in writing—then the buyer is liable to the risk of the loss of the thing sold, or of the damage which may happen to it, although it hath not been delivered to him. And therefore, if a slave thus sold should die, or receive any hurt, or if a building, or part of it, should be consumed by fire, or if lands sold, or any portion of them, should be washed away by a torrent, or be made worse by an inundation, or a storm, which may destroy the trees, the loss in all these cases must be sustained by the buyer, who is obliged to pay the price agreed upon, although he never had possession of the thing; for whatever the accident is, if it happens neither by the fraud nor fault of the seller, he is secure. But, on the other hand, if after the sale any accession is made to the lands by alluvion or otherwise, this increase becomes the gain of the buyer; for it is just that he should receive the profit who must have sustained the loss. But if a slave, who is sold, either runs away, or is stolen, and neither fraud nor negligence can be imputed to the seller, it must be inquired, whether the seller undertook the safe custody of the slave till delivery should be made; if he did, he is answerable for the accident; if he did not, he is secure. The same law takes place in regard to all other animals and things. But when these accidents happen, and the buyer is to sustain the loss, the seller is obliged to make over his right of vindication and condiction; that is, he must transfer to the buyer all right of action, whether real or personal, if necessary; for he who has not delivered the thing sold, is still considered as the proprietor of it. Actions also of theft, or damage done, must be transferred by the seller to the buyer, when the thing sold is stolen, or damaged, before delivery.

§ 4. A sale may be contracted conditionally as well as purely: for instance, when the person who is inclined to sell speaks thus—"If within a certain time you shall approve of the slave Stichus, he shall be yours for so many *aurei.*"

§ 5. Whoever knowingly purchases a place sacred or religious, or a public place, such as a forum or court of justice, he makes a void purchase. But if a man should purchase any of the before-mentioned places, having taken them for profaned or private, being imposed upon by the seller, then such purchaser, not being able to enjoy the possession of what he has bought, may have an action *ex empto* against the seller, and recover the damage suffered by the deceit. The same law also obtains if any person through error should buy a freeman instead of a slave.

Tit. XXV. *De locatione et conductione.*

Location and conduction, *i.e.* letting and hiring, are nearly allied to emption and vendition, *i. e.*, to buying and selling, and are governed by the same rules: for as emption and vendition are contracted as soon as the price of the thing is agreed upon, so location and conduction are contracted when the hire is once fixed by the parties. The locator, or person who lets, is entitled to an action called *actio locati*, if he is aggrieved by the conductor or hirer; and the conductor may have an action called *actio conducti* against the locator.

§ 1. We are willing, that what we have before observed in regard to the sale of a thing, when the price is referred to a third person, should also be understood to have been said of location and conduction, when the quantity of the hire is not agreed upon between the parties, but left to arbitration. And therefore, if a man sends his clothes to a fuller to be scoured, or to a tailor to be mended, and does not previously agree upon any price, in this case location and conduction are not understood to be properly contracted; but an action may be brought by either party *præscriptis verbis*, *i.e.* in words prescribed and adapted to the circumstances of the case.

§ 2. As it was formerly a question whether emption and vendition could be contracted by an exchange of things, so it hath also been doubted whether location and conduction can be said to exist, when one man lends another a particular thing for his use, and receives in return some other thing of which he is also permitted to have the use; and it has been determined that this exchange does not constitute location and conduction, but is a distinct species of contract; for example, if two neighbours have each of them an ox, and each agrees to lend his ox to the other alternately for ten days to do the labours of the field, and the ox of the one dies in the possession of the other, in this case, he who has lost his ox can neither bring the action *locati*, nor *conducti*, nor even the action *commodati;* for the ox was not lent gratuitously; but he may sue by virtue of an action called *præscriptis verbis*, *i.e.*, by an action upon the case.

§ 3. The contract of buying and selling, and that of letting and hiring, are so nearly connected, that in some cases it hath been difficult to distinguish the one from the other, as when lands have been demised to be enjoyed for ever, upon condition that if a certain yearly pension or rent is constantly paid to the proprietor, it shall not be in his power to take these lands from the tenant or his heirs, or from any other person to whom such tenant or his heirs shall have sold them, given them gratuitously, or as a marriage portion, or otherwise disposed of them. But when this contract, concerning which the ancient lawyers had great doubts, was by some thought to be an emption and vendition, and by others a location and conduction, the Zenonian law was enacted, which settled the proper nature of an *emphyteusis*, making it to be neither the one nor the other of the before-mentioned contracts, but declaring it to be supported by its own peculiar covenants, and ordaining that whatever is agreed upon by the parties shall obtain and take place as a contract; and when there is no covenant which declares upon whom the loss of the lands shall fall, that then, if the whole estate happens to be destroyed by a torrent, an earthquake, or any other means, the proprietor must be the sufferer; but if a part only is destroyed, that the loss shall then be borne by the tenant; and this is the law in use.

§ 4. Also, if Titius, for example, should agree with a goldsmith to make a certain number of rings of a particular size and weight, and to furnish the gold, for which Titius should promise him ten *aurei*, as the value both of the workmanship and the gold, it hath been a question whether such a contract would be a buying and selling, or a letting and hiring. Cassius was of opinion that it would be a buying and selling in regard to the matter, and a letting and hiring in regard to the work; but it is now settled that in this case an emption and vendition would only be contracted. But, on the other hand, it is not to be doubted that, if Titius should give his own gold, and agree to pay only for the workmanship, this contract would be a location and conduction.

§ 5. The conductor, or hirer, is not only obliged to observe strictly the covenants of the conduction, but is also bound in equity to perform whatever hath been omitted to be inserted. And whoever has given or promised hire for the use of clothes, silver, horses, &c., is bound to take the same care of them as the most diligent master of a family would take of his own property. But if the hirer does this, and yet loses the things hired by some fortuitous event, he shall not be answerable for the loss.

§ 6. If the conductor, or hirer, dies before the time of the conduction is expired, his heir succeeds to his right, and is entitled to the thing hired for the remainder of the term.

Tit. XXVI. *De societate.*

It is common for persons to enter either into a general partnership or society of all their goods, and this the Greeks emphatically call *κοινωνιαν*, *i. e.*, communion; or into a particular partnership, which regards only some single species of commerce, as that of buying and selling slaves, oil, wine, or corn.

§ 1. If no express agreement has been made by the partners concerning their shares of profit and loss, the loss must be equally borne, and the profit must be equally divided. But if any particular agreement has been made, it must be observed; for it was never yet doubted but that the covenant would be binding, if two persons should agree that two shares of the profit and loss should belong to one partner, and that only the third part of both should belong to the other.

§ 2. But it has been questioned, if Titius and Seius should covenant between themselves, that Titius should receive two parts of the profit, and bear but a third of the loss, and that Seius should bear two parts of the loss, and receive but a third share of the profit, whether such an agreement would be binding? Quintus Mutius was of opinion that such a covenant was contrary to the nature of partnership, and ought not therefore to be ratified; but Servius Sulpitius, whose opinion hath prevailed, thought otherwise, and for this reason, because the labour of some is so highly valuable, that it is but just that they should be admitted into society upon the most advantageous conditions; for no man doubts, but that partnership may be entered into by two persons, when one of them only finds money, inasmuch as it often happens that the work and labour of the other amounts to the value of it, and supplies its place. And also, contrary to the opinion of Mutius, it hath obtained as law, that a partner may by agreement take a share of the profit, and not be accountable for any part of the loss; for Servius thought that this likewise might be done equitably; but it must be so understood that if profit accrues from one species of things, and loss from another, only what remains after the loss is compensated shall be looked upon as profit.

§ 3. It is also a settled point, that if partners expressly mention their shares in one respect only, either solely in regard to gain, or solely in regard to loss, their shares of that which is omitted shall be the same as of that which is mentioned.

§ 4. A partnership lasts as long as the partners persevere in their consent to continue such; and if one of them renounces the partnership the society is dissolved. But if a man renounces with a fraudulent intent, and for no other end, but that he may enjoy the sole benefit of some future fortune, which he expects, his renunciation will not avail; for if a partner in common, as soon as he finds that he has been appointed an heir, should renounce his partnership, that he may possess the inheritance exclusive of all others, he would nevertheless be compelled to divide the inheritance equally with his former partners; yet if an inheritance, which he did not expect, should by accident fall to him after renunciation, the whole would be his own; but those from whom a partner hath separated himself by renouncing possess solely for themselves whatever they acquire after the renunciation of that partner.

§ 5. A partnership is also dissolved by the death of one of the partners; for he who enters into partnership always chooses some certain known person to be his partner upon whom he can depend. And although a partnership is entered into by the consent of many, it is nevertheless dissolved by the death of one, although the rest survive; and this is the law, unless special covenants are made to the contrary at the time of forming the society.

§ 6. Also, if a partnership is entered into on account of some particular commerce, and an end is put to that commerce, the partnership is of course ended.

§ 7. It is likewise manifest that a partnership is dissolved by confiscation; to wit, if all the goods of a partner are confiscated; for when another—for example, the treasurer of the exchequer—succeeds in his place, he is reputed as civilly dead.

§ 8. Also, if a man in partnership, being pressed by his debts, makes a cession or a surrender of his goods, and they are sold to satisfy either public or private demands, the partnership is dissolved. But if the rest of the co-partners should still desire to be in society either with or without this man, the first partnership would not continue, but a new one would commence.

§ 9. It has been a question, whether a partner, like a depositary, is accountable for fraud only, or whether he is also accountable for his negligence? And it now prevails, that he is answerable for all the damages which happen through his fault. And if a man fails in having used the most exact diligence, such a failure is not comprehended under the term *culpa*, or fault; for a partner is not liable to answer damages, if, in regard to the goods of the community, it appears that he has used the same care and diligence towards them, which he has usually observed in keeping his own private property. And it is certain that whoever chooses a negligent man for his partner, can lay the blame upon himself only, and impute his misfortune to his own ill choice.

Tit. XXVII. *De mandato.*

A mandate is framed five ways: either when it is given solely for the benefit of the mandator; or partly for his benefit, and partly for that of the mandatary; or solely for the service of some third person; or partly for the profit of the mandator, and partly for the service of a third person; or partly for the benefit of the mandatary, and partly for the use of a third person. But if a mandate is given solely for the sake of the mandatary, the mandate is useless, for no obligation can arise from it, nor of course any action.

§ 1. A mandate is given solely for the benefit of the mandator, when he requires the mandatary to transact his business, to buy lands, or to become a surety for him.

§ 2. A mandate is given partly for the benefit of the mandator, and partly for the benefit of the mandatary, if the mandator requires you to lend money upon interest to Titius, who would borrow it for the use of the mandator; or if, when you are upon the point of suing a man on account of a fidejussory caution, or a suretyship, he should authorize you at his own risk to sue the principal debtor; or if he should empower you at his own hazard to stipulate for the sum which he owes you from some other person whom he appoints.

§ 3. A mandate is interposed only for the sake of a third person, when the mandator requires the mandatary to perform some office for Titius, to buy lands for him, or to become his bail.

§ 4. A mandate tends to the benefit of the mandator, and also of a third person, when the mandator requires you, who are the mandatary, to transact some affair for the common benefit of both him and Titius, or to buy lands for them both, or to be bound for them.

§ 5. A mandate is given in favour of the mandatary and of a third person, when the mandator requires you to lend money to Titius upon interest; but if you are required to lend money without interest, the mandate can only be in favour of him to whom it is lent.

§ 6. A mandate is given solely for your own benefit, if the mandator requires you rather to make a purchase of lands, than to lend your money upon interest; or, on the contrary, rather to lend your money upon interest, than to buy lands. But a mandate of this species seems rather to be good advice than a mandate, and is therefore not obligatory; for an action of mandate cannot be brought against a man on account of the advice which he has given, although it has not proved beneficial to him to whom it was given, inasmuch as every one is at full liberty to consult his own reason, whether the counsel given to him is expedient or not. And therefore, if you should be advised to employ your money, which now lies dead, either by lending it out at interest, or in making a purchase, and you shall become a loser by following this advice, the adviser would not be liable to an action. And this is so true, that it has even been a question, whether an action of mandate will lie against him who hath required you by mandate to lend money to Titius, who is insolvent. But the opinion of Sabinus hath obtained, and a mandate in this case is now judged to be obligatory; for you would never have trusted Titius, but in obedience to the mandate.

§ 7. A mandate contrary to good manners is not obligatory; as if Titius should command Sempronius to commit theft, or to do some act to the damage or injury of a third person; for although Sempronius should suffer a penalty or punishment in consequence of his obedience to such mandate, he will not be entitled to any action against Titius.

§ 8. He who executes a mandate ought not to exceed the bounds of it; for example, if a mandator should require you to purchase lands, or to be bound for Titius, to the amount of a hundred *aurei;* you ought not to buy the lands at a higher price, or be bound for Titius in a greater sum; for if you exceed the mandate, you will not be entitled to an action for the recovery of the excess. And Cassius and Sabinus were even of opinion, that, although you were willing to bring an action of mandate for no more than the hundred *aurei*, you could not recover them. But it was held by the lawyers of a different school, that the mandatary might sue the mandator for the hundred *aurei;* and this appears to be the more equitable opinion. But if you buy certain lands at a less price than that which the mandator has allowed, you will undoubtedly be entitled to an action of mandate; for if he hath ordered that a hundred *aurei* shall be expended in the purchase of a particular estate, he will certainly be understood to have ordered that the same estate should, if possible, be purchased at a less price.

§ 9. A mandate, properly contracted, becomes null if it is revoked whilst entire; that is, before any act hath been done in consequence of it.

§ 10. A mandate also becomes null if either the mandator or the mandatary dies whilst it continues entire. But it is allowed for the benefit of society, that if a mandator dies, and the mandatary, not knowing of his death, should afterwards execute the mandate, he may bring his action against the heirs of the mandator; for otherwise an unblameable and undoubted want of knowledge would be prejudicial. And in a similar case it hath been determined, that if the debtors of Titius, whose steward has been manumitted, should, without knowledge of the manumission, pay this freedman what was due to Titius, they would be cleared from their debt, and the payment would be good; although by the rigour of the law it would be otherwise, since they had made their payment to another than him to whom it ought to have been made.

§ 11. Every man is at liberty to refuse a mandate; but if it is once accepted, it must be performed, or renounced, as soon as possible, that the mandator may transact the business himself, or by another. But if the renunciation is made so late that the mandator can have no opportunity of transacting this business properly, an action will lie against the mandatary, unless he can show some just cause for his delay in not making a timely renunciation.

§ 12. A mandate may be contracted to transact a particular business at a distant day, or upon condition.

§ 13. In fine, it must be observed, that if a mandate is not gratuitous, it then becomes another species of contract; for if a price is agreed upon, the contract of location and conduction commences. And in general, when a trust or business is undertaken without hire, the contract regards either a mandate, or a deposit; but when there is an agreement for hire, it constitutes location and conduction. And therefore, if a man gives his clothes to a fuller that they may be cleaned, or to a tailor that they may be mended, and there is no agreement or promise made, an action of mandate will lie.

Tit. XXVIII. *De obligationibus quæ quasi ex contractu nascuntur.*

Having already enumerated the various kinds of direct obligations, we will now treat of those which cannot be said properly to arise from a contract, but yet, inasmuch as they take not their origin from anything criminal, seem to arise from an implied or a quasi-contract.

§ 1. When one person transacts the business of another who is absent, they reciprocally obtain a right to certain actions, called *actiones negotiorum gestorum, i.e.*, actions on account of business done: and it is manifest that these can arise from no proper or regular contract; for they take place only when one man assumes the care of the affairs of another without a mandate: and in this case, those persons for whom business is transacted are always bound without their knowledge; and this is permitted for the public good, because the business of those who are absent in a foreign country, and have not committed the administration of their affairs to any particular person, would otherwise be totally neglected: for no man would take this care upon himself, if he could not afterwards bring an action to recover what he had expended. But as the principal is bound to reimburse the agent who has negotiated his affairs properly, so is the agent bound to render a just account of his administration to his principal. And an agent, in this case, is obliged to use the most exact diligence; for it will not suffice, although he proves that he has taken the same care of the affairs of his principal which he usually took of his own, if it can by any means appear that a more diligent man could have acted with greater advantage to his principal.

§ 2. A tutor, although he is subject to an action of tutelage, is not reckoned to be bound by any pact, or agreement; for between a tutor and his pupil there is no express contract. But, because tutors are not subject to an action of malfeasance, they are understood to be bound by an implied or quasi-contract; and thus both tutor and pupil may bring actions reciprocally; the pupil may bring a direct action of tutelage against his tutor, and the tutor, if he has expended his own money in the affairs of his pupil, or has been bound for him, or has mortgaged his own possessions to the creditors, is entitled to the action called *contraria tutelæ*.

§ 3. When a thing happens to be in common among persons who have never entered into a voluntary partnership; as when the same field, or part of an inheritance, is devised, or given generally, between two; in this case the one may be called to answer the other by the action *communi dividundo*, either because the one hath taken to his use the whole produce of the ground, or because the other hath been at the sole expense of maintaining it in good order. But neither of these persons can properly be said to be bound by contract, since they made no agreement between themselves; but, inasmuch as they are exempt from any criminal action, they are accounted as bound by a quasi-contract.

§ 4. And the same law prevails in regard to him who is bound to his co-heir, and is liable to the action *familiæ erciscundæ* for the partition of an universal inheritance.

§ 5. An heir for the same reason cannot properly be said to be bound by contract to a legatary; for the legatary can never be supposed to have entered into any contract either with the heir, or with the deceased: but as the heir cannot be prosecuted by an action of malfeasance, he is presumed to be indebted to the legatary by a quasi-contract.

§ 6. He, to whom another has paid by mistake what was not due, appears to be indebted by quasi-contract; for he is certainly not bound by an express agreement; and, strictly speaking, he might rather be said—as we have before observed—to be bound by the dissolution than by the making of a contract; for he who paid the money with an intent to discharge his debts, seemed rather inclined to dissolve an engagement than to contract one. But, nevertheless, whoever receives money by the mistake of another, is as much bound to repay it as if it had been left to him; and he is therefore liable to an action of condiction.

§ 7. In some cases money paid by mistake, when not due, cannot afterwards be demanded; for the ancient lawyers have delivered it as a maxim, that where an action for double the value of the debt is given upon the denial of it,—as by the law *Aquilia*, and in the case of legacies,—the debtor, who has through error paid money to him to whom it was not due, shall never recover it. But these lawyers would have this rule to take place only in regard to fixed and certain legacies, devised *per damnationem.* But our imperial constitution, which reduced all legacies and trusts to one common nature, hath caused this augmentation *in duplum* after denial to be extended to legacies and trusts in general; yet the privilege of not refunding what is paid by mistake is by our constitution only granted to churches and other holy places, which are honoured on account of religion and piety.

Tit. XXIX. *Per quas personas obligatio acquiritur.*

Having explained the various kinds of obligations which arise from contracts or quasi-contracts, we must now observe, that we acquire obligations not only by means of ourselves, but also by those who are under our power, as by our slaves and our children; and whatever is acquired by our slaves is wholly our own; but that which is acquired by our children under our power, by virtue of their contracts, must be divided according to the decree of our constitution, which gives to the father the usufruct of the thing gained, but reserves the property of it to the son. But a father in bringing an action must act in obedience to our novel constitution.

§ 1. We may also acquire things my means of freemen, and the slaves of others, whom we possess *bonâ fide:* but this we can only do in two cases; to wit, when they have gained an acquisition by their labour, or by virtue of something which belongs to us.

§ 2. We must always acquire in either of the above-named cases by means even of those slaves of whom we have only the usufruct or use.

§ 3. It is certain that a slave, who is in common between two or more, acquires for his masters in proportion to the property which each of them has in him; unless he stipulates, or receives something, in the name of one of them only; as if he had thus stipulated—"Do you promise to give such a particular thing to Titius, my master?" for although it was a doubt in times past whether a slave, when commanded, could stipulate for the sole benefit of one of his masters, yet, since our decision, it has become a settled point—as we have said before—that a slave in this case can acquire for him only who hath ordered the stipulation.

Tit. XXX. *Quibus modis tollitur obligatio.*

An obligation is dissolved by the payment of what is due; or by the payment of one thing for another, if the creditor consents: neither is it material by whom payment is made, whether by the debtor himself, or by another for him; for a debtor becomes free from his debt when another has paid it, either with or without his knowledge, or even against his consent. Also when a principal debtor pays his creditors, then those who have been bound for him are freed from their obligation; and, on the contrary, when a *fide-jussor* or bondsman clears himself from his obligation by payment, he not only becomes free himself, but the principal debtor is also cleared from his debt.

§ 1. An obligation is also dissolved by *acceptilatio*, which is an imaginary payment; for if Titius is willing to remit what is due to him by a verbal contract, it may be done, if the debtor says—"Do you regard what I promised you as accepted and received?" and Titius answers—"I do." An *acceptilatio* may also be made in Greek if it is so worded as to agree with the Latin form; εχεις λαϐων δηναρια τοσα; εχω λαϐων. But the obligations which are thus dissolved are verbal contracts, and no other; and it seems to be a just consequence, that an obligation made by words only may be dissolved by other words of a contrary import. But it is observable, that any species of contract may be deduced to a stipulation, and of course may be dissolved by acceptilation. And note, that as a debt may be paid in part by money, so may it be paid in part also by acceptilation.

§ 2. There is another species of stipulation, called commonly the Aquilian stipulation, by virtue of which every other kind of obligation may be reduced to a stipulation, and may afterwards be dissolved by acceptilation. For the Aquilian stipulation changes all obligations, and was constituted by Gallus Aquilius in the following manner:—"Do you promise," said Aulus Agerius to Numerius Nigidius, "to pay me a sum of money, in lieu of what you were, or shall be, obliged to give me or to perform for my benefit, either simply, at a day to come, or upon condition; and in lieu of those things which, being my property, you have, detain, or possess; or of which you have fraudulently quitted the possession; and for which I may, or shall be, entitled to any species of action, plaint, or prosecution?" Numerius Nigidius answered, "I do"; and, when this was said, Numerius Nigidius asked Aulus Agerius if he regarded the money as accepted and received, which he Numerius had promised? to which Aulus Agerius answered, that he did regard it as accepted and received.

§ 3. An obligation is also dissolved by novation; as when you stipulate with Titius to receive from him what is due to you from Seius. For by the intervention of a new debtor a fresh obligation arises by which the prior obligation is discharged, and transferred to the latter. And sometimes, although the latter stipulation is of no force, yet the prior contract is discharged by the mere act of novation: as if Titius should stipulate to receive a debt which I owe him from a pupil without the authority of his tutor; for in this case the debt is lost, because the first debtor is freed from his debt, and the second obligation is null; but it is not the same if a man stipulates from a slave with a design to make a novation; for then the first debtor remains bound as if there had been no second stipulation. And if you stipulate from the same person a second time, a novation arises if anything new is covenanted in the latter stipulation; as when a condition, a day, or a bondsman is added or taken away. But note that when a condition only is added, novation does not take place till the event happens; and till then the prior obligation continues. It was observed, as a rule, among the ancient lawyers, that a novation arose when a second contract was entered into with an intent to dissolve the former; but it was always a matter of great difficulty to know with what intent the second obligation was made: and the judges, having no positive proof before them, were forced to form their opinions upon presumptions, and according to the circumstances of every particular case. This uncertainty of judging gave rise to our constitution, which enacts that a novation of a former contract shall only take place when it is expressed by the contractors that they covenanted with an intent to make a novation; and that when this is not expressed, the prior contract shall continue valid, and the second be regarded as an accession to it; so that an obligation may remain by virtue of both contracts, according to the determination of our before-named constitution, which may be better known by perusal.

§ 4. We must observe further, that those obligations which are contracted by consent may be dissolved by dissent. For if Titius and Seius have agreed by compact between themselves that Seius shall have a certain estate for a hundred *aurei*, and afterwards before execution, that is, before the price is paid or livery is made of the lands, if the parties dissent from their agreement, they are mutually discharged from it. And the same may be said of location and conduction, and of all other contracts which arise from consent.

BOOK IV.

Tit. I. *De obligationibus, quæ ex delicto nascuntur.*

Having explained in the preceding book the nature of obligations which arise from contracts and quasi-contracts, it follows that we should here treat of those which arise from malfeasance and quasi-malfeasance. The former, as we have shown in the proper place, are divided into four species; but the latter are of one kind only, for they all arise *ex re*, that is, from the crime or malfeasance itself; as from theft, rapine, damage, injury.

§ 1. Theft is a fraudulent subtraction of the thing itself, the use of it, or the possession, for the sake of gain. And this is prohibited by the law of nature.

§ 2. The word *furtum*—theft—is derived from *furvum*—black or dark—because theft is committed privately, and generally in the night; or from *fraus*—fraud; or from *ferendo*, which is of the same import with *auferendo*, and denotes a subtraction or taking away. Or perhaps *furtum* is derived from the Greek, for the Greeks called *fures* φωρας, and φωρας is derived from φωρειν, which signifies to take away.

§ 3. Of theft there are two species, manifest and not manifest; for the thefts called *conceptum* and *oblatum* rather denote the species of action arising on account of theft than the species of theft, as will appear in the next paragraph. A manifest thief, whom the Greeks call επ' αυτοφωρῳ, is he who is taken in the act of thieving, or in the place where he committed it; as if a man, having committed a theft within a house, should be apprehended before he had passed through the outward gate of it; or, having stolen grapes or olives, should be taken in the vineyard or olive orchard. Manifest theft is also further extended: for if the thief is apprehended whilst he is seen to have possession of the thing stolen, or if he is taken in public or in private by the owner or by a stranger at any time before his arrival at the place to which he proposed to carry it, he is guilty of a manifest theft. But if he actually arrives, before apprehension, at the place proposed, then, although the thing stolen is found upon him, he is yet not reputed in law to be a manifest thief. By this description which we have given of manifest theft, it may be clearly understood what is meant by theft not manifest.

§ 4. A theft is called *conceptum—i. e.*, found—when a thing stolen is searched for and found in the possession of some person in the presence of witnesses; and a particular action called *actio concepti* lies against such possessor, although he did not commit the theft. A theft is called *oblatum—i. e.*, offered—when a thing stolen is offered, for instance, to Titius, and found upon him, it having been given to him by Seius, to the intent that it might rather be found upon Titius than upon himself; and in this case a special action, called *actio oblati*, may be brought by Titius against Seius, although Seius was not guilty of the theft. There is also an action called *prohibiti furti*, which lies against him who hinders another to inquire of theft in the presence of witnesses. And further, a penalty was constituted by the edict of the prætor, to be sued by the action *furti non exhibiti* against any man for not having exhibited things stolen, which upon a search were found to have been in his possession. But these four actions are become quite obsolete; for, since a search after things stolen is not now made according to the ancient formalities, these actions have of consequence ceased to be in use; for it is a settled point that all who knowingly have received and concealed a thing stolen, are subject to the penalty of theft not manifest.

§ 5. The penalty of committing a manifest theft is quadruple, whether a thief is free or bond; and the penalty of committing a theft not manifest is double the value of the thing stolen.

§ 6. Theft is committed not only when one man takes the property of another for the sake of appropriating it to himself, but also in a more general sense, when one man uses the property of another against the will of the proprietor. Thus, if a creditor makes use of a pledge, or a depositary of the deposit left with him, or if a man, who hath only the use of a thing for a special purpose, converts it to other uses, a theft is committed. And if any one borrows plate, under pretence of using it at an entertainment of his friends, and then carries it with him into a foreign country; or if a man borrows a horse, and rides it farther than he ought, theft is also committed: and the ancients held this to be law in regard to him who rides a borrowed horse into a field of battle.

§ 7. But it hath nevertheless been adjudged that whoever applies a thing borrowed to other uses than those for which he borrowed it is not guilty of theft, unless the borrower knew that he so applied it contrary to the will of the owner, who would not have permitted such application if he had been apprised of it. But it has also been held, that the borrower in this case is not guilty of theft, if it appears that he thought that the owner would have given his consent. And this is a good distinction; for a theft can never be committed, unless there appears to have been a design and intention of stealing.

§ 8. But if a man imagines that he uses a thing borrowed in some manner contrary to the intention and will of the proprietor, when in reality the proprietor consents that it should be so used, theft is not committed; and from hence arises a question upon the following case. Titius solicited the slave of Mævius to rob his master, and to bring him the things stolen; of this the slave informed his master, who, being willing to discover Titius in the fact, permitted the slave to carry certain things to Titius as stolen; will Titius in this case be subject to an action of theft, or to an action for having corrupted a slave, or to neither? When this was proposed to us as a matter of doubt, and we perceived the altercations which had formerly subsisted among the ancient lawyers upon the same point, some of them allowing of neither of the before-named actions, and others allowing an action of theft only, we therefore, being willing to obviate all subtilities, decreed by our constitution that not only an action of theft might be brought, but also the action *servi corrupti*, which lies for having corrupted a slave. For although the slave became not the worse for the solicitation, and therefore the causes which introduce the action *servi corrupti* do not concur; yet inasmuch as such solicitation was intended to corrupt, it hath therefore pleased us that a penal action should lie against the party soliciting in the same manner as if he had actually succeeded by corrupting the slave; and this we have ordained lest impunity might encourage any evil-disposed persons to make the same attempt upon other slaves, who might have less strength of mind, and be more easily corrupted.

§ 9. A theft may be committed even of free persons; as, for instance, when children, who are under power, are surreptitiously taken from their parents.

§ 10. A man may also possibly commit a theft even of his own property; as when a debtor hath taken away any particular thing which he had left in pledge with his creditor.

§ 11. An action of theft will, in some cases, lie against persons who did not actually commit the theft; it will lie, for example, against those by whose aid and advice the theft was committed; and whoever strikes money out of your hand to the intent that another may pick it up, or whoever so obstructs you as to give an opportunity to his accomplice to take your sheep, oxen, or any part of your property, must be reckoned in the number of aiders and advisers. The ancient lawyers also included him in this number who frightened away a herd from its pasture with a red cloth. But if a man should do any of these acts wantonly, and without an intention of committing theft, then an action can lie only *in factum*, *i. e.*, upon the case, or the fact done: but when Titius commits theft by the aid of Mævius, they are both subject to an action of theft. Theft seems to be committed both by aid and advice, when a man puts a ladder to a window, or breaks open a door or window, to the intent that another may commit theft; or when one man lends another iron bars, or ladders, knowing the bad purposes to which they are to be applied. But it is certain that he who hath afforded no actual assistance, but hath only given his counsel by advising the crime, is not liable to an action of theft.

§ 12. When persons under the power of parents or masters take anything surreptitiously from such parents or masters, a theft is committed, and the thing is looked upon as stolen; so that it cannot be prescribed to by any one, until it hath first reverted into the power of the proprietor; and yet an action of theft will not lie, for between parents and their children, or masters and slaves, no action can arise upon any account. But if the fact was done by the aid and advice of any other, inasmuch as a theft is committed, an action of theft will lie against the aider.

§ 13. An action of theft may be brought by any man who has an interest in the safety of the thing stolen, although he is not the proprietor of it; and the proprietor himself can have no action, unless he has an interest.

§ 14. Hence it follows, that a creditor may bring an action of theft on account of a pledge stolen, although his debtor is solvent, because it may be more expedient for him to rely upon his pledge, than to bring an action against the person of his debtor; and although the debtor himself should have been the taker of the pledge, yet an action of theft will lie against him.

§ 15. If a fuller receives clothes to clean, and they are afterwards stolen from him, the fuller may bring an action of theft, but not the owner; for the owner is reputed to have no interest in their safety, because he has a right of action, called *locati*, against the fuller. But if a thing is stolen from a *bonâ fide* purchaser, he is entitled, like a creditor, to an action of theft, although he is not the proprietor. But an action of theft is not maintainable by the fuller, or any tradesman in similar circumstances, unless he is solvent; that is, unless he is able to pay the owner the full value of the thing lost; for if the fuller is insolvent, then the owner, who cannot recover from the fuller, is allowed to bring an action of theft, having in this case an interest. And note, that whoever is unable to pay the whole of what is due, such person is esteemed insolvent, let the deficiency be ever so small.

§ 16. The ancients were of opinion, that what we have said of a fuller is equally applicable to him to whom something is lent. For as the fuller, by agreeing for a certain price, is obliged to make good the clothes committed to his custody, so is he also, who receives a loan for the sake of using it, under the like necessity of preserving it. But we have amended the law in this point by our decisions, so that it is now at the will of the owner either to bring an action of theft against the thief, or an action on account of the thing lent against the borrower. But if the owner once makes an election of the one, he can never afterwards have recourse to the other; and if he chooses to prosecute the thief, the borrower is altogether free from any action; and if the owner or lender brings a suit against the borrower, he can by no means bring an action against the thief. But the borrower, who is convened on account of the thing lent, may bring an action of theft against the thief, if the owner, who convened him, was apprised that the thing was stolen; but if the owner, either not knowing or doubting of the theft, institutes an action of loan against the borrower, and afterwards upon information is willing to withdraw it, and recur to an action of theft, he shall have liberty, in consideration of his uncertainty, to prosecute the thief without obstacle, if the borrower has not satisfied his demand; but if the borrower has given the owner satisfaction, then the thief is freed from any action of theft which can be brought by the owner; but he is nevertheless subject to the prosecution of the borrower, who has satisfied the owner. But it is most manifest, that if the owner of any particular thing, not knowing that it is stolen, should at first institute an action of loan against the borrower, but should afterwards, upon better information, choose to pursue the thief by an action of theft, the borrower is secure, whatever may be the issue of the action brought against the thief. And this obtains as law, whether the borrower is able to answer the whole, or a part only, of the value of the thing.

§ 17. A depositary is not obliged to make good the thing deposited unless he is himself guilty of some fraud, or malfeasance; and therefore, as a depositary is not obliged to make restitution when the deposit is stolen, and as he has consequently no interest in the conservation of the deposit, he is not allowed to bring an action of theft, which in this case can only be maintained by the owner.

§ 18. It hath been a question whether a person within puberty, who hath taken away the property of another, can be guilty of theft? And it hath been determined, that, inasmuch as theft consists in the intention of defrauding, a person within puberty may be charged with theft, if he is near the age of puberty, and can be proved to have been sensible, that what he did was criminal.

§ 19. An action of theft can only be brought for the penalty, whether double or quadruple; for the owner of the thing stolen may recover the thing itself, either by *vindication* or by *condiction*. An action of *vindication* may be brought against him who hath possession, whether he is the thief or any other; but *condiction* is maintainable only against the thief himself, or his heir; yet it will lie against either of them, whether he is or is not in possession of the thing stolen.

Tit. II. *De vi bonorum raptorum.*

He who takes the property of another by force is liable to an action of theft;—for who can be said to take the property of another more against his will than he who takes it by force? and it hath therefore been rightly observed that such a thief is one of the worst kind;—but the prætor has nevertheless introduced a peculiar action in this case, called *vi bonorum raptorum*, which, if brought within a year after the robbery, enforces the payment of the quadruple value of the thing taken; but if it is brought after the expiration of a year, then the single value only is claimable; and this action is of such a nature that it may be brought for any single thing, though it was of the least value imaginable, if it was taken by force. But the whole quadruple value is not exacted merely for the penalty, as in an action of manifest theft; for in this quadruple value the thing itself is included, so that strictly the penalty is only threefold; but then it is inflicted without distinguishing whether the robber was or was not taken in the actual commission of the fact. For it would be ridiculous that a robber who uses force should be in a better condition than he who is only guilty of a clandestine theft.

§ 1. The action *de vi bonorum raptorum* is only maintainable when there is fraud used as well as force; for if a man, being ignorant of the law, and erroneously thinking any particular thing to be his own, should take it away by force from the possessor, upon a full persuasion that he, as proprietor, could justify such a proceeding, he ought to be acquitted upon this action; neither is he subject, under the before-mentioned circumstances, to an action of theft. But, lest robbers should from hence find out a way of practising their villanies with impunity, it is provided by the imperial constitutions that no man shall be at liberty to take by force any moveable thing or living creature out of the possession of another, although he believes it to be his own; and that whoever offends by forcibly seizing his property, shall forfeit it; and that whoever takes the property of another, imagining it to be his own, shall be obliged, not only to restore the thing itself, but also to pay the value of it as a penalty. And the emperors have thought proper that this should obtain, not only in regard to things moveable and moving, which may be carried away, but also in regard to invasions, or forcible entries, made upon things immoveable, as lands or houses, to the intent that mankind may be deterred from committing any species of rapine.

§ 2. In this action, it is not considered whether the thing taken by force is or is not the property of the complainant; for if he has an interest in it, the action is maintainable; and therefore, if a thing is let, lent, or pledged to Titius, or deposited with him so that he becomes interested in the preservation of it, as he may be even in the case of a deposit if he hath promised to be answerable for its safe custody, or if Titius was a *bonâ fide* possessor or entitled to the usufruct, or has any other right which gives an interest, he may bring this action, not for the recovery of the absolute property, but of that only to which his interest extends. And we may in general affirm, that the same causes which entitle a man to institute an action of theft, when anything hath been privately stolen from him, will also entitle him to bring the action *vi bonorum raptorum*, when force hath been used.

Tit. III. *De lege Aquiliâ.*

The action for injurious damage is given by the law *Aquilia*, which enacts, in the first chapter, that if any man injuriously kills the slave or four-footed beast of another which may be reckoned in the number of his cattle, he shall be condemned to pay the owner the greatest price which the slave or beast might have been sold for at any time within a year, computing backward from the day when the wound was given.

§ 1. As the law does not speak of four-footed beasts in general, but of those only which may be reckoned cattle, we may collect that wild beasts and dogs do not come within the intendment of the law, which can be understood to include only those animals which feed in herds, as horses, mules, asses, sheep, oxen, goats, &c. It hath also been determined that swine are comprised under the term cattle, because they feed in herds; and this Homer testifies in the Odyssey, for which he is quoted by Ælius Marcian in his institutions. "You will find him taking care of the swine, which feed in herds near the Corasian rock, &c." Odyss. b. 13.

§ 2. A man who kills another without having a right or authority so to do, is understood to kill him injuriously; but when there is a right there can be no punishment; and therefore he is not subject to the law who kills a robber or an assassin if there was no other way of avoiding the danger threatened.

§ 3. Neither is he subject to the Aquilian law who hath killed another by accident, if no fault can be found in him. But the law does not punish a man less for damage done by his fault or negligence than for damage done by fraud or design.

§ 4. But if a man, by throwing a javelin for his diversion or exercise, happens to kill a slave who is passing, we must in this case make a distinction; for if the slave is killed by a soldier whilst he is exercising in a place appointed for that purpose, the soldier is guilty of no fault; but if any other person should accidentally kill a slave by throwing a javelin, he is guilty of a fault; and even if a soldier should kill a slave accidentally by throwing a javelin in any other place than that appointed for soldiers to exercise in, he also is guilty of a fault.

§ 5. If a man is lopping a tree, and happens to kill a slave who is passing, the lopper is guilty of a fault if he worked near a public road, or in a way leading to a village, without giving a proper warning by proclamation; but if he made due proclamation, and the other did not take care of himself, the lopper is exempt from fault: and he is equally exempt from fault, although he did not make proclamation, if he worked apart from the high road or in the middle of a field; for a stranger has no right of passage through such places.

§ 6. Also, if a physician, or chirurgeon, who has made an incision in the body of a slave, should afterwards neglect or forsake the cure, by which the death of the slave is occasioned, he is guilty of a fault.

§ 7. The want of skill in a profession is also regarded as a fault; thus a physician, for instance, is culpable, and of course subject to an action, who occasions the death of a slave by an unskilful incision or a rash administration of medicines.

§ 8. If a mule-driver, by reason of unskilfulness, is unable to manage his mules, and a slave is run over by them, the mule-driver is in fault; and if he wants strength to rein them in, when another man is able to do it, he is then equally culpable: and the same may be said of a rider who, through want either of strength or skill, is not able to manage his horse.

§ 9. These words of the law *Aquilia*, "Let him who kills a slave or beast of another forfeit the greatest price which either could have been sold for in that year," are to be understood in the following sense; as thus, if Titius accidentally kills a slave who was then lame, or wanted a limb, or an eye, but had been within the space of a year perfect in all his parts, and very valuable, then Titius shall be obliged to pay not what the slave was worth on the day when he was killed, but what he was worth at any time within a year preceding his death when he was in the fullest vigour. An action therefore upon the law *Aquilia* has always been regarded as penal; for it obliges a man to pay not only the full value of the damage done, but often much more than the full value; and of consequence can by no means pass against the heir of the offender; but it might legally have been transferred against the heir if the condemnation had never exceeded the quantum of the damage.

§ 10. It hath prevailed by construction, though not by virtue of the express words of the law, that not only the value of a slave is to be computed, as we have already mentioned, but that an estimation must be made of whatever further damage is occasioned by his death; as if Titius, for example, should kill a slave at the time when he was instituted an heir, and before he had actually entered upon the heirship at the command of his master; for in this case the loss of the inheritance must be brought into the computation. Also, if a horse or mule is killed by which a pair or set is broken, or if a slave is slain who made one of a company of comedians, an estimation must be made not only according to the value of that slave or animal, but according to the value of those which remain; for if they are damaged, the diminution of their value is also taken into the account.

§ 11. The master of a slave who is killed is at liberty to sue for damages by a private action, founded upon the law *Aquilia*, and at the same time to prosecute the offender publicly for a capital crime.

§ 12. The second chapter of the law *Aquilia* is not in use.

§ 13. By the third chapter of this law, a remedy is given for every other kind of damage; and therefore, if a man wounds a slave, or four-footed animal, which is ranked among cattle, or which is not ranked among cattle, as a dog or wild beast, an action will lie against him by virtue of this third part of the law. A reparation may also be obtained under this chapter for all damage injuriously done to animals in general, or to things inanimate; and the same chapter appoints an action for the recovery of the value of whatever is burned, spoiled, or broken; but the term *ruptum* would alone be sufficient in any of these cases; for in whatever manner a thing is damaged or corrupted, it is understood to be *ruptum*, or spoiled, in some degree; so that whenever a thing is broken, burned, or even torn, bruised, spilled, or in any manner made worse, it may be said to be *ruptum*. It hath also been determined, that if a man intermixes anything with the wine or oil of another, so as to corrupt or impair its natural goodness, he is liable to an action founded upon this chapter of the law *Aquilia*.

§ 14. It is evident, that the first part or chapter of the law subjects every man to an action who, through design or accident, kills the slave or beast of another, and that the third part gives a remedy for any other damage so occasioned. But by this third chapter the person who did the damage is not obliged to pay the highest price which the thing damaged might have been sold for at any time within the year, but only the value of it at any time within thirty days previous to the damage.

§ 15. But it is not said in the third part of the law, that the highest value of the thing damaged shall be recovered by action. But in the opinion of Sabinus, the valuation ought to be made as if the word highest had not been omitted; for when Aquilius the tribune proposed this law, the commonalty of Rome thought it sufficient to insert the word highest in the first chapter.

§ 16. It has been determined, that if a man hath with his own hand or body done damage to another, a direct action will lie by virtue of this law. But when damage is done by any other means, as by imprisoning a slave, or impounding the cattle of another, till they die with hunger; by driving a beast of burden so vehemently as to spoil him; by chasing a herd of cattle till they leap down a precipice; or by persuading a slave to climb a tree, or go down into a well, by which he is killed or maimed; then the action called *utilis* is given, by which reparation may be obtained. And note, that if Titius thrusts the slave of another into the water from the top of a bridge or bank, and the slave is drowned in consequence of the fall, it is plain that Titius occasioned this damage with his own hands, and he is therefore subject to a direct action. But if the damage received was not done by the hand or body of another, and is not corporal, so that neither a direct nor beneficial action can be brought by virtue of the Aquilian law, then in these circumstances an action upon the case or fact will lie against the causer of the damage; and therefore, if any man through compassion should unchain the slave of another, and so promote his escape, a reparation may be obtained against him by an action upon the fact.

Tit. IV. *De injuriis.*

The word *injuria* in a general sense denotes every act which is unjust; but when specially used, it is of the same import with *contumélia*, which takes its derivation from *contémno*, and is in Greek termed ὕβρις: sometimes it signifies a fault, called by the Greeks αδικημα, in which acceptation it is used in the law

Aquilia, when damage injuriously given is spoken of; at other times it signifies iniquity or injustice, which the Greeks call ανομιαν and αδικιαν: therefore, when the prætor or judge pronounces sentence unjustly against any person, such person is said to have suffered an injury.

§ 1. An injury may be done not only by beating and wounding, but also by convitious language, or by seizing the goods of a man, as if he were a debtor, when the person who seized them well knew that nothing was due to him. It is also manifest, that an injury may be committed by writing a defamatory libel, poem, or history, or by maliciously causing another so to do; also by continually soliciting the chastity of a boy, girl, or woman of reputation; and by various other means, which are too numerous to be specified.

§ 2. A man may receive an injury, not only in his own person, but in that of his children under his power, and also in the person of his wife; for this is now the more prevalent opinion: and therefore if an injury is done to Seius's daughter, who is married to Titius, an action may be brought, not only in the name of the daughter, but in the name either of her father or her husband; but if the husband receives an injury, the wife is not allowed to institute a suit in his defence; for it is a maxim, that wives may be defended by their husbands, but not husbands by their wives. And note, that a father-in-law may also commence a suit in the name of his son's wife, on account of an injury done to her, if her husband is under the power of his father.

§ 3. An injury is never understood to be done to a slave, but is reputed to be done to the master, through the person of his slave; but what amounts to an injury in regard to a wife or child does not amount to an injury suffered through the person of a slave; and therefore to constitute an injury by means of the person of a slave, some considerable damage must be done to him, and something which openly affects his master; as if a stranger should beat the slave of another in a cruel manner; for in this case an action would lie; but if a man should only give ill-language to a slave, or strike him with his fist, the master can bring no action upon that account.

§ 4. If an injury is done to the common slave of many masters, the estimation of the injury received is not to be made according to their several proportions of property in the slave, but according to the quality of each master; for it is to them to whom the injury is done.

§ 5. If Titius has the usufruct of a slave, and Mævius the property, then any injury which is done to that slave is understood to be done to Mævius, the proprietor.

§ 6. But if an injury is done to a free person, who is in the service of Titius, Titius can bring no action of injury, but the servant must commence a suit in his own name, unless the person who beat him did it principally for the sake of affronting his master; and in this case Titius may also bring an action of injury. The same law likewise obtains if your servant is the slave of another; for as often as he receives an injury which was intended to affront you, you may yourself bring an action of injury.

§ 7. The punishment of an injury, according to the Twelve Tables, was a return of the like injury, if any limb was broken; but if a blow only was given, or a single bone broken, then the punishment was pecuniary, which was not without effect among the ancients, who lived in great poverty. The prætors afterwards permitted the parties injured to fix their damages at a certain sum, which might serve as a guide to the judge, but not preclude him from lessening the estimate at his discretion. The species of pecuniary punishment which was introduced by the law of the Twelve Tables fell by degrees into desuetude, and that which the prætors gave rise to is now solely in use, and is termed honorary; for the estimation of an injury is either increased or diminished, according to the degree and quality of the person injured; and this distinction of degree is not improperly observed, even in regard to slaves; so that the same injury may be variously estimated, according to the state and condition of him who suffered it; at a higher rate if he had acted as steward or agent to his master, and at a lower estimation if he was a slave of an inferior sort.

§ 8. The law *Cornelia* also speaks of injuries, and hath introduced an action, which lies when a man alleges that he hath been struck or beaten, or that another hath entered forcibly into his house; and any man is allowed in this case to allege a house to be his own, whether it is in reality his, or whether he only hires or borrows it, or even lives in it as a guest.

§ 9. An injury is esteemed atrocious sometimes from the nature of the fact, as when a man is wounded by another, or beaten with a club: sometimes from the place, as when an injury is done in a public theatre, in an open market, or in the presence of the prætor: and sometimes by reason of the rank of the person, as when a magistrate or a senator receives an injury from one of mean condition; or when a parent is injured by his child, or a patron by his freedman; for an injury done to a senator, or to a parent by his child, or to a patron by his freedman, must be atoned for by a heavier punishment than an injury done to a stranger, or a person of low degree. Also the part in which a wound is given may constitute an injury atrocious, as if a man should be wounded in his eye; but it makes no manner of alteration whether such an injury is done to the father of a family or to the son of a family; for the injury will neither be the more nor the less atrocious upon this account.

§ 10. In fine, it must be observed concerning every injury, that the party injured may sue the offending party either criminally or civilly. If the party injured sues civilly, the damage occasioned by the injury must be estimated, and the penalty enjoined accordingly, as we have before noticed; but if he sues criminally, it is the duty of the judge to inflict an extraordinary punishment upon the offender; observing the constitution of Zeno, which permits all persons who have a right to be called illustrious, and of consequence all who enjoy a superior title, either to pursue or defend criminally any action of injury by their proctors; but the tenor of this law will more fully appear by a perusal of the ordinance itself.

§ 11. An action of injury does not only lie against him who hath done an injury by giving a blow, &c., but also against him who by his craft and persuasion hath caused the injury to be done.

§ 12. All right to an action of injury may be lost by dissimulation; and therefore, if a man takes no notice of an injury at the time in which he receives it, he cannot afterwards, although he repents for his former behaviour, commence a suit on account of that injury.

Tit. V. *De obligationibus quæ quasi ex delicto nascuntur.*

If a judge makes a suit his own, by giving an unjust determination, an action of malfeasance will not properly lie against him; but although he is not subject to an action of malfeasance, or of contract, yet as he hath certainly committed a fault, although it was not by design, but through imprudence and want of skill, he may be sued by an action of quasi-malfeasance; and must suffer such a penalty which seems equitable to the conscience of a superior judge.

§ 1. Whoever occupies a chamber from whence anything hath been either thrown or spilt, by which damage is done, he is liable to an action of quasi-malfeasance; and it is not material whether the chamber is the property of the occupier, whether he pays rent for it, or whether he inhabits it gratis: and the reason why such occupier is not suable for a direct malfeasance is, because he is generally sued for the fault of another. Any man is also subject to the same action who hath hung or placed anything in a public road, so as to endanger passengers by the fall of it; in which case a penalty of ten *aurei* is appointed: but when anything hath been thrown or spilt, the action is always for the double of what the damage amounts to. If a freeman is killed by accident, the penalty is fifty *aurei;* but if he only receives some hurt, the quantum of the damage is at the discretion of the judge, who ought to take the fees of the physician into the account, and all other expenses attendant upon the cure, over and above the time which the patient hath lost in his illness, or may lose by being unable to pursue his business.

§ 2. If the son of a family lives separate from his father, and anything is either thrown or spilt from his apartment, or so hung or placed that the fall of it may do damage, it is the opinion of Julian that no action will lie against the father, and that the son only can be sued. The same rule of law is also to be observed in regard to the son of a family who hath acted as a judge, and given an unjust determination.

§ 3. The master of a ship, tavern, or inn, is liable to be sued for a quasi-malfeasance on account of every damage or theft done or committed in any of these places by himself or his servants; for although no action, either of direct malfeasance or of contract, can be brought against the master, yet as he has in some measure been guilty of a fault in employing dishonest persons as his servants, he is therefore subject to a suit for a quasi-malfeasance. But in all these cases the action given is an action upon the fact, which may be brought in favour of an heir, but not against him.

Tit. VI. *De actionibus.*

It now remains that we should treat of actions. An action is nothing more than the right which every man has of bringing an action at law for whatever is due to him.

§ 1. All actions in general, whether they are determinable before judges or arbitrators, may be primarily divided into two kinds, real and personal; for the plaintiff must sue the defendant, either because the defendant is obligated to him by contract, or hath been guilty of some malfeasance; and in this case the action must be personal, in which the plaintiff alleges that his adversary is bound to give or to do something for his service; or some other matter, as the occasion requires: or otherwise, the plaintiff must sue the defendant on account of some corporeal thing when there is no obligation; in which case the action must be real: as, for example, if Sempronius possesses land, which Titius affirms to be his property, the other denying it, Titius must bring a real action against Sempronius for the recovery.

§ 2. Also, if any man brings an action, alleging that he has a right to the usufruct of a field, or house, or a right of driving his cattle, or of drawing water in the land of his neighbour, such action is denominated real. And an action relating to the rights of houses or city estates, which rights are called services, is also of the same kind; as when a man commences a suit, and alleges that he has a right of prospect, a right to raise the height of his house, a right of making a part of it to project, or a right of laying the beams of his building upon his neighbour's walls. There are also contrary actions to these, which relate to usufructs, and the rights of country and city estates; as when the complainant alleges that his adversary is not entitled to the usufruct of a particular ground, or to the right of passage, &c., &c. These actions are also real, but are negative in their nature, and cannot, therefore, be used in regard to things corporeal; for, in respect to things corporeal, the agent or plaintiff is the person out of possession; for a possessor can bring no action: there are, however, many cases in which a possessor may be obliged to act the part of a plaintiff; but we refer the reader to the books of the Digests.

§ 3. The actions of which we have made mention, and all actions of a similar nature, are derived from the civil law; but the prætor, by virtue of his jurisdiction, hath introduced other actions, both real and personal, of which it will be necessary to give some examples: for he often permits a real action to be brought, either by allowing the demandant to allege that he hath acquired by prescription what he hath not so acquired; or, on the contrary, by permitting a former possessor to allege, that his adversary hath not acquired by prescription what in reality he hath so acquired.

§ 4. If any particular thing belonging to one man should be delivered in trust to another, that it might be deposited with him upon some just account, as by reason of a purchase, a gift, a marriage, or a bequest, and it should so happen that such trustee should lose the possession, before he hath gained a property in the thing possessed, he could have no direct action for the recovery of it; inasmuch as real actions are given by the law for the re-vindication of those things only in which a man hath a vested property or dominion. But it being hard that an action should be wanting in such a case, the prætor hath supplied one, in which the person who hath lost his possession is alleged to aver, that he hath a prescriptive right to the thing in question, although he hath not obtained it; and he may thus recover the possession. This action is called *actio Publiciana*, because it was first instituted by the edict of Publicius the prætor.

§ 5. On the contrary, if any man, whilst he is abroad in the service of his country, or a prisoner in the hands of the enemy, should gain a prescriptive title to a thing which belongs to another who was not abroad, then the former proprietor is permitted at any time within a year after the return of the possessor, to bring an action against him, the prescriptive title being rescinded, and the proprietor being allowed to allege that the possessor hath not effectually prescribed, and that therefore the thing in litigation is his own. The same motive of equity hath also induced the prætor to allow the use of this species of action to certain other persons, as we may learn more at large from the Digests.

§ 6. If a debtor disposes of anything by delivering it to some person in order to defraud his creditors, the creditors are then permitted, notwithstanding the delivery, to bring an action for the thing, if they have previously obtained the sentence of the proper magistrate for putting themselves into possession; that is, they are allowed to plead that the thing was not delivered, and of course that it continues to be a part of their debtor's goods.

§ 7. Also the action Serviana, and the action quasi-Serviana, which is called hypothecary, both take their rise from the prætor's jurisdiction. By the action Serviana, a suit may be commenced for the stock and cattle of a farmer, which are obligated as a pledge for the rent of the ground which he farms of his landlord. The action quasi-Serviana is that by which a creditor may sue for a thing pledged or hypothecated to him; and in regard to this action, there is no difference between a pledge and a hypotheque, though in other respects they differ; for by the term pledge is meant that which hath actually been delivered to a creditor, especially if the thing was a moveable; and by the word hypotheque, we comprehend what is obligated to a creditor by a nude agreement only, without a delivery.

§ 8. Personal actions have also been introduced by the prætors, in consequence of their authority; such is the action *de pecuniâ constitutâ;* which much resembles that called *receptitia;* which we have now taken away by our constitution as unnecessary; and whatever advantageous matter it contained, we have added it to the action *de pecuniâ constitutâ.* The prætors have likewise introduced the action concerning the *peculium* of slaves, and the sons of families; and also the actions in which the only question is, whether the plaintiff hath made oath of his debt; they have likewise introduced many others.

§ 9. A suit may be commenced by the action *de pecuniâ constitutâ*, against any person who hath engaged to pay money either for himself or another, without stipulation; but when there is a stipulation, the prætorian action is not wanted; for the performance of the promise may be enforced by the civil law.

§ 10. The prætor hath also given actions *de peculio* against fathers and masters, inasmuch as they are not legally bound by the contracts of their children and slaves; for it is but equity that parents and masters should be condemned to pay to the extent of a *peculium*, which is as it were the patrimony and separate estate of a son, a daughter, or a slave.

§ 11. Also if any man, at the prayer or request of the adverse party, makes oath, that the debt which he sues for is unpaid and due to him, the prætor most justly indulges him with an action upon the fact; in which no inquiry is made whether the debt is due, but whether the oath hath been taken.

§ 12. The prætors have also introduced a great number of penal actions, by virtue of their authority. But to mention some only out of many, they have provided, for instance, an action against him who hath wilfully damaged or erased an edict; against an emancipated son, or a freedman, who hath commenced a suit against his parent or patron, without a previous permission from the proper magistrate; and also against any person, who by force or fraud hath hindered another from appearing to the process of a court of justice. But these are only some instances out of a great number which might be produced.

§ 13. Prejudicial actions are also real; such are those by which it is inquired, whether a man is born free or made free; whether he is a slave or a bastard. But of these actions, that only proceeds from the civil law, by which it is inquired whether a man is free born; the rest all take their rise from the prætor's jurisdiction.

§ 14. Actions being thus divided into real and personal, it is certain that a man cannot sue for his own property by a condiction or a personal action in the following form, viz., "If it appears that the defendant ought to give it me"; for the act of giving implies the conferring of property; and therefore that which is the property of the plaintiff can never be understood to be given to him, or to become more his own than it already is. But, notwithstanding this, in order to show a detestation for thieves and robbers, and to increase the number of actions that may be brought against them, it hath been determined that, besides the double and quadruple penalty to which they are liable, they may be pursued by a condiction for the thing taken, in the very form before recited, "if it appears that they ought to give it." And this is allowed, although the party injured may also bring a real action against them, by which he may demand the thing taken as his own.

§ 15. Real actions are called vindications; and personal actions, in which it is intended that something ought to be done or given, are called condictions; for the word *condicere* was, in our old language, of the same import with *denuntiare*, to denounce: but the term condiction is now improperly used to denote a personal action, by which the plaintiff contends that something ought to be given to him; for denunciations are not in use.

§ 16. Actions are also further divided into those which are given for the sake of obtaining the very thing in dispute; into those which are given for the penalty only; and lastly, into mixed actions, which are given for the recovery both of the thing and the penalty.

§ 17. All real actions are given for the recovery of the thing in litigation; and almost all the personal actions which arise from a contract are also given for the recovery of the thing itself, as the action for a *mutuum*, a *commodatum*, or on account of a stipulation: also the action on account of a deposit, a mandate, partnership, buying and selling, letting and hiring. But when a suit is commenced for a thing deposited by reason of a riot, a fire, or any other calamity, the prætor always gives an action for a double penalty, besides the thing deposited, if the suit is brought against the depositary himself, or against his heir, for fraud; in which case the action is mixed.

§ 18. In cases of malfeasance, some actions are given for the penalty only, and some both for the thing and the penalty; and these are therefore called mixed actions. But in an action of theft, whether manifest or not manifest, nothing more is sued for than the penalty, which in manifest theft is quadruple, and in theft not manifest double; for the owner may recover by a separate action whatever hath been stolen from him, if he alleges that the thing stolen is his own; and he is entitled to this action, not only against the thief, but against any other person who is in possession of his property. The thief may also be sued by a condiction or personal action for the recovery of the thing stolen.

§ 19. An action for goods taken by force is a mixed action, because the value of whatever is taken is included under the quadruple value to be recovered by the action, and thus the penalty is but triple. The action introduced by the law *Aquilia*, on account of damage injuriously done, is also a mixed action; not only when it is given for double value against a man denying the fact, but sometimes when the action is only for single value; as when a man hath killed a slave, who, at the time of his death, was lame, or wanted an eye, but had within the year previous to his decease been free from any defect, and of great price; for in this case the defendant is obliged to pay as much as the slave was worth at any time within the year preceding his death, according to what has already been observed. (B. 4, t. 3.) A mixed action may also be brought against those who have delayed to deliver a legacy or gift in trust, given for the benefit of a church, or any other holy place, till they have been called before a magistrate for that purpose; for then they are compelled to deliver up the thing, or to pay the money bequeathed, and also the value of as much more by way of penalty, and thus they are condemned to pay the double of what was due.

§ 20. There are also some actions which are of a mixed nature, by being in effect as well real as personal; of this sort is the action *familiæ erciscundæ*, which may be brought by co-heirs for the partition of their inheritance; such also is the action *de communi dividundo*, given for the division of any particular thing or things, which, exclusive of an inheritance, are in common; and likewise the action *finium regundorum*, which takes place among those estates which are contiguous. And in these three occasions it is wholly in the power of the judge to give the ground or thing in dispute to either of the parties litigant, and then to oblige the party, if necessity so requires, to recompense his adversary by paying him a sum certain, in amends for any inequality in the adjudication.

§ 21. All actions are for the single, double, triple, or quadruple value of the thing in litigation; for no action extends further.

§ 22. The single value is sued for when an action is given upon a stipulation, a loan, a mandate, the contract of buying and selling, letting and hiring; and also upon other very numerous accounts.

§ 23. The double value is sued for in an action of theft not manifest, of injury, by virtue of the law *Aquilia*, and sometimes in an action of deposit. The double value is likewise sued for in an action brought on account of a slave corrupted, against him by whose advice such a slave hath fled from his master, grown disobedient or luxurious, or become in any manner the worse; and in this action an estimation is to be made of whatever things the slave hath stolen from his master before his flight. An action for the detention of a legacy left to a holy place is also given for double the value, as we have before remarked.

§ 24. A suit may be brought for triple value, when any person inserts a greater sum than is due to him in the libel of convention, to the intent that the officers of any court may exact a larger fee, or sportule, from the defendant; in which case the defendant may obtain the triple value of the extraordinary fee from the plaintiff, including the fee in the triple value. The fees of officers are regulated by our constitution; and it is not to be doubted but that the action called *condictio ex lege* may be given by virtue of that ordinance.

§ 25. A suit may be commenced for quadruple or fourfold

value, by an action for theft manifest, by an action for putting a man in fear, and by an action on account of money given to bring on a litigious suit against some third person, or on account of money given to desist from it. A condiction *ex lege* for the quadruple value arises also from our constitution against those officers of courts of justice who demand anything from the party defendant, contrary to the regulations of the said constitution.

§ 26. But an action of theft not manifest, and an action on account of a slave corrupted, differ from the others of which we have spoken, in that they always enforce a condemnation in double the value; but in an action given by the law *Aquilia* for an injury done, and sometimes in an action of deposit, the double value may be exacted in case of a denial; yet whenever the party defendant makes a confession, then the single value is all which can be recovered. But when a demand is made by an action for a legacy to pious uses, due to any holy place or society, the penalty is not only doubled by the denial of the defendant, but also by any delay of payment which may be adjudged to have given a just cause for citing the defendant before a magistrate; but if the legacy is confessed and paid before any citation issues at the command of the judge, the party complainant must rest satisfied with the single value.

§ 27. An action for putting a man in fear differs also from other actions *in quadruplum*, because it is tacitly implied in the nature of this action, that the party who hath obeyed the command of the judge or magistrate in restoring the things taken may be dismissed; for in all other actions for the fourfold value, every man must be condemned to pay the full penalty, as in the action of theft manifest.

§ 28. The fourth division of actions is into those of good faith, and those of strict right. Those of good faith are the following: viz., actions of buying and selling, letting and hiring; of affairs transacted, of mandate, deposit, partnership, tutelage, loan, mortgage; of the partition of an inheritance, and of the division of any particular thing or things, which belong in common to diverse persons; also actions in prescribed words, which are either estimatory, or derived from commutation; and lastly, that action by virtue of which we demand an inheritance: for although it hath long been doubtful to what class this action belonged, yet it is now clearly determined by our constitution, that the demand of an inheritance is to be numbered among the actions of good faith.

§ 29. The action called *rei uxoriæ*, which was given for the recovery of a marriage portion, was formerly numbered among the actions of good faith; but when, upon finding the action of stipulation to be more full and advantageous, we abrogated the action *rei uxoriæ*, and transferred all its effects, with the addition of many other powers, to the action of stipulation, which is given on account of marriage portions, we then not only thought that this action of stipulation, as far as it related to marriage portions, deserved to be numbered with actions of good faith, but we also added to it, by implication, the full powers of an action of hypotheque; and we have likewise judged it proper, that women, in whose sole behalf we enacted our constitution, should be preferred to all other creditors by mortgage, whenever they themselves sue for their marriage portions.

§ 30. In all actions of good faith a full power is given to the judge of calculating according to the rules of justice and equity how much ought to be restored to the plaintiff; and, of course, when the plaintiff is found to be indebted to the defendant in a less sum, it is in the power of the judge to allow a compensation, and to condemn the defendant in the payment of the difference; and even in actions of strict right the Emperor Marcus introduced a compensation by opposing an exception of fraud: but we have extended compensations much further by our constitution when the debt of the defendant is evident; so that actions of strict right, whether real, personal, or of whatever kind they are, may be diminished by compensation; except only an action of deposit, against which we have not judged it proper to permit any compensation to be alleged, lest the pretence of compensation should give a colour and encouragement to fraud.

§ 31. There are also some actions which we call arbitrary, because they depend entirely upon the arbitration of the judge; for in these, if the party does not obey the legal commands of the court by exhibiting whatever is required, by restoring the thing in litigation, or by paying the value of it, or by giving up a slave in consequence of an action of malfeasance, the judge ought immediately to proceed to condemnation by his definitive sentence. Of these arbitrary actions some are real and some personal: some are real as the action *Publiciana*, *Serviana*, and *quasi-Serviana*, which is likewise called hypothecary: others are personal, as those by which a suit is commenced on account of something done by force, fear, or fraud, or on account of something which was promised to be paid or restored in a certain place; and the action *ad exhibendum*, which was given to the intent that something particular should be exhibited, is also of the same kind: and in all these and the like actions the judge has full power to determine, according to equity and the nature of the thing sued for, in what manner and proportion the plaintiff ought to receive satisfaction.

§ 32. A judge ought always to take as much care as possible so to frame his sentence that it may be given for a thing or sum certain; although the claim upon which the sentence is founded may be for an uncertain sum or quantity.

§ 33. Formerly, if a plaintiff claimed more in his libel than was due or belonged to him, he failed in his cause, that is, he even lost that which really did belong to him; nor was it easy for him to be restored to it by the prætor, unless he was under the age of twenty-five years; for in this, as well as in other cases, it was usual to aid minors if it appeared upon examination that the error was owing to their youth; and whenever an error was such that one of the most knowing of men might have been led into it, then even persons of full age might have been aided by the magistrate; as, for example, if a legatee had demanded his whole legacy, and codicils were afterwards produced by which a part of it was revoked, or new legacies bequeathed to other persons, so that the plaintiff appeared to have demanded more than three-fourths of his legacy; because it was subject to a diminution by the law *Falcidia;* yet in such a case the legatee would be relieved notwithstanding the excess of his demand. It is here necessary to be observed that a man may demand more than what is due to him in four several respects, viz.: in respect to the thing itself; to time; to place; and to the cause. In respect to the thing itself; as when the plaintiff, instead of ten *aurei* which are due to him, demands twenty; or if, when he is in reality the owner but of part of some particular thing, he claims the whole as his own, or a greater share of it than he is entitled to. In respect to time; as when the plaintiff makes his demand before the day of payment, or before the time of the performance of a condition; for as he who does not pay so soon as he ought is always understood to pay less than he ought, so, by a parity of reasoning, whoever commences a suit prematurely demands more than is due. In respect to place; as when any person requires that what was stipulated to be given, or delivered to him at a certain place, should be given or delivered to him at some other place, without taking any notice in his libel of the place specified in the stipulation; as if Titius, for example, should stipulate in these words—"Do you promise to give such a particular thing at Ephesus?" and should afterwards declare simply in his libel that the same thing ought to be given to him at Rome; for Titius would thus be understood to demand more than his due by endeavouring to deprive his debtor of the advantage which he might have had in paying his creditor at Ephesus. And it is upon this account that an arbitrary action is given to him who would demand payment in another place than that which was agreed upon, for in that action the advantage, which might have accrued to the debtor by paying his debt in the place stipulated, is always taken into consideration at the discretion of the judge. This advantage is generally found the greatest in merchandise, as in wine, oil, corn, &c., which in different places bear different prices; and indeed money itself is not lent everywhere at the same interest. But if a man would sue for the performance of a stipulation at Ephesus, or at any other place where it was agreed that the stipulation should be performed, he may legally commence his suit by a pure action, that is, without mentioning the place; and this the prætor allows of, inasmuch as the debtor does not lose any advantage. Next to him who demands more than his due in regard to place, is he who demands more than his due in regard to the cause; as, for instance, if Titius stipulates thus with Sempronius—"Do you promise to give either your slave Stichus, or ten *aurei?*" and then demands from Sempronius either the slave specially, or the money specially; for in this case Titius would be adjudged to have demanded more than his due, the right of election being in Sempronius, by whom the promise was made; and therefore, when Titius sues either for the money specially, or for the slave, he deprives the adverse party of the power of election, and betters his own condition, by making that of his adversary the worse; and it is upon this account that an action has been given, by which the party agent may make his demand conformable to the stipulation, and claim either the slave or the money. And further, if a man should stipulate generally that wine, purple, or a slave, should be given him, and should afterwards sue for the wine of Campania, the purple of Tyre, or the slave Stichus in particular, he would then be adjudged to have demanded more than his due; for the power of election would thus be taken from the adverse party, who was not bound by the stipulation to pay the thing demanded; and although in any of these cases the thing sued for should be of little or no value, yet the demandant would be thought to claim more than his due, because it is often easier for the debtor to pay the thing stipulated, although it may be of greater value than the thing demanded. Such was the law according to the ancient practice, in regard to an over-demand, viz., that the demandant should lose even that which was really due to him. But this law has been greatly restrained by the constitution of Zeno the emperor, and by our own; for if more than is due is demanded in regard to time, the judge must be directed in his proceeding by the constitution of that emperor of glorious memory; but if more is demanded in respect to quantity, or on any other account, then the loss suffered by him upon whom the demand is made, must be recompensed, as we have before declared, by the condemnation of the party agent in triple damages.

§ 34. If a plaintiff sues for less than what he has a claim to, demanding, for instance, only five *aurei*, when ten are due, or the moiety of an estate, when the whole belongs to him, he acts safely by this method; for the judge, in consequence of Zeno's constitution, may nevertheless condemn the adverse party, under the same process, to the payment or delivery of all which appears of right to belong to the plaintiff.

§ 35. When a plaintiff demands one thing instead of another, he risks nothing by the mistake, which he is allowed to correct under one and the same process: as if a litigant should demand the slave Erotes instead of the slave Stichus, or should claim as due by testament what is found to be due upon a stipulation.

§ 36. There are also some actions by which we do not always sue for the whole which is due to us, but for the whole, or less than the whole, as it proves to be most expedient: thus, when a suit is brought against the *peculium* of a son or a slave, if the *peculium* is sufficient to answer the demand, the father or master must be condemned to pay the whole debt; but if the *peculium* is not sufficient, the judge can condemn the defendants only to the extent of its value. We will hereafter explain in its proper place what we mean by the term *peculium*.

§ 37. Also, if a woman commences a suit for the restitution of her marriage portion, the man must be condemned to pay as far as he is able; *i.e.*, as far as his income or faculties will permit; and therefore, if the portion demanded and the faculties of the man are equal, he must be adjudged to satisfy the whole demand; but if his faculties are less than the claim, he must nevertheless be condemned to pay as much as he is able. But the claim of a woman may in this case be lessened by a retention, for the husband is permitted to retain an equivalent for whatever he hath necessarily expended upon the estate given with his wife as a marriage portion; but this will fully appear by a perusal of the Digests, to which the reader is referred.

§ 38. And if any person commences a suit against his parent or patron, or if one partner sues another, the plaintiff can by no means obtain sentence for a greater sum than his adversary is able to pay; and the same is to be observed when a donor is sued on account of his donation.

§ 39. When a compensation is alleged by the defendant, it generally happens that the plaintiff recovers less than his demand; for it is in the power of the judge, as we have before declared, to make an equitable deduction from the demand of the plaintiff of whatever he owes to the defendant, and to condemn the defendant to the payment only of the remainder; as it hath already been observed.

§ 40. Creditors, also, to whom a debtor hath made a cession of his goods, may afterwards, if he hath gained any considerable acquisition, bring a fresh suit against him for as much as he is able to pay, but not more; for it would be inhuman to condemn a man *in solidum*, who hath already been deprived of his whole fortune.

Tit. VII. *Quod cum eo, qui in alienâ potestate est, negotium gestum esse dicitur.*

We have already made mention of the action by which a suit may be brought against the *peculium* or separate estate of a son or a slave, but it is now necessary to speak of it more fully, and also of some other actions, which are given on account of children and slaves against their parents and masters. But inasmuch as the law is almost the same, whether an affair is transacted with a slave, or with him who is under the power of his parent, we will therefore, to avoid being prolix, treat only of slaves and their masters, leaving what we say of them to be understood also of parents and children under power; for whenever there is anything peculiar to be observed in regard to children and parents, we intend to point it out separately.

§ 1. If any business is negotiated by a slave who acts by the command of his master, the prætor will give an action against the master for the whole value of the transaction; for whoever makes a contract with a slave, is presumed to have done it upon a confidence in the master.

§ 2. The prætor also gives two other actions *in solidum* upon the same motive, the one of which is called *exercitoria*, the other *institoria*. The action *exercitoria* takes place when a master hath constituted his slave to be the commander of a vessel, and some contract hath been entered into with such slave merely upon that account; and this action is named *exercitoria*, because he to whom the profits of a ship or vessel appertain is called *exercitor*. The action *institoria* is made use of when a master hath given his slave the management of a shop, or committed any particular affair to his direction, by which some one hath been induced to enter into a contract with such slave; and this action is called *institoria*, because all persons to whom a negotiation is committed are denominated *institores*. The prætor hath likewise been induced, by the same equity, to give these two actions against any man who employs a free person, or the slave of another, in the management of a ship, a warehouse, or any particular affair.

§ 3. The prætor hath also introduced another action called *tributoria*, or tributory; for if a slave, without the command, but with the knowledge, of his master, traffics with the product of his *peculium*, and persons are thus induced to contract with him, the prætor ordains that the merchandise or money arising from his traffic shall be distributed between the master—if he has any just claim—and the rest of the creditors in a rateable proportion; and the master himself is always permitted to make the distribution. But if any creditor complains that too small a share hath been apportioned to him, the prætor will allow him to use the before-named action, which is called *tributoria*, on account of the distribution.

§ 4. The action concerning a *peculium*, and things converted to the profit of the master of a slave, hath likewise been introduced by the prætor; for although a contract hath been entered into by a slave, without the consent of his master, yet, where the money arising from it is converted to the benefit of such master, the master ought to be answerable for the performance of it; and even although the master should receive no emolument from the transaction, yet it is right that he should be answerable for as much as the *peculium* of his slave is found to be worth. But, to be more explicit, we understand that whenever money or any other thing is necessarily used or expended by a slave upon his master's affairs, it is a conversion of it to his benefit; as, for example, if a slave who hath borrowed money should pay the debts of his master, repair his buildings, purchase an estate, provision, or any other thing which is useful; and therefore, if out of ten *aurei* borrowed by a slave he should pay only five to his master's creditors, and squander the rest, the master would nevertheless be condemned to the payment *in solidum* of the five *aurei* which had been expended for his use; but as to the other five, he could be obliged to pay only so much as the *peculium* would answer; and from hence it will appear that if all the ten *aurei* which were borrowed had been converted by the slave to his master's emolument, the lender might have recovered the whole ten from the master; for although it is one and the same action by which a suit is commenced against a *peculium*, and for the recovery of what a slave hath converted to his master's use, yet this action carries with it two different condemnations; and it is for this reason that the judge does not begin to make an estimate of the value of the *peculium* till he has previously examined whether the whole, or any part of the money, arising from the slave's contract, hath been expended for the service of the master: but when the judge proceeds to the valuation of the *peculium*, a deduction is made of whatever the slave owes to his master, or to any other under the power of his master, and the remainder only is understood to be strictly the *peculium*, and chargeable with debts due to strangers. But it sometimes happens that what one slave owes to another under the power of the same master is not deducted; as when the slave, who is the creditor, composes a part of his debtor's *peculium;* for if a slave is indebted to his vicarial slave, this debt cannot be deducted from the *peculium.*

§ 5. It is nevertheless not to be doubted, but that he who hath made a contract with a slave at the command of the master of that slave, and is entitled to the action *institoria* or *exercitoria*, is also entitled to the action *de peculio* and *de in rem verso;* but it would be highly imprudent in any party to relinquish an action by which he could most easily recover his whole demand, and by recurring to another reduce himself to the difficulty of proving that the money he lent to the slave was turned to the use of the master, or that the slave is possessed of a *peculium* sufficient to answer the whole debt. He also to whom the action *tributoria* is given is equally entitled to the action *de peculio* and *de in rem verso;* but it is expedient in some cases to use the one, and in some cases the other; yet it is frequently most expedient to use the action *tributoria*, because in this the condition of the master is not principally regarded; *i. e.*, there is no previous deduction made of what is due to him, his title being esteemed in the same light with that of other creditors; but in the action *de peculio* the debt due to the master is first deducted, and he is condemned only to distribute the remainder among the creditors. Again, in some cases it may be more convenient to commence a suit by the action *de peculio*, because it affects the whole *peculium*, whereas the action *tributoria* regards only so much of it as hath been made use of in traffic; and it is possible that a slave may have trafficked only with a third, a fourth, or some very small part, and that the rest consists of lands, slaves, or money lent at interest. Upon the whole, therefore, it greatly behoves every man to choose that remedy which may be most beneficial to him; but if the creditor of a slave can prove a conversion to the use of the master of that slave, he ought most certainly to commence his suit by the action *de in rem verso*.

§ 6. We understand what we have said concerning a slave and his master to take place equally in regard to children under power and their parents.

§ 7. But children are in some respects particularly regarded by the Macedonian decree of the senate, which prohibits money to be lent them whilst they are under the power of their parents; for creditors are not suffered to bring any action either against the children, even after they are emancipated, or against their parents who emancipated them. This was a caution which the senate thought proper to take, because young heirs, who were loaded with their debts, contracted for the support of luxury, have often endeavoured by private methods to take away the lives of their parents.

§ 8. But, in fine, we must observe that whatever hath been contracted for at the command of a parent or master, and converted to their use, may be recovered by a direct action against the father or master, in the same manner as if the contract had been originally made with them. And it is likewise certain, that he who is liable to the action *institoria* or *exhibitoria* may also be sued by a direct action, inasmuch as the contract is presumed to have been made at his command.

Tit. VIII. *De noxalibus actionibus.*

Noxal actions are given on account of the offences of slaves; as when a slave commits a theft or robbery, or does any other damage or injury. And when the master or owner of a slave is condemned upon this account, it is in his option either to pay the valuation of the damage done, or to deliver up his slave as a recompense.

§ 1. The term *noxa* denotes the slave by whom the malfeasance was done; and by the word *noxia* we understand the malfeasance itself, be it of what kind it will, theft, damage, rapine, or injury.

§ 2. It is with the utmost reason allowable that a master should deliver the slave who is culpable as a full compensation to the party injured; for it was unjust that it should be in the power of slaves to cause their masters to suffer any greater damage than the value of their own bodies would amount to.

§ 3. If a noxal action is given against a master, he may free himself from it by delivering his slave into the possession of the plaintiff, in whom the property in such a slave will become absolutely vested; but if the slave can pay his new master in money the value of the damage, the slave may be manumitted by the assistance of the prætor, although his new master is ever so unwilling.

§ 4. Noxal actions are constituted either by the laws or by the edict of the prætor. They are constituted on account of theft by the law of the Twelve Tables, and on account of damage injuriously done, by virtue of the law *Aquilia.* But on account of injuries and goods taken by force, they are constituted by the edict of the prætor.

§ 5. Every noxal action follows the person of the slave by whom the malfeasance was committed; but as long as he continues under the power of his master, his master only is liable to an action; and if he becomes subject to a new master, then the new master becomes liable; but if the slave is manumitted, he may be prosecuted by a direct action; for then the *noxæ deditio* is extinguished, because no surrender can then be made of him by whom the malfeasance was committed. But, on the contrary, an action which was at first direct may afterwards become noxal; for if a man who is free does any malfeasance, and afterwards becomes a slave—and we have in our first book declared in what cases this may happen—then the action, which was before direct, begins to be a noxal action against his master.

§ 6. Although a slave commits a malfeasance against his master, yet no action is given; for no obligation can arise between a master and his slave: and therefore, if that slave passes under the power of another master, or is manumitted, no action can be brought either against him in his own person or against his new master; from whence it follows that if the slave of another should commit any malfeasance, for example, against Titius, and should afterwards become the slave of the same Titius, the action is extinguished; for it is a maxim that an action becomes extinct whenever it is brought into a state in which it could not have had a commencement: and hence it is, that although a slave, from whom a master hath received damage, should cease to be under the power of that master, yet no action can afterwards be given against such slave; neither can a slave, who hath been aliened or manumitted, bring any action against his late master, by whom he hath been ill-treated.

§ 7. The ancients indeed admitted this law of the forfeiture of the person to take place even in cases in which their children were concerned, whether male or female; but the later ages have rightly thought, that such a rigorous proceeding ought by all means to be exploded; and it hath therefore passed wholly into disuse; for who could suffer a son, and more especially a daughter, to be delivered up as a forfeiture to a stranger? for in the case of a son, the punishment of the father would be greater than that of the son; and in the case of a daughter, the rules of modesty forbid such a practice. It hath therefore prevailed, that noxal actions should only take place in regard to slaves; and in the books of the ancient commentators of the law we find it often repeated, that the sons of a family may themselves be convened for their own misdeeds.

Tit. IX. *Si quadrupes pauperiem fecisse dicatur.*

A noxal action is given by the law of the Twelve Tables whenever any damage is done by brute animals, through wantonness, fright, or furiousness; but if they are delivered up in atonement for the damage done, the defendant must be discharged from the action; for it is thus written in the law of the Twelve Tables:—"If a horse, apt to kick, should strike with his foot; or if an ox, accustomed to gore, should wound any man with his horns, &c." But a noxal action takes place only in regard to those animals which act contrary to their nature; for when the ferocity of a beast is innate, no action can be given; so that if a bear breaks loose from his master, and mischief is done, the person to whom this animal belonged cannot be convened; for he ceased to be the master as soon as the beast escaped. But it is here to be noted, that the word *pauperies* denotes a damage, by which no injury is intended; for an animal which hath no reason cannot be said to have committed an injury. This is what relates to noxal actions.

§ 1. It must be observed that the edict of the Edile prohibits any man to keep a dog, a boar, a bear, or a lion, where there is a public passage or highway; and if this prohibition is disobeyed, and any free man receives hurt, the master of the beast may be condemned in whatever sum seems agreeable to equity in the opinion of the judge; yet in regard to every other damage, the condemnation must be in the double of what the damage amounts to. It is here necessary to inform the student, that not only the Edilitian action, but also an action for the damage, called *pauperies*, may both take place against the same person; for although actions, and more especially those which are penal, concur together on account of the same thing, they are not destructive the one of another.

Tit. X. *De iis, per quos agere possumus.*

Any man may commence a suit either in his own name, or in that of another; as in the name of a proctor, a tutor, or a curator; but anciently, one person could not sue in the name of another, unless in a cause of liberty, tutelage, or where a society was concerned. It was afterwards permitted by the law *Hostilia*, that an action of theft might be brought in the names of those who were captives in the hands of the enemy; who were absent upon the affairs of the republic; or who were under the care of tutors. But as it was found in later times to be highly inconvenient, that any man should be prohibited either from suing, or defending in the name of another, it by degrees became a practice to sue by proctors; for ill health, old age, the necessity of voyaging, and many other cases, continually prevent mankind from being able to prosecute their own affairs in person.

§ 1. It is not necessary to use any certain form of words in appointing a proctor, nor to make the appointment in the presence of the adverse party; for it is generally done even without his knowledge: and note, that whoever is employed either to sue or to defend for another, is understood to be a proctor.

§ 2. We have already explained in the first book of our Institutions how tutors and curators may be appointed.

Tit. XI. *De satisdationibus.*

In taking security, the ancients pursued a different method from that which the moderns have made choice of; for anciently, if a real action was brought, the defendant, or party in possession, was compelled to give security, to the end that, if he lost his cause, and would neither restore the thing itself, nor pay the estimation of it, the demandant might be enabled either to sue such defendant, or the parties bound for him; and this species of caution is termed *judicatum solvi:* nor is it difficult to understand why it is so called; since every demandant stipulated that the thing adjudged to him should be paid. We have already observed, that whoever defended his own cause, was obliged to give security; it is therefore with much greater reason, that the proctor in the cause of another should be compelled to give caution. But if a demandant in a real action had sued in his own name, he was under no necessity of giving security; yet, if he sued only as a proctor, he was obliged to give caution, that his acts would be ratified by his principal, *rem ratam dominum habiturum;* for the danger was, lest the client or party principal should bring a fresh suit for the same thing: and by the words of the edict even tutors and curators were compellable to give caution, as well as proctors, though it was sometimes remitted when tutors or curators were demandants; and such was the practice in regard to real actions.

§ 1. The same rules which were observed in real obtained also in personal actions, in regard to the taking security on the part of the plaintiff; and if the defendant in a personal action proceeded in another's name he was obliged to give caution; for no one was reputed a competent defendant in the cause of another, unless security was given: but whenever any man was convened in a personal action to defend his own cause, he was not compelled to give caution that the thing adjudged should be paid.

§ 2. But at present we observe a very different practice; for if a defendant is now convened, either in a real or personal action, in his own cause, he is not compellable to give security for the payment of the estimation of the suit, but only for his own person; to wit, that he will remain in judgment till the cause is determined: and this security is sometimes given by sureties; sometimes by a promise upon oath, which is called a juratory caution; and sometimes by a simple promise without an oath, according to the quality of the person of the defendant.

§ 3. But if a suit is commenced or defended by a proctor, the proctor of the plaintiff, if he does not either enrol a mandate of appointment in the acts of court, or cause his client to nominate him publicly, is obliged to give security that his client will ratify his proceeding. The same rule is also to be observed, if a tutor, curator, or any person to whom the management of the affairs of others is entrusted, commences a suit by a proctor.

§ 4. But when a party is convened, if he is ready to nominate a proctor, such party may appear in open court, and confirm the nomination by giving the caution *judicatum solvi* under the usual stipulation; or he may appear out of court, and become himself the surety, that his proctor will perform all the covenants in the instrument of caution; and whether the party convened does this in court, or out of court, he is obliged to make his estate chargeable, that his heirs, as well as himself, may be liable to an action. And a further security must likewise be given, that he will either appear in person at the time of pronouncing sentence, or that his sureties, in case of his non-appearance, shall be bound to pay whatever the sentence exacts, if no appeal is interposed.

§ 5. When a defendant does not give an appearance, then any other person who is willing may take upon himself the defence for him; and this may be done either in a real or personal action, without distinction, if the caution *judicatum solvi* is entered into for the payment of the estimation of the suit; for no man—according to the ancient rule already mentioned—can be said to defend the cause of another legally, unless security is given.

§ 6. But all such formalities may be more perfectly learned from the usage and practice of courts.

§ 7. We have judged it expedient that these forms shall obtain not only in Constantinople, but also in all our other provinces, in which a different practice may have hitherto prevailed through the want of knowledge; for it is necessary that all the provinces should be guided by the example of the capital of our dominions, and follow the practice of our royal city.

Tit. XII. *De perpetuis et temporalibus actionibus, et quæ ad hæredes et in hæredes transeunt.*

All those actions which took their rise from the law, the decrees of the senate, or the constitutions, were anciently reputed perpetual; but the later emperors have by their ordinances fixed certain limits both to real and personal actions. Actions given by virtue of the prætor's authority, are generally limited to the space of one year; for such is the duration of his office: but sometimes the prætorian actions are made perpetual; that is, they are extended to the limits introduced by the constitutions; such are those actions which the prætor gives to the possessors of goods, and to others who hold the place of heirs. The action of manifest theft is also perpetual, although it proceeds from the mere authority of the prætor; for it was thought absurd, that this action should determine within the space of a year.

§ 1. But all actions in general, which either the law or the prætor gives against any man, will not also be given against his heirs; for it is a most certain rule of law, that penal actions, arising from a malfeasance, will not lie against the heir of an offender; as, for instance, actions of theft, rapine, injury, or damage injuriously done; but nevertheless these actions will pass to heirs, and are never denied, but in an action of injury, and in other cases of a similar nature; yet sometimes even an action of contract will not lie against an heir, as when a testator acts fraudulently, and nothing comes to the possession of the heir by reason of the fraud: but if the penal actions, of which we have already spoken, are once contested by the principal parties concerned, they will afterwards pass both to and against the heirs of such parties.

§ 2. It remains to be observed, that if the defendant before sentence gives full satisfaction to the plaintiff, it is the duty of the judge to dismiss such defendant, although, at the time of contestation of suit, his cause was so bad, that he deserved to be condemned; and upon this account it was anciently a common saying, that all actions were dismissible.

Tit. XIII. *De exceptionibus.*

It follows, that we should treat of exceptions. Exceptions have been introduced into causes for the defence of the party cited; for it often happens, that a suit, which in itself is just, may yet become unjust, when commenced against a wrong person.

§ 1. If a man who is compelled by fear, or induced by fraud or mistake, makes a promise to Titius, for example, by stipulation; yet it is evident, that he is bound by the civil law, and that Titius may have an efficacious action; but it would be unjust that a condemnation should follow; and therefore the party who made such promise is permitted to plead exceptive matter in bar to the action, by setting forth that the promise was extorted by fear or fraud, or otherwise by alleging the peculiar circumstances of the case, whatever they are; and these are called exceptions *in factum compositæ*, *i.e.*, exceptions on the fact.

§ 2. The same practice prevails if Sempronius, for example, causes Titius to stipulate to repay him money, which Titius never received from him. It is certain, that Sempronius in this case may bring an action, for Titius is bound by the stipulation; yet as it would be unjust that he should be condemned upon that account, he is allowed to defend himself by an exception *pecuniæ non numeratæ*, *i.e.*, on account of money not paid. But by our express constitution we have shortened the time allowed for bringing this exception, as we have already observed in the former book.

§ 3. And further, although a debtor enters into a compact with his creditor, that his creditor shall not sue him, yet the debtor remains bound; for obligations are not to be wholly dissolved by a mere agreement; and therefore an action in this form, *si paret, eum dare oportere*, would be efficacious against the debtor; but as it would be unjust that the debtor should be condemned to make payment, notwithstanding the agreement, he is therefore permitted to defend himself by an exception of compact.

§ 4. If an oath is administered to a debtor at the instance of his creditor, and such debtor swears that nothing is due from him, yet he still remains obligated; but as it would not be right that the plaintiff should afterwards complain of perjury, the debtor may defend himself by alleging his own oath by way of exception. Exceptions of this sort are likewise equally necessary in real actions; as when the party in possession takes an oath at the request of the demandant, and swears that the thing in dispute is his own, and the demandant will nevertheless endeavour to recover it; for although the demandant's allegation is true, viz., that the thing claimed appertains to him, yet it is unjust that the possessor should be condemned.

§ 5. If a man hath been sued either upon a real or personal action, the obligation nevertheless remains; and therefore in strict law he may again be sued upon the same account; but in case of a second suit, he may be relieved, if he alleges by way of exception that the cause hath already been adjudged.

§ 6. It may suffice to have given these instances of exceptions in general; but in how many and in what various cases they are necessary, may be more fully learned from the larger books of the Digests.

§ 7. Some exceptions proceed from the laws themselves, or from those regulations which hold the place of laws; but others take their rise from the authority of the prætor.

§ 8. Some exceptions are called perpetual and peremptory; others are termed temporary and dilatory.

§ 9. The perpetual and peremptory are those which always obstruct the party agent, and destroy the force of the action; of this sort is the exception of fraud, of fear, and of compact, when it is agreed that the money shall not be sued for.

§ 10. Temporary and dilatory exceptions are those which operate for a time, and create delay; such is the exception of an agreement not to pursue a debt within a certain time, as within five years; but at the expiration of that time the creditor may proceed; and therefore those against whom an exception of agreement, or any other similar exception, can be objected, must delay their action, and not sue till the time agreed upon is expired; and it is for this reason that those exceptions are termed dilatory: and formerly, if the party's agent had sued within the time in which it was agreed not to sue, and an exception was interposed, it not only hindered such parties from obtaining in that cause, but it also disabled them from proceeding, even after the expiration of the time agreed on; for they were reputed to have lost their right, by having commenced a temerary suit. But we have been willing to mitigate this rigour, and have decreed, that whoever presumes to commence a suit before the time limited by the agreement, shall be subject to the constitution of Zeno, concerning those who demand more than their due: and if a party agent breaks in upon the time which he has before spontaneously allowed, or contemns the limits which the nature of some actions allow, the party defendant, who suffers such injurious treatment, becomes entitled to twice the time before allowed; and even when that is expired, cannot be obliged to give an appearance, till he has been reimbursed the whole of his expenses; and this we have ordained *in terrorem* that all plaintiffs may be taught to observe the proper time of commencing their suits.

§ 11. Dilatory exceptions may also arise by reason of the person of the party suing; such are those which are made against proctors; as if a suitor should employ a soldier or a woman to act for him: for soldiers are not permitted to appear in any cause, even in behalf of a father, a mother, or a wife, although they obtain the sanction of an imperial rescript, but they are allowed to act in their own affairs without offending against military discipline. But we have put a stop to the exceptions of infamy which were formerly made both against proctors and their constituents, having observed them to be little practised, and fearing, lest by means of such altercations a disquisition into the merits of causes should be retarded.

Tit. XIV. *De replicationibus.*

Sometimes an exception which appears at the first view to be valid is nevertheless not so; and when this happens there is a necessity for an additional allegation in aid of the plaintiff, which is called a replication, because the force of the exception is replicated, that is, unfolded and destroyed by it; as if a creditor should covenant with his debtor not to sue him, and it should afterwards be agreed between them that the creditor may sue; in consequence of which agreement the creditor brings an action, to which the debtor excepts, alleging the agreement of his creditor not to sue him. In this case the exception would be of weight; for, as such an agreement was entered into, it remains good, although a subsequent one was afterwards made to a contrary effect; but as it would be unjust that a creditor should be concluded by the exception, he is allowed to make a replication by reason of the subsequent compact.

§ 1. It also sometimes happens that a replication at first appears to be concludent though it is not so in reality; and when it so happens, then another allegation, called a duplication, must be offered in support of the defendant.

§ 2. And when a duplication carries with it an appearance of justice, but is upon some account injurious to the party agent, he may also in his turn give another allegation, which is termed a triplication.

§ 3. But the great variety of business which continually

occurs often extends the use of all these exceptions much further than we have mentioned; but of these a fuller knowledge may be obtained by a perusal of the larger volumes of the Digests.

§ 4. The exceptions by which a debtor may defend himself are generally allowed to be used by his bondsmen; and this is a right practice: for a demand made upon them is, as it were, a demand upon the debtor himself, who is compellable by an action of mandate to pay over to his sureties whatever they have been obliged to pay upon his account; and therefore, if a creditor hath covenanted with his debtor not to sue him, the bondsmen of such debtor may be aided by an exception of compact, in the same manner as if the promise had been made expressly to them. But there are some exceptions which cannot be made use of in behalf of sureties; for although when a debtor hath made a cession of his goods he may defend himself by alleging that cession as an exception to a suit brought by a creditor, yet the same exception cannot be alleged by the bondsmen; and the reason is evident; for whoever demands sureties hath always this principally in view, that he may be able to recover his debt from those sureties in case of failure in the principal debtor.

Tit. XV. *De interdictis.*

We are now led to treat of interdicts, or of those actions which supply their place. Interdicts were certain forms of words by which the prætor either commanded or prohibited something to be done; and these were chiefly used when any contention arose concerning possession or quasi-possession.

§ 1. The first division of them is into prohibitory, restoratory, and exhibitory interdicts. The prohibitory are those by which the prætor prohibits something to be done, as when he forbids force to be used against a lawful possessor, or against a person who is burying another where he hath a right; or when he forbids an edifice to be raised in a sacred place; or hinders a work from being erected in a public river, or on the banks of it, which may render it less navigable. The restoratory are those interdicts by which the prætor orders something to be restored, as the possession of goods to the universal successor, who has been kept out of possession by one who hath no right; or when the prætor commands possession to be restored to him who hath been forcibly ejected. And the exhibitory interdicts are those by which the prætor commands some exhibit to be made, as of a slave, for example, concerning whose liberty a cause is depending; or of a freedman, from whom a patron would exact the service due to him; or of children to their parent, under whose power they are. Some nevertheless imagine that interdicts can with propriety be only prohibitory, because the word *interdicere* signifies to denounce and prohibit; and that the restoratory and exhibitory interdicts might more properly be called decrees: yet it hath obtained by usage that they should all be termed interdicts, because they are pronounced between two—*inter duos dicuntur*—the demandant and the possessor.

§ 2. The second division of interdicts is into those which are given for the acquisition, the retention, or the recovery, of a possession.

§ 3. An interdict for the acquisition of possession is given to him whom the prætor appoints to be the possessor of the goods of a deceased person. This interdict is called *Quorum bonorum;* and the effect of it is, that it obliges all persons who retain goods in their hands as heirs or possessors to restore such goods to them to whom the possession of them hath been committed by the magistrate: and note, that he is reputed to possess as heir who think and takes himself so to be; and that he is deemed to possess as possessor who, without authority, retains a part or the whole of an inheritance, knowing that the possession does not belong to him. An interdict of acquisition is so called because it is useful to him only who first endeavours to acquire the possession; and therefore this interdict would be useless to any one who had once acquired possession, but afterwards lost it. The interdict called the Salvian interdict is also appointed for the acquisition of possession, and is used by the proprietors of farms, in order to acquire the goods which their tenants have pledged and engaged as a security for the payment of rent.

§ 4. The interdicts *Uti possidetis* and *Utrubi* have been introduced for the sake of retaining possession; for when there is a controversy between the parties concerning property, it is necessary to inquire which of them is in possession, that it may be known who ought to be the demandant; for till the possession is ascertained, an action of demand cannot be instituted; and natural reason teaches us that, when one of the parties is in possession, the other must of course be the demandant in the suit: but as it is by far more advantageous to be the possessor than the demandant, there is generally great contention for the possession; for although the possessor is not in reality the true proprietor, yet the possession will still remain in him, if the plaintiff does not prove the thing in litigation to be his own: and therefore, when the rights of parties are not clear, the sentence is always against the demandant. By the interdict *Uti possidetis*, the possession of a farm or house is contended for; and by the interdict *Utrubi*, the possession of things moveable is disputed. These interdicts anciently differed much in their force and effects; for, by the interdict *Uti possidetis*, that party who was in possession at the time of bringing the interdict prevailed, if he had not obtained the possession from his adversary by force, clandestinely, or precariously; but it was not material in what manner the possessor had obtained the possession from any other person: and by the interdict *Utrubi*, that party prevailed who had been in possession for the greatest part of the year preceding the contest, if he had not acquired that possession clandestinely, precariously, or by force. But the present practice is nevertheless otherwise; for the power of both interdicts in regard to possession is now made equal; so that in any cause instituted either for things moveable or immoveable, that party prevails who was in possession at the time of contesting suit, if it is not made apparent that he gained such possession by force, by clandestine means, or precariously.

§ 5. A man is regarded as a possessor, not only when he is himself in possession, but also when any other who is not under his power holds possession in his name; as, for instance, a farmer or a tenant. Any person may also possess by means of those to whom he hath committed the thing in litigation, either as a deposit or a loan; and this is what is meant by saying that a possession may be retained by any one by means of another, who possesses in his name. It is, moreover, held that a possession may be retained by the mere intention only; for, although a man is neither in possession himself, nor any other for him, but has quitted the possession of certain lands, with an intent to return to them again, he shall nevertheless be deemed to continue in possession. We have already explained, in our second Institution, by what persons any man may acquire possession; and although it may be retained *solo animo*, that is, by an intention only, yet it is indubitable that a mere intention is not sufficient for the acquisition of possession.

§ 6. The interdict for the recovery of possession is generally made use of when any person hath been forcibly ousted from the possession of his house or estate; for the party ousted is then entitled to the interdict *Unde vi*, by which the intruder is compelled to restore him to possession, although he who had been thus forcibly ousted was himself in possession by clandestine means, by force, or precariously. But, as we have before observed, it is provided by the imperial constitutions that whenever any man seizes a thing by force, if it is his own, he shall lose his property in it; and if it belongs to another, he shall be compelled, not only to make restitution, but also to pay the full value to the party who suffered the force. But whoever ousts another of possession by force is likewise subject to the law *Julia, de vi privatâ* or *de vi publicâ:* if the seizing or intrusion was effected without weapons, then the offender is only liable to the law *de vi privatâ;* but if it was effected by an armed force, he is then subject to the law *de vi publicâ*. We comprehend not only shields, swords, and helmets under the term arms, but also clubs and stones.

§ 7. The third division of interdicts is into simple and double interdicts; the simple are those in which there is both a plaintiff and a defendant; and of this sort are all restoratory and exhibitory interdicts: for the plaintiff or demandant is he who requires something to be exhibited or restored, and the defendant is he from whom the exhibition or restitution is required. But of the prohibitory interdicts, some are simple, some double; they are simple when the prætor forbids something to be done in a sacred place, on a public river, or upon the banks of it; and the demandant is he who desires that some act should not be done, and the defendant is he who endeavours to do it. The interdicts *Uti possedetis* and *Utrubi* are instances of the double interdicts; and they are called double, because in these the condition of either litigant is equal, the one not being understood to be more particularly the plaintiff or the defendant than the other, inasmuch as each sustains the part of both.

§ 8. It would be superfluous at this day to speak of the order and ancient effect of interdicts, for when judgments are extraordinary—and at present all judgments are so—an interdict is rendered unnecessary; and judgments are therefore now delivered without interdicts, in the same manner as if a beneficial action was given in consequence of an interdict.

Tit. XVI. *De pœnâ temere litigantium.*

Our legislators and magistrates have ever been careful to hinder mankind from entering into rash and litigious contentions; and we also are studious to effect the same purpose. And that such suits may be the better prevented, the rashness both of plaintiffs and defendants hath been properly restrained by pecuniary punishments, the coercion of an oath, and the fear of infamy.

§ 1. By virtue of one of our constitutions, an oath must be administered to every man against whom an action is brought; for a defendant is not permitted to plead till he hath first sworn that he proceeds as a contradictor, upon a firm belief that his cause is good. But actions lie, in particular cases, for double and triple value against those who have given a negative issue; as when a suit is commenced on account of injurious damage, or for a legacy left to a sacred place, as a church, hospital, &c. There are also actions upon which more than the simple value is recoverable at the time of their commencement; as upon an action of theft manifest, which is for fourfold the value; and upon an action of theft not manifest, which lies for double the value; because, in these, as well as in some other cases, the action is at first given for more than the simple value, whether the defendant denies or confesses the charge brought against him. But the calumny of the plaintiff is also under restraint; for he, too, is compelled by our constitution to swear, that he did not commence the suit with an intention to calumniate, but upon a thorough confidence that he had a good cause; and, what is more, the advocates on both sides are likewise compellable to take a similar oath, the substance of which is set forth in another of our constitutions. This practice hath been introduced in the place of the ancient action of calumny, which compelled the plaintiff to pay the tenth part of his demand as a punishment; but this action is now disused; and instead of it, we have introduced the before-mentioned oath, and have ordained that every rash litigant, who hath failed in his proof, should be compelled to pay his adversary the damages and costs of suit.

§ 2. In some cases the parties condemned become infamous, as in actions of theft, rapine, injury, or fraud. The parties condemned are likewise rendered infamous in an action of tutelage, mandate, or deposit, if it is a direct, and not a contrary, action. An action of partnership has also the same effect; for it is direct in regard to all the partners; and therefore any one of them who is condemned in such action is branded with infamy. But not only those who have been condemned in an action of theft, rapine, injury, or fraud, are rendered infamous, but those also who have bargained to prevent a criminal prosecution; and this is a right practice; for there is a wide difference between a debtor on account of crime, and a debtor upon contract.

§ 3. All actions take their commencement from that part of the prætor's edict, in which he treats *de in jus vocando;* that is, of calling persons into judgment: for the first step to be taken in all matters of controversy is to cite or call the adverse party to appear before the judge, who is to determine the cause. And in the same part of the edict the prætor hath treated parents and patrons, and even the children of patrons and patronesses, with so great a respect, that he does not suffer them to be called into judgment by their children or their freedmen until application hath been first made to him, and leave obtained; and if any man presumes to cite a parent, a patron, or the children of a patron, without such previous permission, he is subject to a penalty of fifty *solidi*.

Tit. XVII. *De officio judicis.*

It now remains that we should inquire into the office and duty of a judge. And it is certain, that it ought to be his principal care never to determine otherwise than the laws, the constitutions, or the customs and usages direct.

§ 1. And therefore, if a suit is commenced by a noxal action, the judge ought always to observe the following form of condemnation, if the defendant deserves to be condemned; *e.g.*, "I condemn Publius Mævius to pay Lucius Titius ten *aurei*, or to deliver up the slave who did the damage."

§ 2. When a cause, commenced upon a real action, is brought before a judge for his determination, and he thinks proper to pronounce against the demandant, the possessor ought then to be acquitted; but if the judge think it just to condemn the possessor, the party condemned must be admonished to restore the very thing which was in dispute, together with all its produce. But if the possessor alleges that he is unable to make an immediate restitution, and petitions for a longer time, without any seeming intention to frustrate the sentence, he is to be indulged; provided always, that he gives caution by a sufficient bondsman for the full payment of the condemnation and costs of suit, if he should fail to make restitution within the time appointed. And if an inheritance is sued for, a judge ought to determine just in the same manner in regard to the profits, as he would in a suit for some particular thing only; for if the defendant appear to have been a possessor *in malâ fide*, then almost the same reasoning prevails in both actions in regard to the profits, whether they were taken by the possessor, or, through negligence, not taken by him; but if the defendant was a possessor *bonâ fide*, then no account is expected, either of fruits consumed, or of fruits not gathered, before the contestation of suit; yet note that, from the time of contestation, all fruits must be accounted for, whether they were gathered and used, or left ungathered, through the negligence of the possessor.

§ 3. If a man proceeds by an action *ad exhibendum*, it is not sufficient that the defendant should exhibit the thing in question, but he must also be answerable for all profits and emoluments accruing from it; that the plaintiff may be in the same state as if his property had been restored to him at the time when he first brought his action; and therefore, if the possessor, during his delay to surrender the thing in dispute, shall gain a prescriptive title to it, yet such possessor shall nevertheless be condemned to restitution; for he shall not be allowed to avail himself of his own delay. And further, it is the duty of the judge to take an account of the profits of the middle time; that is, of the time between contestation and sentence. But, if the defendant declares that he is not able instantly to produce the thing adjudged, and prays a further time, without any appearance of affecting a delay, a term ought to be assigned him, upon his giving caution to make restitution. But if he neither obeys the commands of the magistrate in instantly producing the thing adjudged, nor in giving a sufficient caution for the production of it at a future day, he must then be condemned to pay the full damages, which the demandant hath sustained by not having the thing delivered to him at the commencement of the suit.

§ 4. When a suit is commenced by the action *familiæ erciscundæ*, for the partition of an inheritance, it is the duty of the judge to decree to each heir his respective portion; and if the partition, when made, is more advantageous to the one than to the other, then ought the judge, as we have before observed, to oblige him who has the largest part, to make a full recompense in money to his co-heir: it therefore follows, that every co-heir, who hath taken the profits of an inheritance to his sole use, and consumed them, is liable to be compelled to make a restitution. And this is the law not only when there are two heirs, but also when there are many.

§ 5. The same law is also observed when a suit is brought upon the action *communi dividundo*, for one particular thing only, it being but a part or parcel of an inheritance; as, for example, a field, or any piece of ground, which, if it can be conveniently divided, ought to be adjudged to each claimant in equal portions; and if the share of one is larger than the share of another, the party possessing such large portion must be condemned to make a recompense in money. But if the thing sued for is of such a nature that it cannot be divided, as a slave, or a horse, for example, it must be given entirely to one of the coparceners, who must be ordered to make a satisfaction in money to the other.

§ 6. When the action *finium regundorum* is brought for the determination of boundaries, the judge ought first to examine whether it is absolutely requisite to proceed to an adjudication: but it is in one case undoubtedly necessary; and this happens whenever it becomes expedient that any grounds should be divided by more conspicuous boundaries than they formerly were; for necessity then makes it requisite that a part of one man's ground should be adjudged to another, in which case it is incumbent upon a judge to condemn him whose estate is enlarged to pay an equivalent to the other, whose estate is diminished. It is also by virtue of this action that any one may be prosecuted who hath committed any fraud in relation to boundaries, by either removing stones, or cutting down trees, which supplied the place of landmarks. The same action will also subject any man to condemnation on account of contumacy, if he refuses to suffer his lands to be measured at the command of a judge.

§ 7. And note, that whatever is adjudged by virtue of a sentence proceeding from any of these actions, the same instantly becomes the property of him to whom it was so adjudged.

Tit. XVIII. *De publicis judiciis.*

Public judgments are not introduced by actions, nor are they in anything similar to the other judgments of which we have been treating. They also differ greatly from one another in the manner of being instituted and prosecuted.

§ 1. These judgments are denominated public, or popular, because, in general, they may be sued to execution by any of the people.

§ 2. Of these judgments some are capital, and others not capital. Those we term capital by which a criminal is prohibited from fire and water, or condemned to death, to deportation, or to the mines. The other judgments, by which men are fined and rendered infamous, are public indeed, but yet not capital.

§ 3. The following laws denounce public judgments. The law *Julia majestatis* extends its force against those who have been hardy enough to undertake any enterprise against the emperor or the republic. The penalty of this law is the loss of life, and the very memory of the offender becomes infamous after his death.

§ 4. The law *Julia*, which was made for the suppression of adulteries, not only punishes those men with death who violate the marriage bed of others, but also those who commit acts of detestable lewdness with persons of their own sex. The same law also inflicts a punishment upon all who are guilty of the crime called *stuprum*, which is that of debauching a virgin, or a widow of honest fame, without using force. The punishment of this crime in persons of condition is the confiscation of a moiety of their possessions; but offenders of low degree undergo a corporal chastisement with relegation.

§ 5. The law *Cornelia de sicariis* punishes those who commit murder with death, and also those who carry weapons, called *tela*, with an intent to kill. The term *telum*, according to Caius's interpretation, commonly signifies an arrow made to be shot from a bow; but it is now used to denote any missive weapon, or whatever is thrown from the hand: it therefore follows that a club, a stone, or a piece of iron, may be comprehended under that appellation. The word *telum* is evidently derived from the Greek adverb τηλου, *procul*, because thrown from a distance. And we may trace the same analogy in the Greek word βελος: for what we call *telum*, the Greeks term βελος, from βαλλεσθαι, to throw; and of this we are informed by Xenophon, who writes thus: "Darts also were carried, spears, arrows, slings, and a multitude of stones." Assassins and murderers are called *sicarii*, from *sica*, which signifies a short crooked sword or poniard. The same law also inflicts a capital punishment upon those who practise odious arts, or sell pernicious medicaments, occasioning the death of mankind, as well by poison as by magical incantations.

§ 6. The law *Pompeia de paricidiis* inflicts a new punishment upon those who commit parricide, which is the most execrable of all crimes; and by this law it is ordained that whoever, either publicly or privately, hastens the death of a parent or a child, or of any person comprised under the tie or denomination of a parent, shall be punished as a committer of parricide; and that any one who hath advised, or been privy to the death of any of these persons is also guilty of parricide, although he is a stranger and not related to their family. A criminal, in case of parricide, is neither put to death by the sword, by fire, nor by any other ordinary punishment; for the law directs that he shall be sewed up in a kind of sack, with a dog, a cock, a viper, and an ape, and being put up in this horrid inclosure shall be thrown either into the sea, or an adjacent river, according to the situation of the place where the punishment is inflicted. Thus, whilst he is yet alive, he is deprived of the very elements, so that his living body is denied the benefits of the air, and his dead body the use of the earth. But if a man is guilty of the murder of any other person, related to him either by cognation or affinity, he is only subject to the punishment inflicted by the law *Cornelia de sicariis*.

§ 7. The law *Cornelia de falsis*, which is also called *testamentaria*, punishes any man who knowingly and with a fraudulent intent hath written, signed, dictated, or produced a false will or any other instrument; it also punishes every one who hath made, engraved, or in any manner counterfeited the seal of another. The punishment inflicted by the law upon slaves in these cases is death, but the punishment of free persons is deportation.

§ 8. The law *Julia* concerning public and private force, take place against all who use force, whether they are armed or unarmed; but if proof is made of an armed force, the punishment is deportation by that law; and if the force was not accompanied with arms, the penalty to be inflicted is the confiscation of one third part of the offender's goods. Nevertheless, if a rape is committed upon a virgin, a widow, a nun, or upon any other person, both the ravishers and their accomplices are all equally subject to a capital punishment, according to the decision of our constitution, in which the student may read more at large of this matter.

§ 9. The law *Julia de peculatu* punishes those who have been guilty of theft in regard to public money or anything which is sacred; but if judges themselves, during the time of their acting as such, commit a theft of this kind, their punishment is capital; and the punishment of all those who assist in such a theft, or knowingly receive the money stolen, is also capital. But all other persons who offend against this law are only subject to deportation.

§ 10. The law *Fabia* against plagiaries is also numbered among public judgments; but in consequence of the imperial constitutions the offenders against the law are sometimes punished with death, and sometimes by a milder punishment.

§ 11. There are also other public judgments; such are the Julian laws *de ambitu*, *repetundarum*, *de annonâ*, *de residuis;* which do not punish with death, but inflict other punishments upon those who offend.

§ 12. But it is now time to conclude our Institutions; and we declare it to be our intent that this brief exposition of public judgments should serve only as an index to give a general idea of that knowledge which, through the blessing of God, may be most fully and particularly obtained by perusing the Digests with a diligent attention.

ALPHABETICAL GEOGRAPHICAL INDEX.

ALPHABETICAL INDEX.

The letters G. *and* J. *signify respectively Gaius and Justinian. When the number of the page is not prefixed by either, it refers to matter in the "Outline."*

LONDON: PRINTED BY C. F. ROWORTH, GREAT NEW ST., FETTER LANE, E.C.

www.ingramcontent.com/pod-product-compliance
Lightning Source LLC
LaVergne TN
LVHW091633100826
845152LV00001B/19

* 9 7 8 1 5 8 4 7 7 6 1 2 3 *